STANDARD NORMAL DISTRIBUTION

Area or probability

Entries in the table give the area under the curve between the mean and z standard deviations above the mean. For example, for $z = 1.25$ the area under the curve between the mean and z is .3944.

z	.00	.01	.02	.03	.04	.05	.06	.07	.08	.09
.0	.0000	.0040	.0080	.0120	.0160	.0199	.0239	.0279	.0319	.0359
.1	.0398	.0438	.0478	.0517	.0557	.0596	.0636	.0675	.0714	.0753
.2	.0793	.0832	.0871	.0910	.0948	.0987	.1026	.1064	.1103	.1141
.3	.1179	.1217	.1255	.1293	.1331	.1368	.1406	.1443	.1480	.1517
.4	.1554	.1591	.1628	.1664	.1700	.1736	.1772	.1808	.1844	.1879
.5	.1915	.1950	.1985	.2019	.2054	.2088	.2123	.2157	.2190	.2224
.6	.2257	.2291	.2324	.2357	.2389	.2422	.2454	.2486	.2517	.2549
.7	.2580	.2611	.2642	.2673	.2704	.2734	.2764	.2794	.2823	.2852
.8	.2881	.2910	.2939	.2967	.2995	.3023	.3051	.3078	.3106	.3133
.9	.3159	.3186	.3212	.3238	.3264	.3289	.3315	.3340	.3365	.3389
1.0	.3413	.3438	.3461	.3485	.3508	.3531	.3554	.3577	.3599	.3621
1.1	.3643	.3665	.3686	.3708	.3729	.3749	.3770	.3790	.3810	.3830
1.2	.3849	.3869	.3888	.3907	.3925	.3944	.3962	.3980	.3997	.4015
1.3	.4032	.4049	.4066	.4082	.4099	.4115	.4131	.4147	.4162	.4177
1.4	.4192	.4207	.4222	.4236	.4251	.4265	.4279	.4292	.4306	.4319
1.5	.4332	.4345	.4357	.4370	.4382	.4394	.4406	.4418	.4429	.4441
1.6	.4452	.4463	.4474	.4484	.4495	.4505	.4515	.4525	.4535	.4545
1.7	.4554	.4564	.4573	.4582	.4591	.4599	.4608	.4616	.4625	.4633
1.8	.4641	.4649	.4656	.4664	.4671	.4678	.4686	.4693	.4699	.4706
1.9	.4713	.4719	.4726	.4732	.4738	.4744	.4750	.4756	.4761	.4767
2.0	.4772	.4778	.4783	.4788	.4793	.4798	.4803	.4808	.4812	.4817
2.1	.4821	.4826	.4830	.4834	.4838	.4842	.4846	.4850	.4854	.4857
2.2	.4861	.4864	.4868	.4871	.4875	.4878	.4881	.4884	.4887	.4890
2.3	.4893	.4896	.4898	.4901	.4904	.4906	.4909	.4911	.4913	.4916
2.4	.4918	.4920	.4922	.4925	.4927	.4929	.4931	.4932	.4934	.4936
2.5	.4938	.4940	.4941	.4943	.4945	.4946	.4948	.4949	.4951	.4952
2.6	.4953	.4955	.4956	.4957	.4959	.4960	.4961	.4962	.4963	.4964
2.7	.4965	.4966	.4967	.4968	.4969	.4970	.4971	.4972	.4973	.4974
2.8	.4974	.4975	.4976	.4977	.4977	.4978	.4979	.4979	.4980	.4981
2.9	.4981	.4982	.4982	.4983	.4984	.4984	.4985	.4985	.4986	.4986
3.0	.4986	.4987	.4987	.4988	.4988	.4989	.4989	.4989	.4990	.4990

THIRD EDITION

ESSENTIALS OF STATISTICS FOR BUSINESS AND ECONOMICS

David R. Anderson
University of Cincinnati

Dennis J. Sweeney
University of Cincinnati

Thomas A. Williams
Rochester Institute of Technology

THOMSON

SOUTH-WESTERN

Australia · Canada · Mexico · Singapore · Spain · United Kingdom · United States

THOMSON

SOUTH-WESTERN

Essentials of Statistics for Business and Economics, 3rd Edition

David R. Anderson, Dennis J. Sweeney, Thomas A. Williams

Publisher:
Melissa Acuña

Senior Acquisitions Editor:
Charles E. McCormick, Jr.

Senior Developmental Editor:
Alice C. Denny

Marketing Manager:
Larry Qualls

Senior Production Editor:
Deanna R. Quinn

Media Technology Editor:
Diane Van Bakel

Media Developmental Editor:
Chris Wittmer

Media Production Editor:
Amy Wilson

Manufacturing Coordinator:
Diane Lohman

Internal Design:
Michael H. Stratton

Cover Design:
Paul Neff Design, Casey Gilbertson

Cover Image:
PhotoDisc, Inc.

Production House and Compositor:
BookMasters, Inc.

Printer:
Quebecor World—Versailles

Library of Congress Cataloging-in-Publication Data
Anderson, David Ray
    Essentials of statistics for business and
economics / David R. Anderson, Dennis J.
Sweeney, Thomas A. Williams.—3rd ed.
        p. cm.
    Includes bibliographical references
and index.
    ISBN 0-324-14580-2
    1. Social sciences—Statistical methods.
2. Commercial statistics. 3. Economics—
Statistical methods. 4. Statistics—
Problems, exercises, etc. I. Sweeney,
Dennis J. II. Williams, Thomas Arthur.
III. Title.
HA29.A587 2003
519.5—dc21   2002018700

Brief Contents

Contents

Chapter 8
Interval Estimation 296

Chapter 11
Comparisons Involving Proportions and a Test of Independence 446

Chapter 12
Simple Linear Regression 478

Chapter 13
Multiple Regression 547

Preface

The purpose of *ESSENTIALS OF STATISTICS FOR BUSINESS AND ECONOMICS* is to give students, primarily those in the fields of business administration and economics, a conceptual introduction to the field of statistics and its many applications. The text is applications oriented and written with the needs of the non-mathematician in mind; the mathematical prerequisite is a knowledge of algebra.

Applications of data analysis and statistical methodology are an integral part of the organization and presentation of the text material. The discussion and development of each technique is presented in an application setting, with the statistical results providing insights to decisions and solution to problems.

Although the book is applications oriented, we have taken care to provide sound methodological development and to use notation that is generally accepted for the topic being covered. Hence, students will find that this text provides good preparation for the study of more advanced statistical material. An updated bibliography to guide further study is included as an appendix.

CHANGES IN THE THIRD EDITION

We appreciate the acceptance and positive response to the previous editions of *ESSENTIALS OF STATISTICS FOR BUSINESS AND ECONOMICS*. Accordingly, in making modifications for this new edition, we have maintained the presentation style and readability of those editions. The significant changes in the new edition are summarized here.

Content Revisions

The following list summarizes selected content revisions for the edition.

- A discussion of levels of measurement for data (Chapter 1)
- More material on graphical and tabular descriptive statistics (Chapter 2)
- The use of Minitab and Microsoft® Excel for random sampling (Chapter 7)
- An earlier discussion of the term *margin of error* and additional information on when to use z and when to use t for interval estimation (Chapter 8)
- More emphasis on computing and interpreting p-values (Chapters 9 through 11)
- Formulas for regression computations have been modified to emphasize intuition and deemphasize computational issues (Chapter 12)

New Examples and Exercises Based on Real Data

We have added over 200 new examples and exercises based on real data and recent reference sources of statistical information. Using *The Wall Street Journal, USA Today, Fortune, Barron's*, various websites, and a variety of other sources, we have drawn upon actual studies to develop explanations and to create exercises that demonstrate many uses of statistics in business and economics. We believe that the use of real data helps generate more student interest in the material and enables the student to learn about both the statistical methodology and its application.

New Chapter on Multiple Regression

Given the importance of regression in applied statistics, we have added a new Chapter 13 entitled Multiple Regression. Simple linear regression remains the topic of Chapter 12. In the new chapter, we cover the multiple regression model, the assumptions, testing for significance, and using the estimated regression equation for estimation and prediction. The chapter also includes a section on the use and interpretation of qualitative independent variables.

New Case Problems

We have added six new case problems to this edition, bringing the total number of case problems in the text to twenty-one. The new case problems, which are based on referenced data sets, appear in the chapters on interval estimation and regression. These case problems provide students with the opportunity to analyze somewhat larger data sets and prepare managerial reports based on the results of the analysis.

Minitab and Microsoft® Excel Appendixes

Minitab and Excel Spreadsheet appendixes appear at the end of most chapters. These appendixes provide step-by-step procedures that make it easy for students to use Minitab or Excel to conduct the statistical analysis presented in the chapter. All appendixes have been updated for the latest versions of Minitab and Excel. The Excel appendix for descriptive statistics (Chapter 2) now includes the use of the function wizard, the chart wizard, and the pivot table report. These procedures expose the student to the extensive capabilities of Excel for creating graphical presentations and for developing crosstabulations. New and/or revised appendixes appear at the end of the chapters on descriptive statistics, sampling, interval estimation, hypothesis testing, and comparisons involving proportions.

FEATURES AND PEDAGOGY

We have continued many of the features that appeared in previous editions. Some of the more important ones are noted here.

Statistics in Practice

Each chapter begins with a statistics in practice article that describes an application of the statistical methodology to be covered in the chapter. Statistics in practice have been provided by practitioners at companies such as Procter & Gamble, Mead, Dollar General, Colgate-Palmolive, Alliance Data Systems, Monsanto, and others.

Methods Exercises and Applications Exercises

The end-of-section exercises are split into two parts, Methods and Applications. The Methods exercises require students to use the formulas and make the necessary computations. The Applications exercises require students to use the chapter material in real-world situations. Thus, students first focus on the computational "nuts and bolts," then move on to the subtleties of statistical application and interpretation.

Self-Test Exercises

Certain exercises are identified as self-test exercises. Completely worked-out solutions for those exercises are provided in Appendix E at the back of the book. Students can attempt the self-test exercises and immediately check the solution to evaluate their understanding of the concepts presented in the chapter.

Notes and Comments

At the end of many sections, we provide Notes and Comments designed to give the student additional insights about the statistical methodology and its application. Notes and Comments include warnings about or limitations of the methodology, recommendations for application, brief descriptions of additional technical considerations, and other matters.

Data Sets Accompany the Text

Over 150 data sets are now available on the CD-ROM that is packaged with the text. The data sets are available in both MINITAB and Excel formats. Data set logos are used in the text to identify the data sets that are available on the CD. Data sets for all case problems as well as data sets for larger exercises are also included on the CD.

ANCILLARY TEACHING AND LEARNING MATERIALS

Three print ancillaries are available to students either through their bookstore or for direct purchase through the on-line catalog at **www.swcollege.com.**

- Prepared by Mohammad Ahmadi of the University of Tennessee-Chattanooga, the **Work Book** (ISBN: 0-324-144582-9) provides the student with significant supplementary study materials. It contains an outline, review and list of formulas in each text chapter, sample exercises with step-by-step solutions, exercises with answers, and a series of self-testing questions with answers.
- Another student ancillary is the *Microsoft® Excel Companion for Business Statistics* (ISBN: 0-324-06898-0) by David Eldredge of Murray State University. This manual provides step-by-step instructions for using Excel to solve many of the problems included in introductory business statistics. Directions for Excel 2000 and Excel 97 are included.
- **Solutions Manual** At the request of the instructor, a print version of the Solutions Manual can be packaged with the text for student purchase

The following instructor support materials are available to adopters from the Thomson™ Academic Resource Center at 800-423-0563 or through **www.swcollege.com:**

- **Instructor's Resource CD** (ISBN: 0-324-14584-5)—All instructor ancillaries are provided on a single CD-ROM. Included in this convenient format are:
  - **Solutions Manual**—The Solutions Manual prepared by the authors, includes solutions for all problems in the text.
  - **Instructor's Manual**—The Instructor's Manual also prepared by the authors, contains solutions to all case problems presented in the text.
  - **PowerPoint™ Presentation Slides**—Prepared by John Loucks of St. Edward's University, the presentation slides contain a teaching outline that incorporates graphics to help instructors create even more stimulating lectures. The PowerPoint 97 slides may be adapted using PowerPoint software to facilitate classroom use.
  - **Test Bank** and **ExamView™**—Prepared also by Mohammad Ahmadi, the Test Bank includes multiple choice questions and problems for each chapter. ExamView™ computerized testing software allows instructors to create, edit, store, and print exams.

ACKNOWLEDGMENTS

We would like to acknowledge the work of our reviewers who provided comments and suggestions of ways to continue to improve our text. Thanks to:

Ali Arshad, College of Santa Fe
Timothy M. Bergquist, Northwest Christian College
Habtu Braha, Coppin State College
Robert Cochran, University of Wyoming
Dale DeBoer, University of Colorado, Colorado Springs
Raj Devasagayam, St. Norbert College
Nader D. Ebrahimi, University of New Mexico
H. Robert Gadd, Southern Adventist University
Karen Gutermuth, Virginia Military Institute
Md. Mahbubul Kabir, Lyon College
Gary Nelson, Central Community College, Columbus Campus
Elaine Parks, Laramie County Community College
Charles J. Reichert, University of Wisconsin–Superior
Larry Scheuermann, University of Louisiana, Lafayette
Carlton Scott, University of California–Irvine
Alan D. Smith, Robert Morris College
Stephen L. S. Smith, Gordon College
Wibawa A. Sutanto, Prairie View A&M University
Bennie D. Waller, Francis Marion University
Zhiwei Zhu, University of Louisiana at Lafayette
Charles Zimmerman, Robert Morris College

We continue to owe a debt to our many colleagues and friends for their helpful comments and suggestions in the development of this and earlier editions of our text. Among them are:

Mohammad Ahmadi, University of Tennessee at Chattanooga
Lari Arjomand, Clayton College and State University
Robert Balough, Clarion University
Mike Bourke, Houston Baptist University
James Brannon, University of Wisconsin–Oshkosh
John Bryant, University of Pittsburgh
Peter Bryant, University of Colorado
Terri L. Byczkowski, University of Cincinnati
Robert Carver, Stonehill College
Robert Cochran, University of Wyoming
David W. Cravens, Texas Christian University
Robert Carver, Stonehill College
Robert Collins, Marquette University
Tom Dahlstrom, Eastern College
Gopal Dorai, William Patterson University
Nicholas Farnum, California State University–Fullerton
Donald Gren, Salt Lake Community College
Paul Guy, California State University–Chico
Clifford Hawley, West Virginia University
Alan Humphrey, University of Rhode Island
Ann Hussein, Philadelphia College of Textiles and Science

C. Thomas Innis, University of Cincinnati
Ben Isselhardt, Rochester Institute of Technology
Jeffery Jarrett, University of Rhode Island
Ronald Klimberg, St. Joseph's University
David Krueger, St. Cloud State University
Martin S. Levy, University of Cincinnati
David Lucking-Reiley, Vanderbilt University
Bala Maniam, Sam Houston State University
Don Marx, University of Alaska, Anchorage
Tom McCullough, University of California–Berkeley
Mitchell Muesham, Sam Houston State University
Roger Myerson, Northwestern University
Glenn Nilligan, The Ohio State University
Richard O'Connell, Miami University of Ohio
Alan Olinsky, Bryant College
Ceyhun Ozgur, Valparaiso University
Tom Pray, Rochester Institute of Technology
Harold Rahmlow, St. Joseph's University
H. V. Ramakrishna, Penn State University at Great Valley
Tom Ryan, Case Western Reserve University
Alan Smith, Robert Morris College
Bill Seaver, University of Tennessee
Willbann Terpening, Gonzaga University
David Tufte, University of New Orleans
Ted Tsukahara, St. Mary's College of California
Hroki Tsurumi, Rutgers University
Victor Ukpolo, Austin Peay State University
Ebenge Usip, Youngstown State University
Cindy VanEs, Cornell University
Jack Vaughn, University of Texas–El Paso
Andrew Welki, John Carroll University
Ari Wijetunga, Morehead State University
J. E. Willis, Louisiana State University
Mustafa Yilmaz, Northeastern University
Gary Yoshimoto, St. Cloud State University

A special thanks is owed to our associates from business and industry that supplied the statistics in practice features. We recognize them individually by a credit line in each of the articles. Finally, we are also indebted to our senior acquisitions editor Charles McCormick, Jr., our senior developmental editor Alice Denny, our senior production editor Deanna Quinn, our marketing manager Larry Qualls, and others at South-Western/Thomson Learning for their editorial counsel and support during the preparation of this text.

David R. Anderson
Dennis J. Sweeney
Thomas A. Williams

About the Authors

David R. Anderson.   David R. Anderson is Professor of Quantitative Analysis in the College of Business Administration at the University of Cincinnati. Born in Grand Forks, North Dakota, he earned his B.S., M.S., and Ph.D. degrees from Purdue University. Professor Anderson has served as Head of the Department of Quantitative Analysis and Operations Management and as Associate Dean of the College of Business Administration. In addition, he was the coordinator of the College's first Executive Program.

At the University of Cincinnati, Professor Anderson has taught introductory statistics for business students as well as graduate-level courses in regression analysis, multivariate analysis, and management science. He has also taught statistical courses at the Department of Labor in Washington, D.C. He has been honored with nominations and awards for excellence in teaching and excellence in service to student organizations.

Professor Anderson has coauthored ten textbooks in the areas of statistics, management science, linear programming, and production and operations management. He is an active consultant in the field of sampling and statistical methods.

Dennis J. Sweeney.   Dennis J. Sweeney is Professor of Quantitative Analysis and Founder of the Center for Productivity Improvement at the University of Cincinnati. Born in Des Moines, Iowa, he earned a B.S.B.A. degree from Drake University and his M.B.A. and D.B.A. degrees from Indiana University where he was an NDEA Fellow. During 1978–79, Professor Sweeney worked in the management science group at Procter & Gamble; during 1981–82, he was a visiting professor at Duke University. Professor Sweeney served as Head of the Department of Quantitative Analysis and as Associate Dean of the College of Business Administration at the University of Cincinnati.

Professor Sweeney has published more than thirty articles and monographs in the area of management science and statistics. The National Science Foundation, IBM, Procter & Gamble, Federated Department Stores, Kroger, and Cincinnati Gas & Electric have funded his research, which has been published in *Management Science*, *Operations Research*, *Mathematical Programming*, *Decision Sciences*, and other journals.

Professor Sweeney has coauthored ten textbooks in the areas of statistics, management science, linear programming, and production and operations management.

Thomas A. Williams.   Thomas A. Williams is Professor of Management Science in the College of Business at Rochester Institute of Technology. Born in Elmira, New York, he earned his B.S. degree at Clarkson University. He did his graduate work at Rensselaer Polytechnic Institute, where he received his M.S. and Ph.D. degrees.

Before joining the College of Business at RIT, Professor Williams served for seven years as a faculty member in the College of Business Administration at the University of Cincinnati, where he developed the undergraduate program in Information Systems and then served as its coordinator. At RIT he was the first chairman of the Decision Sciences Department. He teaches courses in management science and statistics, as well as graduate courses in regression and decision analysis.

Professor Williams is the coauthor of eleven textbooks in the areas of management science, statistics, production and operations management, and mathematics. He has been a consultant for numerous *Fortune* 500 companies and has worked on projects ranging from the use of data analysis to the development of large-scale regression models.

DATA AND STATISTICS

CONTENTS

Chapter 1

BUSINESS WEEK*

NEW YORK, NEW YORK

With a global circulation of more than 1 million, *Business Week* is the most widely read business magazine in the world. More than 200 dedicated reporters and editors in 26 bureaus worldwide deliver a variety of articles of interest to the business and economic community. Along with feature articles on current topics, the magazine contains regular sections on International Business, Economic Analysis, Information Processing, and Science & Technology. Information in the feature articles and the regular sections help readers stay abreast of current developments and assess the impact of those developments on business and economic conditions.

Most issues of *Business Week* provide an in-depth report on a topic of current interest. Often, the in-depth reports contain statistical facts and summaries that help the reader understand the business and/or economic information. For example, the January 8, 2001, issue reported statistical information about the top 25 managers of the year; the March 19, 2001, issue contained a report on the banking crisis in Japan; and the June 18, 2001, issue provided a variety of statistics on the top 100 information technology companies. In addition, the weekly *Business Week Investor* provides statistics about the state of the economy, including production indexes, stock prices, mutual funds, and interest rates.

Business Week also uses statistics and statistical information in managing its own business. For example, an annual survey of subscribers helps the company learn about subscriber demographics, reading habits, likely purchases, lifestyles, and so on. *Business Week* managers use the statistical summaries from the survey to

Business Week uses statistical facts and summaries in many of its articles. © 2002 Thomson Learning.

provide better services to subscribers and advertisers. For instance, a recent North American subscriber survey indicated that 90% of *Business Week* subscribers have a personal computer at home and that 64% of *Business Week* subscribers are involved with computer purchases at work. Such statistics alert *Business Week* managers to subscriber interest in articles about new developments in computers. The results of the survey are also made available to potential advertisers. The high percentage of subscribers using personal computers at home and the high percentage of subscribers involved with computer purchases at work would be an incentive for a computer manufacturer to consider advertising in *Business Week*.

In this chapter, we discuss the types of data that are available for statistical analysis and describe how the data are obtained. We introduce descriptive statistics and statistical inference as ways of converting data into meaningful and easily interpreted statistical information.

*The authors are indebted to Charlene Trentham, Research Manager at *Business Week*, for providing this Statistics in Practice.

Frequently, we see the following kinds of statements in newspaper and magazine articles:

- The average price of a movie ticket is $5.60 (*Money,* April 2001).
- Last year less than 40% of stock mutual funds had a positive return (*Forbes Best of the Web,* February 26, 2001).
- E-commerce sites spend an average of $108 to acquire a new customer (*Business 2.0,* March 2000).
- The *Washington Post* reaches 46% of households in the region on weekdays and 61% on Sundays, tops among big city newspapers (*Fortune,* January 10, 2000).
- Stocks account for 75% of the average investor's portfolio (*The Wall Street Journal,* March 27, 2000).
- Nokia, the world's largest and most profitable mobile phone maker, estimated an annual demand for 405 million phones (*Business Week,* June 25, 2001).

The numerical facts in the preceding statements ($5.60, 40%, $108, 46%, 61%, 75%, and 405 million) are called **statistics.** Thus, in everyday usage, the term *statistics* refers to numerical facts. However, the field, or subject, of statistics involves much more than numerical facts. In a broad sense, statistics is the art and science of collecting, analyzing, presenting, and interpreting data. Particularly in business and economics, a major reason for collecting, analyzing, presenting, and interpreting data is to give managers and decision makers a better understanding of the business and economic environment and thus enable them to make more informed and better decisions. In this text, we emphasize the use of statistics for business and economic decision making.

Chapter 1 begins with some illustrations of the applications of statistics in business and economics. In Section 1.2 we define the term *data* and introduce the concept of a data set. This section also introduces key terms such as *variables* and *observations,* discusses the difference between quantitative and qualitative data, and illustrates the difference between cross-sectional and time series data. Section 1.3 discusses how data can be obtained from existing sources or through survey and experimental studies designed to obtain new data. The important role that the Internet now plays in obtaining data is also highlighted. The use of data in developing descriptive statistics and in making statistical inferences is described in Sections 1.4 and 1.5.

1.1   APPLICATIONS IN BUSINESS AND ECONOMICS

In today's global business and economic environment, vast amounts of statistical information are available. The most successful managers and decision makers understand the information and use it effectively. In this section, we provide examples that illustrate some of the uses of statistics in business and economics.

Accounting

Public accounting firms use statistical sampling procedures when conducting audits for their clients. For instance, suppose an accounting firm wants to determine whether the amount of accounts receivable shown on a client's balance sheet fairly represents the actual amount of accounts receivable. Usually the number of individual accounts receivable is so large that reviewing and validating every account would be too time-consuming and expensive. As common practice in such situations, the audit staff selects a subset of the accounts called a sample. After reviewing the accuracy of the sampled accounts, the auditors draw a conclusion as to whether the accounts receivable amount shown on the client's balance sheet is acceptable.

Finance

Financial analysts use a variety of statistical information to guide their investment recommendations. In the case of stocks, the analysts review a variety of financial data including price/earnings ratios and dividend yields. By comparing the information for an individual stock with information about the stock market averages, a financial analyst can begin to draw a conclusion as to whether an individual stock is over- or undervalued. For example, *Barron's* (January 10, 2000) reported that the average price/earnings ratio for the 30 stocks in the Dow Jones Industrial Average was 24.7. Philip Morris had a price/earnings ratio of 9. In this case, the statistical information on price/earnings ratios showed that Philip Morris had a lower price in comparison to its earnings than the average for the Dow Jones stocks. Therefore, a financial analyst might conclude that Philip Morris was underpriced. This and other information about Philip Morris would help the analyst make buy, sell, or hold recommendations for the stock.

Marketing

Electronic scanners at retail checkout counters collect data for a variety of marketing research applications. For example, data suppliers such as ACNielsen and Information Resources, Inc., purchase point-of-sale scanner data from grocery stores, process the data, and then sell statistical summaries of the data to manufacturers. Manufacturers spent an average of $387,325 per product category to obtain this type of scanner data (Scanner Data User Survey, Mercer Management Consulting, Inc., April 1997). Manufacturers also purchase data and statistical summaries on promotional activities such as special pricing and the use of in-store displays. Brand managers can review the scanner statistics and the promotional activity statistics to better understand the relationship between promotional activities and sales. Such analyses help in establishing future marketing strategies for the various products.

Production

With today's emphasis on quality, quality control is an important application of statistics in production. A variety of statistical quality control charts are used to monitor the output of a production process. In particular, an x-bar chart is used to monitor the average output. Suppose, for example, that a machine fills containers with 12 ounces of a soft drink. Periodically, a production worker selects a sample of containers and computes the average number of ounces in the sample containers. This average, or x-bar value, is plotted on an x-bar chart. A plotted value above the chart's upper control limit indicates overfilling, and a plotted value below the chart's lower control limit indicates underfilling. The process is "in control" and allowed to continue as long as the plotted x-bar values fall between the chart's upper and lower control limits. Properly interpreted, an x-bar chart can help determine when adjustments are necessary to correct a production process.

Economics

Economists are frequently asked to provide forecasts about the future of the economy or some aspect of it. They use a variety of statistical information in making such forecasts. For instance, in forecasting inflation rates, economists use statistical information on such indicators as the Producer Price Index, the unemployment rate, and manufacturing capacity utilization. Often these statistical indicators are entered into computerized forecasting models that predict inflation rates.

Applications of statistics such as those described in this section are an integral part of this text. Such examples provide an overview of the breadth of statistical applications. To supplement these examples, practitioners in the fields of business and economics provided Statistics in Practice articles that introduce the material covered in each chapter. The Statistics in Practice applications show the importance of statistics in a wide variety of decision-making situations.

1.2 DATA

Data are the facts and figures collected, analyzed, and summarized for presentation and interpretation. Together, the data collected in a particular study are referred to as the **data set** for the study. Table 1.1 shows a data set containing information for 25 of the shadow stocks tracked by the American Association of Individual Investors. Shadow stocks are common stocks of smaller companies not closely followed by Wall Street analysts.

TABLE 1.1   A DATA SET FOR 25 SHADOW STOCKS

CDfile
Shadow

Company	Exchange	Ticker Symbol	Annual Sales ($ millions)	Earnings per Share ($)	Price/ Earnings Ratio
Advanced Comm. Systems	OTC	ACSC	75.10	0.32	39.10
Ag-Chem Equipment Co.	OTC	AGCH	321.10	0.48	23.40
Aztec Manufacturing Co.	NYSE	AZZ	79.70	1.18	7.80
Cal-Maine Foods, Inc.	OTC	CALM	314.10	0.38	11.70
Chesapeake Utilities	NYSE	CPK	174.50	1.13	16.20
Dataram Corporation	AMEX	DTM	73.10	0.86	11.00
EnergySouth, Inc.	OTC	ENSI	74.00	1.67	13.20
Gencor Industries, Inc.	AMEX	GX	263.30	1.96	4.70
Industrial Scientific	OTC	ISCX	43.50	2.03	11.50
Keystone Consolidated	NYSE	KES	365.70	0.86	9.40
LandCare USA, Inc.	NYSE	GRW	111.40	0.33	29.40
Market Facts, Inc.	OTC	MFAC	126.70	0.98	26.50
Meridian Diagnostics, Inc.	OTC	KITS	36.30	0.46	14.70
Merit Medical Systems	OTC	MMSI	67.20	0.27	24.50
Met-Pro Corporation	NYSE	MPR	61.90	1.01	12.40
Nobility Homes, Inc.	OTC	NOBH	45.80	0.87	14.70
Omega Research, Inc.	OTC	OMGA	27.60	0.11	27.30
Point of Sale Limited	OTC	POSIF	12.30	0.28	25.40
Psychemedics Corp.	AMEX	PMD	17.60	0.13	39.40
Roadhouse Grill, Inc.	OTC	GRLL	118.40	0.26	20.80
Selas Corp. of America	AMEX	SLS	97.10	0.77	10.70
Toymax International, Inc.	OTC	TMAX	104.50	1.08	4.70
VSI Holdings, Inc.	AMEX	VIS	166.80	0.25	21.00
Warrantech Corporation	OTC	WTEC	207.30	0.13	29.80
Webco Industries, Inc.	AMEX	WEB	153.50	0.88	7.50

Source: American Association of Individual Investors Web site, March 1999.

Elements, Variables, and Observations

Elements are the entities on which data are collected. For the data set in Table 1.1, each individual company's stock is an element. With 25 stocks, the data set contains 25 elements. A **variable** is a characteristic of interest for the elements. The data set in Table 1.1 has the following five variables:

- *Exchange:* Where the stock is traded—NYSE (New York Stock Exchange), AMEX (American Stock Exchange), and OTC (Over-the-Counter).
- *Ticker Symbol:* The abbreviation used to identify the stock on the exchange listing.
- *Annual Sales:* Total sales for the company in millions of dollars for the most recent 12 months.
- *Earnings per Share:* Total earnings per share in dollars for the latest 12 months.
- *Price/Earnings Ratio:* Market price per share divided by the most recent 12 months' earnings per share.

Collecting measurements on each variable for every element in a study provides the data. The set of measurements obtained for a particular element is called an **observation.** Referring to Table 1.1, we see that the set of measurements for the first observation (Advanced Comm. Systems) is OTC, ACSC, 75.10, 0.32, and 39.10. The set of measurements for the second observation (Ag-Chem Equipment Co.) is OTC, AGCH, 321.10, 0.48, and 23.40; and so on. Because the data set contains 25 elements, it has 25 observations.

Scales of Measurement

Data collection requires one of the following scales of measurement: nominal, ordinal, interval, and ratio. The scale of measurement determines the amount of information contained in the data and indicates the data summarization and statistical analyses that are most appropriate.

The scale of measurement for a variable is a **nominal scale** when the data are labels or names used to identify an attribute of the element. For example, referring to the data in Table 1.1, we see that the scale of measurement for the exchange variable is nominal because NYSE, AMEX, and OTC are labels used to identify where the company's stock is traded. In cases where the scale of measurement is nominal, a numeric code as well as nonnumeric labels may be used. For example, to facilitate data collection and to prepare the data for entry into a computer database, we might use a numeric code by letting 1 denote the New York Stock Exchange, 2 denote the American Stock Exchange, and 3 denote over-the-counter. In this case the numeric values, 1, 2, and 3 are the labels used to identify where the stock is traded. The scale of measurement is nominal even though the data appear as numeric values.

The scale of measurement for a variable is an **ordinal scale** if the data exhibit the properties of nominal data and the order or rank of the data is meaningful. For example, Eastside Automotive sends customers a questionnaire designed to obtain data on the quality of its automotive repair service. Each customer provides a repair service rating of excellent, good, or poor. Because the data obtained are labels—excellent, good, or poor—the data have the properties of nominal data. In addition, the data can be ranked, or ordered, with respect to the service quality. Data recorded as excellent indicates the best service, followed by good and then poor. Thus, the scale of measurement is ordinal. Note that the ordinal data can also be recorded using a numeric code. For example, we could use 1 for excellent, 2 for good, and 3 for poor to maintain the properties of ordinal data. Thus, data for an ordinal scale may be either nonnumeric or numeric.

The scale of measurement for a variable is an **interval scale** if the data have the properties of ordinal data and the interval between observations is expressed in terms of a fixed unit of measure. Interval data are always numeric. Scholastic Aptitude Test (SAT) scores are an example of interval-scaled data. For example, three students with SAT scores of 1120, 1050, and 970 can be ranked or ordered in terms of best performance to poorest performance. In addition, the differences between the scores are meaningful. For instance, student 1 scored $1120 - 1050 = 70$ points more than student 2, while student 2 scored $1050 - 970 = 80$ points more than student 3.

The scale of measurement for a variable is a **ratio scale** if the data have all the properties of interval data and the ratio of two values is meaningful. Variables such as distance, height, weight, and time use the ratio scale of measurement. A requirement of this scale is that it must contain a zero value that indicates that nothing exists for the variable at the zero point. For example, consider the cost of an automobile. A zero value for the cost would indicate that the automobile has no cost and is free. In addition, if we compare the cost of $30,000 for one automobile to the cost of $15,000 for a second automobile, the ratio property shows that the first automobile is $30,000/$15,000 = 2 times, or twice, the cost of the second automobile.

Qualitative and Quantitative Data

Data can be further classified as either qualitative or quantitative. **Qualitative data** are labels or names used to identify an attribute of each element. Qualitative data use either the nominal or ordinal scale of measurement and may be nonnumeric or numeric. **Quantitative data** are numeric values that indicate how much or how many. Quantitative data use either the interval or ratio scale of measurement.

The statistical method used to summarize data depends upon whether the data are qualitative or quantitative.

A **qualitative variable** is a variable with qualitative data, and a **quantitative variable** is a variable with quantitative data. The statistical analysis appropriate for a particular variable depends upon whether the variable is qualitative or quantitative. If the variable is qualitative, the statistical analysis is rather limited. We can summarize qualitative data by counting the number of observations in each qualitative category or by computing the proportion of the observations in each qualitative category. However, even when the qualitative data have a numeric code, arithmetic operations such as addition, subtraction, multiplication, and division do not provide meaningful results. Section 2.1 provides ways for summarizing qualitative data.

On the other hand, arithmetic operations often provide meaningful results for a quantitative variable. For example, for a quantitative variable, the data may be added and then divided by the number of observations to compute the average value. This average is usually meaningful and easily interpreted. In general, more alternatives for statistical analysis are possible when the data are quantitative. Section 2.2 and Chapter 3 provide ways of summarizing quantitative data.

Cross-Sectional and Time Series Data

For purposes of statistical analysis, distinguishing between cross-sectional data and time series data is important. **Cross-sectional data** are data collected at the same or approximately the same point in time. The data in Table 1.1 are cross-sectional because they describe the five variables for the 25 shadow stocks at the same point in time. **Time series data** are data collected over several time periods. For example, Figure 1.1 is a graph of the

FIGURE 1.1   U.S. CITY AVERAGE PRICE PER GALLON FOR UNLEADED
REGULAR GASOLINE

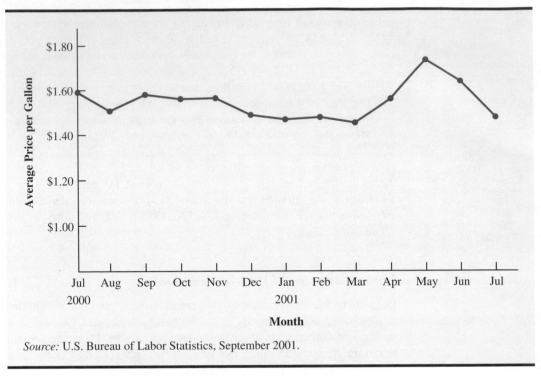

Source: U.S. Bureau of Labor Statistics, September 2001.

U.S. city average price per gallon for unleaded regular gasoline. It shows a rather stable average price per gallon in the $1.45 to $1.60 range over the one-year period with the exception of May–June 2001, when it jumped to $1.73 per gallon. However, by July 2001 it returned to approximately $1.50 per gallon. Most of the statistical methods presented in this text apply to cross-sectional rather than time series data.

NOTES AND COMMENTS

1. An observation is the set of measurements obtained for each element in a data set. Hence, the number of observations is always the same as the number of elements. The number of measurements obtained for each element is equal to the number of variables.

2. Quantitative data may be discrete or continuous. Quantitative data that measure how many are discrete. Quantitative data that measure how much are continuous because they have no separation between the possible data values.

1.3   DATA SOURCES

Data can be collected from existing sources or from surveys and experimental studies designed to obtain new data.

Existing Sources

In some cases, data needed for a particular application may already exist within a firm or organization. All companies maintain a variety of databases about their employees, customers, and business operations. Data on employee salaries, ages, and years of experience can usually be obtained from internal personnel records. Data on sales, advertising expenditures, distribution costs, inventory levels, and production quantities are generally available from other internal records. Most companies also maintain detailed data about their customers. Table 1.2 shows some of the data commonly available from internal company records.

Organizations that specialize in collecting and maintaining data make available substantial amounts of business and economic data. Companies obtain access to these external data sources through leasing arrangements or by purchase. Dun & Bradstreet, Bloomberg, and Dow Jones & Company are three firms that provide extensive business database services to clients. ACNielsen and Information Resources, Inc., built successful businesses collecting and processing data that they sell to advertisers and product manufacturers.

Data are also available from a variety of industry associations and special interest organizations. The Travel Industry Association of America maintains travel-related information such as the number of tourists and travel expenditures by states. Such data would be of interest to firms and individuals in the travel industry. The Graduate Management Admission Council maintains data on test scores, student characteristics, and graduate management education programs. Most of the data from these types of sources are available to qualified users at a modest cost.

The Internet continues to grow as an important source of data and statistical information. Almost all companies have Web sites that provide general information about the company as well as data on sales, number of employees, number of products, product prices, and product specifications. In addition, a number of companies specialize in making information available over the Internet. As a result, one can obtain access to stock quotes, meal prices at restaurants, salary data, and an almost infinite variety of information.

Government agencies are another important source of existing data. For instance, the U.S. Department of Labor maintains considerable data on employment rates, wage rates, size of the labor force, and union membership. Table 1.3 lists selected governmental agencies and some of the data they provide. Most government agencies that collect and process

TABLE 1.2   EXAMPLES OF DATA AVAILABLE FROM INTERNAL COMPANY RECORDS

Source	Some of the Data Typically Available
Employee records	Name, address, social security number, salary, number of vacation days, number of sick days, and bonus
Production records	Part or product number, quantity produced, direct labor cost, and materials cost
Inventory records	Part or product number, number of units on hand, reorder level, economic order quantity, and discount schedule
Sales records	Product number, sales volume, sales volume by region, and sales volume by customer type
Credit records	Customer name, address, phone number, credit limit, and accounts receivable balance
Customer profile	Age, gender, income level, household size, address, and preferences

TABLE 1.3   EXAMPLES OF DATA AVAILABLE FROM SELECTED GOVERNMENT
AGENCIES

Government Agency	Some of the Data Available
Census Bureau *www.census.gov*	Population data, number of households, and household income
Federal Reserve Board *www.federalreserve.gov*	Data on the money supply, installment credit, exchange rates, and discount rates
Office of Management and Budget *www.whitehouse.gov/omb*	Data on revenue, expenditures, and debt of the federal government
Department of Commerce *www.doc.gov*	Data on business activity, value of shipments by industry, level of profits by industry, and growing and declining industries
Bureau of Labor Statistics *www.bls.gov*	Consumer spending, hourly earnings, unemployment rate, safety records, and international statistics

data also make the results available through a Web site. For instance, the U.S. Census Bureau provides a wealth of data at its Web site, *www.census.gov*. Figure 1.2 shows the home page for the Census Bureau.

Statistical Studies

Sometimes the data needed for a particular application are not available through existing sources. In such cases, the data can often be obtained by conducting a statistical study. Statistical studies can be classified as either *experimental* or *observational*.

The largest experimental statistical study ever conducted is believed to be the 1954 Public Health Service experiment for the Salk polio vaccine. Nearly 2 million children in grades 1, 2, and 3 were selected from throughout the United States.

In an experimental study, a variable of interest is first identified. Then one or more other variables are identified and controlled so that data can be obtained about how they influence the variable of interest. For example, a pharmaceutical firm might be interested in conducting an experiment to learn about how a new drug affects blood pressure. Blood pressure is the variable of interest in the study. The dosage level of the new drug is another variable that is hoped to have a causal effect on blood pressure. To obtain data about the effect of the new drug, a sample of individuals is selected. The dosage level of the new drug is controlled, with different groups of individuals being given different dosage levels. Data on blood pressure are collected for each group. Statistical analysis of the experimental data can help determine how the new drug affects blood pressure.

Studies of smokers and nonsmokers are observational studies because researchers do not determine or control who will smoke and who will not smoke.

In nonexperimental, or observational, statistical studies, no attempt is made to control the variables of interest. A survey is perhaps the most common type of observational study. For instance, in a personal interview survey, research questions are first identified. Then a questionnaire is designed and administered to a sample of individuals. Some restaurants use observational studies to obtain data about their customers' opinions of the quality of food, service, atmosphere, and so on. A questionnaire used by the Lobster Pot Restaurant in Redington Shores, Florida, is shown in Figure 1.3. Note that the customers completing the questionnaire are asked to provide ratings for five variables: food quality, friendliness of service, promptness of service, cleanliness, and management. The response categories of excellent, good, satisfactory, and unsatisfactory provide data that enable Lobster Pot's managers to assess the quality of the restaurant's operation.

Managers wanting to use data and statistical analyses as an aid to decision making must be aware of the time and cost required to obtain the data. The use of existing data sources

FIGURE 1.2   U.S. CENSUS BUREAU HOMEPAGE

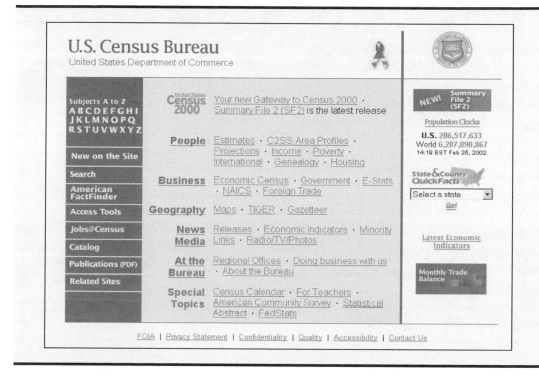

is desirable when data must be obtained in a relatively short period of time. If important data are not readily available from an existing source, the additional time and cost involved in obtaining the data must be taken into account. In all cases, the decision maker should consider the contribution of the statistical analysis to the decision-making process. The cost of data acquisition and the subsequent statistical analysis should not exceed the savings generated by using the information to make a better decision.

Data Acquisition Errors

Managers should always be aware of the possibility of data errors in statistical studies. Using erroneous data can be worse than not using any data at all. An error in data acquisition occurs whenever the data value obtained is not equal to the true or actual value that would have been obtained with a correct procedure. Such errors can occur in a number of ways. For example, an interviewer might make a recording error, such as a transposition in writing the age of a 24-year-old person as 42, or the person answering an interview question might misinterpret the question and provide an incorrect response.

Experienced data analysts take great care in collecting and recording data to ensure that errors are not made. Special procedures can be used to check for internal consistency of the data. For instance, such procedures would indicate that the analyst should review the accuracy of data for a respondent who is shown to be 22 years of age but who reports 20 years of work experience. Data analysts also review data with unusually large and small values, called outliers, which are candidates for possible data errors. In Chapter 3 we present some of the methods statisticians use to identify outliers.

FIGURE 1.3   CUSTOMER OPINION QUESTIONNAIRE USED BY THE LOBSTER POT
RESTAURANT, REDINGTON SHORES, FLORIDA (*Used with permission*)

The
LOBSTER Pot
RESTAURANT

We are happy you stopped by the Lobster Pot Restaurant and want to make sure you will come back. So, if you have a little time, we will really appreciate it if you will fill out this card. Your comments and suggestions are extremely important to us. Thank you!

Server's Name _____

	Excellent	Good	Satisfactory	Unsatisfactory
Food Quality	❑	❑	❑	❑
Friendly Service	❑	❑	❑	❑
Prompt Service	❑	❑	❑	❑
Cleanliness	❑	❑	❑	❑
Management	❑	❑	❑	❑

Comments _____

_____

What prompted your visit to us? _____

_____

Please drop in suggestion box at entrance. Thank you.

Errors often occur during data acquisition. Blindly using any data that happen to be available or using data that were acquired with little care can result in misleading information and bad decisions. Thus, taking steps to acquire accurate data can help ensure reliable and valuable decision-making information.

1.4   DESCRIPTIVE STATISTICS

Most of the statistical information in newspapers, magazines, company reports, and other publications consists of data that are summarized and presented in a form that is easy for the reader to understand. Such summaries of data, which may be tabular, graphical, or numerical, are referred to as **descriptive statistics.**

Refer again to the data set in Table 1.1 where data on 25 shadow stocks are presented. Methods of descriptive statistics can be used to provide summaries of the information in this data set. For example, a tabular summary of the data for the qualitative variable Exchange is shown in Table 1.4. A graphical summary of the same data, called a bar graph, is shown in Figure 1.4. These types of tabular and graphical summaries generally make the data easier to interpret. Referring to Table 1.4 and Figure 1.4, we can see easily that the majority of the stocks in the data set are traded over-the-counter. On a percentage basis, 56%

TABLE 1.4   FREQUENCIES AND PERCENT FREQUENCIES FOR THE EXCHANGE
VARIABLE

Exchange	Frequency	Percent Frequency
New York Stock Exchange (NYSE)	5	20
American Stock Exchange (AMEX)	6	24
Over-the-counter (OTC)	14	56
Totals	25	100

are traded over-the-counter, 24% are traded on the American Stock Exchange, and 20% are traded on the New York Stock Exchange.

A graphical summary of the data for the quantitative variable price/earnings ratio for the shadow stocks, called a histogram, is provided in Figure 1.5. From the histogram, it is easy to see that the price/earnings ratios range from 0.0 to 39.9, with the highest concentrations between 8.0 and 15.9.

In addition to tabular and graphical displays, numerical descriptive statistics are used to summarize data. The most common numerical descriptive statistic is the average, or mean. Using the data on annual sales for the shadow stocks in Table 1.1, we can compute the average annual sales by adding the annual sales for all 25 stocks and dividing the sum by 25. Doing so provides average annual sales of $125.54 million. This average is taken as a measure of the central tendency, or central location, of the data.

In recent years interest has grown in statistical methods that can be used for developing and presenting descriptive statistics. Chapters 2 and 3 are devoted to the tabular, graphical, and numerical methods of descriptive statistics.

FIGURE 1.4   BAR GRAPH FOR THE EXCHANGE VARIABLE

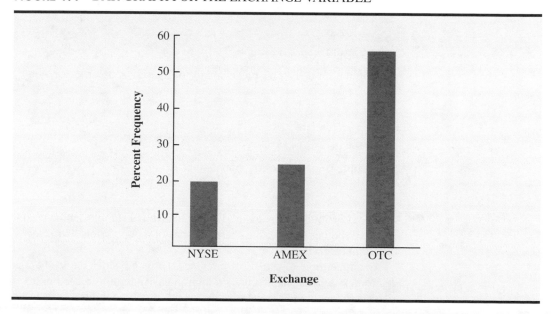

FIGURE 1.5   HISTOGRAM FOR THE PRICE/EARNINGS RATIO

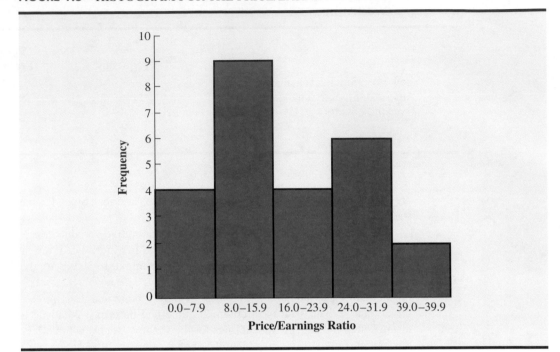

1.5   STATISTICAL INFERENCE

In many situations, data are sought for a large group of elements (individuals, companies, voters, households, products, customers, and so on). Because of time, cost, and other considerations, data are collected from only a small portion of the group. The larger group of elements in a particular study is called the **population,** and the smaller group is called the **sample.** Formally, we use the following definitions.

Population

A population is the set of all elements of interest in a particular study.

Sample

A sample is a subset of the population.

A major contribution of statistics is that data from a sample can be used to make estimates and test hypotheses about the characteristics of a population. This process is referred to as **statistical inference.**

As an example of statistical inference, let us consider the study conducted by Norris Electronics. Norris manufactures a high-intensity lightbulb used in a variety of electrical products. In an attempt to increase the useful life of the lightbulb, the product design group

TABLE 1.5   HOURS UNTIL BURNOUT FOR A SAMPLE OF 200 LIGHTBULBS FOR THE
NORRIS ELECTRONICS EXAMPLE

CDfile
Norris

107	73	68	97	76	79	94	59	98	57
54	65	71	70	84	88	62	61	79	98
66	62	79	86	68	74	61	82	65	98
62	116	65	88	64	79	78	79	77	86
74	85	73	80	68	78	89	72	58	69
92	78	88	77	103	88	63	68	88	81
75	90	62	89	71	71	74	70	74	70
65	81	75	62	94	71	85	84	83	63
81	62	79	83	93	61	65	62	92	65
83	70	70	81	77	72	84	67	59	58
78	66	66	94	77	63	66	75	68	76
90	78	71	101	78	43	59	67	61	71
96	75	64	76	72	77	74	65	82	86
66	86	96	89	81	71	85	99	59	92
68	72	77	60	87	84	75	77	51	45
85	67	87	80	84	93	69	76	89	75
83	68	72	67	92	89	82	96	77	102
74	91	76	83	66	68	61	73	72	76
73	77	79	94	63	59	62	71	81	65
73	63	63	89	82	64	85	92	64	73

has developed a new lightbulb filament. In this case, the population is defined as all lightbulbs that could be produced with the new filament. To evaluate the advantages of the new
filament, 200 bulbs with the new filament were manufactured and tested. Data were collected on the number of hours each lightbulb operated before filament burnout. The data
from this sample are reported in Table 1.5.

Suppose Norris is interested in using the sample data to make an inference about the
average hours of useful life for the population of all lightbulbs that could be produced with
the new filament. Adding the 200 values in Table 1.5 and dividing the total by 200 provides
the sample average lifetime for the lightbulbs: 76 hours. We can use this sample result to
estimate that the average lifetime for the lightbulbs in the population is 76 hours. Figure 1.6
is a graphical summary of the statistical inference process for Norris Electronics.

Whenever statisticians use a sample to estimate population characteristics of interest,
they usually provide a statement of the quality, or precision, associated with the estimate.
For the Norris example, the statistician might state that the estimate of the average lifetime
for the population of new lightbulbs is 76 hours with a margin of error of ± 4 hours. Thus,
an interval estimate of the average lifetime for all lightbulbs produced with the new filament is 72 hours to 80 hours. The statistician can also state how confident he or she is that
the interval from 72 hours to 80 hours contains the population average.

SUMMARY

Statistics is the art and science of collecting, analyzing, presenting, and interpreting data.
Nearly every college student majoring in business or economics is required to take a course
in statistics. We began the chapter by describing typical statistical applications for business
and economics.

FIGURE 1.6   THE PROCESS OF STATISTICAL INFERENCE FOR THE NORRIS
ELECTRONICS EXAMPLE

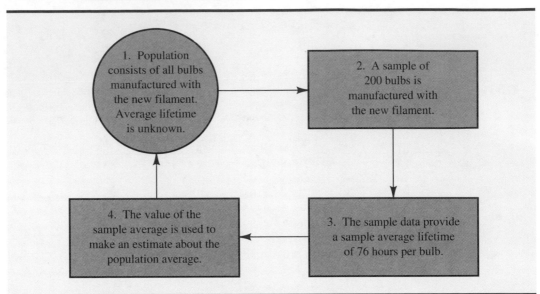

Data are the facts and figures that are collected, analyzed, presented, and interpreted. Four scales of measurement are available for obtaining data on a particular variable: nominal, ordinal, interval, and ratio. The scale of measurement for a variable is nominal when the data are labels or names used to identify an attribute of an element. The scale is ordinal if the data have the properties of nominal data and the order or rank of the data is meaningful. The scale is interval if the data have the properties of ordinal data and the interval between observations is expressed in terms of a fixed unit of measure. Finally, the scale of measurement is ratio if the data have all the properties of interval data and the ratio of two values is meaningful.

For purposes of statistical analysis, data can be classified as qualitative or quantitative. Qualitative data are labels or names used to identify an attribute of each element. Qualitative data use either the nominal or ordinal scale of measurement and may be nonnumeric or numeric. Quantitative data are numeric values that indicate how much or how many. Quantitative data use either the interval or ratio scale of measurement. Ordinary arithmetic operations are meaningful only if the data are quantitative. Therefore, statistical computations used for quantitative data are not always appropriate for qualitative data.

In Sections 1.4 and 1.5 we introduced the topics of descriptive statistics and statistical inference. Descriptive statistics are the tabular, graphical, and numerical methods used to summarize data. Statistical inference is the process of using data obtained from a sample to make estimates or test hypotheses about the characteristics of a population.

GLOSSARY

Statistics   The art and science of collecting, analyzing, presenting, and interpreting data.

Data   The facts and figures collected, analyzed, and interpreted.

Data set   All the data collected in a particular study.

Elements   The entities on which data are collected.

Variable   A characteristic of interest for the elements.

Observation   The set of measurements obtained for a single element.

Nominal scale   A scale of measurement for a variable that uses a label or name to identify an attribute of an element. Nominal data may be nonnumeric or numeric.

Ordinal scale   A scale of measurement for a variable that has the properties of nominal data and can be used to rank or order the data. Ordinal data may be nonnumeric or numeric.

Interval scale   A scale of measurement for a variable that has the properties of ordinal data and the interval between observations is expressed in terms of a fixed unit of measure. Interval data are always numeric.

Ratio scale   A scale of measurement for a variable that has all the properties of interval data and the ratio of two values is meaningful. Ratio data are always numeric.

Qualitative data   Data that are labels or names used to identify an attribute of each element. Qualitative data use the nominal or ordinal scale of measurement and may be nonnumeric or numeric.

Quantitative data   Data that indicate how much or how many of something. Quantitative data use the interval or ratio scale of measurement and are always numeric.

Qualitative variable   A variable with qualitative data.

Quantitative variable   A variable with quantitative data.

Cross-sectional data   Data collected at the same or approximately the same point in time.

Time series data   Data collected at several successive periods of time.

Descriptive statistics   Tabular, graphical, and numerical summaries of data.

Population   The set of all elements of interest in a particular study.

Sample   A subset of the population.

Statistical inference   The process of using data obtained from a sample to make estimates or test hypotheses about the characteristics of a population.

EXERCISES

1. Discuss the differences between statistics as numerical facts and statistics as a discipline or field of study.

SELFtest

2. *Condé Nast Traveler* conducts an annual poll of subscribers in order to determine the best places to stay throughout the world. Table 1.6 is a sample of nine European hotels from one of their polls. The price of a standard double room during the hotel's high season ranges from $ (lowest price) to $$$$ (highest price). The overall score includes subscribers' evaluations of each hotel's rooms, service, restaurants, location/atmosphere, and public areas; a higher overall score corresponds to a higher level of satisfaction.
    a. How many elements are in this data set?
    b. How many variables are in this data set?
    c. Which variables are qualitative and which variables are quantitative?
    d. What type of measurement scale is being used for each of the variables?

SELFtest

3. Refer to Table 1.6.
    a. What is the average number of rooms for the nine hotels?
    b. Compute the average overall score.
    c. What is the percentage of hotels located in England?
    d. What is the percentage of hotels with a room rate of $$?

TABLE 1.6   RATINGS FOR PLACES TO STAY IN EUROPE

CDfile

Hotel

Name of Property	Country	Room Rate	Number of Rooms	Overall Score
Graveteye Manor	England	$$	18	83.6
Villa d'Este	Italy	$$$$	166	86.3
Hotel Prem	Germany	$	54	77.8
Hotel d'Europe	France	$$	47	76.8
Palace Luzern	Switzerland	$$	326	80.9
Royal Crescent Hotel	England	$$$	45	73.7
Hotel Sacher	Austria	$$$	120	85.5
Duc de Bourgogne	Belgium	$	10	76.9
Villa Gallici	France	$$	22	90.6

Source: Condé Nast Traveler, January 2000.

SELFtest

4. *Fortune* magazine provides data on how the 500 largest U.S. industrial corporations rank in terms of revenues and profits. Data for a sample of *Fortune* 500 companies are given in Table 1.7.
   a. How many elements are in this data set?
   b. What is the population?
   c. Compute the average revenue for the sample.
   d. Using the results in part (c), what is the estimate of the average revenues for the population?

5. Consider the data set for the sample of *Fortune* 500 companies in Table 1.7.
   a. How many variables are in the data set?
   b. Which of the variables are qualitative and which are quantitative?
   c. Compute the average profit for the sample.
   d. What percentage of the companies earned a profit over $100 million?
   e. What percentage of the companies have an industry code of 3?

TABLE 1.7   A SAMPLE OF 10 *FORTUNE* 500 COMPANIES

CDfile

Fortune

Company	Revenue ($ millions)	Profit ($ millions)	Industry Code
US Airways Group	8688.0	538.0	3
International Paper	19500.0	213.0	23
Tyson Foods	7414.1	25.1	20
Hewlett-Packard	47061.0	2945.0	13
Intel	26273.0	6068.0	49
Northrup Grumman	8902.0	214.0	2
Seagate Technology	6819.0	−530.0	11
Unisys	7208.4	387.0	10
Westvaco	2904.7	132.0	23
Campbell Soup	7505.0	660.0	20

Source: Fortune, April 26, 1999.

6. Columbia House provides CDs and tapes to its mail-order club members. A Columbia House Music Survey asked new club members to complete an 11-question survey. Some of the questions asked were:
   a. How many CDs and tapes have you bought in the last 12 months?
   b. Are you currently a member of a national mail-order book club? (Yes or No)
   c. What is your age?
   d. Including yourself, how many people (adults and children) are in your household?
   e. What kind of music are you interested in buying? (15 categories were listed, including hard rock, soft rock, adult contemporary, heavy metal, rap, and country)
   Comment on whether each question provides qualitative or quantitative data.

7. A *Barron's* subscriber survey (September 15, 2000) asked subscribers to indicate their employment status. The data were recorded with 1 denoting employed full-time, 2 denoting employed part-time, 3 denoting retired, and 4 denoting unemployed (homemaker, student, etc.).
   a. The variable is employment status. Is it a qualitative or quantitative variable?
   b. What type of measurement scale is being used for this variable?

8. A *Wall Street Journal*/NBC News poll asked 2013 adults, "How satisfied are you with the state of the U.S. economy today?" (*The Wall Street Journal,* December 12, 1997). Response categories were Dissatisfied, Satisfied, and Not Sure.
   a. What was the sample size for this survey?
   b. Are the data qualitative or quantitative?
   c. Would it make more sense to use averages or percentages as a summary of the data for this question?
   d. Of the respondents, 28% said that they were dissatisfied with the state of the U.S. economy. How many individuals provided this response?

9. The Commerce Department reported receiving the following applications for the Malcolm Baldrige National Quality Award: 23 from large manufacturing firms, 18 from large service firms, and 30 from small businesses.
   a. Is type of business a qualitative or quantitative variable?
   b. What percentage of the applications came from small businesses?

10. State whether each of the following variables is qualitative or quantitative and indicate the measurement scale that is appropriate for each.
   a. Age
   b. Gender
   c. Class rank
   d. Make of automobile
   e. Number of people favoring the death penalty

11. State whether each of the following variables is qualitative or quantitative and indicate the measurement scale being used.
   a. Annual sales
   b. Soft drink size (small, medium, large)
   c. Employee classification (GS1 through GS18)
   d. Earnings per share
   e. Method of payment (cash, check, credit card)

12. The Hawaii Visitors Bureau collects data on visitors to Hawaii. The following questions were among 16 asked in a questionnaire handed out to passengers during incoming airline flights in June 2001.
   • This trip to Hawaii is my: 1st, 2nd, 3rd, 4th, etc.
   • The primary reason for this trip is: (10 categories including vacation, convention, honeymoon)

- Where I plan to stay: (11 categories including hotel, apartment, relatives, camping)
- Total days in Hawaii
a. What is the population being studied?
b. Is the use of a questionnaire a good way to reach the population of passengers on incoming airline flights?
c. Comment on each of the four questions in terms of whether it will provide qualitative or quantitative data.

SELFtest

13. Figure 1.7 provides a bar graph summarizing the actual and projected earnings for Volkswagen for the years 1997 to 2002 (*Business Week,* July 23, 2001).
a. Are the data qualitative or quantitative?
b. Are the data times series or cross-sectional?
c. What is the variable of interest?
d. Comment on the trend in Volkswagen's earnings over time. Would you expect to see an increase or decrease in 2003?

14. The following data set provides a snapshot of the financial performance of Ameritech Corporation (*Barron's,* December 29, 1997).

	1993	1994	1995	1996
Earnings per Share	$2.78	$2.13	$3.41	$3.83
Revenues (billions)	$11.87	$12.57	$13.43	$14.92
Net Income (billions)	$1.51	$1.17	$1.89	$2.12
Book Value per Share	$14.35	$10.98	$12.67	$13.98

a. How many variables are there?
b. Are the data qualitative or quantitative?
c. Are they cross-sectional or time series data? Why?

15. Refer again to the data in Table 1.7 for *Fortune* 500 companies (April 26, 1999). Are they cross-sectional or time series data? Why?

FIGURE 1.7   EARNINGS FOR VOLKSWAGEN

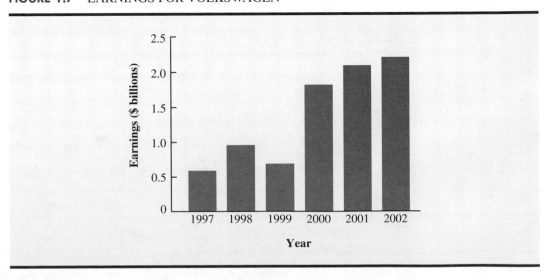

16. The marketing group at your company has come up with a new diet soft drink that it claims will capture a large share of the young adult market.

    a. What data would you want to see before deciding to invest substantial funds in introducing the new product into the marketplace?

    b. How would you expect the data mentioned in part (a) to be obtained?

17. A manager of a large corporation recommends a $10,000 raise be given to keep a valued subordinate from moving to another company. What internal and external sources of data might be used to decide whether such a salary increase is appropriate?

18. In a recent study of causes of death in men 60 years of age and older, a sample of 120 men indicated that 48 died as a result of some form of heart disease.

    a. Develop a descriptive statistic that can be used as an estimate of the percentage of men 60 years of age or older who die from some form of heart disease.

    b. Are the data on cause of death qualitative or quantitative?

    c. Discuss the role of statistical inference in this type of medical research.

19. A *Business Week* North American subscriber study collected data from a sample of 2861 subscribers. Fifty-nine percent of the respondents indicated that their annual income was $75,000 or more and 50% reported having an American Express credit card.

    a. What is the population of interest in this study?

    b. Is annual income a qualitative or quantitative variable?

    c. Is ownership of an American Express card a qualitative or quantitative variable?

    d. Does this study involve cross-sectional or time series data?

    e. Describe any statistical inferences *Business Week* might make on the basis of the survey.

20. A Scanner Data User Survey of 50 companies provided the following findings (Mercer Management Consulting, Inc., April 24, 1997):

    • ACNielsen earned 56% of the dollar-share of the market.

    • The average amount spent on scanner data per category of consumer goods was $387,325.

    • On a scale of 1 (very dissatisfied) to 5 (very satisfied), the average level of overall satisfaction with scanner data was 3.73.

    a. Cite two descriptive statistics.

    b. Make an inference of the overall satisfaction in the population of all users of scanner data.

    c. Make an inference about the average amount spent per category for scanner data for consumer goods.

21. A seven-year medical research study reported that women whose mothers took the drug DES during pregnancy were *twice* as likely to develop tissue abnormalities that might lead to cancer as were women whose mothers did not take the drug.

    a. This study involved the comparison of two populations. What were the populations?

    b. Do you suppose the data were obtained in a survey or an experiment?

    c. For the population of women whose mothers took the drug DES during pregnancy, a sample of 3980 women showed 63 developed tissue abnormalities that might lead to cancer. Provide a descriptive statistic that could be used to estimate the number of women out of 1000 in this population who have tissue abnormalities.

    d. For the population of women whose mothers did not take the drug DES during pregnancy, what is the estimate of the number of women out of 1000 who would be expected to have tissue abnormalities?

    e. Medical studies often use a relatively large sample (in this case, 3980). Why?

22. A firm is interested in testing the advertising effectiveness of a new television commercial. As part of the test, the commercial is shown on a 6:30 P.M. local news program in Denver, Colorado. Two days later, a market research firm conducts a telephone survey to obtain information on recall rates (percentage of viewers who recall seeing the commercial) and impressions of the commercial.

a.   What is the population for this study?

b.   What is the sample for this study?

c.   Why would a sample be used in this situation? Explain.

23.   The ACNielsen organization conducts weekly surveys of television viewing throughout the United States. The ACNielsen statistical ratings indicate the size of the viewing audience for each major network television program. Rankings of the television programs and of the viewing audience market shares for each network are published each week.

a.   What is the ACNielsen organization attempting to measure?

b.   What is the population?

c.   Why would a sample be used for this situation?

d.   What kinds of decisions or actions are based on the ACNielsen studies?

24.   A sample of midterm grades for five students showed the following results: 72, 65, 82, 90, 76. Which of the following statements are correct, and which should be challenged as being too generalized?

a.   The average midterm grade for the sample of five students is 77.

b.   The average midterm grade for all students who took the exam is 77.

c.   An estimate of the average midterm grade for all students who took the exam is 77.

d.   More than half of the students who take this exam will score between 70 and 85.

e.   If five other students are included in the sample, their grades will be between 65 and 90.

DESCRIPTIVE STATISTICS: TABULAR AND GRAPHICAL METHODS

Chapter 2

CONTENTS

COLGATE-PALMOLIVE COMPANY*

NEW YORK, NEW YORK

The Colgate-Palmolive Company started as a small soap and candle shop in New York City in 1806. Today, Colgate-Palmolive is a $9 billion company whose products can be found in more than 200 countries and territories around the world. While best known for its brand names of Colgate, Palmolive, Ajax, and Fab, the company also markets Mennen, Hill's Science Diet, and Hill's Prescription Diet products.

The Colgate-Palmolive Company uses statistics in its quality assurance program for home laundry detergent products. One concern is customer satisfaction with the quantity of detergent in a carton. Every carton in each size category is filled with the same amount of detergent by weight, but the volume of detergent is affected by the density of the detergent powder. For instance, if the powder density is on the heavy side, a smaller volume of detergent is needed to reach the carton's specified weight. As a result, the carton may appear to be underfilled when opened by the consumer.

To control the problem of heavy detergent powder, limits are placed on the acceptable range of powder density. Statistical samples are taken periodically, and the density of each powder sample is measured. Data summaries are then provided for operating personnel so that corrective action can be taken if necessary to keep the density within the desired quality specifications.

A histogram for the densities of 150 samples taken over a one-week period and a frequency distribution are shown in the accompanying figure and table. Density levels above .40 are unacceptably high. The histogram and frequency distribution show that the operation is

Statistical summaries help maintain the quality of these Colgate-Palmolive products. © Joe Higgins/South-Western.

Histogram of Density Data

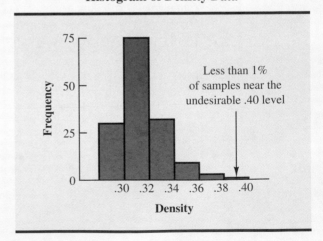

Less than 1% of samples near the undesirable .40 level

---

*The authors are indebted to William R. Fowle, Manager of Quality Assurance, Colgate-Palmolive Company, for providing this Statistics in Practice.

meeting its quality guidelines with all of the densities less than or equal to .40. Managers viewing these statistical summaries would be pleased with the quality of the detergent production process.

In this chapter, you will learn about tabular and graphical methods of descriptive statistics such as frequency distributions, bar graphs, histograms, stem-and-leaf displays, crosstabulations, and others. The goal of these methods is to summarize data so that they can be easily understood and interpreted.

Frequency Distribution of Density Data

Density	Frequency
.29–.30	30
.31–.32	75
.33–.34	32
.35–.36	9
.37–.38	3
.39–.40	1
Total	150

As indicated in Chapter 1, data can be classified as either qualitative or quantitative. **Qualitative data** are labels or names used to identify categories of like items. **Quantitative data** are numerical values that indicate how much or how many.

The purpose of this chapter is to introduce tabular and graphical methods commonly used to summarize both qualitative and quantitative data. Tabular and graphical summaries of data can be found in annual reports, newspaper articles, and research studies. Everyone is exposed to these types of presentations. Hence, it is important to understand how they are prepared and how they should be interpreted. We begin with tabular and graphical methods for summarizing data concerning a single variable. The last section introduces methods for summarizing data when the relationship between two variables is of interest.

Modern statistical software packages provide extensive capabilities for summarizing data and preparing graphical presentations. Minitab and Microsoft Excel are two packages that are widely available. In the chapter appendixes, we show some of their capabilities.

2.1   SUMMARIZING QUALITATIVE DATA

Frequency Distribution

We begin the discussion of how tabular and graphical methods can be used to summarize qualitative data with the definition of a **frequency distribution.**

Frequency Distribution

A frequency distribution is a tabular summary of data showing the number (frequency) of items in each of several nonoverlapping classes.

Let us use the following example to demonstrate the construction and interpretation of a frequency distribution for qualitative data. According to *Beverage Digest,* Coke Classic, Diet Coke, Dr. Pepper, Pepsi-Cola, and Sprite are the five top-selling soft drinks (*The Wall Street Journal Almanac,* 1998). Assume that the data in Table 2.1 show the soft drink selected for a sample of 50 soft drink purchases.

To develop a frequency distribution for these data, we count the number of times each soft drink appears in Table 2.1. Coke Classic appears 19 times, Diet Coke appears 8 times,

TABLE 2.1   DATA FROM A SAMPLE OF 50 SOFT DRINK PURCHASES

CDfile
SoftDrink

Coke Classic	Sprite	Pepsi-Cola
Diet Coke	Coke Classic	Coke Classic
Pepsi-Cola	Diet Coke	Coke Classic
Diet Coke	Coke Classic	Coke Classic
Coke Classic	Diet Coke	Pepsi-Cola
Coke Classic	Coke Classic	Dr. Pepper
Dr. Pepper	Sprite	Coke Classic
Diet Coke	Pepsi-Cola	Diet Coke
Pepsi-Cola	Coke Classic	Pepsi-Cola
Pepsi-Cola	Coke Classic	Pepsi-Cola
Coke Classic	Coke Classic	Pepsi-Cola
Dr. Pepper	Pepsi-Cola	Pepsi-Cola
Sprite	Coke Classic	Coke Classic
Coke Classic	Sprite	Dr. Pepper
Diet Coke	Dr. Pepper	Pepsi-Cola
Coke Classic	Pepsi-Cola	Sprite
Coke Classic	Diet Coke	

Dr. Pepper appears 5 times, Pepsi-Cola appears 13 times, and Sprite appears 5 times. These counts are summarized in the frequency distribution in Table 2.2.

This frequency distribution provides a summary of how the 50 soft drink purchases are distributed across the five soft drinks. This summary provides more insight than the original data shown in Table 2.1. Viewing the frequency distribution, we see that Coke Classic is the leader, Pepsi-Cola is second, Diet Coke is third, and Sprite and Dr. Pepper are tied for fourth. The frequency distribution has provided information about the relative popularity of the five best-selling soft drinks.

TABLE 2.2

FREQUENCY
DISTRIBUTION OF
SOFT DRINK
PURCHASES

Soft Drink	Frequency
Coke Classic	19
Diet Coke	8
Dr. Pepper	5
Pepsi-Cola	13
Sprite	5
Total	50

Relative Frequency and Percent Frequency Distributions

A frequency distribution shows the number (frequency) of items in each of several nonoverlapping classes. However, we are often interested in the proportion, or percentage, of items in each class. The relative frequency of a class is the fraction or proportion of items belonging to a class. For a data set with n observations, the relative frequency of each class is as follows:

Relative Frequency

$$\text{Relative Frequency of a Class} = \frac{\text{Frequency of the Class}}{n} \tag{2.1}$$

The *percent frequency* of a class is the relative frequency multiplied by 100.

A **relative frequency distribution** is a tabular summary of data showing the relative frequency for each class. A **percent frequency distribution** is a tabular summary of data showing the percent frequency for each class. Table 2.3 shows a relative frequency distribution and a percent frequency distribution for the soft drink data. In Table 2.3 we see that the relative frequency for Coke Classic is 19/50 = .38, the relative frequency for Diet Coke

TABLE 2.3   RELATIVE AND PERCENT FREQUENCY DISTRIBUTIONS OF SOFT DRINK
PURCHASES

Soft Drink	Relative Frequency	Percent Frequency
Coke Classic	.38	38
Diet Coke	.16	16
Dr. Pepper	.10	10
Pepsi-Cola	.26	26
Sprite	.10	10
Total	1.00	100

In quality control applications, bar graphs are used to identify the most important causes of problems. When the bars are arranged in descending order of height from left to right with the most frequently occurring cause appearing first, the bar graph is called a pareto diagram. This diagram is named for its founder, Vilfredo Pareto, an Italian economist.

is 8/50 = .16, and so on. From the percent frequency distribution, we see that 38% of the purchases were Coke Classic, 16% of the purchases were Diet Coke, and so on. We can also note that 38% + 26% + 16% = 80% of the purchases were of the top three soft drinks.

Bar Graphs and Pie Charts

A **bar graph** is a graphical device for depicting data that have been summarized in a frequency, relative frequency, or percent frequency distribution. On one axis of the graph (usually the horizontal axis), we specify the labels that are used for the classes (categories) of data. A frequency, relative frequency, or percent frequency scale can be used for the other axis of the graph (usually the vertical axis). Then, using a bar of fixed width drawn above each class label, we extend the length of the bar until we reach the frequency, relative frequency, or percent frequency of the class. For qualitative data, the bars should be separated to emphasize the fact that each class (category) is separate. Figure 2.1 is a bar graph of the frequency distribution for the 50 soft drink purchases. Note how the graphical presentation shows Coke Classic, Pepsi-Cola, and Diet Coke to be the preferred brands.

FIGURE 2.1   BAR GRAPH OF SOFT DRINK PURCHASES

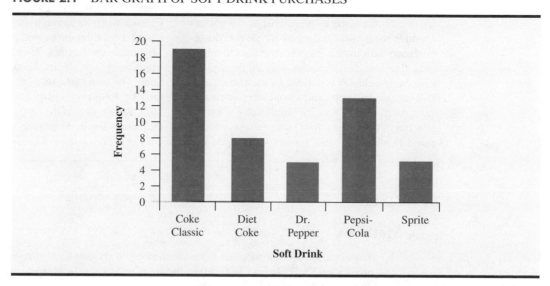

The **pie chart** is another graphical device for presenting relative frequency and percent frequency distributions. To construct a pie chart, we first draw a circle to represent all of the data. Then we use the relative frequencies to subdivide the circle into sectors, or parts, that correspond to the relative frequency for each class. For example, because a circle has 360 degrees and Coke Classic has a relative frequency of .38, the sector of the pie chart labeled Coke Classic consists of .38(360) = 136.8 degrees. The sector of the pie chart labeled Diet Coke consists of .16(360) = 57.6 degrees. Similar calculations for the other classes yield the pie chart in Figure 2.2. The numerical values shown for each sector can be frequencies, relative frequencies, or percent frequencies.

FIGURE 2.2   PIE CHART OF SOFT DRINK PURCHASES

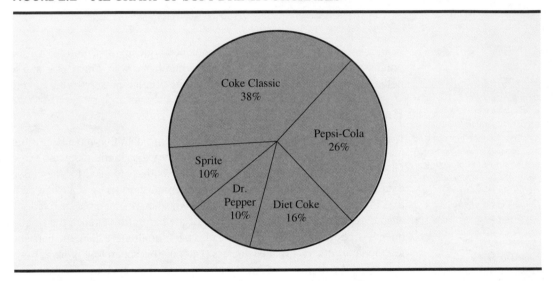

NOTES AND COMMENTS

1. Often the number of classes in a frequency distribution is the same as the number of categories found in the data, as is the case for the soft drink purchase data in this section. The data involve only five soft drinks, and a separate frequency distribution class was defined for each one. Data that included all soft drinks would require many categories, most of which would have a small number of purchases. Most statisticians recommend that classes with smaller frequencies be grouped into an aggregate class called "other." Classes with frequencies of 5 percent or less would most often be treated in this fashion.

2. The sum of the frequencies in any frequency distribution always equals the number of observations. The sum of the relative frequencies in any relative frequency distribution always equals 1.00, and the sum of the percentages in a percent frequency distribution always equals 100.

EXERCISES

Methods

1. The response to a question has three alternatives: A, B, and C. A sample of 120 responses provides 60 A, 24 B, and 36 C. Show the frequency and relative frequency distributions.

2. A partial relative frequency distribution is given.

Class	Relative Frequency
A	.22
B	.18
C	.40
D	

a. What is the relative frequency of class D?
b. The total sample size is 200. What is the frequency of class D?
c. Show the frequency distribution.
d. Show the percent frequency distribution.

SELFtest   3. A questionnaire provides 58 yes, 42 no, and 20 no-opinion answers.
a. In the construction of a pie chart, how many degrees would be in the section of the pie showing the yes answers?
b. How many degrees would be in the section of the pie showing the no answers?
c. Construct a pie chart.
d. Construct a bar graph.

Applications

4. According to Nielsen Media Research, the top four TV shows at 8:00 P.M., April 6, 2000, were Millionaire, Frasier, Chicago Hope, and Charmed (*USA Today,* April 13, 2000). Data for a sample of 50 viewers follow.

CDfile
Nielsen

Millionaire	Millionaire	Millionaire	Frasier	Charmed
Frasier	Frasier	Millionaire	Millionaire	Frasier
Frasier	Millionaire	Millionaire	Chicago Hope	Millionaire
Charmed	Millionaire	Frasier	Chicago Hope	Millionaire
Chicago Hope	Charmed	Frasier	Frasier	Millionaire
Millionaire	Frasier	Millionaire	Millionaire	Chicago Hope
Frasier	Millionaire	Millionaire	Charmed	Chicago Hope
Chicago Hope	Millionaire	Millionaire	Millionaire	Millionaire
Frasier	Frasier	Millionaire	Frasier	Frasier
Millionaire	Millionaire	Chicago Hope	Millionaire	Frasier

a. Are these qualitative or quantitative data?
b. Provide frequency and percent frequency distributions.
c. Construct a bar graph and a pie chart.
d. On the basis of the sample, which show has the largest market share? Which one is second?

5. In alphabetical order, the six most common last names in the United States are Brown, Davis, Johnson, Jones, Smith, and Williams (*Time Almanac 2001*). Assume that a sample of 50 individuals with one of these last names provided the following data.

CDfile
Names

Brown	Williams	Williams	Williams	Brown
Smith	Jones	Smith	Johnson	Smith
Davis	Smith	Brown	Williams	Johnson
Johnson	Smith	Smith	Johnson	Brown
Williams	Davis	Johnson	Williams	Johnson
Williams	Johnson	Jones	Smith	Brown

Johnson	Smith	Smith	Brown	Jones
Jones	Jones	Smith	Smith	Davis
Davis	Jones	Williams	Davis	Smith
Jones	Johnson	Brown	Johnson	Davis

Summarize the data by constructing the following:

a. Relative and percent frequency distributions
b. A bar graph
c. A pie chart
d. Based on these data, what are the three most common last names?

6. The eight best-selling paperback business books in February 2000 are listed in Table 2.4 (*Business Week,* April 3, 2000). Suppose a sample of book purchases in the Denver, Colorado, area provided the following data for these eight books.

7 Habits	Dad	7 Habits	Millionaire	Millionaire	WSJ Guide
Motley	Millionaire	Tax Guide	7 Habits	Dad	Dummies
Millionaire	Motley	Dad	Dad	Parachute	Dad
Dad	7 Habits	WSJ Guide	WSJ Guide	WSJ Guide	7 Habits
Motley	WSJ Guide	Millionaire	7 Habits	Millionaire	Millionaire
Millionaire	7 Habits	Millionaire	7 Habits	Motley	Motley
Motley	7 Habits	Dad	Dad	Dad	Dad
7 Habits	WSJ Guide	Tax Guide	Millionaire	Motley	Tax Guide
Motley	Motley	Millionaire	Millionaire	Dad	Dummies
Millionaire	Millionaire	Millionaire	Dad	Millionaire	Dad

TABLE 2.4

THE EIGHT
BEST-SELLING
PAPERBACK
BUSINESS BOOKS

- *The 7 Habits of Highly Effective People*
- *Investing for Dummies*
- *The Ernst & Young Tax Guide 2000*
- *The Millionaire Next Door*
- *The Motley Fool Investment Guide*
- *Rich Dad, Poor Dad*
- *The Wall Street Journal Guide to Understanding Money and Investing*
- *What Color Is Your Parachute? 2000*

CDfile
BwBooks

SELFtest

a. Construct frequency and percent frequency distributions for the data. Group any books with a frequency of 5% or less in an "other" category.
b. Rank the best-selling books.
c. What percentage of the sales are represented by *The Millionaire Next Door* and *Rich Dad, Poor Dad?*

7. Leverock's Waterfront Steakhouse in Maderia Beach, Florida, uses a questionnaire to ask customers how they rate the server, food quality, cocktails, prices, and atmosphere at the restaurant. Each characteristic is rated on a scale of outstanding (O), very good (V), good (G), average (A), and poor (P). Use descriptive statistics to summarize the following data collected on food quality. What is your feeling about the food quality ratings at the restaurant?

G	O	V	G	A	O	V	O	V	G	O	V	A
V	O	P	V	O	G	A	O	O	O	G	O	V
V	A	G	O	V	P	V	O	O	G	O	O	V
O	G	A	O	V	O	O	G	V	A	G

8. Data for a sample of 55 members of the Baseball Hall of Fame in Cooperstown, New York, are shown here. Each observation indicates the primary position played by the Hall of Famers: pitcher (P), catcher (H), 1st base (1), 2nd base (2), 3rd base (3), shortstop (S), left field (L), center field (C), and right field (R).

L	P	C	H	2	P	R	1	S	S	1	L	P	R	P
P	P	P	R	C	S	L	R	P	C	C	P	P	R	P
2	3	P	H	L	P	1	C	P	P	P	S	1	L	R
R	1	2	H	S	3	H	2	L	P

a. Use frequency and relative frequency distributions to summarize the data.
b. What position provides the most Hall of Famers?
c. What position provides the fewest Hall of Famers?

d. What outfield position (L, C, or R) provides the most Hall of Famers?

e. Compare infielders (1, 2, 3, and S) to outfielders (L, C, and R).

9. Employees at Electronics Associates are on a flextime system; they can begin their working day at 7:00, 7:30, 8:00, 8:30, or 9:00 A.M. The following data represent a sample of the starting times selected by the employees.

| 7:00 | 8:30 | 9:00 | 8:00 | 7:30 | 7:30 | 8:30 | 8:30 | 7:30 | 7:00 |
| 8:30 | 8:30 | 8:00 | 8:00 | 7:30 | 8:30 | 7:00 | 9:00 | 8:30 | 8:00 |

Summarize the data by constructing the following:

a. A frequency distribution

b. A percent frequency distribution

c. A bar graph

d. A pie chart

e. What do the summaries tell you about employee preferences in the flextime system?

10. A 2001 Merrill Lynch Client Satisfaction Survey asked clients to indicate how satisfied they were with their financial consultant. Client responses were coded 1 to 7, with 1 indicating "not at all satisfied" and 7 indicating "extremely satisfied." Assume that the following data are from a sample of 60 responses for a particular financial consultant.

Client

5	7	6	6	7	5	5	7	3	6
7	7	6	6	6	5	5	6	7	7
6	6	4	4	7	6	7	6	7	6
5	7	5	7	6	4	7	5	7	6
6	5	3	7	7	6	6	6	6	5
5	6	6	7	7	5	6	4	6	6

a. Comment on why these are qualitative data.

b. Provide a frequency distribution and a relative frequency distribution for the data.

c. Provide a bar graph.

d. On the basis of your summaries, comment on the clients' overall evaluation of the financial consultant.

2.2   SUMMARIZING QUANTITATIVE DATA

Frequency Distribution

As defined in Section 2.1, a frequency distribution is a tabular summary showing the number (frequency) of items in each of several nonoverlapping classes. This definition holds for quantitative as well as qualitative data. However, with quantitative data we have to be more careful in defining the nonoverlapping classes to be used in the frequency distribution.

For example, consider the quantitative data in Table 2.5. These data provide the time in days required to complete year-end audits for a sample of 20 clients of Sanderson and Clifford, a small public accounting firm. The three steps necessary to define the classes for a frequency distribution with quantitative data are as follow:

1. Determine the number of nonoverlapping classes.

2. Determine the width of each class.

3. Determine the class limits.

Let us demonstrate these steps by developing a frequency distribution for the audit-time data in Table 2.5.

TABLE 2.5

YEAR-END AUDIT
TIMES (IN DAYS)

12	14	19	18
15	15	18	17
20	27	22	23
22	21	33	28
14	18	16	13

Audit

Number of Classes.   Classes are formed by specifying ranges that will be used to group the data. As a general guideline, we recommend using between 5 and 20 classes. For a small number of data items, as few as five or six classes may be used to summarize the data. For a larger number of data items, a larger number of classes is usually required. The goal is to use enough classes to show the variation in the data, but not so many classes that some contain only a few data items. Because the number of data items in Table 2.5 is relatively small ($n = 20$), we chose to develop a frequency distribution with five classes.

Width of the Classes.   The second step in constructing a frequency distribution for quantitative data is to choose a width for the classes. As a general guideline, we recommend that the width be the same for each class. Thus the choices of the number of classes and the width of classes are not independent decisions. A larger number of classes means a smaller class width, and vice versa. To determine an approximate class width, we begin by identifying the largest and smallest data values. Then, once the desired number of classes has been specified, we can use the following expression to determine the approximate class width.

Making the classes the same width reduces the chance of inappropriate interpretations by the user.

$$\text{Approximate Class Width} = \frac{\text{Largest Data Value} - \text{Smallest Data Value}}{\text{Number of Classes}} \quad (2.2)$$

The approximate class width given by equation (2.2) can be rounded to a more convenient value based on the preference of the person developing the frequency distribution. For example, an approximate class width of 9.28 might be rounded to 10 simply because 10 is a more convenient class width to use in constructing and presenting a frequency distribution.

For the data involving the year-end audit times, the largest value is 33 and the smallest value is 12. Because we decided to summarize the data with five classes, using equation (2.2) provides an approximate class width of $(33 - 12)/5 = 4.2$. We therefore decided to use a class width of 5 days in the frequency distribution.

There is no one best frequency distribution for a data set. Different people may construct different, but equally acceptable, frequency distributions. The goal is to reveal the natural grouping and variation in the data.

In practice, the number of classes and the appropriate class width are determined by trial and error. Once a possible number of classes is chosen, equation (2.2) is used to find the approximate class width. The process can be repeated for a different number of classes. Ultimately, the analyst uses judgment to determine the combination of the number of classes and class width that provides the best frequency distribution for summarizing the data.

For the audit-time data in Table 2.5, after deciding to use five classes, each with a width of 5 days, the next task is to specify the class limits for each of the classes.

Class Limits.   Class limits must be chosen so that each data item belongs to one and only one class. The *lower class limit* identifies the smallest possible data value assigned to the class. The *upper class limit* identifies the largest possible data value assigned to the class. In developing frequency distributions for qualitative data, we did not need to specify class limits because each data item naturally fell into a separate class (category). But with quantitative data, such as the audit times in Table 2.5, class limits are necessary to determine where each data value belongs.

Using the audit-time data in Table 2.5, we selected 10 days as the lower class limit and 14 days as the upper class limit for the first class. This class is denoted 10–14 in Table 2.6. The smallest data value, 12, is included in the 10–14 class. We then selected 15 days as the lower class limit and 19 days as the upper class limit of the next class. We continued defining the lower and upper class limits to obtain a total of five classes: 10–14, 15–19, 20–24, 25–29 and 30–34. The largest data value, 33, is included in the 30–34 class. The difference between the lower class limits of adjacent classes is the class width. Using the first two lower class limits of 10 and 15, we see that the class width is $15 - 10 = 5$.

Once the number of classes, class width, and class limits have been determined, a frequency distribution can be obtained by *counting* the number of data values belonging to each class. For example, the data in Table 2.5 show that four values—12, 14, 14, and 13—belong to the 10–14 class. Thus, the frequency for the 10–14 class is 4. Continuing this counting process for the 15–19, 20–24, 25–29, and 30–34 classes provides the frequency distribution in Table 2.6. Using this frequency distribution, we can observe that:

1. The most frequently occurring audit times are in the class of 15–19 days. Eight of the 20 audit times belong to this class.
2. Only one audit required 30 or more days.

Other conclusions are possible, depending on the interests of the person viewing the frequency distribution. The value of a frequency distribution is that it provides insights about the data that are not easily obtained by viewing the data in their original unorganized form.

Class Midpoint.   In some applications, we want to know the midpoints of the classes in a frequency distribution for quantitative data. The **class midpoint** is the value halfway between the lower and upper class limits. For the audit-time data, the five class midpoints are 12, 17, 22, 27, and 32.

Relative Frequency and Percent Frequency Distributions

We define the relative frequency and percent frequency distributions for quantitative data in the same manner as for qualitative data. First, recall that the relative frequency is simply the proportion of the observations belonging to a class. With n observations,

$$\text{Relative Frequency of Class} = \frac{\text{Frequency of the Class}}{n}$$

The percent frequency of a class is the relative frequency multiplied by 100.

Based on the class frequencies in Table 2.6 and with $n = 20$, Table 2.7 shows the relative frequency distribution and percent frequency distribution for the audit-time data. Note that .40 of the audits, or 40%, required from 15 to 19 days. Only .05 of the audits, or 5%, required 30 or more days. Again, additional interpretations and insights can be obtained by using Table 2.7.

TABLE 2.6

FREQUENCY DISTRIBUTION FOR THE AUDIT TIME DATA

Audit Time (days)	Frequency
10–14	4
15–19	8
20–24	5
25–29	2
30–34	1
Total	20

TABLE 2.7   RELATIVE AND PERCENT FREQUENCY DISTRIBUTIONS FOR THE AUDIT-TIME DATA

Audit Time (days)	Relative Frequency	Percent Frequency
10–14	.20	20
15–19	.40	40
20–24	.25	25
25–29	.10	10
30–34	.05	5
Total	1.00	100

FIGURE 2.3   DOT PLOT FOR THE AUDIT-TIME DATA

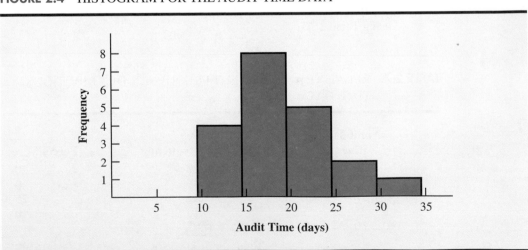

Dot Plot

One of the simplest graphical summaries of data is a **dot plot.** A horizontal axis shows the range of values for the observations. Each observation is represented by a dot placed above the axis. Figure 2.3 is the dot plot for the audit-time data in Table 2.5. The three dots located above 18 on the horizontal axis indicate that three observations have a value of 18. Dot plots show the details of the data and are useful for comparing the distribution of the data for two or more variables.

Histogram

A common graphical presentation of quantitative data is a **histogram.** This graphical summary can be prepared for data that have been previously summarized in either a frequency, relative frequency, or percent frequency distribution. A histogram is constructed by placing the variable of interest on the horizontal axis and the frequency, relative frequency, or percent frequency on the vertical axis. The frequency, relative frequency, or percent frequency of each class is shown by drawing a rectangle whose base is the class interval on the horizontal axis and whose height is the corresponding frequency, relative frequency, or percent frequency.

FIGURE 2.4   HISTOGRAM FOR THE AUDIT-TIME DATA

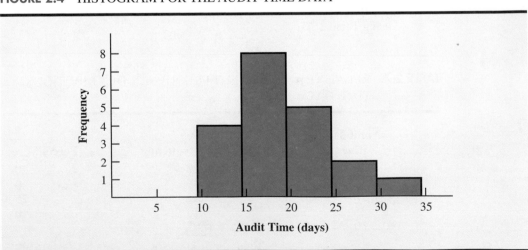

Figure 2.4 is a histogram for the audit-time data. Note that the class with the greatest frequency is shown by the rectangle appearing above the class of 15–19 days. The height of the rectangle shows that the frequency of this class is 8. A histogram for the relative or percent frequency distribution of this data would look the same as the histogram in Figure 2.4 with the exception that the vertical axis would be labeled with relative or percent frequency values.

As Figure 2.4 shows, the adjacent rectangles of a histogram touch one another. Unlike a bar graph, a histogram has no natural separation between the rectangles of adjacent classes. This format is the usual convention for histograms. Because the classes for the audit-time data are stated as 10–14, 15–19, 20–24, 25–29, and 30–34, there appear to be one-unit intervals of 14 to 15, 19 to 20, 24 to 25, and 29 to 30 between the classes. These spaces are eliminated by drawing the vertical lines of the histogram halfway between the class limits. The vertical lines separating the classes for the histogram in Figure 2.4 are located at 14.5, 19.5, 24.5, and 29.5. The first class starts at 9.5 and the last class ends at 34.5 to show all classes have a class width of five. This minor adjustment to eliminate the spaces between classes in a histogram helps show that, even though the data are rounded, all values between the lower limit of the first class and the upper limit of the last class are possible.

Cumulative Distributions

A variation of the frequency distribution that provides another tabular summary of quantitative data is the **cumulative frequency distribution.** The cumulative frequency distribution uses the number of classes, class widths, and class limits that were developed for the frequency distribution. However, rather than showing the frequency of each class, the cumulative frequency distribution shows the number of data items with values *less than or equal to the upper class limit* of each class. The first two columns of Table 2.8 provide the cumulative frequency distribution for the audit-time data.

To understand how the cumulative frequencies are determined, consider the class with the description "less than or equal to 24." The cumulative frequency for this class is simply the sum of the frequencies for all classes with data values less than or equal to 24. For the frequency distribution in Table 2.6, the sum of the frequencies for classes 10–14, 15–19, and 20–24 indicates that there are $4 + 8 + 5 = 17$ data values less than or equal to 24. Hence, the cumulative frequency for this class is 17. In addition, the cumulative frequency

TABLE 2.8   CUMULATIVE FREQUENCY, CUMULATIVE RELATIVE FREQUENCY, AND CUMULATIVE PERCENT FREQUENCY DISTRIBUTIONS FOR THE AUDIT-TIME DATA

Audit Time (days)	Cumulative Frequency	Cumulative Relative Frequency	Cumulative Percent Frequency
Less than or equal to 14	4	.20	20
Less than or equal to 19	12	.60	60
Less than or equal to 24	17	.85	85
Less than or equal to 29	19	.95	95
Less than or equal to 34	20	1.00	100

distribution in Table 2.8 shows that 4 audits were completed in 14 days or less and 19 audits were completed in 29 days or less.

As a final point, we note that a **cumulative relative frequency distribution** shows the proportion of data items, and a **cumulative percent frequency distribution** shows the percentage of data items with values less than or equal to the upper limit of each class. The cumulative relative frequency distribution can be computed either by summing the relative frequencies in the relative frequency distribution or by dividing the cumulative frequencies by the total number of items. Using the latter approach, we found the cumulative relative frequencies in column 3 of Table 2.8 by dividing the cumulative frequencies in column 2 by the total number of items ($n = 20$). The cumulative percent frequencies were again computed by multiplying the relative frequencies by 100. The cumulative relative and percent frequency distributions show that .85 of the audits, or 85%, were completed in 24 days or less, .95 of the audits, or 95%, were completed in 29 days or less, and so on.

Ogive

A graph of a cumulative distribution is called an **ogive.** The data values are shown on the horizontal axis and either the cumulative frequencies, the cumulative relative frequencies, or the cumulative percent frequencies are shown on the vertical axis. Figure 2.5 is the ogive for the cumulative frequencies of the audit-time data in Table 2.8.

The ogive is constructed by plotting a point corresponding to the cumulative frequency of each class. Because the classes for the audit-time data are 10–14, 15–19, 20–24, and so on, there appear to be one-unit gaps from 14 to 15, 19 to 20, and so on. As with the histogram, these gaps are eliminated by plotting points halfway between the classes. Thus, 14.5 is used for the 10–14 class, 19.5 is used for the 15–19 class, and so on. The "less than or equal to 14" class with a cumulative frequency of 4 is shown on the ogive in Figure 2.5 by the point located at 14.5 on the horizontal axis and 4 on the vertical axis. The "less than or equal to 19" class with a cumulative frequency of 12 is shown by the point located at 19.5 on the horizontal axis and 12 on the vertical axis. Note that one additional point is plotted at the left end of the ogive. This point starts the ogive by showing that no data values fall

FIGURE 2.5   OGIVE FOR THE AUDIT-TIME DATA

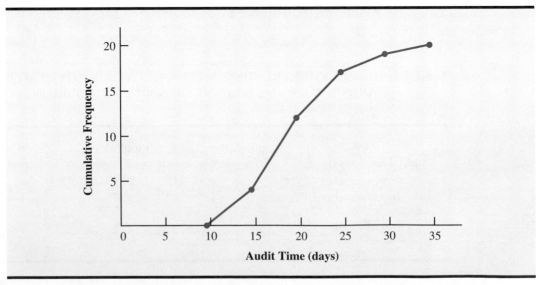

below the 10–14 class. It is plotted at 9.5 on the horizontal axis and 0 on the vertical axis. The plotted points are connected by straight lines to complete the ogive.

NOTES AND COMMENTS

1. The appropriate values for the class limits with quantitative data depend on the level of accuracy of the data. For instance, with the audit-time data of Table 2.5 the limits used were integer values because the data had been rounded to the nearest day. If the data were rounded to the nearest tenth of a day (e.g., 12.3, 14.4, and so on), then the limits would have been stated in tenths of days. For instance, the first class would have been 10.0–14.9. If the data were rounded to the nearest hundredth of a day (e.g., 12.34, 14.45, and so on), the limits would have been stated in hundredths of days. For instance, the first class would have been 10.00–14.99.

2. An *open-end* class is one that has only a lower class limit or an upper class limit. For example, in the audit-time data of Table 2.5, suppose two of the audits had taken 58 and 65 days. Rather than continue with the classes of width 5 with classes 35–39, 40–44, 45–49, and so on, we could simplify the frequency distribution to show an open-end class of "35 or more." This class would have a frequency of 2. Most often the open-end class appears at the upper end of the distribution. Sometimes an open-end class appears at the lower end of the distribution, and occasionally such classes appear at both ends.

3. The last entry in a cumulative frequency distribution is always the total number of observations. The last entry in a cumulative relative frequency distribution is always 1.00 and the last entry in a cumulative percent frequency distribution is always 100.

4. A bar graph and a histogram are essentially the same thing; both are graphical presentations of the data in a frequency distribution. A histogram is just a bar graph with no separation between bars. The separation between bars is appropriate for qualitative data because the data are discrete; no intermediate values are possible. For some quantitative data, a separation between bars is appropriate. Consider, for example, the number of classes in which a college student is enrolled. The data may only assume integer values. Intermediate values such as 1.5, 2.73, and so on are not possible. With continuous quantitative data, such as the audit times in Table 2.5, a separation between bars is not appropriate.

EXERCISES

Methods

11. Consider the following data.

14	21	23	21	16
19	22	25	16	16
24	24	25	19	16
19	18	19	21	12
16	17	18	23	25
20	23	16	20	19
24	26	15	22	24
20	22	24	22	20

a. Develop a frequency distribution using classes of 12–14, 15–17, 18–20, 21–23, and 24–26.

b. Develop a relative frequency distribution and a percent frequency distribution using the classes in part (a).

SELFtest   12. Consider the following frequency distribution.

Class	Frequency
10–19	10
20–29	14
30–39	17
40–49	7
50–59	2

Construct a cumulative frequency distribution and a cumulative relative frequency distribution.

13. Construct a histogram and an ogive for the data in Exercise 12.

14. Consider the following data.

8.9	10.2	11.5	7.8	10.0	12.2	13.5	14.1	10.0	12.2
6.8	9.5	11.5	11.2	14.9	7.5	10.0	6.0	15.8	11.5

a. Construct a dot plot.
b. Construct a frequency distribution.
c. Construct a percent frequency distribution.

Applications

SELFtest   15. A doctor's office staff has studied the waiting times for patients who arrive at the office with a request for emergency service. The following data were collected over a one-month period (the waiting times are in minutes).

2   5   10   12   4   4   5   17   11   8   9   8   12   21   6   8   7   13   18   3

Use classes of 0–4, 5–9, and so on.
a. Show the frequency distribution.
b. Show the relative frequency distribution.
c. Show the cumulative frequency distribution.
d. Show the cumulative relative frequency distribution.
e. What proportion of patients needing emergency service have a waiting time of 9 minutes or less?

16. A sample of 25 computer hardware companies taken from the *Stock Invester Pro* database is shown in Table 2.9.
a. Develop tabular summaries and a histogram for the stock price data. Comment on typical stock prices and the distribution of stock prices.
b. Develop tabular summaries and a histogram for the earnings per share data. Comment on your results.

Spending

17. Mendelsohn Media Research provided survey data on the annual amount of household purchases by families with an annual income of $75,000 or more (*Money,* 2001). Assume that the following data from a sample of 25 households show the dollars spent in the past year on books and magazines.

280	496	382	202	287
266	119	10	385	135
475	255	379	267	24
42	25	283	110	423
160	123	16	243	363

TABLE 2.9   DATA SET FOR 25 COMPUTER HARDWARE COMPANIES

CDfile
Stocks

Company	Stock Price	Institutional Ownership (%)	Price/Book Value	Earnings per Share (Annual $)
Amdahl	12.31	45.4	2.49	−2.49
Auspex Systems	11.00	66.1	2.22	0.85
Compaq Computer	65.50	83.0	6.84	2.01
Data General	35.94	91.5	4.25	1.15
Digi International	15.00	33.4	2.04	−0.89
Digital Equipment Corp.	43.00	58.8	1.92	−2.93
En Pointe Technologies	14.25	11.8	3.47	0.80
Equitrac	16.25	20.9	2.38	0.76
Franklin Electronic Pbls.	12.88	30.8	1.41	0.82
Gateway 2000	39.13	36.0	6.45	1.74
Hewlett-Packard	61.50	50.2	4.35	2.64
Ingram Micro	28.75	14.4	4.53	1.01
Maxwell Technologies	30.50	26.5	8.07	0.46
MicroAge	27.19	76.6	2.16	1.25
Micron Electronics	16.31	18.8	4.48	1.06
Network Computing Devices	11.88	39.8	3.34	0.15
Pomeroy Computer Resource	33.00	56.9	3.29	1.81
Sequent Computer Systems	28.19	57.0	2.65	0.36
Silicon Graphics	27.44	63.0	3.01	0.44
Southern Electronics	15.13	41.9	2.46	0.99
Stratus Computer	55.50	77.2	2.48	2.52
Sun Microsystems	48.00	59.3	7.50	1.67
Tandem Computers	34.25	61.3	3.61	1.02
Tech Data	38.94	82.3	3.80	1.50
Unisys	11.31	34.8	16.64	0.08

Source: Stock Investor Pro, American Association of Individual Investors, August 31, 1997.

    a.   Construct a frequency distribution and relative frequency distribution for the data.

    b.   Provide a histogram.

    c.   Comment on the annual spending on books and magazines for families in the sample.

18.   Wageweb conducts surveys of salary data and presents summaries on its Web site. Using salary data as of January 1, 2000, Wageweb reported that salaries of marketing vice presidents ranged from $85,090 to $190,054 (*Wageweb.com,* April 12, 2000). Assume the following data are a sample of the annual salaries for 50 marketing vice presidents. Data are in thousands of dollars.

CDfile
Wageweb

145	95	148	112	132
140	162	118	170	144
145	127	148	165	138
173	113	104	141	142
116	178	123	141	138
127	143	134	136	137
155	93	102	154	142
134	165	123	124	124
138	160	157	138	131
114	135	151	138	157

a. What are the lowest and highest salaries?

b. Use a class width of $15,000 and prepare tabular summaries of the annual salary data.

c. What proportion of the annual salaries are $135,000 or less?

d. What percentage of the annual salaries are more than $150,000?

e. Prepare a histogram.

19. The data for the numbers of units produced by a production employee during the most recent 20 days are shown here.

160	170	181	156	176
148	198	179	162	150
162	156	179	178	151
157	154	179	148	156

Summarize the data by constructing the following:

a. A frequency distribution

b. A relative frequency distribution

c. A cumulative frequency distribution

d. A cumulative relative frequency distribution

e. An ogive

20. The U.S. Bureau of the Census publishes a variety of information on the U.S. population. Following is the percent frequency distribution of the U.S. population by age as of July 1, 2000 (*The World Almanac and Book of Facts 2000*).

Age	Percent Frequency
0–13	20.0
14–17	5.7
18–24	9.6
25–34	13.6
35–44	16.3
45–54	13.5
55–64	8.7
65 or over	12.6
	100.0

a. What percentage of the population is 34 years old or less?

b. What percentage of the population is over 34 years old?

c. What percentage of the population is between 25 and 54 years old inclusively?

d. The total population is 275 million. How many people are less than 25 years old?

e. Suppose you believe that half the people in the 55–64 class are retired and that approximately all of the people 65 or older are retired. Estimate the number of retired people in the population.

CDfile
Computer

21. The *Nielsen Home Technology Report* provided information about home technology and its usage by persons aged 12 and older. The following data are the hours of personal computer usage during one week for a sample of 50 persons.

4.1	1.5	10.4	5.9	3.4	5.7	1.6	6.1	3.0	3.7
3.1	4.8	2.0	14.8	5.4	4.2	3.9	4.1	11.1	3.5
4.1	4.1	8.8	5.6	4.3	3.3	7.1	10.3	6.2	7.6
10.8	2.8	9.5	12.9	12.1	0.7	4.0	9.2	4.4	5.7
7.2	6.1	5.7	5.9	4.7	3.9	3.7	3.1	6.1	3.1

Summarize the data by constructing the following:
a. A frequency distribution (with class width of 3 hours)
b. A relative frequency distribution
c. A histogram
d. An ogive
e. Comment on what the data indicate about personal computer usage at home.

2.3   EXPLORATORY DATA ANALYSIS: THE STEM-AND-LEAF DISPLAY

The techniques of **exploratory data analysis** consist of simple arithmetic and easy-to-draw graphs that can be used to summarize data quickly. One technique—referred to as a **stem-and-leaf display**—can be used to show both the rank order and shape of a data set simultaneously.

To illustrate the use of a stem-and-leaf display, consider the data in Table 2.10. These data are the result of a 150-question aptitude test given to 50 individuals who were recently interviewed for a position at Haskens Manufacturing. The data values indicate the number of questions answered correctly.

To develop a stem-and-leaf display, we first arrange the leading digits of each data value to the left of a vertical line. To the right of the vertical line, we record the last digit for each data value as we pass through the observations in the order they were recorded. The last digit for each data value is placed on the line corresponding to its first digit as follows:

```
 6 | 9  8
 7 | 2  3  6  3  6  5
 8 | 6  2  3  1  1  0  4  5
 9 | 7  2  2  6  2  1  5  8  8  5  4
10 | 7  4  8  0  2  6  6  0  6
11 | 2  8  5  9  3  5  9
12 | 6  8  7  4
13 | 2  4
14 | 1
```

TABLE 2.10   NUMBER OF QUESTIONS ANSWERED CORRECTLY ON AN APTITUDE TEST

CDfile
ApTest

112	72	69	97	107
73	92	76	86	73
126	128	118	127	124
82	104	132	134	83
92	108	96	100	92
115	76	91	102	81
95	141	81	80	106
84	119	113	98	75
68	98	115	106	95
100	85	94	106	119

With this organization of the data, sorting the digits on each line into rank order is simple. Doing so leads to the stem-and-leaf display shown here.

```
 6 | 8  9
 7 | 2  3  3  5  6  6
 8 | 0  1  1  2  3  4  5  6
 9 | 1  2  2  2  4  5  5  6  7  8  8
10 | 0  0  2  4  6  6  6  7  8
11 | 2  3  5  5  8  9  9
12 | 4  6  7  8
13 | 2  4
14 | 1
```

The numbers to the left of the line (6, 7, 8, 9, 10, 11, 12, 13, and 14) form the *stem,* and each digit to the right of the line is a *leaf.* For example, consider the first line with a stem of 6 and leaves of 8 and 9.

$$6 \mid 8 \quad 9$$

It indicates that two data values have a first digit of 6. The leaves show that the data values are 68 and 69. Similarly, the second line

$$7 \mid 2 \quad 3 \quad 3 \quad 5 \quad 6 \quad 6$$

indicates that six data values have a first digit of 7. The leaves show that the data values are 72, 73, 73, 75, 76, and 76.

To focus on the shape indicated by the stem-and-leaf display, let us use a rectangle to contain the leaves of each stem. Doing so, we obtain the following.

```
 6 | 8  9
 7 | 2  3  3  5  6  6
 8 | 0  1  1  2  3  4  5  6
 9 | 1  2  2  2  4  5  5  6  7  8  8
10 | 0  0  2  4  6  6  6  7  8
11 | 2  3  5  5  8  9  9
12 | 4  6  7  8
13 | 2  4
14 | 1
```

Rotating this page counterclockwise onto its side provides a picture of the data that is similar to a histogram with classes of 60–69, 70–79, 80–89, and so on.

Although the stem-and-leaf display may appear to offer the same information as a histogram, it has two primary advantages.

1. The stem-and-leaf display is easier to construct by hand.
2. Within a class interval, the stem-and-leaf display provides more information than the histogram because the stem-and-leaf shows the actual data values.

In a stretched stem-and-leaf display, whenever a stem value is stated twice, the first value corresponds to leaf values of 0–4, and the second value corresponds to leaf values of 5–9.

Just as a frequency distribution or histogram has no absolute number of classes, neither does a stem-and-leaf display have an absolute number of rows or stems. If we believe that our original stem-and-leaf display has condensed the data too much, we can easily stretch the display by using two or more stems for each leading digit. For example, to use two stems for each leading digit, we would place all data values ending in 0, 1, 2, 3, and 4 on one line and all values ending in 5, 6, 7, 8, and 9 on a second line. The following stretched stem-and-leaf display illustrates this approach.

```
 6 | 8  9
 7 | 2  3  3
 7 | 5  6  6
 8 | 0  1  1  2  3  4
 8 | 5  6
 9 | 1  2  2  2  4
 9 | 5  5  6  7  8  8
10 | 0  0  2  4
10 | 6  6  6  7  8
11 | 2  3
11 | 5  5  8  9  9
12 | 4
12 | 6  7  8
13 | 2  4
13 |
14 | 1
```

Note that values 72, 73, and 73 have leaves in the 0–4 range and are shown with the first stem value of 7. The values 75, 76, and 76 have leaves in the 5–9 range and are shown with the second stem value of 7. This stretched stem-and-leaf display is similar to a frequency distribution with intervals of 65–69, 70–74, 75–79, and so on.

The preceding example showed a stem-and-leaf display for data having up to three digits. Stem-and-leaf displays for data with more than three digits are possible. For example, consider the following data on the number of hamburgers sold by a fast-food restaurant for each of 15 weeks.

1565	1852	1644	1766	1888	1912	2044	1812
1790	1679	2008	1852	1967	1954	1733	

A stem-and-leaf display of these data follows.

Leaf Unit = 10

```
15 | 6
16 | 4  7
17 | 3  6  9
18 | 1  5  5  8
19 | 1  5  6
20 | 0  4
```

A single digit is used to define each leaf in a stem-and-leaf display. The leaf unit indicates how to multiply the stem-and-leaf numbers in order to approximate the original data. Leaf units may be 100, 10, 1, 0.1, and so on.

Note that a single digit is used to define each leaf and that only the first three digits of each observation have been used to construct the display. At the top of the display we have specified Leaf Unit = 10. To illustrate how to interpret the values in the display, consider the first stem, 15, and its associated leaf, 6. Combining these, we obtain the number 156. To reconstruct an approximation of the original observation, we must multiply this number by 10, the value of the *leaf unit*. Thus, $156 \times 10 = 1560$ is an approximation of the original observation used to construct the stem-and-leaf display. Although it is not possible to reconstruct the exact data from this stem-and-leaf display, the convention of using a single digit for each leaf enables stem-and-leaf displays to be constructed for data having a large number of digits. For stem-and-leaf displays where the leaf unit is not shown, the leaf unit is assumed to equal 1.

EXERCISES

Methods

22. Construct a stem-and-leaf display for the following data.

70	72	75	64	58	83	80	82
76	75	68	65	57	78	85	72

SELFtest **23.** Construct a stem-and-leaf display for the following data.

11.3	9.6	10.4	7.5	8.3	10.5	10.0
9.3	8.1	7.7	7.5	8.4	6.3	8.8

24. Construct a stem-and-leaf display for the following data. Use a leaf unit of 10.

1161	1206	1478	1300	1604	1725	1361	1422
1221	1378	1623	1426	1557	1730	1706	1689

Applications

SELFtest **25.** A psychologist developed a new test of adult intelligence. The test was administered to 20 individuals, and the following data were obtained.

114	99	131	124	117	102	106	127	119	115
98	104	144	151	132	106	125	122	118	118

Construct a stem-and-leaf display for the data.

26. The earnings per share data for a sample of 20 companies from the *Business Week* Corporate Scoreboard follow (*Business Week,* November 17, 1997):

Company	Earnings per Share ($)	Company	Earnings per Share ($)
Barnes & Noble	0.78	Hershey Foods	1.97
Citicorp	7.10	Hewlett-Packard	2.82
Compaq Computer	2.16	Humana	0.89
Dana	3.42	Microsoft	2.66
Dell Computer	2.03	Procter & Gamble	2.53
Digital Equipment	1.28	Quaker State	0.41
General Dynamics	4.82	Sara Lee	2.08
Goodyear	0.94	Snap-On Tools	2.38
Harley-Davidson	1.11	Sunstrand	2.53
Heinz	0.98	Xerox	3.95

Develop a stem-and-leaf display for the data. Use a leaf unit of 0.1. Comment on what you learned about the earnings per share for these companies.

27. In a study of job satisfaction, a series of tests was administered to 50 subjects. The following data were obtained; higher scores represent greater dissatisfaction.

JobSat

87	76	67	58	92	59	41	50	90	75	80	81	70
77	69	61	88	46	85	97	50	47	81	87	75	60
65	92	77	71	70	74	53	43	61	89	84	83	70
46	84	76	78	64	69	76	78	67	74	64		

Construct a stem-and-leaf display for the data.

28. Periodically *Barron's* publishes earnings forecasts for the companies listed in the Dow Jones Industrial Average. The following are the 2000 forecasts of price/earnings (P/E) ratios for these companies implied by *Barron's* earnings forecasts (*Barron's,* February 14, 2000).

PEforcast

Company	2000 P/E Forecast	Company	2000 P/E Forecast
AT&T	23	Honeywell	13
Alcoa	15	IBM	28
American Express	25	Intel	37
Boeing	16	International Paper	14
Caterpillar	13	Johnson & Johnson	23
Citigroup	17	McDonald's	23
Coca-Cola	39	Merck	25
Disney	47	Microsoft	60
Dupont	18	Minnesota Mining	19
Eastman Kodak	11	J. P. Morgan	11
Exxon/Mobil	22	Philip Morris	5
General Electric	37	Procter & Gamble	26
General Motors	8	SBC Comm.	19
Hewlett-Packard	36	United Technologies	14
Home Depot	48	Wal-Mart	40

   a. Develop a stem-and-leaf display for the data.
   b. Use the results of the stem-and-leaf display to develop a frequency distribution and percent frequency distribution.

2.4   CROSSTABULATIONS AND SCATTER DIAGRAMS

Crosstabulations and scatter diagrams are used to summarize data in a way that reveals the relationship between variables.

Thus far in this chapter, we have focused on tabular and graphical methods that are used to summarize the data for *one variable at a time*. Often a manager or decision maker is interested in tabular and graphical methods that will assist in the understanding of the *relationship between two variables*. Crosstabulation and scatter diagrams are two such methods.

Crosstabulation

Crosstabulation is a method that can be used to summarize the data for two variables simultaneously. Let us illustrate the use of a crosstabulation by considering the following application. Zagat's Restaurant Review is a service that provides data on restaurants located throughout the world. Data on a variety of variables such as the restaurant's quality rating and typical meal price are reported. Quality rating is a qualitative variable with rating categories of good, very good, and excellent. Meal price is a quantitative variable that generally ranges from $10 to $49. The quality rating and the meal price data were collected for a sample of 300 restaurants located in the Los Angeles area. Table 2.11 shows the data for the first 10 restaurants.

A crosstabulation of the data for this application is shown in Table 2.12. The left and top margin labels define the classes for the two variables. In the left margin, the row labels (good, very good, and excellent) correspond to the three classes of the quality rating variable. In the top margin, the column labels ($10–19, $20–29, $30–39, and $40–49) correspond to the four classes of the meal price variable. Each restaurant in the sample provides a quality rating and a meal price. Thus, each restaurant in the sample is associated with a cell appearing in one of the rows and one of the columns of the crosstabulation. For ex-

TABLE 2.11   QUALITY RATING AND MEAL PRICE FOR LOS ANGELES RESTAURANTS

CDfile
Restaurant

Restaurant	Quality Rating	Meal Price ($)
1	Good	18
2	Very Good	22
3	Good	28
4	Excellent	38
5	Very Good	33
6	Good	28
7	Very Good	19
8	Very Good	11
9	Very Good	23
10	Good	13
.	.	.
.	.	.
.	.	.

TABLE 2.12   CROSSTABULATION OF QUALITY RATING AND MEAL PRICE FOR 300 LOS ANGELES RESTAURANTS

Quality Rating	Meal Price				
	$10–19	$20–29	$30–39	$40–49	Total
Good	42	40	2	0	84
Very Good	34	64	46	6	150
Excellent	2	14	28	22	66
Total	78	118	76	28	300

ample, restaurant 5 is identified as having a very good quality rating and a meal price of $33. This restaurant belongs to the cell in row 2 and column 3 of Table 2.12. In constructing a crosstabulation, we simply count the number of restaurants that belong to each of the cells in the crosstabulation table.

In reviewing Table 2.12, we see that the greatest number of restaurants in the sample (64) have a very good rating and a meal price in the $20–29 range. Only two restaurants have an excellent rating and a meal price in the $10–19 range. Similar interpretations of the other frequencies can be made. In addition, note that the right and bottom margins of the crosstabulation provide the frequency distributions for quality rating and meal price separately. From the frequency distribution in the right margin, we see that data on quality ratings show 84 good restaurants, 150 very good restaurants, and 66 excellent restaurants. Similarly, the bottom margin shows the frequency distribution for the meal price variable.

The value of a crosstabulation is that it provides insight about the relationship between the variables. From the results in Table 2.12, higher meal prices appear to be associated with the higher quality restaurants and the lower meal prices appear to be associated with the lower quality restaurants.

Converting the entries in the table into row percentages or column percentages can afford additional insight about the relationship between the variables. For row percentages, the results of dividing each frequency in Table 2.12 by its corresponding row total are shown in Table 2.13. For example, the percentage in the first row and first column, 50.0, is calculated by dividing 42 by 84 and multiplying by 100 (42/84 × 100 = 50.0%). Of the restaurants with the lowest (good) quality rating, we see that the greatest percentages are for the less expensive restaurants (50.0% have $10–19 meal prices and 47.6% have $20–29 meal prices). Of the restaurants with the highest (excellent) quality rating, we see that the greatest

TABLE 2.13   ROW PERCENTAGES FOR EACH QUALITY RATING CATEGORY

Quality Rating	Meal Price				
	$10–19	$20–29	$30–39	$40–49	Total
Good	50.0	47.6	2.4	0.0	100
Very Good	22.7	42.7	30.6	4.0	100
Excellent	3.0	21.2	42.4	33.4	100

TABLE 2.14   SAMPLE DATA FOR THE STEREO AND SOUND EQUIPMENT STORE

Week	Number of Commercials x	Sales ($100s) y
1	2	50
2	5	57
3	1	41
4	3	54
5	4	54
6	1	38
7	5	63
8	3	48
9	4	59
10	2	46

CDfile

Stereo

percentages are for the more expensive restaurants (42.4% have $30–39 meal prices and 33.4% have $40–49 meal prices). Thus, we continue to see that the more expensive meals are associated with the higher quality restaurants.

Crosstabulation is widely used for examining the relationship between two variables. In practice, final reports for many statistical surveys include a large number of crosstabulation tables. In the Los Angeles restaurant sample, the crosstabulation is based on one qualitative variable (quality rating) and one quantitative variable (meal price). Crosstabulations can also be developed when both variables are qualitative and when both variables are quantitative.

Scatter Diagram

A **scatter diagram** is a graphical presentation of the relationship between two quantitative variables. As an illustration of a scatter diagram, consider the situation of a stereo and sound equipment store in San Francisco. On 10 occasions during the past three months, the store has used weekend television commercials to promote sales at its stores. The manager wants to investigate whether a relationship can be demonstrated between the number of commercials shown and the sales at the store during the following week. Sample data for the 10 weeks with sales in hundreds of dollars are shown in Table 2.14.

Figure 2.6 is the scatter diagram for the data in Table 2.14. The number of commercials (x) is shown on the horizontal axis and the sales (y) are shown on the vertical axis. For week 1, $x = 2$ and $y = 50$. A point with those coordinates is plotted on the scatter diagram. Similar points are plotted for the other nine weeks. Note that on two of the weeks, one commercial was shown, on two of the weeks two commercials were shown, and so on.

The completed scatter diagram in Figure 2.6 indicates a positive relationship between the number of commercials and sales. Higher sales are associated with a higher number of commercials. The relationship is not perfect in that all points are not on a straight line. However, the general pattern of the points suggests that the overall relationship is positive.

Some general scatter diagram patterns and the types of relationships they suggest are shown in Figure 2.7. The top left panel depicts a positive relationship similar to the one for the number of commercials and sales example. In the top right panel, the scatter diagram shows no apparent relationship between the variables. The bottom panel depicts a negative relationship where y tends to decrease as x increases.

FIGURE 2.6   SCATTER DIAGRAM FOR THE STEREO AND SOUND EQUIPMENT STORE

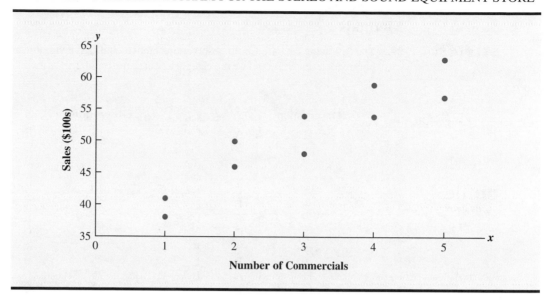

FIGURE 2.7   TYPES OF RELATIONSHIPS DEPICTED BY SCATTER DIAGRAMS

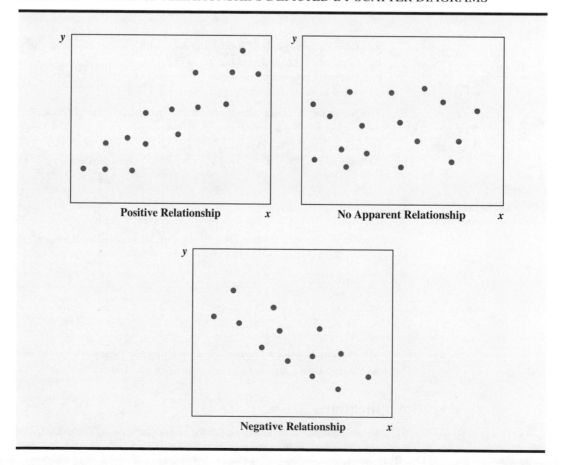

EXERCISES

Methods

29. The following data are for 30 observations on two qualitative variables, x and y. The categories for x are A, B, and C; the categories for y are 1 and 2.

CDfile

Crosstab

Observation	x	y	Observation	x	y
1	A	1	16	B	2
2	B	1	17	C	1
3	B	1	18	B	1
4	C	2	19	C	1
5	B	1	20	B	1
6	C	2	21	C	2
7	B	1	22	B	1
8	C	2	23	C	2
9	A	1	24	A	1
10	B	1	25	B	1
11	A	1	26	C	2
12	B	1	27	C	2
13	C	2	28	A	1
14	C	2	29	B	1
15	C	2	30	B	2

   a. Develop a crosstabulation for the data, with x in the rows and y in the columns.
   b. Compute the row percentages.
   c. Compute column percentages.
   d. What is the relationship, if any, between x and y?

30. The following 20 observations are for two quantitative variables, x and y.

CDfile

Scatter

Observation	x	y	Observation	x	y
1	−22	22	11	−37	48
2	−33	49	12	34	−29
3	2	8	13	9	−18
4	29	−16	14	−33	31
5	−13	10	15	20	−16
6	21	−28	16	−3	14
7	−13	27	17	−15	18
8	−23	35	18	12	17
9	14	−5	19	−20	−11
10	3	−3	20	−7	−22

   a. Develop a scatter diagram for the relationship between x and y.
   b. What is the relationship, if any, between x and y?

Applications

31. Compute column percentages for the restaurant data in Table 2.12. What is the relationship between quality rating and meal price?

SELFtest   **32.** Table 2.15 provides financial data for a sample of 36 companies whose stock is traded on the New York Stock Exchange (*Investor's Business Daily,* April 7, 2000). EPS Rating is a measure of growth in earnings per share for the company. The data on Sales/Margins/ROE is a composite rating based on a company's sales growth rate, its profit margins, and its return on equity (ROE).

   a. Prepare a crosstabulation of the data on Sales/Margins/ROE (rows) and EPS Rating (columns). Use classes of 0–19, 20–39, 40–59, 60–79, and 80–99 for EPS Rating.

   b. Compute row percentages and comment on any relationship between the variables.

TABLE 2.15   FINANCIAL DATA FOR A SAMPLE OF 36 COMPANIES

CDfile

IBD

Company	EPS Rating	Relative Price Strength	Industry Group Relative Strength	Sales/Margins/ ROE
Advo	81	74	B	A
Alaska AirGp	58	17	C	B
Alliant Tech	84	22	B	B
Atmos Engy	21	9	C	E
Bank of Am.	87	38	C	A
Bowater PLC	14	46	C	D
Callaway Golf	46	62	B	E
Central Parking	76	18	B	C
Dean Foods	84	7	B	C
Dole Food	70	54	E	C
Elec. Data Sys	72	69	A	B
Fed. Dept. Stor.	79	21	D	B
Gateway	82	68	A	A
Goodyear	21	9	E	D
Hanson PLC	57	32	B	B
ICN Pharm.	76	56	A	D
Jefferson plt	80	38	D	C
Kroger	84	24	D	A
Mattel	18	20	E	D
McDermott	6	6	A	C
Monaco	97	21	D	A
Murphy Oil	80	62	B	B
Nordstrom	58	57	B	C
NYMAGIC	17	45	D	D
Office Depot	58	40	B	B
Payless Shoes	76	59	B	B
Praxair	62	32	C	B
Reebok	31	72	C	E
Safeway	91	61	D	A
Teco Energy	49	48	D	B
Texaco	80	31	D	C
US West	60	65	B	A
United Rental	98	12	C	A
Wachovia	69	36	E	B
Winnebago	83	49	D	A
York Intl.	28	14	D	B

Source: Investor's Business Daily, April 7, 2000.

33. Refer to the data in Table 2.15.
    a. Prepare a crosstabulation of the data on Sales/Margins/ROE and Industry Group Relative Strength.
    b. Prepare a frequency distribution for the data on Sales/Margins/ROE.
    c. Prepare a frequency distribution for the data on Industry Group Relative Strength.
    d. How has the crosstabulation helped in preparing the frequency distributions in parts (c) and (d)?

34. Refer to the data in Table 2.15.
    a. Prepare a scatter diagram of the data for EPS Rating and Relative Price Strength.
    b. Comment on the relationship, if any, between the variables. The meaning of the EPS Rating is described in Exercise 32. Relative Price Strength is a measure on the change in the stock's price over the past 12 months. Higher values indicate greater strength.

35. The following data show the hotel revenue and the gaming revenue, in millions of dollars, for 10 Las Vegas casino hotels (*Cornell Hotel and Restaurant Administration Quarterly*, October 1997).

Casino

Company	Hotel Revenue ($ millions)	Gaming Revenue ($ millions)
Boyd Gaming	303.5	548.2
Circus Circus Enterprises	664.8	664.8
Grand Casinos	121.0	270.7
Hilton Corp. Gaming Div.	429.6	511.0
MGM Grand, Inc.	373.1	404.7
Mirage Resorts	670.9	782.8
Primadonna Resorts	66.4	130.7
Rio Hotel & Casino	105.8	105.5
Sahara Gaming	102.4	148.7
Station Casinos	135.8	358.5

a. Develop a scatter diagram of the data on Hotel Revenue and Gaming Revenue.
b. Comment on the relationship, if any, between the variables.

SUMMARY

A set of data, even if modest in size, is often difficult to interpret directly in the form in which it is gathered. Tabular and graphical methods provide procedures for organizing and summarizing data so that patterns are revealed and the data are more easily interpreted. Frequency distributions, relative frequency distributions, percent frequency distributions, bar graphs, and pie charts were presented as tabular and graphical procedures for summarizing qualitative data. Frequency distributions, relative frequency distributions, percent frequency distributions, dot plots, histograms, cumulative frequency distributions, cumulative relative frequency distributions, cumulative percent frequency distributions, and ogives were presented as ways of summarizing quantitative data. A stem-and-leaf display was presented as an exploratory data analysis technique that can be used to summarize quantitative data. Crosstabulation was presented as a tabular method for summarizing data for two variables. The scatter diagram was introduced as a graphical method for showing the relationship between two quantitative variables. Figure 2.8 presents the tabular and graphical methods presented in this chapter.

FIGURE 2.8   TABULAR AND GRAPHICAL METHODS FOR SUMMARIZING DATA

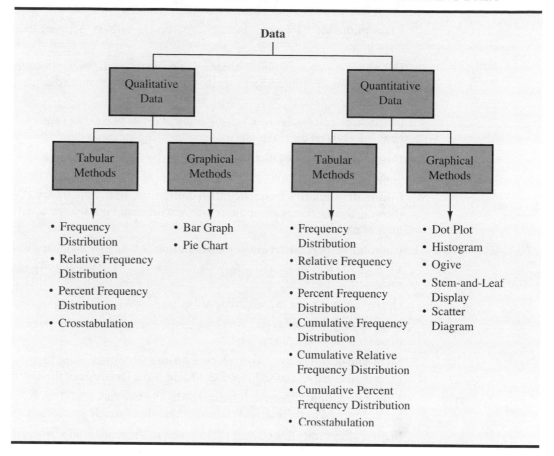

With large data sets, computer software packages are essential in constructing tabular and graphical summaries of data. In the two chapter appendixes, we show how Minitab and Microsoft Excel can be used for this purpose.

GLOSSARY

Qualitative data   Data that are labels or names used to identify categories of like items.

Quantitative data   Data that indicate how much or how many.

Frequency distribution   A tabular summary of data showing the number (frequency) of items in each of several nonoverlapping classes.

Relative frequency distribution   A tabular summary of data showing the fraction or proportion of data items in each of several nonoverlapping classes.

Percent frequency distribution   A tabular summary of data showing the percentage of items in each of several nonoverlapping classes.

Bar graph   A graphical device for depicting data that have been summarized in a frequency distribution, relative frequency distribution, or percent frequency distribution.

Pie chart   A graphical device for presenting data summaries based on subdivision of a circle into sectors that correspond to the relative frequency for each class.

Class midpoint   The point in each class that is halfway between the lower and upper class limits.

Dot plot   A simple graphical summary of data with each observation represented by a dot placed above a horizontal axis that shows the distribution of the data values.

Histogram   A graphical presentation of a frequency distribution, relative frequency distribution, or percent frequency distribution of quantitative data constructed by placing the class intervals on the horizontal axis and the frequencies on the vertical axis.

Cumulative frequency distribution   A tabular summary of quantitative data showing the number of items with values less than or equal to the upper class limit of each class.

Cumulative relative frequency distribution   A tabular summary of quantitative data showing the fraction or proportion of items with values less than or equal to the upper class limit of each class.

Cumulative percent frequency distribution   A tabular summary of quantitative data showing the percentage of items with values less than or equal to the upper class limit of each class.

Ogive   A graph of a cumulative distribution.

Exploratory data analysis   Methods that use simple arithmetic and easy-to-draw graphs to summarize data quickly.

Stem-and-leaf display   An exploratory data analysis technique that simultaneously rank orders quantitative data and provides insight about the shape of the distribution.

Crosstabulation   A tabular summary of data for two variables. The classes for one variable are represented by the rows; the classes for the other variable are represented by the columns.

Scatter diagram   A graphical presentation of the relationship between two quantitative variables. One variable is shown on the horizontal axis and the other variable is shown on the vertical axis.

KEY FORMULAS

Relative Frequency

$$\frac{\text{Frequency of the Class}}{n} \tag{2.1}$$

Approximate Class Width

$$\frac{\text{Largest Data Value} - \text{Smallest Data Value}}{\text{Number of Classes}} \tag{2.2}$$

SUPPLEMENTARY EXERCISES

36.   *Autodata* and *USA Today* research provided data on the best-selling vehicle models for March 2000 (*USA Today*, April 4, 2000). Among those listed were Chevrolet Silverado/C/K pickup, Ford F-Series pickup, Ford Taurus, Honda Accord, and Toyota Camry. Data from a sample of 50 vehicle purchases are presented in Table 2.16.

TABLE 2.16   DATA FOR 50 VEHICLE PURCHASES

Vehicles

Silverado	Taurus	Accord	F-Series	Silverado
F-Series	Accord	Silverado	Camry	Taurus
Silverado	F-Series	Camry	Silverado	F-Series
Taurus	F-Series	Taurus	F-Series	Camry
Taurus	F-Series	F-Series	Accord	Camry
Silverado	Silverado	Silverado	Silverado	Taurus
Camry	Silverado	Accord	F-Series	F-Series
Taurus	F-Series	Accord	Camry	Accord
F-Series	Silverado	F-Series	F-Series	Taurus
Camry	Silverado	F-Series	F-Series	F-Series

    a. Develop a frequency and percent frequency distribution.
    b. What are the two top-selling vehicles?
    c. Show a pie chart.

37. Each of the *Fortune* 1000 companies belongs to one of several industry classifications (*Fortune*, April 17, 2000). A sample of 20 companies with their corresponding classification follows.

Company	Industry Classification	Company	Industry Classification
IBP	Food	Borden	Food
Intel	Electronics	McDonnell Douglas	Aerospace
Coca-Cola	Beverage	Morton International	Chemicals
Union Carbide	Chemicals	Quaker Oats	Food
General Electric	Electronics	PepsiCo	Beverage
Motorola	Electronics	Maytag	Electronics
Kellogg	Food	Textron	Aerospace
Dow Chemical	Chemicals	Sara Lee	Food
Campbell Soup	Food	Harris	Electronics
Ralston Purina	Food	Eaton	Electronics

    a. Provide a frequency distribution showing the number of companies in each industry.
    b. Provide a percent frequency distribution.
    c. Provide a bar graph for the data.

38. During 1998 and 1999, *Time* magazine carried cover stories on the following movies: *Blair Witch Project, Phantom Menace, Beloved, Primary Colors,* and *Truman Show. Time* keeps track of mail received on its cover stories; the number of pieces of mail received on these movies was 159, 89, 85, 57, and 51 respectively (*Time*, September 27, 1999).
    a. Develop a percent frequency distribution for the mail data.
    b. Develop a pie chart.
    c. The cover stories on the *Blair Witch Project* and *Phantom Menace* were run in 1999; the others were run in 1998. What percent of the mail pertained to 1999 cover stories?

TABLE 2.17   SALES IN HEALTH CARE SERVICES FOR THE THIRD QUARTER 1997

Beverly Ent.	805	Novacare	357
Coventry	307	Phycor	284
Express Scripts	320	Quest Diag.	374
Healthsouth	748	Quorum Health	393
Horizon	445	Sun Healthcare	486
Humana	1968	Tenet Healthcare	2331
Int. Health	472	U. Wisconsin	389
Lab. Corp. Am.	377	Univ. Health	362
Manor Care	274	Vencor	845
Medpartners	1614	Wellpoint	1512

Source: Business Week, November 17, 1997.

39. The data in Table 2.17 represent sales in millions of dollars for 20 companies in the health care services industry during the third quarter 1997 (*Business Week,* November 17, 1997).
   a. Construct a frequency distribution to summarize the data. Use a class width of 500.
   b. Develop a relative frequency distribution.
   c. Construct a cumulative frequency distribution.
   d. Construct a cumulative relative frequency distribution.
   e. Construct a histogram as a graphical representation.

40. The closing prices of 40 common stocks follow (*Barron's,* September 3, 2001).

Comstock

29.63	34.00	43.25	8.75	37.88	8.63	7.63	30.38	35.25	19.38
9.25	16.50	38.00	53.38	16.63	1.25	48.38	18.00	9.38	9.25
10.00	25.02	18.00	8.00	28.50	24.25	21.63	18.50	33.63	31.13
32.25	29.63	79.38	11.38	38.88	11.50	52.00	14.00	9.00	33.50

   a. Construct frequency and relative frequency distributions.
   b. Construct cumulative frequency and cumulative relative frequency distributions.
   c. Construct a histogram.
   d. Using your summaries, make comments and observations about the price of common stock.

41. Ninety-four new shadow stocks were reported by the American Association of Individual Investors (*AAII Journal,* February 1997). The term *shadow* indicates stocks for small to medium-sized firms not followed closely by the major brokerage houses. Information on where the stock was traded—New York Stock Exchange (NYSE), American Stock Exchange (AMEX), and over-the-counter (OTC)—the earnings per share, and the price/earnings ratio was provided for the following sample of 20 shadow stocks.

Shadow

Stock	Exchange	Earnings per Share ($)	Price/ Earnings Ratio
Chemi-Trol	OTC	.39	27.30
Candie's	OTC	.07	36.20
TST/Impreso	OTC	.65	12.70
Unimed Pharm.	OTC	.12	59.30
Skyline Chili	AMEX	.34	19.30

Stock	Exchange	Earnings per Share ($)	Price/ Earnings Ratio
Cyanotech	OTC	.22	29.30
Catalina Light.	NYSE	.15	33.20
DDL Elect.	NYSE	.10	10.20
Euphonix	OTC	.09	49.70
Mesa Labs	OTC	.37	14.40
RCM Tech.	OTC	.47	18.60
Anuhco	AMEX	.70	11.40
Hello Direct	OTC	.23	21.10
Hilite Industries	OTC	.61	7.80
Alpha Tech.	OTC	.11	34.60
Wegener Group	OTC	.16	24.50
U.S. Home & Garden	OTC	.24	8.70
Chalone Wine	OTC	.27	44.40
Eng. Support Sys.	OTC	.89	16.70
Int. Remote Imaging	AMEX	.86	4.70

a. Provide frequency and relative frequency distributions for the exchange data. Where are most shadow stocks listed?

b. Provide frequency and relative frequency distributions for the earnings per share and price/earnings ratio data. Use classes of .00–.19, .20–.39, and so on, for the earnings per share data and classes of 0.0–9.9, 10.0–19.9, and so on for the price/earnings ratio data. What observations and comments can you make about the shadow stocks?

42. A state-by-state listing of per capita personal income for 1998 follows.

Ala.	21,500	Ky.	21,551	N.D.	21,708
Alaska	25,771	La.	21,385	Ohio	25,239
Ariz.	23,152	Maine	23,002	Okla.	21,056
Ark.	20,393	Md.	30,023	Ore.	24,775
Calif.	27,579	Mass.	32,902	Penn.	26,889
Colo.	28,821	Mich.	25,979	R.I.	26,924
Conn.	37,700	Minn.	27,667	S.C.	21,387
Del.	29,932	Miss.	18,998	S.D.	22,201
D.C.	37,325	Mo.	24,447	Tenn.	23,615
Fla.	25,922	Mont.	20,427	Texas	25,028
Ga.	25,106	Neb.	24,786	Utah	21,096
Hawaii	26,210	Nev.	27,360	Vt.	24,217
Idaho	21,080	N.H.	29,219	Va.	27,489
Ill.	28,976	N.J.	33,953	Wash.	28,066
Ind.	24,302	N.M.	20,008	W. Va.	19,373
Iowa	24,007	N.Y.	31,679	Wis.	25,184
Kan.	25,049	N.C.	24,122	Wyo.	23,225

Source: Bureau of Economic Analysis, *Current Population Survey*, March 2000.

Develop a frequency distribution, a relative frequency distribution, and a histogram.

43. The conclusion from a 40-state poll conducted by the Joint Council on Economic Education is that students do not learn enough economics. The findings were based on test results from 11th- and 12th-grade students who took a 46-question, multiple-choice test on basic economic concepts such as profit and the law of supply and demand. The following table gives sample data on the number of questions answered correctly.

12	10	16	24	12	14	18	23
31	14	15	19	17	9	19	28
24	16	21	13	20	12	22	18
22	18	30	16	26	18	16	14
8	25	22	15	33	24	17	19

Summarize these data using the following:
a. A stem-and-leaf display
b. A frequency distribution
c. A relative frequency distribution
d. A cumulative frequency distribution
e. On the basis of these data, do you agree with the claim that students are not learning enough economics? Explain.

44. The daily high and low temperatures for 20 cities follow (*USA Today,* May 9, 2000).

CDfile
HighLow

City	High	Low	City	High	Low
Athens	75	54	Melbourne	66	50
Bangkok	92	74	Montreal	64	52
Cairo	84	57	Paris	77	55
Copenhagen	64	39	Rio de Janeiro	80	61
Dublin	64	46	Rome	81	54
Havana	86	68	Seoul	64	50
Hong Kong	81	72	Singapore	90	75
Johannesburg	61	50	Sydney	68	55
London	73	48	Tokyo	79	59
Manila	93	75	Vancouver	57	43

a. Prepare a stem-and-leaf display for the high temperatures.
b. Prepare a stem-and-leaf display for the low temperatures.
c. Compare the stem-and-leaf displays from parts (a) and (b) and make some comments about the differences between daily high and low temperatures.
d. Use the stem-and-leaf display from part (a) to determine the number of cities having a high temperature of 80 degrees or above.
e. Provide frequency distributions for both high and low temperature data.

45. Refer to the data set for high and low temperatures for 20 cities in Exercise 44.
a. Develop a scatter diagram to show the relationship between the two variables, high temperature and low temperature.
b. Comment on the relationship between high and low temperature.

46. A study of job satisfaction was conducted for four occupations. Job satisfaction was measured using an 18-item questionnaire with each question receiving a response score of 1 to 5, with higher scores indicating greater satisfaction. The sum of the 18 scores provides the job satisfaction score for each individual in the sample. The data are as follows.

<table>
<tr><th>Occupation</th><th>Satisfaction Score</th><th>Occupation</th><th>Satisfaction Score</th><th>Occupation</th><th>Satisfaction Score</th></tr>
<tr><td>Lawyer</td><td>42</td><td>Physical Therapist</td><td>78</td><td>Systems Analyst</td><td>60</td></tr>
<tr><td>Physical Therapist</td><td>86</td><td>Systems Analyst</td><td>44</td><td>Physical Therapist</td><td>59</td></tr>
<tr><td>Lawyer</td><td>42</td><td>Systems Analyst</td><td>71</td><td>Cabinetmaker</td><td>78</td></tr>
<tr><td>Systems Analyst</td><td>55</td><td>Lawyer</td><td>50</td><td>Physical Therapist</td><td>60</td></tr>
<tr><td>Lawyer</td><td>38</td><td>Lawyer</td><td>48</td><td>Physical Therapist</td><td>50</td></tr>
<tr><td>Cabinetmaker</td><td>79</td><td>Cabinetmaker</td><td>69</td><td>Cabinetmaker</td><td>79</td></tr>
<tr><td>Lawyer</td><td>44</td><td>Physical Therapist</td><td>80</td><td>Systems Analyst</td><td>62</td></tr>
<tr><td>Systems Analyst</td><td>41</td><td>Systems Analyst</td><td>64</td><td>Lawyer</td><td>45</td></tr>
<tr><td>Physical Therapist</td><td>55</td><td>Physical Therapist</td><td>55</td><td>Cabinetmaker</td><td>84</td></tr>
<tr><td>Systems Analyst</td><td>66</td><td>Cabinetmaker</td><td>64</td><td>Physical Therapist</td><td>62</td></tr>
<tr><td>Lawyer</td><td>53</td><td>Cabinetmaker</td><td>59</td><td>Systems Analyst</td><td>73</td></tr>
<tr><td>Cabinetmaker</td><td>65</td><td>Cabinetmaker</td><td>54</td><td>Cabinetmaker</td><td>60</td></tr>
<tr><td>Lawyer</td><td>74</td><td>Systems Analyst</td><td>76</td><td>Lawyer</td><td>64</td></tr>
<tr><td>Physical Therapist</td><td>52</td><td></td><td></td><td></td><td></td></tr>
</table>

CDfile
OccupSat

a. Provide a crosstabulation of occupation and job satisfaction score.
b. Compute the row percentages for your crosstabulation in part (a).
c. What observations can you make concerning the level of job satisfaction for these occupations?

47. Do larger companies generate more revenue? The following data show the number of employees and annual revenue for a sample of 20 *Fortune* 1000 companies (*Fortune*, April 17, 2000).

CDfile
RevEmps

<table>
<tr><th>Company</th><th>Employees</th><th>Revenue ($ millions)</th><th>Company</th><th>Employees</th><th>Revenue ($ millions)</th></tr>
<tr><td>Sprint</td><td>77,600</td><td>19,930</td><td>American Financial</td><td>9,400</td><td>3,334</td></tr>
<tr><td>Chase Manhattan</td><td>74,801</td><td>33,710</td><td>Fluor</td><td>53,561</td><td>12,417</td></tr>
<tr><td>Computer Sciences</td><td>50,000</td><td>7,660</td><td>Phillips Petroleum</td><td>15,900</td><td>13,852</td></tr>
<tr><td>Wells Fargo</td><td>89,355</td><td>21,795</td><td>Cardinal Health</td><td>36,000</td><td>25,034</td></tr>
<tr><td>Sunbeam</td><td>12,200</td><td>2,398</td><td>Borders Group</td><td>23,500</td><td>2,999</td></tr>
<tr><td>CBS</td><td>29,000</td><td>7,510</td><td>MCI Worldcom</td><td>77,000</td><td>37,120</td></tr>
<tr><td>Time Warner</td><td>69,722</td><td>27,333</td><td>Consolidated Edison</td><td>14,269</td><td>7,491</td></tr>
<tr><td>Steelcase</td><td>16,200</td><td>2,743</td><td>IBP</td><td>45,000</td><td>14,075</td></tr>
<tr><td>Georgia-Pacific</td><td>57,000</td><td>17,796</td><td>Super Value</td><td>50,000</td><td>17,421</td></tr>
<tr><td>Toro</td><td>1,275</td><td>4,673</td><td>H&R Block</td><td>4,200</td><td>1,669</td></tr>
</table>

a. Prepare a scatter diagram to show the relationship between the variables Revenue and Employees.
b. Comment on any relationship between the variables.

48. A survey of commercial buildings served by the Cincinnati Gas & Electric Company was concluded in 1992 (CG&E Commercial Building Characteristics Survey, November 25,

1992). One question asked what main heating fuel was used and another asked the year the commercial building was constructed. A partial crosstabulation of the findings follows.

Year Constructed	Fuel Type				
	Electricity	Natural Gas	Oil	Propane	Other
1973 or before	40	183	12	5	7
1974–1979	24	26	2	2	0
1980–1986	37	38	1	0	6
1987–1991	48	70	2	0	1

    a. Complete the crosstabulation by showing the row totals and column totals.
    b. Show the frequency distributions for year constructed and for fuel type.
    c. Prepare a crosstabulation showing column percentages.

49. Table 2.18 contains a portion of the data on the file named Fortune on the CD-ROM at the back of the book. It provides data on stockholders' equity, market value, and profits for a sample of 50 *Fortune* 500 companies (*Fortune,* April 26, 1999).
    a. Prepare a crosstabulation for the variables stockholders' equity and profit. Use classes of 0–200, 200–400, . . . , 1000–1200 for profit, and classes of 0–1200, 1200–2400, . . . , 4800–6000 for stockholders' equity.
    b. Compute the row percentages for your crosstabulation in part (a).
    c. What relationship, if any, do you notice between profit and stockholders' equity?

50. Refer to the data set in Table 2.18.
    a. Prepare a crosstabulation for the variables market value and profit.
    b. Compute the row percentages for your crosstabulation in part (a).
    c. Comment on any relationship between the variables.

TABLE 2.18   DATA FOR A SAMPLE OF 50 *FORTUNE* 500 COMPANIES

CDfile
Fortune

Company	Stockholders' Equity ($1000s)	Market Value ($1000s)	Profit ($1000s)
AGCO	982.1	372.1	60.6
AMP	2698.0	12017.6	2.0
Apple Computer	1642.0	4605.0	309.0
Baxter International	2839.0	21743.0	315.0
Bergen Brunswick	629.1	2787.5	3.1
Best Buy	557.7	10376.5	94.5
Charles Schwab	1429.0	35340.6	348.5
.	.	.	.
.	.	.	.
.	.	.	.
Walgreen	2849.0	30324.7	511.0
Westvaco	2246.4	2225.6	132.0
Whirlpool	2001.0	3729.4	325.0
Xerox	5544.0	35603.7	395.0

51. Refer to the data set in Table 2.18.
    a. Prepare a scatter diagram to show the relationship between the variables profit and stockholders' equity.
    b. Comment on any relationship between the variables.
52. Refer to the data set in Table 2.18.
    a. Prepare a scatter diagram to show the relationship between the variables market value and stockholders' equity.
    b. Comment on any relationship between the variables.

Case Problem   CONSOLIDATED FOODS

Consolidated Foods operates a chain of supermarkets in New Mexico, Arizona, and California. A promotional campaign has advertised the chain's offering of a credit card policy whereby Consolidated Foods' customers have the option of paying for their purchases with credit cards, such as Visa and MasterCard, in addition to the usual options of cash or personal check. The policy is being implemented on a trial basis with the hope that the credit card option will encourage customers to make larger purchases.

After the first month of operation, a random sample of 100 customers was selected over a one-week period. Data were collected on the method of payment and how much was spent by each of the 100 customers. A portion of the sample data are shown in Table 2.19. Prior to the new credit card policy, approximately 50% of Consolidated Foods' customers paid in cash and approximately 50% paid by personal check.

TABLE 2.19   PURCHASE AMOUNT AND METHOD OF PAYMENT FOR A SAMPLE
OF 100 CONSOLIDATED FOODS CUSTOMERS

Customer	Amount ($)	Method of Payment
1	28.58	Check
2	52.04	Check
3	7.41	Cash
4	11.17	Cash
5	43.79	Credit Card
6	48.95	Check
7	57.59	Check
8	27.60	Check
9	26.91	Credit Card
10	9.00	Cash
·	·	·
·	·	·
·	·	·
95	18.09	Cash
96	54.84	Check
97	41.10	Check
98	43.14	Check
99	3.31	Cash
100	69.77	Credit Card

Managerial Report

Use the tabular and graphical methods of descriptive statistics to summarize the sample data in the data set Consolid. Your report should contain summaries such as the following.

1. A frequency and relative frequency distribution for the method of payment.
2. A bar graph or pie chart for the method of payment.
3. Frequency and relative frequency distributions for the amount spent in each method of payment.
4. Histograms and/or stem-and-leaf plots for the amount spent in each method of payment.
5. A crosstabulation for the variables method of payment and amount spent.

What preliminary insights do you have about the amounts spent and method of payment at Consolidated Foods?

Appendix 2.1   USING MINITAB FOR TABULAR AND GRAPHICAL METHODS

Minitab has extensive capabilities for constructing tabular and graphical summaries of data. In this appendix we show how Minitab can be used to construct several graphical summaries and the tabular summary of a crosstabulation. The graphical methods presented are the dot plot, the histogram, the stem-and-leaf display, and the scatter diagram.

Dot Plot

CDfile
Audit

We use the audit-time data in Table 2.5 to demonstrate. The data have been entered into column C1 of a Minitab worksheet. The following steps will generate the dot plot shown in Figure 2.3.

Step 1. Select the **Graph** pull-down menu
Step 2. Choose **Dotplot**
Step 3. When the Dotplot dialog box appears:
        Enter C1 in the **Variables** box
        Click **OK**

Histogram

CDfile
Audit

We show how to construct a histogram with frequencies on the vertical axis using the audit-time data in Table 2.5. The data have been entered into column C1 of a Minitab worksheet. The following steps will generate the histogram shown in Figure 2.4.

Step 1. Select the **Graph** pull-down menu
Step 2. Choose **Histogram**
Step 3. When the Histogram dialog box appears:
        Enter C1 in row 1 of the **Graph variables** box
        Select **Bar** under **Display** and **Graph** under **For each** in the **Data display** box
        Select **Options**
Step 4. When the Histogram Options dialog box appears:
        Select **Frequency** under **Type of Histogram**
        Select **CutPoint** under **Type of Intervals**

Select **Midpoint/cutpoint positions** under **Definition of Intervals** and enter 10:35/5 in the box[1]

Click **OK**

Step 5. When the Histogram dialog box appears:

Click **OK**

Stem-and-Leaf Display

ApTest

We use the aptitude test data in Table 2.10 to demonstrate the construction of a stem-and-leaf display. The data have been entered into column C1 of a Minitab worksheet. The following steps will generate the stretched stem-and-leaf display shown in Section 2.3.

Step 1. Select the **Graph** pull-down menu

Step 2. Choose **Stem-and-Leaf**

Step 3. When the Stem-and-Leaf dialog box appears:

Enter C1 in the **Variables** box

Click **OK**

Scatter Diagram

Stereo

We use the stereo and sound equipment store data in Table 2.14 to demonstrate the construction of a scatter diagram. The weeks are numbered from 1 to 10 in column C1, the data for number of commercials have been entered into column C2, and the data for sales have been entered into column C3 of a Minitab worksheet. The following steps will generate the scatter diagram shown in Figure 2.6.

Step 1. Select the **Graph** pull-down menu

Step 2. Choose **Plot**

Step 3. When the Plot dialog box appears:

Enter C3 under **Y** and C2 under **X** in the **Graph variables** section

Select **Symbol** under **Display** and **Point** under **For each** in the **Data display** section

Click **OK**

Crosstabulation

Restaurant

We use the data from Zagat's restaurant review, part of which is shown in Table 2.11, to demonstrate. The restaurants are numbered from 1 to 300 in column C1 of the Minitab worksheet. The quality ratings are in column C2, and the meal prices are in column C3.

Minitab can only create a crosstabulation for qualitative variables and meal price is a quantitative variable. So we have to first code the meal price data by specifying the category (class) to which each meal price belongs. The following steps will code the meal price data to create four categories of meal price in column C4: $10–19, $20–29, $30–39, and $40–49.

Step 1. Select the **Manip** pull-down menu

Step 2. Choose **Code**

Step 3. Choose **Numeric to Text**

Step 4. When the Code-Numeric to Text dialog box appears:

Enter C3 in the **Code data from columns** box

---

[1]The entry 10:35/5 indicates that 10 is the lowest value for the histogram, 35 is the highest value for the histogram, and 5 is the class width.

> Enter C4 in the **Into columns** box
> Enter 10:19 in the first **Original values** box and $10–19 in the adjacent **New** box
> Enter 20:29 in the second **Original values** box and $20–29 in the adjacent **New** box
> Enter 30:39 in the third **Original values** box and $30–39 in the adjacent **New** box
> Enter 40:49 in the fourth **Original values** box and $40–49 in the adjacent **New** box
> Click **OK**

For each meal price in column C3 the associated meal price category will now appear in column 4. We can now develop a crosstabulation for quality rating and the meal price categories by using the data in columns 2 and 4. The following steps will create a crosstabulation containing the same information as shown in Table 2.12.

Step 1. Select the **Stat** pull-down menu
Step 2. Choose **Tables**
Step 3. Choose **Cross Tabulation**
Step 4. When the Cross Tabulation dialog box appears:
> Enter C2 C4 in the **Classification variables** box
> Select **Counts**
> Click **OK**

Appendix 2.2   USING EXCEL FOR TABULAR AND GRAPHICAL METHODS

Excel has extensive capabilities for constructing tabular and graphical summaries of data. Three of the most powerful tools available are the Function Wizard, The Chart Wizard, and the PivotTable Report.

Functions and the Function Wizard

Excel provides a variety of functions that are useful for statistical analysis. If you know what function you want and how to use it, you can simply enter the function directly into a cell of an Excel worksheet. If not, Excel provides a Function Wizard to help in identifying the functions available and in using them.

Function Wizard. To access the Function Wizard click f_x on the standard toolbar or select the **Insert** pull-down menu and choose f_x Function. The **Paste Function** dialog box will then appear (See Figure 2.9). The **Function category** box shows a list of the categories of Excel functions; we have selected **Statistical** in Figure 2.9. With Statistical highlighted, a list of all the statistical functions available is displayed in the **Function name** box. Here, we have highlighted the COUNTIF function. Once a function has been highlighted, the proper form for the function along with a brief description appears below the Function category and Function name boxes. To obtain assistance in properly using the function, click **OK.**

Frequency Distributions.   We show how the COUNTIF function can be used to construct a frequency distribution for the data on soft drink purchases in Table 2.1. Refer to Figure 2.10 as we describe the tasks involved. The formula worksheet (shows the functions and formulas used) is in the background and the value worksheet (shows the results obtained using the functions and formulas) is in the foreground.

FIGURE 2.9   EXCEL'S PASTE FUNCTION DIALOG BOX

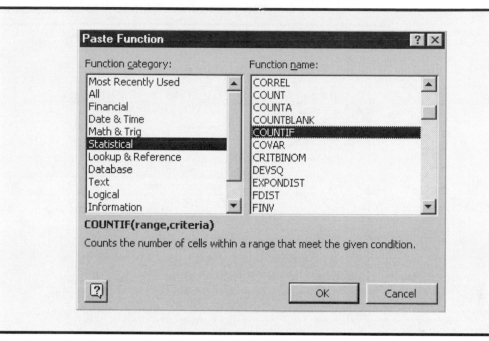

The label "Brand Purchased" and the data for the 50 soft drink purchases have been entered into cells A1:A51. We have also entered a label and the soft drink names into cells C1:C6. Excel's COUNTIF function can be used to count the number of times each soft drink appears in cells A2:A51. The following steps utilize the Function Wizard to produce the frequency distribution in the foreground of Figure 2.10.

Step 1. Select cell **D2,** access the Function Wizard, and choose **COUNTIF** from the list
of statistical functions
Step 2. Click **OK**
Step 3. When the COUNTIF dialog box appears:
Enter $A$2:$A$51 in the **Range** box
Enter C2 in the **Criteria** box
Click **OK**
Step 4. Copy cell D2 to cells D3:D6

The formula worksheet in the background of Figure 2.10 shows the cell formulas inserted by applying these steps. The value worksheet, in the foreground of Figure 2.10, shows the values computed using these cell formulas; we see that the Excel worksheet shows the same frequency distribution that we developed in Table 2.2.

If you are familiar with the COUNTIF function, and do not need the assistance of the Function Wizard, you can enter the formulas directly into cells D2:D6. For instance, to count the number of times that Coke Classic appears, enter the following formula into cell D2:

$$=COUNTIF(\$A\$2:\$A\$51,C2)$$

To count the number of times the other soft drinks appear, copy the formula into cells D3:D6.

FIGURE 2.10   FREQUENCY DISTRIBUTION FOR SOFT DRINK PURCHASES
CONSTRUCTED USING EXCEL'S COUNTIF FUNCTION

Note: Rows 11–44 are hidden.

	A	B	C	D	E
1	Brand Purchased		Soft Drink	Frequency	
2	Coke Classic		Coke Classic	=COUNTIF($A$2:$A$51,C2)	
3	Diet Coke		Diet Coke	=COUNTIF($A$2:$A$51,C3)	
4	Pepsi-Cola		Dr. Pepper	=COUNTIF($A$2:$A$51,C4)	
5	Diet Coke		Pepsi-Cola	=COUNTIF($A$2:$A$51,C5)	
6	Coke Classic		Sprite	=COUNTIF($A$2:$A$51,C6)	
7	Coke Classic				
8	Dr. Pepper				
9	Diet Coke				
10	Pepsi-Cola				
45	Pepsi-Cola				
46	Pepsi-Cola				
47	Pepsi-Cola				
48	Coke Classic				
49	Dr. Pepper				
50	Pepsi-Cola				
51	Sprite				
52					

	A	B	C	D	E
1	Brand Purchased		Soft Drink	Frequency	
2	Coke Classic		Coke Classic	19	
3	Diet Coke		Diet Coke	8	
4	Pepsi-Cola		Dr. Pepper	5	
5	Diet Coke		Pepsi-Cola	13	
6	Coke Classic		Sprite	5	
7	Coke Classic				
8	Dr. Pepper				
9	Diet Coke				
10	Pepsi-Cola				
45	Pepsi-Cola				
46	Pepsi-Cola				
47	Pepsi-Cola				
48	Coke Classic				
49	Dr. Pepper				
50	Pepsi-Cola				
51	Sprite				
52					

Many more of Excel's functions will be demonstrated in future chapter appendixes. Depending on the complexity of the function, we will either enter it directly into the appropriate cell or utilize the Function Wizard.

Chart Wizard

Excel's Chart Wizard has extensive capabilities for developing graphical presentations. It is a tool that allows us to go beyond what can be done with functions and formulas alone. We show how it can be used to construct bar graphs, histograms, and scatter diagrams.

CDfile
SoftDrink

Bar Graphs and Histograms.   Here we show how the Chart Wizard can be used to construct bar graphs and histograms. Let us start by developing a bar graph for the soft drink data; we constructed a frequency distribution in Figure 2.10. The chart we are going to develop is an extension of that worksheet. Refer to Figure 2.11 as we describe the tasks involved. The value worksheet from Figure 2.10 is in the background; the chart developed using the Chart Wizard is in the foreground.

FIGURE 2.11   BAR GRAPH OF SOFT DRINK PURCHASES CONSTRUCTED USING EXCEL'S CHART WIZARD

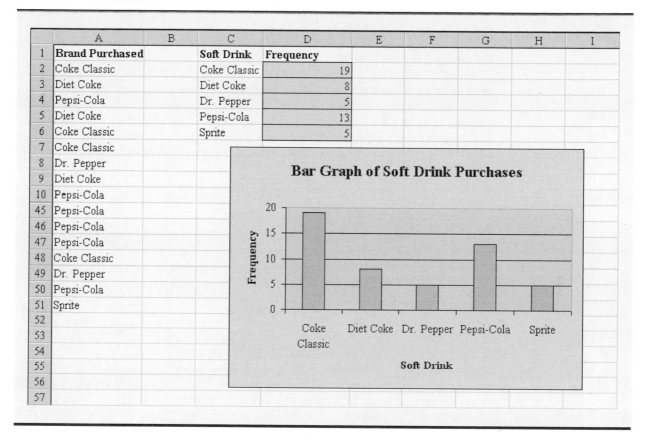

The following steps describe how to use Excel's Chart Wizard to construct a bar graph for the soft drink data using the frequency distribution appearing in cells C1:D6.

Step 1. Select cells C1:D6

Step 2. Select the **Chart Wizard** button on the Standard toolbar (or select the **Insert** pull-down menu and choose the **Chart** option)

Step 3. When the Chart Wizard–Step 1 of 4–Chart Type dialog box appears:
Choose **Column** in the **Chart type** list
Choose **Clustered Column** from the **Chart sub-type** display
Select **Next**

Step 4. When the Chart Wizard–Step 2 of 4–Chart Source Data dialog box appears:
Select **Next**

Step 5. When the Chart Wizard–Step 3 of 4–Chart Options dialog box appears:
Select the **Titles** tab
Enter **Bar Graph of Soft Drink Purchases** in the **Chart title** box
Enter **Soft Drink** in the **Category (X) axis** box
Enter **Frequency** in the **Values (Y) axis** box
Select the **Legend** tab and then
Remove the check in the **Show legend** Box
Select **Next**

Step 6. When the Chart Wizard–Step 4 of 4–Chart Location dialog box appears:
> Specify a location for the new chart (We used the current worksheet by selecting **As object in**)
> Select **Finish**

The resulting bar graph (chart) is shown in Figure 2.11.[2]

Excel's Chart Wizard can produce a pie chart for the soft drink data in a similar fashion. The major difference is that in Step 3 we would choose Pie in the Chart type list.

As we stated in a note and comment at the end of Section 2.2, a histogram is essentially the same as a bar graph with no separation between the bars. Figure 2.12 shows the audit-time data with a frequency distribution in the background and a bar graph developed using the Chart Wizard (using the same steps just described) in the foreground. Because the adjacent bars in a histogram must touch, we need to edit the column chart (the bar graph) in order to eliminate the gap between each of the bars. The following steps accomplish this process.

Step 1. Right click on any bar in the column chart to produce a list of options
Step 2. Choose **Format Data Series**
Step 3. When the Format Data Series dialog box appears:
> Select the **Options** tab
> Enter **0** in the **Gap width** box
> Click **OK**

CDfile
Stereo

Scatter Diagram.   We use the stereo and sound equipment store data in Table 2.14 to demonstrate the use of Excel's Chart Wizard to construct a scatter diagram. Refer to Figure 2.13 as we describe the tasks involved. The data are in the background and the scatter diagram produced by the Chart Wizard is in the foreground. The following steps will produce the scatter diagram.

Step 1. Select cells B1:C11
Step 2. Select the **Chart Wizard** button on the standard toolbar (or select the **Insert** pull-down menu and choose the **Chart** option)
Step 3. When the Chart Wizard–Step 1 of 4–Chart Type dialog box appears:
> Choose **XY (Scatter)** in the **Chart type:** display
> Select **Next**
Step 4. When the Chart Wizard–Step 2 of 4–Chart Source Data dialog box appears:
> Select **Next**
Step 5. When the Chart Wizard–Step 3 of 4–Chart Options dialog box appears:
> Select the **Titles** tab
> Enter **Scatter Diagram for the Stereo and Sound Equipment Store** in the **Chart title** box
> Enter **No. of Commercials** in the **Value (X) axis** box
> Enter **Sales Volume** in the **Value (Y) axis** box
> Select the **Legend** tab
> Remove the check in the **Show legend** box
> Select **Next**

---

[2]Resizing an Excel chart is not difficult. First, select the chart. Small black squares, called sizing handles, will appear on the chart border. Click on the sizing handles and drag them to resize the figure to your preference.

FIGURE 2.12   HISTOGRAM CONSTRUCTED USING EXCEL FOR THE AUDIT-TIME DATA

	A	B	C	D	E	F	G	H	I	J
1	Audit Time		Audit Time	Frequency						
2	12		10-14	4						
3	15		15-19	8						
4	20		20-24	5						
5	22		25-29	2						
6	14		30-34	1						
7	14									
8	15									
9	27									
10	21									
11	18									
12	19									
13	18									
14	22									
15	33									
16	16									
17	18									
18	17									
19	23									
20	28									
21	13									
22										

Histogram for Audit-Time Data

Step 6. When the Chart Wizard–Step 4 of 4–Chart Location dialog box appears:
Specify a location for the new chart (We used the current worksheet by se-
lecting **As object in**)
Select **Finish**

PivotTable Report

Excel's PivotTable Report provides a valuable tool for managing data sets involving more than one variable. We will illustrate its use by showing how to develop a crosstabulation.

CDfile
Restaurant

Crosstabulation.   We will illustrate the construction of a crosstabulation using the restaurant data in Figure 2.14. Labels have been entered in row 1 and the data for each of the 300 restaurants have been entered into cells A2:C301.

The crosstabulation shown in Table 2.12 has three rows under the heading Quality Rating, corresponding to the three quality categories, Good, Very Good, and Excellent. Unless we specify differently, the PivotTable Report will order the labels alphabetically causing the quality ratings to be listed in the order Excellent, Good, and Very Good. Because we want the quality ratings in the order Good, Very Good, Excellent, we must change the default order for the PivotTable Report. The following steps will do so:

Step 1. Select the **Tools** pull-down menu
Step 2. Choose **Options**

FIGURE 2.13 SCATTER DIAGRAM FOR STEREO AND SOUND EQUIPMENT STORE USING EXCEL'S CHART WIZARD

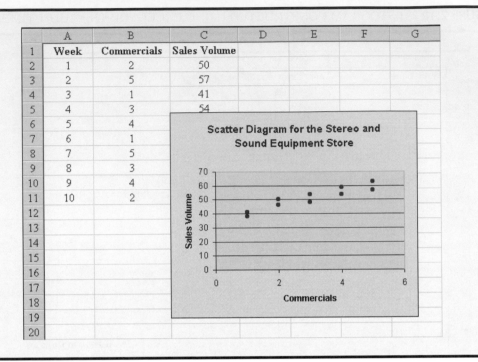

FIGURE 2.14 EXCEL WORKSHEET CONTAINING RESTAURANT DATA

Restaurant

Note: Rows 12–291 are hidden.

	A	B	C	D
1	Restaurant	Quality Rating	Meal Price ($)	
2	1	Good	18	
3	2	Very Good	22	
4	3	Good	28	
5	4	Excellent	38	
6	5	Very Good	33	
7	6	Good	28	
8	7	Very Good	19	
9	8	Very Good	11	
10	9	Very Good	23	
11	10	Good	13	
292	291	Very Good	23	
293	292	Very Good	24	
294	293	Excellent	45	
295	294	Good	14	
296	295	Good	18	
297	296	Good	17	
298	297	Good	16	
299	298	Good	15	
300	299	Very Good	38	
301	300	Very Good	31	
302				

Step 3. When the Options dialog box appears:

Select the **Custom lists** tab (see Figure 2.15)

In the **List entries** box, type **Good** and press Enter; type **Very Good** and press Enter; and type **Excellent**

Select **Add**

Click **OK**

We are now ready to use the PivotTable Report to construct a crosstabulation of the data for quality rating and meal price. Starting with the worksheet in Figure 2.14, the following steps are necessary:

Step 1. Select the **Data** pull down menu

Step 2. Choose the **PivotTable and PivotChart** Report

Step 3. When the PivotTable and PivotChart Wizard–Step 1 of 3 dialog box appears:

Choose **Microsoft Excel list or database**

Choose **PivotTable**

Select **Next**

Step 4. When the PivotTable and PivotChart Wizard–Step 2 of 3 dialog box appears:

Enter A1:C301 in the **Range** box

Select **Next**

FIGURE 2.15   DIALOG BOX FOR CHANGING SORT ORDER IN EXCEL PIVOTTABLE

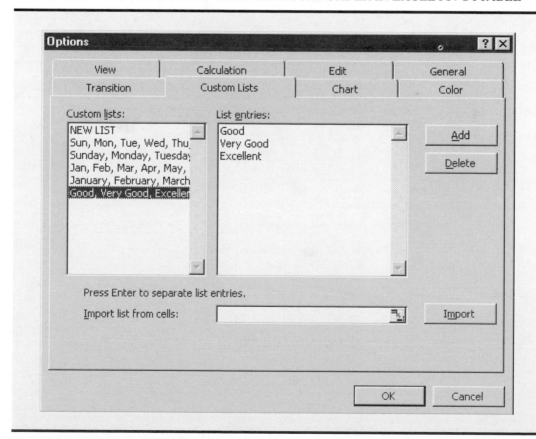

Step 5. When the PivotTable and PivotChart Wizard–Step 3 of 3 dialog box appears:
    Select **New Worksheet**
    Click the **Layout** button
Step 6. When the PivotTable and PivotChart Wizard–Layout diagram appears (see Figure 2.16):
    Drag the **QualityRating** field button to the **ROW** section of the diagram
    Drag the **Meal Price ($)** field button to the **COLUMN** section of the diagram
    Drag the **Restaurant** field button to the **DATA** section of the diagram
    Double click the **Sum of Restaurant** field button in the DATA section
    When the PivotTable Field dialog box appears:
      Choose **Count** under **Summarize by**
      Click **OK** (Figure 2.17 shows the completed layout diagram)
    Click **OK**
Step 7. When the PivotTable and PivotChart Wizard–Step 3 of 3 dialog box reappears:
    Select **Finish**

A portion of the output generated by Excel is shown in Figure 2.18. Note that the output that appears in columns D through AK has been hidden so the results can be shown in a reasonably sized figure. The row labels (Good, Very Good, and Excellent) and row totals (84, 150, 66, and 300) that appear in Figure 2.18 are the same as the row labels and row totals shown in Table 2.12. But, in Figure 2.18, one column is designated for each possible value of meal price. For example, column B contains a count of restaurants with a $10 meal price, column C contains a count of restaurants with an $11 meal price, and so on. To view

FIGURE 2.16 PIVOTTABLE AND PIVOTCHART WIZARD-LAYOUT DIAGRAM

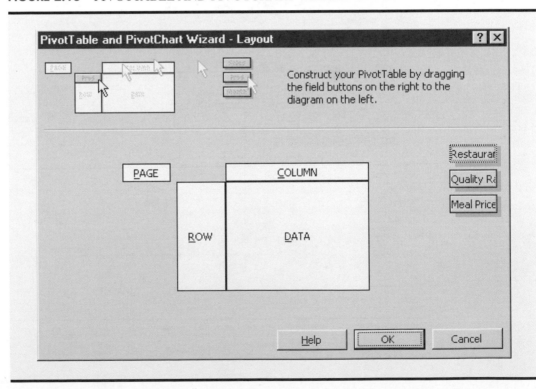

FIGURE 2.17   COMPLETED LAYOUT DIAGRAM

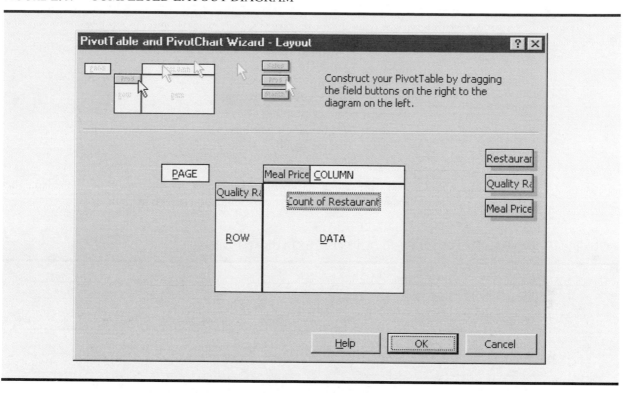

FIGURE 2.18   INITIAL PIVOTTABLE REPORT OUTPUT (COLUMNS D:AK ARE HIDDEN.)

	A	B	C	AL	AM	AN	AO
1							
2							
3	Count of Restaurant	Meal Price ($) ▾					
4	Quality Rating ▾	10	11	47	48	Grand Total	
5	Good	6	4			84	
6	Very Good	1	4		1	150	
7	Excellent			2	2	66	
8	Grand Total	7	8	2	3	300	
9							
10							
11							
12							
13							
14							
15		PivotTable		✕			
16		PivotTable ▾					
17							
18							
19							
20							

the PivotTable Report in a form similar to that shown in Table 2.12, we must group the columns into four price categories: $10–19, $20–29, $30–39, and $40–49. The steps necessary to group the columns for the worksheet shown in Figure 2.18 follow.

Step 1. Right click on Meal Price ($) in cell B3 of the PivotTable
Step 2. Select **Group and Outline**
Choose **Group**
Step 3. When the **Grouping** dialog box appears
Enter 10 in the **Starting at** box
Enter 49 in the **Ending at** box
Enter 10 in the **By** box
Click **OK**

The revised PivotTable output is shown in Figure 2.19. It is the final PivotTable. Note that it provides the same information as the crosstabulation shown in Table 2.12.

FIGURE 2.19   FINAL PIVOTTABLE REPORT FOR RESTAURANT DATA

	A	B	C	D	E	F	G
1							
2							
3	Count of Restaurant	Meal Price ($) ▼					
4	Quality Rating ▼	10-19	20-29	30-39	40-49	Grand Total	
5	Good	42	40	2		84	
6	Very Good	34	64	46	6	150	
7	Excellent	2	14	28	22	66	
8	Grand Total	78	118	76	28	300	
9							
10							
11							
12							
13							
14							
15			PivotTable ✕				
16			PivotTable ▼				
17							
18							
19							
20							

DESCRIPTIVE STATISTICS: NUMERICAL METHODS

CONTENTS

SMALL FRY DESIGN*

SANTA ANA, CALIFORNIA

Founded in 1997, Small Fry Design is a toy and accessory company that designs and imports products for infants. The company's product line includes teddy bears, mobiles, musical toys, rattles, and security blankets, and features high-quality soft toy designs with an emphasis on color, texture, and sound. The products are designed in the United States and manufactured in China.

Small Fry Design uses independent representatives to sell the products to infant furnishing retailers, children's accessory and apparel stores, gift shops, upscale department stores, and major catalog companies. Currently, Small Fry Design products are distributed in more than 1000 retail outlets throughout the United States.

Cash flow management is one of the most critical activities in the day-to-day operation of this young company. Ensuring sufficient incoming cash to meet both current and ongoing debt obligations can mean the difference between business success and failure. A critical factor in cash flow management is the analysis and control of accounts receivable. By measuring the average age and dollar value of outstanding invoices, management can predict cash availability and monitor changes in the status of accounts receivable. The company has set the following goals: the average age for outstanding invoices should not exceed 45 days and the dollar value of invoices more than 60 days old should not exceed 5% of the dollar value of all accounts receivable.

In a recent summary of accounts receivable status, the following descriptive statistics were provided for the age of outstanding invoices:

Mean	40 days
Median	35 days
Mode	31 days

Small Fry Design's bumble bee and blanket products.
© Photo courtesy of Small Fry Design.

Interpretation of these statistics shows that the mean or average age of an invoice is 40 days. The median shows that half of the invoices have been outstanding 35 days or more. The mode of 31 days is the most frequent invoice age indicating that the most common length of time an invoice has been outstanding is 31 days. The statistical summary also showed that only 3% of the dollar value of all accounts receivable was over 60 days old. Based on the statistical information, management was satisfied that accounts receivable and incoming cash flow were under control.

In this chapter, you will learn how to compute and interpret some of the statistical measures used by Small Fry Design. In addition to the mean, median, and mode, you will learn about other descriptive statistics such as the range, variance, standard deviation, percentiles, and correlation. These numerical measures assist in the understanding and interpretation of data.

---

*The authors are indebted to John A. McCarthy, president of Small Fry Design, for providing this Statistics in Practice.

In Chapter 2 we discussed tabular and graphical methods used to summarize data. These procedures are effective in written reports and as visual aids for presentations to individuals or groups. In this chapter, we present several numerical methods of descriptive statistics that provide additional alternatives for summarizing data.

We start by considering data sets consisting of a single variable. The numerical measures of location and dispersion are computed by using the n data values. If the data set contains more than one variable, each single variable numerical measure can be computed separately. In the two-variable case, we will also develop measures of the relationship between the variables.

Several numerical measures of location, dispersion, and association are introduced. If the measures are computed using data from a sample, they are called **sample statistics.** If the measures are computed using data from a population, they are called **population parameters.**

3.1   MEASURES OF LOCATION

Mean

Perhaps the most important numerical measure of location is the **mean,** or average value, for a variable. The mean provides a measure of central location for the data. If the data are from a sample, the mean is denoted by $\bar{x}$; if the data are from a population, the mean is denoted by the Greek letter μ.

In statistical formulas, it is customary to denote the value of variable x for the first observation by x_1, the value of variable x for the second observation by x_2, and so on. In general, the value of variable x for the ith observation is denoted by x_i. For a sample with n observations, the formula for the sample mean is as follows.

Sample Mean

$$\bar{x} = \frac{\Sigma x_i}{n} \qquad (3.1)$$

In the preceding formula, the numerator is the sum of the values of the n observations. That is,

$$\Sigma x_i = x_1 + x_2 + \cdots + x_n$$

The Greek letter Σ is the summation sign.

To illustrate the computation of a sample mean, let us consider the following class-size data for a sample of five college classes.

$$46 \quad 54 \quad 42 \quad 46 \quad 32$$

We use the notation x_1, x_2, x_3, x_4, x_5 to represent the number of students in each of the five classes.

$$x_1 = 46 \qquad x_2 = 54 \qquad x_3 = 42 \qquad x_4 = 46 \qquad x_5 = 32$$

Hence, to compute the sample mean, we write

$$\bar{x} = \frac{\Sigma x_i}{n} = \frac{x_1 + x_2 + x_3 + x_4 + x_5}{5} = \frac{46 + 54 + 42 + 46 + 32}{5} = 44$$

The sample mean class size is 44 students.

Another illustration of the computation of a sample mean is given in the following situation. Suppose that a college placement office sent a questionnaire to a sample of business school graduates requesting information on monthly starting salaries. Table 3.1 shows the collected data. The mean monthly starting salary for the sample of 12 business college graduates is computed as

$$\bar{x} = \frac{\Sigma x_i}{n} = \frac{x_1 + x_2 + \cdots + x_{12}}{12}$$

$$= \frac{2850 + 2950 + \cdots + 2880}{12}$$

$$= \frac{35{,}280}{12} = 2940$$

Equation (3.1) shows how the mean is computed for a sample with n observations. The formula for computing the mean of a population is the same, but we use different notation to indicate that we are working with the entire population. The number of observations in the population is denoted by N and the symbol for the population mean is μ.

Population Mean

$$\mu = \frac{\Sigma x_i}{N} \tag{3.2}$$

Median

The **median** is another measure of central location for data. The median is the value in the middle when the data are arranged in ascending order. With an odd number of observations, the median is the middle value. An even number of observations has no middle value. In this

TABLE 3.1   MONTHLY STARTING SALARIES FOR A SAMPLE OF 12 BUSINESS
SCHOOL GRADUATES

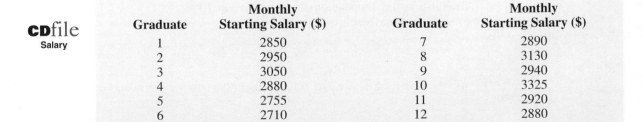

CDfile
Salary

Graduate	Monthly Starting Salary ($)	Graduate	Monthly Starting Salary ($)
1	2850	7	2890
2	2950	8	3130
3	3050	9	2940
4	2880	10	3325
5	2755	11	2920
6	2710	12	2880

case, we follow the convention of defining the median to be the average of the two middle values. For convenience the definition of the median is restated as follows.

Median

Arrange the data in ascending order (smallest value to largest value).

(a) For an odd number of observations, the median is the middle value.
(b) For an even number of observations, the median is the average of the two middle values.

Let us apply this definition to compute the median class size for the sample of five college classes. Arranging the data in ascending order provides the following list.

$$32 \quad 42 \quad 46 \quad 46 \quad 54$$

Because $n = 5$ is odd, the median is the middle value. Thus the median class size is 46 students. Even though this data set has two values of 46, each observation is treated separately when we arrange the data in ascending order.

Suppose we also compute the median starting salary for the business college graduates. We first arrange the data in Table 3.1 in ascending order.

$$2710 \quad 2755 \quad 2850 \quad 2880 \quad 2880 \quad \underbrace{2890 \quad 2920}_{\text{Middle Two Values}} \quad 2940 \quad 2950 \quad 3050 \quad 3130 \quad 3325$$

Because $n = 12$ is even, we identify the middle two values: 2890 and 2920. The median is the average of these values.

$$\text{Median} = \frac{2890 + 2920}{2} = 2905$$

The median is the measure of location most often reported for annual income and property value data because a few extremely large incomes or property values can inflate the mean. In such cases, the median is a better measure of central location.

Although the mean is the more commonly used measure of central location, in some situations the median is preferred. The mean is influenced by extremely small and large values. For instance, suppose that one of the graduates (see Table 3.1) had a starting salary of $10,000 per month (maybe the individual's family owns the company). If we change the highest monthly starting salary in Table 3.1 from $3325 to $10,000 and recompute the mean, the sample mean changes from $2940 to $3496. The median of $2905, however, is unchanged, because $2890 and $2920 are still the middle two values. With the extremely high starting salary included, the median provides a better measure of central location than the mean. We can generalize to say that whenever data have extreme values, the median is often the preferred measure of central location.

Mode

A third measure of location is the **mode.** The mode is defined as follows.

Mode

The mode is the value that occurs with greatest frequency.

To illustrate the identification of the mode, consider the sample of five class sizes. The only value that occurs more than once is 46. Because this value, occurring with a frequency of 2, has the greatest frequency, it is the mode. As another illustration, consider the sample of starting salaries for the business school graduates. The only monthly starting salary that occurs more than once is $2880. Because this value has the greatest frequency, it is the mode.

Situations can arise for which the greatest frequency occurs at two or more different values. In these instances more than one mode exists. If the data have exactly two modes, we say that the data are *bimodal*. If data have more than two modes, we say that the data are *multimodal*. In multimodal cases the mode is almost never reported; listing three or more modes would not be particularly helpful in describing a location for the data.

Percentiles

A **percentile** provides information about how the data are spread over the interval from the smallest value to the largest value. For data that do not have numerous repeated values, the pth percentile divides the data into two parts. Approximately p percent of the observations have values less than the pth percentile; approximately $(100 - p)$ percent of the observations have values greater than the pth percentile. The pth percentile is formally defined as follows.

Percentile

The pth percentile is a value such that *at least p* percent of the observations are less than or equal to this value and *at least* $(100 - p)$ percent of the observations are greater than or equal to this value.

Colleges and universities frequently report admission test scores in terms of percentiles. For instance, suppose an applicant obtains a raw score of 54 on the verbal portion of an admission test. How this student performed in relation to other students taking the same test may not be readily apparent. However, if the raw score of 54 corresponds to the 70th percentile, we know that approximately 70% of the students scored lower than this individual and approximately 30% of the students scored higher than this individual.

The following procedure can be used to compute the pth percentile.

Calculating the pth Percentile

Following these steps makes it easy to calculate percentiles.

Step 1. Arrange the data in ascending order (smallest value to largest value).
Step 2. Compute an index i

$$i = \left(\frac{p}{100}\right)n$$

where p is the percentile of interest and n is the number of observations.
Step 3. (a) If *i is not an integer, round up.* The next integer *greater* than i denotes the position of the pth percentile.
(b) If *i is an integer,* the pth percentile is the average of the values in positions i and $i + 1$.

As an illustration of this procedure, let us determine the 85th percentile for the starting salary data in Table 3.1.

Step 1. Arrange the data in ascending order.

2710   2755   2850   2880   2880   2890   2920   2940   2950   3050   3130   3325

Step 2.

$$i = \left(\frac{p}{100}\right)n = \left(\frac{85}{100}\right)12 = 10.2$$

Step 3. Because i is not an integer, *round up*. The position of the 85th percentile is the next integer greater than 10.2, the 11th position.

Returning to the data, we see that the 85th percentile is the value in the 11th position, or 3130.

As another illustration of this procedure, let us consider the calculation of the 50th percentile. Applying step 2, we obtain

$$i = \left(\frac{50}{100}\right)12 = 6$$

Because i is an integer, step 3(b) states that the 50th percentile is the average of the sixth and seventh values; thus the 50th percentile is $(2890 + 2920)/2 = 2905$. Note that the *50th percentile is also the median.*

Quartiles

Quartiles are just specific percentiles; thus, the steps for computing percentiles can be applied directly in the computation of quartiles.

It is often desirable to divide data into four parts, with each part containing approximately one-fourth, or 25%, of the observations. Figure 3.1 shows a data set divided into four parts. The division points are referred to as the **quartiles** and are defined as

Q_1 = first quartile, or 25th percentile

Q_2 = second quartile, or 50th percentile (also the median)

Q_3 = third quartile, or 75th percentile.

FIGURE 3.1   LOCATION OF THE QUARTILES

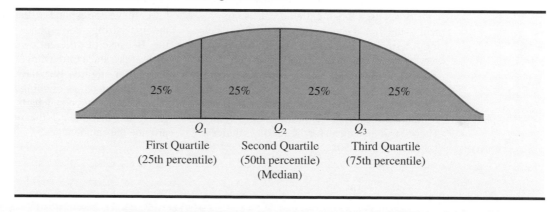

The monthly starting salary data are again arranged in ascending order. Q_2, the second quartile (median), has already been identified as 2905.

2710 2755 2850 2880 2880 2890 2920 2940 2950 3050 3130 3325

The computations of Q_1 and Q_3 require the use of the rule for finding the 25th and 75th percentiles. Those calculations follow.

For Q_1,

$$i = \left(\frac{p}{100}\right)n = \left(\frac{25}{100}\right)12 = 3$$

Because i is an integer, step 3(b) indicates that the first quartile, or 25th percentile, is the average of the third and fourth values; thus, $Q_1 = (2850 + 2880)/2 = 2865$.

For Q_3,

$$i = \left(\frac{p}{100}\right)n = \left(\frac{75}{100}\right)12 = 9$$

Again, because i is an integer, step 3(b) indicates that the third quartile, or 75th percentile, is the average of the ninth and tenth values; thus, $Q_3 = (\$2950 + \$3050)/2 = \$3000$.

The quartiles have divided the data into four parts, with each part consisting of 25% of the observations.

2710 2755 2850 | 2880 2880 2890 | 2920 2940 2950 | 3050 3130 3325

$Q_1 = 2865$ \qquad\qquad $Q_2 = 2905$ \qquad\qquad $Q_3 = 3000$
(Median)

We have defined the quartiles as the 25th, 50th, and 75th percentiles. Thus, we have computed the quartiles in the same way as the other percentiles. However, other conventions are sometimes used to compute quartiles and the actual values reported may vary slightly depending on the convention used. Nevertheless, the objective of all procedures for computing quartiles is to divide data into roughly four equal parts.

NOTES AND COMMENTS

1. It is better to use the median than the mean as a measure of central location when a data set contains extreme values. Another measure, sometimes used when extreme values are present, is the *trimmed mean*. It is obtained by deleting the smallest and largest values from a data set, then computing the mean of the remaining values. For example, the 5% trimmed mean is obtained by removing the smallest 5% and the largest 5% of the data values from a data set, then computing the mean of the remaining values. The 5% trimmed mean for the starting salaries in Table 3.1 is 2924.50.

2. An alternative to the quartile for dividing a data set into four equal parts has been developed by proponents of exploratory data analysis. The lower hinge corresponds to the first quartile, and the upper **hinge** corresponds to the third quartile. Because of different computational procedures, the values of the hinges and the quartiles may differ slightly. But, they can both be correctly interpreted as dividing a data set into approximately four equal parts. For the starting salary data in Table 3.1, the hinges and quartiles provide the same values.

EXERCISES

Methods

1. Consider the sample of size 5 with data values of 10, 20, 12, 17, and 16. Compute the mean and median.

2. Consider the sample of size 6 with data values of 10, 20, 21, 17, 16, and 12. Compute the mean and median.

SELFtest 3. Consider the sample of size 8 with data values of 27, 25, 20, 15, 30, 34, 28, and 25. Compute the 20th, 25th, 65th, and 75th percentiles.

4. Consider a sample with the data values of 53, 55, 70, 58, 64, 57, 53, 69, 57, 68, and 53. Compute the mean, median, and mode.

Applications

CDfile

AcctSal

5. According to a salary survey conducted by the National Association of Colleges and Employers, bachelor's degree candidates in accounting received starting offers averaging $34,500 per year (Bureau of Labor Statistics, *Occupational Outlook Handbook*, 2000–01 Edition). A sample of 30 students who graduated in 2000 with a bachelor's degree in accounting resulted in the following starting salaries. Data are in thousands of dollars.

36.8	34.9	35.2	37.2	36.2
35.8	36.8	36.1	36.7	36.6
37.3	38.2	36.3	36.4	39.0
38.3	36.0	35.0	36.7	37.9
38.3	36.4	36.5	38.4	39.4
38.8	35.4	36.4	37.0	36.4

   a. What is the mean starting salary?
   b. What is the median starting salary?
   c. What is the mode?
   d. What is the first quartile?
   e. What is the third quartile?

6. More and more investors are turning to discount brokers to save money when buying and selling shares of stock. The American Association of Individual Investors conducts an annual survey of discount brokers. Shown in Table 3.2 are the commissions charged by a sample of 20 discount brokers for two types of trades: 500 shares at $50 per share and 1000 shares at $5 per share.
   a. Compute the mean, median, and mode for the commission charged on a trade of 500 shares at $50 per share.
   b. Compute the mean, median, and mode for the commission charged on a trade of 1000 shares at $5 per share.
   c. Which costs the most: trading 500 shares at $50 per share or trading 1000 shares at $5 per share?
   d. Does the cost of a transaction seem to be related to the amount of the transaction? For example, the amount of the transaction when trading 500 shares at $50 per share is $25,000.

TABLE 3.2 COMMISSIONS CHARGED BY DISCOUNT BROKERS

	Commission ($)	
Broker	**500@$50**	**1000@$5**
AcuTrade	38.00	48.00
Bank of San Francisco	140.00	79.50
Burke Christensen & Lewis	34.00	34.00
Bush Burns Securities	35.00	35.00
Charles Schwab	155.00	90.00
Downstate Discount	55.00	60.00
Dreyfus Lion Account	154.50	88.50
First Union Brokerage	140.00	90.00
Levitt & Levitt	35.00	70.00
Max Ule	195.00	70.00
Mongerson & Co	95.00	66.00
Quick & Reilly	119.50	60.50
Scottsdale Securities, Inc.	50.00	63.00
Seaport Securities Corp.	50.00	70.00
St. Louis Discount	66.00	64.00
Summit Financial Services	95.00	60.50
T. Rowe Price Brokerage	134.00	80.00
Unified Financial Services	154.00	90.00
Wall Street Access	45.00	45.00
Your Discount Broker	55.00	70.00

Source: AAII Journal, January 2000.

CDfile
Discount

7. The average person spends 45 minutes a day listening to recorded music (*The Des Moines Register,* December 5, 1997). The following data were obtained for the number of minutes spent listening to recorded music for a sample of 30 individuals.

CDfile
Music

88.3	4.3	4.6	7.0	9.2
0.0	99.2	34.9	81.7	0.0
85.4	0.0	17.5	45.0	53.3
29.1	28.8	0.0	98.9	64.5
4.4	67.9	94.2	7.6	56.6
52.9	145.6	70.4	65.1	63.6

a. Compute the mean and mode.
b. Do these data appear to be consistent with the average reported by the newspaper?
c. Compute the median.
d. Compute the first and third quartiles.
e. Compute and interpret the 40th percentile.

SELFtest

8. Millions of Americans get up each morning and telecommute to work from offices in their home. Following is a sample of age data for individuals working at home.

28	54	20	46	25	48	53	27	26	37
40	36	42	25	27	33	18	40	45	25

a. Compute the mean and mode.
b. The median age of the population of all adults is 35.5 years (*The New York Times Almanac, 2001*). Use the median age of the preceding data to comment on whether the at-home workers tend to be younger or older than the population of all adults.

    c. Compute the first and third quartiles.

    d. Compute and interpret the 32nd percentile.

9. Media Matrix collected data showing the most popular Web sites when browsing at home and at work (*Business 2.0*, January 2000). The following data show the number of unique visitors (in 1000s) for the top 25 Web sites when browsing at home.

CDfile
Websites

Web Site	Unique Visitors (thousands)
about.com	5538
altavista.com	7391
amazon.com	7986
angelfire.com	8917
aol.com	23863
bluemountainarts.com	6786
ebay.com	8296
excite.com	10479
geocities.com	15321
go.com	14330
hotbot.com	5760
hotmail.com	11791
icq.com	5052
looksmart.com	5984
lycos.com	9950
microsoft.com	15593
msn.com	23505
netscape.com	14470
passport.com	11299
real.com	6785
snap.com	5730
tripod.com	7970
xoom.com	5652
yahoo.com	26796
zdnet.com	5133

    a. Compute the mean and median.

    b. Do you think it would be better to use the mean or the median as the measure of central tendency for these data? Explain.

    c. Compute the first and third quartiles.

    d. Compute and interpret the 85th percentile.

10. The *Los Angeles Times* regularly reports the air quality index for various areas of Southern California. Index ratings of 0–50 are considered good, 51–100 moderate, 101–200 unhealthy, 201–275 very unhealthy, and over 275 hazardous. Recent air quality indexes for Pomona were 28, 42, 58, 48, 45, 55, 60, 49, and 50.

    a. Compute the mean, median, and mode for the data. Should the Pomona air quality index be considered good?

    b. Compute the 25th percentile and 75th percentile for the Pomona air quality data.

11. The following data represent the number of automobiles arriving at a toll booth during 20 intervals, each of 10-minute duration. Compute the mean, median, mode, first quartile, and third quartile for the data.

26	26	58	24	22	22	15	33	19	27
21	18	16	20	34	24	27	30	31	33

12. In automobile mileage and gasoline-consumption testing, 13 automobiles were road tested for 300 miles in both city and country driving conditions. The following data were recorded for miles-per-gallon performance.

City: 16.2   16.7   15.9   14.4   13.2   15.3   16.8   16.0   16.1   15.3   15.2   15.3   16.2
Highway: 19.4   20.6   18.3   18.6   19.2   17.4   17.2   18.6   19.0   21.1   19.4   18.5   18.7

Use the mean, median, and mode to make a statement about the difference in performance for city and country driving.

13. A sample of 15 college seniors showed the following credit hours taken during the final term of the senior year:

     15   21   18   16   18   21   19   15   14   18   17   20   18   15   16

    a. What are the mean, median, and mode for credit hours taken? Compute and interpret.
    b. Compute the first and third quartiles.
    c. Compute and interpret the 70th percentile.

14. Because of recent technological advances, today's digital cameras produce better-looking pictures than did their predecessors a year ago. The following data show the street price, maximum picture capacity, and battery life (minutes) for 20 of the latest models (*PC World*, January 2000).

CDfile
Cameras

Camera	Price ($)	Maximum Picture Capacity	Battery Life (minutes)
Agfa Ephoto CL30	349	36	25
Canon PowerShot A50	499	106	75
Canon PowerShot Pro70	999	96	118
Epson PhotoPC 800	699	120	99
Fujifilm DX-10	299	30	229
Fujifilm MX-2700	699	141	124
Fujifilm MX-2900 Zoom	899	141	88
HP PhotoSmart C200	299	80	68
Kodak DC215 Zoom	399	54	159
Kodak DC265 Zoom	899	180	186
Kodak DC280 Zoom	799	245	143
Minolta Dimage EX Zoom 1500	549	105	38
Nikon Coolpix 950	999	32	88
Olympus D-340R	299	122	161
Olympus D-450 Zoom	499	122	62
Richo RDC-500	699	99	56
Sony Cybershot DSC-F55	699	63	69
Sony Mavica MVC-FD73	599	40	186
Sony Mavica MVC-FD88	999	40	88
Toshiba PDR-M4	599	124	142

    a. Compute the mean price.
    b. Compute the mean maximum picture capacity.
    c. Compute the mean battery life.
    d. If you had to select one camera from this list, what camera would you choose? Explain.

3.2   MEASURES OF VARIABILITY

In addition to measures of location, it is often desirable to consider measures of variability, or dispersion. For example, suppose that you are a purchasing agent for a large manufacturing firm and that you regularly place orders with two different suppliers. After several months of operation, you find that the mean number of days required to fill orders is indeed about 10 days for both of the suppliers. The histograms summarizing the number of working days required to fill orders from the suppliers are shown in Figure 3.2. Although the mean number of days is roughly 10 for both suppliers, do the two suppliers have the same degree of reliability in terms of making deliveries on schedule? Note the dispersion, or variability, in the histograms. Which supplier would you prefer?

For most firms, receiving materials and supplies on schedule is important. The seven- or eight-day deliveries shown for J.C. Clark Distributors might be viewed favorably; however, a few of the slow 13- to 15-day deliveries could be disastrous in terms of keeping a workforce busy and production on schedule. This example illustrates a situation in which the variability in the delivery times may be an overriding consideration in selecting a supplier. For most purchasing agents, the lower variability shown for Dawson Supply, Inc., would make Dawson the preferred supplier.

We turn now to a discussion of some commonly used measures of variability.

Range

Perhaps the simplest measure of variability is the **range.**

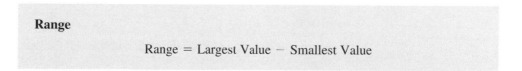

Range

$$\text{Range} = \text{Largest Value} - \text{Smallest Value}$$

FIGURE 3.2   HISTORICAL DATA SHOWING THE NUMBER OF DAYS REQUIRED TO FILL ORDERS

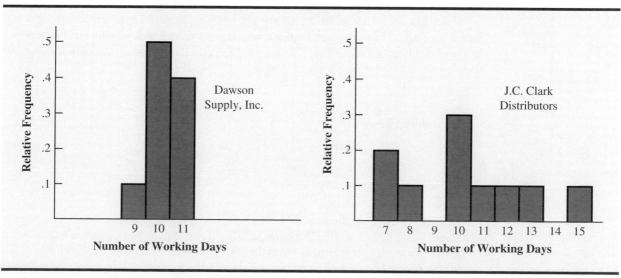

Let us refer to the data on monthly starting salaries for business school graduates in Table 3.1. The largest starting salary is 3325 and the smallest is 2710. The range is 3325 − 2710 = 615.

The range is easy to compute, but it is sensitive to just two data values: the largest and smallest.

Although the range is the easiest of the measures of variability to compute, it is seldom used as the only measure because of its sensitivity to just two of the observations. Suppose one of the graduates had a starting salary of $10,000. In this case, the range would be 10,000 − 2710 = 7290 rather than 615. This large value for the range would not be particularly descriptive of the variability in the data because 11 of the 12 starting salaries are closely grouped between 2710 and 3130.

Interquartile Range

A measure of variability that overcomes the dependency on extreme values is the **interquartile range (IQR).** This measure of variability is simply the difference between the third quartile, Q_3, and the first quartile, Q_1. In other words, the interquartile range is the range for the middle 50% of the data.

Interquartile Range

$$IQR = Q_3 - Q_1 \tag{3.3}$$

For the data on monthly starting salaries, the quartiles are $Q_3 = 3000$ and $Q_1 = 2865$. Thus, the interquartile range is 3000 − 2865 = 135.

Variance

The **variance** is a measure of variability that utilizes all the data. The variance is based on the difference between the value of each observation (x_i) and the mean. The difference between each x_i and the mean ($\bar{x}$ for a sample, μ for a population) is called a *deviation about the mean.* For a sample, a deviation about the mean is written ($x_i - \bar{x}$); for a population, it is written ($x_i - \mu$). In the computation of the variance, the deviations about the mean are *squared.*

If the data are for a population, the average of the squared deviations is called the *population variance.* The population variance is denoted by the Greek symbol σ^2. For a population of N observations and with μ denoting the population mean, the definition of the population variance is as follows.

Population Variance

$$\sigma^2 = \frac{\Sigma(x_i - \mu)^2}{N} \tag{3.4}$$

In most statistical applications, the data being analyzed is a sample. When we compute a sample variance, we are often interested in using it to estimate the population variance σ^2. Although a detailed explanation is beyond the scope of this text, it can be shown that if the sum of the squared deviations about the sample mean is divided by $n - 1$, and not n, the resulting sample variance provides an unbiased estimate of the population variance. For this reason, the *sample variance,* denoted by s^2, is defined as follows.

Sample Variance

$$s^2 = \frac{\Sigma(x_i - \bar{x})^2}{n - 1} \tag{3.5}$$

To illustrate the computation of the sample variance, we use the data on class size for the sample of five college classes as presented in Section 3.1. A summary of the data, including the computation of the deviations about the mean and the squared deviations about the mean, is shown in Table 3.3. The sum of squared deviations about the mean is $\Sigma(x_i - \bar{x})^2 = 256$. Hence, with $n - 1 = 4$, the sample variance is

$$s^2 = \frac{\Sigma(x_i - \bar{x})^2}{n - 1} = \frac{256}{4} = 64$$

Before moving on, let us note that the units associated with the sample variance often cause confusion. Because the values being summed in the variance calculation, $(x_i - \bar{x})^2$, are squared, the units associated with the sample variance are also squared. For instance, the sample variance for the class-size data is $s^2 = 64$ (students)^2. The squared units associated with variance make it difficult to obtain an intuitive understanding and interpretation of the numerical value of the variance. We recommend that you think of the variance as a measure useful in comparing the amount of variability for two or more variables. In a comparison of the variables, the one with the larger variance has the most variability. Further interpretation of the value of the variance may not be necessary.

As another illustration of computing a sample variance, consider the starting salaries listed in Table 3.1 for the 12 business school graduates. In Section 3.1, we showed that the sample mean starting salary was 2940. The computation of the sample variance ($s^2 = 27{,}440.91$) is shown in Table 3.4.

Note that in Tables 3.3 and 3.4 we show both the sum of the deviations about the mean and the sum of the squared deviations about the mean. For any data set, the sum

TABLE 3.3   COMPUTATION OF DEVIATIONS AND SQUARED DEVIATIONS ABOUT THE MEAN FOR THE CLASS-SIZE DATA

Number of Students in Class (x_i)	Mean Class Size ($\bar{x}$)	Deviation About the Mean ($x_i - \bar{x}$)	Squared Deviation About the Mean ($x_i - \bar{x})^2$
46	44	2	4
54	44	10	100
42	44	−2	4
46	44	2	4
32	44	−12	144
		0	256
		$\Sigma(x_i - \bar{x})$	$\Sigma(x_i - \bar{x})^2$

TABLE 3.4   COMPUTATION OF THE SAMPLE VARIANCE FOR THE STARTING
SALARY DATA

Monthly Salary (x_i)	Sample Mean $(\bar{x})$	Deviation About the Mean $(x_i - \bar{x})$	Squared Deviation About the Mean $(x_i - \bar{x})^2$
2850	2940	−90	8,100
2950	2940	10	100
3050	2940	110	12,100
2880	2940	−60	3,600
2755	2940	−185	34,225
2710	2940	−230	52,900
2890	2940	−50	2,500
3130	2940	190	36,100
2940	2940	0	0
3325	2940	385	148,225
2920	2940	−20	400
2880	2940	−60	3,600
		0	301,850
		$\Sigma(x_i - \bar{x})$	$\Sigma(x_i - \bar{x})^2$

Using equation (3.5),

$$s^2 = \frac{\Sigma(x_i - \bar{x})^2}{n - 1} = \frac{301,850}{11} = 27,440.91$$

of the deviations about the mean will *always equal zero*. Note that in Tables 3.3 and 3.4, $\Sigma(x_i - \bar{x}) = 0$. The positive deviations and negative deviations always cancel each other, causing the sum of the deviations about the mean to equal zero.

Standard Deviation

The **standard deviation** is defined as the positive square root of the variance. Following the notation we adopted for a sample variance and a population variance, we use s to denote the sample standard deviation and σ to denote the population standard deviation. The standard deviation is derived from the variance in the following way.

Standard Deviation

$$\text{Sample Standard Deviation} = s = \sqrt{s^2} \qquad (3.6)$$

$$\text{Population Standard Deviation} = \sigma = \sqrt{\sigma^2} \qquad (3.7)$$

Recall that the sample variance for the sample of class sizes in five college classes is $s^2 = 64$. Thus the sample standard deviation is $s = \sqrt{64} = 8$. For the data set on starting salaries, the sample standard deviation is $s = \sqrt{27,440.91} = 165.65$.

The standard deviation is easier to interpret than the variance because standard deviation is measured in the same units as the data.

What is gained by converting the variance to its corresponding standard deviation? Recall that the units associated with the variance are squared. For example, the sample variance for the starting salary data of business school graduates is $s^2 = 27,440.91$ (dollars)^2. Because the standard deviation is simply the square root of the variance, the units of the variance, dollars squared, are converted to dollars in the standard deviation. Thus, the standard deviation of the starting salary data is $165.65. In other words, the standard deviation is measured in the same units as the original data. For this reason the standard deviation is more easily compared to the mean and other statistics that are measured in the same units as the original data.

Coefficient of Variation

The coefficient of variation is a relative measure of variability; it measures the standard deviation relative to the mean.

In some situations we may be interested in a descriptive statistic that indicates how large the standard deviation is in relation to the mean. This measure is called the **coefficient of variation** and is computed as follows.

Coefficient of Variation

$$\frac{\text{Standard Deviation}}{\text{Mean}} \times 100 \tag{3.8}$$

For the class-size data, we found a sample mean of 44 and a sample standard deviation of 8. The coefficient of variation is $(8/44) \times 100 = 18.2$. In words, the coefficient of variation tells us that the sample standard deviation is 18.2% of the value of the sample mean. For the starting salary data with a sample mean of 2940 and a sample standard deviation of 165.65, the coefficient of variation, $(165.65/2940) \times 100 = 5.6$, tells us the sample standard deviation is only 5.6% of the value of the sample mean. In general, the coefficient of variation is a useful statistic for comparing the variability of variables that have different standard deviations and different means.

NOTES AND COMMENTS

1. Statistical software packages and spreadsheets can be used to develop the descriptive statistics presented in this chapter. After the data have been entered into a worksheet, a few simple commands can be used to generate the desired output. In Appendixes 3.1 and 3.2, we show how Minitab and Excel can be used to develop descriptive statistics.

2. The standard deviation is a commonly used measure of the risk associated with investing in stock and stock funds (*Business Week*, January 17, 2000). It provides a measure of how monthly returns fluctuate around the long-run average return.

3. Rounding the value of the sample mean $\bar{x}$ and the values of the squared deviations $(x_i - \bar{x})^2$ may introduce errors when a calculator is used in the computation of the variance and standard deviation. To reduce rounding errors, we recommend carrying at least six significant digits during intermediate calculations. The resulting variance or standard deviation can then be rounded to fewer digits.

4. An alternative formula for the computation of the sample variance is

$$s^2 = \frac{\Sigma x_i^2 - n\bar{x}^2}{n - 1}$$

where $\Sigma x_i^2 = x_1^2 + x_2^2 + \cdots + x_n^2$.

EXERCISES

Methods

15. Consider the sample of size 5 with data values of 10, 20, 12, 17, and 16. Compute the range and interquartile range.

16. Consider the sample of size 5 with data values of 10, 20, 12, 17, and 16. Compute the variance and standard deviation.

SELFtest   **17.** Consider the sample of size 8 with data values of 27, 25, 20, 15, 30, 34, 28, and 25. Compute the range, interquartile range, variance, and standard deviation.

Applications

SELFtest   **18.** A bowler's scores for six games were 182, 168, 184, 190, 170, and 174. Using these data as a sample, compute the following descriptive statistics.
  a. Range
  b. Variance
  c. Standard deviation
  d. Coefficient of variation

19. *PC World* provided ratings for the top 15 notebook PCs (*PC World*, February 2000). A 100-point scale was used to provide an overall rating for each notebook tested in the study. A score in the 90s is exceptional, while one in the 70s is above average. The overall ratings for the 15 notebooks tested are shown here.

CDfile
Notebook

Notebook	Overall Rating
AMS Tech Roadster 15CTA380	67
Compaq Armada M700	78
Compaq Prosignia Notebook 150	79
Dell Inspiron 3700 C466GT	80
Dell Inspiron 7500 R500VT	84
Dell Latitude Cpi A366XT	76
Enpower ENP-313 Pro	77
Gateway Solo 9300LS	92
HP Pavillion Notebook PC	83
IBM ThinkPad I Series 1480	78
Micro Express NP7400	77
Micron TransPort NX PII-400	78
NEC Versa SX	78
Sceptre Soundx 5200	73
Sony VAIO PCG-F340	77

Compute the range, interquartile range, variance, and standard deviation.

20. The *Los Angeles Times* regularly reports the air quality index for various areas of Southern California. A sample of air quality index values for Pomona provided the following data: 28, 42, 58, 48, 45, 55, 60, 49, and 50.
  a. Compute the range and interquartile range.
  b. Compute the sample variance and sample standard deviation.
  c. A sample of air quality index readings for Anaheim provided a sample mean of 48.5, a sample variance of 136, and a sample standard deviation of 11.66. What comparisons can you make between the air quality in Pomona and that in Anaheim on the basis of these descriptive statistics?

21. The Davis Manufacturing Company has just completed five weeks of operation using a new process that is supposed to increase productivity. The numbers of parts produced each week are 410, 420, 390, 400, and 380. Compute the sample variance and sample standard deviation.

22. Assume that the following data were used to construct the histograms of the number of days required to fill orders for Dawson Supply, Inc., and J. C. Clark Distributors (see Figure 3.2).

Dawson Supply Days for Delivery: 11   10   9   10   11   11   10   11   10   10
Clark Distributors Days for Delivery: 8   10   13   7   10   11   10   7   15   12

Use the range and standard deviation to support the previous observation that Dawson Supply provides the more consistent and reliable delivery times.

23. Police records show the following numbers of daily crime reports for a sample of days during the winter months and a sample of days during the summer months.

Crime

Winter	Summer
18	28
20	18
15	24
16	32
21	18
20	29
12	23
16	38
19	28
20	18

a. Compute the range and interquartile range for each period.
b. Compute the variance and standard deviation for each period.
c. Compute the coefficient of variation for each period.
d. Compare the variability of the two periods.

24. The American Association of Individual Investors conducts an annual survey of discount brokers (*AAII Journal,* January 1997). Shown in Table 3.2 are the commissions charged by a sample of 20 discount brokers for two types of trades: 500 shares at $50 per share and 1000 shares at $5 per share.
a. Compute the range and interquartile range for each type of trade.
b. Compute the variance and standard deviation for each type of trade.
c. Compute the coefficient of variation for each type of trade.
d. Compare the variability of cost for the two types of trades.

25. A production department uses a sampling procedure to test the quality of newly produced items. The department employs the following decision rule at an inspection station: If a sample of 14 items has a variance of more than .005, the production line must be shut down for repairs. Suppose the following data have just been collected:

3.43   3.45   3.43   3.48   3.52   3.50   3.39
3.48   3.41   3.38   3.49   3.45   3.51   3.50

Should the production line be shut down? Why or why not?

26. The following times were recorded by the quarter-mile and mile runners of a university track team (times are in minutes).

Quarter-mile Times:	.92	.98	1.04	.90	.99
Mile Times:	4.52	4.35	4.60	4.70	4.50

After viewing this sample of running times, one of the coaches commented that the quarter-milers turned in the more consistent times. Use the standard deviation and the coefficient of variation to summarize the variability in the data. Does the use of the coefficient of variation indicate that the coach's statement should be qualified?

3.3   MEASURES OF RELATIVE LOCATION AND DETECTING OUTLIERS

We have described several measures of location and variability for data. The mean is the most widely used measure of location, whereas the standard deviation and variance are the most widely used measures of variability. Using only the mean and the standard deviation, we also can learn much about the relative location of items in a data set.

z-Scores

By using the mean and standard deviation, we can determine the relative location of any observation. Suppose we have a sample of *n* observations, with the values denoted by x_1, $x_2, \ldots, x_n$. In addition, assume that the sample mean, $\bar{x}$, and the sample standard deviation, s, have been computed. Associated with each value, x_i, is another value called its **z-score.** Equation (3.9) shows how the z-score is computed for each x_i.

---

z-Score

$$z_i = \frac{x_i - \bar{x}}{s} \qquad (3.9)$$

where

z_i = the z-score for x_i
$\bar{x}$ = the sample mean
s = the sample standard deviation

The z-score is often called the *standardized value.* The standardized value or z-score, z_i, can be interpreted as the *number of standard deviations x_i is from the mean $\bar{x}$.* For example, $z_1 = 1.2$ would indicate that x_1 is 1.2 standard deviations greater than the sample mean. Similarly, $z_2 = -.5$ would indicate that x_2 is .5, or 1/2, standard deviation less than the sample mean. A z-score greater than zero occurs for observations with a value greater than the mean, and a z-score less than zero occurs for observations with a value less than the mean. A z-score of zero indicates that the value of the observation is equal to the mean.

The z-score for any observation can be interpreted as a measure of the relative location of the observation in a data set. Thus, observations in two different data sets with the same z-score can be said to have the same relative location in terms of being the same number of standard deviations from the mean.

The z-scores for the class-size data are shown in Table 3.5. Recall that the sample mean, $\bar{x} = 44$, and sample standard deviation, $s = 8$, have been computed previously. The z-score of -1.50 for the fifth observation shows it is farthest from the mean; it is 1.50 standard deviations below the mean.

Chebyshev's Theorem

Chebyshev's theorem enables us to make statements about the proportion of data values that must be within a specified number of standard deviations from the mean.

> **Chebyshev's Theorem**
>
> At least $(1 - 1/z^2)$ of the data values must be within z standard deviations of the mean, where z is any value greater than 1.

Some of the implications of this theorem, with $z = 2$, 3, and 4 standard deviations, follow.

- At least .75, or 75%, of the data values must be within $z = 2$ standard deviations of the mean.
- At least .89, or 89%, of the data values must be within $z = 3$ standard deviations of the mean.
- At least .94, or 94%, of the data values must be within $z = 4$ standard deviations of the mean.

For an example using Chebyshev's theorem, assume that the midterm test scores for 100 students in a college business statistics course had a mean of 70 and a standard deviation of 5. How many students had test scores between 60 and 80? How many students had test scores between 58 and 82?

For the test scores between 60 and 80, we note that 60 is two standard deviations below the mean and 80 is two standard deviations above the mean. Using Chebyshev's theorem, we see that at least .75, or at least 75%, of the observations must have values within two standard deviations of the mean. Thus, at least 75 of the 100 students must have scored between 60 and 80.

For the test scores between 58 and 82, we see that $(58 - 70)/5 = -2.4$ indicates 58 is 2.4 standard deviations below the mean and that $(82 - 70)/5 = +2.4$ indicates 82 is

TABLE 3.5 z-SCORES FOR THE CLASS-SIZE DATA

Number of Students in Class (x_i)	Deviation About the Mean $(x_i - \bar{x})$	z-score $\left(\dfrac{x_i - \bar{x}}{s}\right)$	
46	2	$2/8 =$	$.25$
54	10	$10/8 =$	1.25
42	-2	$-2/8 =$	$-.25$
46	2	$2/8 =$	$.25$
32	-12	$-12/8 =$	-1.50

Chebyshev's theorem requires z > 1, but z need not be an integer. Exercise 27 involves noninteger values of z greater than 1.

2.4 standard deviations above the mean. Applying Chebyshev's theorem with $z = 2.4$, we have

$$\left(1 - \frac{1}{z^2}\right) = \left[1 - \frac{1}{(2.4)^2}\right] = .826$$

At least 82.6% of the students must have test scores between 58 and 82.

Empirical Rule

The empirical rule is based on the normal probability distribution, which will be discussed in Chapter 6.

One of the advantages of Chebyshev's theorem is that it applies to any data set regardless of the shape of the distribution of the data. In practical applications, however, many data sets exhibit a mound-shaped or bell-shaped distribution like the one shown in Figure 3.3. When the data are believed to approximate this distribution, the **empirical rule** can be used to determine the percentage of data values that must be within a specified number of standard deviations of the mean.

Empirical Rule

For data having a bell-shaped distribution:

- Approximately 68% of the data values will be within one standard deviation of the mean.
- Approximately 95% of the data values will be within two standard deviations of the mean.
- Almost all of the data values will be within three standard deviations of the mean.

For example, liquid detergent cartons are filled automatically on a production line. Filling weights frequently have a bell-shaped distribution. If the mean filling weight is

FIGURE 3.3   A MOUND-SHAPED OR BELL-SHAPED DISTRIBUTION

16 ounces and the standard deviation is .25 ounces, we can use the empirical rule to draw the following conclusions.

- Approximately 68% of the filled cartons will have weights between 15.75 and 16.25 ounces (that is, within one standard deviation of the mean).
- Approximately 95% of the filled cartons will have weights between 15.50 and 16.50 ounces (that is, within two standard deviations of the mean).
- Almost all filled cartons will have weights between 15.25 and 16.75 ounces (that is, within three standard deviations of the mean).

Detecting Outliers

Sometimes a data set will have one or more observations with unusually large or unusually small values. Extreme values such as these are called **outliers.** Experienced statisticians take steps to identify outliers and then review each one carefully. An outlier may be a data value for which the data have been incorrectly recorded. If so, it can be corrected before further analysis. An outlier may also be from an observation that was incorrectly included in the data set; if so, it can be removed. Finally, an outlier may just be an unusual data value that has been recorded correctly and belongs in the data set. In such cases the item should remain.

It is a good idea to check for outliers before making decisions based on data analysis. Errors are often made in recording data and entering data into the computer. Outliers should not necessarily be deleted, but their accuracy and appropriateness should be verified.

Standardized values (z-scores) can be used to help identify outliers. Recall that the empirical rule allows us to conclude that for data with a bell-shaped distribution, almost all the data values will be within three standard deviations of the mean. Hence, in using z-scores to identify outliers, we recommend treating any data value with a z-score less than -3 or greater than $+3$ as an outlier. Such items can then be reviewed for accuracy and to determine whether they belong in the data set.

Refer to the z-scores for the class-size data in Table 3.5. The z-score of -1.50 shows the fifth item is farthest from the mean. However, this standardized value is well within the -3 to $+3$ guideline for outliers. Thus, the z-scores show that outliers are not present in the class-size data.

NOTES AND COMMENTS

1. Chebyshev's theorem is applicable for any data set and can be used to state the minimum number of data values that will be within a certain number of standard deviations of the mean. If the data set is known to be approximately bell-shaped, more can be said. For instance, the empirical rule allows us to say that *approximately* 95% of the data values will be within two standard deviations of the mean; Chebyshev's theo-rem allows us to conclude only that at least 75% of the data values will be in that interval.

2. Before analyzing a data set, statisticians usually make a variety of checks to ensure the validity of data. In a large study it is not uncommon for errors to be made in recording data values or in entering the values at a computer. Identifying outliers is one tool used to check the validity of the data.

EXERCISES

Methods

SELFtest   **27.** Consider a sample with a mean of 30 and a standard deviation of 5. Use Chebyshev's theorem to determine the proportion, or percentage, of the data within each of the following ranges.

   a. 20 to 40   **b.** 15 to 45   **c.** 22 to 38   **d.** 18 to 42   **e.** 12 to 48

28. Data that have a bell-shaped distribution have a mean of 30 and a standard deviation of 5. Use the empirical rule to determine the proportion, or percentage, of data within each of the following ranges.

    a. 20 to 40   **b.** 15 to 45   **c.** 25 to 35

29. Consider the sample of size 5 with data values of 10, 20, 12, 17, and 16. Compute the z-score for each of the five data values.

30. Consider a sample with a mean of 500 and a standard deviation of 100. What is the z-score for each of the data values 520, 650, 500, 450, and 280?

Applications

31. The results of a national survey of 1154 adults showed that on average, adults sleep 6.9 hours per day during the workweek (2000 Omnibus Sleep in America Poll). Suppose that the standard deviation is 1.2 hours.

    a. Use Chebyshev's theorem to calculate the percentage of individuals who sleep between 4.5 and 9.3 hours per day.

    b. Use Chebyshev's theorem to calculate the percentage of individuals who sleep between 3.9 and 9.9 hours per day.

    c. Assume that the number of hours of sleep is bell-shaped. Use the empirical rule to calculate the percentage of individuals who sleep between 4.5 and 9.3 hours per day. How does this result compare to the value that you obtained using Chebyshev's theorem in part (a)?

32. According to ACNielsen, kids aged 12 to 17 watched an average of 3 hours of television per day for the broadcast year that ended in August (*Barron's,* November 8, 1999). Suppose that the standard deviation is 1 hour and that the distribution of the time spent watching television has a bell-shaped distribution.

    a. What percentage of kids aged 12 to 17 watches television between 2 and 3 hours per day?

    b. What percentage of kids aged 12 to 17 watches television between 1 and 4 hours per day?

    c. What percentage of kids aged 12 to 17 watches television more than 4 hours per day?

33. Suppose that IQ scores have a bell-shaped distribution with a mean of 100 and a standard deviation of 15.

    a. What percentage of people should have an IQ score between 85 and 115?

    b. What percentage of people should have an IQ score between 70 and 130?

    c. What percentage of people should have an IQ score of more than 130?

    d. A person with an IQ score of more than 145 is considered a genius. Does the empirical rule support this statement? Explain.

34. The average labor cost for color TV repair in Chicago is $90.06 (*The Wall Street Journal,* January 2, 1998). Suppose the standard deviation is $20.

    a. What is the z-score for a repair job with a labor cost of $71?

    b. What is the z-score for a repair job with a labor cost of $168?

    c. Interpret the z-scores in parts (a) and (b). Comment on whether either should be considered an outlier.

35. Wageweb conducts surveys of salary data and presents summaries on its Web site. Using salary data as of January 1, 2000, Wageweb reported that salaries of benefits managers ranged from $50,935 to $79,577 (Wageweb.com, April 12, 2000). Assume the following data are a sample of the annual salaries for 30 benefits managers (data are in thousands of dollars).

CDfile
Wageweb

57.7	64.4	62.1	59.1	71.1
63.0	64.7	61.2	66.8	61.8
64.2	63.3	62.2	61.2	59.4
63.0	66.7	60.3	74.0	62.8
68.7	63.8	59.2	60.3	56.6
59.3	69.5	61.7	58.9	63.1

a. Compute the mean and standard deviation for the sample data.

b. Using the mean and standard deviation computed in part (a) as estimates of the mean and standard deviation of salary for the population of benefits managers, use Chebyshev's theorem to determine the percentage of benefits managers with an annual salary between $55,000 and $71,000.

c. Develop a histogram for the sample data. Does it appear reasonable to assume that the distribution of annual salary can be approximated by a bell-shaped distribution?

d. Assume that the distribution of annual salary is bell-shaped. Using the mean and standard deviation computed in part (a) as estimates of the mean and standard deviation of salary for the population of benefits managers, use the empirical rule to determine the percentage of benefits managers with an annual salary between $55,000 and $71,000. Compare your answer with the value computed in part (b).

e. Do the sample data contain any outliers?

36. A sample of 10 National Basketball Association (NBA) scores provided the following data (*USA Today,* April 14, 2000).

CDfile
NBA

Winning Team	Points Scored	Losing Team	Points Scored	Winning Margin
Philadelphia	93	Washington	84	9
Charlotte	119	Atlanta	87	32
Milwaukee	101	Cleveland	100	1
Indiana	77	Toronto	73	4
Seattle	110	Minnesota	83	27
Boston	95	Orlando	91	4
Detroit	90	Miami	73	17
New York	91	New Jersey	89	2
Utah	102	L.A. Clippers	93	9
Phoenix	122	Vancouver	116	6

a. Compute the mean and standard deviation for the number of points scored by the winning team.

b. Assume that the number of points scored by the winning team for all NBA games is bell-shaped. Using the mean and standard deviation computed in part (a) as estimates of the mean and standard deviation of the points scored for the population of all NBA games, estimate the percentage of all NBA games in which the winning team will score 100 or more points. Estimate the percentage of games in which the winning team will score more than 114 points.

c. Compute the mean and standard deviation for the winning margin. Do the winning margin data contain any outliers? Explain.

37. *Consumer Review* posts reviews and ratings of a variety of products on the Internet. The following is a sample of 20 speaker systems and the ratings posted on January 2, 1998 (see *www.audioreview.com*). The ratings are on a scale of 1 to 5, with 5 being best.

CDfile
Speakers

Speaker	Rating	Speaker	Rating
Infinity Kappa 6.1	4.00	ACI Sapphire III	4.67
Allison One	4.12	Bose 501 Series	2.14
Cambridge Ensemble II	3.82	DCM KX-212	4.09
Dynaudio Contour 1.3	4.00	Eosone RSF1000	4.17
Hsu Rsch. HRSW12V	4.56	Joseph Audio RM7si	4.88
Legacy Audio Focus	4.32	Martin Logan Aerius	4.26
Mission 73li	4.33	Omni Audio SA 12.3	2.32
PSB 400i	4.50	Polk Audio RT12	4.50
Snell Acoustics D IV	4.64	Sunfire True Subwoofer	4.17
Thiel CS1.5	4.20	Yamaha NS-A636	2.17

a. Compute the mean and the median.
b. Compute the first and third quartiles.
c. Compute the standard deviation.
d. What are the z-scores associated with the Allison One and the Omni Audio SA 12.3?
e. Do the data contain any outliers? Explain.

3.4   EXPLORATORY DATA ANALYSIS

In Chapter 2 we introduced the stem-and-leaf display as a technique of exploratory data analysis. Recall that exploratory data analysis enables us to use simple arithmetic and easy-to-draw pictures to summarize data. In this section we continue exploratory data analysis by considering five-number summaries and box plots.

Five-Number Summary

In a **five-number summary,** the following five numbers are used to summarize the data.

1. Smallest value
2. First quartile (Q_1)
3. Median (Q_2)
4. Third quartile (Q_3)
5. Largest value

The easiest way to develop a five-number summary is to first place the data in ascending order. Then it is easy to identify the smallest value, the three quartiles, and the largest value. The monthly starting salaries shown in Table 3.1 for a sample of 12 business school graduates are repeated here in ascending order.

2710 2755 2850 | 2880 2880 2890 | 2920 2940 2950 | 3050 3130 3325

$Q_1 = 2865$ $Q_2 = 2905$ $Q_3 = 3000$
                    (Median)

The median of 2905 and the quartiles $Q_1 = 2865$ and $Q_3 = 3000$ were computed in Section 3.1. A review of the preceding data shows a smallest value of 2710 and a largest value of 3325. Thus the five-number summary for the salary data is 2710, 2865, 2905, 3000, 3325. Approximately one-fourth, or 25%, of the observations are between adjacent numbers in a five-number summary.

Box Plot

A **box plot** is a graphical summary of data based on a five-number summary. A key to the development of a box plot is the computation of the median and the quartiles, Q_1 and Q_3. The interquartile range, IQR $= Q_3 - Q_1$, is also used. Figure 3.4 is the box plot for the monthly starting salary data. The steps used to construct the box plot follow.

Box plots provide another way to identify outliers. But they do not necessarily identify the same values as those with a z-score less than −3 or greater than +3. Either, or both, procedures may be used. All you are trying to do is identify values that may not belong in the data set.

1. A box is drawn with the ends of the box located at the first and third quartiles. For the salary data, $Q_1 = 2865$ and $Q_3 = 3000$. This box contains the middle 50% of the data.
2. A vertical line is drawn in the box at the location of the median (2905 for the salary data). Thus the median line divides the data into two equal parts.
3. By using the interquartile range, IQR $= Q_3 - Q_1$, limits are located. The limits for the box plot are located 1.5(IQR) below Q_1 and 1.5(IQR) above Q_3. For the salary data, IQR $= Q_3 - Q_1 = 3000 - 2865 = 135$. Thus, the limits are 2865 − 1.5(135) = 2662.5 and 3000 + 1.5(135) = 3202.5. Data outside these limits are considered *outliers*.
4. The dashed lines in Figure 3.4 are called *whiskers*. The whiskers are drawn from the ends of the box to the smallest and largest data values *inside the limits* computed in step 3. Thus the whiskers end at salary values of 2710 and 3130.
5. Finally, the location of each outlier is shown with the symbol *. In Figure 3.4 we see one outlier, 3325.

In Figure 3.4 we have included lines showing the location of the limits. These lines were drawn to show how the limits are computed and where they are located for the salary data. Although the limits are always computed, generally they are not drawn on the box plots. Figure 3.5 shows the usual appearance of a box plot for the salary data.

FIGURE 3.4   BOX PLOT OF THE STARTING SALARY DATA WITH LINES SHOWING THE LOWER AND UPPER LIMITS

FIGURE 3.5   BOX PLOT OF THE STARTING SALARY DATA

NOTES AND COMMENTS

1. When using a box plot, we may or may not identify the same outliers as the ones we select when using z-scores less than -3 and greater than $+3$. However, the objective of both approaches is simply to identify items that should be reviewed to ensure the validity of the data. Outliers identified by either procedure should be reviewed.

2. An advantage of the exploratory data analysis procedures is that they are easy to use; few numerical calculations are necessary. We simply sort the items into ascending order and identify the median and quartiles Q_1 and Q_3 to obtain the five-number summary. The limits and the box plot can then easily be determined. It is not necessary to compute the mean and the standard deviation for the data.

3. In Appendix 3.1, we show how to construct a box plot for the starting salary data using Minitab. The box plot obtained looks just like the one in Figure 3.5, but turned on its side.

EXERCISES

Methods

38. Consider the sample of size 8 with data values of 27, 25, 20, 15, 30, 34, 28, and 25. Provide the five-number summary for the data.

39. Show the box plot for the data in Exercise 38.

SELFtest   **40.** Show the five-number summary and the box plot for the following data: 5, 15, 18, 10, 8, 12, 16, 10, and 6.

41. A data set has a first quartile of 42 and a third quartile of 50. Compute the lower and upper limits. Should a data value of 65 be considered an outlier?

Applications

42. A goal of management is to earn as much as possible relative to the capital invested in the company. Return on equity—the ratio of net income to stockholders' equity—provides one measure of success in this effort. Shown here are the return on equity percentages for 25 companies (*Standard & Poor's Stock Reports,* November 1997).

CDfile
ReEquity

9.0	19.6	22.9	41.6	11.4
15.8	52.7	17.3	12.3	5.1
17.3	31.1	9.6	8.6	11.2
12.8	12.2	14.5	9.2	16.6
5.0	30.3	14.7	19.2	6.2

a. Provide a five-number summary.
b. Compute the lower and upper limits.
c. Do there appear to be outliers? How would this information be helpful to a financial analyst?
d. Show a box plot.

SELFtest   43. Annual sales, in millions of dollars, for 21 pharmaceutical companies follow.

8408	1374	1872	8879	2459	11413
608	14138	6452	1850	2818	1356
10498	7478	4019	4341	739	2127
3653	5794	8305			

a. Provide a five-number summary.
b. Compute the lower and upper limits.
c. Do there appear to be outliers?
d. Johnson & Johnson's sales are the largest in the list at $14,138 million. Suppose a data entry error (a transposition) had been made and the sales had been entered as $41,138 million. Would the method of detecting outliers in part (c) identify this problem and allow for correction of the data entry error?
e. Show a box plot.

44. Corporate share repurchase programs are often touted as a benefit for shareholders. But, Robert Gabele, director of insider research for First Call/Thomson Financial, notes that many companies undertake these programs solely to acquire stock for the companies' incentive options for top managers. Across all companies, existing stock options in 1998 represented 6.2% of all common shares outstanding. The following data show the number of shares covered by option grants and the number of shares outstanding for 15 companies. *Bloomberg* identified these companies as the ones that would need to repurchase the highest percentage of outstanding shares to cover their option grants (*Bloomberg Personal Finance,* January/February 2000).

CDfile
Options

Company	Shares of Option Grants Outstanding (millions)	Common Shares Outstanding (millions)
Adobe Systems	20.3	61.8
Apple Computer	52.7	160.9
Applied Materials	109.1	375.4
Autodesk	15.7	58.9
Best Buy	44.2	203.8
Cendant	183.3	718.1
Dell Computer	720.8	2540.9
Fruit of the Loom	14.2	66.9
ITT Industries	18.0	87.9
Merrill Lynch	89.9	365.5
Novell	120.2	335.0
Parametric Technology	78.3	269.3
Reebok International	12.8	56.1
Silicon Graphics	52.6	188.8
Toys R Us	54.8	247.6

a. What are the mean and median number of shares of option grants outstanding?
b. What are the first and third quartiles for the number of shares of option grants outstanding?

   c.   Are there any outliers for the number of shares of option grants outstanding? Show a box plot.

   d.   Compute the mean percentage of the ratio of the number of shares of option grants outstanding to the number of common shares outstanding. How does this percentage compare to the 1998 percentage of 6.2% reported for all companies?

45.   The Highway Loss Data Institute's Injury and Collision Loss Experience report rates car models on the basis of the number of insurance claims filed after accidents. Index ratings near 100 are considered average. Lower ratings are better, indicating a safer car model. Shown are ratings for 20 midsize cars and 20 small cars.

CDfile
Injury

Midsize cars:	81	91	93	127	68	81	60	51	58	75
	100	103	119	82	128	76	68	81	91	82
Small cars:	73	100	127	100	124	103	119	108	109	113
	108	118	103	120	102	122	96	133	80	140

Summarize the data for the midsize and small cars separately.

   a.   Provide a five-number summary for midsize cars and for small cars.

   b.   Show the box plots.

   c.   Make a statement about what your summaries indicate about the safety of midsize cars in comparison to small cars.

46.   Birinyi Associates, Inc., conducted a survey of stock markets around the world to assess their performance during 1997. Table 3.6 summarizes the findings for a sample of 30 countries.

   a.   What are the mean and median percentage changes for these countries?

   b.   What are the first and third quartiles?

   c.   Are there any outliers? Show a box plot.

   d.   What percentile would you report for the United States?

TABLE 3.6   PERCENT CHANGE IN VALUE FOR WORLD STOCK MARKETS

CDfile
World

Country	Percent Change	Country	Percent Change
Argentina	24.70	India	18.60
Australia	7.91	Israel	27.91
Bahrain	49.67	Japan	−21.19
Barbados	48.29	Lithuania	16.82
Bermuda	51.92	Mexico	54.92
Brazil	44.84	Namibia	6.52
Chile	12.80	Nigeria	−7.97
Colombia	69.60	Panama	59.40
Croatia	−1.07	Poland	2.27
Czech Republic	−3.25	Russia	125.89
Ecuador	5.37	Slovenia	18.71
Estonia	62.34	Sri Lanka	15.49
Finland	32.31	Taiwan	18.08
Germany	47.11	Turkey	254.45
Greece	59.19	United States	22.64

Source: The Wall Street Journal, January 2, 1998.

3.5   MEASURES OF ASSOCIATION BETWEEN TWO VARIABLES

Thus far we have examined numerical methods used to summarize the data for *one variable at a time*. Often a manager or decision maker is interested in the *relationship between two variables*. In this section we present covariance and correlation as descriptive measures of the relationship between two variables.

We begin by reconsidering the application concerning a stereo and sound equipment store in San Francisco as presented in Section 2.4. The store's manager wants to determine the relationship between the number of weekend television commercials shown and the sales at the store during the following week. Sample data with sales expressed in hundreds of dollars are provided in Table 3.7 with one observation for each week ($n = 10$). The scatter diagram in Figure 3.6 shows a positive relationship, with higher sales (y) associated with a greater number of commercials (x). In fact, the scatter diagram suggests that a straight line could be used as a linear approximation of the relationship. In the following discussion, we introduce **covariance** as a descriptive measure of the linear association between two variables.

Covariance

For a sample of size n with the observations (x_1, y_1), (x_2, y_2) and so on, the *sample covariance* is defined as follows:

Sample Covariance

$$s_{xy} = \frac{\Sigma(x_i - \bar{x})(y_i - \bar{y})}{n - 1} \tag{3.10}$$

This formula pairs each x_i with a y_i. We then sum the products obtained by multiplying the deviation of each x_i from its sample mean $\bar{x}$ by the deviation of the corresponding y_i from its sample mean $\bar{y}$; this sum is then divided by $n - 1$.

TABLE 3.7   SAMPLE DATA FOR THE STEREO AND SOUND EQUIPMENT STORE

CDfile
Stereo

Week	Number of Commercials x	Sales Volume ($100s) y
1	2	50
2	5	57
3	1	41
4	3	54
5	4	54
6	1	38
7	5	63
8	3	48
9	4	59
10	2	46

FIGURE 3.6   SCATTER DIAGRAM FOR THE STEREO AND SOUND EQUIPMENT STORE

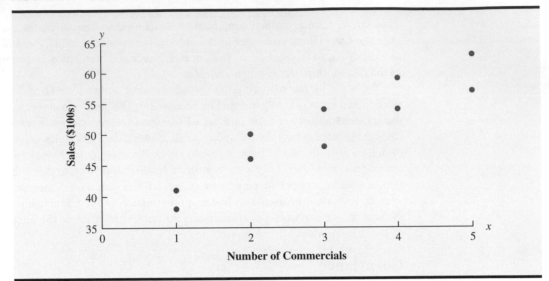

Number of Commercials

To measure the strength of the linear relationship between the number of commercials x and the sales volume y in the stereo and sound equipment store problem, we use equation (3.10) to compute the sample covariance. The calculations in Table 3.8 show the computation of $\Sigma(x_i - \bar{x})(y_i - \bar{y})$. Note that $\bar{x} = 30/10 = 3$ and $\bar{y} = 510/10 = 51$. Using equation (3.10), we obtain a sample covariance of

$$s_{xy} = \frac{\Sigma(x_i - \bar{x})(y_i - \bar{y})}{n - 1} = \frac{99}{9} = 11$$

The formula for computing the covariance of a population of size N is similar to equation (3.10), but we use different notation to indicate that we are working with the entire population.

Population Covariance

$$\sigma_{xy} = \frac{\Sigma(x_i - \mu_x)(y_i - \mu_y)}{N} \tag{3.11}$$

In equation (3.11) we use the notation μ_x for the population mean of the variable x and μ_y for the population mean of the variable y. The population covariance σ_{xy} is defined for a population of size N.

Interpretation of the Covariance

To aid in the interpretation of the sample covariance, consider Figure 3.7. It is the same as the scatter diagram of Figure 3.6 with a vertical dashed line at $\bar{x} = 3$ and a horizontal dashed line at $\bar{y} = 51$. Four quadrants have been identified on the graph. Points in quadrant I correspond to x_i greater than $\bar{x}$ and y_i greater than $\bar{y}$, points in quadrant II correspond

TABLE 3.8   CALCULATIONS FOR THE SAMPLE COVARIANCE

x_i	y_i	$x_i - \bar{x}$	$y_i - \bar{y}$	$(x_i - \bar{x})(y_i - \bar{y})$
2	50	-1	-1	1
5	57	2	6	12
1	41	-2	-10	20
3	54	0	3	0
4	54	1	3	3
1	38	-2	-13	26
5	63	2	12	24
3	48	0	-3	0
4	59	1	8	8
2	46	-1	-5	5
Totals 30	510	0	0	99

$$s_{xy} = \frac{\Sigma(x_i - \bar{x})(y_i - \bar{y})}{n - 1} = \frac{99}{10 - 1} = 11$$

to x_i less than $\bar{x}$ and y_i greater than $\bar{y}$, and so on. Thus, the value of $(x_i - \bar{x})(y_i - \bar{y})$ must be positive for points in quadrant I, negative for points in quadrant II, positive for points in quadrant III, and negative for points in quadrant IV.

The covariance is a measure of the linear association between two variables.

If the value of s_{xy} is positive, the points that have had the greatest influence on s_{xy} must be in quadrants I and III. Hence, a positive value for s_{xy} is indicative of a positive linear association between x and y; that is, as the value of x increases, the value of y increases. If the value of s_{xy} is negative, however, the points that have had the greatest influence on s_{xy} are in quadrants II and IV. Hence, a negative value for s_{xy} indicates a negative linear association between x and y; that is, as the value of x increases, the value of y decreases. Finally,

FIGURE 3.7   PARTITIONED SCATTER DIAGRAM FOR THE STEREO AND SOUND EQUIPMENT STORE

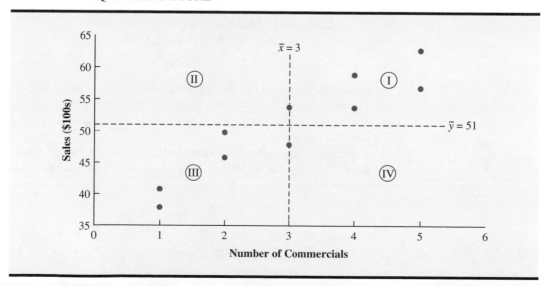

if the points are evenly distributed across all four quadrants, the value of s_{xy} will be close to zero, indicating no linear association between x and y. Figure 3.8 shows the values of s_{xy} that can be expected with three different types of scatter diagrams.

Referring again to Figure 3.7, we see that the scatter diagram for the stereo and sound equipment store follows the pattern in the top panel of Figure 3.8. As we should expect, the value of the sample covariance is positive with $s_{xy} = 11$.

From the preceding discussion, it might appear that a large positive value for the covariance indicates a strong positive linear relationship and that a large negative value indicates a strong negative linear relationship. However, one problem with using covariance as a measure of the strength of the linear relationship is that the value we obtain for the covariance depends on the units of measurement for x and y. For example, suppose we are interested in the relationship between height x and weight y for individuals. Clearly the strength of the relationship should be the same whether we measure height in feet or inches. When height is measured in inches, however, we get much larger numerical values for $(x_i - \bar{x})$ than we get when it is measured in feet. Thus, with height measured in inches, we would obtain a larger value for the numerator $\Sigma(x_i - \bar{x})(y_i - \bar{y})$ in equation (3.10)—and hence a larger covariance—when in fact there is no difference in the relationship. A measure of the relationship between two variables that avoids this difficulty is the **correlation coefficient.**

Correlation Coefficient

For sample data, the Pearson product moment correlation coefficient is defined as follows.

Pearson Product Moment Correlation Coefficient: Sample Data

$$r_{xy} = \frac{s_{xy}}{s_x s_y} \tag{3.12}$$

where

r_{xy} = sample correlation coefficient

s_{xy} = sample covariance

s_x = sample standard deviation of x

s_y = sample standard deviation of y

Equation (3.12) shows that the Pearson product moment correlation coefficient for sample data (commonly referred to more simply as the *sample correlation coefficient*) is computed by dividing the sample covariance by the product of the standard deviation of x and the standard deviation of y.

Let us now compute the sample correlation coefficient for the stereo and sound equipment store. Using the data in Table 3.7, we can compute the sample standard deviations for the two variables.

$$s_x = \sqrt{\frac{\Sigma(x_i - \bar{x})^2}{n - 1}} = \sqrt{\frac{20}{9}} = 1.4907$$

$$s_y = \sqrt{\frac{\Sigma(y_i - \bar{y})^2}{n - 1}} = \sqrt{\frac{566}{9}} = 7.9303$$

FIGURE 3.8   INTERPRETATION OF SAMPLE COVARIANCE

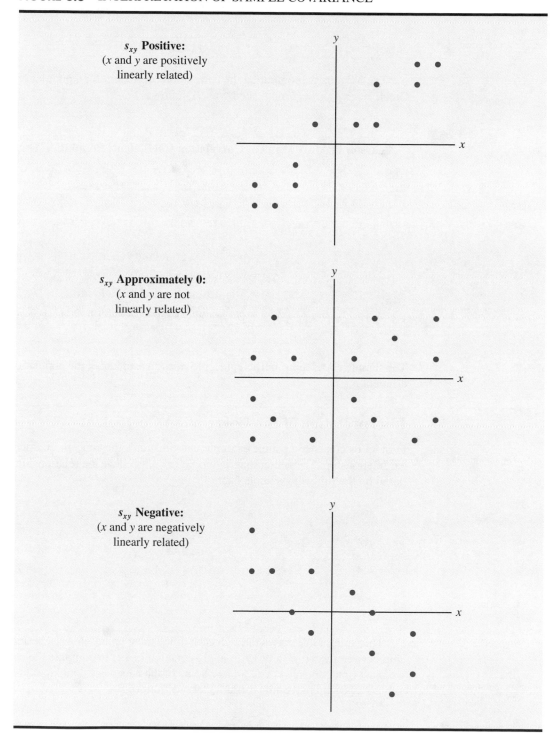

Now, because $s_{xy} = 11$, the sample correlation coefficient equals

$$r_{xy} = \frac{s_{xy}}{s_x s_y} = \frac{11}{(1.4907)(7.9303)} = +.93$$

The formula for computing the correlation coefficient for a population, denoted by the Greek letter ρ_{xy} (rho, pronounced "row"), follows.

Pearson Product Moment Correlation Coefficient: Population Data

$$\rho_{xy} = \frac{\sigma_{xy}}{\sigma_x \sigma_y} \qquad (3.13)$$

where

ρ_{xy} = population correlation coefficient
σ_{xy} = population covariance
σ_x = population standard deviation for x
σ_y = population standard deviation for y

The sample correlation coefficient r_{xy} provides an estimate of the population correlation coefficient ρ_{xy}.

Interpretation of the Correlation Coefficient

First let us consider a simple example that illustrates the concept of a perfect positive linear relationship. The scatter diagram in Figure 3.9 depicts the relationship between x and y based on the following sample data.

x_i	y_i
5	10
10	30
15	50

The straight line drawn through each of the three points shows a perfect linear relationship between x and y. In order to apply equation (3.12) to compute the sample correlation we must first compute s_{xy}, s_x, and s_y. Some of the necessary computations are contained in Table 3.9. Using the results in Table 3.9, we find

$$s_{xy} = \frac{\Sigma(x_i - \bar{x})(y_i - \bar{y})}{n - 1} = \frac{200}{2} = 100$$

$$s_x = \sqrt{\frac{\Sigma(x_i - \bar{x})^2}{n - 1}} = \sqrt{\frac{50}{2}} = 5$$

FIGURE 3.9   SCATTER DIAGRAM DEPICTING A PERFECT POSITIVE LINEAR
RELATIONSHIP

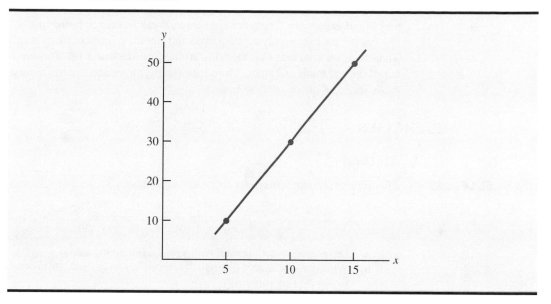

$$s_y = \sqrt{\frac{\Sigma(y_i - \bar{y})^2}{n - 1}} = \sqrt{\frac{800}{2}} = 20$$

$$r_{xy} = \frac{s_{xy}}{s_x s_y} = \frac{100}{5(20)} = 1$$

Thus, we see that the value of the sample correlation coefficient is 1.

　　　In general, it can be shown that if all the points in a data set fall on a positively sloped straight line, the value of the sample correlation coefficient is $+1$; that is, a sample correlation coefficient of $+1$ corresponds to a perfect positive linear relationship between x and y. Moreover, if the points in the data set are on a straight line having negative slope, the value of the sample correlation coefficient is -1; that is, a sample correlation coefficient of -1 corresponds to a perfect negative linear relationship between x and y.

　　　Let us now suppose that a certain data set shows a positive linear relationship between x and y, but the relationship is not perfect. The value of r_{xy} will be less than 1, indicating

The correlation coefficient ranges from −1 to +1. Values close to −1 or +1 indicate a strong linear relationship. The closer the correlation is to zero the weaker the relationship.

TABLE 3.9   COMPUTATIONS USED IN CALCULATING THE SAMPLE
CORRELATION COEFFICIENT

	x_i	y_i	$x_i - \bar{x}$	$(x_i - \bar{x})^2$	$y_i - \bar{y}$	$(y_i - \bar{y})^2$	$(x_i - \bar{x})(y_i - \bar{y})$
	5	10	−5	25	−20	400	100
	10	30	0	0	0	0	0
	15	50	5	25	20	400	100
Totals	30	90	0	50	0	800	200

$\bar{x} = 10$ $\bar{y} = 30$

that the points in the scatter diagram are not all on a straight line. As the points in a data set deviate more and more from a perfect positive linear relationship, the value of r_{xy} becomes smaller and smaller. A value of r_{xy} equal to zero indicates no linear relationship between x and y, and values of r_{xy} near zero indicate a weak linear relationship.

For the data set involving the stereo and sound equipment store, recall that $r_{xy} = +.93$. Therefore, we conclude that there is a strong positive linear relationship between the number of commercials and sales. More specifically, an increase in the number of commercials is associated with an increase in sales.

EXERCISES

Methods

SELFtest   **47.** Five observations taken for two variables follow.

x_i	4	6	11	3	16
y_i	50	50	40	60	30

     a. Develop a scatter diagram with x on the horizontal axis.
     b. What does the scatter diagram developed in part (a) indicate about the relationship between the two variables?
     c. Compute and interpret the sample covariance for the data.
     d. Compute and interpret the sample correlation coefficient for the data.

48. Five observations taken for two variables follow.

x_i	6	11	15	21	27
y_i	6	9	6	17	12

     a. Develop a scatter diagram for these data.
     b. What does the scatter diagram indicate about a possible relationship between x and y?
     c. Compute and interpret the sample covariance for the data.
     d. Compute and interpret the sample correlation coefficient for the data.

Applications

49. A high school guidance counselor collected the following data about the grade point averages (GPA) and the SAT mathematics test scores for six seniors.

GPA	2.7	3.5	3.7	3.3	3.6	3.0
SAT	450	560	700	620	640	570

     a. Develop a scatter diagram for the data with GPA on the horizontal axis.
     b. Does there appear to be any relationship between the GPA and the SAT mathematics test score? Explain.
     c. Compute and interpret the sample covariance for the data.
     d. Compute the sample correlation coefficient for the data. What does this value tell us about the relationship between the two variables?

50. A department of transportation's study on driving speed and mileage for midsize automobiles resulted in the following data.

Driving Speed	30	50	40	55	30	25	60	25	50	55
Mileage	28	25	25	23	30	32	21	35	26	25

Compute and interpret the sample correlation coefficient for these data.

51. *PC World* provided ratings for the top 15 notebook PCs (*PC World,* February 2000). The performance score is a measure of how fast a PC can run a mix of common business applications in comparison to their baseline machine. For example, a PC with a performance score of 200 is twice as fast as the baseline machine. A 100-point scale was used to provide an overall rating for each notebook tested in the study. A score in the 90s is exceptional, while one in the 70s is above average. The performance scores and the overall ratings for the 15 notebooks are shown.

CDfile
PCs

Notebook	Performance Score	Overall Rating
AMS Tech Roadster 15CTA380	115	67
Compaq Armada M700	191	78
Compaq Prosignia Notebook 150	153	79
Dell Inspiron 3700 C466GT	194	80
Dell Inspiron 7500 R500VT	236	84
Dell Latitude Cpi A366XT	184	76
Enpower ENP-313 Pro	184	77
Gateway Solo 9300LS	216	92
HP Pavillion Notebook PC	185	83
IBM ThinkPad I Series 1480	183	78
Micro Express NP7400	189	77
Micron TransPort NX PII-400	202	78
NEC Versa SX	192	78
Sceptre Soundx 5200	141	73
Sony VAIO PCG-F340	187	77

    a. Compute the sample correlation coefficient.

    b. What does the sample correlation coefficient tell about the relationship between the performance score and the overall rating?

52. The Dow Jones Industrial Average (DJIA) and the Standard & Poor's 500 (S&P) Index are both used as measures of overall movement in the stock market. The DJIA is based on the price movements of 30 large companies; the S&P 500 is an index composed of 500 stocks. Some say the S&P 500 is a better measure of stock market performance because it is broader based. The closing price for the DJIA and the S&P 500 for 10 weeks, beginning with February 11, 2000, are shown (*Barron's,* April 17, 2000).

CDfile
DowS&P

Date	Dow Jones	S&P 500
February 11	10425	1387
February 18	10220	1346
February 25	9862	1333
March 3	10367	1409
March 10	9929	1395
March 17	10595	1464
March 24	11113	1527
March 31	10922	1499
April 7	11111	1516
April 14	10306	1357

    a. Compute the sample correlation coefficient for these data.

    b. Are they poorly correlated, or do they have a close association?

53. The daily high and low temperatures for 20 cities follow (*USA Today,* May 9, 2000). What is the correlation between the high and low temperatures?

HighLow

City	High	Low
Athens	75	54
Bangkok	92	74
Cairo	84	57
Copenhagen	64	39
Dublin	64	46
Havana	86	68
Hong Kong	81	72
Johannesburg	61	50
London	73	48
Manila	93	75
Melbourne	66	50
Montreal	64	52
Paris	77	55
Rio de Janeiro	80	61
Rome	81	54
Seoul	64	50
Singapore	90	75
Sydney	68	55
Tokyo	79	59
Vancouver	57	43

3.6　THE WEIGHTED MEAN AND WORKING WITH GROUPED DATA

In Section 3.1, we presented the mean as one of the most important measures of descriptive statistics. The formula for the mean of a sample with n observations is restated as follows.

$$\bar{x} = \frac{\Sigma x_i}{n} = \frac{x_1 + x_2 + \cdots + x_n}{n} \tag{3.14}$$

In this formula, each x_i is given equal importance or weight. Although this practice is most common, in some instances, the mean is computed by giving each observation a weight that reflects its importance. A mean computed in this manner is referred to as a **weighted mean.**

Weighted Mean

The weighted mean is computed as follows:

Weighted Mean

$$\bar{x} = \frac{\Sigma w_i x_i}{\Sigma w_i} \tag{3.15}$$

where

$$x_i = \text{value of observation } i$$
$$w_i = \text{weight for observation } i$$

When the data are from a sample, equation (3.15) provides the weighted sample mean. When the data come from a population, μ replaces $\bar{x}$ and (3.15) provides the weighted population mean.

As an example of the need for a weighted mean, consider the following sample of five purchases of a raw material over the past three months.

Purchase	Cost per Pound ($)	Number of Pounds
1	3.00	1200
2	3.40	500
3	2.80	2750
4	2.90	1000
5	3.25	800

Note that the cost per pound has varied from $2.80 to $3.40 and the quantity purchased has varied from 500 to 2500 pounds. Suppose that a manager has asked for information about the mean cost per pound of the raw material. Because the quantities ordered vary, we must use the formula for a weighted mean. The five cost-per-pound data values are $x_1 = 3.00$, $x_2 = 3.40$, $x_3 = 2.80$, $x_4 = 2.90$, and $x_5 = 3.25$. The mean cost per pound is found by weighting each cost by its corresponding quantity. For this example, the weights are $w_1 = 1200$, $w_2 = 500$, $w_3 = 2500$, $w_4 = 1000$, and $w_5 = 800$. Using (3.15), the weighted mean is calculated as follows:

$$\bar{x} = \frac{1200(3.00) + 500(3.40) + 2500(2.80) + 1000(2.90) + 800(3.25)}{1200 + 500 + 2500 + 1000 + 800}$$

$$= \frac{17,800}{6000} = 2.967$$

Thus, the weighted mean computation shows that the mean cost per pound for the raw material is $2.967. Note that using (3.14) rather than the weighted mean formula would have provided misleading results. In this case, the mean of the five cost-per-pound values is $(3.00 + 3.40 + 2.80 + 2.90 + 3.25)/5 = 15.35/5 = \$3.07$, which overstates the actual mean cost per pound.

Computing a grade point average is a good example of the use of a weighted mean.

The choice of weights for a particular weighted mean computation depends upon the application. An example that is well known to college students is the computation of a grade point average (GPA). In this computation, the data values generally used are 4 for an A grade, 3 for a B grade, 2 for a C grade, 1 for a D grade, and 0 for an F grade. The weights are the number of credits hours earned for each grade. Exercise 56 at the end of this section provides an example of this weighted mean computation. In other weighted mean computations, quantities such as pounds, dollars, and/or volume are frequently used as weights. In any case, when data values vary in importance, the analyst must choose the weight that best reflects the importance of each data value in the determination of the mean.

Grouped Data

In most cases, measures of location and variability are computed by using the individual data values. Sometimes, however, we have data in only a grouped or frequency distribution form. In the following discussion, we show how the weighted mean formula can be used to obtain approximations of the mean, variance, and standard deviation for **grouped data.**

In Section 2.2 we provided a frequency distribution of the time in days required to complete year-end audits for the public accounting firm of Sanderson and Clifford. The frequency distribution of audit times based on a sample of 20 clients appears in Table 3.10. Based on this frequency distribution, what is the sample mean audit time?

To compute the mean using only the grouped data, we treat the midpoint of each class as being representative of the items in the class. Let M_i denote the midpoint for class i and let f_i denote the frequency of class i. The weighted mean formula (3.15) is then used with the data values denoted as M_i and the weights given by the frequencies f_i. In this case, the denominator of (3.15) is the sum of the frequencies, which is the sample size n. That is, $\Sigma f_i = n$. Thus, the equation for the sample mean for grouped data is as follows.

Sample Mean for Grouped Data

$$\bar{x} = \frac{\Sigma f_i M_i}{n} \tag{3.16}$$

where

$$M_i = \text{the midpoint for class } i$$
$$f_i = \text{the frequency for class } i$$
$$n = \Sigma f_i = \text{the sample size}$$

With the class midpoints, M_i, halfway between the class limits, the first class of 10–14 in Table 3.10 has a midpoint at $(10 + 14)/2 = 12$. The five class midpoints and the weighted mean computation for the audit time data are summarized in Table 3.11. As can be seen, the sample mean audit time is 19 days.

To compute the variance for grouped data, we use a slightly altered version of the formula for the variance provided in equation (3.5). In equation (3.5), the squared deviations of the data about the sample mean $\bar{x}$ were written $(x_i - \bar{x})^2$. However, with grouped data, the values are not known. In this case, we treat the class midpoint, M_i, as being representative of the x_i values in the corresponding class. Thus the squared deviations about the sample mean, $(x_i - \bar{x})^2$, are replaced by $(M_i - \bar{x})^2$. Then, just as we did with the sample mean calculations for grouped data, we weight each value by the frequency of the class, f_i. The sum of the squared deviations about the mean for all the data is approximated by $\Sigma f_i(M_i - \bar{x})^2$.

TABLE 3.10   FREQUENCY DISTRIBUTION OF AUDIT TIMES

Audit Time (days)	Frequency
10–14	4
15–19	8
20–24	5
25–29	2
30–34	1
Total	20

TABLE 3.11   COMPUTATION OF THE SAMPLE MEAN AUDIT TIME FOR GROUPED DATA

Audit Time (days)	Class Midpoint (M_i)	Frequency (f_i)	$f_i M_i$
10–14	12	4	48
15–19	17	8	136
20–24	22	5	110
25–29	27	2	54
30–34	32	1	32
		20	380

$$\text{Sample mean } \bar{x} = \frac{\Sigma f_i M_i}{n} = \frac{380}{20} = 19 \text{ days}$$

The term $n - 1$ rather than n appears in the denominator in order to make the sample variance the estimate of the population variance σ^2. Thus, the following formula is used to obtain the sample variance for grouped data.

Sample Variance for Grouped Data

$$s^2 = \frac{\Sigma f_i(M_i - \bar{x})^2}{n - 1} \tag{3.17}$$

The calculation of the sample variance for audit times based on the grouped data from Table 3.10 is shown in Table 3.12. Thus, $s^2 = 30$.

The standard deviation for grouped data is simply the square root of the variance for grouped data. For the audit time data, the sample standard deviation is $s = \sqrt{30} = 5.48$.

TABLE 3.12   COMPUTATION OF THE SAMPLE VARIANCE OF AUDIT TIMES FOR GROUPED DATA (SAMPLE MEAN $\bar{x} = 19$)

Audit Time (days)	Class Midpoint (M_i)	Frequency (f_i)	Deviation $(M_i - \bar{x})$	Squared Deviation $(M_i - \bar{x})^2$	$f_i(M_i - \bar{x})^2$
10–14	12	4	−7	49	196
15–19	17	8	−2	4	32
20–24	22	5	3	9	45
25–29	27	2	8	64	128
30–34	32	1	13	169	169
		20			570
					$\Sigma f_i(M_i - \bar{x})^2$

$$\text{Sample variance } s^2 = \frac{\Sigma f_i(M_i - \bar{x})^2}{n - 1} = \frac{570}{19} = 30$$

Before closing this section on computing measures of location and dispersion for grouped data, we note that the formulas (3.16) and (3.17) are for a sample. Population summary measures are computed similarly. The grouped data formulas for a population mean and variance follow.

Population Mean for Grouped Data

$$\mu = \frac{\sum f_i M_i}{N} \tag{3.18}$$

Population Variance for Grouped Data

$$\sigma^2 = \frac{\sum f_i (M_i - \mu)^2}{N} \tag{3.19}$$

NOTES AND COMMENTS

1. An alternative formula for the computation of the sample variance for grouped data is

$$s^2 = \frac{\sum f_i M_i^2 - n\bar{x}^2}{n - 1}$$

where $\sum f_i M_i^2 = f_1 M_1^2 + f_2 M_2^2 + \cdots + f_k M_k^2$ and k is the number of classes used to group the data. Using this formula may ease the computations slightly.

2. In computations of descriptive statistics for grouped data, the class midpoints approximate the data values in each class. The descriptive statistics for grouped data approximate the descriptive statistics that would result from using the original data directly. We therefore recommend computing descriptive statistics from the original data rather than from grouped data whenever possible.

EXERCISES

Methods

54. Consider the following data and corresponding weights.

x_i	Weight (w_i)
3.2	6
2.0	3
2.5	2
5.0	8

  a. Compute the weighted mean for the data.
  b. Compute the sample mean of the four data values without weighting. Note the difference in the results provided by the two computations.

SELFtest 55. Consider the sample data in the following frequency distribution.

Class	Midpoint	Frequency
3–7	5	4
8–12	10	7
13–17	15	9
18–22	20	5

    a. Compute the sample mean.
    b. Compute the sample variance and sample standard deviation.

Applications

SELFtest 56. The grade point average for college students is based on a weighted mean computation. For most colleges, the grades are given the following data values: A (4), B (3), C (2), D (1), and F (0). After 60 credit hours of course work, a student at State University has earned 9 credit hours of A, 15 credit hours of B, 33 credit hours of C, and 3 credit hours of D.
    a. Compute the student's grade point average.
    b. Students at State University must have a 2.5 grade point average for their first 60 credit hours of course work in order to be admitted to the business college. Will this student be admitted?

57. *Bloomberg Personal Finance* (July/August 2001) included the following companies in its recommended investment portfolio. For a portfolio value of $25,000, the amounts shown are the recommended amounts allocated to each stock.

Company	Portfolio	Estimated Growth Rate	Dividend Yield
Citigroup	$3000	15%	1.21%
General Electric	5500	14	1.48
Kimberly-Clark	4200	12	1.72
Oracle	3000	25	0.00
Pharmacia	3000	20	0.96
SBC Communications	3800	12	2.48
WorldCom	2500	35	0.00

    a. Using the portfolio dollar amounts as the weights, what is the weighted average estimated growth rate for the portfolio?
    b. What is the weighted average dividend yield for the portfolio?

58. A service station has recorded the following frequency distribution for the number of gallons of gasoline sold per car in a sample of 680 cars.

Gasoline (gallons)	Frequency
0–4	74
5–9	192
10–14	280
15–19	105
20–24	23
25–29	6
Total	680

Compute the mean, variance, and standard deviation for these grouped data. If the service station expects to service about 120 cars on a given day, what is an estimate of the total number of gallons of gasoline that will be sold?

59. A survey of subscribers to *Fortune* magazine asked the following question: "How many of the last four issues have you read or looked through?" Suppose that the following frequency distribution summarizes 500 responses.

Number Read	Frequency
0	15
1	10
2	40
3	85
4	350
Total	500

a. What is the mean number of issues read by a *Fortune* subscriber?
b. What is the standard deviation of the number of issues read?

SUMMARY

In this chapter we introduced several descriptive statistics that can be used to summarize the location and variability of data. Unlike the tabular and graphical procedures introduced in Chapter 2, the measures introduced in this chapter summarize the data in terms of numerical values. When the numerical values obtained are for a sample, they are called sample statistics. When the numerical values obtained are for a population, they are called population parameters. Some of the notation used for sample statistics and population parameters follow.

	Sample Statistic	Population Parameter
Mean	$\bar{x}$	μ
Variance	s^2	σ^2
Standard deviation	s	σ
Covariance	s_{xy}	σ_{xy}
Correlation	r_{xy}	ρ_{xy}

As measures of central location, we defined the mean, median, and mode. Then the concept of percentiles was used to describe other locations in the data set. Next, we presented the range, interquartile range, variance, standard deviation, and coefficient of variation as measures of variability or dispersion. We then described how the mean and standard deviation could be used together, applying the empirical rule and Chebyshev's theorem, to provide more information about the distribution of data and to identify outliers.

In Section 3.4 we showed how to develop a five-number summary and a box plot to provide simultaneous information about the location, variability, and shape of the distribution. In Section 3.5 we introduced covariance and the correlation coefficient as measures of association between two variables. In the final section, we showed how to compute a weighted mean and how to calculate a mean, variance, and standard deviation for grouped data.

The descriptive statistics we have discussed can be developed using statistical software packages and spreadsheets. In Appendix 3.1 we show how to develop most of the descriptive statistics introduced in the chapter using Minitab. In Appendix 3.2, we demonstrate the use of Excel for the same purpose.

GLOSSARY

Sample statistic   A numerical value used as a summary measure for a sample (e.g., the sample mean, $\bar{x}$, the sample variance, s^2, and the sample standard deviation, s).

Population parameter   A numerical value used as a summary measure for a population of data (e.g., the population mean, μ, the population variance, σ^2, and the population standard deviation, σ).

Mean   A measure of central location for a data set. It is computed by summing all the data values and dividing by the number of observations.

Median   A measure of central location. It is the value in the middle when the data are arranged in ascending order.

Mode   A measure of location, defined as the value that occurs with greatest frequency.

Percentile   A value such that at least p percent of the observations are less than or equal to this value and at least $(100 - p)$ percent of the observations are greater than or equal to this value. The 50th percentile is the median.

Quartiles   The 25th, 50th, and 75th percentiles are the first quartile, the second quartile (median), and third quartile, respectively. The quartiles can be used to divide the data set into four parts, with each part containing approximately 25% of the data.

Hinges   The value of the lower hinge is approximately the first quartile, or 25th percentile. The value of the upper hinge is approximately the third quartile, or 75th percentile. The values of the hinges and quartiles may differ slightly because of differing computational conventions, but their objective is to divide the data into four equal parts.

Range   A measure of variability, defined to be the largest value minus the smallest value.

Interquartile range (IQR)   A measure of variability, defined to be the difference between the third and first quartiles.

Variance   A measure of variability based on the squared deviations of the data values about the mean.

Standard deviation   A measure of variability computed by taking the positive square root of the variance.

Coefficient of variation   A measure of relative variability computed by dividing the standard deviation by the mean and multiplying by 100.

z-score   A value computed by dividing the deviation about the mean $(x_i - \bar{x})$ by the standard deviation s. A z-score is referred to as a standardized value and denotes the number of standard deviations x_i is from the mean.

Chebyshev's theorem   A theorem applying to any data set that can be used to make statements about the proportion of observations that must be within a specified number of standard deviations of the mean.

Empirical rule   A rule that can be used to compute the percentage of data values that must be within one, two, and three standard deviations of the mean for data having a bell-shaped distribution.

Outlier   An unusually small or unusually large data value.

Five-number summary   An exploratory data analysis technique that uses five numbers to summarize the data: smallest value, first quartile, median, third quartile, and largest value.

Box plot   A graphical summary of data based on a five-number summary.

Covariance   A numerical measure of linear association between two variables. Positive values indicate a positive relationship; negative values indicate a negative relationship.

Correlation coefficient   A numerical measure of linear association between two variables that takes values between -1 and $+1$. Values near $+1$ indicate a strong positive linear relationship, values near -1 indicate a strong negative linear relationship, and values near zero indicate lack of a linear relationship.

Weighted mean   The mean for a data set obtained by assigning each observation a weight that reflects its importance within the data set.

Grouped data   Data available in class intervals as summarized by a frequency distribution. Individual values of the original data are not available.

KEY FORMULAS

Sample Mean

$$\bar{x} = \frac{\Sigma x_i}{n} \tag{3.1}$$

Population Mean

$$\mu = \frac{\Sigma x_i}{N} \tag{3.2}$$

Interquartile Range

$$IQR = Q_3 - Q_1 \tag{3.3}$$

Population Variance

$$\sigma^2 = \frac{\Sigma(x_i - \mu)^2}{N} \tag{3.4}$$

Sample Variance

$$s^2 = \frac{\Sigma(x_i - \bar{x})^2}{n - 1} \tag{3.5}$$

Standard Deviation

$$\text{Sample Standard Deviation} = s = \sqrt{s^2} \tag{3.6}$$

$$\text{Population Standard Deviation} = \sigma = \sqrt{\sigma^2} \tag{3.7}$$

Coefficient of Variation

$$\frac{\text{Standard Deviation}}{\text{Mean}} \times 100 \tag{3.8}$$

z-score

$$z_i = \frac{x_i - \bar{x}}{s} \tag{3.9}$$

Sample Covariance

$$s_{xy} = \frac{\Sigma(x_i - \bar{x})(y_i - \bar{y})}{n - 1} \tag{3.10}$$

Pearson Product Moment Correlation Coefficient: Sample Data

$$r_{xy} = \frac{s_{xy}}{s_x s_y} \tag{3.12}$$

Weighted Mean

$$\bar{x} = \frac{\Sigma w_i x_i}{\Sigma w_i} \tag{3.15}$$

Sample Mean for Grouped Data

$$\bar{x} = \frac{\Sigma f_i M_i}{n} \tag{3.16}$$

Sample Variance for Grouped Data

$$s^2 = \frac{\Sigma f_i (M_i - \bar{x})^2}{n - 1} \tag{3.17}$$

Population Mean for Grouped Data

$$\mu = \frac{\Sigma f_i M_i}{N} \tag{3.18}$$

Population Variance for Grouped Data

$$\sigma^2 = \frac{\Sigma f_i (M_i - \mu)^2}{N} \tag{3.19}$$

SUPPLEMENTARY EXERCISES

60. The average American spends \$65.88 per month dining out (*The Des Moines Register*, December 5, 1997). A sample of young adults provided the following dining out expenditures (in dollars) over the past month.

CDfile
Eat

253	101	245	467	131	0	225
80	113	69	198	95	129	124
11	178	104	161	0	118	151
55	152	134	169			

a. Compute the mean, median, and mode.
b. Considering your results in part (a), do these young adults seem to spend about the same as an average American eating out?
c. Compute the first and third quartiles.
d. Compute the range and interquartile range.
e. Compute the variance and standard deviation.
f. Are there any outliers?

61. The total annual compensation for a board member at one of the nation's 100 biggest public companies is based in part on the cash retainer, an annual payment for serving on the board. In addition to the cash retainer, a board member may receive a stock retainer, a stock grant, a stock option, and a fee for attending board meetings. The total compensation can easily exceed $100,000 even with an annual retainer as low as $15,000. The following data show the cash retainer for a sample of 20 of the nation's biggest public companies (*USA Today*, April 17, 2000).

CDfile
Retainer

Company	Cash Retainer ($1000s)
American Express	64
Bank of America	36
Boeing	26
Chevron	35
Dell Computer	40
DuPont	35
ExxonMobil	40
Ford Motor	30
General Motors	60
International Paper	36
Kroger	28
Lucent Technologies	50
Motorola	20
Procter & Gamble	55
Raytheon	40
Sears Roebuck	30
Texaco	15
United Parcel Service	55
Wal-Mart Stores	25
Xerox	40

Compute the following descriptive statistics.
a. Mean, median, and mode
b. The first and third quartiles
c. The range and interquartile range
d. The variance and the standard deviation
e. Coefficient of variation

62. A survey conducted to assess the ability of computer manufacturers to handle problems quickly (*PC Computing*, November 1997) obtained the following results.

Company	Days to Resolve Problems	Company	Days to Resolve Problems
Compaq	13	Gateway	21
Packard Bell	27	Digital	27
Quantex	11	IBM	12

Company	Days to Resolve Problems	Company	Days to Resolve Problems
Dell	14	Hewlett-Packard	14
NEC	14	AT&T	20
AST	17	Toshiba	37
Acer	16	Micron	17

    a. What are the mean and median number of days needed to resolve problems?

    b. What are the variance and standard deviation?

    c. Which manufacturer holds the best record?

    d. What is the z-score for Packard Bell?

    e. What is the z-score for IBM?

    f. Are there any outliers?

63. The following data show home mortgage loan amounts handled by one loan officer at the Westwood Savings and Loan Association. Data are in thousands of dollars.

CDfile
Mortgage

52.0	68.5	63.0	57.5	64.0	42.5	55.9	73.2	67.5	66.2
55.2	60.9	53.8	58.4	43.0	61.0	63.5	55.4	63.5	50.2
69.0	68.1	60.5	75.5	60.5	82.0	70.5	81.6	72.5	74.8

    a. Find the mean, median, and mode.

    b. Find the first and third quartiles.

64. According to Forrester Research, Inc., approximately 19% of Internet users play games online. The following data show the number of unique users (in thousands) for the month of March for 10 game sites (*The Wall Street Journal,* April 17, 2000).

Site	Unique Users
AOLGames.aol	9416
extremelotto.com	3955
freelotto.com	12901
gamesville.com	4844
iwin.com	7410
prizecentral.com	4899
shockwave.com	5582
speedyclick.com	6628
uproar.com	8821
webstakes.com	7499

Using these data, compute the mean, median, variance, and standard deviation.

65. The typical household income for a sample of 20 cities follow (*Places Rated Almanac,* 2000). Data are in thousands of dollars.

CDfile
Income

City	Income
Akron, OH	74.1
Atlanta, GA	82.4
Birmingham, AL	71.2
Bismark, ND	62.8

(continued)

City	Income
Cleveland, OH	79.2
Columbia, SC	66.8
Danbury, CT	132.3
Denver, CO	82.6
Detroit, MI	85.3
Fort Lauderdale, FL	75.8
Hartford, CT	89.1
Lancaster, PA	75.2
Madison, WI	78.8
Naples, FL	100.0
Nashville, TN	77.3
Philadelphia, PA	87.0
Savannah, GA	67.8
Toledo, OH	71.2
Trenton, NJ	106.4
Washington, DC	97.4

a. Compute the mean and standard deviation for the sample data.
b. Using the mean and standard deviation computed in part (a) as estimates of the mean and standard deviation of household income for the population of all cities, use Chebyshev's theorem to determine the range within which 75% of the household incomes for the population of all cities must fall.
c. Assume that the distribution of household income is bell-shaped. Using the mean and standard deviation computed in part (a) as estimates of the mean and standard deviation of household income for the population of all cities, use the empirical rule to determine the range within which 95% of the household incomes for the population of all cities must fall. Compare your answer with the value in part (b).
d. Does the sample data contain any outliers?

66. Public transportation and the automobile are two methods an employee can use to get to work each day. Samples of times recorded for each method are shown. Times are in minutes.

Public Transportation:	28	29	32	37	33	25	29	32	41	34
Automobile:	29	31	33	32	34	30	31	32	35	33

a. Compute the sample mean time to get to work for each method.
b. Compute the sample standard deviation for each method.
c. On the basis of your results from parts (a) and (b), which method of transportation should be preferred? Explain.
d. Develop a box plot for each method. Does a comparison of the box plots support your conclusion in part (c)?

67. Final examination scores for 25 statistics students follow.

56	77	84	82	42	61	44	95	98	84
93	62	96	78	88	58	62	79	85	89
89	97	53	76	75					

a. Provide a five-number summary.
b. Provide a box plot.

68. The following data show the total yardage accumulated during the NCAA college football season for a sample of 20 receivers.

744	652	576	1112	971	451	1023	852	809	596
941	975	400	711	1174	1278	820	511	907	1251

CDfile
Exam

a. Provide a five-number summary.
b. Provide a box plot.
c. Identify any outliers.

69. The typical household income and typical home price for a sample of 20 cities follow (*Places Rated Almanac,* 2000). Data are in thousands of dollars.

Cities

City	Income	Home Price
Bismark, ND	62.8	92.8
Columbia, SC	66.8	116.7
Savannah, GA	67.8	108.1
Birmingham, AL	71.2	130.9
Toledo, OH	71.2	101.1
Akron, OH	74.1	114.9
Lancaster, PA	75.2	125.9
Fort Lauderdale, FL	75.8	145.3
Nashville, TN	77.3	125.9
Madison, WI	78.8	145.2
Cleveland, OH	79.2	135.8
Atlanta, GA	82.4	126.9
Denver, CO	82.6	161.9
Detroit, MI	85.3	145.0
Philadelphia, PA	87.0	151.5
Hartford, CT	89.1	162.1
Washington, DC	97.4	191.9
Naples, FL	100.0	173.6
Trenton, NJ	106.4	168.1
Danbury, CT	132.3	234.1

a. What is the value of the sample covariance? Does it indicate a positive or a negative linear relationship?
b. What is the sample correlation coefficient?

70. *Road & Track* provided the following sample of the tire ratings and load-carrying capacity of automobiles tires.

Tire Rating	Load-Carrying Capacity
75	853
82	1047
85	1135
87	1201
88	1235
91	1356
92	1389
93	1433
105	2039

a. Develop a scatter diagram for the data with tire rating on the *x*-axis.
b. What is the sample correlation coefficient and what does it tell you about the relationship between tire rating and load-carrying capacity?

71. In Exercise 6, we computed a variety of descriptive statistics for two types of trades made by discount brokers: 500 shares at $50 per share, and 1000 shares at $5 per share. Table 3.2

shows the commissions charged on each of these trades by a sample of 20 discount brokers (*AAII Journal,* January 1997). Compute the covariance and the correlation coefficient
for the two types of trades. What did you learn about the relationship?

72. The following data show the trailing 52-weeks primary share earnings and book values as
    reported by 10 companies (*The Wall Street Journal,* March 13, 2000).

Company	Book Value	Earnings
Am Elec	25.21	2.69
Columbia En	23.20	3.01
Con Ed	25.19	3.13
Duke Energy	20.17	2.25
Edison Int'l	13.55	1.79
Enron Cp.	7.44	1.27
Peco	13.61	3.15
Pub Sv Ent	21.86	3.29
Southn Co.	8.77	1.86
Unicom	23.22	2.74

    a. Develop a scatter diagram for the data with book value on the *x*-axis.
    b. What is the sample correlation coefficient and what does it tell you about the rela-
       tionship between the earnings per share and the book value?

73. The days to maturity for a sample of five money market funds are shown here. The dollar
    amounts invested in the funds are provided. Use the weighted mean to determine the mean
    number of days to maturity for dollars invested in these five money market funds.

Days to Maturity	Dollar Value ($ millions)
20	20
12	30
7	10
5	15
6	10

74. A forecasting technique referred to as moving averages uses the average or mean of the
    most recent *n* periods to forecast the next value for time series data. With a three-period
    moving average, the most recent three periods of data are used in the forecast computa-
    tion. Consider a product with the following demand for the first three months of the cur-
    rent year: January (800 units), February (750 units), and March (900 units).
    a. What is the three-month moving average forecast for April?
    b. A variation of this forecasting technique is called weighted moving averages. The
       weighting allows the more recent time series data to receive more weight or more im-
       portance in the computation of the forecast. For example, a weighted three-month
       moving average might give a weight of 3 to data one month old, a weight of 2 to data
       two months old, and a weight of 1 to data three months old. Use this data to provide a
       three-month weighted moving average forecast for April.

75. The dividend yield is the percentage of the value of a share of stock that will be paid as an
    annual dividend to the stockholder. A sample of six stocks held by Innis Investments had
    the following dividend yields (*Barron's,* January 5, 1998). The amount Innis has invested
    in each stock is also shown. What is the mean dividend yield for the portfolio?

Company	Dividend Yield	Amount Invested ($)
Apple Computer	0.00	5500
Chevron	2.98	9200
Eastman Kodak	2.77	4300
Exxon	2.65	6000
Merck	1.58	3000
Sears	2.00	2000

76. Dinner check amounts at La Maison French Restaurant have the frequency distribution shown as follows. Compute the mean, variance, and standard deviation for the data.

Dinner Check ($)	Frequency
25–34	2
35–44	6
45–54	4
55–64	4
65–74	2
75–84	2
Total	20

77. Automobiles traveling on a highway with a posted speed limit of 55 miles per hour are checked for speed by a state police radar system. Following is a frequency distribution of speeds.

Speed (miles per hour)	Frequency
45–49	10
50–54	40
55–59	150
60–64	175
65–69	75
70–74	15
75–79	10
Total	475

a. What is the mean speed of the automobiles traveling on this highway?
b. Compute the variance and the standard deviation.

Case Problem 1   CONSOLIDATED FOODS, INC.

Consolidated Foods, Inc., operates a chain of supermarkets in New Mexico, Arizona, and California. (See Case Problem, Chapter 2). Table 3.13 shows a portion of the data on dollar amounts and method of payment for a sample of 100 customers. Consolidated's managers requested the sample be taken to learn about payment practices of the stores' customers. In particular, managers wanted to learn about how a new credit card payment option was related to the customers' purchase amounts.

TABLE 3.13   PURCHASE AMOUNT AND METHOD OF PAYMENT FOR A SAMPLE OF 100 CONSOLIDATED FOODS CUSTOMERS

CDfile

Consolid

Customer	Amount ($)	Method of Payment
1	28.58	Check
2	52.04	Check
3	7.41	Cash
4	11.17	Cash
5	43.79	Credit Card
6	48.95	Check
7	57.59	Check
8	27.60	Check
9	26.91	Credit Card
10	9.00	Cash
.	.	.
.	.	.
.	.	.
95	18.09	Cash
96	54.84	Check
97	41.10	Check
98	43.14	Check
99	3.31	Cash
100	69.77	Credit Card

Managerial Report

Use the methods of descriptive statistics presented in Chapter 3 to summarize the sample data. Provide summaries of the dollar purchase amounts for cash customers, personal check customers, and credit card customers separately. Your report should contain the following summaries and discussions.

1. A comparison and interpretation of means and medians.
2. A comparison and interpretation of measures of variability such as the range and standard deviation.
3. The identification and interpretation of the five-number summaries for each method of payment.
4. Box plots for each method of payment.

Use the summary section of your report to provide a discussion of what you have learned about the method of payment and the amounts of payments for Consolidated Foods customers.

Case Problem 2   NATIONAL HEALTH CARE ASSOCIATION

The National Health Care Association faces a projected shortage of nurses in the health care profession. To learn the current degree of job satisfaction among nurses, the association sponsored a study of hospital nurses throughout the country. As part of this study, a sample of 50 nurses indicated their degree of satisfaction with their work, their pay, and their opportunities for promotion. Each of the three aspects of satisfaction was measured on a scale from 0 to 100, with larger values for higher degrees of satisfaction. The data collected

TABLE 3.14   SATISFACTION SCORE DATA FOR A SAMPLE OF 50 NURSES

Nurse	Hospital	Work	Pay	Promotion
1	Private	74	47	63
2	VA	72	76	37
3	University	75	53	92
4	Private	89	66	62
5	University	69	47	16
6	Private	85	56	64
7	University	89	80	64
8	Private	88	36	47
9	University	88	55	52
10	Private	84	42	66
·	·	·	·	·
45	University	79	59	41
46	University	84	53	63
47	University	87	66	49
48	VA	84	74	37
49	VA	95	66	52
50	Private	72	57	40

also showed the type of hospital employing the nurses. The types of hospitals were private (P), Veterans Administration (VA), and University (U). A portion of the data is shown in Table 3.14. The complete data set can be found on the data disk in the file named Health.

Managerial Report

Use methods of descriptive statistics to summarize the data. Present the summaries that will be beneficial in communicating the results to others. Discuss your findings. Specifically, comment on the following questions.

1. On the basis of the entire data set and the three job satisfaction variables, what aspect of the job is most satisfying for the nurses? What appears to be the least satisfying? In what area(s), if any, do you feel improvements should be made? Discuss.
2. On the basis of descriptive measures of variability, what measure of job satisfaction appears to generate the greatest difference of opinion among the nurses? Explain.
3. What can be learned about the types of hospitals? Does any particular type of hospital seem to have better levels of job satisfaction than the other types? Do your results suggest any recommendations for learning about and/or improving job satisfaction? Discuss.
4. What additional descriptive statistics and insights can you use to learn about and possibly improve job satisfaction?

Case Problem 3   BUSINESS SCHOOLS OF ASIA-PACIFIC

The pursuit of a higher education degree in business is now international. A survey shows that more and more Asians choose the Master of Business Administration degree route to corporate success (*Asia, Inc.*, September 1997). The number of applicants for MBA courses at Asia-Pacific schools increases about 30% a year. In 1997, the 74 business schools in the Asia-Pacific region reported a record 170,000 applications for the 11,000 full-time MBA degrees to be awarded in 1999. A main reason for the surge in demand is that an MBA can greatly enhance earning power.

Across the region, thousands of Asians show an increasing willingness to temporarily shelve their careers and spend two years in pursuit of a theoretical business qualification. Courses in these schools are notoriously tough and include economics, banking, marketing, behavioral sciences, labor relations, decision making, strategic thinking, business law, and more. *Asia, Inc.* provided the data set in Table 3.15, which shows some of the characteristics of the leading Asia-Pacific business schools.

Managerial Report

Use the methods of descriptive statistics to summarize the data in Table 3.15. Discuss your findings.

1. Include a summary for each variable in the data set. Make comments and interpretations based on maximums and minimums, as well as the appropriate means and proportions. What new insights do these descriptive statistics provide concerning Asia-Pacific business schools?
2. Summarize the data to compare the following:
   a. Any difference between local and foreign tuition costs.
   b. Any difference between mean starting salaries for schools requiring and not requiring work experience.
   c. Any difference between starting salaries for schools requiring and not requiring English tests.
3. Present any additional graphical and numerical summaries that will be beneficial in communicating the data in Table 3.15 to others.

Appendix 3.1   DESCRIPTIVE STATISTICS WITH MINITAB

In this appendix, we describe how to use Minitab to develop descriptive statistics. Table 3.1 listed the starting salaries for 12 business school graduates. Panel A of Figure 3.10 shows the descriptive statistics obtained by using Minitab to summarize these data. Definitions of the headings in Panel A follow.

N	number of data values
Mean	mean
Median	median
StDev	standard deviation
Min	minimum data value
Max	maximum data value
Q1	first quartile
Q3	third quartile

We have discussed, in a note, the numerical measure labeled TrMean and not discussed SEMean. TrMean refers to the *trimmed mean*. The trimmed mean indicates the central location of the data after removing the effect of the smallest and largest data values in the data set. Minitab provides the 5% trimmed mean; the smallest 5% of the data values and the

TABLE 3.15   DATA FOR 25 ASIA-PACIFIC BUSINESS SCHOOLS

Business School	Full-Time Enrollment	Students per Faculty	Local Tuition ($)	Foreign Tuition ($)	Age	% Foreign	GMAT	English Test	Work Experience	Starting Salary ($)
Melbourne Business School	200	5	24,420	29,600	28	47	Yes	No	Yes	71,400
University of New South Wales (Sydney)	228	4	19,993	32,582	29	28	Yes	No	Yes	65,200
Indian Institute of Management (Ahmedabad)	392	5	4,300	4,300	22	0	No	No	No	7,100
Chinese University of Hong Kong	90	5	11,140	11,140	29	10	Yes	No	No	31,000
International University of Japan (Niigata)	126	4	33,060	33,060	28	60	Yes	Yes	No	87,000
Asian Institute of Management (Manila)	389	5	7,562	9,000	25	50	Yes	No	No	22,800
Indian Institute of Management (Bangalore)	380	5	3,935	16,000	23	1	Yes	No	No	7,500
National University of Singapore	147	6	6,146	7,170	29	51	Yes	Yes	Yes	43,300
Indian Institute of Management (Calcutta)	463	8	2,880	16,000	23	0	No	No	No	7,400
Australian National University (Canberra)	42	2	20,300	20,300	30	80	Yes	Yes	Yes	46,600
Nanyang Technological University (Singapore)	50	5	8,500	8,500	32	20	Yes	No	Yes	49,300
University of Queensland (Brisbane)	138	17	16,000	22,800	32	26	No	No	Yes	49,600
Hong Kong University of Science and Technology	60	2	11,513	11,513	26	37	Yes	No	Yes	34,000
Macquarie Graduate School of Management (Sydney)	12	8	17,172	19,778	34	27	No	No	Yes	60,100
Chulalongkorn University (Bangkok)	200	7	17,355	17,355	25	6	Yes	No	Yes	17,600
Monash Mt. Eliza Business School (Melbourne)	350	13	16,200	22,500	30	30	Yes	Yes	Yes	52,500
Asian Institute of Management (Bangkok)	300	10	18,200	18,200	29	90	No	Yes	Yes	25,000
University of Adelaide	20	19	16,426	23,100	30	10	No	No	Yes	66,000
Massey University (Palmerston North, New Zealand)	30	15	13,106	21,625	37	35	No	Yes	Yes	41,400
Royal Melbourne Institute of Technology Business Graduate School	30	7	13,880	17,765	32	30	No	Yes	Yes	48,900
Jammalal Bajaj Institute of Management Studies (Bombay)	240	9	1,000	1,000	24	0	No	No	Yes	7,000
Curtin Institute of Technology (Perth)	98	15	9,475	19,097	29	43	Yes	No	Yes	55,000
Lahore University of Management Sciences	70	14	11,250	26,300	23	2.5	No	No	No	7,500
Universiti Sains Malaysia (Penang)	30	5	2,260	2,260	32	15	No	Yes	Yes	16,000
De La Salle University (Manila)	44	17	3,300	3,600	28	3.5	Yes	No	Yes	13,100

FIGURE 3.10   DESCRIPTIVE STATISTICS AND BOX PLOT PROVIDED BY MINITAB

Panel A: Descriptive Statistics

N	Mean	Median	TrMean	StDev	SEMean
12	2940.0	2905.0	2924.5	165.7	47.8

Min	Max	Q1	Q3		
2710.0	3325.0	2857.5	3025.0		

Panel B: Box Plot

largest 5% of the data values are removed. The 5% trimmed mean is found by computing the mean for the middle 90% of the data. SEMean, which is the *standard error of the mean,* is computed by dividing the standard deviation by the square root of N. The interpretation and use of this measure are discussed in Chapter 7 when we introduce the topics of sampling and sampling distributions.

Although the numerical measures of range, interquartile range, variance, and coefficient of variation do not appear on the Minitab output, these values can be easily computed if desired from the results in Figure 3.10 by the following formulas.

$$\text{Range} = \text{Max} - \text{Min}$$
$$\text{IQR} = Q_3 - Q_1$$
$$\text{Variance} = (\text{StDev})^2$$
$$\text{Coefficient of Variation} = (\text{StDev}/\text{Mean}) \times 100$$

Finally, note that Minitab's quartiles $Q_1 = 2857.5$ and $Q_3 = 3025$ are slightly different from the quartiles $Q_1 = 2865$ and $Q_3 = 3000$ computed in Section 3.1. The different conventions* used to identify the quartiles explain this variation. Hence, the values of Q_1 and Q_3 provided by one convention may not be identical to the values of Q_1 and Q_3 provided by another convention. Any differences tend to be negligible, however, and the results provided should not mislead the user in making the usual interpretations associated with quartiles.

Let us now see how the statistics in Figure 3.10 are generated. The starting salary data have been entered into column C2 (the second column) of a Minitab worksheet. The following steps will then generate the descriptive statistics.

CDfile
Salary

---

*With the n observations arranged in ascending order (smallest value to largest value), Minitab uses the positions given by $(n + 1)/4$ and $3(n + 1)/4$ to locate Q_1 and Q_3, respectively. When a position is fractional, Minitab interpolates between the two adjacent ordered data values to determine the corresponding quartile.

Step 1. Select the **Stat** pull-down menu
Step 2. Choose **Basic Statistics**
Step 3. Choose **Display Descriptive Statistics**
Step 4. When the Display Descriptive Statistics dialog box appears:
        Enter C2 in the **Variables** box
        Click **OK**

Panel B of Figure 3.10 is a box plot provided by Minitab. The box drawn from the first to the third quartiles contains the middle 50% of the data. The line within the box locates the median. The asterisk indicates an outlier at 3325.

The following steps generate the box plot shown in panel B of Figure 3.10.

Step 1. Select the **Graph** pull-down menu
Step 2. Choose **Boxplot**
Step 3. When the Boxplot dialog box appears:
        Enter C2 under **Y** in the **Graph variables** box
        Click **OK**

CDfile
Stereo

Figure 3.11 shows the covariance and correlation output that Minitab provided for the stereo and sound equipment store data in Table 3.7. In the covariance portion of the figure, Commerci denotes the number of weekend television commercials and Sales denotes the sales during the following week. The value in column Commerci and row Sales, 11, is the sample covariance as computed in Section 3.5. The value in column Commerci and row Commerci, 2.22222, is the sample variance for the number of commercials, and the value in column Sales and row Sales, 62.88889, is the sample variance for sales. The sample correlation coefficient, 0.930, is shown in the correlation portion of the output. Note: The interpretation and use of the p-value provided in the output are discussed in Chapter 9.

Let us now describe how to obtain the information in Figure 3.11. We entered the data for the number of commercials into column C2 and the data for sales into column C3 of a Minitab worksheet. The steps necessary to generate the covariance output in the first three rows of Figure 3.11 follow.

Step 1. Select the **Stat** pull-down menu
Step 2. Choose **Basic Statistics**
Step 3. Choose **Covariance**
Step 4. When the Covariance dialog box appears:
        Enter C2 C3 in the **Variables** box
        Click **OK**

FIGURE 3.11   COVARIANCE AND CORRELATION PROVIDED BY MINITAB FOR THE NUMBER OF COMMERCIALS AND SALES DATA

```
Covariances: Commercials, Sales

             Commerci      Sales
Commerci      2.22222
Sales        11.00000    62.88889


Correlations: Commercials, Sales

Pearson correlation of Commercials and Sales = 0.930
P-Value = 0.000
```

To obtain the correlation output in Figure 3.11, only one change is necessary in the steps for obtaining the covariance. In step 3, the **Correlation** option is selected.

Appendix 3.2   DESCRIPTIVE STATISTICS WITH EXCEL

Excel can be used to generate the descriptive statistics discussed in this chapter. We show how Excel can be used to generate several measures of location and variability for a single variable and to generate the covariance and correlation coefficient as measures of association between two variables.

Using Excel Functions

CDfile
Salary

Excel provides functions for computing the mean, median, mode, sample variance, and sample standard deviation. We illustrate the use of these Excel functions by computing the mean, median, mode, sample variance, and sample standard deviation for the starting salary data in Table 3.1. Refer to Figure 3.12 as we describe the steps involved. The data have been entered in column B.

Excel's AVERAGE function can be used to compute the mean by entering the following formula into cell E1:

$$=\text{AVERAGE(B2:B13)}$$

FIGURE 3.12   USING EXCEL FUNCTIONS FOR COMPUTING THE MEAN, MEDIAN, MODE, VARIANCE, AND STANDARD DEVIATION

	A	B	C	D	E	F
1	Graduate	Starting Salary		Mean	=AVERAGE(B2:B13)	
2	1	2850		Median	=MEDIAN(B2:B13)	
3	2	2950		Mode	=MODE(B2:B13)	
4	3	3050		Variance	=VAR(B2:B13)	
5	4	2880		Standard Deviation	=STDEV(B2:B13)	
6	5	2755				

	A	B	C	D	E	F
1	Graduate	Starting Salary		Mean	2940	
2	1	2850		Median	2905	
3	2	2950		Mode	2880	
4	3	3050		Variance	27440.909	
5	4	2880		Standard Deviation	165.65	
6	5	2755				
7	6	2710				
8	7	2890				
9	8	3130				
10	9	2940				
11	10	3325				
12	11	2920				
13	12	2880				
14						

Row	Graduate	Starting Salary
7	6	2710
8	7	2890
9	8	3130
10	9	2940
11	10	3325
12	11	2920
13	12	2880
14		

Similarly, the formulas =MEDIAN(B2:B13), =MODE(B2:B13), =VAR(B2:B13), and =STDEV(B2:B13) are entered into cells E2:E5, respectively, to compute the median, mode, variance, and standard deviation. The worksheet in the foreground shows that the values computed using the Excel functions are the same as we computed earlier in the chapter.

Excel also provides functions that can be used to compute the covariance and correlation coefficient. But, you must be careful when using these functions because the covariance function treats the data as if it were a population and the correlation function treats the data as if it were a sample. Thus, the result obtained using Excel's covariance function must be adjusted to provide the sample covariance. We show here how these functions can be used to compute the sample covariance and the sample correlation coefficient for the stereo and sound equipment store data in Table 3.7. Refer to Figure 3.13 as we present the steps involved.

CDfile

Stereo

Excel's covariance function, COVAR, can be used to compute the population covariance by entering the following formula into cell F1:

$$=COVAR(B2:B11,C2:C11)$$

Similarly, the formula =CORREL(B2:B11,C2:C11) is entered into cell F2 to compute the sample correlation coefficient. The worksheet in the foreground shows the values computed using the Excel functions. Note that the value of the sample correlation coefficient (.93) is the same as computed using equation (3.12). However, the result provided by the Excel COVAR function, 9.9, was obtained by treating the data as if it were a population. Thus, we must adjust the Excel result of 9.9 to obtain the sample covariance. The adjustment is rather simple. First, note that the formula for the population covariance, equation (3.11), requires dividing by the total number of observations in the data set. But, the formula for the sample covariance, equation (3.10), requires dividing by the total number of observations minus 1. So, to use the Excel result of 9.9 to compute the sample covariance, we simply multiply 9.9 by $n/(n-1)$. Because $n = 10$, we obtain

$$s_{xy} = \left(\frac{10}{9}\right)9.9 = 11$$

Thus, the sample covariance for the stereo and sound equipment data is 11.

Using Excel's Descriptive Statistics Tool

As we already demonstrated, Excel provides statistical functions to compute descriptive statistics for a data set. These functions can be used to compute one statistic at a time (e.g., mean, variance, etc.). Excel also provides a variety of Data Analysis Tools. One of these tools, called Descriptive Statistics, allows the user to compute a variety of descriptive statistics at once. We show here how it can be used to compute descriptive statistics for the starting salary data in Table 3.1. Refer to Figure 3.14 as we describe the steps involved.

Step 1. Select the **Tools** pull-down menu
Step 2. Choose **Data Analysis**
Step 3. Choose **Descriptive Statistics** from the list of Analysis Tools
Step 4. When the Descriptive Statistics dialog box appears:
        Enter B1:B13 in the **Input Range** box
        Select **Grouped By Columns**
        Select **Labels in First Row**
        Select **Output Range**

FIGURE 3.13   USING EXCEL FUNCTIONS FOR COMPUTING COVARIANCE AND CORRELATION

	A	B	C	D	E	F	G
1	Week	Commercials	Sales		Covariance	=COVAR(B2:B11,C2:C11)	
2	1	2	50		Correlation	=CORREL(B2:B11,C2:C11)	
3	2	5	57				
4	3	1	41				
5	4	3	54				
6	5	4	54				
7	6	1	38				
8	7	5	63				
9	8	3	48				
10	9	4	59				
11	10	2	46				
12							

	A	B	C	D	E	F	G
1	Week	Commercials	Sales		Covariance	9.90	
2	1	2	50		Correlation	0.93	
3	2	5	57				
4	3	1	41				
5	4	3	54				
6	5	4	54				
7	6	1	38				
8	7	5	63				
9	8	3	48				
10	9	4	59				
11	10	2	46				
12							
13							

> Enter D1 in the **Output Range** box (to identify the upper left-hand corner of the section of the worksheet where the descriptive statistics will appear)
>
> Click **OK**

Cells D1:E15 of Figure 3.14 show the descriptive statistics provided by Excel. The boldface entries are the descriptive statistics we have covered in this chapter. The descriptive statistics that are not boldface are either covered subsequently in the text or discussed in more advanced texts.

FIGURE 3.14   USING EXCEL'S DESCRIPTIVE STATISTICS TOOL

	A	B	C	D	E	F
1	Graduate	Starting Salary		*Starting Salary*		
2	1	2850				
3	2	2950		**Mean**	2940	
4	3	3050		Standard Error	47.82	
5	4	2880		**Median**	2905	
6	5	2755		**Mode**	2880	
7	6	2710		**Standard Deviation**	165.65	
8	7	2890		**Sample Variance**	27440.91	
9	8	3130		Kurtosis	1.72	
10	9	2940		Skewness	1.09	
11	10	3325		**Range**	615	
12	11	2920		**Minimum**	2710	
13	12	2880		**Maximum**	3325	
14				**Sum**	35280	
15				**Count**	12	
16						

INTRODUCTION TO PROBABILITY

Chapter 4

CONTENTS

MORTON INTERNATIONAL*

CHICAGO, ILLINOIS

Morton International is a company with businesses in salt, household products, rocket motors, and specialty chemicals. Carstab Corporation, a subsidiary of Morton International, produces specialty chemicals and offers a variety of chemicals designed to meet the unique specifications of its customers. For one particular customer, Carstab produced an expensive catalyst used in chemical processing. Some, but not all, of the lots produced by Carstab met the customer's specifications for the product.

Carstab's customer agreed to test each lot after receiving it and determine whether the catalyst would perform the desired function. Lots that did not pass the customer's test would be returned to Carstab. Over time, Carstab found that the customer was accepting 60% of the lots and returning 40%. In probability terms, each Carstab shipment to the customer had a .60 probability of being accepted and a .40 probability of being returned.

Neither Carstab nor its customer was pleased with these results. In an effort to improve service, Carstab explored the possibility of duplicating the customer's test prior to shipment. However, the high cost of the special testing equipment made that alternative infeasible. Carstab's chemists then proposed a new, relatively low-cost test designed to indicate whether a lot would pass the customer's test. The probability question of interest was: What is the probability that a lot will pass the customer's test if it has passed the new Carstab test?

A sample of lots was produced and subjected to the new Carstab test. Only lots that passed the new test

Morton Salt: "When It Rains It Pours." © Joe Higgins/ South-Western.

were sent to the customer. Probability analysis of the data indicated that if a lot passed the Carstab test, it had a .909 probability of passing the customer's test and being accepted. Alternatively, if a lot passed the Carstab test, it had only a .091 probability of being returned. The probability analysis provided key supporting evidence for the adoption and implementation of the new testing procedure at Carstab. The new test resulted in an immediate improvement in customer service and a substantial reduction in shipping and handling costs for returned lots.

The probability of a lot being accepted by the customer after passing the new Carstab test is called a conditional probability. In this chapter, you will learn how to compute this and other probabilities that are helpful in decision making.

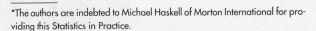

*The authors are indebted to Michael Haskell of Morton International for providing this Statistics in Practice.

Managers often base their decisions on an analysis of uncertainties such as the following:

1. What are the chances that sales will decrease if we increase prices?
2. What is the likelihood a new assembly method will increase productivity?
3. How likely is it that the project will be finished on time?
4. What is the chance that a new investment will be profitable?

Some of the earliest work on probability originated in a series of letters between Pierre de Fermat and Blaise Pascal in the 1650s.

Probability is a numerical measure of the likelihood that an event will occur. Thus, probabilities could be used as measures of the degree of uncertainty associated with the four events previously listed. If probabilities were available, we could determine the likelihood of each event occurring.

Probability values are always assigned on a scale from 0 to 1. A probability near zero indicates an event is unlikely to occur; a probability near 1 indicates an event is almost certain to occur. Other probabilities between 0 and 1 represent degrees of likelihood that an event will occur. For example, if we consider the event "rain tomorrow," we understand that when the weather report indicates "a near-zero probability of rain," it means almost no chance of rain. However, if a .90 probability of rain is reported, we know that rain is likely to occur. A .50 probability indicates that rain is just as likely to occur as not. Figure 4.1 depicts the view of probability as a numerical measure of the likelihood of an event occurring.

4.1   EXPERIMENTS, COUNTING RULES, AND ASSIGNING PROBABILITIES

In discussing probability, we define an **experiment** to be a process that generates well-defined outcomes. On any single repetition of an experiment, one and only one of the possible experimental outcomes will occur. Several examples of experiments and their associated outcomes follow.

Experiment	Experimental Outcomes
Toss a coin	Head, tail
Select a part for inspection	Defective, nondefective
Conduct a sales call	Purchase, no purchase
Roll a die	1, 2, 3, 4, 5, 6
Play a football game	Win, lose, tie

FIGURE 4.1   PROBABILITY AS A NUMERICAL MEASURE OF THE LIKELIHOOD OF AN EVENT OCCURRING

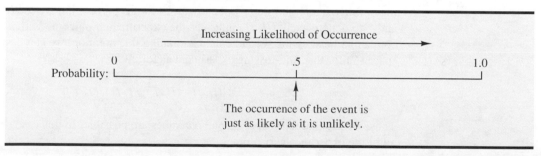

By specifying all possible experimental outcomes, we identify the **sample space** for an experiment.

Sample Space

The sample space for an experiment is the set of all experimental outcomes.

Experimental outcomes are also called sample points.

An experimental outcome is also called a **sample point** to identify it as an element of the sample space.

Consider the first experiment in the preceding table—tossing a coin. The upward face of the coin—a head or a tail—determines the experimental outcomes (sample points). If we let S denote the sample space, we can use the following notation to describe the sample space.

$$S = \{\text{Head, Tail}\}$$

The sample space for the second experiment in the table—selecting a part for inspection—can be described as follows:

$$S = \{\text{Defective, Nondefective}\}$$

Both of the experiments just described have two experimental outcomes (sample points). However, suppose we consider the fourth experiment listed in the table—rolling a die. The possible experimental outcomes, defined as the number of dots appearing on the upward face of the die, are the six points in the sample space for this experiment.

$$S = \{1, 2, 3, 4, 5, 6\}$$

Counting Rules, Combinations, and Permutations

Being able to identify and count the experimental outcomes is a necessary step in assigning probabilities. We now discuss three useful counting rules.

Multiple-Step Experiments.   The first counting rule applies to multiple-step experiments. Consider the experiment of tossing two coins. Let the experimental outcomes be defined in terms of the sequence of heads and tails appearing on the upward faces of the two coins. How many experimental outcomes are possible for this experiment? The experiment of tossing two coins can be thought of as a two-step experiment in which step 1 is the tossing of the first coin and step 2 is the tossing of the second coin. If we use H to denote a head and T to denote a tail, (H, H) indicates the experimental outcome with a head on the first coin and a head on the second coin. Continuing this notation, we can describe the sample space (S) for this coin-tossing experiment as follows:

$$S = \{(H, H), (H, T), (T, H), (T, T)\}$$

Thus, we see that four experimental outcomes are possible. In this case, we can easily list all of the experimental outcomes.

The counting rule for multiple-step experiments makes it possible to determine the number of experimental outcomes without listing them.

A Counting Rule for Multiple-Step Experiments

If an experiment can be described as a sequence of k steps with n_1 possible outcomes on the first step, n_2 possible outcomes on the second step, and so on, then the total number of experimental outcomes is given by $(n_1)(n_2) \ldots (n_k)$.

Viewing the experiment of tossing two coins as a sequence of first tossing one coin ($n_1 = 2$) and then tossing the other coin ($n_2 = 2$), we can see from the counting rule that there are $(2)(2) = 4$ distinct experimental outcomes. As shown, they are $S = \{(H, H), (H, T), (T, H), (T, T)\}$. The number of experimental outcomes in an experiment involving tossing six coins is $(2)(2)(2)(2)(2)(2) = 64$.

Without the tree diagram, one might think only three experimental outcomes are possible for two tosses of a coin: 0 heads, 1 head, and 2 heads.

A **tree diagram** provides a graphical representation that helps in visualizing a multiple-step experiment. Figure 4.2 shows a tree diagram for the experiment of tossing two coins. The sequence of steps moves from left to right through the tree. Step 1 corresponds to tossing the first coin and step 2 corresponds to tossing the second coin. For each step, the two possible outcomes are head or tail. Note that for each possible outcome at step 1, two branches correspond to the two possible outcomes at step 2. Each of the points on the right end of the tree corresponds to an experimental outcome. Each path through the tree from the leftmost node to one of the nodes at the right side of the tree corresponds to a unique sequence of outcomes.

Let us now see how the counting rule for multiple-step experiments can be used in the analysis of a capacity expansion project faced by the Kentucky Power & Light Company

FIGURE 4.2   TREE DIAGRAM FOR THE EXPERIMENT OF TOSSING TWO COINS

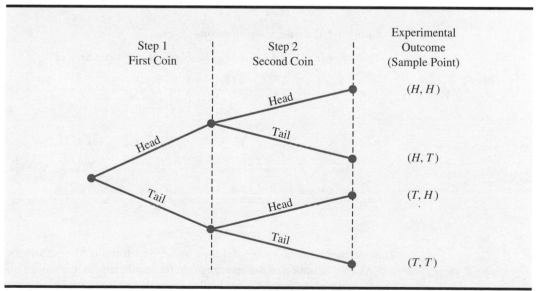

(KP&L). KP&L is starting a project designed to increase the generating capacity of one of its plants in northern Kentucky. The project is divided into two sequential stages or steps: stage 1 (design) and stage 2 (construction). Even though each stage will be scheduled and controlled as closely as possible, management cannot predict beforehand the exact time required to complete each stage of the project. An analysis of similar construction projects revealed completion times for the design stage of 2, 3, or 4 months and completion times for the construction stage of 6, 7, or 8 months. In addition, because of the critical need for additional electrical power, management set a goal of 10 months for the completion of the entire project.

Because this project has three possible completion times for the design stage (step 1) and three possible completion times for the construction stage (step 2), the counting rule for multiple-step experiments can be applied here to determine a total of (3)(3) = 9 experimental outcomes. To describe the experimental outcomes, we use a two-number notation; for instance, (2, 6) indicates that the design stage is completed in 2 months and the construction stage is completed in 6 months. This experimental outcome results in a total of 2 + 6 = 8 months to complete the entire project. Table 4.1 summarizes the nine experimental outcomes for the KP&L problem. The tree diagram in Figure 4.3 shows how the nine outcomes (sample points) occur.

The counting rule and tree diagram help the project manager identify the experimental outcomes and determine the possible project completion times. From the information in Figure 4.3, we see that the project will be completed in 8 to 12 months, with six of the nine experimental outcomes providing the desired completion time of 10 months or less. Even though identifying the experimental outcomes may be helpful, we need to consider how probability values can be assigned to the experimental outcomes before making an assessment of the probability that the project will be completed within the desired 10 months.

Combinations.　A second useful counting rule allows one to count the number of experimental outcomes when the experiment involves selecting n objects from a (usually larger) set of N objects. It is called the counting rule for combinations.

Counting Rule for Combinations

The number of combinations of N objects taken n at a time is

$$C_n^N = \binom{N}{n} = \frac{N!}{n!(N-n)!} \qquad (4.1)$$

where
$$N! = N(N-1)(N-2)\cdots(2)(1)$$
$$n! = n(n-1)(n-2)\cdots(2)(1)$$

and, by definition,
$$0! = 1$$

The notation ! means *factorial;* for example, 5 factorial is 5! = (5)(4)(3)(2)(1) = 120.

As an illustration of the counting rule for combinations, consider a quality control procedure in which an inspector randomly selects two of five parts to test for defects. In a group

TABLE 4.1   EXPERIMENTAL OUTCOMES (SAMPLE POINTS) FOR THE KP&L PROJECT

Completion Time (months)

Stage 1 Design	Stage 2 Construction	Notation for Experimental Outcome	Total Project Completion Time (months)
2	6	(2, 6)	8
2	7	(2, 7)	9
2	8	(2, 8)	10
3	6	(3, 6)	9
3	7	(3, 7)	10
3	8	(3, 8)	11
4	6	(4, 6)	10
4	7	(4, 7)	11
4	8	(4, 8)	12

FIGURE 4.3   TREE DIAGRAM FOR THE KP&L PROJECT

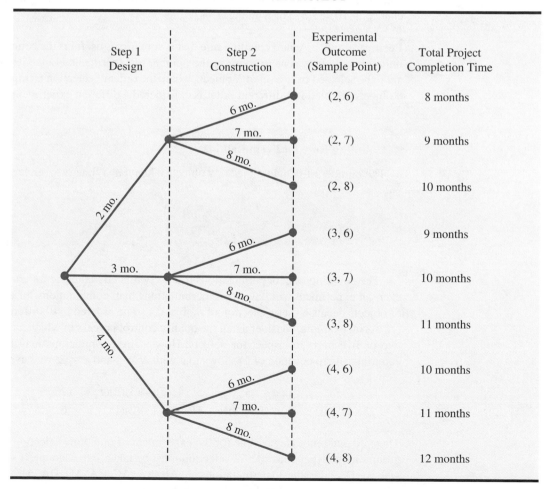

In sampling from a finite population of size N, the counting rule for combinations is used to find the number of different samples of size n that can be selected.

of five parts, how many combinations of two parts can be selected? The counting rule in equation (4.1) shows that with $N = 5$ and $n = 2$, we have

$$C_2^5 = \binom{5}{2} = \frac{5!}{2!(5-2)!} = \frac{(5)(4)(3)(2)(1)}{(2)(1)(3)(2)(1)} = \frac{120}{12} = 10$$

Thus, 10 outcomes are possible for the experiment of randomly selecting two parts from a group of five. If we label the five parts as A, B, C, D, and E, the 10 combinations or experimental outcomes can be identified as AB, AC, AD, AE, BC, BD, BE, CD, CE, and DE.

As another example, consider that the Ohio lottery system uses the random selection of six integers from a group of 47 to determine the weekly lottery winner. The counting rule for combinations, equation (4.1), can be used to determine the number of ways six different integers can be selected from a group of 47.

$$\binom{47}{6} = \frac{47!}{6!(47-6)!} = \frac{47!}{6!41!} = \frac{(47)(46)(45)(44)(43)(42)}{(6)(5)(4)(3)(2)(1)} = 10,737,573$$

The counting rule for combinations shows that the chance of winning the lottery is slim.

The counting rule for combinations tells us that more than 10 million experimental outcomes are possible in the lottery drawing. An individual who buys a lottery ticket has 1 chance in 10,737,573 of winning.

Permutations.　A third counting rule that is sometimes useful is the counting rule for permutations. It allows one to compute the number of experimental outcomes when n objects are to be selected from a set of N objects where the order of selection is important. The same n objects selected in a different order is considered a different experimental outcome.

Counting Rule for Permutations

The number of permutations of N objects taken n at a time is given by

$$P_n^N = n!\binom{N}{n} = \frac{N!}{(N-n)!} \tag{4.2}$$

The counting rule for permutations is closely related to the one for combinations; however, an experiment will have more permutations than combinations for the same number of objects because every selection of n objects can be ordered in $n!$ different ways.

As an example, consider again the quality control process in which an inspector selects two of five parts to inspect for defects. How many permutations may be selected? The counting rule in equation (4.2) shows that with $N = 5$ and $n = 2$, we have

$$P_2^5 = \frac{5!}{(5-2)!} = \frac{5!}{3!} = \frac{(5)(4)(3)(2)(1)}{(3)(2)(1)} = \frac{120}{6} = 20$$

Thus, 20 outcomes are possible for the experiment of randomly selecting two parts from a group of five when the order of selection must be taken into account. If we label the parts A, B, C, D, and E, the 20 permutations are AB, BA, AC, CA, AD, DA, AE, EA, BC, CB, BD, DB, BE, EB, CD, DC, CE, EC, DE, and ED.

Assigning Probabilities

Now let us see how probabilities can be assigned to experimental outcomes. The three approaches most frequently used are the classical, relative frequency, and subjective methods. Regardless of the method used, two **basic requirements for assigning probabilities** must be met.

Basic Requirements for Assigning Probabilities

1. The probability assigned to each experimental outcome must be between 0 and 1, inclusively. If we let E_i denote the ith experimental outcome and $P(E_i)$ its probability, then this requirement can be written as

$$0 \leq P(E_i) \leq 1 \text{ for all } i \tag{4.3}$$

2. The sum of the probabilities for all the experimental outcomes must equal 1. For n experimental outcomes, this requirement can be written as

$$P(E_1) + P(E_2) + \cdots + P(E_n) = 1 \tag{4.4}$$

The **classical method** of assigning probabilities is appropriate when all the experimental outcomes are equally likely. If n experimental outcomes are possible, a probability of $1/n$ is assigned to each experimental outcome. When using this approach, the two basic requirements for assigning probabilities are automatically satisfied.

For an example, consider the experiment of tossing a fair coin. The two experimental outcomes—head and tail—are equally likely. Because one of the two equally likely outcomes is a head, the probability of observing a head is 1/2, or .50. Similarly, the probability of observing a tail is also 1/2, or .50.

As another example, consider the experiment of rolling a die. It would seem reasonable to conclude that the six possible outcomes are equally likely, and hence each outcome is assigned a probability of 1/6. If $P(1)$ denotes the probability that one dot appears on the upward face of the die, then $P(1) = 1/6$. Similarly, $P(2) = 1/6$. $P(3) = 1/6$, $P(4) = 1/6$, $P(5) = 1/6$, and $P(6) = 1/6$. Note that these probabilities satisfy the two basic requirements of equations (4.3) and (4.4) because each of the probabilities is greater than or equal to zero and they sum to one.

The **relative frequency method** of assigning probabilities is appropriate when data are available to estimate the proportion of the time the experimental outcome will occur if the experiment is repeated a large number of times. As an example consider a study of waiting times in the X-ray department for a local hospital. A clerk recorded the number of patients waiting for service at 9:00 A.M. on 20 successive days, and obtained the following results.

Number Waiting	Number of Days Outcome Occurred
0	2
1	5
2	6
3	4
4	3
Total	20

These data show that on 2 of the 20 days, zero patients were waiting for service; on 5 of the days, one patient was waiting for service; and so on. Using the relative frequency method, we would assign a probability of 2/20 = .10 to the experimental outcome of zero patients waiting for service, 5/20 = .25 to the experimental outcome of one patient waiting, 6/20 = .30 to two patients waiting, 4/20 = .20 to three patients waiting, and 3/20 = .15 to four patients waiting. As with the classical method, using the relative frequency method automatically satisfies the two basic requirements of equations (4.3) and (4.4).

The **subjective method** of assigning probabilities is most appropriate when one cannot realistically assume that the experimental outcomes are equally likely and when little relevant data are available. When the subjective method is used to assign probabilities to the experimental outcomes, we may use any information available, such as our experience or intuition. After considering all available information, a probability value that expresses our *degree of belief* (on a scale from 0 to 1) that the experimental outcome will occur is specified. Because subjective probability expresses a person's degree of belief, it is personal. Using the subjective method, different people can be expected to assign different probabilities to the same experimental outcome.

The subjective method requires extra care to ensure that the two basic requirements of equations (4.3) and (4.4) are satisfied. Regardless of a person's degree of belief, the probability value assigned to each experimental outcome must be between 0 and 1, inclusive, and the sum of all the probabilities for the experimental outcomes must equal one.

Consider the case in which Tom and Judy Elsbernd just made an offer to purchase a house. Two outcomes are possible:

$$E_1 = \text{their offer is accepted}$$
$$E_2 = \text{their offer is rejected}$$

Judy believes that the probability their offer will be accepted is .8; thus, Judy would set $P(E_1) = .8$ and $P(E_2) = .2$. Tom, however, believes that the probability that their offer will be accepted is .6; hence, Tom would set $P(E_1) = .6$ and $P(E_2) = .4$. Note that Tom's probability estimate for E_1 reflects a greater pessimism that their offer will be accepted.

Both Judy and Tom assigned probabilities that satisfy the two basic requirements. The fact that their probability estimates differ emphasizes the personal nature of the subjective method.

Bayes' theorem (see Section 4.5) provides a means for combining subjectively determined prior probabilities with probabilities obtained by other means to obtain revised, or posterior, probabilities.

Even in business situations where either the classical or the relative frequency approach can be applied, managers may want to provide subjective probability estimates. In such cases, the best probability estimates often are obtained by combining the estimates from the classical or relative frequency approach with subjective probability estimates.

Probabilities for the KP&L Project

To perform further analysis on the KP&L project, we must develop probabilities for each of the nine experimental outcomes listed in Table 4.1. On the basis of experience and judgment, management concluded that the experimental outcomes were not equally likely. Hence, the classical method of assigning probabilities could not be used. Management then decided to conduct a study of the completion times for similar projects undertaken by KP&L over the past three years. The results of a study of 40 similar projects are summarized in Table 4.2.

TABLE 4.2   COMPLETION RESULTS FOR 40 KP&L PROJECTS

Completion Time (months)			Number of Past Projects Having These
Stage 1 Design	**Stage 2 Construction**	**Sample Point**	**Completion Times**
2	6	(2, 6)	6
2	7	(2, 7)	6
2	8	(2, 8)	2
3	6	(3, 6)	4
3	7	(3, 7)	8
3	8	(3, 8)	2
4	6	(4, 6)	2
4	7	(4, 7)	4
4	8	(4, 8)	6
		Total	40

After reviewing the results of the study, management decided to employ the relative frequency method of assigning probabilities. Management could have provided subjective probability estimates, but felt that the current project was quite similar to the 40 previous projects. Thus, the relative frequency method was judged best.

In using the data in Table 4.2 to compute probabilities, we note that outcome (2, 6)— stage 1 completed in 2 months and stage 2 completed in 6 months—occurred six times in the 40 projects. We can use the relative frequency method to assign a probability of 6/40 = .15 to this outcome. Similarly, outcome (2, 7) also occurred in six of the 40 projects, providing a 6/40 = .15 probability. Continuing in this manner, we obtain the probability assignments for the sample points of the KP&L project shown in Table 4.3. Note that $P(2, 6)$ represents the probability of the sample point (2, 6), $P(2, 7)$ represents the probability of the sample point (2, 7), and so on.

TABLE 4.3   PROBABILITY ASSIGNMENTS FOR THE KP&L PROJECT BASED ON THE RELATIVE FREQUENCY METHOD

Sample Point	Project Completion Time	Probability of Sample Point
(2, 6)	8 months	$P(2, 6) = 6/40 = $ .15
(2, 7)	9 months	$P(2, 7) = 6/40 = $ .15
(2, 8)	10 months	$P(2, 8) = 2/40 = $ .05
(3, 6)	9 months	$P(3, 6) = 4/40 = $ .10
(3, 7)	10 months	$P(3, 7) = 8/40 = $ .20
(3, 8)	11 months	$P(3, 8) = 2/40 = $ .05
(4, 6)	10 months	$P(4, 6) = 2/40 = $ .05
(4, 7)	11 months	$P(4, 7) = 4/40 = $ .10
(4, 8)	12 months	$P(4, 8) = 6/40 = $ .15
	Total	1.00

NOTES AND COMMENTS

1. In statistics, the notion of an experiment differs somewhat from the notion of an experiment in the physical sciences. In the physical sciences, researchers usually conduct an experiment in a laboratory or a controlled environment in order to learn about cause and effect. In statistical experiments, probability determines outcomes. Even though the experiment is repeated in exactly the same way, an entirely different outcome may occur. Because of this influence of probability on the outcome, the experiments of statistics are sometimes called *random experiments*.

2. When drawing a random sample without replacement from a population of size N, the counting rule for combinations is used to find the number of different samples of size n that can be selected.

EXERCISES

Methods

1. An experiment has three steps with three outcomes possible for the first step, two outcomes possible for the second step, and four outcomes possible for the third step. How many experimental outcomes exist for the entire experiment?

SELFtest

2. How many ways can three items be selected from a group of six items? Use the letters A, B, C, D, E, and F to identify the items, and list each of the different combinations of three items.

3. How many permutations of three items can be selected from a group of six? Use the letters A, B, C, D, E, and F to identify the items, and list each of the permutations of items B, D, and F.

4. Consider the experiment of tossing a coin three times.
   a. Develop a tree diagram for the experiment.
   b. List the experimental outcomes.
   c. What is the probability for each experimental outcome?

5. Suppose an experiment has five equally likely outcomes: E_1, E_2, E_3, E_4, E_5. Assign probabilities to each outcome and show that the conditions in equations (4.3) and (4.4) are satisfied. What method did you use?

SELFtest

6. An experiment with three outcomes has been repeated 50 times, and it was learned that E_1 occurred 20 times. E_2 occurred 13 times, and E_3 occurred 17 times. Assign probabilities to the outcomes. What method did you use?

7. A decision maker has subjectively assigned the following probabilities to the four outcomes of an experiment: $P(E_1) = .10$, $P(E_2) = .15$, $P(E_3) = .40$, and $P(E_4) = .20$. Are these valid probability assignments? Explain.

Applications

8. In the city of Milford, applications for zoning changes go through a two-step process: a review by the planning commission and a final decision by the city council. At step 1 the planning commission reviews the zoning change request and makes a positive or negative recommendation concerning the change. At step 2 the city council reviews the planning commission's recommendation and then votes to approve or to disapprove the zoning change. Suppose the developer of an apartment complex submits an application for a zoning change. Consider the application process as an experiment.
   a. How many sample points are there for this experiment? List the sample points.
   b. Construct a tree diagram for the experiment.

SELFtest   **9.** Simple random sampling uses a sample of size n from a population of size N to obtain data that can be used to make inferences about the characteristics of a population. Suppose we have a population of 50 bank accounts and want to take a random sample of four accounts in order to learn about the population. How many different random samples of four accounts are possible?

SELFtest   **10.** The availability of venture capital provided a big boost in funds available to companies in recent years. According to Venture Economics (*Investor's Business Daily*, April 28, 2000), 2,374 venture capital disbursements were made in 1999. Of these 1,434 were to companies in California, 390 were to companies in Massachusetts, 217 were to companies in New York, and 112 were to companies in Colorado. Twenty-two percent of the companies receiving funds were in the early stages of development and 55% of the companies were in an expansion stage.

Suppose you want to randomly choose one of these companies to learn about how they used the funds.

    a. What is the probability the company chosen will be from California?

    b. What is the probability the company chosen will not be from one of the four states mentioned?

    c. What is the probability the company will not be in the early stages of development?

    d. Assuming the companies in the early stages of development were evenly distributed across the country, how many Massachusetts companies receiving venture capital funds were in their early stages of development?

    e. The total amount of funds invested was $32.4 billion. Estimate the amount that went to Colorado.

11. Strom Construction has made bids on two contracts. The owner has identified the possible outcomes and subjectively assigned the following probabilities.

Experimental Outcome	Obtain Contract 1	Obtain Contract 2	Probability
1	Yes	Yes	.15
2	Yes	No	.15
3	No	Yes	.30
4	No	No	.25

    a. Are these valid probability assignments? Why or why not?

    b. What, if anything, needs to be done to make the probability assignments valid?

12. The Powerball lottery is played twice each week in 21 states and the District of Columbia. To play Powerball a participant must purchase a ticket for $1 and then select five numbers from the digits 1 through 49 and a Powerball number from the digits 1 though 42. To determine the winning numbers for each game, lottery officials draw five white balls out of a drum with 49 white balls, and one red ball out of a drum with 42 red balls. To win the jackpot, a participant's numbers must match the numbers on the five white balls in any order and the number on the red Powerball. In August 2001, four winners shared a jackpot of $295 million by matching the numbers 8-17-22-42-47 plus the Powerball number of 21. In addition to the jackpot, a variety of other prizes are awarded each time the game is played. For instance, a prize of $100,000 is paid if the participant's five numbers match the numbers on the five white balls (*www.powerball.com,* August 31, 2001).

    a. Compute the number of ways the first five numbers can be selected.

    b. What is the probability of winning a prize of $100,000 by matching the numbers on the five white balls?

    c. What is the probability of winning the Powerball jackpot?

13. A company that manufactures toothpaste is studying five different package designs. Assuming that one design is just as likely to be selected by a consumer as any other design, what selection probability would you assign to each of the package designs? In an actual experiment, 100 consumers were asked to pick the design they preferred. The following data were obtained. Do the data appear to confirm the belief that one design is just as likely to be selected as another? Explain.

Design	Number of Times Preferred
1	5
2	15
3	30
4	40
5	10

4.2 EVENTS AND THEIR PROBABILITIES

In the introduction to this chapter we used the term *event* much as it would be used in everyday language. Then, in Section 4.1, we introduced the concept of an experiment and its associated experimental outcomes or sample points. Sample points and events provide the foundation for the study of probability. As a result, we must now introduce the formal definition of an **event** as it relates to sample points. Doing so will provide the basis for determining the probability of an event.

Event

An *event* is a collection of sample points.

For an example, let us return to the KP&L project and assume that the project manager is interested in the event that the entire project can be completed in 10 months or less. Referring to Table 4.3, we see that six sample points—(2, 6), (2, 7), (2, 8), (3, 6), (3, 7), and (4, 6)—provide a project completion time of 10 months or less. Let C denote the event that the project is completed in 10 months or less; we write

$$C = \{(2, 6), (2, 7), (2, 8), (3, 6), (3, 7), (4, 6)\}$$

Event C is said to occur if *any one* of these six sample points appears as the experimental outcome.

Other events that might be of interest to KP&L management include the following.

L = The event that the project is completed in *less* than 10 months
M = The event that the project is completed in *more* than 10 months

Using the information in Table 4.3, we see that these events consist of the following sample points.

$$L = \{(2, 6), (2, 7), (3, 6)\}$$
$$M = \{(3, 8), (4, 7), (4, 8)\}$$

A variety of additional events can be defined for the KP&L project, but in each case the event must be identified as a collection of sample points for the experiment.

Given the probabilities of the sample points shown in Table 4.3, we can use the following definition to compute the probability of any event that KP&L management might want to consider.

Probability of an Event

The probability of any event is equal to the sum of the probabilities of the sample points in the event.

Using this definition, we calculate the probability of a particular event by adding the probabilities of the sample points (experimental outcomes) that make up the event. We can now compute the probability that the project will take 10 months or less to complete. Because this event is given by $C = \{(2, 6), (2, 7), (2, 8), (3, 6), (3, 7), (4, 6)\}$, the probability of event C, denoted $P(C)$, is given by

$$P(C) = P(2, 6) + P(2, 7) + P(2, 8) + P(3, 6) + P(3, 7) + P(4, 6)$$

Refer to the sample point probabilities in Table 4.3; we have

$$P(C) = .15 + .15 + .05 + .10 + .20 + .05 = .70$$

Similarly, because the event that the project is completed in less than 10 months is given by $L = \{(2, 6), (2, 7), (3, 6)\}$, the probability of this event is given by

$$P(L) = P(2, 6) + P(2, 7) + P(3, 6)$$
$$= .15 + .15 + .10 = .40$$

Finally, for the event that the project is completed in more than 10 months, we have $M = \{(3, 8), (4, 7), (4, 8)\}$ and thus

$$P(M) = P(3, 8) + P(4, 7) + P(4, 8)$$
$$= .05 + .10 + .15 = .30$$

Using these probability results, we can now tell KP&L management that there is a .70 probability that the project will be completed in 10 months or less, a .40 probability that the project will be completed in less than 10 months, and a .30 probability that the project will be completed in more than 10 months. This procedure of computing event probabilities can be repeated for any event of interest to the KP&L management.

Any time that we can identify all the sample points of an experiment and assign probabilities to each, we can compute the probability of an event using the definition. However, in many experiments, the large number of sample points makes the identification of the sample points, as well as the determination of their associated probabilities, extremely cumbersome, if not impossible. In the remaining sections of this chapter, we present some basic probability relationships that can be used to compute the probability of an event without knowledge of all the sample point probabilities.

NOTES AND COMMENTS

1. The sample space, S, is an event. Because it contains all the experimental outcomes, it has a probability of 1; that is, $P(S) = 1$.
2. When the classical method is used to assign probabilities, the assumption is that the experimental outcomes are equally likely. In such cases, the probability of an event can be computed by counting the number of experimental outcomes in the event and dividing the result by the total number of experimental outcomes.

EXERCISES

Methods

14. An experiment has four equally likely outcomes: E_1, E_2, E_3, and E_4.
    a. What is the probability that E_2 occurs?
    b. What is the probability that any two of the outcomes occur (e.g., E_1 or E_3)?
    c. What is the probability that any three of the outcomes occur (e.g., E_1 or E_2 or E_4)?

SELFtest   **15.** Consider the experiment of selecting a card from a deck of 52 cards. Each card corresponds to a sample point with a 1/52 probability.
    a. List the sample points in the event an ace is selected.
    b. List the sample points in the event a club is selected.
    c. List the sample points in the event a face card (jack, queen, or king) is selected.
    d. Find the probabilities associated with each of the events in (a), (b), and (c).

16. Consider the experiment of rolling a pair of dice. Suppose that we are interested in the sum of the face values showing on the dice.
    a. How many sample points are possible? (Hint: Use the counting rule for multiple-step experiments.)
    b. List the sample points.
    c. What is the probability of obtaining a value of 7?
    d. What is the probability of obtaining a value of 9 or greater?
    e. Because each roll has six possible even values (2, 4, 6, 8, 10, and 12) and only five possible odd values (3, 5, 7, 9, and 11), the dice should show even values more often than odd values. Do you agree with this statement? Explain.
    f. What method did you use to assign the probabilities requested?

Applications

SELFtest   **17.** Refer to the KP&L sample points and sample point probabilities in Table 4.3.
    a. The design stage (stage 1) will run over budget if it takes four months to complete. List the sample points in the event the design stage is over budget.
    b. What is the probability that the design stage is over budget?
    c. The construction stage (stage 2) will run over budget if it takes eight months to complete. List the sample points in the event the construction stage is over budget.
    d. What is the probability that the construction stage is over budget?
    e. What is the probability that both stages are over budget?

18. Suppose that a manager of a large apartment complex provides the following subjective probability estimates about the number of vacancies that will exist next month.

Vacancies	Probability
0	.05
1	.15
2	.35
3	.25
4	.10
5	.10

List the sample points in each of the following events and provide the probability of the event.
  a. No vacancies
  b. At least four vacancies
  c. Two or fewer vacancies

19. The manager of a furniture store sells from 0 to 4 china hutches each week. On the basis of past experience, the following probabilities are assigned to sales of 0, 1, 2, 3, or 4 hutches: $P(0) = .08$; $P(1) = .18$; $P(2) = .32$; $P(3) = .30$; and $P(4) = .12$.
  a. Are these valid probability assignments? Why or why not?
  b. Let A be the event that 2 or fewer are sold in one week. Find $P(A)$.
  c. Let B be the event that 4 or more are sold in one week. Find $P(B)$.

20. *Fortune* magazine publishes an annual issue containing information on *Fortune* 500 companies. The following data show the six states with the largest number of *Fortune* 500 companies as well as the number of companies headquartered in those states (*Fortune*, April 17, 2000).

State	Number of Companies
New York	56
California	53
Texas	43
Illinois	37
Ohio	28
Pennsylvania	28

Suppose a *Fortune* 500 company is chosen for a follow-up questionnaire. What are the probabilities of the following events?
  a. Let N be the event the company is headquartered in New York. Find $P(N)$.
  b. Let T be the event the company is headquartered in Texas. Find $P(T)$.
  c. Let B be the event the company is headquartered in one of these six states. Find $P(B)$.

21. A survey of 50 students at Tarpon Springs College about the number of extracurricular activities resulted in the data shown.

Number of Activities	Frequency
0	8
1	20
2	12
3	6
4	3
5	1

a. Let A be the event that a student participates in at least 1 activity. Find $P(A)$.
b. Let B be the event that a student participates in 3 or more activities. Find $P(B)$.
c. What is the probability that a student participates in exactly 2 activities?

4.3   SOME BASIC RELATIONSHIPS OF PROBABILITY

Complement of an Event

Given an event A, the **complement of A** is defined to be the event consisting of all sample points that are *not* in A. The complement of A is denoted by A^c. Figure 4.4 is a diagram, known as a **Venn diagram**, which illustrates the concept of a complement. The rectangular area represents the sample space for the experiment and as such contains all possible sample points. The circle represents event A and contains only the sample points that belong to A. The shaded region of the rectangle contains all sample points not in event A, and is by definition the complement of A.

In any probability application, either event A or its complement A^c must occur. Therefore, we have

$$P(A) + P(A^c) = 1$$

Solving for $P(A)$, we obtain the following result.

> **Computing Probability Using the Complement**
> $$P(A) = 1 - P(A^c) \tag{4.5}$$

Equation (4.5) shows that the probability of an event A can be computed easily if the probability of its complement, $P(A^c)$, is known.

As an example, consider the case of a sales manager who, after reviewing sales reports, states that 80% of new customer contacts result in no sale. By allowing A to denote the event of a sale and A^c to denote the event of no sale, the manager is stating that $P(A^c) = .80$. Using equation (4.5), we see that

$$P(A) = 1 - P(A^c) = 1 - .80 = .20$$

We can conclude that a new customer contact has a .20 probability of resulting in a sale.

FIGURE 4.4   COMPLEMENT OF EVENT A IS SHADED

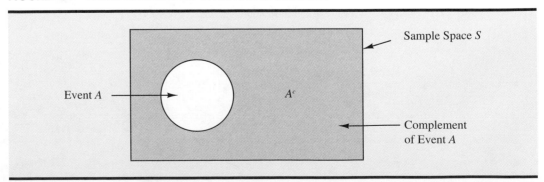

In another example, a purchasing agent states a .90 probability that a supplier will send a shipment that is free of defective parts. Using the complement, we can conclude that there is a $1 - .90 = .10$ probability that the shipment will contain defective parts.

Addition Law

The addition law is helpful when we are interested in knowing the probability that at least one of two events occurs. That is, with events A and B we are interested in knowing the probability that event A or event B or both occur.

Before we present the addition law, we need to discuss two concepts related to the combination of events: the *union* of events and the *intersection* of events. Given two events A and B, the **union of A and B** is defined as follows.

Union of Two Events

The union of A and B is the event containing *all* sample points belonging to A *or* B *or both*. The union is denoted by $A \cup B$.

The Venn diagram in Figure 4.5 depicts the union of events A and B. Note that the two circles contain all the sample points in event A as well as all the sample points in event B. The fact that the circles overlap indicates that some sample points are contained in both A and B.

The definition of the **intersection of A and B** follows.

Intersection of Two Events

Given two events A and B, the intersection of A and B is the event containing the sample points belonging to *both A and B*. The intersection is denoted by $A \cap B$.

The Venn diagram depicting the intersection of the two events is shown in Figure 4.6. The area where the two circles overlap is the intersection; it contains the sample points that are in both A and B.

Let us now continue with a discussion of the addition law. The **addition law** provides a way to compute the probability of event A or B or both A and B occurring. In other words,

FIGURE 4.5   UNION OF EVENTS A AND B IS SHADED

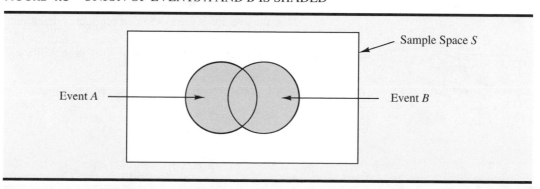

FIGURE 4.6   INTERSECTION OF EVENTS *A* AND *B* IS SHADED

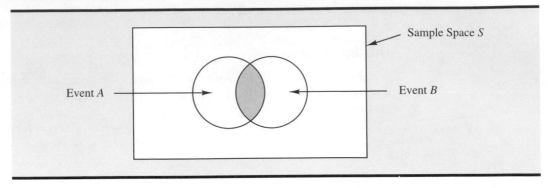

the addition law is used to compute the probability of the union of two events. The addition law is written as follows.

Addition Law

$$P(A \cup B) = P(A) + P(B) - P(A \cap B) \qquad (4.6)$$

To understand the addition law intuitively, note that the first two terms in the addition law, $P(A) + P(B)$, account for all the sample points in $A \cup B$. However, because the sample points in the intersection $A \cap B$ are in both A and B, when we compute $P(A) + P(B)$, we are in effect counting each of the sample points in $A \cap B$ twice. We correct for this over-counting by subtracting $P(A \cap B)$.

As an example of an application of the addition law, let us consider the case of a small assembly plant with 50 employees. Each worker is expected to complete work assignments on time and in such a way that the assembled product will pass a final inspection. On occasion, some of the workers fail to meet the performance standards by completing work late and/or assembling a defective product. At the end of a performance evaluation period, the production manager found that 5 of the 50 workers had completed work late, 6 of the 50 workers had assembled a defective product, and 2 of the 50 workers had both completed work late *and* assembled a defective product.

Let

$$L = \text{the event that the work is completed late}$$
$$D = \text{the event that the assembled product is defective}$$

The relative frequency information leads to the following probabilities.

$$P(L) = \frac{5}{50} = .10$$

$$P(D) = \frac{6}{50} = .12$$

$$P(L \cap D) = \frac{2}{50} = .04$$

After reviewing the performance data, the production manager decided to assign a poor performance rating to any employee whose work was either late or defective; thus the event of interest is $L \cup D$. What is the probability that the production manager assigned an employee a poor performance rating?

Note that the probability question is about the union of two events. Specifically, we want to know $P(L \cup D)$. Using equation (4.6), we have

$$P(L \cup D) = P(L) + P(D) - P(L \cap D)$$

Knowing values for the three probabilities on the right side of this expression, we can write

$$P(L \cup D) = .10 + .12 - .04 = .18$$

This calculation indicates a .18 probability that a randomly selected employee received a poor performance rating.

As another example of the addition law, consider a recent study conducted by the personnel manager of a major computer software company. The study showed that 30% of the employees who left the firm within two years did so primarily because they were dissatisfied with their salary, 20% left because they were dissatisfied with their work assignments, and 12% of the former employees indicated dissatisfaction with *both* their salary and their work assignments. What is the probability that an employee who leaves within two years does so because of dissatisfaction with salary, dissatisfaction with the work assignment, or both?

Let

S = the event that the employee leaves because of salary

W = the event that the employee leaves because of work assignment

We have $P(S) = .30$, $P(W) = .20$, and $P(S \cap W) = .12$. Using equation (4.6), the addition law, we have

$$P(S \cup W) = P(S) + P(W) - P(S \cap W) = .30 + .20 - .12 = .38.$$

We find a .38 probability that an employee leaves for salary or work assignment reasons.

Before we conclude our discussion of the addition law, let us consider a special case that arises for **mutually exclusive events.**

Mutually Exclusive Events

Two events are said to be mutually exclusive if the events have no sample points in common.

Events A and B are mutually exclusive if, when one event occurs, the other cannot occur. Thus, a requirement for A and B to be mutually exclusive is that their intersection must contain no sample points. The Venn diagram depicting two mutually exclusive events A and B is shown in Figure 4.7. In this case $P(A \cap B) = 0$ and the addition law can be written as follows.

Addition Law for Mutually Exclusive Events

$$P(A \cup B) = P(A) + P(B)$$

FIGURE 4.7 MUTUALLY EXCLUSIVE EVENTS

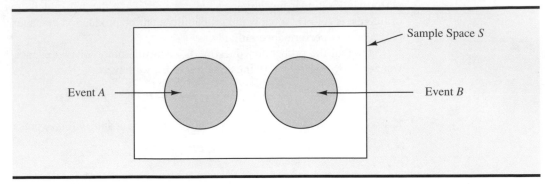

EXERCISES

Methods

22. Suppose that we have a sample space with five equally likely experimental outcomes: E_1, E_2, E_3, E_4, E_5. Let

$$A = \{E_1, E_2\}$$
$$B = \{E_3, E_4\}$$
$$C = \{E_2, E_3, E_5\}$$

   a. Find $P(A)$, $P(B)$, and $P(C)$.
   b. Find $P(A \cup B)$. Are A and B mutually exclusive?
   c. Find A^c, C^c, $P(A^c)$, and $P(C^c)$.
   d. Find $A \cup B^c$ and $P(A \cup B^c)$.
   e. Find $P(B \cup C)$.

SELFtest   **23.** Suppose that we have a sample space $S = \{E_1, E_2, E_3, E_4, E_5, E_6, E_7\}$, where $E_1, E_2, \ldots,$ E_7 denote the sample points. The following probability assignments apply: $P(E_1) = .05$, $P(E_2) = .20$, $P(E_3) = .20$, $P(E_4) = .25$, $P(E_5) = .15$, $P(E_6) = .10$, and $P(E_7) = .05$. Let

$$A = \{E_1, E_4, E_6\}$$
$$B = \{E_2, E_4, E_7\}$$
$$C = \{E_2, E_3, E_5, E_7\}$$

   a. Find $P(A)$, $P(B)$, and $P(C)$.
   b. Find $A \cup B$ and $P(A \cup B)$.
   c. Find $A \cap B$ and $P(A \cap B)$.
   d. Are events A and C mutually exclusive?
   e. Find B^c and $P(B^c)$.

Applications

24. Clarkson University surveyed alumni to learn more about what they think of Clarkson. One part of the survey asked respondents to indicate whether their overall experience at Clarkson fell short of expectations, met expectations, or surpassed expectations. The results showed that 4% of the respondents did not provide a response, 26% said that their experience fell short of expectations, and 65% of the respondents said that their experience met expectations (*Clarkson Magazine*, Summer 2001).

   a. If we chose an alumnus at random, what is the probability that he or she would say their experience surpassed expectations?

   b. If we chose an alumnus at random, what is the probability that he or she would say their experience met or surpassed expectations?

25. Data on the 30 largest bond funds provided one-year and five-year percentage returns for the period ending March 31, 2000 (*The Wall Street Journal*, April 10, 2000). Suppose we consider a one-year return in excess of 2% to be high and a five-year return in excess of 44% to be high. One-half of the funds had a one-year return in excess of 2%, 12 of the funds had a five-year return in excess of 44%, and six of the funds had a one-year return in excess of 2% and a five-year return in excess of 44%.

   a. Find the probability of a fund having a high one-year return, the probability of a fund having a high five-year return, and the probability of a fund having both a high one-year return and a high five-year return.

   b. What is the probability that a fund has a high one-year return or a high five-year return or both?

   c. What is the probability that a fund has neither a high one-year return nor a high five-year return?

26. Data on the 30 largest stock and balanced funds provided one-year and five-year percentage returns for the period ending March 31, 2000 (*The Wall Street Journal*, April 10, 2000). Suppose we consider a one-year return in excess of 50% to be high and a five-year return in excess of 300% to be high. Nine of the funds had one-year returns in excess of 50%, seven of the funds had five-year returns in excess of 300%, and five of the funds had both one-year returns in excess of 50% and five-year returns in excess of 300%.

   a. What is the probability of a high one-year return and what is the probability of a high five-year return?

   b. What is the probability of both a high one-year return and a high five-year return?

   c. What is the probability of neither a high one-year return nor a high five-year return?

27. A 2001 preseason NCAA college football poll asked the question, Will the Big Ten or the Pac-10 have a team in this year's national championship game, the Rose Bowl? Of the 13,429 respondents, 2961 said the Big Ten would, 4494 said the Pac-10 would, and 6823 said neither the Big Ten nor the Pac-10 would have a team in the Rose Bowl (*www.yahoo.com*, August 30, 2001).

   a. What is the probability that a respondent said neither the Big Ten nor the Pac-10 will have a team in the Rose Bowl?

   b. What is the probability that a respondent said either the Big Ten or the Pac-10 will have a team in the Rose Bowl?

   c. Find the probability that a respondent said both the Big Ten and the Pac-10 would have a team in the Rose Bowl.

SELFtest **28.** A survey of magazine subscribers showed that 45.8% rented a car during the past 12 months for business reasons, 54% rented a car during the past 12 months for personal reasons, and 30% rented a car during the past 12 months for both business and personal reasons.

   a. What is the probability that a subscriber rented a car during the past 12 months for business or personal reasons?

   b. What is the probability that a subscriber did not rent a car during the past 12 months for either business or personal reasons?

29. High school seniors with strong academic records apply to the nation's most selective colleges in greater numbers each year. Because the number of slots remains relatively stable, some colleges reject more early applicants. The University of Pennsylvania received 2851 applications for early admission. Of this group, it admitted 1033 students, rejected 854 outright, and deferred 964 to the regular admissions pool. Penn admitted about 18% of the applicants in the regular admissions pool for a total class size (number of early admissions plus number of regular admissions) of 2375 students (*USA Today*, January 24, 2001). Let *E*, *R*, and *D* represent the events that a student who applies for early admission is admitted, rejected outright, or deferred to the regular admissions pool; and let *A* represent the event that a student in the regular admissions pool is admitted.

a.   Use the data to estimate $P(E)$, $P(R)$, and $P(D)$.
b.   Are events *E* and *D* mutually exclusive? Find $P(E \cap D)$.
c.   For the 2375 students admitted to Penn, what is the probability that a randomly selected student was accepted for early admission?
d.   Are events *E* and *A* mutually exclusive?
e.   Suppose a student applies to Penn for early admission. What is the probability the student will be admitted for early admission or be accepted for admission in the regular admission pool?

4.4   CONDITIONAL PROBABILITY

Often, the probability of an event is influenced by whether a related event has occurred. Suppose we have an event *A* with probability $P(A)$. If we obtain new information and learn that a related event, denoted by *B*, has occurred, we will want to take advantage of this information by calculating a new probability for event *A*. This new probability of event *A* is called a **conditional probability** and is written $P(A \mid B)$. We use the notation | to indicate that we are considering the probability of event *A* *given* the condition that event *B* has occurred. Hence, the notation $P(A \mid B)$ reads "the probability of *A* given *B*."

As an illustration of the application of conditional probability, consider the situation of the promotion status of male and female officers of a major metropolitan police force in the eastern United States. The police force consists of 1200 officers, 960 men and 240 women. Over the past two years, 324 officers on the police force received promotions. The specific breakdown of promotions for male and female officers is shown in Table 4.4.

After reviewing the promotion record, a committee of female officers raised a discrimination case on the basis that 288 male officers had received promotions but only 36 female officers had received promotions. The police administration argued that the relatively low number of promotions for female officers was due not to discrimination, but to the fact that relatively few females are members of the police force. Let us show how conditional probability could be used to analyze the discrimination charge.

Let

$$M = \text{event an officer is a man}$$
$$W = \text{event an officer is a woman}$$
$$A = \text{event an officer is promoted}$$
$$A^c = \text{event an officer is not promoted}$$

TABLE 4.4   PROMOTION STATUS OF POLICE OFFICERS OVER THE PAST TWO YEARS

	Men	Women	Totals
Promoted	288	36	324
Not Promoted	672	204	876
Totals	960	240	1200

Dividing the data values in Table 4.4 by the total of 1200 officers enables us to summarize the available information with the following probability values.

$$P(M \cap A) = 288/1200 = .24 = \text{probability that a randomly selected officer}$$
$$\text{is a man } and \text{ is promoted}$$

$$P(M \cap A^c) = 672/1200 = .56 = \text{probability that a randomly selected officer}$$
$$\text{is a man } and \text{ is not promoted}$$

$$P(W \cap A) = 36/1200 = .03 = \text{probability that a randomly selected officer}$$
$$\text{is a woman } and \text{ is promoted}$$

$$P(W \cap A^c) = 204/1200 = .17 = \text{probability that a randomly selected officer}$$
$$\text{is a woman } and \text{ is not promoted}$$

Because each of these values gives the probability of the intersection of two events, the probabilities are called **joint probabilities.** Table 4.5, which provides a summary of the probability information for the police officer promotion situation, is referred to as a *joint probability table.*

The values in the margins of the joint probability table provide the probabilities of each event separately. That is, $P(M) = .80$, $P(W) = .20$, $P(A) = .27$, and $P(A^c) = .73$. These probabilities are referred to as *marginal probabilities* because of their location in the margins of the joint probability table. We note that the marginal probabilities are found by summing the joint probabilities in the corresponding row or column of the joint probability table. For instance, the marginal probability of being promoted is $P(A) = P(M \cap A) + P(W \cap A) = .24 + .03 = .27$. From the marginal probabilities, we see that 80% of the force is male, 20% of the force is female, 27% of all officers received promotions, and 73% were not promoted.

Let us begin the conditional probability analysis by computing the probability that an officer is promoted given that the officer is a man. In conditional probability notation, we are attempting to determine $P(A \mid M)$. To calculate $P(A \mid M)$, we first realize that this notation simply means that we are considering the probability of the event A (promotion) given that the condition designated as event M (the officer is a man) is known to exist. Thus $P(A \mid M)$ tells us that we are now concerned only with the promotion status of the 960 male officers. Because 288 of the 960 male officers received promotions, the probability of being promoted given that the officer is a man is $288/960 = .30$. In other words, given that an officer is a man, that officer had a 30% chance of receiving a promotion over the past two years.

This procedure was easy to apply because the values in Table 4.4 show the number of officers in each category. We now want to demonstrate how conditional probabilities such

TABLE 4.5   JOINT PROBABILITY TABLE FOR PROMOTIONS

Joint probabilities appear in the body of the table.	Men (*M*)	Women (*W*)	Totals
Promoted (*A*)	.24	.03	.27
Not Promoted (*A^c*)	.56	.17	.73
Totals	.80	.20	1.00

Marginal probabilities appear in the margins of the table.

as $P(A \mid M)$ can be computed directly from related event probabilities rather than the frequency data of Table 4.4.

We have shown that $P(A \mid M) = 288/960 = .30$. Let us now divide both the numerator and denominator of this fraction by 1200, the total number of officers in the study.

$$P(A \mid M) = \frac{288}{960} = \frac{288/1200}{960/1200} = \frac{.24}{.80} = .30$$

We now see that the conditional probability $P(A \mid M)$ can be computed as $.24/.80$. Refer to the joint probability table (Table 4.5). Note in particular that $.24$ is the joint probability of A and M; that is, $P(A \cap M) = .24$. Also note that $.80$ is the marginal probability that a randomly selected officer is a man; that is, $P(M) = .80$. Thus, the conditional probability $P(A \mid M)$ can be computed as the ratio of the joint probability $P(A \cap M)$ to the marginal probability $P(M)$.

$$P(A \mid M) = \frac{P(A \cap M)}{P(M)} = \frac{.24}{.80} = .30$$

The fact that conditional probabilities can be computed as the ratio of a joint probability to a marginal probability provides the following general formula for conditional probability calculations for two events A and B.

Conditional Probability

$$P(A \mid B) = \frac{P(A \cap B)}{P(B)} \tag{4.7}$$

or

$$P(B \mid A) = \frac{P(A \cap B)}{P(A)} \tag{4.8}$$

The Venn diagram in Figure 4.8 is helpful in obtaining an intuitive understanding of conditional probability. The circle on the right shows that event B has occurred; the portion of the circle that overlaps with event A denotes the event $(A \cap B)$. We know that once event B has occurred, the only way that we can also observe event A is for the event $(A \cap B)$ to occur. Thus, the ratio $P(A \cap B)/P(B)$ provides the conditional probability that we will observe event A given event B has already occurred.

Let us return to the issue of discrimination against the female officers. The marginal probability in row 1 of Table 4.5 shows that the probability of promotion of an officer is $P(A) = .27$ (regardless of whether that officer is male or female). However, the critical issue in the discrimination case involves the two conditional probabilities $P(A \mid M)$ and $P(A \mid W)$. That is, what is the probability of a promotion *given* that the officer is a man, and what is the probability of a promotion given that the officer is a woman? If these two probabilities are equal, a discrimination argument has no basis because the chances of a promotion are the same for male and female officers. However, a difference in the two conditional probabilities will support the position that male and female officers are treated differently in promotion decisions.

We have already determined that $P(A \mid M) = .30$. Let us now use the probability values in Table 4.5 and the basic relationship of conditional probability in equation (4.7) to

FIGURE 4.8   CONDITIONAL PROBABILITY

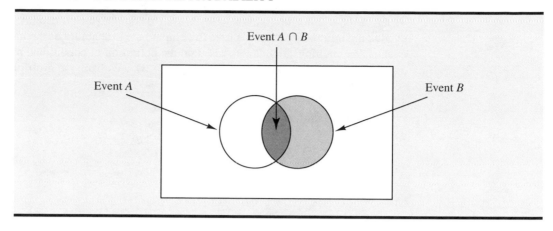

compute the probability that an officer is promoted given that the officer is a woman; that is, $P(A \mid W)$. Using equation (4.7), with W replacing B, we obtain

$$P(A \mid W) = \frac{P(A \cap W)}{P(W)} = \frac{.03}{.20} = .15$$

What conclusion do you draw? The probability of a promotion given that the officer is a man is .30, twice the .15 probability of a promotion given that the officer is a woman. Although the use of conditional probability does not in itself prove that discrimination exists in this case, the conditional probability values support the argument presented by the female officers.

Independent Events

In the preceding illustration, $P(A) = .27$, $P(A \mid M) = .30$, and $P(A \mid W) = .15$. We see that the probability of a promotion (event A) is affected or influenced by whether the officer is a man or a woman. Particularly, because $P(A \mid M) \neq P(A)$, we would say that events A and M are dependent events. That is, the probability of event A (promotion) is altered or affected by knowing that event M (the officer is a man) has occurred. Similarly, with $P(A \mid W) \neq P(A)$, we would say that events A and W are *dependent events*. However, if the probability of event A is not changed by the occurrence of event M—that is, $P(A \mid M) = P(A)$—we would say that events A and M are **independent events.** This situation leads to the following definition of the independence of two events.

Independent Events

Two events A and B are independent if

$$P(A \mid B) = P(A) \tag{4.9}$$

or

$$P(B \mid A) = P(B) \tag{4.10}$$

Otherwise, the events are dependent.

Multiplication Law

Whereas the addition law of probability is used to compute the probability of a union of two events, the multiplication law is used to compute the probability of the intersection of two events. The multiplication law is based on the definition of conditional probability. Using equations (4.7) and (4.8) and solving for $P(A \cap B)$, we obtain the **multiplication law.**

Multiplication Law

$$P(A \cap B) = P(B)P(A \mid B) \qquad\qquad (4.11)$$

or

$$P(A \cap B) = P(A)P(B \mid A) \qquad\qquad (4.12)$$

To illustrate the use of the multiplication law, consider a newspaper circulation department where it is known that 84% of the households in a particular neighborhood subscribe to the daily edition of the paper. If we let D denote the event that a household subscribes to the daily edition, $P(D) = .84$. In addition, it is known that the probability that a household that already holds a daily subscription also subscribes to the Sunday edition (event S) is .75; that is, $P(S \mid D) = .75$. What is the probability that a household subscribes to both the Sunday and daily editions of the newspaper? Using the multiplication law, we compute the desired $P(S \cap D)$ as

$$P(S \cap D) = P(D)P(S \mid D) = .84(.75) = .63$$

We now know that 63% of the households subscribe to both the Sunday and daily editions.

Before concluding this section, let us consider the special case of the multiplication law when the events involved are independent. Recall that events A and B are independent whenever $P(A \mid B) = P(A)$ or $P(B \mid A) = P(B)$. Hence, using equations (4.11) and (4.12) for the special case of independent events, we obtain the following multiplication law.

Multiplication Law for Independent Events

$$P(A \cap B) = P(A)P(B) \qquad\qquad (4.13)$$

To compute the probability of the intersection of two independent events, we simply multiply the corresponding probabilities. Note that the multiplication law for independent events provides another way to determine whether A and B are independent. That is, if $P(A \cap B) = P(A)P(B)$, then A and B are independent; if $P(A \cap B) \neq P(A)P(B)$, then A and B are dependent.

As an application of the multiplication law for independent events, consider the situation of a service station manager who knows from past experience that 80% of the customers use a credit card when they purchase gasoline. What is the probability that the next two customers purchasing gasoline will each use a credit card? If we let

A = the event that the first customer uses a credit card

B = the event that the second customer uses a credit card

then the event of interest is $A \cap B$. Given no other information, we can reasonably assume that A and B are independent events. Thus,

$$P(A \cap B) = P(A)P(B) = (.80)(.80) = .64$$

To summarize this section, we note that our interest in conditional probability is motivated by the fact that events are often related. In such cases, we say the events are dependent and the conditional probability formulas in equations (4.7) and (4.8) must be used to compute the event probabilities. If two events are not related, they are independent; in this case neither event's probability is affected by whether the other event occurred.

NOTES AND COMMENTS

Do not confuse the notion of mutually exclusive events with that of independent events. Two events with nonzero probabilities cannot be both mutually exclusive and independent. If one mutu-ally exclusive event is known to occur, the other cannot occur; thus, the probability of the other event occurring is reduced to zero. They are therefore dependent.

EXERCISES

Methods

SELFtest   **30.** Suppose that we have two events, A and B, with $P(A) = .50$, $P(B) = .60$, and $P(A \cap B) = .40$.
   a. Find $P(A \mid B)$.
   b. Find $P(B \mid A)$.
   c. Are A and B independent? Why or why not?

31. Assume that we have two events, A and B, that are mutually exclusive. Assume further that we know $P(A) = .30$ and $P(B) = .40$.
   a. What is $P(A \cap B)$?
   b. What is $P(A \mid B)$?
   c. A student in statistics argues that the concepts of mutually exclusive events and independent events are really the same, and that if events are mutually exclusive they must be independent. Do you agree with this statement? Use the probability information in this problem to justify your answer.
   d. What general conclusion would you make about mutually exclusive and independent events given the results of this problem?

Applications

32. A Daytona Beach nightclub has the following data on the age and marital status of 140 customers.

		Marital Status	
		Single	Married
Age	Under 30	77	14
	30 or Over	28	21

a. Develop a joint probability table for these data.
b. Use the marginal probabilities to comment on the age of customers attending the club.
c. Use the marginal probabilities to comment on the marital status of customers attending the club.
d. What is the probability of finding a customer who is single and under the age of 30?
e. If a customer is under 30, what is the probability that he or she is single?
f. Is marital status independent of age? Explain, using probabilities.

SELFtest   33. In a survey of MBA students, the following data were obtained on "students' first reason for application to the school in which they matriculated."

| | | **Reason for Application** | | | |
		School Quality	**School Cost or Convenience**	**Other**	**Totals**
Enrollment	**Full Time**	421	393	76	890
Status	**Part Time**	400	593	46	1039
	Totals	821	986	122	1929

a. Develop a joint probability table for these data.
b. Use the marginal probabilities of school quality, cost/convenience, and other to comment on the most important reason for choosing a school.
c. If a student goes full time, what is the probability that school quality is the first reason for choosing a school?
d. If a student goes part time, what is the probability that school quality is the first reason for choosing a school?
e. Let A denote the event that a student is full time and let B denote the event that the student lists school quality as the first reason for applying. Are events A and B independent? Justify your answer.

34. The following table shows the distribution of blood types in the general population (Hoxworth Blood Center, Cincinnati, Ohio).

	A	**B**	**AB**	**O**
Rh+	34%	9%	4%	38%
Rh−	6%	2%	1%	6%

a. What is the probability a person will have type O blood?
b. What is the probability a person will be Rh−?
c. What is the probability a married couple will both be Rh−?
d. What is the probability a married couple will both have type AB blood?
e. What is the probability a person will be Rh− given she or he has type O blood?
f. What is the probability a person will have type B blood given he or she is Rh+?

35. "Since 1950, the January Barometer has predicted the annual course of the stock market with amazing accuracy" (*1998 Stock Trader's Almanac*). Over the 48 years from 1950 through 1997, the stock market has been up in January 31 times; it has been up for the year 36 times; and it has been up for the year and up for January 29 times.

a. Estimate the probability the stock market will be up in January.
b. Estimate the probability the stock market will be up for the year.
c. What is the probability the stock market will be up for the year given it is up in January?
d. Do the probabilities suggest that the stock market's January performance and its annual performance are independent events? Explain.

36. A study of job satisfaction was conducted for four occupations: cabinetmaker, lawyer, physical therapist, and systems analyst. Job satisfaction was measured on a scale of 0–100. The data obtained are summarized in the following crosstabulation.

Occupation	Satisfaction Score				
	Under 50	50–59	60–69	70–79	80–89
Cabinetmaker	0	2	4	3	1
Lawyer	6	2	1	1	0
Physical Therapist	0	5	2	1	2
Systems Analyst	2	1	4	3	0

a. Develop a joint probability table.
b. What is the probability one of the participants studied had a satisfaction score in the 80s?
c. What is the probability of a satisfaction score in the 80s given the study participant was a physical therapist?
d. What is the probability one of the participants studied was a lawyer?
e. What is the probability one of the participants was a lawyer and received a score under 50?
f. What is the probability of a satisfaction score under 50 given a person is a lawyer?
g. What is the probability of a satisfaction score of 70 or higher?

37. A purchasing agent placed rush orders for a particular raw material with two different suppliers, A and B. If neither order arrives in four days, the production process must be shut down until at least one of the orders arrives. The probability that supplier A can deliver the material in four days is .55. The probability that supplier B can deliver the material in four days is .35.
a. What is the probability that both suppliers will deliver the material in four days? Because two separate suppliers are involved, we are willing to assume independence.
b. What is the probability that at least one supplier will deliver the material in four days?
c. What is the probability that the production process will be shut down in four days because of a shortage of raw material (that is, both orders are late)?

38. A survey of 1035 workers by the Institute for the Future and the Gallup Organization found that workers are being inundated by messages (*The Cincinnati Enquirer*, November 2, 1998). The study indicated that each worker gets an average of 190 messages per day. The following table shows the breakdown by type of message.

Source	Daily Messages	Source	Daily Messages
Telephone	52	E-mail	30
Voice mail	22	Interoffice mail	18
U.S. mail	18	Fax	15
Post-it note	11	Phone msg. slip	10
Pager	4	Overnight courier	4
Cellular phone	3	U.S. Express mail	3

   a. For any particular worker, what is the probability the next message will be on the telephone?

   b. For the next two messages, what is the probability the first will be via e-mail and the second will be via fax?

   c. What is the probability the next message received will be via telephone call or interoffice mail?

4.5   BAYES' THEOREM

In the discussion of conditional probability, we indicated that revising probabilities when new information is obtained is an important phase of probability analysis. Often, we begin the analysis with initial or **prior probability** estimates for specific events of interest. Then, from sources such as a sample, a special report, or a product test, we obtain additional information about the events. Given this new information, we update the prior probability values by calculating revised probabilities, referred to as **posterior probabilities. Bayes' theorem** provides a means for making these probability calculations. The steps in this probability revision process are shown in Figure 4.9.

As an application of Bayes' theorem, consider a manufacturing firm that receives shipments of parts from two different suppliers. Let A_1 denote the event that a part is from supplier 1 and A_2 denote the event that a part is from supplier 2. Currently, 65% of the parts purchased by the company are from supplier 1 and the remaining 35% are from supplier 2. Hence, if a part is selected at random, we would assign the prior probabilities $P(A_1) = .65$ and $P(A_2) = .35$.

The quality of the purchased parts varies with the source of supply. Historical data suggest that the quality ratings of the two suppliers are as shown in Table 4.6. If we let G denote the event that a part is good and B denote the event that a part is bad, the information in Table 4.6 provides the following conditional probability values.

$$P(G \mid A_1) = .98 \quad P(B \mid A_1) = .02$$
$$P(G \mid A_2) = .95 \quad P(B \mid A_2) = .05$$

The tree diagram in Figure 4.10 depicts the process of the firm receiving a part from one of the two suppliers and then discovering that the part is good or bad as a two-step experiment. We see that four experimental outcomes are possible; two correspond to the part being good and two correspond to the part being bad.

Each of the experimental outcomes is the intersection of two events, so we can use the multiplication rule to compute the probabilities. For instance,

$$P(A_1, G) = P(A_1 \cap G) = P(A_1)P(G \mid A_1)$$

FIGURE 4.9   PROBABILITY REVISION USING BAYES' THEOREM

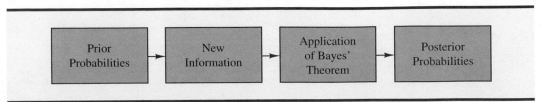

TABLE 4.6   HISTORICAL QUALITY LEVELS OF TWO SUPPLIERS

	Percentage Good Parts	Percentage Bad Parts
Supplier 1	98	2
Supplier 2	95	5

The process of computing these joint probabilities can be depicted in what is called a probability tree (see Figure 4.11). From left to right through the tree, the probabilities for each branch at step 1 are prior probabilities and the probabilities for each branch at step 2 are conditional probabilities. To find the probabilities of each experimental outcome, we simply multiply the probabilities on the branches leading to the outcome. Each of these joint probabilities is shown in Figure 4.11 along with the known probabilities for each branch.

Suppose now that the parts from the two suppliers are used in the firm's manufacturing process and that a machine breaks down because it attempts to process a bad part. Given the information that the part is bad, what is the probability that it came from supplier 1 and what is the probability that it came from supplier 2? With the information in the probability tree (Figure 4.11), Bayes' theorem can be used to answer these questions.

Letting B denote the event that the part is bad, we are looking for the posterior probabilities $P(A_1 \mid B)$ and $P(A_2 \mid B)$. From the law of conditional probability, we know that

$$P(A_1 \mid B) = \frac{P(A_1 \cap B)}{P(B)} \qquad (4.14)$$

Referring to the probability tree, we see that

$$P(A_1 \cap B) = P(A_1)P(B \mid A_1) \qquad (4.15)$$

FIGURE 4.10   TREE DIAGRAM FOR TWO-SUPPLIER EXAMPLE

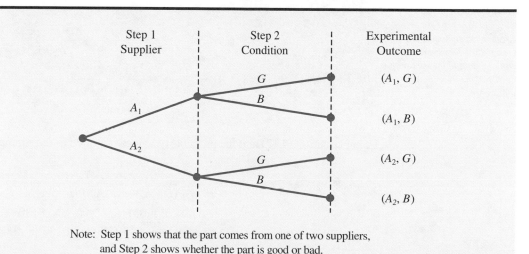

Note: Step 1 shows that the part comes from one of two suppliers,
       and Step 2 shows whether the part is good or bad.

FIGURE 4.11   PROBABILITY TREE FOR TWO-SUPPLIER EXAMPLE

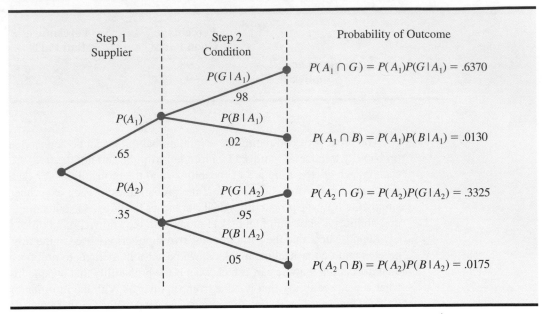

To find $P(B)$, we note that event B can occur in only two ways: $(A_1 \cap B)$ and $(A_2 \cap B)$. Therefore, we have

$$P(B) = P(A_1 \cap B) + P(A_2 \cap B)$$
$$= P(A_1)P(B \mid A_1) + P(A_2)P(B \mid A_2) \tag{4.16}$$

Substituting from equations (4.15) and (4.16) into equation (4.14) and writing a similar result for $P(A_2 \mid B)$, we obtain Bayes' theorem for the case of two events.

The Reverend Thomas Bayes (1702–1761), a Presbyterian minister, is credited with the original work leading to the version of Bayes' theorem in use today.

Bayes' Theorem (Two-Event Case)

$$P(A_1 \mid B) = \frac{P(A_1)P(B \mid A_1)}{P(A_1)P(B \mid A_1) + P(A_2)P(B \mid A_2)} \tag{4.17}$$

$$P(A_2 \mid B) = \frac{P(A_2)P(B \mid A_2)}{P(A_1)P(B \mid A_1) + P(A_2)P(B \mid A_2)} \tag{4.18}$$

Using equation (4.17) and the probability values provided in the example, we have

$$P(A_1 \mid B) = \frac{P(A_1)P(B \mid A_1)}{P(A_1)P(B \mid A_1) + P(A_2)P(B \mid A_2)}$$
$$= \frac{(.65)(.02)}{(.65)(.02) + (.35)(.05)} = \frac{.0130}{.0130 + .0175}$$
$$= \frac{.0130}{.0305} = .4262$$

In addition, using equation (4.18), we find $P(A_2 \mid B)$.

$$P(A_2 \mid B) = \frac{(.35)(.05)}{(.65)(.02) + (.35)(.05)}$$

$$= \frac{.0175}{.0130 + .0175} = \frac{.0175}{.0305} = .5738$$

Note that in this application we started with a probability of .65 that a part selected at random was from supplier 1. However, given information that the part is bad, the probability that the part is from supplier 1 drops to .4262. In fact, if the part is bad, it has better than a 50–50 chance that it came from supplier 2; that is, $P(A_2 \mid B) = .5738$.

Bayes' theorem is applicable when the events for which we want to compute posterior probabilities are mutually exclusive and their union is the entire sample space.* For the case of n mutually exclusive events $A_1, A_2, \ldots, A_n$, whose union is the entire sample space, Bayes' theorem can be used to compute any posterior probability $P(A_i \mid B)$ as shown below.

Bayes' Theorem

$$P(A_i \mid B) = \frac{P(A_i)P(B \mid A_i)}{P(A_1)P(B \mid A_1) + P(A_2)P(B \mid A_2) + \cdots + P(A_n)P(B \mid A_n)} \qquad (4.19)$$

With prior probabilities $P(A_1)$, $P(A_2)$, $\ldots$, $P(A_n)$ and the appropriate conditional probabilities $P(B \mid A_1)$, $P(B \mid A_2)$, $\ldots$, $P(B \mid A_n)$, equation (4.19) can be used to compute the posterior probability of the events $A_1, A_2, \ldots, A_n$.

Tabular Approach

A tabular approach is helpful in conducting the Bayes' theorem calculations. Such an approach is shown in Table 4.7 for the parts supplier problem. The computations shown there are done in the following steps.

Step 1. Prepare the following three columns:
   Column 1—The mutually exclusive events A_i for which posterior probabilities are desired.
   Column 2—The prior probabilities $P(A_i)$ for the events.
   Column 3—The conditional probabilities $P(B \mid A_i)$ of the new information B *given* each event.

Step 2. In column 4, compute the joint probabilities $P(A_i \cap B)$ for each event and the new information B by using the multiplication law. These joint probabilities are found by multiplying the prior probabilities in column 2 by the corresponding conditional probabilities in column 3; that is, $P(A_i \cap B) = P(A_i)P(B \mid A_i)$.

Step 3. Sum the joint probabilities in column 4. The sum is the probability of the new information, $P(B)$. Thus we see in Table 4.7 that there is a .0130 probability that the part came from supplier 1 and is bad, and a .0175 probability that the part came from supplier 2 and is bad. Because these are the only two ways in which a bad part can be obtained, the sum .0130 + .0175 shows an overall probability of .0305 of finding a bad part from the combined shipments of the two suppliers.

*If the union of events is the entire sample space, the events are said to be *collectively exhaustive.*

TABLE 4.7   SUMMARY OF BAYES' THEOREM CALCULATIONS FOR THE
TWO-SUPPLIER PROBLEM

(1) Events A_i	(2) Prior Probabilities $P(A_i)$	(3) Conditional Probabilities $P(B \mid A_i)$	(4) Joint Probabilities $P(A_i \cap B)$	(5) Posterior Probabilities $P(A_i \mid B)$
A_1	.65	.02	.0130	.0130/.0305 = .4262
A_2	.35	.05	.0175	.0175/.0305 = .5738
	1.00		$P(B) = .0305$	1.0000

Step 4. In column 5, compute the posterior probabilities using the basic relationship of conditional probability.

$$P(A_i \mid B) = \frac{P(A_i \cap B)}{P(B)}$$

Note that the joint probabilities $P(A_i \cap B)$ are in column 4 and the probability $P(B)$ is the sum of column 4.

NOTES AND COMMENTS

1. Bayes' theorem is used extensively in decision analysis. The prior probabilities are often subjective estimates provided by a decision maker. Sample information is obtained and posterior probabilities are computed for use in choosing the best decision.

2. An event and its complement are mutually exclusive, and their union is the entire sample space. Thus, Bayes' theorem is always applicable for computing posterior probabilities of an event and its complement.

EXERCISES

Methods

SELFtest

39. The prior probabilities for events A_1 and A_2 are $P(A_1) = .40$ and $P(A_2) = .60$. It is also known that $P(A_1 \cap A_2) = 0$. Suppose $P(B \mid A_1) = .20$ and $P(B \mid A_2) = .05$.
  a. Are A_1 and A_2 mutually exclusive? Explain.
  b. Compute $P(A_1 \cap B)$ and $P(A_2 \cap B)$.
  c. Compute $P(B)$.
  d. Apply Bayes' theorem to compute $P(A_1 \mid B)$ and $P(A_2 \mid B)$.

40. The prior probabilities for events A_1, A_2, and A_3 are $P(A_1) = .20$, $P(A_2) = .50$, and $P(A_3) = .30$. The conditional probabilities of event B given A_1, A_2, and A_3 are $P(B \mid A_1) = .50$, $P(B \mid A_2) = .40$, and $P(B \mid A_3) = .30$.
  a. Compute $P(B \cap A_1)$, $P(B \cap A_2)$, and $P(B \cap A_3)$.
  b. Apply Bayes' theorem, equation (4.19), to compute the posterior probability $P(A_2 \mid B)$.
  c. Use the tabular approach to applying Bayes' theorem to compute $P(A_1 \mid B)$, $P(A_2 \mid B)$, and $P(A_3 \mid B)$.

Applications

41. A consulting firm submitted a bid for a large research project. The firm's management initially felt they had a 50–50 chance of getting the project. However, the agency to which the bid was submitted subsequently requested additional information on the bid. Past experience indicates that for 75% of the successful bids and 40% of the unsuccessful bids the agency requested additional information.
    a. What is the prior probability of the bid being successful (that is, prior to the request for additional information)?
    b. What is the conditional probability of a request for additional information given that the bid will ultimately be successful?
    c. Compute the posterior probability that the bid will be successful given a request for additional information.

SELFtest 42. A local bank reviews its credit card policy with the intention of recalling some of its credit cards. In the past approximately 5% of cardholders defaulted, leaving the bank unable to collect the outstanding balance. Hence, management established a prior probability of .05 that any particular cardholder will default. The bank further found that the probability of missing a monthly payment is .20 for customers who do not default. Of course, the probability of missing a monthly payment for those who default is 1.
    a. Given that a customer missed a monthly payment, compute the posterior probability that the customer will default.
    b. The bank would like to recall its card if the probability that a customer will default is greater than .20. Should the bank recall its card if the customer misses a monthly payment? Why or why not?

43. Small cars get better gas mileage, but they are not as safe as bigger cars. Small cars accounted for 18% of the vehicles on the road, but accidents involving small cars led to 11,898 fatalities during a recent year (*Reader's Digest*, May, 2000). Assume the probability a small car is involved in an accident is .18. The probability of an accident involving a small car leading to a fatality is .128 and the probability of an accident not involving a small car leading to a fatality is .05. Suppose you learn of an accident involving a fatality. What is the probability a small car was involved?

44. A city's professional basketball team plays at home, and its professional hockey team plays away on the same night. A professional basketball team has a .641 probability of winning a home game, and a professional hockey team has a .462 probability of winning an away game. Historically, when both teams play on the same night, the chance that the next morning's leading sports story will be about the basketball game is 60% and the chance that it will be about the hockey game is 40%. Suppose that on the morning after these games the newspaper's leading sports story begins with the headline "We Win!!" What is the probability that the story is about the basketball team?

45. In an article about investment growth, *Money* magazine reported that drug stocks show powerful long-term trends and offer investors unparalleled potential for strong and steady gains. The federal Health Care Financing Administration supports this conclusion through its forecast that annual prescription drug expenditures will reach $366 billion by 2010, up from $117 billion in 2000. Many individuals age 65 and older rely heavily on prescription drugs. For this group, 82% take prescription drugs regularly, 55% take three or more prescriptions regularly, and 40% currently use five or more prescriptions. In contrast, 49% of people under age 65 take prescription drugs regularly, with 17% taking three or more prescriptions regularly and 28% using five or more prescriptions (*Money*, September 2001). The U.S. Census Bureau reports that of the 281,421,906 people in the United States, 34,991,753 are age 65 years and older (U.S. Census Bureau, Census 2000).

   a. Compute the probability that a person in the United States is age 65 or older.

   b. Compute the probability that a person takes prescription drugs regularly.

   c. Compute the probability that a person is age 65 or older and takes five or more prescriptions.

   d. Given a person uses five or more prescriptions, compute the probability that the person is age 65 or older.

SUMMARY

In this chapter we introduced basic probability concepts and illustrated how probability analysis can be used to provide helpful information for decision making. We described how probability can be interpreted as a numerical measure of the likelihood that an event will occur. In addition, we saw that the probability of an event can be computed either by summing the probabilities of the experimental outcomes (sample points) comprising the event or by using the relationships established by the addition, conditional probability, and multiplication laws of probability. For cases in which additional information is available, we showed how Bayes' theorem can be used to obtain revised or posterior probabilities.

GLOSSARY

Probability   A numerical measure of the likelihood that an event will occur.

Experiment   A process that generates well-defined outcomes.

Sample space   The set of all experimental outcomes.

Sample point   An element of the sample space. A sample point represents an experimental outcome.

Tree diagram   A graphical representation helpful in identifying the sample points of an experiment involving multiple steps.

Basic requirements for assigning probabilities   Two requirements that restrict the manner in which probability assignments can be made: (1) for each experimental outcome E_i we must have $0 \leq P(E_i) \leq 1$; (2) considering all experimental outcomes, we must have $P(E_1) + P(E_2) + \cdots + P(E_n) = 1$.

Classical method   A method of assigning probabilities that is appropriate when the experimental outcomes are equally likely.

Relative frequency method   A method of assigning probabilities that is appropriate when data are available to estimate the proportion of times an experimental outcome will occur in the long run.

Subjective method   A method of assigning probabilities on the basis of judgment.

Event   A collection of sample points.

Complement of A   The event consisting of all sample points that are not in A.

Venn diagram   A graphical representation for showing symbolically the sample space and operations involving events. The sample space is represented by a rectangle and events are represented as circles within the sample space.

Union of A and B   The event containing all sample points belonging to A or B or both. The union is denoted $A \cup B$.

Intersection of A and B   The event containing all sample points belonging to both A and B. The intersection is denoted $A \cap B$.

Addition law   A probability law used to compute the probability of the union of two events. It is $P(A \cup B) = P(A) + P(B) - P(A \cap B)$. For mutually exclusive events, $P(A \cap B) = 0$, in this case the addition law reduces to $P(A \cup B) = P(A) + P(B)$.

Mutually exclusive events   Events that have no sample points in common; that is, $A \cap B$ is empty and $P(A \cap B) = 0$.

Conditional probability   The probability of an event given that another event has occurred. The conditional probability of A given B is $P(A \mid B) = P(A \cap B)/P(B)$.

Joint probability   The probability of two events both occurring; that is, the probability of the intersection of two events.

Independent events   Two events A and B where $P(A \mid B) = P(A)$ or $P(B \mid A) = P(B)$; that is, the events have no influence on each other.

Multiplication law   A probability law used to compute the probability of the intersection of two events. It is $P(A \cap B) = P(B)P(A \mid B)$ or $P(A \cap B) = P(A)P(B \mid A)$. For independent events it reduces to $P(A \cap B) = P(A)P(B)$.

Prior probabilities   Initial estimates of the probabilities of events.

Posterior probabilities   Revised probabilities of events based on additional information.

Bayes' theorem   A method used to compute posterior probabilities.

KEY FORMULAS

Counting Rule for Combinations

$$C_n^N = \binom{N}{n} = \frac{N!}{n!(N-n)!} \tag{4.1}$$

Counting Rule for Permutations

$$P_n^N = n!\binom{N}{n} = \frac{N!}{(N-n)!} \tag{4.2}$$

Computing Probability Using the Complement

$$P(A) = 1 - P(A^c) \tag{4.5}$$

Addition Law

$$P(A \cup B) = P(A) + P(B) - P(A \cap B) \tag{4.6}$$

Conditional Probability

$$P(A \mid B) = \frac{P(A \cap B)}{P(B)} \tag{4.7}$$

$$P(B \mid A) = \frac{P(A \cap B)}{P(A)} \tag{4.8}$$

Multiplication Law

$$P(A \cap B) = P(B)P(A \mid B) \tag{4.11}$$

$$P(A \cap B) = P(A)P(B \mid A) \tag{4.12}$$

Multiplication Law for Independent Events

$$P(A \cap B) = P(A)P(B) \tag{4.13}$$

Bayes' Theorem

$$P(A_i \mid B) = \frac{P(A_i)P(B \mid A_i)}{P(A_1)P(B \mid A_1) + P(A_2)P(B \mid A_2) + \cdots + P(A_n)P(B \mid A_n)} \tag{4.19}$$

SUPPLEMENTARY EXERCISES

46. In a *Business Week*/Harris Poll, 1035 adults were asked about their attitudes toward business (*Business Week*, September 11, 2000). One question asked: "How would you rate large U.S. companies on making good products and competing in a global environment?" The responses were: excellent—18%, pretty good—50%, only fair—26%, poor—5%, and don't know/no answer—1%.
   a. What is the probability that a respondent rated U.S. companies pretty good or excellent?
   b. How many respondents rated U.S. companies poor?
   c. How many respondents did not know or didn't answer?

47. A financial manager just made two new investments—one in the oil industry and one in municipal bonds. After a one-year period, each of the investments will be classified as either successful or unsuccessful. Consider the making of the two investments as an experiment.
   a. How many sample points exist for this experiment?
   b. Show a tree diagram and list the sample points.
   c. Let O = the event that the oil industry investment is successful and M = the event that the municipal bond investment is successful. List the sample points in O and in M.
   d. List the sample points in the union of the events ($O \cup M$).
   e. List the sample points in the intersection of the events ($O \cap M$).
   f. Are events O and M mutually exclusive? Explain.

48. A survey of American opinion asked: Are you satisfied or dissatisfied with the state of the U.S. economy today? (*The Wall Street Journal*, June 27, 1997). The following table provides the responses for all adults and the distribution by age groups.

	Satisfied (%)	Dissatisfied (%)	Other (%)
All Adults	61	37	2
18–34	64	35	1
35–49	58	41	1
50–64	57	40	3
65+	70	26	4

   a. What is the probability a respondent is satisfied?
   b. Which age groups report a higher level of satisfaction than the average for all adults?
   c. What is the probability a respondent 65 or older did not indicate they were satisfied?

49. A study of 31,000 hospital administrators in New York State found that 4% of the admissions led to treatment-caused injuries. One-seventh of these treatment-caused injuries resulted in death, and one-fourth were caused by negligence. Malpractice claims were filed

in one out of 7.5 cases involving negligence, and payments were made in one out of every two claims.

a.   What is the probability a person admitted to the hospital will suffer a treatment-caused injury due to negligence?

b.   What is the probability a person admitted to the hospital will die from a treatment-caused injury due to negligence?

c.   In the case of a negligent treatment-caused injury, what is the probability a malpractice claim will be paid?

50.   A telephone survey obtained the following data to determine viewer response to a new television show.

Rating	Frequency
Poor	4
Below average	8
Average	11
Above average	14
Excellent	13

a.   What is the probability that a randomly selected viewer will rate the new show as average or better?

b.   What is the probability that a randomly selected viewer will rate the new show below average or worse?

51.   *Business Week* surveyed its subscribers concerning the number of cars they owned or leased. Responses were obtained to three questions: How many cars do you own? How many cars do you lease? How many cars do you have (owned or leased)? Table 4.8 contains the results obtained from 932 households (*Business Week* 1996 Worldwide Subscriber Study). In interpreting the table note that the third row shows that 401 households own two cars, 47 households lease two cars, and 447 households have two cars (owned and/or leased).

a.   What is the probability a household leases one car?

b.   What is the probability a household owns two or fewer cars?

c.   What is the probability a household has three or more cars?

d.   What is the probability a household does not own or lease a car?

TABLE 4.8   NUMBER OF CARS OWNED OR LEASED, AND TOTAL NUMBER OF CARS PER HOUSEHOLD

	Number of Households		
Cars	Own	Lease	Have
0	65	708	19
1	242	168	168
2	401	47	447
3	149	9	186
4 or more	75	0	112
Total	932	932	932

52. A GMAC MBA new-matriculants survey provided the following data for 2018 students.

		Applied to More Than One School	
		Yes	No
Age Group	23 and under	207	201
	24–26	299	379
	27–30	185	268
	31–35	66	193
	36 and over	51	169

a. For a randomly selected MBA student, prepare a joint probability table for the experiment consisting of observing the student's age and whether the student applied to one or more schools.
b. What is the probability that a randomly selected applicant is 23 or under?
c. What is the probability that a randomly selected applicant is older than 26?
d. What is the probability that a randomly selected applicant applied to more than one school?

53. Refer again to the data from the GMAC new-matriculants survey in Exercise 52.
a. Given that a person applied to more than one school, what is the probability that the person is 24–26 years old?
b. Given that a person is in the 36-and-over age group, what is the probability that the person applied to more than one school?
c. What is the probability that a person is 24–26 years old *or* applied to more than one school?
d. Suppose a person is known to have applied to only one school. What is the probability that the person is 31 or more years old?
e. Is the number of schools applied to independent of age? Explain.

54. An IBD/TIPP poll was conducted to learn about attitudes toward investment and retirement (*Investor's Business Daily*, May 5, 2000). One question asked male and female respondents how important they felt level of risk was in choosing a retirement investment. The following joint probability table was constructed from the data provided. Important means the respondent said level of risk was either important or very important.

	Male	Female	Total
Important	.22	.27	.49
Not Important	.28	.23	.51
Total	.50	.50	1.00

a. What is the probability a survey respondent will say level of risk is important?
b. What is the probability a male respondent will say level of risk is important?
c. What is the probability a female respondent will say level of risk is important?
d. Is level of risk independent of the gender of the respondent? Why or why not?
e. Do male and female attitudes toward risk differ?

55. A large consumer goods company has been running a television advertisement for one of its soap products. A survey was conducted. On the basis of this survey, probabilities were assigned to the following events.

$$B = \text{individual purchased the product}$$
$$S = \text{individual recalls seeing the advertisement}$$
$$B \cap S = \text{individual purchased the product and recalls seeing the advertisement}$$

The probabilities assigned were $P(B) = .20$, $P(S) = .40$, and $P(B \cap S) = .12$.

   a. What is the probability of an individual's purchasing the product given that the individual recalls seeing the advertisement? Does seeing the advertisement increase the probability that the individual will purchase the product? As a decision maker, would you recommend continuing the advertisement (assuming that the cost is reasonable)?
   b. Assume that individuals who do not purchase the company's soap product buy from its competitors. What would be your estimate of the company's market share? Would you expect that continuing the advertisement will increase the company's market share? Why or why not?
   c. The company has also tested another advertisement and assigned it values of $P(S) = .30$ and $P(B \cap S) = .10$. What is $P(B \mid S)$ for this other advertisement? Which advertisement seems to have had the bigger effect on customer purchases?

56. Cooper Realty is a small real estate company located in Albany, New York, specializing primarily in residential listings. They recently became interested in determining the likelihood of one of their listings being sold within a certain number of days. An analysis of company sales of 800 homes in previous years produced the following data.

		Days Listed Until Sold			
		Under 30	31–90	Over 90	Total
Initial Asking Price	Under $150,000	50	40	10	100
	$150,000–$199,999	20	150	80	250
	$200,000–$250,000	20	280	100	400
	Over $250,000	10	30	10	50
	Total	100	500	200	800

   a. If A is defined as the event that a home is listed for over 90 days before being sold, estimate the probability of A.
   b. If B is defined as the event that the initial asking price is under $150,000, estimate the probability of B.
   c. What is the probability of $A \cap B$?
   d. Assuming that a contract just signed to list a home has an initial asking price of less than $150,000, what is the probability that the home will take Cooper Realty more than 90 days to sell?
   e. Are events A and B independent?

57. A company studied the number of lost-time accidents occurring at its Brownsville, Texas, plant. Historical records show that 6% of the employees suffered lost-time accidents last year. Management believes that a special safety program will reduce such accidents to 5% during the current year. In addition, it estimates that 15% of employees who had lost-time accidents last year will experience a lost-time accident during the current year.

   a. What percentage of the employees will experience lost-time accidents in both years?
   b. What percentage of the employees will suffer at least one lost-time accident over the two-year period?

58. The Dallas IRS auditing staff, concerned with identifying potentially fraudulent tax returns, believes that the probability of finding a fraudulent return given that the return contains deductions for contributions exceeding the IRS standard is .20. Given that the deductions for contributions do not exceed the IRS standard, the probability of a fraudulent return decreases to .02. If 8% of all returns exceed the IRS standard for deductions due to contributions, what is the best estimate of the percentage of fraudulent returns?

59. An oil company purchased an option on land in Alaska. Preliminary geologic studies assigned the following prior probabilities.

$$P(\text{high-quality oil}) = .50$$
$$P(\text{medium-quality oil}) = .20$$
$$P(\text{no oil}) = .30$$

  a. What is the probability of finding oil?
  b. After 200 feet of drilling on the first well, a soil test is taken. The probabilities of finding the particular type of soil identified by the test follow.

$$P(\text{soil} \mid \text{high-quality oil}) = .20$$
$$P(\text{soil} \mid \text{medium-quality oil}) = .80$$
$$P(\text{soil} \mid \text{no oil}) = .20$$

  How should the firm interpret the soil test? What are the revised probabilities, and what is the new probability of finding oil?

60. A Bayesian approach can be used to revise probabilities that a prospect field will produce oil. In one case, geological assessment indicates a 25% chance that the field will produce oil. Further, there is an 80% chance that a particular well will produce oil given that oil is present in the prospect field.
  a. Suppose that one well is drilled on the field and it comes up dry. What is the probability that the prospect field will produce oil?
  b. If two wells come up dry, what is the probability that the field will produce oil?
  c. The oil company would like to keep looking as long as the chances of finding oil are greater than 1%. How many dry wells must be drilled before the field will be abandoned?

Case Problem   HAMILTON COUNTY JUDGES

Hamilton County judges try thousands of cases per year. In an overwhelming majority of the cases disposed, the verdict stands as rendered. However, some cases are appealed, and of those appealed, some of the cases are reversed. Kristen DelGuzzi of *The Cincinnati Enquirer* conducted a study of cases handled by Hamilton County judges over the years 1994 through 1996 (*The Cincinnati Enquirer*, January 11, 1998). Shown in Table 4.9 are the results for 182,908 cases handled (disposed) by 38 judges in Common Pleas Court, Domestic Relations Court, and Municipal Court. Two of the judges (Dinkelacker and Hogan) did not serve in the same court for the entire three-year period.

The purpose of the newspaper's study was to evaluate the performance of the judges. Appeals are often the result of mistakes made by judges, and the newspaper wanted to know which judges were doing a good job and which were making too many mistakes. You have been called in to assist in the data analysis. Use your knowledge of probability and conditional probability to help with the ranking of the judges. You also may be able to analyze the likelihood of appeal and reversal for cases handled by different courts.

TABLE 4.9 TOTAL CASES DISPOSED, APPEALED, AND REVERSED IN HAMILTON COUNTY COURTS DURING 1994 THROUGH 1996

Common Pleas Court

Judge	Total Cases Disposed	Appealed Cases	Reversed Cases
Fred Cartolano	3037	137	12
Thomas Crush	3372	119	10
Patrick Dinkelacker	1258	44	8
Timothy Hogan	1954	60	7
Robert Kraft	3138	127	7
William Mathews	2264	91	18
William Morrissey	3032	121	22
Norbert Nadel	2959	131	20
Arthur Ney, Jr.	3219	125	14
Richard Niehaus	3353	137	16
Thomas Nurre	3000	121	6
John O'Connor	2969	129	12
Robert Ruehlman	3205	145	18
J. Howard Sundermann	955	60	10
Ann Marie Tracey	3141	127	13
Ralph Winkler	3089	88	6
Total	43945	1762	199

Domestic Relations Court

Judge	Total Cases Disposed	Appealed Cases	Reversed Cases
Penelope Cunningham	2729	7	1
Patrick Dinkelacker	6001	19	4
Deborah Gaines	8799	48	9
Ronald Panioto	12970	32	3
Total	30499	106	17

Municipal Court

Judge	Total Cases Disposed	Appealed Cases	Reversed Cases
Mike Allen	6149	43	4
Nadine Allen	7812	34	6
Timothy Black	7954	41	6
David Davis	7736	43	5
Leslie Isaiah Gaines	5282	35	13
Karla Grady	5253	6	0
Deidra Hair	2532	5	0
Dennis Helmick	7900	29	5
Timothy Hogan	2308	13	2
James Patrick Kenney	2798	6	1
Joseph Luebbers	4698	25	8
William Mallory	8277	38	9
Melba Marsh	8219	34	7
Beth Mattingly	2971	13	1
Albert Mestemaker	4975	28	9
Mark Painter	2239	7	3
Jack Rosen	7790	41	13
Mark Schweikert	5403	33	6
David Stockdale	5371	22	4
John A. West	2797	4	2
Total	108464	500	104

Managerial Report

Prepare a report with your rankings of the judges. Also, include an analysis of the likelihood of appeal and case reversal in the three courts. At a minimum, your report should include the following:

1. The probability of cases being appealed and reversed in the three different courts.
2. The probability of a case being appealed for each judge.
3. The probability of a case being reversed for each judge.
4. The probability of reversal given an appeal for each judge.
5. Rank the judges within each court. State the criteria you used and provide a rationale for your choice.

DISCRETE PROBABILITY DISTRIBUTIONS

Chapter 5

CONTENTS

CITIBANK*

LONG ISLAND CITY, NEW YORK

Citibank, a division of Citigroup, makes available a wide range of financial services, including checking and savings accounts, loans and mortgages, insurance, and investment services, within the framework of a unique strategy for delivering those services called Citibanking. Citibanking entails a consistent brand identity all over the world, consistent product offerings, and high-level customer service. Citibanking lets you manage your money anytime, anywhere, anyway you choose. Whether you need to save for the future or borrow for today, you can do it all at Citibank.

Citibanking's state-of-the-art automatic teller machines (ATMs) located in Citicard Banking Centers (CBCs), let customers do all their banking in one place with the touch of a finger, 24 hours a day, 7 days a week. More than 150 different banking functions from deposits to managing investments can be performed with ease. Citibanking ATMs are so much more than just cash machines that customers today use them for 80% of their transactions.

Each Citibank CBC operates as a waiting line system with randomly arriving customers seeking service at one of the ATMs. If all ATMs are busy, the arriving customers wait in line. Periodic CBC capacity studies are used to analyze customer waiting times and to determine whether additional ATMs are needed.

Data collected by Citibank showed that the random customer arrivals followed a probability distribution known as the Poisson probability distribution. Using the Poisson probability distribution, Citibank can compute probabilities for the number of customers arriving at a CBC during any time period and make decisions con-

A Citibank ATM in Manhattan. © PhotoDisc, Inc./GettyOne Imagery.

cerning the number of ATMs needed. For example, let x = the number of customers arriving during a one-minute period. Assuming that a particular CBC has a mean arrival rate of 2 customers per minute, the following table shows the probabilities for the number of customers arriving during a one-minute period.

x	Probability
0	.1353
1	.2707
2	.2707
3	.1804
4	.0902
5 or more	.0527

Discrete probability distributions, such as the one used by Citibank, are the topic of this chapter. In addition to the Poisson probability distribution, you will learn about the binomial and hypergeometric probability distributions and how they can be used to provide helpful probability information.

*The authors are indebted to Ms. Stacey Karter, Citibank, for providing this Statistics in Practice.

In this chapter we continue the study of probability by introducing the concepts of random variables and probability distributions. The focus of this chapter is discrete probability distributions. Three special discrete probability distributions—the binomial, Poisson, and hypergeometric—are covered.

5.1   RANDOM VARIABLES

In Chapter 4 we defined the concept of an experiment and its associated experimental outcomes. A random variable provides a means for describing experimental outcomes using numerical values.

Random variables must assume numerical values.

> **Random Variable**
>
> A **random variable** is a numerical description of the outcome of an experiment.

In effect, a random variable associates a numerical value with each possible experimental outcome. The particular numerical value of the random variable depends on the outcome of the experiment. A random variable can be classified as being either *discrete* or *continuous* depending on the numerical values it assumes.

Discrete Random Variables

A random variable that may assume either a finite number of values or an infinite sequence of values such as 0, 1, 2, . . . is referred to as a **discrete random variable.** For example, consider the experiment of an accountant taking the certified public accountant (CPA) examination. The examination has four parts. We can define a random variable as x = the number of parts of the CPA examination passed. It is a discrete random variable because it may assume the finite number of values 0, 1, 2, 3, or 4.

As another example of a discrete random variable, consider the experiment of cars arriving at a tollbooth. The random variable of interest is x = the number of cars arriving during a one-day period. The possible values for x come from the sequence of integers 0, 1, 2, and so on. Hence, x is a discrete random variable assuming one of the values in this infinite sequence.

Although many experiments have outcomes that are naturally described by numerical values, others do not. For example, a survey question might ask an individual to recall the message in a recent television commercial. This experiment would have two possible outcomes: the individual cannot recall the message and the individual can recall the message. We can still describe these experimental outcomes numerically by defining the discrete random variable x as follows: let x = 0 if the individual cannot recall the message and x = 1 if the individual can recall the message. The numerical values for this random variable are arbitrary (we could have used 5 and 10), but they are acceptable in terms of the definition of a random variable—namely, x is a random variable because it provides a numerical description of the outcome of the experiment.

Table 5.1 provides some additional examples of discrete random variables. Note that in each example the discrete random variable assumes a finite number of values or an infinite sequence of values such as 0, 1, 2, ... Discrete random variables such as these are discussed in detail in this chapter.

Continuous Random Variables

A random variable that may assume any numerical value in an interval or collection of intervals is called a **continuous random variable.** Experimental outcomes based on measurement scales such as time, weight, distance, and temperature can be described by

TABLE 5.1 EXAMPLES OF DISCRETE RANDOM VARIABLES

Experiment	Random Variable (x)	Possible Values for the Random Variable
Contact five customers	Number of customers who place an order	0, 1, 2, 3, 4, 5
Inspect a shipment of 50 radios	Number of defective radios	0, 1, 2, $\cdots$, 49, 50
Operate a restaurant for one day	Number of customers	0, 1, 2, 3, $\cdots$
Sell an automobile	Gender of the customer	0 if male; 1 if female

continuous random variables. For example, consider an experiment of monitoring incoming telephone calls to the claims office of a major insurance company. Suppose the random variable of interest is x = the time between consecutive incoming calls in minutes. This random variable may assume any value in the interval $x \geq 0$. Actually, an infinite number of values are possible for x, including values such as 1.26 minutes, 2.751 minutes, 4.3333 minutes, and so on. As another example, consider a 90-mile section of interstate highway I-75 north of Atlanta, Georgia. For an emergency ambulance service located in Atlanta, we might define the random variable as x = number of miles to the location of the next traffic accident along this section of I-75. In this case, x would be a continuous random variable assuming any value in the interval $0 \leq x \leq 90$. Additional examples of continuous random variables are listed in Table 5.2. Note that each example describes a random variable that may assume any value in an interval of values. Continuous random variables and their probability distributions will be the topic of Chapter 6.

TABLE 5.2 EXAMPLES OF CONTINUOUS RANDOM VARIABLES

Experiment	Random Variable (x)	Possible Values for the Random Variable
Operate a bank	Time between customer arrivals in minutes	$x \geq 0$
Fill a soft drink can (max = 12.1 ounces)	Number of ounces	$0 \leq x \leq 12.1$
Construct a new library	Percentage of project complete after six months	$0 \leq x \leq 100$
Test a new chemical process	Temperature when the desired reaction takes place (min 150° F; max 212° F)	$150 \leq x \leq 212$

NOTES AND COMMENTS

One way to determine whether a random variable is discrete or continuous is to think of the values of the random variable as points on a line segment. Choose two points representing values of the random variable. If the entire line segment between the two points also represents possible values for the random variable, then the random variable is continuous.

EXERCISES

Methods

SELFtest   1. Consider the experiment of tossing a coin twice.
    a. List the experimental outcomes.
    b. Define a random variable that represents the number of heads occurring on the two tosses.
    c. Show what value the random variable would assume for each of the experimental outcomes.
    d. Is this random variable discrete or continuous?

2. Consider the experiment of a worker assembling a product.
    a. Define a random variable that represents the time in minutes required to assemble the product.
    b. What values may the random variable assume?
    c. Is the random variable discrete or continuous?

Applications

SELFtest   3. Three students schedule interviews for summer employment at the Brookwood Institute. In each case, the interview results in either an offer for a position or no offer. Experimental outcomes are defined in terms of the results of the three interviews.
    a. List the experimental outcomes.
    b. Define a random variable that represents the number of offers made. Is the random variable continuous?
    c. Show the value of the random variable for each of the experimental outcomes.

4. Suppose we know home mortgage rates for 12 Florida lending institutions. Assume that the random variable of interest is the number of lending institutions in this group that offers a 30-year fixed rate of 8.5% or less. What values may this random variable assume?

5. To perform a certain type of blood analysis, lab technicians must perform two procedures. The first procedure requires either 1 or 2 separate steps, and the second procedure requires either 1, 2, or 3 steps.
    a. List the experimental outcomes associated with performing the blood analysis.
    b. If the random variable of interest is the total number of steps required to do the complete analysis (both procedures), show what value the random variable will assume for each of the experimental outcomes.

6. Listed is a series of experiments and associated random variables. In each case, identify the values that the random variable can assume and state whether the random variable is discrete or continuous.

Experiment	Random Variable (x)
a. Take a 20-question examination	Number of questions answered correctly
b. Observe cars arriving at a tollbooth for one hour	Number of cars arriving at tollbooth
c. Audit 50 tax returns	Number of returns containing errors
d. Observe an employee's work	Number of nonproductive hours in an eight-hour workday
e. Weigh a shipment of goods	Number of pounds

5.2   DISCRETE PROBABILITY DISTRIBUTIONS

The **probability distribution** for a random variable describes how probabilities are distributed over the values of the random variable. For a discrete random variable x, the probability distribution is defined by a **probability function,** denoted by $f(x)$. The probability function provides the probability for each value of the random variable.

As an illustration of a discrete random variable and its probability distribution, consider the sales of automobiles at DiCarlo Motors in Saratoga, New York. Over the past 300 days of operation, sales data show 54 days with no automobiles sold, 117 days with one automobile sold, 72 days with two automobiles sold, 42 days with three automobiles sold, 12 days with four automobiles sold, and 3 days with five automobiles sold. Suppose we consider the experiment of selecting a day of operation at DiCarlo Motors and define the random variable of interest as $x = $ the number of automobiles sold during a day. From historical data, we know x is a discrete random variable that can assume the values 0, 1, 2, 3, 4, or 5. In probability function notation, $f(0)$ provides the probability of zero automobiles sold, $f(1)$ provides the probability of one automobile sold, and so on. Because historical data show 54 of 300 days with zero automobiles sold, we assign the value $54/300 = .18$ to $f(0)$, indicating that the probability of zero automobiles being sold during a day is .18. Similarly, because 117 of 300 days had one automobile sold, we assign the value $117/300 = .39$ to $f(1)$, indicating that the probability of exactly one automobile being sold during a day is .39. Continuing in this way for the other values of the random variable, we compute the values for $f(2)$, $f(3)$, $f(4)$, and $f(5)$ as shown in Table 5.3, the probability distribution for the number of automobiles sold during a day at DiCarlo Motors.

A primary advantage of defining a random variable and its probability distribution is that once the probability distribution is known, it is relatively easy to determine the probability of a variety of events that may be of interest to a decision maker. For example, using the probability distribution for DiCarlo Motors as shown in Table 5.3, we see that the most probable number of automobiles sold during a day is one with a probability of $f(1) = .39$. In addition, there is an $f(3) + f(4) + f(5) = .14 + .04 + .01 = .19$ probability of selling three or more automobiles during a day. These probabilities, plus others the decision maker may ask about, provide information that can help the decision maker understand the process of selling automobiles at DiCarlo Motors.

TABLE 5.3   PROBABILITY DISTRIBUTION FOR THE NUMBER OF AUTOMOBILES SOLD DURING A DAY AT DICARLO MOTORS

x	$f(x)$
0	.18
1	.39
2	.24
3	.14
4	.04
5	.01
Total	1.00

In the development of a probability function for any discrete random variable, the following two conditions must be satisfied.

These conditions are the analogs to the two basic requirements for assigning probabilities to experimental outcomes presented in Chapter 4.

Required Conditions for a Discrete Probability Function

$$f(x) \geq 0 \qquad\qquad (5.1)$$

$$\Sigma f(x) = 1 \qquad\qquad (5.2)$$

Table 5.3 shows that the probabilities for the random variable x satisfy equation (5.1); $f(x)$ is greater than or equal to 0 for all values of x. In addition, because the probabilities sum to 1, equation (5.2) is satisfied. Thus, the DiCarlo Motors probability function is a valid discrete probability function.

We can also present probability distributions graphically. In Figure 5.1 the values of the random variable x for DiCarlo Motors are shown on the horizontal axis and the probability associated with these values is shown on the vertical axis.

In addition to tables and graphs, a formula that gives the probability function, $f(x)$, for every value of x is often used to describe probability distributions. The simplest example of a discrete probability distribution given by a formula is the **discrete uniform probability distribution.** Its probability function is given.

Discrete Uniform Probability Function

$$f(x) = 1/n \qquad\qquad (5.3)$$

where

$n =$ the number of values the random variable may assume

For example, suppose that for the experiment of rolling a die we define the random variable x to be the number of dots on the upward face. There are $n = 6$ possible values for the random variable; $x = 1, 2, 3, 4, 5, 6$. Thus, the probability function for this random variable is

$$f(x) = 1/6 \qquad x = 1, 2, 3, 4, 5, 6$$

The possible values of the random variable and the associated probabilities are shown.

x	$f(x)$
1	1/6
2	1/6
3	1/6
4	1/6
5	1/6
6	1/6

FIGURE 5.1   GRAPHICAL REPRESENTATION OF THE PROBABILITY DISTRIBUTION
FOR THE NUMBER OF AUTOMOBILES SOLD DURING A DAY AT
DICARLO MOTORS

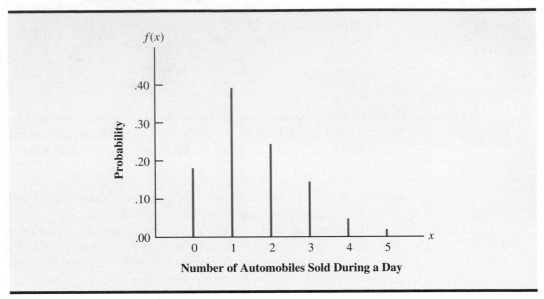

Number of Automobiles Sold During a Day

Note that the values of the random variable are equally likely.

As another example, consider the random variable x with the following discrete probability distribution.

x	$f(x)$
1	1/10
2	2/10
3	3/10
4	4/10

This probability distribution can be defined by the formula

$$f(x) = \frac{x}{10} \qquad \text{for } x = 1, 2, 3, \text{ or } 4$$

Evaluating $f(x)$ for a given value of the random variable will provide the associated probability. For example, using the preceding probability function, we see that $f(2) = 2/10$ provides the probability that the random variable assumes a value of 2.

The more widely used discrete probability distributions generally are specified by formulas. Three important cases are the binomial, Poisson, and hypergeometric probability distributions; they are discussed later in the chapter.

EXERCISES

Methods

SELFtest   **7.** The probability distribution of the random variable x is shown as follows.

x	$f(x)$
20	.20
25	.15
30	.25
35	.40

    a. Is this a valid probability distribution?
    b. What is the probability that $x = 30$?
    c. What is the probability that x is less than or equal to 25?
    d. What is the probability that x is greater than 30?

Applications

SELFtest   **8.** The following data were collected by counting the number of operating rooms in use at Tampa General Hospital over a 20-day period: On 3 of the days only one operating room was used, on 5 of the days two were used, on 8 of the days three were used, and on 4 days all four of the hospital's operating rooms were used.
    a. Use the relative frequency approach to construct a probability distribution for the number of operating rooms in use on any given day.
    b. Draw a graph of the probability distribution.
    c. Show that your probability distribution satisfies the required conditions for a valid discrete probability distribution.

  9. Nationally, 38% of fourth-graders cannot read an age-appropriate book. The following data show the number of children, by age, identified as learning disabled under special education. Most of these children have reading problems that should be identified and corrected before third grade. Current federal law prohibits most children from receiving extra help from special education programs until they fall behind by approximately two years' worth of learning, and that typically means third grade or later (*USA Today*, September 6, 2001).

Age	Number of Children
6	37,369
7	87,436
8	160,840
9	239,719
10	286,719
11	306,533
12	310,787
13	302,604
14	289,168

TABLE 5.4   PERCENT FREQUENCY DISTRIBUTION OF JOB SATISFACTION SCORES
FOR INFORMATION SYSTEMS EXECUTIVES AND MIDDLE MANAGERS

Job Satisfaction Score	IS Senior Executives (%)	IS Middle Managers (%)
1	5	4
2	9	10
3	3	12
4	42	46
5	41	28

Suppose that we want to select a sample of children identified as learning disabled under special education for a special program designed to improve reading ability. Let x be a random variable indicating the age of one randomly selected child.

a.   Use the data to develop a probability distribution for x. Specify the values for the random variable and the corresponding values for the probability function $f(x)$.

b.   Draw a graph of the probability distribution.

c.   Show that the probability distribution satisfies equations (5.1) and (5.2).

10.   Table 5.4 shows the percent frequency distributions of job satisfaction scores for a sample of information systems (IS) senior executives and IS middle managers (*Computerworld*, May 26, 1997). The scores range from a low of 1 (very dissatisfied) to a high of 5 (very satisfied).

a.   Develop a probability distribution for the job satisfaction score of a senior executive.

b.   Develop a probability distribution for the job satisfaction score of a middle manager.

c.   What is the probability a senior executive will report a job satisfaction score of 4 or 5?

d.   What is the probability a middle manager is very satisfied?

e.   Compare the overall job satisfaction of senior executives and middle managers.

11.   A technician services mailing machines at companies in the Phoenix area. Depending on the type of malfunction, the service call can take one, two, three, or four hours. The different types of malfunctions occur at about the same frequency.

a.   Develop a probability distribution for the duration of a service call.

b.   Draw a graph of the probability distribution.

c.   Show that your probability distribution satisfies the conditions required for a discrete probability function.

d.   What is the probability a service call will take three hours?

e.   A service call has just come in, but the type of malfunction is unknown. It is 3:00 P.M. and service technicians usually get off at 5:00 P.M. What is the probability the service technician will have to work overtime to fix the machine today?

12.   The director of admissions at Lakeville Community College subjectively assessed a probability distribution for x, the number of entering students, as follows.

x	$f(x)$
1000	.15
1100	.20
1200	.30
1300	.25
1400	.10

a. Is this probability distribution valid?
b. What is the probability of 1200 or fewer entering students?

13. A psychologist determined that the number of hours required to obtain the trust of a new patient is either one, two, or three. Let x be a random variable indicating the time in hours required to gain the patient's trust. The following probability function has been proposed.

$$f(x) = \frac{x}{6} \qquad \text{for } x = 1, 2, \text{ or } 3$$

a. Is this probability function valid? Explain.
b. What is the probability that it takes exactly two hours to gain the patient's trust?
c. What is the probability that it takes at least two hours to gain the patient's trust?

14. The following table is a partial probability distribution for the MRA Company's projected profits (x = profit in thousands of dollars) for the first year of operation (the negative value denotes a loss).

x	$f(x)$
−100	.10
0	.20
50	.30
100	.25
150	.10
200	

a. What is the proper value for $f(200)$? What is your interpretation of this value?
b. What is the probability that MRA will be profitable?
c. What is the probability that MRA will make at least $100,000?

5.3   EXPECTED VALUE AND VARIANCE

Expected Value

The **expected value,** or mean, of a random variable is a measure of the central location for the random variable. The formula for the expected value of a discrete random variable x follows.

The expected value is a weighted average of the values the random variable may assume. The weights are the probabilities.

Expected Value of a Discrete Random Variable

$$E(x) = \mu = \Sigma x f(x) \tag{5.4}$$

Both the notations $E(x)$ and μ are used to denote the expected value of a random variable.

Equation (5.4) shows that to compute the expected value of a discrete random variable, we must multiply each value of the random variable by the corresponding probability $f(x)$ and then add the resulting products. Using the DiCarlo Motors automobile sales example from Section 5.2, we show the calculation of the expected value for the number of automobiles sold during a day in Table 5.5. The sum of the entries in the $xf(x)$ column shows

TABLE 5.5   CALCULATION OF THE EXPECTED VALUE FOR THE NUMBER
OF AUTOMOBILES SOLD DURING A DAY AT DICARLO MOTORS

x	$f(x)$	$xf(x)$
0	.18	$0(.18) =$ .00
1	.39	$1(.39) =$ .39
2	.24	$2(.24) =$ .48
3	.14	$3(.14) =$ .42
4	.04	$4(.04) =$ .16
5	.01	$5(.01) =$ .05
		1.50

$$E(x) = \mu = \Sigma xf(x)$$

The expected value does not have to be a value the random variable can assume.

that the expected value is 1.50 automobiles per day. We therefore know that although sales of 0, 1, 2, 3, 4, or 5 automobiles are possible on any one day, over time DiCarlo can antici-pate selling an average of 1.50 automobiles per day. Assuming 30 days of operation during a month, we can use the expected value of 1.50 to anticipate average monthly sales of $30(1.50) = 45$ automobiles.

Variance

Even though the expected value provides the mean value for the random variable, we often need a measure of variability, or dispersion. Just as we used the variance in Chapter 3 to summarize the variability in data, we now use **variance** to summarize the variability in the values of a random variable. The formula for the variance of a discrete random variable follows.

The variance is a weighted average of the squared deviations of a random variable from its mean. The weights are the probabilities.

Variance of a Discrete Random Variable

$$\text{Var}(x) = \sigma^2 = \Sigma(x - \mu)^2 f(x) \tag{5.5}$$

As equation (5.5) shows, an essential part of the variance formula is the deviation, $x - \mu$, which measures how far a particular value of the random variable is from the expected value, or mean, μ. In computing the variance of a random variable, the deviations are squared and then weighted by the corresponding value of the probability function. The sum of these weighted squared deviations for all values of the random variable is referred to as the *variance*. The notations $\text{Var}(x)$ and σ^2 are both used to denote the variance of a random variable.

The calculation of the variance for the probability distribution of the number of auto-mobiles sold during a day at DiCarlo Motors is summarized in Table 5.6. We see that the variance is 1.25. The **standard deviation,** σ, is defined as the positive square root of the variance. Thus, the standard deviation for the number of automobiles sold during a day is

$$\sigma = \sqrt{1.25} = 1.118$$

TABLE 5.6 CALCULATION OF THE VARIANCE FOR THE NUMBER OF AUTOMOBILES SOLD DURING A DAY AT DICARLO MOTORS

x	$x - \mu$	$(x - \mu)^2$	$f(x)$	$(x - \mu)^2 f(x)$
0	$0 - 1.50 = -1.50$	2.25	.18	$2.25(.18) = $ .4050
1	$1 - 1.50 = -.50$	.25	.39	$.25(.39) = $ .0975
2	$2 - 1.50 = .50$	.25	.24	$.25(.24) = $ .0600
3	$3 - 1.50 = 1.50$	2.25	.14	$2.25(.14) = $ .3150
4	$4 - 1.50 = 2.50$	6.25	.04	$6.25(.04) = $ .2500
5	$5 - 1.50 = 3.50$	12.25	.01	$12.25(.01) = $ .1225
				1.2500

$$\sigma^2 = \Sigma(x - \mu)^2 f(x)$$

The standard deviation is measured in the same units as the random variable ($\sigma = 1.118$ automobiles) and therefore is often preferred in describing the variability of a random variable. The variance σ^2 is measured in squared units and is thus more difficult to interpret.

EXERCISES

Methods

15. The following table provides a probability distribution for the random variable x.

x	$f(x)$
3	.25
6	.50
9	.25

    a. Compute $E(x)$, the expected value of x.
    b. Compute σ^2, the variance of x.
    c. Compute σ, the standard deviation of x.

SELFtest   **16.** The following table provides a probability distribution for the random variable y.

y	$f(y)$
2	.20
4	.30
7	.40
8	.10

    a. Compute $E(y)$.
    b. Compute Var(y) and σ.

Applications

17. A volunteer ambulance service handles zero to five service calls on any given day. The probability distribution for the number of service calls follows.

Number of Service Calls	Probability
0	.10
1	.15
2	.30
3	.20
4	.15
5	.10

    a. What is the expected number of service calls?

    b. What is the variance in the number of service calls? What is the standard deviation?

SELFtest   18. *The Statistical Abstract of the United States,* 1997, shows that the average number of television sets per household is 2.3. Assume that the probability distribution for the number of television sets per household in New Orleans is as shown in the following table.

x	$f(x)$
0	.01
1	.23
2	.41
3	.20
4	.10
5	.05

    a. Compute the expected value of the number of television sets per household and compare it with the average reported in the *Statistical Abstract.*

    b. What are the variance and standard deviation of the number of television sets per household?

19. The actual shooting records of four basketball teams showed the probability of making a 2-point basket was .50 and the probability of making a 3-point basket was .39.

    a. What is the expected value of a 2-point shot for these teams?

    b. What is the expected value of a 3-point shot for these teams?

    c. If the probability of making a 2-point basket is greater than the probability of making a 3-point basket, why do coaches allow some players to shoot the 3-point shot if they have the opportunity? Use expected value to explain your answer.

20. The probability distribution for damage claims paid by the Newton Automobile Insurance Company on collision insurance follows.

Payment ($)	Probability
0	.90
400	.04
1000	.03
2000	.01
4000	.01
6000	.01

a. Use the expected collision payment to determine the collision insurance premium that would enable the company to break even.

b. The insurance company charges an annual rate of $260 for the collision coverage. What is the expected value of the collision policy for a policyholder? (Hint: It is the expected payments from the company minus the cost of coverage.) Why does the policyholder purchase a collision policy with this expected value?

21. The following probability distributions of job satisfaction scores for a sample of information systems (IS) senior executives and IS middle managers range from a low of 1 (very dissatisfied) to a high of 5 (very satisfied) (*Computerworld*, May 26, 1997).

	Probability	
Job Satisfaction Score	IS Senior Executives	IS Middle Managers
1	.05	.04
2	.09	.10
3	.03	.12
4	.42	.46
5	.41	.28

a. What is the expected value of the job satisfaction score for senior executives?

b. What is the expected value of the job satisfaction score for middle managers?

c. Compute the variance of job satisfaction scores for executives and middle managers.

d. Compute the standard deviation of job satisfaction scores for both probability distributions.

e. Compare the overall job satisfaction of senior executives and middle managers.

22. The demand for a product of Carolina Industries varies greatly from month to month. The probability distribution in the following table, based on the past two years of data, shows the company's monthly demand.

Unit Demand	Probability
300	.20
400	.30
500	.35
600	.15

a. If the company bases monthly orders on the expected value of the monthly demand, what should Carolina's monthly order quantity be for this product?

b. Assume that each unit demanded generates $70 in revenue and that each unit ordered costs $50. How much will the company gain or lose in a month if it places an order based on your answer to part (a) and the actual demand for the item is 300 units?

23. According to a survey, 95% of subscribers to *The Wall Street Journal Interactive Edition* have a computer at home. For those households, the probability distributions for the number of laptop and desktop computers are given (*The Wall Street Journal Interactive Edition Subscriber Study*, 1999).

	Probability	
Number of Computers	Laptop	Desktop
0	.47	.06
1	.45	.56
2	.06	.28
3	.02	.10

a. What is the expected value of the number of computers per household for each type of computer?
b. What is the variance of the number of computers per household for each type of computer?
c. Make some comparisons between the number of laptops and the number of desktops owned by the *Journal's* subscribers.

24. The J. R. Ryland Computer Company is considering a plant expansion that will enable the company to begin production of a new computer product. The company's president must determine whether to make the expansion a medium- or large-scale project. An uncertainty is the demand for the new product, which for planning purposes may be low demand, medium demand, or high demand. The probability estimates for demand are .20, .50, and .30, respectively. Letting x and y indicate the annual profit in thousands of dollars, the firm's planners have developed the following profit forecasts for the medium- and large-scale expansion projects.

		Medium-Scale Expansion Profit		Large-Scale Expansion Profit	
		x	$f(x)$	y	$f(y)$
	Low	50	.20	0	.20
Demand	Medium	150	.50	100	.50
	High	200	.30	300	.30

a. Compute the expected value for the profit associated with the two expansion alternatives. Which decision is preferred for the objective of maximizing the expected profit?
b. Compute the variance for the profit associated with the two expansion alternatives. Which decision is preferred for the objective of minimizing the risk or uncertainty?

5.4   BINOMIAL PROBABILITY DISTRIBUTION

The binomial probability distribution is a discrete probability distribution that has many applications. It is associated with a multiple-step experiment that we call the binomial experiment.

A Binomial Experiment

A **binomial experiment** has the following four properties.

> **Properties of a Binomial Experiment**
> 1. The experiment consists of a sequence of n identical trials.
> 2. Two outcomes are possible on each trial. We refer to one outcome as a *success* and the other outcome as a *failure*.
> 3. The probability of a success, denoted by p, does not change from trial to trial. Consequently, the probability of a failure, denoted by $1 - p$, does not change from trial to trial.
> 4. The trials are independent.

Jakob Bernoulli (1654–1705), the first of the Bernoulli family of Swiss mathematicians, published a treatise on probability that contained the theory of permutations and combinations, as well as the Binomial Theorem.

If properties 2, 3, and 4 are present, we say the trials are generated by a Bernoulli process. If, in addition, property 1 is present, we say we have a *binomial experiment*. Figure 5.2 depicts one possible sequence of outcomes of a binomial experiment involving eight trials. This case presents the possibility of five successes and three failures.

In a binomial experiment, our interest is in the *number of successes occurring in the n trials*. If we let x denote the number of successes occurring in the n trials, we see that x can assume the values of $0, 1, 2, 3, \ldots, n$. Because the number of values is finite, x is a *discrete* random variable. The probability distribution associated with this random variable is called the **binomial probability distribution.** For example, consider the experiment of tossing a coin five times and on each toss observing whether the coin lands with a head or a tail on its upward face. Suppose we are interested in counting the number of heads appearing over the five tosses. Does this experiment have the properties of a binomial experiment? What is the random variable of interest? Note that:

1. The experiment consists of five identical trials; each trial involves the tossing of one coin.
2. Two outcomes are possible for each trial: a head or a tail. We can designate head a success and tail a failure.
3. The probability of a head and the probability of a tail are the same for each trial, with $p = .5$ and $1 - p = .5$.
4. The trials or tosses are independent because the outcome on any one trial is not affected by what happens on other trials or tosses.

Thus, the properties of a binomial experiment are satisfied. The random variable of interest is $x =$ the number of heads appearing in the five trials. In this case, x can assume the values of 0, 1, 2, 3, 4, or 5.

As another example, consider an insurance salesperson who visits 10 randomly selected families. The outcome associated with each visit is classified as a success if the family purchases an insurance policy and a failure if the family does not. From past experience, the salesperson knows the probability that a randomly selected family will purchase an insurance policy is .10. Checking the properties of a binomial experiment, we observe that:

1. The experiment consists of 10 identical trials; each trial involves contacting one family.
2. Two outcomes are possible on each trial: the family purchases a policy (success) or the family does not purchase a policy (failure).
3. The probabilities of a purchase and a nonpurchase are assumed to be the same for each sales call, with $p = .10$ and $1 - p = .90$.
4. The trials are independent because the families are randomly selected.

FIGURE 5.2   DIAGRAM OF AN EIGHT-TRIAL BINOMIAL EXPERIMENT

Because the four assumptions are satisfied, this example is a binomial experiment. The random variable of interest is the number of sales obtained in contacting the 10 families. In this case, x can assume the values of 0, 1, 2, 3, 4, 5, 6, 7, 8, 9, and 10.

Property 3 of the binomial experiment is called the *stationarity assumption* and is sometimes confused with property 4, independence of trials. To see how they differ, consider again the case of the salesperson calling on families to sell insurance policies. If, as the day wore on, the salesperson got tired and lost enthusiasm, the probability of success (selling a policy) might drop to .05, for example, by the tenth call. In such a case, property 3 (stationarity) would not be satisfied, and we would not have a binomial experiment. Even if property 4 held—that is, the purchase decisions of each family were made independently—it would not be a binomial experiment if property 3 was not satisfied.

In applications involving binomial experiments, a special mathematical formula, called the **binomial probability function,** can be used to compute the probability of x successes in the n trials. Using probability concepts introduced in Chapter 4, we will show in the context of an illustrative problem how the formula can be developed.

Martin Clothing Store Problem

Let us consider the purchase decisions of the next three customers who enter the Martin Clothing Store. On the basis of past experience, the store manager estimates the probability that any one customer will make a purchase is .30. What is the probability that two of the next three customers will make a purchase?

Using a tree diagram (Figure 5.3), we can see that the experiment of observing the three customers each making a purchase decision has eight possible outcomes. Using S to denote success (a purchase) and F to denote failure (no purchase), we are interested in experimental outcomes involving two successes in the three trials (purchase decisions). Next, let us verify that the experiment involving the sequence of three purchase decisions can be viewed as a binomial experiment. Checking the four requirements for a binomial experiment, we note that:

1. The experiment can be described as a sequence of three identical trials, one trial for each of the three customers who will enter the store.
2. Two outcomes—the customer makes a purchase (success) or the customer does not make a purchase (failure)—are possible for each trial.
3. The probability that the customer will make a purchase (.30) or will not make a purchase (.70) is assumed to be the same for all customers.
4. The purchase decision of each customer is independent of the decisions of the other customers.

FIGURE 5.3   TREE DIAGRAM FOR THE MARTIN CLOTHING STORE PROBLEM

First Customer	Second Customer	Third Customer	Experimental Outcome	Value of x
		S	(S, S, S)	3
	S	F	(S, S, F)	2
S	F	S	(S, F, S)	2
		F	(S, F, F)	1
	S	S	(F, S, S)	2
F		F	(F, S, F)	1
	F	S	(F, F, S)	1
		F	(F, F, F)	0

S = Purchase
F = No purchase
x = Number of customers making a purchase

Hence, the properties of a binomial experiment are present.

The number of experimental outcomes resulting in exactly x successes in n trials can be computed from the following formula.*

Number of Experimental Outcomes Providing Exactly x Successes in n Trials

$$\binom{n}{x} = \frac{n!}{x!(n-x)!} \tag{5.6}$$

where

$$n! = n(n-1)(n-2)\cdots(2)(1)$$

and

$$0! = 1$$

---

*This formula, introduced in Chapter 4, determines the number of combinations of n objects selected x at a time. For the binomial experiment, this combinatorial formula provides the number of experimental outcomes (sequences of n trials) resulting in x successes.

Now let us return to the Martin Clothing Store experiment involving three customer purchase decisions. Equation (5.6) can be used to determine the number of experimental outcomes involving two purchases; that is, the number of ways of obtaining $x = 2$ successes in the $n = 3$ trials. From equation (5.6) we have

$$\binom{n}{x} = \binom{3}{2} = \frac{3!}{2!(3-2)!} = \frac{(3)(2)(1)}{(2)(1)(1)} = \frac{6}{2} = 3$$

Equation (5.6) shows that three of the experimental outcomes yield two successes. From Figure 5.3 we see these three outcomes are denoted by (S, S, F), (S, F, S), (F, S, S).

Using equation (5.6) to determine how many experimental outcomes have three successes (purchases) in the three trials, we obtain

$$\binom{n}{x} = \binom{3}{3} = \frac{3!}{3!(3-3)!} = \frac{3!}{3!0!} = \frac{(3)(2)(1)}{3(2)(1)(1)} = \frac{6}{6} = 1$$

From Figure 5.3 we see that the one experimental outcome with three successes is identified by (S, S, S).

We know that equation (5.6) can be used to determine the number of experimental outcomes that result in x successes. But, if we are to determine the probability of x successes in n trials, we must also know the probability associated with each of these experimental outcomes. Because the trials of a binomial experiment are independent, we can simply multiply the probabilities associated with each trial outcome to find the probability of a particular sequence of successes and failures.

The probability of purchases by the first two customers and no purchase by the third customer, denoted (S, S, F), is given by

$$pp(1 - p)$$

With a .30 probability of a purchase on any one trial, the probability of a purchase on the first two trials and no purchase on the third is given by

$$(.30)(.30)(.70) = (.30)^2(.70) = .063$$

Two other sequences of outcomes result in two successes and one failure. The probabilities for all three sequences involving two successes follow.

Trial Outcomes				Probability of
1st Customer	**2nd Customer**	**3rd Customer**	**Experimental Outcome**	**Experimental Outcome**
Purchase	Purchase	No purchase	(S, S, F)	$pp(1-p) = p^2(1-p)$ $= (.30)^2(.70) = .063$
Purchase	No purchase	Purchase	(S, F, S)	$p(1-p)p = p^2(1-p)$ $= (.30)^2(.70) = .063$
No purchase	Purchase	Purchase	(F, S, S)	$(1-p)pp = p^2(1-p)$ $= (.30)^2(.70) = .063$

Observe that all three experimental outcomes with two successes have exactly the same probability This observation holds in general. In any binomial experiment, all sequences of trial outcomes yielding x successes in n trials have the *same probability* of occurrence. The probability of each sequence of trials yielding x successes in n trials follows.

$$\text{Probability of a Particular}$$
$$\text{Sequence of Trial Outcomes} \qquad\qquad\qquad\qquad (5.7)$$
$$\text{with } x \text{ Successes in } n \text{ Trials } = p^x(1 - p)^{(n-x)}$$

For the Martin Clothing Store, this formula shows that any experimental outcome with two successes has a probability of $p^2(1 - p)^{(3-2)} = p^2(1 - p)^1 = (.30)^2(.70)^1 = .063$.

Because equation (5.6) shows the number of outcomes in a binomial experiment with x successes and equation (5.7) gives the probability for each sequence involving x successes, we combine equations (5.6) and (5.7) to obtain the following binomial probability function.

Binomial Probability Function

$$f(x) = \binom{n}{x} p^x (1 - p)^{(n-x)} \qquad\qquad\qquad (5.8)$$

where

$$f(x) = \text{the probability of } x \text{ successes in } n \text{ trials}$$
$$n = \text{the number of trials}$$
$$\binom{n}{x} = \frac{n!}{x!(n - x)!}$$
$$p = \text{the probability of a success on any one trial}$$
$$(1 - p) = \text{the probability of a failure on any one trial}$$

In the Martin Clothing Store example, let us compute the probability that no customer makes a purchase, exactly one customer makes a purchase, exactly two customers make a purchase, and all three customers make a purchase. The calculations are summarized in Table 5.7, which gives the probability distribution of the number of customers making a purchase. Figure 5.4 is a graph of this probability distribution.

The binomial probability function can be applied to *any* binomial experiment. If we are satisfied that a situation has the properties of a binomial experiment and if we know the values of n, p, and $(1 - p)$, we can use equation (5.8) to compute the probability of x successes in the n trials.

If we consider variations of the Martin experiment, such as 10 customers rather than three entering the store, the binomial probability function given by equation (5.8) is still applicable. Suppose we have a binomial experiment with $n = 10$, $x = 4$, and $p = .30$. The probability of making exactly four sales to 10 potential customers entering the store is

$$f(4) = \frac{10!}{4!6!}(.30)^4(.70)^6 = .2001$$

TABLE 5.7   PROBABILITY DISTRIBUTION FOR THE NUMBER OF CUSTOMERS MAKING A PURCHASE

x	$f(x)$
0	$\dfrac{3!}{0!3!}(.30)^0(.70)^3 = \ .343$
1	$\dfrac{3!}{1!2!}(.30)^1(.70)^2 = \ .441$
2	$\dfrac{3!}{2!1!}(.30)^2(.70)^1 = \ .189$
3	$\dfrac{3!}{3!0!}(.30)^3(.70)^0 = \ \underline{.027}$
	1.000

Using Tables of Binomial Probabilities

Tables have been developed that give the probability of x successes in n trials for a binomial experiment. The tables are generally easy to use and quicker than (5.8). Table 5 of Appendix B provides such a table of binomial probabilities. A portion of this table appears in Table 5.8. To use this table, we must specify the values of n, p, and x for the binomial experiment of interest. In the example at the top of Table 5.8, we see that the probability of $x = 3$ successes in a binomial experiment with $n = 10$ and $p = .40$ is .2150. You can use equation (5.8) to verify that you would obtain the same answer if you used the binomial probability function directly.

FIGURE 5.4   GRAPHICAL REPRESENTATION OF THE PROBABILITY DISTRIBUTION FOR THE NUMBER OF CUSTOMERS MAKING A PURCHASE

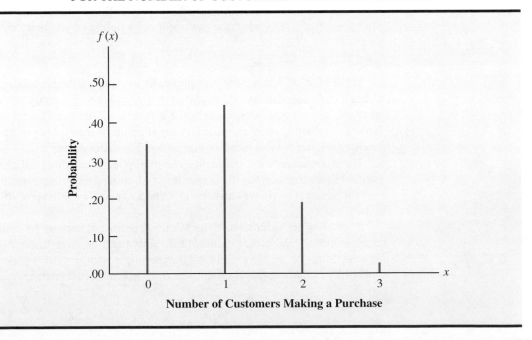

TABLE 5.8   SELECTED VALUES FROM THE BINOMIAL PROBABILITY TABLE
EXAMPLE: $n = 10$, $x = 3$, $p = .40$; $f(3) = .2150$

						p					
n	x	.05	.10	.15	.20	.25	.30	.35	.40	.45	.50
9	0	.6302	.3874	.2316	.1342	.0751	.0404	.0207	.0101	.0046	.0020
	1	.2985	.3874	.3679	.3020	.2253	.1556	.1004	.0605	.0339	.0176
	2	.0629	.1722	.2597	.3020	.3003	.2668	.2162	.1612	.1110	.0703
	3	.0077	.0446	.1069	.1762	.2336	.2668	.2716	.2508	.2119	.1641
	4	.0006	.0074	.0283	.0661	.1168	.1715	.2194	.2508	.2600	.2461
	5	.0000	.0008	.0050	.0165	.0389	.0735	.1181	.1672	.2128	.2461
	6	.0000	.0001	.0006	.0028	.0087	.0210	.0424	.0743	.1160	.1641
	7	.0000	.0000	.0000	.0003	.0012	.0039	.0098	.0212	.0407	.0703
	8	.0000	.0000	.0000	.0000	.0001	.0004	.0013	.0035	.0083	.0176
	9	.0000	.0000	.0000	.0000	.0000	.0000	.0001	.0003	.0008	.0020
10	0	.5987	.3487	.1969	.1074	.0563	.0282	.0135	.0060	.0025	.0010
	1	.3151	.3874	.3474	.2684	.1877	.1211	.0725	.0403	.0207	.0098
	2	.0746	.1937	.2759	.3020	.2816	.2335	.1757	.1209	.0763	.0439
	3	.0105	.0574	.1298	.2013	.2503	.2668	.2522	**.2150**	.1665	.1172
	4	.0010	.0112	.0401	.0881	.1460	.2001	.2377	.2508	.2384	.2051
	5	.0001	.0015	.0085	.0264	.0584	.1029	.1536	.2007	.2340	.2461
	6	.0000	.0001	.0012	.0055	.0162	.0368	.0689	.1115	.1596	.2051
	7	.0000	.0000	.0001	.0008	.0031	.0090	.0212	.0425	.0746	.1172
	8	.0000	.0000	.0000	.0001	.0004	.0014	.0043	.0106	.0229	.0439
	9	.0000	.0000	.0000	.0000	.0000	.0001	.0005	.0016	.0042	.0098
	10	.0000	.0000	.0000	.0000	.0000	.0000	.0000	.0001	.0003	.0010

With modern calculators, these tables are almost unnecessary. It is easy to evaluate (5.8) directly.

Now let us use Table 5.8 to verify the probability of four successes in 10 trials for the Martin Clothing Store problem. Note that the value of $f(4) = .2001$ can be read directly from the table of binomial probabilities, with $n = 10$, $x = 4$, and $p = .30$.

Even though the tables of binomial probabilities are relatively easy to use, it is impossible to have tables that show all possible values of n and p that might be encountered in a binomial experiment. However, with today's calculators, using (5.8) to calculate the desired probability is not difficult, especially if the number of trials is not large. In the exercises, you should practice using (5.8) to compute the binomial probabilities unless the problem specifically requests that you use the binomial probability table.

Statistical software packages such as Minitab and spreadsheet packages such as Excel also provide a capability for computing binomial probabilities. Consider the Martin Clothing Store example with $n = 10$ and $p = .30$. Figure 5.5 shows the binomial probabilities generated by Minitab for all possible values of x. Note that these values are the same as those found in the $p = .30$ column of Table 5.8. Appendix 5.1 gives the step-by-step procedure for using Minitab to generate the output in Figure 5.5. Appendix 5.2 describes how Excel can be used to compute binomial probabilities.

Expected Value and Variance for the Binomial Probability Distribution

In Section 5.3 we provided formulas for computing the expected value and variance of a discrete random variable. In the special case where the random variable has a binomial probability distribution with a known number of trials n and a known probability of success

FIGURE 5.5 MINITAB OUTPUT SHOWING BINOMIAL PROBABILITIES
FOR THE MARTIN CLOTHING STORE PROBLEM

x	P(X = x)
0.00	0.0282
1.00	0.1211
2.00	0.2335
3.00	0.2668
4.00	0.2001
5.00	0.1029
6.00	0.0368
7.00	0.0090
8.00	0.0014
9.00	0.0001
10.00	0.0000

p, the general formulas for the expected value and variance can be simplified. The results follow.

Expected Value and Variance for the Binomial Probability Distribution

$$E(x) = \mu = np \qquad (5.9)$$
$$\text{Var}(x) = \sigma^2 = np(1 - p) \qquad (5.10)$$

For the Martin Clothing Store problem with three customers, we can use equation (5.9) to compute the expected number of customers who will make a purchase.

$$E(x) = np = 3(.30) = .9$$

Suppose that for the next month the Martin Clothing Store forecasts 1000 customers will enter the store. What is the expected number of customers who will make a purchase? The answer is $\mu = np = (1000)(.3) = 300$. Thus, to increase the expected number of sales, Martin's must induce more customers to enter the store and/or somehow increase the probability that any individual customer will make a purchase after entering.

For the Martin Clothing Store problem with three customers, we see that the variance and standard deviation for the number of customers making a purchase are

$$\sigma^2 = np(1 - p) = 3(.3)(.7) = .63$$
$$\sigma = \sqrt{.63} = .79$$

In quality control, the np chart and lot acceptance sampling are excellent examples of the use of the binomial distribution.

For the next 1000 customers entering the store, the variance and standard deviation for the number of customers who will make a purchase are

$$\sigma^2 = np(1 - p) = 1000(.3)(.7) = 210$$
$$\sigma = \sqrt{210} = 14.49$$

NOTES AND COMMENTS

1. The binomial tables in Appendix B show values of p only up to and including $p = .50$. It would appear that such tables cannot be used when the probability of success exceeds $p = .50$. However, they can be used by noting that the probability of $n - x$ failures is also the probability of x successes. When the probability of success is greater than $p = .50$, one can compute the probability of $n - x$ failures instead. The probability of failure, $1 - p$, will be less than .50 when $p > .50$.

2. Some sources present binomial tables in a cumulative form. In using such tables, one must subtract to find the probability of x successes in n trials. For example, $f(2) = P(x \leq 2) - P(x \leq 1)$. Our tables provide these probabilities directly. To compute cumulative probabilities using our tables, one simply sums the individual probabilities. For example, to compute $P(x \leq 2)$ using our tables, we sum $f(0) + f(1) + f(2)$.

EXERCISES

Methods

SELFtest **25.** Consider a binomial experiment with two trials and $p = .4$.

    a. Draw a tree diagram showing it as a two-trial experiment (see Figure 5.3).
    b. Compute the probability of one success, $f(1)$.
    c. Compute $f(0)$.
    d. Compute $f(2)$.
    e. Compute the probability of at least one success.
    f. Compute the expected value, variance, and standard deviation.

26. Consider a binomial experiment with $n = 10$ and $p = .10$.

    a. Compute $f(0)$.
    b. Compute $f(2)$.
    c. Compute $P(x \leq 2)$.
    d. Compute $P(x \geq 1)$.
    e. Compute $E(x)$.
    f. Compute Var(x) and σ.

27. Consider a binomial experiment with $n = 20$ and $p = .70$. Use the binomial tables (Table 5 of Appendix B) for the following calculations.

    a. Compute $f(12)$.
    b. Compute $f(16)$.
    c. Compute $P(x \geq 16)$.
    d. Compute $P(x \leq 15)$.
    e. Compute $E(x)$.
    f. Compute Var(x) and σ.

Applications

28. The 1999 Youth and Money Survey, sponsored by the American Savings Education Council, the Employee Benefit Research Institute, and Mathew Greenwald & Associates, talked to 1000 students ages 16–22 about personal finance. The survey found that 33% of the students have their own credit card.

    a. In a sample of six students, what is the probability that two will have their own credit card?
    b. In a sample of six students, what is the probability that at least two will have their own credit card?
    c. In a sample of 10 students, what is the probability that none will have their own credit card?

29. According to a *Business Week*/Harris Poll of 1035 adults, 40% of those surveyed agreed strongly with the proposition that business has too much power over American life (*Business Week,* September 11, 2000). Assume this percentage is representative of the American population and that a sample of 20 individuals has been taken from a cross-section of the American population to learn about the role of business in their lives. What is the probability that at least five of these individuals will feel that business has too much power over American life?

SELFtest

30. When a new machine is functioning properly, only 3% of the items produced are defective. Assume that we will randomly select two parts produced on the machine and that we are interested in the number of defective parts found.
  a. Describe the conditions under which this situation would be a binomial experiment.
  b. Draw a tree diagram similar to Figure 5.3 showing this problem as a two-trial experiment.
  c. How many experimental outcomes result in exactly one defect being found?
  d. Compute the probabilities associated with finding no defects, exactly one defect, and two defects.

31. Five percent of American truck drivers are women (*Statistical Abstract of the United States,* 1997). Suppose 10 truck drivers are selected randomly to be interviewed about quality of work conditions.
  a. Is the selection of the 10 drivers a binomial experiment? Explain.
  b. What is the probability that two of the drivers will be women?
  c. What is the probability that none will be women?
  d. What is the probability that at least one will be a woman?

32. Military radar and missile detection systems are designed to warn a country against enemy attacks. A reliability question is whether a detection system will be able to identify an attack and issue a warning. Assume that a particular detection system has a .90 probability of detecting a missile attack. Use the binomial probability distribution to answer the following questions.
  a. What is the probability that a single detection system will detect an attack?
  b. If two detection systems are installed in the same area and operate independently, what is the probability that at least one of the systems will detect the attack?
  c. If three systems are installed, what is the probability that at least one of the systems will detect the attack?
  d. Would you recommend that multiple detection systems be used? Explain.

33. Fifty percent of Americans think we are in a recession, even though technically we have not had two straight quarters of negative growth (*Business Week,* July 30, 2001). For a sample of 20 Americans, make the following calculations.
  a. Compute the probability that exactly 12 people think we are in a recession.
  b. Compute the probability that no more than five people think we are in a recession.
  c. How many people would you expect to say we are in a recession?
  d. Compute the variance and standard deviation of the number of people who think we are in a recession.

34. Forty percent of business travelers carry either a cell phone or a laptop (*USA Today,* September 12, 2000). For a sample of 15 business travelers, make the following calculations.
  a. Compute the probability three of the travelers have a cell phone or laptop.
  b. Compute the probability that 12 of the travelers have neither a cell phone nor a laptop.
  c. Compute the probability that at least three of the travelers have a cell phone or a laptop.

35. A university found that 20% of its students withdraw without completing the introductory statistics course. Assume that 20 students have registered for the course this quarter.
  a. What is the probability that two or fewer will withdraw?
  b. What is the probability that exactly four will withdraw?

    c.   What is the probability that more than three will withdraw?

    d.   What is the expected number of withdrawals?

36. For the special case of a binomial random variable, we stated that the variance could be computed using the formula $\sigma^2 = np(1 - p)$. For the Martin Clothing Store problem data in Table 5.7, we found $\sigma^2 = np(1 - p) = .63$. Use the general definition of variance for a discrete random variable, equation (5.5), and the data in Table 5.7 to verify that the variance is in fact .63.

37. Twenty-nine percent of lawyers and judges are women (*Statistical Abstract of the United States,* 1997). In a jurisdiction with 30 lawyers and judges, what is the expected number of women? What are the variance and standard deviation?

5.5   POISSON PROBABILITY DISTRIBUTION

The Poisson probability distribution is often used to model arrival rates in waiting line situations.

In this section we consider a discrete random variable that is often useful in estimating the number of occurrences over a specified interval of time or space. For example, the random variable of interest might be the number of arrivals at a car wash in one hour, the number of repairs needed in 10 miles of highway, or the number of leaks in 100 miles of pipeline. If the following two properties are satisfied, the number of occurrences is a random variable described by the **Poisson probability distribution.**

Properties of a Poisson Experiment

1. The probability of an occurrence is the same for any two intervals of equal length.
2. The occurrence or nonoccurrence in any interval is independent of the occurrence or nonoccurrence in any other interval.

The **Poisson probability function** is defined by equation (5.11).

Poisson Probability Function

$$f(x) = \frac{\mu^x e^{-\mu}}{x!}$$

(5.11)

where

$f(x)$ = the probability of x occurrences in an interval

μ = expected value or mean number of occurrences in an interval

e = 2.71828

Siméon Poisson taught mathematics at the Ecole Polytechnique in Paris from 1802 to 1808. In 1837, he published a work entitled, "Researches on the probability of criminal and civil verdicts," which includes a discussion of what later became known as the Poisson distribution.

Before we consider a specific example to see how the Poisson distribution can be applied, note that the number of occurrences, x, has no upper limit. It is a discrete random variable that may assume an infinite sequence of values ($x = 0, 1, 2, \ldots$).

An Example Involving Time Intervals

Bell Labs uses the Poisson distribution to model the arrival of phone calls.

Suppose that we are interested in the number of arrivals at the drive-up teller window of a bank during a 15-minute period on weekday mornings. If we can assume that the probability of a car arriving is the same for any two time periods of equal length and that the arrival or nonarrival of a car in any time period is independent of the arrival or nonarrival in any other time period, the Poisson probability function is applicable. Suppose these assumptions are satisfied and an analysis of historical data shows that the average number of cars arriving in a 15-minute period of time is 10; in this case, the following probability function applies.

$$f(x) = \frac{10^x e^{-10}}{x!}$$

The random variable here is x = number of cars arriving in any 15-minute period.

If management wanted to know the probability of exactly five arrivals in 15 minutes, we would set $x = 5$ and thus obtain

$$\text{Probability of Exactly} \atop \text{5 Arrivals in 15 Minutes} = f(5) = \frac{10^5 e^{-10}}{5!} = .0378$$

Although this probability was determined by evaluating the probability function with $\mu = 10$ and $x = 5$, it is often easier to refer to tables for the Poisson probability distribution. These tables provide probabilities for specific values of x and μ. We included such a table as Table 7 of Appendix B. For convenience, we reproduced a portion of this table as Table 5.9. Note that to use the table of Poisson probabilities, we need know only the values of x and μ. From Table 5.9 we see that the probability of five arrivals in a 15-minute period is found by locating the value in the row of the table corresponding to $x = 5$ and the column of the table corresponding to $\mu = 10$. Hence, we obtain $f(5) = .0378$.

Our illustration involves a 15-minute period, but other time periods can be used. Suppose we want to compute the probability of one arrival in a 3-minute period. Because 10 is the expected number of arrivals in a 15-minute period, we see that $^{10}/_{15} = ^2/_3$ is the expected number of arrivals in a 1-minute period and that $(2/3)(3 \text{ minutes}) = 2$ is the expected number of arrivals in a 3-minute period. Thus, the probability of x arrivals in a 3-minute time period with $\mu = 2$ is given by the following Poisson probability function.

$$f(x) = \frac{2^x e^{-2}}{x!}$$

Suppose now we want to compute the probability of one arrival in a 3-minute period.

$$\text{Probability of Exactly} \atop \text{1 Arrival in 3 Minutes} = f(1) = \frac{2^1 e^{-2}}{1!} = .2707$$

An Example Involving Length or Distance Intervals

Let us illustrate an application not involving time intervals in which the Poisson probability distribution is useful. Suppose we are concerned with the occurrence of major defects in a highway one month after resurfacing. We will assume that the probability of a defect is the same for any two highway intervals of equal length and that the occurrence or nonoccurrence of a defect in any one interval is independent of the occurrence or nonoccurrence of a defect in any other interval. Hence, the Poisson probability distribution can be applied.

TABLE 5.9   SELECTED VALUES FROM THE POISSON PROBABILITY TABLES
EXAMPLE: $\mu = 10, x = 5; f(5) = .0378$

					μ					
x	9.1	9.2	9.3	9.4	9.5	9.6	9.7	9.8	9.9	10
0	.0001	.0001	.0001	.0001	.0001	.0001	.0001	.0001	.0001	.0000
1	.0010	.0009	.0009	.0008	.0007	.0007	.0006	.0005	.0005	.0005
2	.0046	.0043	.0040	.0037	.0034	.0031	.0029	.0027	.0025	.0023
3	.0140	.0131	.0123	.0115	.0107	.0100	.0093	.0087	.0081	.0076
4	.0319	.0302	.0285	.0269	.0254	.0240	.0226	.0213	.0201	.0189
5	.0581	.0555	.0530	.0506	.0483	.0460	.0439	.0418	.0398	**.0378**
6	.0881	.0851	.0822	.0793	.0764	.0736	.0709	.0682	.0656	.0631
7	.1145	.1118	.1091	.1064	.1037	.1010	.0982	.0955	.0928	.0901
8	.1302	.1286	.1269	.1251	.1232	.1212	.1191	.1170	.1148	.1126
9	.1317	.1315	.1311	.1306	.1300	.1293	.1284	.1274	.1263	.1251
10	.1198	.1210	.1219	.1228	.1235	.1241	.1245	.1249	.1250	.1251
11	.0991	.1012	.1031	.1049	.1067	.1083	.1098	.1112	.1125	.1137
12	.0752	.0776	.0799	.0822	.0844	.0866	.0888	.0908	.0928	.0948
13	.0526	.0549	.0572	.0594	.0617	.0640	.0662	.0685	.0707	.0729
14	.0342	.0361	.0380	.0399	.0419	.0439	.0459	.0479	.0500	.0521
15	.0208	.0221	.0235	.0250	.0265	.0281	.0297	.0313	.0330	.0347
16	.0118	.0127	.0137	.0147	.0157	.0168	.0180	.0192	.0204	.0217
17	.0063	.0069	.0075	.0081	.0088	.0095	.0103	.0111	.0119	.0128
18	.0032	.0035	.0039	.0042	.0046	.0051	.0055	.0060	.0065	.0071
19	.0015	.0017	.0019	.0021	.0023	.0026	.0028	.0031	.0034	.0037
20	.0007	.0008	.0009	.0010	.0011	.0012	.0014	.0015	.0017	.0019
21	.0003	.0003	.0004	.0004	.0005	.0006	.0006	.0007	.0008	.0009
22	.0001	.0001	.0002	.0002	.0002	.0002	.0003	.0003	.0004	.0004
23	.0000	.0001	.0001	.0001	.0001	.0001	.0001	.0001	.0002	.0002
24	.0000	.0000	.0000	.0000	.0000	.0000	.0000	.0001	.0001	.0001

Suppose we learn that major defects one month after resurfacing occur at the average rate of two per mile. Let us find the probability of no major defects in a particular 3-mile section of the highway. Because we are interested in an interval with a length of 3 miles, $\mu = (2 \text{ defects/mile})(3 \text{ miles}) = 6$ represents the expected number of major defects over the 3-mile section of highway. Using equation (5.11), the probability of no major defects is $f(0) = 6^0 e^{-6}/0! = .0025$. Thus, it is unlikely that no major defects will occur in the 3-mile section. In fact, this example indicates a $1 - .0025 = .9975$ probability of at least one major defect in the 3-mile highway section.

EXERCISES

Methods

38.   Consider a Poisson probability distribution with $\mu = 3$.
    a.   Write the appropriate Poisson probability function.
    b.   Compute $f(2)$.
    c.   Compute $f(1)$.
    d.   Compute $P(x \geq 2)$.

SELFtest

39. Consider a Poisson probability distribution with an average number of occurrences per time period of two.
   a. Write the appropriate Poisson probability function.
   b. What is the average number of occurrences in three time periods?
   c. Write the appropriate Poisson probability function to determine the probability of x occurrences in three time periods.
   d. Compute the probability of two occurrences in one time period.
   e. Compute the probability of six occurrences in three time periods.
   f. Compute the probability of five occurrences in two time periods.

Applications

SELFtest

40. Phone calls arrive at the rate of 48 per hour at the reservation desk for Regional Airways.
   a. Compute the probability of receiving three calls in a 5-minute interval of time.
   b. Compute the probability of receiving exactly 10 calls in 15 minutes.
   c. Suppose no calls are currently on hold. If the agent takes 5 minutes to complete the current call, how many callers do you expect to be waiting by that time? What is the probability that none will be waiting?
   d. If no calls are currently being processed, what is the probability that the agent can take 3 minutes for personal time without being interrupted by a call?

41. During the period of time phone-in registrations are being taken at a local university, calls come in at the rate of one every 2 minutes.
   a. What is the expected number of calls in 1 hour?
   b. What is the probability of three calls in 5 minutes?
   c. What is the probability of no calls in a 5-minute period?

42. More than 50 million guests stayed at bed and breakfasts (B&Bs) last year. The Web site for the Bed and Breakfast Inns of North America (*www.bestInns.net*), which averages approximately seven visitors per minute, enables many B&Bs to attract guests without waiting years to be mentioned in guidebooks (*Time,* September 2001).
   a. What is the probability of no Web site visitors in a 1-minute period?
   b. What is the probability of two or more Web site visitors in a 1-minute period?
   c. What is the probability of one or more Web site visitors in a 30-second period?
   d. What is the probability of five or more Web site visitors in a 1-minute period?

43. Airline passengers arrive randomly and independently at the passenger-screening facility at a major international airport. The mean arrival rate is 10 passengers per minute.
   a. What is the probability of no arrivals in a 1-minute period?
   b. What is the probability that three or fewer passengers arrive in a 1-minute period?
   c. What is the probability of no arrivals in a 15-second period?
   d. What is the probability of at least one arrival in a 15-second period?

44. Investment activities for subscribers to *The Wall Street Journal Interactive Edition* show that the average number of security transactions per year is approximately 15 (*The Wall Street Journal* Subscriber Study, 1999). Assume that a particular investor makes transactions at this rate. Furthermore, assume that the probability of a transaction for this investor is the same for any two months and transactions in one month are independent of transactions in any other month. Answer the following questions.
   a. What is the mean number of transactions per month?
   b. What is the probability of no stock transactions during a month?
   c. What is the probability of exactly one stock transaction during a month?
   d. What is the probability of more than one stock transaction during a month?

45. The National Safety Council reported that air bag-related fatalities dropped to 18 in the year 2000 (*www.nsc.org*).

    a. What is the average number of air bag-related fatalities per month?

    b. What is the probability of no air bag-related fatalities in a typical month?

    c. What is the probability of two or more air bag-related fatalities in a typical month?

5.6 HYPERGEOMETRIC PROBABILITY DISTRIBUTION

The hypergeometric probability distribution is closely related to the binomial probability distribution. The two probability distributions differ in two key ways: With the hypergeometric distribution, the trials are not independent, and the probability of success changes from trial to trial.

In the usual notation for the hypergeometric probability distribution, r denotes the number of elements in the population of size N labeled success, and $N - r$ denotes the number of elements in the population labeled failure. The **hypergeometric probability function** is used to compute the probability that in a random selection of n elements, selected without replacement, we obtain x elements labeled success and $n - x$ elements labeled failure. For this result to occur, we must obtain x successes from the r successes in the population and $n - x$ failures from the $N - r$ failures. The following hypergeometric probability function provides $f(x)$, the probability of obtaining x successes in a sample of size n.

Hypergeometric Probability Function

$$f(x) = \frac{\binom{r}{x}\binom{N - r}{n - x}}{\binom{N}{n}} \qquad \text{for } 0 \leq x \leq r \qquad (5.12)$$

where

$$f(x) = \text{probability of } x \text{ successes in } n \text{ trials}$$
$$n = \text{number of trials}$$
$$N = \text{number of elements in the population}$$
$$r = \text{number of elements in the population labeled success}$$

Note that $\binom{N}{n}$ represents the number of ways a sample of size n can be selected from a population of size N; $\binom{r}{x}$ represents the number of ways that x successes can be selected from a total of r successes in the population; and $\binom{N - r}{n - x}$ represents the number of ways that $n - x$ failures can be selected from a total of $N - r$ failures in the population.

To illustrate the computations involved in using equation (5.12), let us consider the problem of selecting two people from a five-member committee to send to a Las Vegas convention. Assume that the five-member committee consists of three women and two men. To determine the probability of randomly selecting two women, we can use equation (5.12) with $n = 2$, $N = 5$, $r = 3$, and $x = 2$.

$$f(2) = \frac{\binom{3}{2}\binom{2}{0}}{\binom{5}{2}} = \frac{\left(\frac{3!}{2!1!}\right)\left(\frac{2!}{2!0!}\right)}{\left(\frac{5!}{2!3!}\right)} = \frac{3}{10} = .30$$

Suppose we learn later that three committee members will be allowed to make the trip. If we use $n = 3$, $N = 5$, $r = 3$, and $x = 2$, the probability that exactly two of the three members will be women is

$$f(2) = \frac{\binom{3}{2}\binom{2}{1}}{\binom{5}{2}} = \frac{\left(\frac{3!}{2!1!}\right)\left(\frac{2!}{1!1!}\right)}{\left(\frac{5!}{2!3!}\right)} = \frac{6}{10} = .60$$

As another illustration, suppose a population consists of 10 items, four of which are classified as defective and six of which are classified as nondefective. What is the probability that a random selection of size three will provide two defective items? For this problem we can think of obtaining a defective item as a "success." Using equation (5.12) with $n = 3$, $N = 10$, $r = 4$, and $x = 2$, we can compute $f(2)$ as follows.

$$f(2) = \frac{\binom{4}{2}\binom{6}{1}}{\binom{10}{3}} = \frac{\left(\frac{4!}{2!2!}\right)\left(\frac{6!}{1!5!}\right)}{\left(\frac{10!}{3!7!}\right)} = \frac{36}{120} = .30$$

EXERCISES

Methods

SELFtest

46. Suppose $N = 10$ and $r = 3$. Compute the hypergeometric probabilities for the following values of n and x.
    a. $n = 4$, $x = 1$
    b. $n = 2$, $x = 2$
    c. $n = 2$, $x = 0$
    d. $n = 4$, $x = 2$

47. Suppose $N = 15$ and $r = 4$. What is the probability of $x = 3$ for $n = 10$?

Applications

48. According to *Beverage Digest*, Coke Classic and Pepsi ranked number one and number two in sales (*The Wall Street Journal Almanac*, 1998). Assume that in a group of 10 individuals, six preferred Coke Classic and four preferred Pepsi. A random sample of three of these individuals is selected.
    a. What is the probability that exactly two preferred Coke Classic?
    b. What is the probability that the majority (either two or three) preferred Pepsi?

49. Blackjack, or "twenty-one" as it is frequently called, is a popular gambling game played in Las Vegas casinos. A player is dealt two cards. Face cards (jacks, queens, and kings) and tens have a point value of 10. Aces have a point value of 1 or 11. A 52-card deck has 16 cards with a point value of 10 (jacks, queens, kings, and tens) and four aces.
   a. What is the probability that both cards dealt are aces or 10-point cards?
   b. What is the probability that both of the cards are aces?
   c. What is the probability that both of the cards have a point value of 10?
   d. A blackjack is a 10-point card and an ace for a value of 21. Use your answers to parts (a), (b), and (c) to determine the probability that a player is dealt blackjack. (Hint: Part (d) is not a hypergeometric problem. Develop your own logical relationship as to how the hypergeometric probabilities from parts (a), (b), and (c) can be combined to answer this question.)

SELFtest   **50.** Axline Computers manufactures personal computers at two plants, one in Texas and the other in Hawaii. The Texas plant has 40 employees; the Hawaii plant has 20. A random sample of 10 employees is to be asked to fill out a benefits questionnaire.
   a. What is the probability that none of the employees are at the plant in Hawaii?
   b. What is the probability that one of the employees is at the plant in Hawaii?
   c. What is the probability that two or more of the employees are at the plant in Hawaii?
   d. What is the probability that nine of the employees are at the plant in Texas?

51. Of the 25 students (14 boys and 11 girls) in the sixth-grade class at St. Andrew School, five students were absent Thursday.
   a. What is the probability that two of the absent students were girls?
   b. What is the probability that two of the absent students were boys?
   c. What is the probability that all of the absent students were boys?
   d. What is the probability that none of the absent students were boys?

52. A shipment of 10 items has two defective and eight nondefective items. In the inspection of the shipment, a sample of items will be selected and tested. If a defective item is found, the shipment of 10 items will be rejected.
   a. If a sample of three items is selected, what is the probability that the shipment will be rejected?
   b. If a sample of four items is selected, what is the probability that the shipment will be rejected?
   c. If a sample of five items is selected, what is the probability that the shipment will be rejected?
   d. If management would like a .90 probability of rejecting a shipment with two defective and eight nondefective items, how large a sample would you recommend?

SUMMARY

A random variable provides a numerical description of the outcome of an experiment. The probability distribution for a random variable describes how the probabilities are distributed over the values the random variable can assume. For any discrete random variable x, the probability distribution is defined by a probability function, denoted by $f(x)$, which provides the probability associated with each value of the random variable. Once the probability function is defined, we can compute the expected value, variance, and standard deviation for the random variable.

The binomial probability distribution can be used to determine the probability of x successes in n trials whenever the experiment has the following properties:

1. The experiment consists of a sequence of n identical trials.
2. Two outcomes are possible on each trial, one called success and the other failure.

3. The probability of a success p does not change from trial to trial. Consequently, the probability of failure, $1 - p$, does not change from trial to trial.
4. The trials are independent.

When the four properties hold, a binomial probability function can be used to determine the probability of obtaining x successes in n trials. Formulas were also presented for the mean and variance of the binomial probability distribution.

The Poisson probability distribution is used when it is desirable to determine the probability of x occurrences over an interval of time or space. The following assumptions are necessary for the Poisson distribution to be applicable.

1. The probability of an occurrence of the event is the same for any two intervals of equal length.
2. The occurrence or nonoccurrence of the event in any interval is independent of the occurrence or nonoccurrence of the event in any other interval.

A third discrete probability distribution, the hypergeometric, was introduced in Section 5.6. Like the binomial, it is used to compute the probability of x successes in n trials. But, in contrast to the binomial, the probability of success changes from trial to trial.

GLOSSARY

Random variable   A numerical description of the outcome of an experiment.

Discrete random variable   A random variable that may assume either a finite number of values or an infinite sequence of values.

Continuous random variable   A random variable that may assume any numerical value in an interval or collection of intervals.

Probability distribution   A description of how the probabilities are distributed over the values of the random variable.

Probability function   A function, denoted by $f(x)$, that provides the probability that x assumes a particular value for a discrete random variable.

Discrete uniform probability distribution   A probability distribution for which each possible value of the random variable has the same probability.

Expected value   A measure of the mean, or central location, of a random variable.

Variance   A measure of the variability, or dispersion, of a random variable.

Standard deviation   The positive square root of the variance.

Binomial experiment   An experiment having the four properties stated at the beginning of Section 5.4.

Binomial probability distribution   A probability distribution showing the probability of x successes in n trials of a binomial experiment.

Binomial probability function   The function used to compute binomial probabilities.

Poisson probability distribution   A probability distribution showing the probability of x occurrences of an event over a specified interval of time or space.

Poisson probability function   The function used to compute Poisson probabilities.

Hypergeometric probability function   The function used to compute the probability of x successes in n trials when the trials are dependent.

KEY FORMULAS

Discrete Uniform Probability Function

$$f(x) = 1/n \tag{5.3}$$

where

$$n = \text{the number of values the random variable may assume}$$

Expected Value of a Discrete Random Variable

$$E(x) = \mu = \Sigma x f(x) \tag{5.4}$$

Variance of a Discrete Random Variable

$$\text{Var}(x) = \sigma^2 = \Sigma(x - \mu)^2 f(x) \tag{5.5}$$

Number of Experimental Outcomes Providing Exactly x Successes in n Trials

$$\binom{n}{x} = \frac{n!}{x!(n - x)!} \tag{5.6}$$

Binomial Probability Function

$$f(x) = \binom{n}{x} p^x (1 - p)^{(n-x)} \tag{5.8}$$

Expected Value for the Binomial Probability Distribution

$$E(x) = \mu = np \tag{5.9}$$

Variance for the Binomial Probability Distribution

$$\text{Var}(x) = \sigma^2 = np(1 - p) \tag{5.10}$$

Poisson Probability Function

$$f(x) = \frac{\mu^x e^{-\mu}}{x!} \tag{5.11}$$

Hypergeometric Probability Function

$$f(x) = \frac{\binom{r}{x}\binom{N - r}{n - x}}{\binom{N}{n}} \qquad \text{for } 0 \leq x \leq r \tag{5.12}$$

SUPPLEMENTARY EXERCISES

53. A *Wall Street Journal*/NBC News poll asked 2004 adults how they felt about their opportunities for career advancement (*The Wall Street Journal*, September 19, 1997). Twenty-three percent indicated they were very satisfied; 38% indicated they were somewhat satisfied; 3% indicated they were not sure; 18% indicated they were somewhat dissatisfied; and 18% indicated they were very dissatisfied. Let x be a random variable representing level of satisfaction. We let $x = 5$ for very satisfied, $x = 4$ for somewhat satisfied, $x = 3$ for not sure, $x = 2$ for somewhat dissatisfied, and $x = 1$ for very dissatisfied.
    a. Use the preceding numerical values to develop a probability distribution for level of satisfaction with opportunities for career advancement.
    b. Compute the expected level of satisfaction. Does a higher score indicate more or less satisfaction?
    c. Compute the variance and standard deviation for the satisfaction scores.

54. An opinion survey of 1009 adults was conducted by Louis Harris & Associates, Inc. (*Business Week*, December 29, 1997). Table 5.10 shows the probability distribution of responses to a question concerning the stock market's valuation.
    a. Show that the probability distribution in Table 5.10 satisfies the properties of all probability distributions.
    b. What are the expected value and variance of the probability distribution of opinions?
    c. Comment on whether people think the stock market is overvalued.

55. The budgeting process for a midwestern college resulted in expense forecasts for the coming year (in millions of dollars) of $9, $10, $11, $12, and $13. Because the actual expenses are unknown, the following respective probabilities are assigned: .3, .2, .25, .05, and .2.
    a. Show the probability distribution for the expense forecast.
    b. What is the expected value of the expense forecast for the coming year?
    c. What is the variance in the expense forecast for the coming year?
    d. If income projections for the year are estimated at $12 million, comment on the financial position of the college.

56. Kristen DelGuzzi conducted a study of Hamilton County judges and courts over a three-year period (*The Cincinnati Enquirer*, January 11, 1998). One finding was that 4% of the cases decided in Common Pleas Court were appealed.
    a. If 20 cases are heard on a particular day, what is the probability that three will be appealed?
    b. If 20 cases are heard on a particular day, what is the probability none will be appealed?
    c. It is not unusual for 1200 cases to be heard in a month. What is the expected number of appeals?
    d. If 1200 cases are heard in a month, what are the variance and standard deviation of the number of appeals?

TABLE 5.10   PROBABILITY DISTRIBUTION OF RESPONSES CONCERNING STOCK MARKET'S VALUATION

Market Valuation	Random Variable (x)	Probability $f(x)$
Very undervalued	1	0.02
Somewhat undervalued	2	0.06
Fairly valued	3	0.28
Somewhat overvalued	4	0.54
Very overvalued	5	0.10

57. A company is planning to interview Internet users to learn how its proposed Web site will be received by different age groups. According to the Bureau of the Census 40% of individuals aged 18 to 54, and 12% of individuals aged 55 and over use the Internet (*Statistical Abstract of the United States,* 2000).
    a. How many people from the 18–54 age group must be contacted to find an expected number of at least 10 Internet users?
    b. How many people from the 55-and-over age group must be contacted to find an expected number of at least 10 Internet users?
    c. If you contact the number of 18- to 54-year-old people suggested in part (a), what is the standard deviation of the number who will be Internet users?
    d. If you contact the number of 55-and-over people suggested in part (b), what is the standard deviation of the number who will be Internet users?

58. Many companies use a quality control technique called *acceptance sampling* to monitor incoming shipments of parts, raw materials, and so on. In the electronics industry, component parts are commonly shipped from suppliers in large lots. Inspection of a sample of *n* components can be viewed as the *n* trials of a binomial experiment. The outcome for each component tested (trial) will be that the component is classified as good or defective. Reynolds Electronics accepts a lot from a particular supplier if the defective components in the lot do not exceed 1%. Suppose a random sample of five items from a recent shipment is tested.
    a. Assume that 1% of the shipment is defective. Compute the probability that no items in the sample are defective.
    b. Assume that 1% of the shipment is defective. Compute the probability that exactly one item in the sample is defective.
    c. What is the probability of observing one or more defective items in the sample if 1% of the shipment is defective?
    d. Would you feel comfortable accepting the shipment if one item were found to be defective? Why or why not?

59. The unemployment rate is 4.1% (*Barron's,* September 4, 2000). Assume that 100 employable people are selected randomly.
    a. What is the expected number of people who are unemployed?
    b. What is the variance and standard deviation of the number of people who are unemployed?

60. In December 1997, the U.S. Department of Justice issued an injunction against Microsoft Corporation for bundling its Internet Explorer® Web browser with its Windows 95® operating system (*Fortune,* February 2, 1998). Public opinion was divided on whether Microsoft was a monopoly. In a *Fortune* poll, 41% of respondents agreed with the statement, "Microsoft is a monopoly." Suppose a sample of 800 people has been taken.
    a. How many would you expect to agree that Microsoft is a monopoly?
    b. What is the standard deviation of the number of respondents who believe Microsoft is a monopoly?
    c. What is the standard deviation of the number of respondents who do not believe Microsoft is a monopoly?

61. Cars arrive at a car wash randomly and independently; the probability of an arrival is the same for any two time intervals of equal length. The mean arrival rate is 15 cars per hour. What is the probability that 20 or more cars will arrive during any given hour of operation?

62. A new automated production process has had an average of 1.5 breakdowns per day. Because of the cost associated with a breakdown, management is concerned about the possibility of having three or more breakdowns during a day. Assume that breakdowns occur randomly, that the probability of a breakdown is the same for any two time intervals of equal length, and that breakdowns in one period are independent of breakdowns in other periods. What is the probability of having three or more breakdowns during a day?

63. A regional director responsible for business development in the state of Pennsylvania is concerned about the number of small business failures. If the mean number of small business failures per month is 10, what is the probability that exactly four small businesses will fail during a given month? Assume that the probability of a failure is the same for any two months and that the occurrence or nonoccurrence of a failure in any month is independent of failures in any other month.

64. Customer arrivals at a bank are random and independent; the probability of an arrival in any 1-minute period is the same as the probability of an arrival in any other 1-minute period. Answer the following questions, assuming a mean arrival rate of three customers per minute.
   a. What is the probability of exactly three arrivals in a 1-minute period?
   b. What is the probability of at least three arrivals in a 1-minute period?

65. A deck of playing cards contains 52 cards, four of which are aces. What is the probability that the deal of a five-card hand provides:
   a. A pair of aces?
   b. Exactly one ace?
   c. No aces?
   d. At least one ace?

66. Through the week ending September 16, 2001, Tiger Woods was the leading money winner on the PGA Tour, with total earnings of $5,517,777. Of the top 10 money winners, seven players used a Titleist brand golf ball (*www.pgatour.com*). Suppose that we randomly select two of the top 10 money winners.
   a. What is the probability that exactly one uses a Titleist golf ball?
   b. What is the probability that both use Titleist golf balls?
   c. What is the probability that neither uses a Titleist golf ball?

Appendix 5.1 DISCRETE PROBABILITY DISTRIBUTIONS WITH MINITAB

Statistical packages such as Minitab offer a relatively easy and efficient procedure for computing binomial probabilities. In this appendix, we show the step-by-step procedure for determining the binomial probabilities for the Martin Clothing Store problem in Section 5.4. Recall that the desired binomial probabilities are based on $n = 10$ and $p = .30$. Before beginning the Minitab routine, the user must enter the desired values of the random variable x into a column of the worksheet. We entered the values 0, 1, 2, . . . , 10 in column 1 (see Figure 5.5) to generate the entire binomial probability distribution. The Minitab steps to obtain the desired binomial probabilities follow.

   Step 1. Select the **Calc** pull-down menu
   Step 2. Choose **Probability Distributions**
   Step 3. Choose **Binomial**
   Step 4. When the Binomial Distribution dialog box appears:
               Select **Probability**
               Enter 10 in the **Number of trials** box
               Enter .3 in the **Probability of success** box
               Enter C1 in the **Input column** box
               Click **OK**

The Minitab output with the binomial probabilities will appear as shown in Figure 5.5.
   Minitab provides Poisson probabilities in a similar manner. The only differences are in step 3, where the Poisson option would be selected, and step 4, where the **Mean** would be entered rather than the number of trials and the probability of success.

Appendix 5.2   DISCRETE PROBABILITY DISTRIBUTIONS WITH EXCEL

Excel provides functions for computing probabilities for the binomial, Poisson, and hyper-geometric distributions introduced in this chapter. The Excel function for computing bino-mial probabilities is BINOMDIST. It has four arguments: x (the number of successes), n (the number of trials), p (the probability of success), and cumulative. FALSE is used for the fourth argument (cumulative) if we want the probability of x successes, and TRUE is used for the fourth argument if we want the cumulative probability of x or fewer successes. Here we show how to compute the probabilities of 0 through 10 successes in the Martin Cloth-ing Store problem of Section 5.4 (see Figure 5.5).

As we describe the worksheet development refer to Figure 5.6; the formula worksheet is in the background, and the value worksheet is in the foreground. We entered the number

FIGURE 5.6   EXCEL WORKSHEET FOR COMPUTING BINOMIAL PROBABILITIES

	A	B	C	D
1	Number of Trials (*n*)	10		
2	Probability of Success (*p*)	0.3		
3				
4		*x*	*f(x)*	
5		0	=BINOMDIST(B5,$B$1,$B$2,FALSE)	
6		1	=BINOMDIST(B6,$B$1,$B$2,FALSE)	
7		2	=BINOMDIST(B7,$B$1,$B$2,FALSE)	
8		3	=BINOMDIST(B8,$B$1,$B$2,FALSE)	
9		4	=BINOMDIST(B9,$B$1,$B$2,FALSE)	
10		5	=BINOMDIST(B10,$B$1,$B$2,FALSE)	
11		6	=BINOMDIST(B11,$B$1,$B$2,FALSE)	
12		7	=BINOMDIST(B12,$B$1,$B$2,FALSE)	
13		8	=BINOMDIST(B13,$B$1,$B$2,FALSE)	
14		9	=BINOMDIST(B14,$B$1,$B$2,FALSE)	
15		10	=BINOMDIST(B15,$B$1,$B$2,FALSE)	
16				

	A	B	C	D
1	Number of Trials (*n*)	10		
2	Probability of Success (*p*)	0.3		
3				
4		*x*	*f(x)*	
5		0	0.0282	
6		1	0.1211	
7		2	0.2335	
8		3	0.2668	
9		4	0.2001	
10		5	0.1029	
11		6	0.0368	
12		7	0.0090	
13		8	0.0014	
14		9	0.0001	
15		10	0.0000	
16				

of trials (10) into cell B1, the probability of success into cell B2, and the values for the random variable into cells B5:B15. The following steps will generate the desired probabilities:

Step 1. Use the BINOMDIST function to compute the probability of $x = 0$ by entering the following formula into cell C5:

$$=BINOMDIST(B5,\$B\$1,\$B\$2,FALSE)$$

Step 2. Copy the formula in cell C5 into cells C6:C15.

The value worksheet in the foreground of Figure 5.6 shows that the probabilities obtained are the same as in Figure 5.5. Poisson and hypergeometric probabilities can be computed in a similar fashion. The POISSON and HYPERGEOMDIST functions are used. Excel's function wizard can help the user in entering the proper arguments for these functions (see Appendix 2.2).

CONTINUOUS PROBABILITY DISTRIBUTIONS

Chapter 6

CONTENTS

PROCTER & GAMBLE*

CINCINNATI, OHIO

Procter & Gamble (P&G) is in the consumer products business worldwide. P&G produces and markets such products as detergents, disposable diapers, over-the-counter pharmaceuticals, dentifrices, bar soaps, mouthwashes, and paper towels. It has the leading brand in more categories than any other consumer products company.

As a leader in the application of statistical methods in decision making, P&G employs people with diverse academic backgrounds: engineering, statistics, operations research, and business. The major quantitative technologies for which these people provide support are probabilistic decision and risk analysis, advanced simulation, quality improvement, and quantitative methods (e.g., linear programming, regression analysis, probability analysis).

The Industrial Chemicals Division of P&G is a major supplier of fatty alcohols derived from natural substances such as coconut oil and from petroleum-based derivatives. The division wanted to know the economic risks and opportunities of expanding its fatty-alcohol production facilities, and P&G's experts in probabilistic decision and risk analysis were called in to help. After structuring and modeling the problem, they determined that the key to profitability was the cost difference between the petroleum- and coconut-based raw materials. Future costs were unknown, but the analysts were able to represent them with the following continuous random variables.

x = the coconut oil price per pound
   of fatty alcohol

and

y = the petroleum raw material price per
   pound of fatty alcohol

Because the key to profitability was the difference between these two random variables, a third random variable, $d = x - y$, was used in the analysis. Experts were

Some of Procter & Gamble's many well-known products.
© Joe Higgins/South-Western.

interviewed to determine the probability distribution for x and y. In turn, this information was used to develop a probability distribution for the difference in prices d. This continuous probability distribution showed a .90 probability that the price difference would be \$.0655 or less and a .50 probability that the price difference would be \$.035 or less. In addition, there was only a .10 probability that the price difference would be \$.0045 or less.[†]

The Industrial Chemicals Division thought that being able to quantify the impact of raw material price differences was key to reaching a consensus. The probabilities obtained were used in a sensitivity analysis of the raw material price difference. The analysis yielded sufficient insight to form the basis for a recommendation to management.

The use of continuous random variables and their probability distributions was helpful to P&G in analyzing the economic risks associated with its fatty-alcohol production. In this chapter, you will gain an understanding of continuous random variables and their probability distributions including one of the most important probability distributions in statistics, the normal distribution.

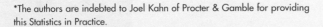

*The authors are indebted to Joel Kahn of Procter & Gamble for providing this Statistics in Practice.

†The price differences stated here have been modified to protect proprietary data.

In the preceding chapter we discussed discrete random variables and their probability distributions. In this chapter we turn to the study of continuous random variables. Specifically, we discuss three continuous probability distributions: the uniform, the normal, and the exponential.

A fundamental difference separates discrete and continuous random variables in terms of how probabilities are computed. For a discrete random variable, the probability function $f(x)$ provides the probability that the random variable assumes a particular value. With continuous random variables the counterpart of the probability function is the **probability density function,** also denoted by $f(x)$. The difference is that the probability density function does not directly provide probabilities. However, the area under the graph of $f(x)$ corresponding to a given interval does provide the probability that the continuous random variable x assumes a value in that interval. So when we compute probabilities for continuous random variables we are computing the probability that the random variable assumes any value in an interval.

One of the implications of the definition of probability for continuous random variables is that the probability of any particular value of the random variable is zero, because the area under the graph of $f(x)$ at any particular point is zero. In Section 6.1 we demonstrate these concepts for a continuous random variable that has a uniform probability distribution.

Much of the chapter is devoted to describing and showing applications of the normal probability distribution. The normal probability distribution is of major importance; it is used extensively in statistical inference. The chapter closes with a discussion of the exponential probability distribution.

6.1   UNIFORM PROBABILITY DISTRIBUTION

Whenever the probability is proportional to the length of the interval, the random variable is uniformly distributed.

Consider the random variable x that represents the flight time of an airplane traveling from Chicago to New York. Suppose the flight time can be any value in the interval from 120 minutes to 140 minutes. Because the random variable x can assume any value in that interval, x is a continuous rather than a discrete random variable. Let us assume that sufficient actual flight data are available to conclude that the probability of a flight time within any 1-minute interval is the same as the probability of a flight time within any other 1-minute interval contained in the larger interval from 120 to 140 minutes. With every 1-minute interval being equally likely, the random variable x is said to have a **uniform probability distribution.** The probability density function, which defines the uniform probability distribution for the flight-time random variable, is

$$f(x) = \begin{cases} 1/20 & \text{for } 120 \leq x \leq 140 \\ 0 & \text{elsewhere} \end{cases}$$

Figure 6.1 is a graph of this probability density function. In general, the uniform probability density function for a random variable x is defined by the following formula.

Uniform Probability Density Function

$$f(x) = \begin{cases} \dfrac{1}{b-a} & \text{for } a \leq x \leq b \\ 0 & \text{elsewhere} \end{cases} \tag{6.1}$$

For the flight-time random variable, $a = 120$ and $b = 140$.

FIGURE 6.1   UNIFORM PROBABILITY DENSITY FUNCTION FOR FLIGHT TIME

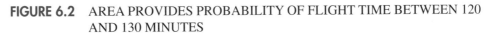

As noted in the introduction, for a continuous random variable, we consider probability only in terms of the likelihood that a random variable assumes a value within a specified interval. In the flight-time example, an acceptable probability question is: What is the probability that the flight time is between 120 and 130 minutes? That is, what is $P(120 \leq x \leq 130)$? Because the flight time must be between 120 and 140 minutes and because the probability is described as being uniform over this interval, we feel comfortable saying $P(120 \leq x \leq 130) = .50$. In the following subsection we show that this probability can be computed as the area under the graph of $f(x)$ from 120 to 130 (see Figure 6.2).

Area as a Measure of Probability

Let us make an observation about the graph in Figure 6.2. Consider the area under the graph of $f(x)$ in the interval from 120 to 130. The area is rectangular, and the area of a rectangle is simply the width multiplied by the height. With the width of the interval equal to $130 - 120 = 10$ and the height equal to the value of the probability density function $f(x) = 1/20$, we have area = width × height = $10(1/20) = 10/20 = .50$.

What observation can you make about the area under the graph of $f(x)$ and probability? They are identical! Indeed, this observation is valid for all continuous random variables.

FIGURE 6.2   AREA PROVIDES PROBABILITY OF FLIGHT TIME BETWEEN 120
AND 130 MINUTES

Once a probability density function $f(x)$ has been identified, the probability that x takes a value between some lower value x_1 and some higher value x_2 can be found by computing the area under the graph of $f(x)$ over the interval from x_1 to x_2.

Given the uniform probability distribution for flight time and using the interpretation of area as probability, we can answer any number of probability questions about flight times. For example, what is the probability of a flight time between 128 and 136 minutes? The width of the interval is $136 - 128 = 8$. With the uniform height of $f(x) = 1/20$, we see that $P(128 \le x \le 136) = 8(1/20) = .40$.

Note that $P(120 \le x \le 140) = 20(1/20) = 1$. That is, the total area under the graph of $f(x)$ is equal to 1. This property holds for all continuous probability distributions and is the analog of the condition that the sum of the probabilities must equal 1 for a discrete probability function. For a continuous probability density function, we must also require that $f(x) \ge 0$ for all values of x. This requirement is the analog of the requirement that $f(x) \ge 0$ for discrete probability functions.

Two major differences stand out between the treatment of continuous random variables and the treatment of their discrete counterparts.

To see that the probability of any single point is 0, refer to Figure 6.2 and compute the probability of a single point, say, x = 125. P(x = 125) = P(125 ≤ x ≤ 125) = 0(1/20) = 0.

1. We no longer talk about the probability of the random variable assuming a particular value. Instead, we talk about the probability of the random variable assuming a value within some given interval.
2. The probability of the random variable assuming a value within some given interval from x_1 to x_2 is defined to be the area under the graph of the probability density function between x_1 and x_2. It implies that the probability of a continuous random variable assuming any particular value exactly is zero, because the area under the graph of $f(x)$ at a single point is zero.

The calculation of the expected value and variance for a continuous random variable is analogous to that for a discrete random variable. However, because the computational procedure involves integral calculus, we leave the derivation of the appropriate formulas to more advanced texts.

For the uniform continuous probability distribution introduced in this section, the formulas for the expected value and variance are

$$E(x) = \frac{a + b}{2}$$

$$\text{Var}(x) = \frac{(b - a)^2}{12}$$

In these formulas, a is the smallest value and b is the largest value that the random variable may assume.

Applying these formulas to the uniform probability distribution for flight times from Chicago to New York, we obtain

$$E(x) = \frac{(120 + 140)}{2} = 130$$

$$\text{Var}(x) = \frac{(140 - 120)^2}{12} = 33.33$$

The standard deviation of flight times can be found by taking the square root of the variance. Thus, $\sigma = 5.77$ minutes.

NOTES AND COMMENTS

1. For a continuous random variable the probability of any particular value is zero; thus, $P(a \leq x \leq b) = P(a < x < b)$. This result shows that the probability of a random variable assuming a value in any interval is the same whether or not the endpoints are included.

2. To see more clearly why the height of a probability density function is not a probability, think about a random variable with the following uniform probability distribution.

$$f(x) = \begin{cases} 2 & \text{for } 0 \leq x \leq .5 \\ 0 & \text{elsewhere} \end{cases}$$

The height of the probability density function, $f(x)$, is 2 for values of x between 0 and .5. However, we know probabilities can never be greater than 1. Thus, we see that $f(x)$ cannot be interpreted as the probability of x.

EXERCISES

Methods

SELFtest

1. The random variable x is known to be uniformly distributed between 1.0 and 1.5.
   a. Show the graph of the probability density function.
   b. Compute $P(x = 1.25)$.
   c. Compute $P(1.0 \leq x \leq 1.25)$.
   d. Compute $P(1.20 < x < 1.5)$.

2. The random variable x is known to be uniformly distributed between 10 and 20.
   a. Show the graph of the probability density function.
   b. Compute $P(x < 15)$.
   c. Compute $P(12 \leq x \leq 18)$.
   d. Compute $E(x)$.
   e. Compute $\text{Var}(x)$.

Applications

3. Delta Airlines quotes a flight time of 2 hours, 5 minutes for its flights from Cincinnati to Tampa. Suppose we believe that actual flight times are uniformly distributed between 2 hours and 2 hours, 20 minutes.
   a. Show the graph of the probability density function for flight times.
   b. What is the probability that the flight will be no more than five minutes late?
   c. What is the probability that the flight will be more than 10 minutes late?
   d. What is the expected flight time?

SELFtest

4. Most computer languages have a function that can be used to generate random numbers. In Excel, the RAND function can be used to generate random numbers between 0 and 1. If we let x denote a random number generated using RAND, then x is a continuous random variable with the following probability density function.

$$f(x) = \begin{cases} 1 & \text{for } 0 \leq x \leq 1 \\ 0 & \text{elsewhere} \end{cases}$$

   a. Graph the probability density function.
   b. What is the probability of generating a random number between .25 and .75?

    c. What is the probability of generating a random number with a value less than or equal to .30?

    d. What is the probability of generating a random number with a value greater than .60?

5. The driving distance for the top 60 women golfers on the LPGA tour is between 238.9 and 261.2 yards (*Golfweek,* December 6, 1997). Assume that the driving distance for these women is uniformly distributed over this interval.

    a. Give a mathematical expression for the probability density function of driving distance.

    b. What is the probability the driving distance for one of these women is less than 250 yards?

    c. What is the probability the driving distance for one of these women is at least 255 yards?

    d. What is the probability the driving distance for one of these women is between 245 and 260 yards?

    e. How many of these women drive the ball at least 250 yards?

6. The label on a bottle of liquid detergent shows contents to be 12 ounces per bottle. The production operation fills the bottle uniformly according to the following probability density function.

$$f(x) = \begin{cases} 8 & \text{for } 11.975 \le x \le 12.100 \\ 0 & \text{elsewhere} \end{cases}$$

    a. What is the probability that a bottle will be filled with between 12 and 12.05 ounces?

    b. What is the probability that a bottle will be filled with 12.02 or more ounces?

    c. Quality control accepts a bottle that is filled to within .02 ounces of the number of ounces shown on the container label. What is the probability that a bottle of this liquid detergent will fail to meet the quality control standard?

7. Suppose we are interested in bidding on a piece of land and we know there is one other bidder.* The seller has announced that the highest bid in excess of $10,000 will be accepted. Assume that the competitor's bid x is a random variable that is uniformly distributed between $10,000 and $15,000.

    a. Suppose you bid $12,000. What is the probability that your bid will be accepted?

    b. Suppose you bid $14,000. What is the probability that your bid will be accepted?

    c. What amount should you bid to maximize the probability that you get the property?

    d. Suppose you know someone who is willing to pay you $16,000 for the property. Would you consider bidding less than the amount in part (c)? Why or why not?

6.2   NORMAL PROBABILITY DISTRIBUTION

The most important probability distribution for describing a continuous random variable is the **normal probability distribution.** The normal probability distribution has been used in a wide variety of practical applications in which the random variables are heights and weights of people, test scores, scientific measurements, amounts of rainfall, and so on. It is also widely used in statistical inference, which is the major topic of the remainder of this book. In such applications, the normal probability distribution provides a description of the likely results obtained through sampling.

Abraham de Moivre, a French mathematician, published The Doctrine of Chances *in 1733. He derived the normal probability distribution.*

---

*This exercise is based on a problem suggested to us by Professor Roger Myerson of Northwestern University.

Normal Curve

The form, or shape, of the normal probability distribution is illustrated by the bell-shaped curve in Figure 6.3. The probability density function that defines the bell-shaped curve of the normal probability distribution follows.

Normal Probability Density Function

$$f(x) = \frac{1}{\sigma\sqrt{2\pi}}\, e^{-(x-\mu)^2/2\sigma^2} \qquad (6.2)$$

where

μ = mean

σ = standard deviation

π = 3.14159

e = 2.71828

We make several observations about the characteristics of the normal probability distribution.

The normal curve has two parameters, μ and σ. They determine the location and shape of the normal probability distribution.

1. The entire family of normal probability distributions is differentiated by its mean μ and its standard deviation σ.
2. The highest point on the normal curve is at the mean, which is also the median and mode of the distribution.
3. The mean of the distribution can be any numerical value: negative, zero, or positive. Three normal distributions with the same standard deviation but three different means (-10, 0, and 20) are shown here.

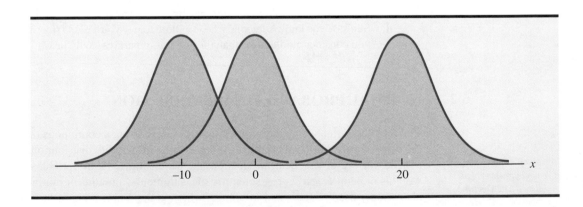

4. The normal probability distribution is symmetric, with the shape of the curve to the left of the mean a mirror image of the shape of the curve to the right of the mean. The tails of the curve extend to infinity in both directions and theoretically never touch the horizontal axis.

FIGURE 6.3   BELL-SHAPED CURVE FOR THE NORMAL PROBABILITY DISTRIBUTION

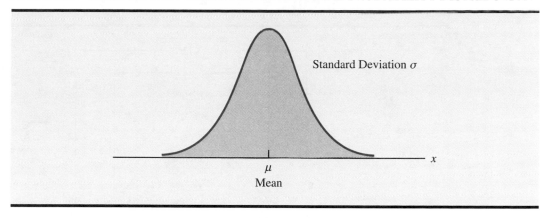

5. The standard deviation determines how flat and wide the curve is. Larger values of the standard deviation result in wider, flatter curves, showing more variability in the data. Two normal distributions with the same mean but with different standard deviations are shown here.

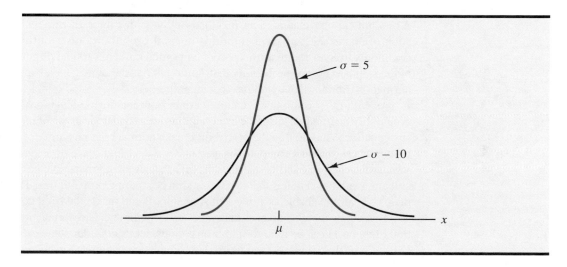

6. Probabilities for the normal random variable are given by areas under the curve. The total area under the curve for the normal probability distribution is 1 (this is true for all continuous probability distributions). Because the distribution is symmetric, the area under the curve to the left of the mean is .50 and the area under the curve to the right of the mean is .50.
7. The percentage of values in some commonly used intervals are:
    a. 68.26% of the values of a normal random variable are within plus or minus one standard deviation of its mean.
    b. 95.44% of the values of a normal random variable are within plus or minus two standard deviations of its mean.

These percentages are the basis for the empirical rule introduced in Section 3.3.

    c. 99.72% of the values of a normal random variable are within plus or minus three standard deviations of its mean.

Figure 6.4 shows properties (a), (b), and (c) graphically.

FIGURE 6.4   AREAS UNDER THE CURVE FOR ANY NORMAL PROBABILITY
DISTRIBUTION

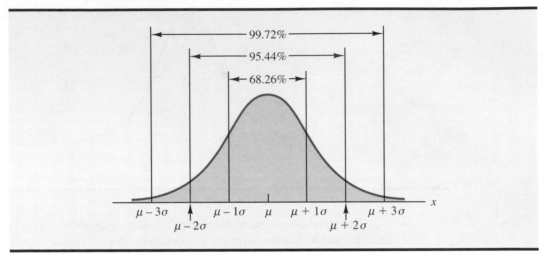

Standard Normal Probability Distribution

A random variable that has a normal distribution with a mean of zero and a standard deviation of one is said to have a **standard normal probability distribution.** The letter z is commonly used to designate this particular normal random variable. Figure 6.5 is the graph of the standard normal probability distribution. It has the same general appearance as other normal distributions, but with the special properties of $\mu = 0$ and $\sigma = 1$.

For the normal probability density function, the height of the curve varies and calculus is required to compute the areas that represent probability.

As with other continuous random variables, probability calculations with any normal probability distribution are made by computing areas under the graph of the probability density function. Thus, to find the probability that a normal random variable is within any specific interval, we must compute the area under the normal curve over that interval. For the standard normal probability distribution, areas under the normal curve have been computed and are available in tables that can be used in computing probabilities. Table 6.1 is such a table; it is also available as Table 1 of Appendix B and inside the front cover of this text.

Given a z value, we use the standard normal table to find the appropriate probability (an area under the curve).

To see how the table of areas under the curve for the standard normal probability distribution (Table 6.1) can be used to find probabilities, let us consider some examples. Later, we will see how this same table can be used to compute probabilities for any normal distribution.

FIGURE 6.5   THE STANDARD NORMAL PROBABILITY DISTRIBUTION

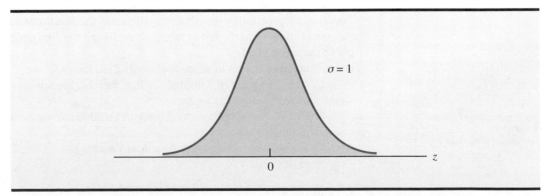

TABLE 6.1   AREAS, OR PROBABILITIES, FOR THE STANDARD NORMAL DISTRIBUTION

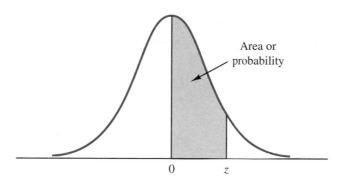

z	.00	.01	.02	.03	.04	.05	.06	.07	.08	.09
.0	.0000	.0040	.0080	.0120	.0160	.0199	.0239	.0279	.0319	.0359
.1	.0398	.0438	.0478	.0517	.0557	.0596	.0636	.0675	.0714	.0753
.2	.0793	.0832	.0871	.0910	.0948	.0987	.1026	.1064	.1103	.1141
.3	.1179	.1217	.1255	.1293	.1331	.1368	.1406	.1443	.1480	.1517
.4	.1554	.1591	.1628	.1664	.1700	.1736	.1772	.1808	.1844	.1879
.5	.1915	.1950	.1985	.2019	.2054	.2088	.2123	.2157	.2190	.2224
.6	.2257	.2291	.2324	.2357	.2389	.2422	.2454	.2486	.2517	.2549
.7	.2580	.2611	.2642	.2673	.2704	.2734	.2764	.2794	.2823	.2852
.8	.2881	.2910	.2939	.2967	.2995	.3023	.3051	.3078	.3106	.3133
.9	.3159	.3186	.3212	.3238	.3264	.3289	.3315	.3340	.3365	.3389
1.0	.3413	.3438	.3461	.3485	.3508	.3531	.3554	.3577	.3599	.3621
1.1	.3643	.3665	.3686	.3708	.3729	.3749	.3770	.3790	.3810	.3830
1.2	.3849	.3869	.3888	.3907	.3925	.3944	.3962	.3980	.3997	.4015
1.3	.4032	.4049	.4066	.4082	.4099	.4115	.4131	.4147	.4162	.4177
1.4	.4192	.4207	.4222	.4236	.4251	.4265	.4279	.4292	.4306	.4319
1.5	.4332	.4345	.4357	.4370	.4382	.4394	.4406	.4418	.4429	.4441
1.6	.4452	.4463	.4474	.4484	.4495	.4505	.4515	.4525	.4535·	.4545
1.7	.4554	.4564	.4573	.4582	.4591	.4599	.4608	.4616	.4625	.4633
1.8	.4641	.4649	.4656	.4664	.4671	.4678	.4686	.4693	.4699	.4706
1.9	.4713	.4719	.4726	.4732	.4738	.4744	.4750	.4756	.4761	.4767
2.0	.4772	.4778	.4783	.4788	.4793	.4798	.4803	.4808	.4812	.4817
2.1	.4821	.4826	.4830	.4834	.4838	.4842	.4846	.4850	.4854	.4857
2.2	.4861	.4864	.4868	.4871	.4875	.4878	.4881	.4884	.4887	.4890
2.3	.4893	.4896	.4898	.4901	.4904	.4906	.4909	.4911	.4913	.4916
2.4	.4918	.4920	.4922	.4925	.4927	.4929	.4931	.4932	.4934	.4936
2.5	.4938	.4940	.4941	.4943	.4945	.4946	.4948	.4949	.4951	.4952
2.6	.4953	.4955	.4956	.4957	.4959	.4960	.4961	.4962	.4963	.4964
2.7	.4965	.4966	.4967	.4968	.4969	.4970	.4971	.4972	.4973	.4974
2.8	.4974	.4975	.4976	.4977	.4977	.4978	.4979	.4979	.4980	.4981
2.9	.4981	.4982	.4982	.4983	.4984	.4984	.4985	.4985	.4986	.4986
3.0	.4986	.4987	.4987	.4988	.4988	.4989	.4989	.4989	.4990	.4990

To begin, let us see how we can compute the probability that the z value for the standard normal random variable will be between .00 and 1.00; that is, $P(.00 \leq z \leq 1.00)$. The darkly shaded region in the following graph shows this probability.

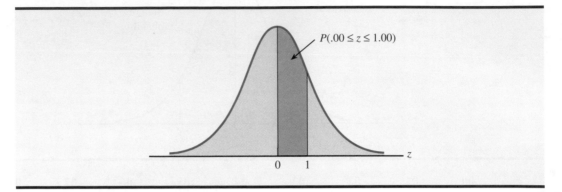

The entries in Table 6.1 give the area under the standard normal curve between the mean, $z = 0$, and a specified value of z (see the graph at the top of the table). In this case, we are interested in the area between $z = 0$ and $z = 1.00$. Thus, we must find the entry in the table corresponding to $z = 1.00$. First, we find 1.0 in the left column of the table and then find .00 in the top row of the table. By looking in the body of the table, we find that the 1.0 row and the .00 column intersect at the value of .3413. We have found the desired probability: $P(.00 \leq z \leq 1.00) = .3413$. A portion of Table 6.1 showing these steps follows.

z	.00	.01	.02
.			
.			
.			
.9	.3159	.3186	.3212
1.0	.3413	.3438	.3461
1.1	.3643	.3665	.3686
1.2	.3849	.3869	.3888
.			
.			
.			

$P(.00 \leq z \leq 1.00)$

Using the same approach, we can find $P(.00 \leq z \leq 1.25)$. By first locating the 1.2 row and then moving across to the .05 column, we find $P(.00 \leq z \leq 1.25) = .3944$.

As another example of the use of the table of areas for the standard normal distribution, we compute the probability of obtaining a z value between $z = -1.00$ and $z = 1.00$; that is, $P(-1.00 \leq z \leq 1.00)$.

Note that we already used Table 6.1 to show that the probability of a z value between $z = .00$ and $z = 1.00$ is .3413, and recall that the normal probability distribution is *symmetric*. Thus, the probability of a z value between $z = .00$ and $z = -1.00$ is the same as the probability of a z value between $z = .00$ and $z = +1.00$. Hence, the probability of a z value between $z = -1.00$ and $z = +1.00$ is

$$P(-1.00 \leq z \leq .00) + P(.00 \leq z \leq 1.00) = .3413 + .3413 = .6826$$

This probability is shown graphically in the following figure.

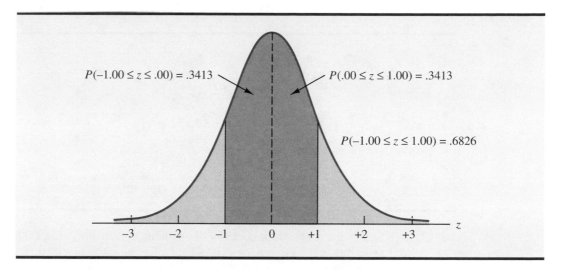

These probability calculations are the basis for observation 7 on page 233.

In a similar manner, we can use the values in Table 6.1 to show that the probability of a z value between -2.00 and $+2.00$ is $.4772 + .4772 = .9544$ and that the probability of a z value between -3.00 and $+3.00$ is $.4986 + .4986 = .9972$. Because we know that the total probability or total area under the curve for any continuous random variable must be 1.0000, the probability $.9972$ tells us that the value of z will almost always be between -3.00 and $+3.00$.

Next, we compute the probability of obtaining a z value of at least 1.58; that is, $P(z \geq 1.58)$. First, we use the $z = 1.5$ row and the $.08$ column of Table 6.1 to find that $P(.00 \leq z \leq 1.58) = .4429$. Now, because the normal probability distribution is symmetric, we know that 50% of the area under the curve must be to the right of the mean (i.e., $z = 0$) and 50% of the area under the curve must be to the left of the mean. If $.4429$ is the area between the mean and $z = 1.58$, then the area or probability corresponding to $z \geq 1.58$ must be $.5000 - .4429 = .0571$. This probability is shown in the following figure.

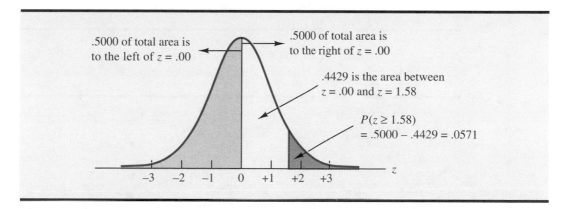

As another illustration, consider the probability that the random variable z assumes a value of $-.50$ or larger; that is, $P(z \geq -.50)$. To make this computation, we note that the probability we are seeking can be written as the sum of two probabilities: $P(z \geq -.50) = P(-.50 \leq z \leq .00) + P(z \geq 0.00)$. We have previously seen that $P(z \geq .00) = .50$. Also, we know that since the normal distribution is symmetric, $P(-.50 \leq z \leq .00) = P(.00 \leq z \leq .50)$.

Referring to Table 6.1, we find that $P(.00 \leq z \leq .50) = .1915$. Therefore $P(z \geq -.50) = .1915 + .5000 = .6915$. The following graph shows this probability.

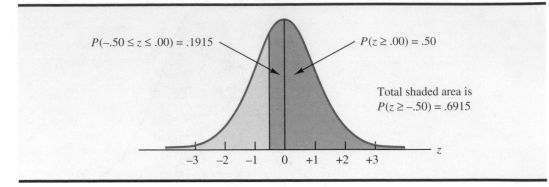

Next, we compute the probability of obtaining a z value between 1.00 and 1.58; that is, $P(1.00 \leq z \leq 1.58)$. From our previous examples, we know that there is a .3413 probability of a z value between $z = 0.00$ and $z = 1.00$ and that there is a .4429 probability of a z value between $z = 0.00$ and $z = 1.58$. Hence, there must be a $.4429 - .3413 = .1016$ probability of a z value between $z = 1.00$ and $z = 1.58$. Thus, $P(1.00 \leq z \leq 1.58) = .1016$. This situation is shown graphically in the following figure.

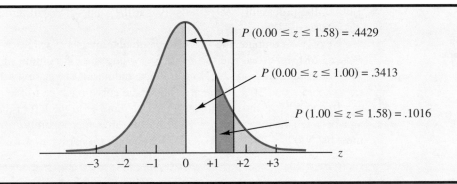

As a final illustration, let us find a z value such that the probability of obtaining a larger z value is .10. The following figure shows this situation graphically.

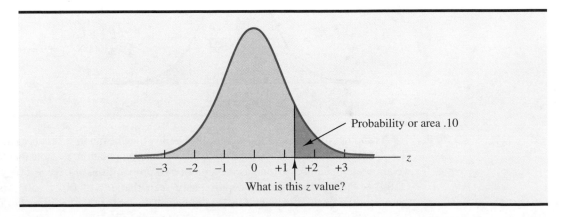

This problem is the inverse of those in the preceding examples. Previously, we specified the z value of interest and then found the corresponding probability, or area. In this example, we are given the probability and asked to find the corresponding z value. To do so, we use the table of probabilities for the standard normal probability distribution (Table 6.1) somewhat differently.

Given a probability, we can use the standard normal table in an inverse fashion to find the corresponding z value.

Recall that the body of Table 6.1 gives the area under the curve between the mean and a particular z value. We have been given the information that the area in the upper tail of the curve is .10. Hence, we must determine how much of the area is between the mean and the z value of interest. Because we know that .5000 of the area is to the right of the mean, $.5000 - .1000 = .4000$ must be the area under the curve between the mean and the desired z value. Scanning the body of the table, we find .3997 as the probability value closest to .4000. The section of the table providing this result follows.

z	.06	.07	.08	.09
.				
.				
.				
1.0	.3554	.3577	.3599	.3621
1.1	.3770	.3790	.3810	.3830
1.2	.3962	.3980	.3997	.4015
1.3	.4131	.4147	.4162	.4177
1.4	.4279	.4292	.4306	.4319
.				
.				
.				

Area value in body
of table closest to .9000

Reading the z value from the left-most column and the top row of the table, we find that the corresponding z value is 1.28. Thus, an area of approximately .4000 (actually .3997) will be between the mean and $z = 1.28$.* In terms of the question originally asked, the probability is approximately .10 that the z value will be larger than 1.28.

The examples illustrate that the table of areas for the standard normal probability distribution can be used to find probabilities associated with values of the standard normal random variable z. Two types of questions can be asked. The first type of question specifies a value, or values, for z and asks us to use the table to determine the corresponding areas, or probabilities. The second type of question provides an area, or probability, and asks us to use the table to determine the corresponding z value. Thus, we need to be flexible in using the standard normal probability table to answer the desired probability question. In most cases, sketching a graph of the standard normal probability distribution and shading the appropriate area or probability helps to visualize the situation and aids in determining the correct answer.

Computing Probabilities for Any Normal Probability Distribution

The reason for discussing the standard normal distribution so extensively is that probabilities for all normal distributions are computed by using the standard normal distribution. That is, when we have a normal distribution with any mean μ and any standard deviation

---

*We could use interpolation in the body of the table to get a better approximation of the z value that corresponds to an area of .4000. Doing so to provide one more decimal place of accuracy would yield a z value of 1.282. However, in most practical situations, sufficient accuracy is obtained by simply using the table value closest to the desired probability.

σ, we answer probability questions about the distribution by first converting to the standard normal distribution. Then we can use Table 6.1 and the appropriate z values to find the desired probabilities. The formula used to convert any normal random variable x with mean μ and standard deviation σ to the standard normal distribution follows.

The formula for the standard normal random variable is similar to the formula we introduced in Chapter 3 for computing z-scores for a data set.

Converting to the Standard Normal Distribution

$$z = \frac{x - \mu}{\sigma} \tag{6.3}$$

A value of x equal to its mean μ results in $z = (\mu - \mu)/\sigma = 0$. Thus, we see that a value of x equal to its mean μ corresponds to a value of z at its mean 0. Now suppose that x is one standard deviation greater than its mean; that is, $x = \mu + \sigma$. Applying equation (6.3), we see that the corresponding z value is $z = [(\mu + \sigma) - \mu]/\sigma = \sigma/\sigma = 1$. Thus, a value of x that is one standard deviation greater than its mean corresponds to $z = 1$. In other words, we can interpret z as the number of standard deviations that the normal random variable x is from its mean μ.

To see how this conversion enables us to compute probabilities for any normal distribution, suppose we have a normal distribution with $\mu = 10$ and $\sigma = 2$. What is the probability that the random variable x is between 10 and 14? Using equation (6.3) we see that at $x = 10$, $z = (x - \mu)/\sigma = (10 - 10)/2 = 0$ and that at $x = 14$, $z = (14 - 10)/2 = 4/2 = 2$. Thus, the answer to our question about the probability of x being between 10 and 14 is given by the equivalent probability that z is between 0 and 2 for the standard normal distribution. In other words, the probability that we are seeking is the probability that the random variable x is between its mean and two standard deviations greater than the mean. Using $z = 2.00$ and Table 6.1, we see that the probability is .4772. Hence the probability that x is between 10 and 14 is .4772.

Grear Tire Company Problem

We turn now to an application of the normal probability distribution. Suppose the Grear Tire Company has just developed a new steel-belted radial tire that will be sold through a national chain of discount stores. Because the tire is a new product, Grear's managers believe that the mileage guarantee offered with the tire will be an important factor in the acceptance of the product. Before finalizing the tire mileage guarantee policy, Grear's managers want probability information about the number of miles the tires will last.

From actual road tests with the tires, Grear's engineering group estimates the mean tire mileage is $\mu = 36,500$ miles and that the standard deviation is $\sigma = 5000$. In addition, the data collected indicate a normal distribution is a reasonable assumption. What percentage of the tires can be expected to last more than 40,000 miles? In other words, what is the probability that the tire mileage will exceed 40,000? This question can be answered by finding the area of the darkly shaded region in Figure 6.6.

At $x = 40,000$, we have

$$z = \frac{x - \mu}{\sigma} = \frac{40,000 - 36,500}{5000} = \frac{3500}{5000} = .70$$

Refer now to the bottom of Figure 6.6. We see that a value of $x = 40,000$ on the Grear Tire normal distribution corresponds to a value of $z = .70$ on the standard normal distribution. Using Table 6.1, we see that the area between the mean and $z = .70$ is .2580. Referring again

FIGURE 6.6   GREAR TIRE COMPANY MILEAGE DISTRIBUTION

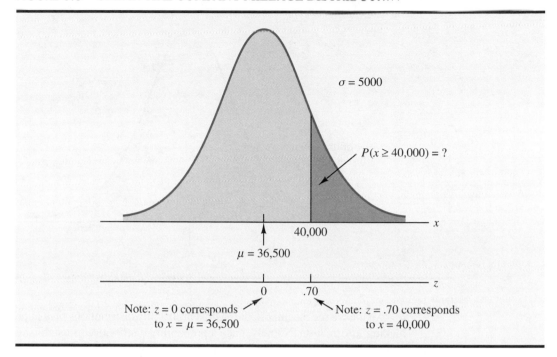

to Figure 6.6, we see that the area between $x = 36,500$ and $x = 40,000$ on the Grear Tire normal distribution is the same. Thus, $.5000 - .2580 = .2420$ is the probability that x will exceed 40,000. We can conclude that about 24.2% of the tires will exceed 40,000 in mileage.

Let us now assume that Grear is considering a guarantee that will provide a discount on replacement tires if the original tires do not exceed the mileage stated in the guarantee. What should the guaranteed mileage be if Grear wants no more than 10% of the tires to be eligible for the discount guarantee? This question is interpreted graphically in Figure 6.7.

According to Figure 6.7, 40% of the area must be between the mean and the unknown guaranteed mileage. We look up .4000 in the body of Table 6.1 and see that this area is at approximately 1.28 standard deviations to the left of the mean. That is, $z = -1.28$ is the value of the standard normal random variable corresponding to the desired mileage guarantee on the Grear Tire normal distribution. To find the value of x corresponding to $z = -1.28$, we have

$$z = \frac{x - \mu}{\sigma} = -1.28$$

$$x - \mu = -1.28\sigma$$

$$x = \mu - 1.28\sigma$$

With $\mu = 36,500$ and $\sigma = 5000$,

$$x = 36,500 - 1.28(5000) = 30,100$$

With the guarantee set at 30,000 miles, the actual percentage eligible for the guarantee will be 9.68%.

Thus, a guarantee of 30,100 miles will meet the requirement that approximately 10% of the tires will be eligible for the guarantee. Perhaps, with this information, the firm will set its tire mileage guarantee at 30,000 miles.

FIGURE 6.7 GREAR'S DISCOUNT GUARANTEE

Again, we see the important role that probability distributions play in providing decision-making information. Namely, once a probability distribution is established for a particular application, it can be used quickly and easily to obtain probability information about the problem. Probability does not make a decision recommendation directly, but it provides information that helps the decision maker better understand the risks and uncertainties associated with the problem. Ultimately, this information may assist the decision maker in reaching a good decision.

EXERCISES

Methods

8. Using Figure 6.4 as a guide, sketch a normal curve for a random variable x that has a mean of $\mu = 100$ and a standard deviation of $\sigma = 10$. Label the horizontal axis with values of 70, 80, 90, 100, 110, 120, and 130.

9. A random variable is normally distributed with a mean of $\mu = 50$ and a standard deviation of $\sigma = 5$.

    a. Sketch a normal curve for the probability density function. Label the horizontal axis with values of 35, 40, 45, 50, 55, 60, and 65. Figure 6.4 shows that the normal curve almost touches the horizontal axis at three standard deviations below and at three standard deviations above the mean (in this case at 35 and 65).

    b. What is the probability the random variable will assume a value between 45 and 55?

    c. What is the probability the random variable will assume a value between 40 and 60?

10. Draw a graph for the standard normal distribution. Label the horizontal axis at values of $-3, -2, -1, 0, 1, 2,$ and 3. Then use the table of probabilities for the standard normal distribution to compute the following probabilities.

    a. $P(0 \leq z \leq 1)$

    b. $P(0 \leq z \leq 1.5)$

    c. $P(0 < z < 2)$

    d. $P(0 < z < 2.5)$

11. Given that z is a standard normal random variable, compute the following probabilities.

    a. $P(-1 \leq z \leq 0)$

    b. $P(-1.5 \leq z \leq 0)$

    c. $P(-2 < z < 0)$

    d. $P(-2.5 \leq z \leq 0)$

    e. $P(-3 \leq z \leq 0)$

12. Given that z is a standard normal random variable, compute the following probabilities.

    a. $P(0 \leq z \leq .83)$

    b. $P(-1.57 \leq z \leq 0)$

    c. $P(z > 44)$

    d. $P(z \geq -.23)$

    e. $P(z < 1.20)$

    f. $P(z \leq -.71)$

SELFtest   13. Given that z is a standard normal random variable, compute the following probabilities.

    a. $P(-1.98 \leq z \leq .49)$

    b. $P(.52 \leq z \leq 1.22)$

    c. $P(-1.75 \leq z \leq -1.04)$

14. Given that z is a standard normal random variable, find z for each situation.

    a. The area between 0 and z is .4750.

    b. The area between 0 and z is .2291.

    c. The area to the right of z is .1314.

    d. The area to the left of z is .6700.

SELFtest   15. Given that z is a standard normal random variable, find z for each situation.

    a. The area to the left of z is .2119.

    b. The area between $-z$ and z is .9030.

    c. The area between $-z$ and z is .2052.

    d. The area to the left of z is .9948.

    e. The area to the right of z is .6915.

16. Given that z is a standard normal random variable, find z for each situation.

    a. The area to the right of z is .01.

    b. The area to the right of z is .025.

    c. The area to the right of z is .05.

    d. The area to the right of z is .10.

Applications

17. The average amount parents and children spent per child on back-to-school clothes in Autumn 2001 was $527 (CNBC, September 5, 2001). Assume the standard deviation is $160 and that the amount spent is normally distributed.

    a. What is the probability that the amount spent on a randomly selected child is more than $700?

    b. What is the probability that the amount spent on a randomly selected child is less than $100?

    c. What is the probability that the amount spent on a randomly selected child is between $450 and $700?

    d. What is the probability that the amount spent on a randomly selected child is no more than $300?

SELFtest

18. The average time a subscriber spends reading *The Wall Street Journal* is 49 minutes (*The Wall Street Journal* Subscriber Study, 1996). Assume the standard deviation is 16 minutes and that the times are normally distributed.
    a. What is the probability a subscriber will spend at least 60 minutes reading the *Journal*?
    b. What is the probability a subscriber will spend no more than 30 minutes reading the *Journal*?
    c. For the 10% who spend the most time reading the *Journal,* how much time do they spend?

19. The average amount of precipitation in Dallas, Texas, during the month of April is 3.5 inches (*The World Almanac,* 2000). Assume that a normal distribution applies and that the standard deviation is .8 inches.
    a. What percentage of the time does the amount of rainfall in April exceed 5 inches?
    b. What percentage of the time is the amount of rainfall in April less than 3 inches?
    c. A month is classified as extremely wet if the amount of rainfall is in the upper 10% for that month. How much precipitation must fall before a month of April is classified as extremely wet?

20. According to a survey, subscribers to *The Wall Street Journal Interactive Edition* spend an average of 27 hours per week using the computer at work (*WSJ.com* Subscriber Study, 1999). Assume the normal distribution applies and that the standard deviation is 8 hours.
    a. What is the probability a randomly selected subscriber spends fewer than 11 hours using the computer at work?
    b. What percentage of the subscribers spends more than 40 hours per week using the computer at work?
    c. A person is classified as a heavy user if he or she is in the upper 20% in terms of hours of usage. How many hours must a subscriber use the computer in order to be classified as a heavy user?

21. A person must score in the upper 2% of the population on an IQ test to qualify for membership in Mensa, the international high-IQ society (*US Airways Attache,* September, 2000). If IQ scores are normally distributed with a mean of 100 and a standard deviation of 15, what score must a person get to qualify for Mensa?

22. According to the Bureau of Labor Statistics, the average weekly pay for a U.S. production worker was $441.84 in 1998 (*The World Almanac,* 2000). Assume that available data indicate that wages are normally distributed with a standard deviation of $90.
    a. What is the probability that a worker earns between $400 and $500?
    b. How much does a production worker have to earn to be in the top 20% of wage earners?
    c. For a randomly selected production worker, what is the probability the worker earns less than $250 per week?

23. The time needed to complete a final examination in a particular college course is normally distributed with a mean of 80 minutes and a standard deviation of 10 minutes. Answer the following questions.
    a. What is the probability of completing the exam in one hour or less?
    b. What is the probability that a student will complete the exam in more than 60 minutes but less than 75 minutes?
    c. Assume that the class has 60 students and that the examination period is 90 minutes in length. How many students do you expect will be unable to complete the exam in the allotted time?

24. The daily trading volumes (millions of shares) for stocks traded on the New York Stock Exchange for 12 days in August and September are shown here (*Barron's,* August 7, 2000, September 4, 2000, and September 11, 2000).

917	983	1,046
944	723	783
813	1,057	766
836	992	973

The probability distribution of trading volume is approximately normal.
a. Compute the mean and standard deviation for the daily trading volume to use as estimates of the population mean and standard deviation.
b. What is the probability that on a particular day the trading volume will be less than 800 million shares?
c. What is the probability that trading volume will exceed 1 billion shares?
d. If the exchange wants to issue a press release on the top 5% of trading days, what volume will trigger a release?

25. The average ticket price for a Washington Redskins football game was $81.89 for the 2001 season (*USA Today,* September 6, 2001). With the additional costs of parking, food, drinks, and souvenirs, the average cost for a family of four to attend a game totaled $442.54. Assume the normal distribution applies and that the standard deviation is $65.
a. What is the probability that a family of four will spend more than $400?
b. What is the probability that a family of four will spend $300 or less?
c. What is the probability that a family of four will spend between $400 and $500?

6.3   EXPONENTIAL PROBABILITY DISTRIBUTION

A continuous probability distribution that is useful in describing the time it takes to complete a task is the **exponential probability distribution.** The exponential random variable can be used to describe such things as the time between arrivals at a car wash, the time required to load a truck, the distance between major defects in a highway, and so on. The exponential probability density function is defined as follows.

Exponential Probability Density Function

$$f(x) = \frac{1}{\mu} e^{-x/\mu} \qquad \text{for } x \geq 0, \mu > 0 \qquad (6.4)$$

As an example of the exponential probability distribution, suppose that $x =$ the time it takes to load a truck at the Schips loading dock follows such a distribution. If the mean, or average, time to load a truck is 15 minutes ($\mu = 15$), the appropriate probability density function is

$$f(x) = \frac{1}{15} e^{-x/15}$$

Figure 6.8 is the graph of this probability density function.

Computing Probabilities for the Exponential Distribution

As with any continuous probability distribution, the area under the curve corresponding to an interval provides the probability that the random variable assumes a value in that interval. In the Schips loading dock example, the probability that loading a truck will take

FIGURE 6.8   EXPONENTIAL PROBABILITY DISTRIBUTION FOR THE SCHIPS
LOADING DOCK EXAMPLE

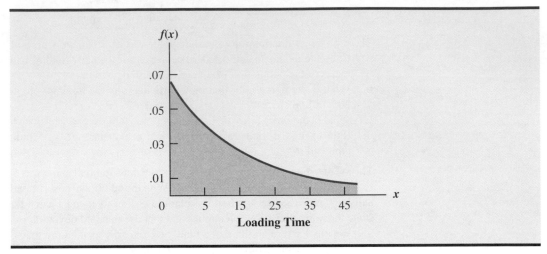

In waiting line applications, the exponential distribution is often used for service time.

6 minutes or less ($x \leq 6$) is defined to be the area under the curve in Figure 6.8 from $x = 0$ to $x = 6$. Similarly, the probability that loading a truck will take 18 minutes or less ($x \leq 18$) is the area under the curve from $x = 0$ to $x = 18$. Note also that the probability that loading a truck will take between 6 minutes and 18 minutes ($6 \leq x \leq 18$) is given by the area under the curve from $x = 6$ to $x = 18$.

To compute exponential probabilities such as those just described, we use the following formula. It provides the cumulative probability of obtaining a value for the exponential random variable of less than or equal to some specific value of x, denoted by x_0.

Exponential Distribution: Cumulative Probabilities

$$P(x \leq x_0) = 1 - e^{-x_0/\mu} \tag{6.5}$$

For the Schips loading dock example, $x =$ loading time and $\mu = 15$, which gives us

$$P(x \leq x_0) = 1 - e^{-x_0/15}$$

Hence, the probability that loading a truck will take 6 minutes or less is

$$P(x \leq 6) = 1 - e^{-6/15} = .3297$$

Figure 6.9 shows the area or probability for a loading time of 6 minutes or less.
Using equation (6.5), we calculate the probability of loading a truck in 18 minutes or less.

$$P(x \leq 18) = 1 - e^{-18/15} = .6988$$

Thus, the probability that loading a truck will take between 6 minutes and 18 minutes is equal to $.6988 - .3297 = .3691$. Probabilities for any other interval can be computed similarly.

FIGURE 6.9   PROBABILITY OF A LOADING TIME OF SIX MINUTES OR LESS

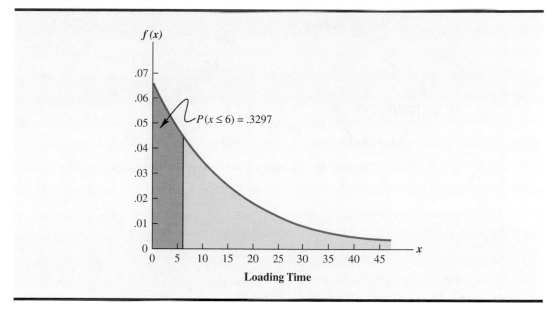

Relationship Between the Poisson and Exponential Distributions

In Section 5.5 we introduced the Poisson distribution as a discrete probability distribution that is often useful in examining the number of occurrences of an event over a specified interval of time or space. Recall that the Poisson probability function is

$$f(x) = \frac{\mu^x e^{-\mu}}{x!}$$

where

$$\mu = \text{expected value or mean number of}$$
$$\text{occurrences over a specified interval}$$

The continuous exponential probability distribution is related to the discrete Poisson distribution. If the Poisson distribution provides an appropriate description of the number of occurrences per interval, the exponential distribution provides a description of the length of the interval between occurrences.

If arrivals follow a Poisson distribution, the time between arrivals must follow an exponential distribution.

To illustrate this relationship, suppose the number of cars that arrive at a car wash during one hour is described by a Poisson probability distribution with a mean of 10 cars per hour. The Poisson probability function that gives the probability of x arrivals per hour is

$$f(x) = \frac{10^x e^{-10}}{x!}$$

Because the average number of arrivals is 10 cars per hour, the average time between cars arriving is

$$\frac{1 \text{ hour}}{10 \text{ cars}} = .1 \text{ hour/car}$$

Thus, the corresponding exponential distribution that describes the time between the arrivals has a mean of $\mu = .1$ hour per car; as a result, the appropriate exponential probability density function is

$$f(x) = \frac{1}{.1} e^{-x/.1} = 10e^{-10x}$$

EXERCISES

Methods

26. Consider the following exponential probability density function.

$$f(x) = \frac{1}{8} e^{-x/8} \qquad \text{for } x \geq 0$$

   a. Compute $P(x \leq 6)$.
   b. Compute $P(x \leq 4)$.
   c. Compute $P(x \geq 6)$.
   d. Compute $P(4 \leq x \leq 6)$.

SELFtest 27. Consider the following exponential probability density function.

$$f(x) = \frac{1}{3} e^{-x/3} \qquad \text{for } x \geq 0$$

   a. Write the formula for $P(x \leq x_0)$.
   b. Compute $P(x \leq 2)$.
   c. Compute $P(x \geq 3)$.
   d. Compute $P(x \leq 5)$.
   e. Compute $P(2 \leq x \leq 5)$.

Applications

28. *Internet Magazine* monitors Internet service providers (ISPs) and provides statistics on their performance. The average time to download a Web page for free ISPs is approximately 20 seconds for European Web pages (*Internet Magazine,* January, 2000). Assume the time to download a Web page follows an exponential distribution.
   a. What is the probability it will take less than 10 seconds to download a Web page?
   b. What is the probability it will take more than 30 seconds to download a Web page?
   c. What is the probability it will take between 10 and 30 seconds to download a Web page?

SELFtest 29. The time between arrivals of vehicles at a particular intersection follows an exponential probability distribution with a mean of 12 seconds.
   a. Sketch this exponential probability distribution.
   b. What is the probability that the time between vehicle arrivals is 12 seconds or less?
   c. What is the probability that the time between vehicle arrivals is 6 seconds or less?
   d. What is the probability of 30 or more seconds between vehicle arrivals?

30. The lifetime (hours) of an electronic device is a random variable with the following exponential probability density function.

$$f(x) = \frac{1}{50} e^{-x/50} \qquad \text{for } x \geq 0$$

    a. What is the mean lifetime of the device?

    b. What is the probability that the device will fail in the first 25 hours of operation?

    c. What is the probability that the device will operate 100 or more hours before failure?

31. Sparagowski & Associates conducted a study of service times at the drive-up window of fast-food restaurants. The average time between placing an order and receiving the order at McDonald's restaurants was 2.78 minutes (*The Cincinnati Enquirer,* July 9, 2000). Waiting times, such as these, frequently follow an exponential distribution.

    a. What is the probability that a customer's service time is less than 2 minutes?

    b. What is the probability that a customer's service time is more than 5 minutes?

    c. What is the probability that a customer's service time is more than 2.78 minutes?

32. According to *Barron's* 1998 Primary Reader Survey, the average annual number of investment transactions for a subscriber is 30 (*www.barronsmag.com,* July 28, 2000). Suppose the number of transactions in a year follows the Poisson probability distribution.

    a. Show the probability distribution for the time between investment transactions.

    b. What is the probability of no transactions during the month of January for a particular subscriber?

    c. What is the probability that the next transaction will occur within the next half month for a particular subscriber?

SUMMARY

This chapter extended the discussion of probability distributions to the case of continuous random variables. The major conceptual difference between discrete and continuous probability distributions involves the method of computing probabilities. With discrete distributions, the probability function $f(x)$ provides the probability that the random variable x assumes various values. With continuous probability distributions, the probability density function $f(x)$ does not provide probability values directly. Instead, probabilities are given by areas under the curve or graph of the probability density function $f(x)$. Because the area under the curve above a single point is zero, we observe that the probability of any particular value is zero for a continuous random variable.

    Three continuous probability distributions—the uniform, normal, and exponential distributions—were treated in detail. The normal probability distribution is used widely in statistical inference and will be used extensively throughout the remainder of the text.

GLOSSARY

Probability density function   A function used to compute probabilities for a continuous random variable. The area under the graph of a probability density function over an interval represents probability.

Uniform probability distribution   A continuous probability distribution for which the probability that the random variable will assume a value in any interval is the same for all intervals of equal length.

Normal probability distribution   A continuous probability distribution. Its probability density function is bell shaped and determined by its mean μ and standard deviation σ.

Standard normal probability distribution   A normal distribution with a mean of zero and a standard deviation of one.

Exponential probability distribution   A continuous probability distribution that is useful in computing probabilities for the time it takes to complete a task.

KEY FORMULAS

Uniform Probability Density Function

$$f(x) = \begin{cases} \dfrac{1}{b-a} & \text{for } a \leq x \leq b \\ 0 & \text{elsewhere} \end{cases} \tag{6.1}$$

Normal Probability Density Function

$$f(x) = \frac{1}{\sigma\sqrt{2\pi}} e^{-(x-\mu)^2/2\sigma^2} \tag{6.2}$$

Converting to the Standard Normal Distribution

$$z = \frac{x-\mu}{\sigma} \tag{6.3}$$

Exponential Probability Density Function

$$f(x) = \frac{1}{\mu} e^{-x/\mu} \qquad \text{for } x \geq 0, \mu > 0 \tag{6.4}$$

Exponential Distribution: Cumulative Probabilities

$$P(x \leq x_0) = 1 - e^{-x_0/\mu} \tag{6.5}$$

SUPPLEMENTARY EXERCISES

33. A business executive, transferred from Chicago to Atlanta, needs to sell her house in Chicago quickly. The executive's employer offered to buy the house for $210,000, but the offer expires at the end of the week. The executive does not currently have a better offer, but can afford to leave the house on the market for another month. From conversations with her realtor, the executive believes the price she will get by leaving the house on the market for another month is uniformly distributed between $200,000 and $225,000.

    a. If she leaves the house on the market for another month, what is the mathematical expression for the probability density function of the sales price?

    b. If she leaves it on the market for another month, what is the probability she will get at least $215,000 for the house?

    c. If she leaves it on the market for another month, what is the probability she will get less than $210,000?

    d. Should the executive leave the house on the market for another month? Why or why not?

34. Sixty-eight percent of the debt owed by American families is home mortgage or equity credit (*Federal Reserve Bulletin,* January 1997). The median amount of mortgage debt for families with the head of the household under 35 years old is $63,000. Assume the amount of mortgage debt for this group is normally distributed and the standard deviation is $15,000.

    a. What is the mean amount of mortgage debt for this group?

    b. How much mortgage debt do the 10% with the smallest debt have?

    c. What percent of these families have mortgage debt in excess of $80,000?

    d. The upper 5% of mortgage debt is in excess of what amount?

35. Motorola used the normal distribution to determine the probability of defects and the number of defects expected in a production process (*APICS—The Performance Advantage,* July 1991). Assume a production process produces units with a mean weight of 10 ounces. Calculate the probability of a defect and the expected number of defects for a 1000-unit production run in the following situations.

   a. The process standard deviation is .15, and the process control is set at plus or minus one standard deviation. Units with weights less than 9.85 or greater than 10.15 ounces will be classified as defects.

   b. Through process design improvements, the process standard deviation can be reduced to .05. Assume the process control remains the same, with weights less than 9.85 or greater than 10.15 ounces being classified as defects.

   c. What is the advantage of reducing process variation thereby setting process control limits at a greater number of standard deviations from the mean?

36. The average annual amount American households spend for daily transportation is $6312 (*Money,* August 2001). Assume that the amount spent is normally distributed.

   a. Suppose you learn that 5% of American households spend less than $1000 for daily transportation. What is the standard deviation of the amount spent?

   b. What is the probability that a household spends between $4000 and $6000?

   c. What is the amount spent by the 3% of households with the highest daily transportation cost?

37. The sales of High-Brite Toothpaste are believed to be approximately normally distributed, with a mean of 10,000 tubes per week and a standard deviation of 1500 tubes per week.

   a. What is the probability that more than 12,000 tubes will be sold in any given week?

   b. To have a .95 probability that the company will have sufficient stock to cover the weekly demand, how many tubes should be produced?

38. Ward Doering Auto Sales is considering offering a special service contract that will cover the total cost of any service work required on leased vehicles. From experience, the company manager estimates that yearly service costs are approximately normally distributed, with a mean of $150 and a standard deviation of $25.

   a. If the company offers the service contract to customers for a yearly charge of $200, what is the probability that any one customer's service costs will exceed the contract price of $200?

   b. What is Ward's expected profit per service contract?

39. The Asian currency crisis of late 1997 and early 1998 was expected to lead to substantial job losses in the United States as inexpensive imports flooded markets. California was expected to be especially hard hit. The Economic Policy Institute estimated that the mean number of job losses in California would be 126,681 (*St. Petersburg Times,* January 24, 1998). Assume the number of jobs lost in California is normally distributed with the mean equal to the estimate and a standard deviation of 30,000.

   a. What is the probability the number of lost jobs is between 80,000 and 150,000?

   b. What is the probability the number of lost jobs will be less than 50,000?

   c. What cutoff value will provide a .95 probability that the number of lost jobs will not exceed the value?

40. Assume that the test scores from a college admissions test are normally distributed, with a mean of 450 and a standard deviation of 100.

   a. What percentage of the people taking the test score between 400 and 500?

   b. Suppose someone receives a score of 630. What percentage of the people taking the test score better? What percentage score worse?

   c. If a particular university will not admit anyone scoring below 480, what percentage of the persons taking the test would be acceptable to the university?

41. According to *Advertising Age,* the average base salary for women working as copywriters in advertising firms is higher than the average base salary for men. The average base salary for women is $67,000 and the average base salary for men is $65,500 (*Working Woman,* July/August 2000). Assume salaries are normally distributed and that the standard deviation is $7000 for both men and women.

    a. What is the probability of a woman receiving a salary in excess of $75,000?

    b. What is the probability of a man receiving a salary in excess of $75,000?

    c. What is the probability of a woman receiving a salary below $50,000?

    d. How much would a woman have to make to have a higher salary than 99% of her male counterparts?

42. A machine fills containers with a particular product. The standard deviation of filling weights is known from past data to be .6 ounce. If only 2% of the containers hold less than 18 ounces, what is the mean filling weight for the machine? That is, what must μ equal? Assume the filling weights have a normal distribution.

43. The time in minutes for which a student uses a computer terminal at the computer center of a major university follows an exponential probability distribution with a mean of 36 minutes. Assume a student arrives at the terminal just as another student is beginning to work on the terminal.

    a. What is the probability that the wait for the second student will be 15 minutes or less?

    b. What is the probability that the wait for the second student will be between 15 and 45 minutes?

    c. What is the probability that the second student will have to wait an hour or more?

44. The Web site for the Bed and Breakfast Inns of North America (*www.bestinns.net*) gets approximately seven visitors per minute (*Time,* September 2001). Suppose the number of Web site visitors per minute follows a Poisson probability distribution.

    a. What is the mean time between visits to the Web site?

    b. Show the exponential probability density function for the time between Web site visits.

    c. What is the probability no one will access the Web site in a 1-minute period?

    d. What is the probability no one will access the Web site in a 12-second period?

45. The average travel time to work for New York City residents is 36.5 minutes (*Time Almanac,* 2001).

    a. Assume the exponential probability distribution is applicable and show the probability density function for the travel time to work for a typical New Yorker.

    b. What is the probability it will take a typical New Yorker between 20 and 40 minutes to travel to work?

    c. What is the probability it will take the typical New Yorker more than 40 minutes to travel to work?

46. The time (in minutes) between telephone calls at an insurance claims office has the following exponential probability distribution.

$$f(x) = .50e^{-.50x} \qquad \text{for } x \geq 0$$

    a. What is the mean time between telephone calls?

    b. What is the probability of having 30 seconds or less between telephone calls?

    c. What is the probability of having 1 minute or less between telephone calls?

    d. What is the probability of having 5 or more minutes without a telephone call?

Appendix 6.1   CONTINUOUS PROBABILITY DISTRIBUTIONS WITH MINITAB

Let us demonstrate the Minitab procedure for computing continuous probabilities by referring to the Grear Tire Company problem where tire mileage was described by a normal probability distribution with $\mu = 36,500$ and $\sigma = 5000$. One question asked was: What is the probability that the tire mileage will exceed 40,000 miles?

For continuous probability distributions, Minitab gives a cumulative probability; that is, Minitab gives the probability that the random variable will assume a value less than or equal to a specified constant. For the Grear tire mileage question, Minitab can be used to determine the cumulative probability that the tire mileage will be less than or equal to 40,000 miles. (The specified constant in this case is 40,000.) After obtaining the cumulative probability from Minitab, we must subtract it from 1 to determine the probability that the tire mileage will exceed 40,000 miles.

Prior to using Minitab to compute a probability, one must enter the specified constant into a column of the worksheet. For the Grear tire mileage question we entered the specified constant of 40,000 into column C1 of the Minitab worksheet. The steps in using Minitab to compute the cumulative probability of the normal random variable assuming a value less than or equal to 40,000 follow.

Step 1. Select the **Calc** pull-down menu
Step 2. Choose **Probability Distributions**
Step 3. Choose **Normal**
Step 4. When the Normal Distribution dialog box appears:
        Select **Cumulative probability**
        Enter 36500 in the **Mean** box
        Enter 5000 in the **Standard deviation** box
        Enter C1 in the **Input column** box (the column containing 40,000)
        Click **OK**

After the user clicks **OK,** Minitab prints the cumulative probability that the normal random variable assumes a value less than or equal to 40,000. Minitab shows that this probability is .7580. Because we are interested in the probability that the tire mileage will be greater than 40,000, the desired probability is $1 - .7580 = .2420$.

A second question in the Grear Tire Company problem was: What mileage guarantee should Grear set to ensure that no more than 10% of the tires qualify for the guarantee? Here we are given a probability and want to find the corresponding value for the random variable. Minitab uses an inverse calculation routine to find the value of the random variable associated with a given cumulative probability. First, we must enter the cumulative probability into a column of the Minitab worksheet (say C1). In this case, the desired cumulative probability is .10. Then, the first three steps of the Minitab procedure are as already listed. In step 4, we select **Inverse cumulative probability** instead of **Cumulative probability** and complete the remaining parts of the step. Minitab then displays the mileage guarantee of 30,100 miles.

Minitab is capable of computing probabilities for other continuous probability distributions, including the exponential probability distribution. To compute exponential probabilities, follow the procedure shown previously for the normal probability distribution and choose the **Exponential** option in step 3. Step 4 is as shown, with the exception that entering the standard deviation is not required. Output for cumulative probabilities and inverse cumulative probabilities is identical to that described for the normal probability distribution.

Appendix 6.2 CONTINUOUS PROBABILITY DISTRIBUTIONS WITH EXCEL

Excel has the capability of computing probabilities for several continuous probability distributions, including the normal and exponential probability distributions. In this appendix, we describe how Excel can be used to compute probabilities for any normal probability distribution. The procedures for the exponential and other continuous probability distributions are similar to the one we describe for the normal probability distribution.

Let us return to the Grear Tire Company problem where the tire mileage was described by a normal probability distribution with $\mu = 36,500$ and $\sigma = 5000$. Assume we are interested in the probability that tire mileage will exceed 40,000 miles.

Excel's NORMDIST function provides cumulative probabilities for a normal probability distribution. The general form of the function is NORMDIST (x, μ, σ, cumulative). For the fourth argument, TRUE is specified if a cumulative probability is desired. Thus, to compute the cumulative probability that the tire mileage will be less than or equal to 40,000 miles we would enter the following formula into any cell of an Excel worksheet:

$$=\text{NORMDIST}(40000,36500,5000,\text{TRUE})$$

At this point, .7580 will appear in the cell where the formula was entered, indicating that the probability of tire mileage being less than or equal to 40,000 miles is .7580. Therefore, the probability that tire mileage will exceed 40,000 miles is $1 - .7580 = .2420$.

Excel's NORMINV function uses an inverse computation to find the x value corresponding to a given cumulative probability. For instance, suppose we want to find the guaranteed mileage Grear should offer so that no more than 10% of the tires will be eligible for the guarantee. We would enter the following formula into any cell of an Excel worksheet:

$$=\text{NORMINV}(.1,36500,5000)$$

At this point, 30092 will appear in the cell where the formula was entered indicating that the probability of a tire not lasting 30,092 miles is .10.

The Excel function for computing exponential probabilities is EXPONDIST. Using it is straightforward. But, if one needs help specifying the proper values for the arguments, Excel's function wizard can be used (see Appendix 2.2).

SAMPLING AND SAMPLING DISTRIBUTIONS

CONTENTS

MEADWESTVACO CORPORATION*

STAMFORD, CONNECTICUT

MeadWestvaco Corporation is a leading producer of packaging, coated and specialty papers, consumer and office products, and specialty chemicals. It has more than 30,000 employees. It operates worldwide in 33 countries, with customers located in 98 countries. MeadWestvaco holds a leading position in paper production, with an annual capacity of 1.8 million tons. The company's products include textbook paper, glossy magazine paper, beverage packaging systems, and office products. MeadWestvaco's internal consulting group uses sampling to provide a variety of information that enables the company to obtain significant productivity benefits and remain competitive.

For example, MeadWestvaco maintains large woodland holdings, which supply the trees, or raw material, for many of the company's products. Managers need reliable and accurate information about the timberlands and forests to evaluate the company's ability to meet its future raw material needs. What is the present volume in the forests? What is the past growth of the forests? What is the projected future growth of the forests? With answers to these important questions, MeadWestvaco's managers can develop plans for the future including long-term planting and harvesting schedules for the trees.

How does MeadWestvaco obtain the information it needs about its vast forest holdings? Data collected from sample plots throughout the forests are the basis for learning about the population of trees owned by the company. To identify the sample plots, the timberland holdings are first divided into three sections based on location and types of trees. Using maps and random numbers, MeadWestvaco analysts identify random samples of $\frac{1}{5}$ to $\frac{1}{7}$ acre plots in each section of the forest. MeadWestvaco foresters collect data from these sample plots to learn about the forest population.

Random sampling of its forest holdings enables MeadWestvaco Corporation to meet future raw material needs. © Walter Hodges/CORBIS.

Foresters throughout the organization participate in the field data collection process. Periodically, two-person teams gather information on each tree in every sample plot. The sample data are entered into the company's continuous forest inventory (CFI) computer system. Reports from the CFI system include a number of frequency distribution summaries containing statistics on types of trees, present forest volume, past forest growth rates, and projected future forest growth and volume. Sampling and the associated statistical summaries of the sample data provide the reports that are essential for the effective management of MeadWestvaco 's forests and timberlands.

In this chapter you will learn about simple random sampling and the sample selection process. In addition, you will learn how statistics such as the sample mean and sample proportion are used to estimate the population mean and population proportion. The important concept of a sampling distribution is also introduced.

*The authors are indebted to Dr. Edward P. Winkofsky for providing this Statistics in Practice.

In Chapter 1, we defined a *population* and a *sample* as two important aspects of a statistical study. The definitions are restated here.

1. A *population* is the set of all the elements of interest in a study.
2. A *sample* is a subset of the population.

The purpose of *statistical inference* is to develop estimates and test hypotheses about the characteristics of a population using information contained in a sample. Let us begin by citing two situations in which sampling gives a manager or decision maker information about a population.

1. A tire manufacturer developed a new tire designed to provide an increase in mileage over the firm's current line of tires. To estimate the mean number of miles provided by the new tires, the manufacturer selected a sample of 120 new tires for testing. The test results provided a sample mean of 36,500 miles. Hence, an estimate of the mean tire mileage for the population of new tires was 36,500 miles.
2. Members of a political party were considering supporting a particular candidate for election to the U.S. Senate, and party leaders wanted an estimate of the proportion of registered voters favoring the candidate. The time and cost associated with contacting every individual in the population of registered voters were prohibitive. Hence, a sample of 400 registered voters was selected and 160 of the 400 voters indicated a preference for the candidate. An estimate of the proportion of the population of registered voters favoring the candidate was $160/400 = .40$.

The preceding examples show how sampling and the sample results can be used to develop estimates of population characteristics. Note that in the tire mileage example, collecting the data on tire life involves wearing out each tire tested. Clearly it is not feasible to test every tire in the population; a sample is the only realistic way to obtain the desired tire mileage data. In the example involving the election, contacting every registered voter in the population is theoretically possible, but the time and cost in doing so are prohibitive; thus, a sample of registered voters is preferred.

A sample mean provides an estimate of a population mean, and a sample proportion provides an estimate of a population proportion. With estimates such as these, some sampling error can be expected. A key point in this chapter is that statistical methods can be used to make probability statements about the size of the sampling error.

The examples illustrate some of the reasons for using samples. However, it is important to realize that sample results provide only *estimates* of the values of the population characteristics. That is, we do not expect the sample mean of 36,500 miles to exactly equal the mean mileage for all tires in the population, nor do we expect exactly 40% of the population of registered voters to favor the candidate. The reason is simply that the sample contains only a portion of the population. With proper sampling methods, the sample results will provide "good" estimates of the population characteristics. But how good can we expect the sample results to be? Fortunately, statistical procedures are available for answering this question.

In this chapter we show how simple random sampling can be used to select a sample from a population. We then show how data obtained from a simple random sample can be used to compute estimates of a population mean, a population standard deviation, and a population proportion. In addition, we introduce the important concept of a sampling distribution. As we show, knowledge of the appropriate sampling distribution is what enables us to make statements about the goodness of the sample results. The last section discusses some alternatives to simple random sampling that are often employed in practice.

7.1   THE ELECTRONICS ASSOCIATES SAMPLING PROBLEM

The director of personnel for Electronics Associates, Inc. (EAI), wants to develop a profile of the company's 2500 managers. The characteristics to be identified include the mean annual salary for the managers and the proportion of managers who completed the company's management training program.

Using the 2500 managers as the population for this study, we can find the annual salary and the training program status for each individual by referring to the firm's personnel records. The data file containing this information for all 2500 managers in the population is on the disk at the back of the book.

Using the EAI data set and the formulas presented in Chapter 3, we compute the population mean and the population standard deviation for the annual salary data.

$$\text{Population mean:} \quad \mu = \$51,800$$
$$\text{Population standard deviation:} \quad \sigma = \$4000$$

The data for the training program status show that 1500 of the 2500 managers completed the training program. Letting p denote the proportion of the population having completed the training program, we see that $p = 1500/2500 = .60$.

A **parameter** is a numerical characteristic of a population. The population mean annual salary ($\mu = \$51,800$), the population standard deviation of annual salary ($\sigma = \$4000$), and the population proportion having completed the training program ($p = .60$) are parameters of the population of EAI managers.

Now, suppose that the necessary information on all the EAI managers was not readily available in the company's database. Employee records for recent hires might not be on the computer. Perhaps only the salary information (and not the training program status) is in the employee's record. Or, maybe the employee records at some locations are on the computer, but records at other locations are not. For whatever reason, it is often the case that it is not possible, or is perhaps too costly, to collect and process information on all elements of a population. In such cases, information from a sample can often be used to develop estimates of the population parameters of interest.

Often the cost of collecting information from a sample is substantially less than from a population, especially when personal interviews must be conducted to collect the information.

The question we now consider is how the firm's director of personnel can obtain estimates of the population parameters of interest by using a sample of managers rather than all 2500 managers in the population. Suppose that a sample of 30 managers will be used. Clearly, the time and the cost of developing a profile would be substantially less for 30 managers than for the entire population. If the personnel director could be assured that a sample of 30 managers would provide adequate information about the population of 2500 managers, working with a sample would be preferable to working with the entire population. Let us explore the possibility of using a sample for the EAI study by first considering how we can identify a sample of 30 managers.

7.2   SIMPLE RANDOM SAMPLING

Several methods can be used to select a sample from a population; one of the most common is **simple random sampling.** The definition of a simple random sample and the process of selecting a simple random sample depend on whether the population is *finite* or *infinite*. Because the EAI sampling problem involves a finite population of 2500 managers, we first consider sampling from a finite population.

Sampling from a Finite Population

A simple random sample of size n from a finite population of size N is defined as follows.

Simple Random Sample (Finite Population)

A simple random sample of size n from a finite population of size N is a sample selected such that each possible sample of size n has the same probability of being selected.

One procedure for selecting a simple random sample from a finite population is to choose the elements for the sample one at a time in such a way that, at each step, each of the elements in the remaining population has the same probability of being selected. Sampling n elements in this way will satisfy the definition of a simple random sample from a finite population.

Computer-generated random numbers can also be used to implement the random sample selection process. Excel provides a function for generating random numbers in its worksheets.

To select a simple random sample from the finite population of EAI managers, we first assign each manager a number. For example, we can assign the managers the numbers 1 to 2500 in the order that their names appear in the EAI personnel file. Next, we refer to the table of random numbers shown in Table 7.1. Using the first row of the table, each digit, 6, 3, 2, . . . , is a random digit with an equal chance of occurring. Because the largest number in the population list of EAI managers, 2500, has four digits, we will select random numbers from the table in sets or groups of four digits. Even though we may start the selection of random numbers anywhere in the table and move systematically in a direction of our choice, we will use the first row of Table 7.1 and move from left to right. The four-digit random numbers are

The random numbers in the table are shown in groups of five for readability.

| 6327 | 1599 | 8671 | 7445 | 1102 | 1514 | 1807 |

Because the numbers in the table are random, these four-digit numbers are equally probable or equally likely.

We can now use these four-digit random numbers to give each manager in the population an equal chance of being included in the random sample. The first number, 6327, is

TABLE 7.1   RANDOM NUMBERS

63271	59986	71744	51102	15141	80714	58683	93108	13554	79945
88547	09896	95436	79115	08303	01041	20030	63754	08459	28364
55957	57243	83865	09911	19761	66535	40102	26646	60147	15702
46276	87453	44790	67122	45573	84358	21625	16999	13385	22782
55363	07449	34835	15290	76616	67191	12777	21861	68689	03263
69393	92785	49902	58447	42048	30378	87618	26933	40640	16281
13186	29431	88190	04588	38733	81290	89541	70290	40113	08243
17726	28652	56836	78351	47327	18518	92222	55201	27340	10493
36520	64465	05550	30157	82242	29520	69753	72602	23756	54935
81628	36100	39254	56835	37636	02421	98063	89641	64953	99337
84649	48968	75215	75498	49539	74240	03466	49292	36401	45525
63291	11618	12613	75055	43915	26488	41116	64531	56827	30825
70502	53225	03655	05915	37140	57051	48393	91322	25653	06543
06426	24771	59935	49801	11082	66762	94477	02494	88215	27191
20711	55609	29430	70165	45406	78484	31639	52009	18873	96927
41990	70538	77191	25860	55204	73417	83920	69468	74972	38712
72452	36618	76298	26678	89334	33938	95567	29380	75906	91807
37042	40318	57099	10528	09925	89773	41335	96244	29002	46453
53766	52875	15987	46962	67342	77592	57651	95508	80033	69828
90585	58955	53122	16025	84299	53310	67380	84249	25348	04332
32001	96293	37203	64516	51530	37069	40261	61374	05815	06714
62606	64324	46354	72157	67248	20135	49804	09226	64419	29457
10078	28073	85389	50324	14500	15562	64165	06125	71353	77669
91561	46145	24177	15294	10061	98124	75732	00815	83452	97355
13091	98112	53959	79607	52244	63303	10413	63839	74762	50289

greater than 2500. It does not correspond to one of the numbered managers in the population, and hence is discarded. The second number, 1599, is between 1 and 2500. Thus the first manager selected for the random sample is number 1599 on the list of EAI managers. Continuing this process, we ignore the numbers 8671 and 7445 before identifying managers number 1102, 1514, and 1807 to be included in the random sample. This process continues until the simple random sample of 30 EAI managers has been obtained.

In implementing the simple random sample selection process, it is possible that a random number used previously may appear again in the table before the sample of 30 EAI managers has been selected. Because we do not want to select a manager more than one time, any previously used random numbers are ignored because the corresponding manager is already included in the sample. Selecting a sample in this manner is referred to as **sampling without replacement.** If we had selected the sample such that previously used random numbers were acceptable and specific managers could be included in the sample two or more times, we would be **sampling with replacement.** Sampling with replacement is a valid way of identifying a simple random sample. However, sampling without replacement is the sampling procedure used most often. When we refer to simple random sampling, we will assume that the sampling is without replacement.

Sampling from an Infinite Population

In practice, a population being studied is usually considered infinite if it involves an ongoing process that makes listing or counting every element in the population impossible.

Many sampling situations in business and economics involve finite populations, but in some situations the population is either infinite or so large that for practical purposes it must be treated as infinite. In sampling from an infinite population, we must use a new definition of a simple random sample. In addition, because the elements in an infinite population cannot be listed and numbered, we must use a different process for selecting the sample.

Suppose we want to estimate the average time between placing an order and receiving food for customers at a fast-food restaurant during the 11:30 A.M. to 1:30 P.M. lunch period. If we consider the population as being all possible customer visits, we see that it would not be feasible to develop a list of all possible visits. In fact, if we define the population as being all customer visits that could conceivably occur during the lunch period, we can consider the population as being infinite. Our task is to select a simple random sample of n customers from this population. The definition of a simple random sample from an infinite population follows.

Simple Random Sample (Infinite Population)

A simple random sample from an infinite population is a sample selected such that the following conditions are satisfied.

1. Each element selected comes from the same population.
2. Each element is selected independently.

For infinite populations, a sample selection procedure must be specially devised to select the items independently and thus avoid a selection bias that gives higher selection probabilities to certain types of elements.

For the problem of selecting a simple random sample of customer visits at a fast-food restaurant, we find that the first condition as defined is satisfied by any customer visit occurring during the 11:30 A.M. to 1:30 P.M. lunch period while the restaurant is operating with its regular staff under "normal" operating conditions. The second condition is satisfied by ensuring that the selection of a particular customer does not influence the selection of any other customer. That is, the customers are selected independently.

A well-known fast-food restaurant has implemented a simple random sampling procedure for just such a situation. The sampling procedure is based on the fact that some customers present discount coupons for special prices on sandwiches, drinks, french fries, and so on. Whenever a customer presents a discount coupon, the next customer served is selected for the sample. Because the customers present discount coupons randomly and independently, the firm is satisfied that the sampling plan satisfies the two conditions for a simple random sample from an infinite population. Note that the customers presenting the coupons are not selected for the sample because their purchase behavior may not be the same as typical customers.

NOTES AND COMMENTS

1. Finite populations are often defined by lists such as organization membership rosters, student enrollment records, credit card account lists, inventory product numbers, and so on. Infinite populations are often defined by an ongoing process whereby the elements of the population consist of items generated as though the process would operate indefinitely under the same conditions. In such cases, it is impossible to obtain a list of all elements in the population. For example, populations consisting of all possible parts to be manufactured, all possible customer visits, all possible bank transactions, and so on are classified as infinite populations.

2. The number of different simple random samples of size n that can be selected from a finite population of size N is

$$\frac{N!}{n!(N-n)!}$$

In this formula, $N!$ and $n!$ are the factorial computations discussed in Chapter 4. For the EAI problem with $N = 2500$ and $n = 30$, this expression can be used to show that approximately 2.75×10^{69} different simple random samples of 30 EAI managers can be obtained.

3. Computers can be used to generate random numbers for selecting random samples. For example, given the EAI population of 2500 managers, Excel's function =RANDBETWEEN (1,2500) can be used to generate random numbers between 1 and 2500. These computer-generated random numbers can then be used to identify the random sample of 30 managers the same way we used the random numbers from Table 7.1.

EXERCISES

Methods

SELFtest

1. Consider a finite population with five elements labeled A, B, C, D, and E. Ten possible simple random samples of size 2 can be selected.
   a. List the 10 samples beginning with AB, AC, and so on.
   b. Using simple random sampling, what is the probability that each sample of size 2 is selected?
   c. Assume random number 1 corresponds to A, random number 2 corresponds to B, and so on. List the simple random sample of size 2 that will be selected by using the random digits 8 0 5 7 5 3 2.

2. Assume a finite population contains 350 elements. Using the last three digits of each of the following five-digit random numbers (601, 022, 448, . . .), determine the first four elements that will be selected for the simple random sample.

   98601   73022   83448   02147   34229   27553   84147   93289   14209

Applications

SELFtest

3. *Fortune* publishes data on sales, profits, assets, stockholders' equity, market value, and earnings per share for the 500 largest U.S. industrial corporations (*Fortune* 500, 2000). Assume that you want to select a simple random sample of 10 corporations from the *Fortune* 500 list. Use the last three digits in column 9 of Table 7.1, beginning with 554. Read down the column and identify the numbers of the 10 corporations that would be selected.

4. Ten companies with widely held stocks are shown here (*USA Today,* September 6, 2000).

AT&T	IBM
America Online	Johnson & Johnson
Cisco Systems	Microsoft
General Electric	Motorola
Intel	Pfizer

   a. Assume that a random sample of five of these companies will be selected for an in-depth study of common business practices in large corporations. Beginning with the first random digit in Table 7.1 and reading down the column, use the single-digit random numbers to select a simple random sample of five companies to be used in the study.
   b. According to the second point in Notes and Comments, how many different simple random samples of size 5 can be selected from the list of 10 companies?

5. A student government organization is interested in estimating the proportion of students who favor a mandatory "pass-fail" grading policy for elective courses. A list of names and addresses of the 645 students enrolled during the current quarter is available from the registrar's office. Using three-digit random numbers in row 10 of Table 7.1 and moving across the row from left to right, identify the first 10 students who would be selected using simple random sampling. The three-digit random numbers begin with 816, 283, and 610.

6. The *County and City Data Book,* published by the Bureau of the Census, lists information on 3139 counties throughout the United States. Assume that a national study will collect data from 30 randomly selected counties. Use four-digit random numbers from the last column of Table 7.1 to identify the numbers corresponding to the first five counties selected for the sample. Ignore the first digits and begin with the four-digit random numbers 9945, 8364, 5702, and so on.

7. Assume that we want to identify a simple random sample of 12 of the 372 doctors practicing in a particular city. The doctors' names are available from a local medical organization. Use the eighth column of five-digit random numbers in Table 7.1 to identify the 12 doctors for the sample. Ignore the first two random digits in each five-digit grouping of the random numbers. This process begins with random number 108 and proceeds down the column of random numbers.

8. The following table provides the NCAA football top 25 teams at the beginning of the 2000 season (*Sports Illustrated,* August 14, 2000). Use the ninth column of the random numbers in Table 7.1, beginning with 13554, to select a simple random sample of six football teams. Begin with team 13 and use the first two digits in each row of the ninth column for your selection process. Which six football teams are selected for the simple random sample?

1. Nebraska	8. Clemson
2. Florida State	9. Texas
3. Alabama	10. Miami
4. Michigan	11. Florida
5. Wisconsin	12. Virginia Tech
6. Kansas State	13. Washington
7. Georgia	14. Tennessee

15. TCU	21. Illinois
16. Purdue	22. Ohio State
17. Mississippi	23. Oklahoma
18. USC	24. Colorado State
19. Penn State	25. Colorado
20. Southern Miss	

9. *Business Week* provided performance data and annual ratings for 895 mutual funds (*Business Week,* February 3, 1997). Assume that a simple random sample of 12 of the 895 mutual funds will be selected for a follow-up study on the performance of mutual funds. Use the fourth column of the random numbers in Table 7.1, beginning with 51102, to select the simple random sample of 12 mutual funds. Begin with mutual fund 511 and use the first three digits in each row of the fourth column for your selection process. What are the numbers of the 12 mutual funds in the simple random sample?

10. Indicate whether the following populations should be considered finite or infinite.
    a. All registered voters in the state of California.
    b. All television sets that could be produced by the Allentown, Pennsylvania, plant of the TV-M Company.
    c. All orders that could be processed by a mail-order firm.
    d. All emergency telephone calls that could come into a local police station.
    e. All components that Fibercon, Inc., produced on the second shift on May 17.

7.3   POINT ESTIMATION

Now that we have described how to select a simple random sample, let us return to the EAI problem. A simple random sample of 30 managers and the corresponding data on annual salary and management training program participation are as shown in Table 7.2. The notation x_1, x_2, and so on is used to denote the annual salary of the first manager in the sample,

TABLE 7.2   ANNUAL SALARY AND TRAINING PROGRAM STATUS FOR A SIMPLE RANDOM SAMPLE OF 30 EAI MANAGERS

Annual Salary ($)	Management Training Program	Annual Salary ($)	Management Training Program
$x_1 = 49,094.30$	Yes	$x_{16} = 51,766.00$	Yes
$x_2 = 53,263.90$	Yes	$x_{17} = 52,541.30$	No
$x_3 = 49,643.50$	Yes	$x_{18} = 44,980.00$	Yes
$x_4 = 49,894.90$	Yes	$x_{19} = 51,932.60$	Yes
$x_5 = 47,621.60$	No	$x_{20} = 52,973.00$	Yes
$x_6 = 55,924.00$	Yes	$x_{21} = 45,120.90$	Yes
$x_7 = 49,092.30$	Yes	$x_{22} = 51,753.00$	Yes
$x_8 = 51,404.40$	Yes	$x_{23} = 54,391.80$	No
$x_9 = 50,957.70$	Yes	$x_{24} = 50,164.20$	No
$x_{10} = 55,109.70$	Yes	$x_{25} = 52,973.60$	No
$x_{11} = 45,922.60$	Yes	$x_{26} = 50,241.30$	No
$x_{12} = 57,268.40$	No	$x_{27} = 52,793.90$	No
$x_{13} = 55,688.80$	Yes	$x_{28} = 50,979.40$	Yes
$x_{14} = 51,564.70$	No	$x_{29} = 55,860.90$	Yes
$x_{15} = 56,188.20$	No	$x_{30} = 57,309.10$	No

the annual salary of the second manager in the sample, and so on. Participation in the management training program is indicated by Yes in the management training program column.

To estimate the value of a population parameter, we compute a corresponding characteristic of the sample, referred to as a **sample statistic.** For example, to estimate the population mean μ and the population standard deviation σ for the annual salary of EAI managers, we simply use the data in Table 7.2 to calculate the corresponding sample statistics: the sample mean $\bar{x}$ and the sample standard deviation s. Using the formulas for a sample mean and a sample standard deviation presented in Chapter 3, the sample mean is

$$\bar{x} = \frac{\Sigma x_i}{n} = \frac{1,554,420}{30} = \$51,814.00$$

and the sample standard deviation is

$$s = \sqrt{\frac{\Sigma(x_i - \bar{x})^2}{n - 1}} = \sqrt{\frac{325,009,260}{29}} = \$3347.72$$

In addition, by computing the proportion of managers in the sample who responded Yes, we can estimate the proportion of managers in the population who have completed the management training program. Table 7.2 shows that 19 of the 30 managers in the sample have completed the training program. Thus, the sample proportion, denoted by $\bar{p}$, is given by

$$\bar{p} = \frac{19}{30} = .63$$

This value is used as an estimate of the population proportion p.

By making the preceding computations, we have performed the statistical procedure called *point estimation*. In point estimation we use the data from the sample to compute a value of a sample statistic that serves as an estimate of a population parameter. Using the terminology of point estimation, we refer to $\bar{x}$ as the **point estimator** of the population mean μ, s as the *point estimator* of the population standard deviation σ, and $\bar{p}$ as the *point estimator* of the population proportion p. The actual numerical value obtained for $\bar{x}$, s, or $\bar{p}$ in a particular sample is called the **point estimate** of the parameter. Thus, for the sample of 30 EAI managers, $51,814.00 is the point estimate of μ, $3,347.72 is the point estimate of σ, and .63 is the point estimate of p. Table 7.3 summarizes the sample results and compares the point estimates to the actual values of the population parameters.

As Table 7.3 shows, none of the point estimates are exactly equal to the corresponding population parameters. This variation is to be expected because only a sample and not a census of the entire population is being used to develop the estimate. The absolute value of the difference between an unbiased point estimate and the corresponding population parameter is called the **sampling error.*** For a sample mean, sample standard deviation, and sample proportion, the sampling errors are $|\bar{x} - \mu|$, $|s - \sigma|$, and $|\bar{p} - p|$, respectively. Thus, for the EAI sample, the values of the sampling errors are $|\$51,814 - \$51,800| = \$14$ for the sample mean, $|\$3,347.72 - \$4000.00| = \$652.28$ for the sample standard deviation, and $|.63 - .60| = .03$ for the sample proportion.

Sampling error is the result of using a subset of the population (the sample), and not the entire population.

---

*Technically the difference between the point estimate and the population parameter is called sampling error only when the point estimator is unbiased. The point estimators ($\bar{x}$, s, and $\bar{p}$) used here are unbiased.

TABLE 7.3   SUMMARY OF POINT ESTIMATES OBTAINED FROM A SIMPLE RANDOM
SAMPLE OF 30 EAI MANAGERS

Population Parameter	Parameter Value	Point Estimator	Point Estimate
μ = Population mean annual salary	$51,800.00	$\bar{x}$ = Sample mean annual salary	$51,814.00
σ = Population standard deviation for annual salary	$4,000.00	s = Sample standard deviation for annual salary	$3,347.72
p = Population proportion having completed the management training program	.60	$\bar{p}$ = Sample proportion having completed the management training program	.63

We were able to compute the sampling errors here because the population parameters were known. However, in an actual sampling application we will not be able to calculate the sampling error exactly because the value of the population parameter will not be known. We will show how statisticians analyze the sample data in order to make probability statements about the size of the sampling error.

NOTES AND COMMENTS

In our discussion of point estimators, we use $\bar{x}$ to denote a sample mean and $\bar{p}$ to denote a sample proportion. Our use of $\bar{p}$ is based on the fact that the sample proportion is also a *sample mean*. For instance, suppose that in a sample of size n with data values $x_1, x_2, \ldots, x_n$, we let $x_i = 1$ when a characteristic of interest is present for the ith observation and $x_i = 0$ when the characteristic is not present. Then the sample proportion is computed by $\Sigma x_i/n$, which is the formula for a sample mean. We also like the consistency of using the bar over the letter to remind the reader that the sample proportion $\bar{p}$ estimates the population proportion just as the sample mean $\bar{x}$ estimates the population mean. Some texts use $\hat{p}$ instead of $\bar{p}$ to denote the sample proportion.

EXERCISES

Methods

SELFtest   **11.**   The following data are from a simple random sample.

$$5 \quad 8 \quad 10 \quad 7 \quad 10 \quad 14$$

    a.   What is the point estimate of the population mean?
    b.   What is the point estimate of the population standard deviation?

12.   A survey question for a sample of 150 individuals yielded 75 Yes responses, 55 No responses, and 20 No Opinions.
    a.   What is the point estimate of the proportion in the population who respond Yes?
    b.   What is the point estimate of the proportion in the population who respond No?

Applications

SELFtest

13. A simple random sample of five months of sales data provided the following information:

Month:	1	2	3	4	5
Units Sold:	94	100	85	94	92

    a. Develop a point estimate of the population mean number of units sold per month.
    b. Develop a point estimate of the population standard deviation.

14. A sample of 784 children ages 9 to 14 were asked about cash provided by their parents (*Consumer Reports,* January 1997). The responses were as follows.

Source of Cash	Frequency
Allowance only	149
Handouts & chores plus an allowance	219
Handouts & chores but no allowance	251
Nothing	165
Total	784

    a. Develop a point estimate of the proportion of children who receive an allowance as their only source of cash.
    b. Develop a point estimate of the proportion of children who receive cash as handouts and for chores, but nothing in the form of an allowance.
    c. Considering all sources, develop a point estimate of the proportion of children who receive at least some cash from their parents.

15. *Appliance Magazine* provided estimates of the life expectancy of household appliances (*USA Today,* September 5, 2000). A simple random sample of 10 VCRs shows the following useful life in years.

    6.5   8.0   6.2   7.4   7.0   8.4   9.5   4.6   5.0   7.4

    a. Develop a point estimate of the population mean life expectancy for VCRs.
    b. Develop a point estimate of the population standard deviation for life expectancy of VCRs.

16. The U.S. Department of Transportation reports statistics on how frequently major airline flights arrive at or before their scheduled arrival times (*Associated Press,* September 8, 2000). Assume that the estimated proportion of flights arriving on time for an airline is based on a sample of 1400 flights. If 1117 of the flights arrive on time, develop a point estimate of the proportion of all flights that arrive on time.

17. A Louis Harris poll used a survey of 1008 adults to learn about how people feel about the economy (*Business Week,* August 7, 2000). Responses were as follow:

    595 adults   The economy is growing.
    332 adults   The economy is staying about the same.
      81 adults   The economy is shrinking.

Develop a point estimate of the following population parameters.
    a. The proportion of all adults who feel the economy is growing.
    b. The proportion of all adults who feel the economy is staying about the same.
    c. The proportion of all adults who feel the economy is shrinking.

7.4   INTRODUCTION TO SAMPLING DISTRIBUTIONS

In the preceding section we used a simple random sample of 30 EAI managers to develop point estimates of the mean and standard deviation of annual salary for the population of all EAI managers as well as the proportion of the managers in the population who completed the company's management training program. Suppose we select another simple random sample of 30 EAI managers, and an analysis of the data from the second sample provides the following information.

$$\text{Sample Mean } \bar{x} = \$52,669.70$$
$$\text{Sample Standard Deviation } s = \$4,239.07$$
$$\text{Sample Proportion } \bar{p} = .70$$

These results show that different values of $\bar{x}$, s, and $\bar{p}$ have been obtained with the second sample. A second simple random sample cannot be expected to contain the same elements as the first. Let us imagine carrying out the same process of selecting a new simple random sample of 30 managers over and over again, each time computing values of $\bar{x}$, s, and $\bar{p}$. In this way we could begin to identify the variety of values that these point estimators can have. To illustrate, we repeated the simple random sampling process for the EAI problem until we obtained 500 samples of 30 managers each and the corresponding $\bar{x}$, s, and $\bar{p}$ values. A portion of the results is shown in Table 7.4. Table 7.5 gives the frequency and relative frequency distributions for the 500 $\bar{x}$ values. Figure 7.1 is the relative frequency histogram for the $\bar{x}$ values.

The concept of a sampling distribution is one of the most important topics in this chapter. The ability to understand the material in subsequent chapters depends heavily on the ability to understand and use the sampling distributions presented in this chapter.

Recall that in Chapter 5 we defined a random variable as a numerical description of the outcome of an experiment. If we consider the process of selecting a simple random sample as an experiment, the sample mean $\bar{x}$ is the numerical description of the outcome of the experiment. Thus, the sample mean $\bar{x}$ is a random variable. As a result, just like other random variables, $\bar{x}$ has a mean or expected value, a variance, and a probability distribution. Because the various possible values of $\bar{x}$ are the result of different simple random samples, the probability distribution of $\bar{x}$ is called the **sampling distribution** of $\bar{x}$. Knowledge of this sampling distribution and its properties will enable us to make probability statements about how close the sample mean $\bar{x}$ is to the population mean μ.

Let us return to Figure 7.1. We would need to enumerate every possible sample of 30 managers and compute each sample mean to completely determine the sampling

TABLE 7.4   VALUES OF $\bar{x}$, s, AND $\bar{p}$ FROM 500 SIMPLE RANDOM SAMPLES
OF 30 EAI MANAGERS

Sample Number	Sample Mean ($\bar{x}$)	Sample Standard Deviation (s)	Sample Proportion ($\bar{p}$)
1	51,814.00	3,347.72	.63
2	52,669.70	4,239.07	.70
3	51,780.30	4,433.43	.67
4	51,587.90	3,985.32	.53
.	.	.	.
.	.	.	.
.	.	.	.
500	51,752.00	3,857.82	.50

TABLE 7.5   FREQUENCY DISTRIBUTION OF $\bar{x}$ FROM 500 SIMPLE RANDOM SAMPLES OF 300 EAI MANAGERS

Mean Annual Salary ($)	Frequency	Relative Frequency
49,500.00–49,999.99	2	.004
50,000.00–50,499.99	16	.032
50,500.00–50,999.99	52	.104
51,000.00–51,499.99	101	.202
51,500.00–51,999.99	133	.266
52,000.00–52,499.99	110	.220
52,500.00–52,999.99	54	.108
53,000.00–53,499.99	26	.052
53,500.00–53,999.99	6	.012
Totals	500	1.000

distribution of $\bar{x}$. However, the histogram of 500 $\bar{x}$ values gives an approximation of this sampling distribution. From the approximation we observe the bell-shaped appearance of the distribution. We note that the estimate of the population mean provided by $\bar{x}$ could be off by more than $2000. But we also note that the largest concentration of the $\bar{x}$ values and the mean of the 500 $\bar{x}$ values is near the population mean $\mu = \$51,800$. We will describe the properties of the sampling distribution of $\bar{x}$ more fully in the next section.

The 500 values of the sample standard deviation s and the 500 values of the sample proportion $\bar{p}$ are summarized by the relative frequency histograms in Figures 7.2 and 7.3. As in

FIGURE 7.1   RELATIVE FREQUENCY HISTOGRAM OF $\bar{x}$ VALUES FROM 500 SIMPLE RANDOM SAMPLES OF SIZE 30 EACH

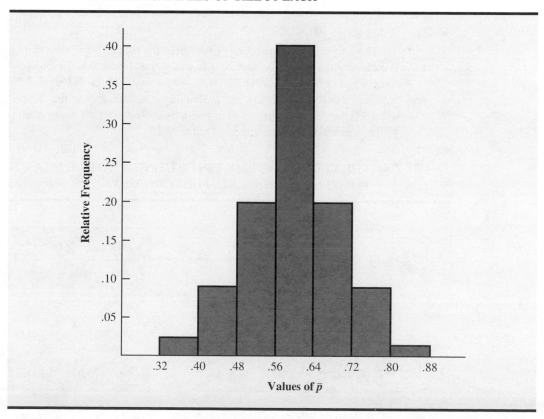

the case of $\bar{x}$, both s and $\bar{p}$ are random variables that provide numerical descriptions of the outcome of a simple random sample. If every possible sample of size 30 were selected from the population and if a value of s and a value of $\bar{p}$ were computed for each sample, the resulting probability distributions would be called the sampling distribution of s and the sampling distribution of $\bar{p}$, respectively. The relative frequency histograms of the 500 sample values, Figures 7.2 and 7.3, provide a general idea of the appearance of these two sampling distributions.

In practice, we select only one simple random sample from the population. We repeated the sampling process 500 times in this section simply to illustrate that many different samples are possible and that the different samples generate a variety of values for the sample statistics $\bar{x}$, s, and $\bar{p}$. The probability distribution of any particular sample statistic is called the sampling distribution of the statistic. In Section 7.5 we show the characteristics of the sampling distribution of $\bar{x}$. In Section 7.6 we show the characteristics of the sampling distribution of $\bar{p}$.

7.5 SAMPLING DISTRIBUTION OF $\bar{x}$

One of the most common statistical procedures is the use of a sample mean $\bar{x}$ to make inferences about a population mean μ. This process is shown in Figure 7.4. On each repetition of the process, we can anticipate obtaining a different value for the sample mean $\bar{x}$. The probability distribution for all possible values of the sample mean $\bar{x}$ is called the sampling distribution of the sample mean $\bar{x}$.

> **Sampling Distribution of $\bar{x}$**
>
> The sampling distribution of $\bar{x}$ is the probability distribution of all possible values of the sample mean, $\bar{x}$.

The purpose of this section is to describe the properties of the sampling distribution of $\bar{x}$, including the expected value or mean of $\bar{x}$, the standard deviation of $\bar{x}$, and the shape or form of the sampling distribution itself. As we shall see, knowledge of the sampling distribution of $\bar{x}$ will enable us to make probability statements about the sampling error involved when $\bar{x}$ is used to estimate μ. Let us begin by considering the mean of all possible $\bar{x}$ values, which is referred to as the expected value of $\bar{x}$.

FIGURE 7.4 THE STATISTICAL PROCESS OF USING A SAMPLE MEAN TO MAKE INFERENCES ABOUT A POPULATION MEAN

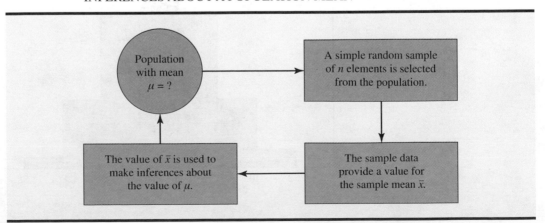

Expected Value of $\bar{x}$

In the EAI sampling problem we saw that different simple random samples result in a variety of values for the sample mean $\bar{x}$. Because many different values of the random variable $\bar{x}$ are possible, we are often interested in the mean of all possible values of $\bar{x}$ that can be generated by the various simple random samples. The mean of the $\bar{x}$ random variable is the expected value of $\bar{x}$. Let $E(\bar{x})$ represent the expected value of $\bar{x}$ and μ represent the mean of the population from which we are sampling. It can be shown that with simple random sampling, $E(\bar{x})$ and μ are equal.

The expected value of $\bar{x}$ equals the mean of the population from which the sample is drawn.

Expected Value of $\bar{x}$

$$E(\bar{x}) = \mu \qquad (7.1)$$

where

$$E(\bar{x}) = \text{the expected value of } \bar{x}$$
$$\mu = \text{the population mean}$$

This result shows that with simple random sampling, the expected value or mean for $\bar{x}$ is equal to the mean of the population. In Section 7.1 we saw that the mean annual salary for the population of EAI managers is $\mu = \$51{,}800$. Thus, according to equation (7.1), the mean of all possible sample means for the EAI study is also $51,800.

When the expected value of a point estimator equals the population parameter, we say the point estimator is unbiased. Thus, equation (7.1) shows that $\bar{x}$ is an unbiased estimator of the population mean μ. **Unbiasedness** is a desirable property of point estimators.

Standard Deviation of $\bar{x}$

Let us define the standard deviation of the sampling distribution of $\bar{x}$. We will use the following notation.

$$\sigma_{\bar{x}} = \text{the standard deviation of the sampling distribution of } \bar{x}$$
$$\sigma = \text{the standard deviation of the population}$$
$$n = \text{the sample size}$$
$$N = \text{the population size}$$

It can be shown that with simple random sampling, the standard deviation of $\bar{x}$ depends on whether the population is finite or infinite. The two formulas for the standard deviation of $\bar{x}$ follow.

Standard Deviation of $\bar{x}$

Finite Population	*Infinite Population*
$\sigma_{\bar{x}} = \sqrt{\dfrac{N-n}{N-1}}\left(\dfrac{\sigma}{\sqrt{n}}\right)$	$\sigma_{\bar{x}} = \dfrac{\sigma}{\sqrt{n}}$ (7.2)

In comparing the two formulas in (7.2), we see that the factor $\sqrt{(N - n)/(N - 1)}$ is required for the finite population case but not for the infinite population case. This factor is commonly referred to as the **finite population correction factor.** In many practical sampling situations, we find that the population involved, although finite, is "large," whereas the sample size is relatively "small." In such cases the finite population correction factor $\sqrt{(N - n)/(N - 1)}$ is close to 1. As a result, the difference between the values of the standard deviation of $\bar{x}$ for the finite and infinite population cases becomes negligible. Then, $\sigma_{\bar{x}} = \sigma/\sqrt{n}$ becomes a good approximation to the standard deviation of $\bar{x}$ even though the population is finite. This observation leads to the following general guideline, or rule of thumb, for computing the standard deviation of $\bar{x}$.

Use the Following Expression to Calculate the Standard Deviation of $\bar{x}$

$$\sigma_{\bar{x}} = \frac{\sigma}{\sqrt{n}} \tag{7.3}$$

whenever

1. The population is infinite; or
2. The population is finite *and* the sample size is less than or equal to 5% of the population size; that is, $n/N \le .05$.

Problem 21 shows that when $n/N \le .05$, the finite population correction factor has little effect on the value of $\sigma_{\bar{x}}$.

In cases where $n/N > .05$, the finite population version of (7.2) should be used in the computation of $\sigma_{\bar{x}}$. Unless otherwise noted, throughout the text we will assume that the population size is "large," $n/N \le .05$, and (7.3) can be used to compute $\sigma_{\bar{x}}$.

Now let us return to the EAI study and determine the standard deviation of all possible sample means that can be generated with samples of 30 EAI managers. In Section 7.1 we saw that the population standard deviation for the annual salary data is $\sigma = 4000$. In this case the population is finite, with $N = 2500$. However, with a sample size of 30, we have $n/N = 30/2500 = .012$. Following the rule of thumb given in (7.3), we can ignore the finite population correction factor and use equation (7.3) to compute the standard deviation of $\bar{x}$.

$$\sigma_{\bar{x}} = \frac{\sigma}{\sqrt{n}} = \frac{4000}{\sqrt{30}} = 730.30$$

Later we will see that the value of $\sigma_{\bar{x}}$ is helpful in determining how far the sample mean may be from the population mean. Because of the role that $\sigma_{\bar{x}}$ plays in computing possible sampling errors when $\bar{x}$ is used as an estimate of μ, $\sigma_{\bar{x}}$ is referred to as the **standard error** of the mean.

Central Limit Theorem

The final step in identifying the characteristics of the sampling distribution of $\bar{x}$ is to determine the form of the probability distribution of $\bar{x}$. We consider two cases: one in which the population distribution is unknown and one in which the population distribution is known to be normally distributed.

The central limit theorem applies to any population. Thus, it can be used to describe the sampling distribution of $\bar{x}$ even when the population distribution is unknown.

When the population distribution is unknown, we rely on one of the most important theorems in statistics—the **central limit theorem.** A statement of the central limit theorem as it applies to the sampling distribution of $\bar{x}$ follows.

Central Limit Theorem

In selecting simple random samples of size n from a population, the sampling distribution of the sample mean $\bar{x}$ can be approximated by a *normal probability distribution* as the sample size becomes large.

Figure 7.5 shows how the central limit theorem works for three different populations; each column refers to one of the populations. The top panel of the figure shows that none of the populations are normal. However, note what begins to happen to the sampling distribution of $\bar{x}$ as the sample size is increased. When the samples are of size 2, we see that the sampling distribution of $\bar{x}$ begins to take on an appearance different from that of the population distribution. For samples of size 5, we see all three sampling distributions beginning to take on a bell-shaped appearance. Finally, the samples of size 30 show all three sampling distributions to be approximately normal. Thus, for sufficiently large samples, the sampling distribution of $\bar{x}$ can be approximated by a normal probability distribution. However, how large must the sample size be before we can assume that the central limit theorem applies? Statistical researchers have investigated this question by studying the sampling distribution of $\bar{x}$ for a variety of populations and a variety of sample sizes. General statistical practice is to assume that for most applications, the sampling distribution of $\bar{x}$ can be approximated by a normal probability distribution whenever the sample size is 30 or more. In effect, a sample size of 30 or more is assumed to satisfy the large-sample condition of the central limit theorem. This observation is so important that we restate it.

The sampling distribution of $\bar{x}$ can be approximated by a normal probability distribution whenever the sample size is large. The large-sample condition can be assumed for simple random samples of size 30 or more.

The central limit theorem is the key to identifying the approximate form of the sampling distribution of $\bar{x}$ whenever the population distribution is unknown. However, we may encounter some sampling situations in which the population is assumed or believed to have a normal probability distribution. When this condition occurs, the following result identifies the form of the sampling distribution of $\bar{x}$.

Whenever the population has a normal probability distribution, the sampling distribution of $\bar{x}$ has a normal probability distribution for any sample size.

In summary, if we use a large ($n \geq 30$) simple random sample, the central limit theorem enables us to conclude that the sampling distribution of $\bar{x}$ can be approximated by a normal probability distribution. When the simple random sample is small ($n < 30$), the sampling distribution of $\bar{x}$ can be considered normal only if we are willing to assume that the population has a normal probability distribution.

FIGURE 7.5   ILLUSTRATION OF THE CENTRAL LIMIT THEOREM
                 FOR THREE POPULATIONS

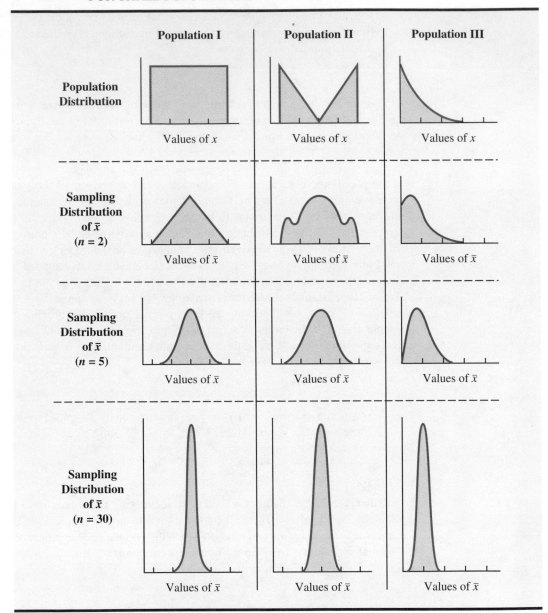

Sampling Distribution of $\bar{x}$ for the EAI Problem

For the EAI study we have shown that $E(\bar{x}) = 51{,}800$ and $\sigma_{\bar{x}} = 730.30$. Because we are using a simple random sample of 30 managers, the central limit theorem enables us to conclude that the sampling distribution of $\bar{x}$ is approximately normal as shown in Figure 7.6.

FIGURE 7.6   SAMPLING DISTRIBUTION OF $\bar{x}$ FOR THE MEAN ANNUAL SALARY
OF A SIMPLE RANDOM SAMPLE OF 30 EAI MANAGERS

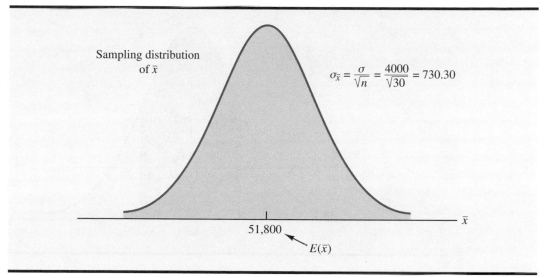

Practical Value of the Sampling Distribution of $\bar{x}$

Whenever a simple random sample is selected and the value of the sample mean $\bar{x}$ is used to estimate the value of the population mean μ, we cannot expect the sample mean to exactly equal the population mean. As stated earlier, the absolute value of the difference between the value of the sample mean $\bar{x}$ and the value of the population mean μ, $|\bar{x} - \mu|$, is called the *sampling error*. The practical reason we are interested in the sampling distribution of $\bar{x}$ is that it can be used to provide probability information about the size of the sampling error. To demonstrate this use, let us return to the EAI problem.

Suppose the personnel director believes the sample mean will be an acceptable estimate of the population mean if the sample mean is within $500 of the population mean. However, it is not possible to guarantee that the sample mean will be within $500 of the population mean. Indeed, Table 7.5 and Figure 7.1 show that some of the 500 sample means differed by more than $2000 from the population mean. So we must think of the personnel director's request in probability terms. That is, the personnel director is concerned with the following question: What is the probability that the sample mean computed using a simple random sample of 30 EAI managers will be within $500 of the population mean?

Because we have identified the properties of the sampling distribution of $\bar{x}$ (see Figure 7.6), we will use this distribution to answer the probability question. Refer to the sampling distribution of $\bar{x}$ shown again in Figure 7.7. The personnel director is asking about the probability that the sample mean is between $51,300 and $52,300. If the value of the sample mean $\bar{x}$ is in this interval, the value of $\bar{x}$ will be within $500 of the population mean. The appropriate probability is given by the darkly shaded area of the sampling distribution shown in Figure 7.7. Because the sampling distribution is normal, with mean 51,800 and

FIGURE 7.7   THE PROBABILITY OF A SAMPLE MEAN BEING WITHIN $500
OF THE POPULATION MEAN

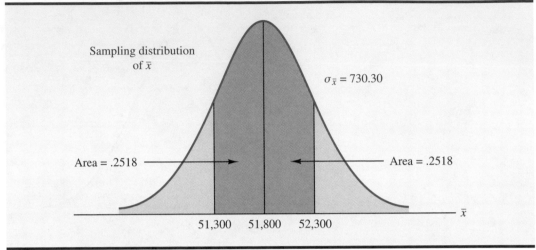

standard deviation 730.30, we can use the standard normal probability distribution table to find the area or probability. At $\bar{x} = 51{,}300$, we have

$$z = \frac{51{,}300 - 51{,}800}{730.30} = -.68$$

Referring to the standard normal probability distribution table, we find an area between $z = 0$ and $z = -.68$ of .2517. Similar calculations for $\bar{x} = 52{,}300$ show an area between $z = 0$ and $z = +.68$ of .2517. Thus, the probability of the value of the sample mean being between 51,300 and 52,300 is $.2517 + .2517 = .5034$.

The sampling distribution of $\bar{x}$ can be used to provide probability information about how close the sample mean $\bar{x}$ is to the population mean μ.

The preceding computations show that a simple random sample of 30 EAI managers has a .5034 probability of providing a sample mean $\bar{x}$ that is within $500 of the population mean. Thus, there is a $1 - .5034 = .4966$ probability that the sampling error will be more than $500. In other words, a simple random sample of 30 EAI managers has roughly a 50–50 chance of providing a sample mean within the allowable $500. Perhaps a larger sample size should be considered. Let us explore this possibility by considering the relationship between the sample size and the sampling distribution of $\bar{x}$.

Relationship Between the Sample Size and the Sampling Distribution of $\bar{x}$

Suppose that in the EAI sampling problem we select a simple random sample of 100 EAI managers instead of the 30 originally considered. Intuitively, it would seem that with more data provided by the larger sample size, the sample mean based on $n = 100$ should provide a better estimate of the population mean than the sample mean based on $n = 30$. To see how much better, let us consider the relationship between the sample size and the sampling distribution of $\bar{x}$.

First note that $E(\bar{x}) = \mu$ regardless of the sample size. Thus, the mean of all possible values of $\bar{x}$ is equal to the population mean μ regardless of the sample size n. However, note that the standard error of the mean, $\sigma_{\bar{x}} = \sigma/\sqrt{n}$, is related to the square root of the sample size. Whenever the sample size is increased, the standard error of the mean $\sigma_{\bar{x}}$ decreases. With $n = 30$, the standard error of the mean for the EAI problem is 730.30. However, with the increase in the sample size to $n = 100$, the standard error of the mean is decreased to

$$\sigma_{\bar{x}} = \frac{\sigma}{\sqrt{n}} = \frac{4000}{\sqrt{100}} = 400$$

The sampling distributions of $\bar{x}$ with $n = 30$ and $n = 100$ are shown in Figure 7.8. Because the sampling distribution with $n = 100$ has a smaller standard error, the values of $\bar{x}$ have less variation and tend to be closer to the population mean than the values of $\bar{x}$ with $n = 30$.

We can use the sampling distribution of $\bar{x}$ for the case with $n = 100$ to compute the probability that a simple random sample of 100 EAI managers will provide a sample mean that is within \$500 of the population mean. Because the sampling distribution is normal, with mean 51,800 and standard deviation 400, we can use the standard normal probability distribution table to find the area or probability. At $\bar{x} = 51,300$ (Figure 7.9), we have

$$z = \frac{51,300 - 51,800}{400} = -1.25$$

Referring to the standard normal probability distribution table, we find an area between $z = 0$ and $z = -1.25$ of .3944. With a similar calculation for $\bar{x} = 52,300$, we see that the probability of the value of the sample mean being between 51,300 and 52,300 is .3944 + .3944 = .7888. Thus, by increasing the sample size from 30 to 100 EAI managers, we increased the probability that the sampling error will be \$500 or less; that is, the probability of obtaining a sample mean within \$500 of the population mean increases from .5036 to .7888.

The important point in this discussion is that as the sample size is increased, the standard error of the mean decreases. As a result, the larger sample size provides a higher probability that the sample mean is within a specified distance of the population mean.

FIGURE 7.8   A COMPARISON OF THE SAMPLING DISTRIBUTIONS OF $\bar{x}$ FOR SIMPLE RANDOM SAMPLES OF $n = 30$ AND $n = 100$ EAI MANAGERS

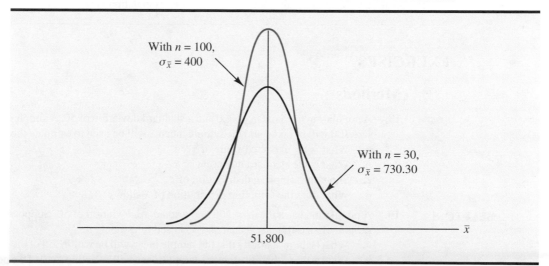

FIGURE 7.9   THE PROBABILITY OF A SAMPLE MEAN BEING WITHIN $500 OF THE POPULATION MEAN WHEN A SIMPLE RANDOM SAMPLE OF 100 EAI MANAGERS IS USED

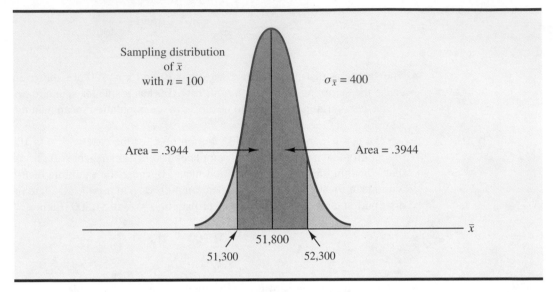

NOTES AND COMMENTS

1. In presenting the sampling distribution of $\bar{x}$ for the EAI problem, we took advantage of the fact that the population mean $\mu = 51,800$ and the population standard deviation $\sigma = 4000$ were known. However, usually the values of the population mean μ and the population standard deviation σ that are needed to determine the sampling distribution of $\bar{x}$ will be unknown. In Chapter 8 we will show how the sample mean $\bar{x}$ and the sample standard deviation s are used when μ and σ are unknown.

2. The theoretical proof of the central limit theorem requires independent observations in the sample. This condition is met for infinite populations and for finite populations where sampling is done with replacement. Although the central limit theorem does not directly address sampling without replacement from finite populations, general statistical practice applies the findings of the central limit theorem when the population size is large.

EXERCISES

Methods

18. A population has a mean of 200 and a standard deviation of 50. A simple random sample of size 100 will be taken and the sample mean $\bar{x}$ will be used to estimate the population mean.
    a. What is the expected value of $\bar{x}$?
    b. What is the standard deviation of $\bar{x}$?
    c. Show the sampling distribution of $\bar{x}$.
    d. What does the sampling distribution of $\bar{x}$ show?

SELFtest   19. A population has a mean of 200 and a standard deviation of 50. Suppose a simple random sample of size 100 is selected and $\bar{x}$ is used to estimate μ.
    a. What is the probability that the sample mean will be within ± 5 of the population mean?
    b. What is the probability that the sample mean will be within ± 10 of the population mean?

20. Assume the population standard deviation is $\sigma = 25$. Compute the standard error of the mean, $\sigma_{\bar{x}}$, for sample sizes of 50, 100, 150, and 200. What can you say about the size of the standard error of the mean as the sample size is increased?

21. Suppose a simple random sample of size 50 is selected from a population with $\sigma = 10$. Find the value of the standard error of the mean in each of the following cases (use the finite population correction factor if appropriate).
    a. The population size is infinite.
    b. The population size is $N = 50,000$.
    c. The population size is $N = 5000$.
    d. The population size is $N = 500$.

22. A population has a mean of 400 and a standard deviation of 50. The probability distribution of the population is unknown.
    a. A researcher will use simple random samples of either 10, 20, 30, or 40 items to collect data about the population. With which of these sample-size alternatives will we be able to use a normal probability distribution to describe the sampling distribution of $\bar{x}$? Explain.
    b. Show the sampling distribution of $\bar{x}$ for the instances in which the normal probability distribution is appropriate.

23. A large population has a mean of 100 and a standard deviation of 16. What is the probability that a sample mean will be within ± 2 of the population mean for each of the following sample sizes?
    a. $n = 50$
    b. $n = 100$
    c. $n = 200$
    d. $n = 400$
    e. What is the advantage of a larger sample size?

Applications

24. Refer to the EAI sampling problem. Suppose a simple random sample of 60 managers is used.
    a. Sketch the sampling distribution of $\bar{x}$ when simple random samples of size 60 are used.
    b. What happens to the sampling distribution of $\bar{x}$ if simple random samples of size 120 are used?
    c. What general statement can you make about what happens to the sampling distribution of $\bar{x}$ as the sample size is increased? Does this generalization seem logical? Explain.

SELFtest   25. In the EAI sampling problem (see Figure 7.7), we showed that for $n = 30$, there was .5034 probability of obtaining a sample mean within $\pm \$500$ of the population mean.
    a. What is the probability that $\bar{x}$ is within $\$500$ of the population mean if a sample of size 60 is used?
    b. Answer part (a) for a sample of size 120.

26. The mean sales price per unit for a product sold in the United States is $1.20. Use this as the population mean price per unit, and assume that the population standard deviation is $\sigma = .10$. Suppose that a random sample of 50 retail stores will be selected, and a sample mean price per unit will be computed for data collected from the 50 retail stores.
    a. Show the sampling distribution of the sample mean $\bar{x}$ where $\bar{x}$ is the sample mean price per unit for the 50 retail stores.
    b. What is the probability that the simple random sample will provide a sample mean within 2 cents, .02, of the population mean?
    c. What is the probability that the simple random sample will provide a sample mean within 1 cent, .01, of the population mean?

27. The College Board American College Testing Program reported a population mean SAT score of $\mu = 1017$ (*The New York Times*, 2000 Almanac). Assume that the population standard deviation is $\sigma = 100$.
   a. What is the probability that a random sample of 75 students will provide a sample mean SAT score within 10 of the population mean?
   b. What is the probability a random sample of 75 students will provide a sample mean SAT score within 20 of the population mean?

28. The mean annual starting salary for marketing majors is $34,000 (*Time*, May 8, 2000). Assume that for the population of graduates with a marketing major, the mean annual starting salary is $\mu = 34,000$, and the standard deviation is $\sigma = 2000$.
   a. What is the probability that a simple random sample of marketing majors will have a sample mean within ±$250 of the population mean for each of the following sample sizes: 30, 50, 100, 200 and 400?
   b. What is the advantage of a larger sample size when attempting to estimate the population mean?

29. The mean monthly rental for a two-bedroom apartment in Atlanta is $982 (*Elle*, September 1998). Assume that the population mean is $982 and the population standard deviation is $210.
   a. What is the probability that a simple random sample of 40 two-bedroom apartments will provide a sample mean monthly rental within ±$100 of the population mean?
   b. What is the probability that a simple random sample of 40 two-bedroom apartments will provide a sample mean monthly rental within ±$25 of the population mean?
   c. Discuss the results in parts (a) and (b).

30. The population mean for the price of a new one-family home is $166,500 (U.S. Bureau of the Census, *New One-Family Houses Sold*, 1997). Assume that the population standard deviation is $42,000 and that a sample of 100 new one-family homes will be selected.
   a. Show the sampling distribution of the sample mean price for new homes based on the sample of 100.
   b. What is the probability that the sample mean for the 100 new homes will be within $10,000 of the population mean?
   c. Repeat part (b) for values of $5000, $2500, and $1000.
   d. To estimate the population mean price to within ±$2500 or ±$1000, what would you recommend?

31. *Money* magazine reported that the average price of a gallon of gasoline in the United States during the first quarter of 2001 was $1.46 (*Money*, August 2001). Assume the price reported by *Money* is the population mean, and the population standard deviation is $\sigma = \$.15$.
   a. What is the probability that the mean price for a sample of 30 gas stations is within $.03 of the population mean?
   b. What is the probability that the mean price for a sample of 50 gas stations is within $.03 of the population mean?
   c. What is the probability that the mean price for a sample 100 gas stations is within $.03 of the population mean?
   d. Would you recommend a sample size of 30, 50, or 100 to have at least a .95 probability that the sample mean is within $.03 of the population mean?

32. To estimate the mean age for a population of 4000 employees, a simple random sample of
    40 employees is selected.
    a. Would you use the finite population correction factor in calculating the standard error
       of the mean? Explain.
    b. If the population standard deviation is $\sigma = 8.2$ years, compute the standard error both
       with and without the finite population correction factor. What is the rationale for ig-
       noring the finite population correction factor whenever $n/N \leq .05$?
    c. What is the probability that the sample mean age of the employees will be within
       ± 2 years of the population mean age?

7.6   SAMPLING DISTRIBUTION OF $\bar{p}$

In many situations in business and economics, we use the sample proportion $\bar{p}$ to make
statistical inferences about the population proportion p. This process is depicted in Figure 7.10. On each repetition of the process, we can anticipate obtaining a different value
for the sample proportion $\bar{p}$. The probability distribution for all possible values of the
sample proportion $\bar{p}$ is called the sampling distribution of the sample proportion $\bar{p}$.

Sampling Distribution of $\bar{p}$

The sampling distribution of $\bar{p}$ is the probability distribution of all possible values of
the sample proportion $\bar{p}$.

To determine how close the sample proportion $\bar{p}$ is to the population proportion p,
we need to understand the properties of the sampling distribution of $\bar{p}$: the expected
value of $\bar{p}$, the standard deviation of $\bar{p}$, and the shape or form of the sampling distribution of $\bar{p}$.

FIGURE 7.10   THE STATISTICAL PROCESS OF USING A SAMPLE PROPORTION
TO MAKE INFERENCES ABOUT A POPULATION PROPORTION

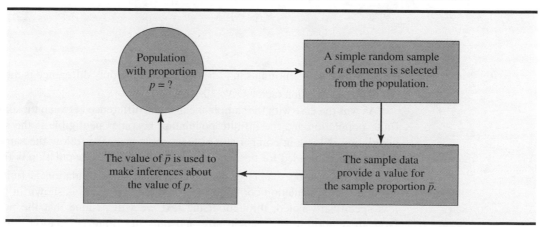

Expected Value of $\bar{p}$

The expected value of $\bar{p}$, the mean of all possible values of $\bar{p}$, can be expressed as follows.

Expected Value of $\bar{p}$

$$E(\bar{p}) = p \tag{7.4}$$

where

$$E(\bar{p}) = \text{the expected value of } \bar{p}$$
$$p = \text{the population proportion}$$

Equation (7.4) shows that the mean of all possible $\bar{p}$ values is equal to the population proportion p. Thus, $\bar{p}$ is an unbiased estimator of p. Recall that in Section 7.1 we noted that $p = .60$ for the EAI population, where p is the proportion of the population of managers who had participated in the company's management training program. Thus, the expected value of $\bar{p}$ for the EAI sampling problem is .60.

Standard Deviation of $\bar{p}$

The standard deviation of $\bar{p}$ is referred to as the **standard error** of the proportion. Just as we found for the sample mean $\bar{x}$, the standard deviation of $\bar{p}$ depends on whether the population is finite or infinite. The two formulas for computing the standard deviation of $\bar{p}$ follow.

Standard Deviation of $\bar{p}$

Finite Population	*Infinite Population*
$\sigma_{\bar{p}} = \sqrt{\dfrac{N-n}{N-1}}\sqrt{\dfrac{p(1-p)}{n}}$	$\sigma_{\bar{p}} = \sqrt{\dfrac{p(1-p)}{n}}$ (7.5)

Comparing the two formulas in (7.5), we see that the only difference is the use of the finite population correction factor $\sqrt{(N-n)/(N-1)}$.

As was the case with the sample mean $\bar{x}$, the difference between the expressions for the finite population and the infinite population becomes negligible if the size of the finite population is large in comparison to the sample size. We follow the same rule of thumb that we recommended for the sample mean. That is, if the population is finite with $n/N \leq .05$, we will use $\sigma_{\bar{p}} = \sqrt{p(1-p)/n}$. However, if the population is finite and if $n/N > .05$, the finite population correction factor should be used, as shown in (7.5). Again, unless specifically noted, throughout the text we will assume that the population size is large in relation to the sample size and thus the finite population correction factor is unnecessary.

For the EAI study we know that the population proportion of managers who have participated in the management training program is $p = .60$. With $n/N = 30/2500 = .012$, we can ignore the finite population correction factor when we compute the standard deviation of $\bar{p}$. For the simple random sample of 30 managers, $\sigma_{\bar{p}}$ is

$$\sigma_{\bar{p}} = \sqrt{\frac{p(1 - p)}{n}} = \sqrt{\frac{.60(1 - .60)}{30}} = .0894$$

Form of the Sampling Distribution of $\bar{p}$

Now that we know the mean and standard deviation of $\bar{p}$, we want to consider the form of the sampling distribution of $\bar{p}$. Applying the central limit theorem as it relates to $\bar{p}$ produces the following result.

> The sampling distribution of $\bar{p}$ can be approximated by a normal probability distribution whenever the sample size is large.

With $\bar{p}$, the sample size can be considered large* whenever the following two conditions are satisfied.

$$np \geq 5$$
$$n(1 - p) \geq 5$$

Recall that for the EAI sampling problem we know that the population proportion of managers who have participated in the training program is $p = .60$. With a simple random sample of size 30, we have $np = 30(.60) = 18$ and $n(1 - p) = 30(.40) = 12$. Thus, the sampling distribution of $\bar{p}$ can be approximated by a normal probability distribution as shown in Figure 7.11.

Practical Value of the Sampling Distribution of $\bar{p}$

Whenever a simple random sample is selected and the value of the sample proportion $\bar{p}$ is used to estimate the value of the population proportion p, we anticipate some sampling error. In this case, the sampling error is the absolute value of the difference between the value of the sample proportion $\bar{p}$ and the value of the population proportion p. The practical value of the sampling distribution of $\bar{p}$ is that it can be used to provide probability information about the sampling error.

Suppose, in the EAI problem, the personnel director wants to know the probability of obtaining a value of $\bar{p}$ that is within .05 of the population proportion of EAI managers who have participated in the training program. That is, what is the probability of obtaining a sample with a sample proportion $\bar{p}$ between .55 and .65? The darkly shaded area in Figure 7.12 shows this probability. Using the fact that the sampling distribution of $\bar{p}$ can be approximated by

---

*For values of p near .50, sample sizes as small as 10 permit a normal approximation. But, with very small or very large values of p much larger samples are needed. For example, with $p = .05$ a sample of size 100 is needed.

FIGURE 7.11 SAMPLING DISTRIBUTION OF $\bar{p}$ FOR THE PROPORTION OF EAI MANAGERS WHO PARTICIPATED IN THE MANAGEMENT TRAINING PROGRAM

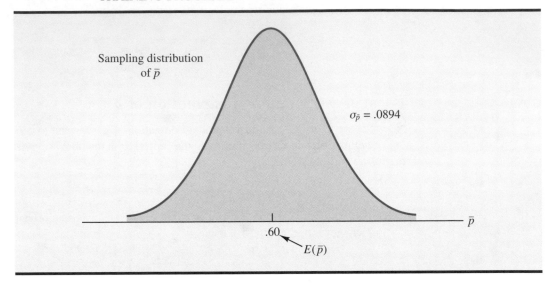

a normal probability distribution with a mean of .60 and a standard deviation of $\sigma_{\bar{p}} = .0894$, we find that the standard normal random variable corresponding to $\bar{p} = .55$ has a value of $z = (.55 - .60)/.0894 = -.56$. Referring to the standard normal probability distribution table, we see that the area between $z = -.56$ and $z = 0$ is .2123. Similarly, at $\bar{p} = .65$ we find an area between $z = 0$ and $z = .56$ of .2123. Thus, the probability of selecting a sample that provides a sample proportion $\bar{p}$ within .05 of the population proportion p is $.2123 + .2123 = .4246$.

FIGURE 7.12 SAMPLING DISTRIBUTION OF $\bar{p}$ FOR THE EAI SAMPLING PROBLEM

If we consider increasing the sample size to $n = 100$, the standard error of the proportion becomes

$$\sigma_{\bar{p}} = \sqrt{\frac{.60(1 - .60)}{100}} = .0490$$

With a sample size of 100 EAI managers, the probability of the sample proportion having a value within .05 of the population proportion can now be computed. Because the sampling distribution is approximately normal, with mean .60 and standard error .0490, we can use the standard normal probability distribution table to find the area or probability. At $\bar{p}$ = .55, we have $z = (.55 - .60)/.0490 = -1.02$. Referring to the standard normal probability distribution table, we see that the area between $z = -1.02$ and $z = 0$ is .3461. Similarly, at .65 the area between $z = 0$ and $z = 1.02$ is .3461. Thus, if the sample size is increased from 30 to 100, the probability that the sample proportion $\bar{p}$ is within .05 of the population proportion p will increase to $.3461 + .3461 = .6922$. Thus, the probability that the sampling error will be less than or equal to .05 has increased.

EXERCISES

Methods

33. A simple random sample of size 100 is selected from a population with $p = .40$.
   a. What is the expected value of $\bar{p}$?
   b. What is the standard deviation of $\bar{p}$?
   c. Show the sampling distribution of $\bar{p}$.
   d. What does the sampling distribution of $\bar{p}$ show?

SELFtest **34.** A population proportion is .40. A simple random sample of size 200 will be taken and the sample proportion $\bar{p}$ will be used to estimate the population proportion.
   a. What is the probability that the sample proportion will be within $\pm.03$ of the population proportion?
   b. What is the probability that the sample proportion will be within $\pm.05$ of the population proportion?

35. Assume that the population proportion is .55. Compute the standard error of the proportion, $\sigma_{\bar{p}}$, for sample sizes of 100, 200, 500, and 1000. What can you say about the size of the standard error of the proportion as the sample size is increased?

36. The population proportion is .30. What is the probability that a sample proportion will be within $\pm.04$ of the population proportion for each of the following sample sizes?
   a. $n = 100$
   b. $n = 200$
   c. $n = 500$
   d. $n = 1000$
   e. What is the advantage of a larger sample size?

Applications

SELFtest **37.** The president of Doerman Distributors, Inc., believes that 30% of the firm's orders come from first-time customers. A simple random sample of 100 orders will be used to estimate the proportion of first-time customers.
   a. Assume that the president is correct and $p = .30$. What is the sampling distribution of $\bar{p}$ for this study?

    b. What is the probability that the sample proportion $\bar{p}$ will be between .20 and .40?

    c. What is the probability that the sample proportion will be between .25 and .35?

38. The Grocery Manufacturers of America reported that 76% of consumers read the ingredients listed on a product's label. Assume the population proportion is $p = .76$ and a sample of 400 consumers is selected from the population.

    a. Show the sampling distribution of the sample proportion $\bar{p}$ where $\bar{p}$ is the proportion of the sampled consumers who read the ingredients listed on a product's label.

    b. What is the probability that the sample proportion will be within $\pm.03$ of the population proportion?

    c. Answer part (b) for a sample of 750 consumers.

39. *Time*/CNN voter polls monitored public opinion for the presidential candidates during the 2000 presidential election campaign. One *Time*/CNN poll conducted by Yankelovich Partners, Inc., used a sample of 589 likely voters (*Time,* June 26, 2000). Assume the population proportion for a presidential candidate is $p = .50$. Let $\bar{p}$ be the sample proportion of likely voters favoring the presidential candidate.

    a. Show the sampling distribution of $\bar{p}$.

    b. What is the probability the *Time*/CNN poll will provide a sample proportion within $\pm.04$ of the population proportion?

    c. What is the probability the *Time*/CNN poll will provide a sample proportion within $\pm.03$ of the population proportion?

    d. What is the probability the *Time*/CNN poll will provide a sample proportion within $\pm.02$ of the population proportion?

40. Although most people believe breakfast is the most important meal of the day, 25% of adults skip breakfast (*U.S. News & World Report,* November 10, 1997). Assume the population proportion is $p = .25$, and $\bar{p}$ is the sample proportion of adults who skip breakfast based on a sample of 200 adults.

    a. Show the sampling distribution of $\bar{p}$.

    b. What is the probability that the sample proportion will be within $\pm.03$ of the population proportion?

    c. What is the probability that the sample proportion will be within $\pm.05$ of the population proportion?

41. The *Democrat and Chronicle* reported that 25% of the flights arriving at the San Diego airport during the first five months of 2001 were late (*Democrat and Chronicle,* July 23, 2001). Assume the population proportion is $p = .25$.

    a. Show the sampling distribution of $\bar{p}$, the proportion of late flights in a sample of 1000 flights.

    b. What is the probability that the sample proportion will be within $\pm.03$ of the population proportion if a sample of size 1000 is selected?

    c. Answer part (b) for a sample of 500 flights.

42. Assume that 15% of the parts produced in an assembly line operation are defective, but that the firm's production manager is not aware of this situation. Assume further that 50 parts are tested by the quality assurance department to determine the quality of the assembly operation. Let $\bar{p}$ be the sample proportion found defective by the quality assurance test.

    a. Show the sampling distribution for $\bar{p}$.

    b. What is the probability that the sample proportion will be within $\pm.03$ of the population proportion that is defective?

    c. If the test shows $\bar{p} = .10$ or more, the assembly line operation will be shut down to check for the cause of the defects. What is the probability that the sample of 50 parts will lead to the conclusion that the assembly line should be shut down?

43. The Food Marketing Institute found that 17% of households spend more than $100 per week on groceries. Assume the population proportion is $p = .17$ and a simple random sample of 800 households will be selected from the population.

    a. Show the sampling distribution of $\bar{p}$, the sample proportion of households spending more than $100 per week on groceries.

    b. What is the probability that the sample proportion will be within $\pm.02$ of the population proportion?

    c. Answer part (b) for a sample of 1600 households.

7.7   SAMPLING METHODS

This section provides a brief introduction to sampling methods other than simple random sampling.

We have described the simple random sampling procedure and discussed the properties of the sampling distributions of $\bar{x}$ and $\bar{p}$ when simple random sampling is used. However, simple random sampling is not the only sampling method available. Such methods as stratified random sampling, cluster sampling, and systematic sampling provide advantages over simple random sampling in some situations. In this section we briefly introduce some of these alternative sampling methods.

Stratified Random Sampling

In **stratified random sampling,** the elements in the population are first divided into groups called *strata,* such that each element in the population belongs to one and only one stratum. The basis for forming the strata, such as department, location, age, industry type, and so on, is at the discretion of the designer of the sample. However, the best results are obtained when the elements within each stratum are as much alike as possible. Figure 7.13 is a diagram of a population divided into *H* strata.

Stratified random sampling works best when the variance among elements in each stratum is relatively small.

After the strata are formed, a simple random sample is taken from each stratum. Formulas are available for combining the results for the individual stratum samples into one estimate of the population parameter of interest. The value of stratified random sampling depends on how homogeneous the elements are within the strata. If elements within strata are alike, the strata will have low variances. Thus relatively small sample sizes can be used to obtain good estimates of the strata characteristics. If strata are homogeneous, the stratified random sampling procedure provides results just as precise as those of simple random sampling by using a smaller total sample size.

FIGURE 7.13   DIAGRAM FOR STRATIFIED RANDOM SAMPLING

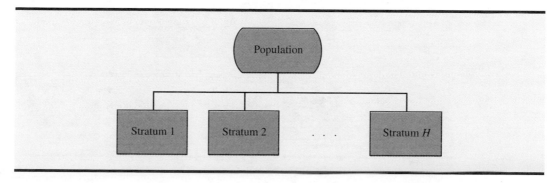

Cluster Sampling

In **cluster sampling,** the elements in the population are first divided into separate groups called *clusters*. Each element of the population belongs to one and only one cluster (see Figure 7.14). A simple random sample of the clusters is then taken. All elements within each sampled cluster form the sample. Cluster sampling tends to provide the best results when the elements within the clusters are not alike. In the ideal case, each cluster is a representative small-scale version of the entire population. The value of cluster sampling depends on how representative each cluster is of the entire population. If all clusters are alike in this regard, sampling a small number of clusters will provide good estimates of the population parameters.

One of the primary applications of cluster sampling is area sampling, where clusters are city blocks or other well-defined areas. Cluster sampling generally requires a larger total sample size than either simple random sampling or stratified random sampling. However, it can result in cost savings because of the fact that when an interviewer is sent to a sampled cluster (e.g., a city-block location), many sample observations can be obtained in a relatively short time. Hence, a larger sample size may be obtainable with a significantly lower total cost.

Systematic Sampling

In some sampling situations, especially those with large populations, it is time-consuming to select a simple random sample by first finding a random number and then counting or searching through the list of the population until the corresponding element is found. An alternative to simple random sampling is **systematic sampling.** For example, if a sample size of 50 is desired from a population containing 5000 elements, we will sample one element for every 5000/50 = 100 elements in the population. A systematic sample for this case involves selecting randomly one of the first 100 elements from the population list. Other sample elements are identified by starting with the first sampled element and then selecting every 100th element that follows in the population list. In effect, the sample of 50 is identified by moving systematically through the population and identifying every 100th element after the first randomly selected element. The sample of 50 usually will be easier to identify in this way than it would be if simple random sampling were used. Because the first element selected is a random choice, a systematic sample is usually assumed to have the properties of a simple random sample. This assumption is especially applicable when the list of elements in the population is a random ordering of the elements.

FIGURE 7.14   DIAGRAM FOR CLUSTER SAMPLING

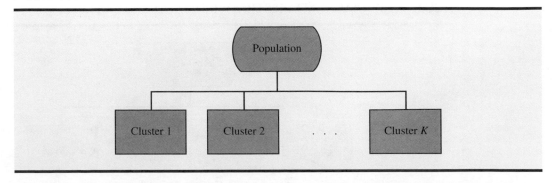

Convenience Sampling

The sampling methods discussed thus far are referred to as *probability sampling* techniques. Elements selected from the population have a known probability of being included in the sample. The advantage of probability sampling is that the sampling distribution of the appropriate sample statistic generally can be identified. Formulas such as the ones for simple random sampling presented in this chapter can be used to determine the properties of the sampling distribution. Then the sampling distribution can be used to make probability statements about the sampling error associated with the results.

Convenience sampling is a *nonprobability sampling* technique. As the name implies, the sample is identified primarily by convenience. Elements are included in the sample without prespecified or known probabilities of being selected. For example, a professor conducting research at a university may use student volunteers to constitute a sample simply because they are readily available and will participate as subjects for little or no cost. Similarly, an inspector may sample a shipment of oranges by selecting oranges haphazardly from among several crates. Labeling each orange and using a probability method of sampling would be impractical. Samples such as wildlife captures and volunteer panels for consumer research are also convenience samples.

Convenience samples have the advantage of relatively easy sample selection and data collection; however, it is impossible to evaluate the "goodness" of the sample in terms of its representativeness of the population. A convenience sample may provide good results or it may not; no statistically justified procedure allows a probability analysis and inference about the quality of the sample results. Sometimes researchers apply statistical methods designed for probability samples to a convenience sample, arguing that the convenience sample can be treated as though it were a probability sample. However, this argument cannot be supported, and we should be cautious in interpreting the results of convenience samples that are used to make inferences about populations.

Judgment Sampling

One additional nonprobability sampling technique is **judgment sampling.** In this approach, the person most knowledgeable on the subject of the study selects elements of the population that he or she feels are most representative of the population. Often this method is a relatively easy way of selecting a sample. For example, a reporter may sample two or three senators, judging that those senators reflect the general opinion of all senators. However, the quality of the sample results depends on the judgment of the person selecting the sample. Again, great caution is warranted in drawing conclusions based on judgment samples used to make inferences about populations.

NOTES AND COMMENTS

We recommend using probability sampling methods: simple random sampling, stratified random sampling, cluster sampling, or systematic sampling. For these methods, formulas are available for evaluating the "goodness" of the sample results in terms of the closeness of the results to the population characteristics being estimated. An evaluation of the goodness cannot be made with convenience or judgment sampling. Thus, great care should be used in interpreting the results based on nonprobability sampling methods.

SUMMARY

In this chapter we presented the concepts of simple random sampling and sampling distributions. We demonstrated how a simple random sample can be selected and how the data collected for the sample can be used to develop point estimates of population parameters. Because different simple random samples provide a variety of different values for the point estimators, point estimators such as $\bar{x}$ and $\bar{p}$ are random variables. The probability distribution of such a random variable is called a sampling distribution. In particular, we described the sampling distributions of the sample mean $\bar{x}$ and the sample proportion $\bar{p}$.

In considering the characteristics of the sampling distributions of $\bar{x}$ and $\bar{p}$, we stated that $E(\bar{x}) = \mu$ and $E(\bar{p}) = p$. After developing the standard deviation or standard error formulas for these estimators, we showed how the central limit theorem provided the basis for using a normal probability distribution to approximate these sampling distributions in the large-sample case. Rules of thumb were given for determining when large-sample conditions were satisfied. Other sampling methods including stratified random sampling, cluster sampling, systematic sampling, convenience sampling, and judgment sampling were discussed.

GLOSSARY

Parameter   A numerical characteristic of a population, such as a population mean μ, a population standard deviation σ, a population proportion p, and so on.

Simple random sampling   Finite population: a sample selected such that each possible sample of size n has the same probability of being selected. Infinite population: a sample selected such that each element comes from the same population and the elements are selected independently.

Sampling without replacement   Once an element has been included in the sample, it is removed from the population and cannot be selected a second time.

Sampling with replacement   Once an element has been included in the sample, it is returned to the population. A previously selected element can be selected again and therefore may appear in the sample more than once.

Sample statistic   A sample characteristic, such as a sample mean $\bar{x}$, a sample standard deviation s, a sample proportion $\bar{p}$, and so on. The value of the sample statistic is used to estimate the value of the corresponding population parameter.

Point estimator   The sample statistic, such as $\bar{x}$, s, or $\bar{p}$, that provides the point estimate of the population parameter.

Point estimate   The value of a point estimator used in a particular instance as an estimate of a population parameter.

Sampling error   The absolute value of the difference between an unbiased point estimator and the corresponding population parameter. For a sample mean, sample standard deviation, and sample proportion, the sampling errors are $|\bar{x} - \mu|$, $|s - \sigma|$, and $|\bar{p} - p|$, respectively.

Sampling distribution   A probability distribution consisting of all possible values of a sample statistic.

Unbiasedness   A property of a point estimator that is present when the expected value of the point estimator is equal to the population parameter it estimates.

Finite population correction factor   The term $\sqrt{(N - n)/(N - 1)}$ that is used in the formulas for $\sigma_{\bar{x}}$ and $\sigma_{\bar{p}}$ whenever a finite population, rather than an infinite population, is being sampled. The generally accepted rule of thumb is to ignore the finite population correction factor whenever $n/N < .05$.

Standard error   The standard deviation of a point estimator.

Central limit theorem   A theorem that enables one to use the normal probability distribution to approximate the sampling distribution of $\bar{x}$ and $\bar{p}$ whenever the sample size is large.

Stratified random sampling   A probability sampling method in which the population is first divided into strata and a simple random sample is then taken from each stratum.

Cluster sampling   A probability sampling method in which the population is first divided into clusters and then a simple random sample of the clusters is taken.

Systematic sampling   A probability sampling method in which we randomly select one of the first k elements and then select every kth element thereafter.

Convenience sampling   A nonprobability method of sampling whereby elements are selected for the sample on the basis of convenience.

Judgment sampling   A nonprobability method of sampling whereby elements are selected for the sample based on the judgment of the person doing the study.

KEY FORMULAS

Expected Value of $\bar{x}$

$$E(\bar{x}) = \mu \tag{7.1}$$

Standard Deviation of $\bar{x}$ (Standard Error)

Finite Population   *Infinite Population*

$$\sigma_{\bar{x}} = \sqrt{\frac{N-n}{N-1}}\left(\frac{\sigma}{\sqrt{n}}\right) \qquad\qquad \sigma_{\bar{x}} = \frac{\sigma}{\sqrt{n}} \tag{7.2}$$

Expected Value of $\bar{p}$

$$E(\bar{p}) = p \tag{7.4}$$

Standard Deviation of $\bar{p}$ (Standard Error)

Finite Population   *Infinite Population*

$$\sigma_{\bar{p}} = \sqrt{\frac{N-n}{N-1}}\sqrt{\frac{p(1-p)}{n}} \qquad\qquad \sigma_{\bar{p}} = \sqrt{\frac{p(1-p)}{n}} \tag{7.5}$$

SUPPLEMENTARY EXERCISES

44.   *Business Week's* Corporate Scoreboard provides quarterly data on sales, profits, net income, return on equity, price/earnings ratio, and earnings per share for 899 companies (*Business Week,* August 14, 2000). The companies can be numbered 1 to 899 in the order they appear on the Corporate Scoreboard list. Begin at the bottom of the second column of random digits in Table 7.1. Ignoring the first two digits in each group and using three-digit random numbers beginning with 112, read *up* the column to identify the number of (from 1 to 899) the first eight companies to be included in a simple random sample.

45. The mean television viewing time for teens is three hours per day (*Barron's,* November 8, 1999). Assume the population mean is $\mu = 3$ and the population standard deviation is $\sigma = 1.2$ hours. Suppose a sample of 50 teens will be used to monitor television viewing time. Let $\bar{x}$ denote the sample mean viewing time.

    a. Show the sampling distribution of $\bar{x}$.

    b. What is the probability the sample mean will be within $\pm.25$ hours of the population mean?

46. The mean travel time to work for individuals in Chicago is 31.5 minutes (*1998 Information Please Almanac*). Assume the population mean is $\mu = 31.5$ minutes and the population standard deviation is $\sigma = 12$ minutes. A sample of 50 Chicago residents is selected.

    a. Show the sampling distribution of $\bar{x}$ where $\bar{x}$ is the sample mean travel time to work for the 50 Chicago residents.

    b. What is the probability that the sample mean will be within ± 1 minute of the population mean?

    c. What is the probability that the sample mean will be within ± 3 minutes of the population mean?

47. The U.S. Bureau of Labor Statistics reported the mean hourly wage rate for individuals in executive, administrative, and managerial occupations is $24.07 (*The Wall Street Journal Almanac 1998*). Assume the population mean is $\mu = \$24.07$ and the population standard deviation is $\sigma = \$4.80$. A sample of 120 individuals in executive, administrative, and managerial occupations will be selected.

    a. What is the probability that the sample mean will be within $\pm\$0.50$ of the population mean?

    b. What is the probability that the sample mean will be within $\pm\$1.00$ of the population mean?

48. The average annual salary for federal government employees in Indiana during 1999 was $41,979 (*The World Almanac 2001*). Use this figure as the population mean and assume the population standard deviation is $\sigma = \$5000$. Suppose that a random sample of 50 federal government employees will be selected from the population.

    a. What is the value of the standard error of the mean?

    b. What is the probability that the sample mean will be more than $41,979?

    c. What is the probability the sample mean will be within $1000 of the population mean?

    d. How would the probability in part (c) change if the sample size were increased to 100?

49. Three firms have inventories that differ in size. Firm A has an inventory of 2000 items, firm B has an inventory of 5000 items, and firm C has an inventory of 10,000 items. The population standard deviation for the cost of the items in each firm's inventory is $\sigma = 144$. A statistical consultant recommends that each firm take a sample of 50 items from its inventory to provide statistically valid estimates of the average cost per item. Managers of the small firm state that because it has the smallest population, it should be able to obtain the data from a much smaller sample than that required by the larger firms. However, the consultant states that to obtain the same standard error and thus the same precision in the sample results, all firms should use the same sample size regardless of population size.

    a. Using the finite population correction factor, compute the standard error for each of the three firms given a sample of size 50.

    b. What is the probability that for each firm the sample mean $\bar{x}$ will be within ± 25 of the population mean μ?

50. A researcher reports survey results by stating that the standard error of the mean is 20. The population standard deviation is 500.

    a. How large was the sample used in this survey?

    b. What is the probability that the point estimate was within ± 25 of the population mean?

51. A production process is checked periodically by a quality control inspector. The inspector selects simple random samples of 30 finished products and computes the sample mean product weights $\bar{x}$. If test results over a long period of time show that 5% of the x values are over 2.1 pounds and 5% are under 1.9 pounds, what are the mean and the standard deviation for the population of products produced with this process?

52. As of June 13, 2001, 30.5% of individual investors were bullish on the stock market short term (*AAII Journal,* July 2001). Answer the following questions assuming a sample of 200 individual investors is used.
    a. Show the sampling distribution of $\bar{p}$, the sample proportion of individual investors who are bullish on the market short term.
    b. What is the probability that the sample proportion will be within $\pm.04$ of the population proportion?
    c. What is the probability that the sample proportion will be within $\pm.02$ of the population proportion?

53. A market research firm conducts telephone surveys with a 40% historical response rate. What is the probability that in a new sample of 400 telephone numbers, at least 150 individuals will cooperate and respond to the questions? In other words, what is the probability that the sample proportion will be at least $150/400 = .375$?

54. According to ORC International, 71% of Internet users connect their computers to the Internet by normal telephone lines (*USA Today,* January 18, 2000). Assume a population proportion $p = .71$.
    a. What is the probability that a sample proportion from a simple random sample of 350 Internet users will be within $\pm.05$ of the population proportion?
    b. What is the probability that a sample proportion from a simple random sample of 350 Internet users will be .75 or greater?

55. The proportion of individuals insured by the All-Driver Automobile Insurance Company who have received at least one traffic ticket during a five-year period is .15.
    a. Show the sampling distribution of $\bar{p}$ if a random sample of 150 insured individuals is used to estimate the proportion having received at least one ticket.
    b. What is the probability that the sample proportion will be within $\pm.03$ of the population proportion?

56. Lori Jeffrey is a successful sales representative for a major publisher of college textbooks. Historically, Lori obtains a book adoption on 25% of her sales calls. Viewing her sales calls for one month as a sample of all possible sales calls, assume that a statistical analysis of the data yields a standard error of the proportion of .0625.
    a. How large was the sample used in this analysis? That is, how many sales calls did Lori make during the month?
    b. Let $\bar{p}$ indicate the sample proportion of book adoptions obtained during the month. Show the sampling distribution $\bar{p}$.
    c. Using the sampling distribution of $\bar{p}$, compute the probability that Lori will obtain book adoptions on 30% or more of her sales calls during a one-month period.

Appendix 7.1   RANDOM SAMPLING WITH MINITAB

If a list of the elements in a population is available in a Minitab file, Minitab can be used to select a simple random sample. For example, a list of the top 100 metropolitan areas in the United States and Canada are provided in column 1 of the data set MetAreas (*Places Rated Almanac—The Millennium Edition 2000*). Column 2 contains the overall rating of each metropolitan area. The first 10 metropolitan areas in the data set and their corresponding ratings are shown in Table 7.6.

TABLE 7.6   OVERALL RATING FOR THE FIRST 10 METROPOLITAN AREAS IN THE DATA SET METAREAS

CDfile

MetAreas

Metropolitan Area	Rating
Albany, NY	64.18
Albuquerque, NM	66.16
Appleton, WI	60.56
Atlanta, GA	69.97
Austin, TX	71.48
Baltimore, MD	69.75
Birmingham, AL	69.59
Boise City, ID	68.36
Boston, MA	68.99
Buffalo, NY	66.10

Suppose that you would like to select a simple random sample of 30 metropolitan areas in order to do an in-depth study of the cost of living in the United States and Canada. The following steps can be used to select the sample.

Step 1. Select the **Calc** pull-down menu

Step 2. Choose **Random Data**

Step 3. Choose **Sample From Columns**

Step 4. When the Sample From Columns dialog box appears:

Enter 30 in the **Sample __** box

Enter C1 C2 in the **Sample 30 rows from column(s)** box

Enter C3 C4 in the **Store samples in** box

Step 5. Click **OK**

The random sample of 30 metropolitan areas appears in columns C3 and C4.

Appendix 7.2   RANDOM SAMPLING WITH EXCEL

If a list of the elements in a population is available in an Excel file, Excel can be used to select a simple random sample. For example, a list of the top 100 metropolitan areas in the United States and Canada are provided in column A of the data set MetAreas (*Places Rated Almanac—The Millennium Edition 2000*). Column B contains the overall rating of each metropolitan area. The first 10 metropolitan areas in the data set and their corresponding ratings are shown in Table 7.6. Assume that you would like to select a simple random sample of 30 metropolitan areas in order to do an in-depth study of the cost of living in the United States and Canada.

The rows of any Excel data set can be placed in a random order by adding an extra column to the data set and filling the column with random numbers using the =RAND() function. Then using Excel's sort ascending capability on the random number column, the rows of the data set will be reordered randomly. The random sample of size *n* appears in the first *n* rows of the reordered data set.

In the MetAreas data set, labels are in row 1 and the 100 metropolitan areas are in rows 2 to 101. The following steps can be used to select a simple random sample of 30 metropolitan areas.

Step 1. Enter =RAND() in cell C2
Step 2. Copy cell C2 to cells C3:C101
Step 3. Select any cell in Column C
Step 4. Click the **Sort Ascending** button on the tool bar

The random sample of 30 metropolitan areas appears in rows 2 to 31 of the reordered data set. The random numbers in column C are no longer necessary and can be deleted if desired.

Chapter 8

INTERVAL ESTIMATION

CONTENTS

DOLLAR GENERAL CORPORATION*

GOODLETTSVILLE, TENNESSEE

Dollar General Corporation was founded in 1939 as a dry goods wholesale company. After World War II, the company began opening retail locations in rural south-central Kentucky. Today Dollar General Corporation operates more than 4300 stores across the middle and southeastern United States. Emphasizing small-store convenience, Dollar General markets health and beauty aids, cleaning supplies, housewares, stationery, apparel, shoes, and domestic items at everyday low prices.

Being in an inventory-intense business with more than 20,000 products, Dollar General made the decision to adopt the LIFO (last-in, first-out) method of inventory valuation. This method matches current costs against current revenues, which minimizes the effect of radical price changes on profit and loss results. In addition, the LIFO method reduces net income and thereby income taxes during periods of inflation. LIFO also brings disposable cash generated from sales in line with income and allows for the replacement of inventory at current costs.

Accounting practices require that a LIFO index be established for inventory under the LIFO method of valuation. For example, a LIFO index of 1.028 indicates that the company's inventory value at current costs reflects a 2.8% increase due to inflation over the most recent one-year period.

The establishment of a LIFO index requires that the year-end inventory count for each product be valued at the current year-end cost and at the preceding year-end cost. To avoid counting the inventory of every product in more than 4300 retail locations, a random sample of 800 products is selected from 100 retail locations and three warehouses. Physical inventories for the sampled

This store in the Cleveland area is one of more than 4300 Dollar General Stores. © Jim Baron/The Image Finders.

products are taken at the end of the year. Accounting personnel then provide the current-year and preceding-year costs needed to construct the LIFO index.

For a recent year, the LIFO index was 1.030. However, because this index is a sample estimate of the population's LIFO index, a statement about the precision of the estimate was required. On the basis of the sample results and a 95% confidence level, the margin of error was computed to be .006. Thus, the interval from 1.024 to 1.036 provides the 95% confidence interval estimate of the population LIFO index. This precision was judged to be good.

In this chapter you will learn how to compute the margin of error associated with a sample mean and a sample proportion. Then, you will learn how to use this information to construct and interpret confidence interval estimates of a population mean and a population proportion. You will also learn how to determine the sample size needed to ensure that the margin of error will be within acceptable limits.

*The authors are indebted to Robert S. Knaul, Controller, Dollar General Corporation, for providing this Statistics in Practice.

In Chapter 7 we stated that a point estimator is a sample statistic used to estimate a population parameter. For instance, the sample mean $\bar{x}$ is a point estimator of the population mean μ, and the sample proportion $\bar{p}$ is a point estimator of the population proportion p. Because a point estimator does not provide information about how close the estimate is to the population parameter, statisticians usually prefer to construct an **interval estimate** by subtracting and adding a value, called the **margin of error,** to a point estimate.

$$\text{Point Estimate} \pm \text{Margin of Error}$$

This chapter focuses on the development of interval estimates for a population mean μ and a population proportion p. An interval estimate of the population mean is

$$\bar{x} \pm \text{Margin of Error}$$

and an interval estimate of a population proportion is

$$\bar{p} \pm \text{Margin of Error}$$

The inclusion of the margin of error term provides a measure of the precision associated with the estimate. As we shall see, much of the work in constructing an interval estimate is in determining a value for the margin of error that will provide the desired precision. The sampling distribution of $\bar{x}$ and the sampling distribution of $\bar{p}$ presented in Chapter 7 play important roles in this regard.

8.1   INTERVAL ESTIMATION OF A POPULATION MEAN: LARGE-SAMPLE CASE

In this section we show how a simple random sample can be used to develop an interval estimate of a population mean in the large sample case ($n \geq 30$). We begin with a situation in which the population standard deviation σ can be assumed *known*. We then consider the case where it cannot be; in this case σ is estimated by the sample standard deviation s.

CJW Estimation Problem

The development of an interval estimate of a population mean can be illustrated by considering the monthly customer service survey conducted by CJW, Inc. CJW provides a Web site for accepting customer orders and providing follow-up service over the Internet. The company prides itself on providing easy online ordering, timely delivery, and prompt response to customer inquiries. Good customer service is critical to the ongoing success of the company.

CJW's quality assurance team uses a customer service survey to measure satisfaction with its Web site and online customer service. Each month, the team sends a questionnaire to a random sample of customers who placed an order or requested service during the previous month. The questionnaire asks customers to rate their satisfaction with such things as ease of placing orders, timely delivery, accurate order filling, and technical advice. The team summarizes each customer's questionnaire with an overall satisfaction score x that ranges from 0 (worst possible score) to 100 (best possible score). A sample mean customer satisfaction score $\bar{x}$ is then computed.

The sample mean satisfaction score provides a point estimate of the mean satisfaction score μ for the population of all CJW customers. With this timely measure of customer service, CJW can promptly take corrective action if a low customer satisfaction score results. The company has conducted this satisfaction survey for a number of months, and has consistently obtained an estimate near 20 for the standard deviation of satisfaction scores. Based on this historical data, CJW now assumes a known value of $\sigma = 20$ for the population standard deviation.

During the most recent month, the quality assurance team surveyed 100 customers ($n = 100$) and obtained a sample mean satisfaction score of $\bar{x} = 82$. This sample mean satisfaction score provides a point estimate of the population mean satisfaction score, μ. In the discussion that follows, we show how to compute a margin of error for this estimate and hence develop an interval estimate.

Sampling Error

Any time a sample mean is used to provide a point estimate of a population mean, someone may ask: How good is the estimate? The "how good" question is a way of asking about the error involved when the value of $\bar{x}$ is used as a point estimate of μ. As we noted in Chapter 7, the absolute value of the difference between an unbiased point estimator and the population parameter is called the **sampling error.** For the case of a sample mean estimating a population mean, the sampling error is defined as follows:

$$\text{Sampling Error} = |\bar{x} - \mu| \tag{8.1}$$

In practice, the value of the sampling error cannot be determined exactly because the population mean μ is unknown. However, the sampling distribution of $\bar{x}$ can be used to make probability statements about the sampling error, which we will illustrate using the CJW example.

The central limit theorem applies to any population. Thus, the methodology presented in this section can be used even if the population distribution is unknown.

With a sample size $n = 100$ and a population standard deviation $\sigma = 20$, the central limit theorem introduced in Chapter 7 enables us to conclude that the sampling distribution of $\bar{x}$ can be approximated by a normal distribution with a mean μ and a standard deviation $\sigma_{\bar{x}} = \sigma/\sqrt{n} = 20/\sqrt{100} = 2$. This sampling distribution is shown in Figure 8.1. Because the sampling distribution shows how values of $\bar{x}$ are distributed around μ, the sampling distribution provides information about the possible differences between $\bar{x}$ and μ. This information provides the basis for a probability statement about the sampling error.

Using the tables of areas for the standard normal probability distribution, we find that 95% of the values of a normally distributed random variable are within ± 1.96 standard deviations of the mean. Because the sampling distribution of $\bar{x}$ can be approximated by a normal distribution, 95% of all $\bar{x}$ values must be within $\pm 1.96\sigma_{\bar{x}}$ of the mean μ. In the CJW example, $1.96\sigma_{\bar{x}} = 1.96(2) = 3.92$. Thus, we can conclude that 95% of the sample means that can be obtained using a sample size $n = 100$ will be within ± 3.92 of the population mean μ.

The location of the sample means that differ from μ by 3.92 or less is shown in Figure 8.2. Note that if a sample mean falls in the region denoted by "95% of all $\bar{x}$ values," it provides a sampling error $|\bar{x} - \mu|$ of 3.92 or less. However, if a sample mean appears in either the lower tail or the upper tail of the sampling distribution, the sampling error $|\bar{x} - \mu|$ will be greater than 3.92. Therefore we can make the following probability statement about the sampling error for the CJW problem.

There is a .95 probability that the sample mean will provide a sampling error of 3.92 or less.

This probability statement, or **precision statement,** tells CJW about the likely size of the sampling error if the sample mean from a simple random sample of 100 customers is used

FIGURE 8.1   SAMPLING DISTRIBUTION OF THE SAMPLE MEAN SATISFACTION
SCORE FROM SIMPLE RANDOM SAMPLES OF 100 CUSTOMERS

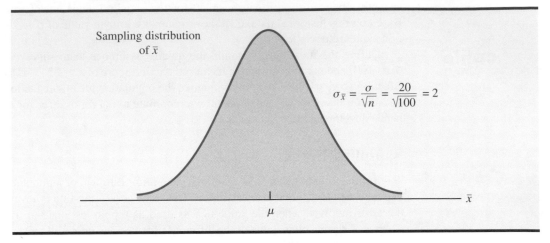

Sampling distribution
of $\bar{x}$

$$\sigma_{\bar{x}} = \frac{\sigma}{\sqrt{n}} = \frac{20}{\sqrt{100}} = 2$$

μ

$\bar{x}$

to estimate the population mean. The value 3.92, which provides an upper limit on the sampling error 95% of the time, is referred to as the *margin of error.*

σ Assumed Known

Let us show how we can use the precision statement to develop a confidence interval estimate of a population mean. We start with the case in which the population standard deviation can be assumed known. The general form of an interval estimate of a population mean takes the following form:

$$\bar{x} \pm \text{Margin of Error}$$

FIGURE 8.2   SAMPLING DISTRIBUTION OF $\bar{x}$ SHOWING THE LOCATION OF SAMPLE
MEANS THAT PROVIDE A SAMPLING ERROR OF 3.92 OR LESS

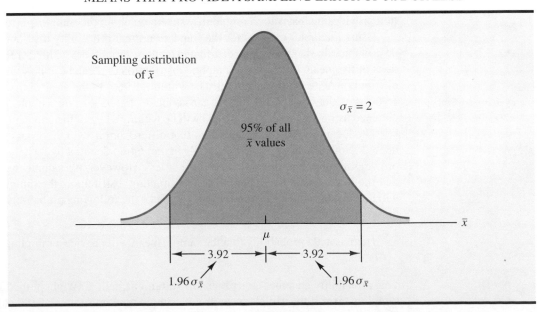

Sampling distribution
of $\bar{x}$

$\sigma_{\bar{x}} = 2$

95% of all
$\bar{x}$ values

μ

$\bar{x}$

3.92   3.92

$1.96\,\sigma_{\bar{x}}$ $1.96\,\sigma_{\bar{x}}$

Let us now develop such an interval estimate for the CJW example. The CJW sample of $n = 100$ customers meets the large-sample condition of $n \geq 30$. In addition, prior customer surveys provided data that enabled CJW to assume that the population standard deviation is known with $\sigma = 20$. For the most recent CJW survey of $n = 100$ customers, the sample mean is $\bar{x} = 82$. We have shown that using the .95 probability precision statement, the margin of error is 3.92. Thus, 82 ± 3.92 provides an interval estimate of the population mean. Subtracting and adding the margin of error, we obtain $82 - 3.92 = 78.08$ as the lower limit and $82 + 3.92 = 85.92$ as the upper limit of the interval estimate.

To better interpret an interval estimate of a population mean μ, let us consider the values of the sample mean $\bar{x}$ that could be obtained if we took three *different* random samples, each consisting of 100 CJW customers. The first sample mean might turn out to have the value shown as $\bar{x}_1$ in Figure 8.3. In this case, Figure 8.3 shows that the interval formed by subtracting 3.92 from $\bar{x}$ and adding 3.92 to $\bar{x}_1$ includes the population mean μ. Now consider what happens if the second sample mean turns out to have the value shown as $\bar{x}_2$ in Figure 8.3. Although this sample mean differs from the first sample mean, we see that the interval formed by subtracting 3.92 from $\bar{x}_2$ and adding 3.92 to $\bar{x}_2$ also includes the population mean μ. However, consider what happens if the third sample mean turns out to have the value shown as $\bar{x}_3$ in Figure 8.3. In this case, the interval formed by subtracting 3.92 from $\bar{x}_3$ and adding 3.92 to $\bar{x}_3$ does not include the population mean μ. Because $\bar{x}_3$ falls in the upper tail of the distribution and is farther than 3.92 from μ, subtracting and adding 3.92 to $\bar{x}_3$ forms an interval that does not include μ.

FIGURE 8.3   INTERVALS FORMED FROM SELECTED SAMPLE MEANS AT LOCATIONS $\bar{x}_1$, $\bar{x}_2$, AND $\bar{x}_3$

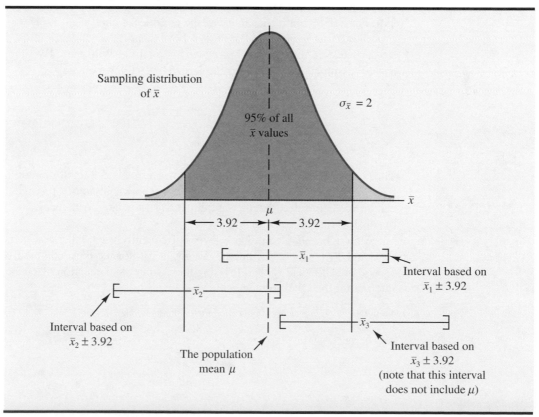

*This discussion provides
insight as to why the
interval is called a 95%
confidence interval.*

Any sample mean $\bar{x}$ that is within the shaded region of Figure 8.3 will provide an interval that contains the population mean μ. Because 95% of all possible sample means are in the shaded region, 95% of all intervals formed by subtracting 3.92 from $\bar{x}$ and adding 3.92 to $\bar{x}$ will include the population mean μ. Thus we are *95% confident* that the interval constructed from $\bar{x} - 3.92$ to $\bar{x} + 3.92$ will include the population mean μ. Because 95% of all possible sample means provide an interval that includes the population mean, the interval is established at the 95% **confidence level.** The value .95 is referred to as the **confidence coefficient,** and the interval estimate $\bar{x} \pm 3.92$ is called a 95% confidence interval.

The general procedure for developing an interval estimate of a population mean whenever we have a large sample and the population standard deviation is assumed known follows.

Interval Estimate of a Population Mean: Large-Sample Case ($n \geq 30$) with σ Assumed Known

$$\bar{x} \pm z_{\alpha/2} \frac{\sigma}{\sqrt{n}} \tag{8.2}$$

where $(1 - \alpha)$ is the confidence coefficient and $z_{\alpha/2}$ is the z value providing an area $\alpha/2$ in the upper tail of the standard normal probability distribution.

Let us use expression (8.2) to construct a 95% confidence interval for the CJW problem. For a 95% confidence interval, the confidence coefficient is $(1 - \alpha) = .95$ and thus, $\alpha = .05$. Using the tables of areas for the standard normal distribution, an area of $\alpha/2 = .05/2 = .025$ in the upper tail provides $z_{.025} = 1.96$. With the CJW sample mean $\bar{x} = 82$, $\sigma = 20$ assumed known, and a sample size $n = 100$, we obtain

$$82 \pm 1.96 \frac{20}{\sqrt{100}}$$

$$82 \pm 3.92$$

Thus, using expression (8.2), the margin of error is 3.92 and the confidence interval is $82 - 3.92 = 78.08$ to $82 + 3.92 = 85.92$. As shown previously, this result means that CJW can be 95% confident that the sampling error associated with using $\bar{x} = 82$ as an estimate of μ is less than or equal to 3.92.

Although a 95% confidence level is frequently used, other confidence levels such as 90% and 99% may be considered. Values of $z_{\alpha/2}$ for the most commonly used confidence levels* are shown in Table 8.1. Using these values and equation (8.2), the 90% confidence interval for the CJW problem is

$$82 \pm 1.645 \frac{20}{\sqrt{100}}$$

$$82 \pm 3.29$$

---

*The standard normal probability table provides z values with two decimal places. However, it is general practice to use z values with three decimal places for the confidence levels of 90%, 95%, and 99%.

TABLE 8.1   VALUES OF $z_{\alpha/2}$ FOR THE MOST COMMONLY USED CONFIDENCE LEVELS

Confidence Level	α	$\alpha/2$	$z_{\alpha/2}$
90%	.10	.05	1.645
95%	.05	.025	1.960
99%	.01	.005	2.576

Thus, at 90% confidence, the margin of error is 3.29 and the confidence interval is $82 - 3.29 = 78.71$ to $82 + 3.29 = 85.29$. Similarly, the 99% confidence interval is

$$82 \pm 2.576 \frac{20}{\sqrt{100}}$$

$$82 \pm 5.15$$

Thus, at 99% confidence, the margin of error is 5.15 and the confidence interval is $82 - 5.15 = 76.85$ to $82 + 5.15 = 87.15$.

Comparing the results for the 90%, 95%, and 99% confidence levels, we see that in order to have a higher degree of confidence, the margin of error and thus the width of the confidence interval must be larger.

σ Estimated by s

With the population standard deviation σ unknown, we use the sample standard deviation s to estimate σ.

A difficulty in using expression (8.2) to compute an interval estimate of a population mean arises because many applications provide no basis for assuming that the population standard deviation is known. In such cases, the sample standard deviation s is used to estimate σ. In the large-sample case ($n \geq 30$), the following formula can be used to develop an interval estimate of a population mean.*

> **Interval Estimate of a Population Mean: Large-Sample Case ($n \geq 30$) with σ Estimated by s**
>
> $$\bar{x} \pm z_{\alpha/2} \frac{s}{\sqrt{n}} \tag{8.3}$$
>
> where s is the sample standard deviation, $(1 - \alpha)$ is the confidence coefficient, and $z_{\alpha/2}$ is the z-value providing an area of $\alpha/2$ in the upper tail of the standard normal probability distribution.

To illustrate this interval estimation procedure, let us consider a sampling study designed to estimate the credit card debt of U.S. households. A sample of 85 households provided the credit card balances shown in Table 8.2. With $n = 85$, we have the large-sample case. In addition, because no historical data are available about credit card balances per household, the population standard deviation σ will be estimated by the sample standard

---

*The proof of applicability for this interval is based on both the central limit theorem and the fact that s^2 converges to σ^2 as the sample size increases. Use of expression (8.3) does not require knowledge of the population probability distribution.

TABLE 8.2　CREDIT CARD BALANCES FOR A SAMPLE OF 85 HOUSEHOLDS

CDfile
Balance

9619	5994	3344	7888	7581	9980
5364	4652	13627	3091	12545	8718
8348	5376	968	943	7959	8452
7348	5998	4714	8762	2563	4935
381	7530	4334	1407	6787	5938
2998	3678	4911	6644	5071	5266
1686	3581	1920	7644	9536	10658
1962	5625	3780	11169	4459	3910
4920	5619	3478	7979	8047	7503
5047	9032	6185	3258	8083	1582
6921	13236	1141	8660	2153	
5759	4447	7577	7511	8003	
8047	609	4667	14442	6795	
3924	414	5219	4447	5915	
3470	7636	6416	6550	7164	

deviation s. Let us develop a 95% confidence interval estimate of the population mean credit card balance per household.

First, we use the data in Table 8.2 to compute the sample mean $\bar{x} = \$5900$ and the sample standard deviation $s = \$3058$. At 95% confidence, $z_{\alpha/2} = z_{.025} = 1.96$. With a sample size of $n = 85$, expression (8.3) shows

$$5900 \pm 1.96\,\frac{3058}{\sqrt{85}}$$

$$5900 \pm 650$$

Hence, the margin of error is $650 and the 95% confidence interval estimate of the population mean is $5900 - 650 = \$5250$ to $5900 + 650 = \$6550$. We can be 95% confident that the population mean credit card balance for all households falls between $5250 and $6550.

In Chapter 7, we pointed out that $\sigma_{\bar{x}} = \sigma/\sqrt{n}$ is the standard error of the mean. Minitab provides an estimate of the standard error of the mean by using s to estimate σ.

Minitab, Excel, and other software packages provide easy computations of confidence intervals for the large-sample case when s is used to estimate σ. The procedures used by Minitab and Excel are described in Appendixes 8.1 and 8.2. The results of the Minitab interval estimation procedure are shown in Figure 8.4. The sample of 85 households provides a sample mean credit card balance of $5900, a sample standard deviation of $3058, a standard error of the mean of $332, and a 95% confidence interval of $5250 to $6550.

FIGURE 8.4　MINITAB CONFIDENCE INTERVAL FOR THE CREDIT CARD BALANCE SURVEY

Variable	N	Mean	StDev	SE Mean	95.0% CI
Balance	85	5900	3058	332	(5250, 6550)

NOTES AND COMMENTS

1. In developing an interval estimate of the population mean, we specify the desired confidence coefficient $(1 - \alpha)$ before selecting the sample. Thus, prior to selecting the sample, we conclude that there is a $1 - \alpha$ probability that the confidence interval we eventually compute will contain the population mean μ. However, once the sample is taken, the sample mean $\bar{x}$ is computed, and the particular interval estimate is determined, the resulting interval may or may not contain μ. If $1 - \alpha$ is reasonably large, we can be confident that the resulting interval will contain μ because we know that if we use this procedure repeatedly, $100(1 - \alpha)$ percent of all possible intervals developed in this way will contain μ.

2. In practical applications, the population standard deviation σ is rarely known. However, his-

torical data, theoretical, or other reasons may provide the user with good information about the value of σ. If this value of σ is believed to be better than an estimate of σ that can be obtained by using a sample standard deviation s, expression (8.2) should be used for the large-sample case with σ assumed known.

3. The sample size n appears in the denominator of the interval estimation expressions (8.2) and (8.3). Thus, if a particular sample size provides too wide an interval to be of any practical use, we may want to consider increasing the sample size. With n in the denominator, a larger sample size will provide a smaller margin of error, a narrower interval, and a greater precision. The procedure for determining the size of a simple random sample necessary to obtain a desired precision is discussed in Section 8.3.

EXERCISES

Methods

1. A simple random sample of 40 items resulted in a sample mean of 25. The population standard deviation is $\sigma = 5$.

    a. What is the standard error of the mean, $\sigma_{\bar{x}}$?

    b. At a 95% probability, what is the margin of error?

SELFtest   **2.** A simple random sample of 50 items resulted in a sample mean of 32 and a sample standard deviation of 6.

    a. Provide a 90% confidence interval for the population mean.

    b. Provide a 95% confidence interval for the population mean.

    c. Provide a 99% confidence interval for the population mean.

3. A sample of 60 items resulted in a sample mean of 80 and a sample standard deviation of 15.

    a. Compute the 95% confidence interval for the population mean.

    b. Assume that the same sample mean and sample standard deviation were obtained from a sample of 120 items. Provide a 95% confidence interval for the population mean.

    c. What is the effect of a larger sample size on the interval estimate of a population mean?

4. A 95% confidence interval for a population mean was reported to be 122 to 130. If the sample mean is 126 and the sample standard deviation is 16.07, what sample size was used in this study?

Applications

SELFtest   **5.** In an effort to estimate the mean amount spent per customer for dinner at a major Atlanta restaurant, data were collected for a sample of 49 customers. Assume a population standard deviation of $5.

    a. At 95% confidence, what is the margin of error?

    b. If the sample mean is $24.80, what is the 95% confidence interval for the population mean?

6. Mean weekly earnings of individuals working in various industries were reported in *The New York Times 1998 Almanac*. The mean weekly earnings for individuals in the service industry were $369. Assume that this result was based on a sample of 250 service individuals and that the sample standard deviation was $50. Compute the 95% confidence interval for the population mean weekly earnings for individuals working in the service industry.

7. The undergraduate grade point average (GPA) for students admitted to the top graduate business schools was 3.37 (*Best Graduate Schools, U.S. News and World Report*, 2001 Edition). Assume this estimate was based on a sample of 120 students admitted to the top schools. Using past years' data, the population standard deviation can be assumed known with $\sigma = .28$. What is the 95% confidence interval estimate of the mean undergraduate GPA for students admitted to the top graduate business schools?

8. The National Association of Independent Colleges and Universities reported that students graduating from public colleges and universities carry an average debt of $12,000 upon graduation (*Kiplinger's Personal Finance Magazine*, November 1998). Assume that this average or mean amount is based on a sample of 245 students and that, based on past studies, the population standard deviation for the debt upon graduation is $2200.
   a. Develop a 90% confidence interval estimate of the population mean.
   b. Develop a 95% confidence interval estimate of the population mean.
   c. Develop a 99% confidence interval estimate of the population mean.
   d. Discuss what happens to the width of the confidence interval as the confidence level is increased. Does this result seem reasonable? Explain.

CDfile
Workers

9. A summary of the mean hourly pay for production workers was reported in *The Wall Street Journal*, November 25, 1997. A sample of 60 hourly pay rates for production workers is contained in the data set Workers.
   a. Use Workers to develop a point estimate of the mean hourly pay rate for the population of production workers.
   b. What is the sample standard deviation?
   c. What is the 95% confidence interval for the mean hourly pay rate for the population of production workers?

10. Nielsen Media Research reports the household mean television viewing time during the 8 P.M. to 11 P.M. time period is 7.75 hours per week (*The World Almanac 2000*). Assuming a sample size of 180 households and a sample standard deviation of 3.45 hours, what is the 95% confidence interval estimate of the mean television viewing time per week during the 8 P.M. to 11 P.M. time period?

11. The International Air Transport Association surveys business travelers to develop quality ratings for transatlantic gateway airports. The maximum possible rating is 10. Suppose a simple random sample of 50 business travelers is selected and each traveler is asked to provide a rating for the Miami International Airport. The ratings obtained from the sample of 50 business travelers follow.

Miami

6	4	6	8	7	7	6	3	3	8	10	4	8
7	8	7	5	9	5	8	4	3	8	5	5	4
4	4	8	4	5	6	2	5	9	9	8	4	8
9	9	5	9	7	8	3	10	8	9	6		

Develop a 95% confidence interval estimate of the population mean rating for Miami.

12. Thirty fast-food restaurants including Wendy's, McDonald's, and Burger King were visited during the summer of 2000 (*The Cincinnati Enquirer*, July 9, 2000). During each visit, the customer went to the drive-through and ordered a basic meal such as a "combo" meal

FastFood

or a sandwich, fries, and shake. The time between pulling up to the message board and receiving the filled order was recorded. The times in minutes for the 30 visits are as follows:

0.9	1.0	1.2	2.2	1.9	3.6	2.8	5.2	1.8	2.1
6.8	1.3	3.0	4.5	2.8	2.3	2.7	5.7	4.8	3.5
2.6	3.3	5.0	4.0	7.2	9.1	2.8	3.6	7.3	9.0

    a. Provide a point estimate of the population mean drive-through time at fast-food restaurants.
    b. At 95% confidence, what is the margin of error?
    c. What is the 95% confidence interval estimate of the population mean?

8.2   INTERVAL ESTIMATION OF A POPULATION MEAN: SMALL-SAMPLE CASE

The interval estimation procedures developed in Section 8.1 were based on large-sample theory and the use of the central limit theorem. In such cases, the sampling distribution of $\bar{x}$ can be approximated by a normal probability distribution regardless of the population. As a result, the large-sample procedures do not require any assumption about the distribution of the population.

The methodology presented in this section is based on the assumption that the population has a normal distribution.

    In this section we show how to develop an interval estimate of a population mean for the small-sample case ($n < 30$). With a small sample, the sampling distribution of $\bar{x}$ depends on the distribution of the population. The interval estimation procedures that follow are based on the assumption that the population has a normal distribution. If this assumption is appropriate, the methodology presented in this section can be used to compute an interval estimate of a population mean. However, if this assumption is not appropriate, we recommend increasing the sample size to $n \geq 30$ in order to use the large-sample procedures presented in Section 8.1.

    In the small-sample case, we begin with the situation where the population standard deviation σ is assumed known. We then consider the case where the population standard deviation σ is estimated by the sample standard deviation s.

σ Assumed Known

We begin by making the assumption that the population is normally distributed and the population standard deviation σ is assumed known. Under these conditions, the sampling distribution of $\bar{x}$ is normally distributed with mean μ and standard deviation $\sigma_{\bar{x}} = \sigma/\sqrt{n}$ for any sample size. Thus, given that the sampling distribution of $\bar{x}$ is a normal distribution, the small-sample interval estimation procedure with σ assumed known is identical to the large-sample interval estimation procedure presented in Section 8.1. This procedure is stated as follows:

Interval Estimate of a Population Mean: Small-Sample Case ($n < 30$) with σ Assumed Known

Assumption: The population has a normal probability distribution.

$$\bar{x} \pm z_{\alpha/2} \frac{\sigma}{\sqrt{n}} \tag{8.4}$$

where $(1 - \alpha)$ is the confidence coefficient and $z_{\alpha/2}$ is the z-value providing an area of $\alpha/2$ in the upper tail of the standard normal probability distribution

---

With σ assumed known, $z_{\alpha/2}$ based on the desired confidence level, the sample size n and the sample mean $\bar{x}$, expression (8.4) can be used to compute an interval estimate of the population mean. Because this computation is identical to the computation made in Section 8.1, we shall not present a new numerical example here.

σ Estimated by s

We begin by making the assumption that the population has a normal distribution. Without any basis for assuming that the population standard deviation σ is known, the sample standard deviation s is used to estimate σ. Under these conditions, the interval estimation procedure is based on a probability distribution known as the *t* **distribution.**

William Sealy Gosset, writing under the name "Student," is the founder of the t distribution. Gosset, an Oxford graduate in mathematics, worked for the Guinness Brewery in Dublin, Ireland. He developed a new small-sample theory of statistics while working on small-scale materials and temperature experiments in the brewery.

The *t* distribution is a family of similar probability distributions, with a specific *t* distribution depending on a parameter known as the **degrees of freedom.** The *t* distribution with one degree of freedom is unique, as is the *t* distribution with two degrees of freedom, with three degrees of freedom, and so on. As the number of degrees of freedom increases, the difference between the *t* distribution and the standard normal probability distribution becomes smaller and smaller. Figure 8.5 shows *t* distributions with 10 and 20 degrees of freedom and their relationship to the standard normal probability distribution. Note that a *t* distribution with more degrees of freedom exhibits less variability and more closely resembles the standard normal probability distribution. Note also that the mean of the *t* distribution is zero.

As the degrees of freedom increase, the t distribution approaches the standard normal distribution. In fact, standard normal distribution z values can be found in the infinite degrees of freedom row of the t distribution table.

We place a subscript on *t* to indicate the area in the upper tail of the *t* distribution. For example, just as we used $z_{.025}$ to indicate the *z* value providing a .025 area in the upper tail of a standard normal probability distribution, we will use $t_{.025}$ to indicate a .025 area in the upper tail of a *t* distribution. In general, we will use the notation $t_{\alpha/2}$ to represent a *t* value with an area of $\alpha/2$ in the upper tail of the *t* distribution. See Figure 8.6.

Table 8.3 contains a table for the *t* distribution. This table also appears inside the front cover of the text. Note, for example, that for a *t* distribution with 10 degrees of freedom, $t_{.025} = 2.228$. Similarly, for a *t* distribution with 20 degrees of freedom, $t_{.025} = 2.086$. As the degrees of freedom continue to increase, $t_{.025}$ approaches $z_{.025} = 1.96$.

FIGURE 8.5   COMPARISON OF THE STANDARD NORMAL DISTRIBUTION WITH *t* DISTRIBUTIONS HAVING 10 AND 20 DEGREES OF FREEDOM

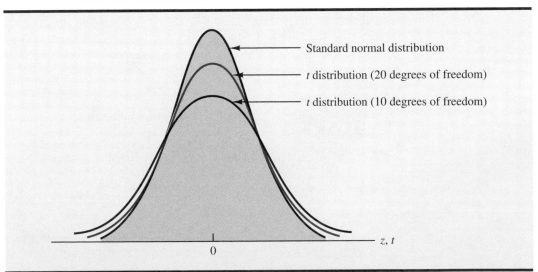

FIGURE 8.6 t DISTRIBUTION WITH $\alpha/2$ AREA OR PROBABILITY IN THE UPPER TAIL

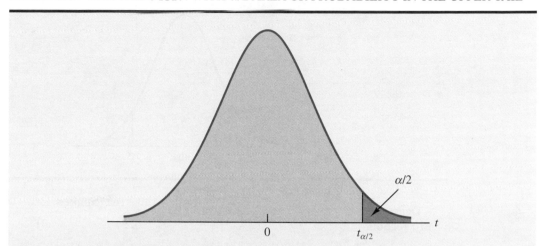

Now that we have an idea of what the t distribution is, let us see how it is used to develop an interval estimate of a population mean. Assume that the population has a normal probability distribution and use the sample standard deviation s to estimate the population standard deviation σ. The following interval estimation procedure is applicable.

Interval Estimate of a Population Mean: Small-Sample Case ($n < 30$) with σ Estimated by s

Assumption: The population has a normal probability distribution.

$$\bar{x} \pm t_{\alpha/2} \frac{s}{\sqrt{n}} \tag{8.5}$$

where s is the sample standard deviation, $(1 - \alpha)$ is the confidence coefficient, and $t_{\alpha/2}$ is the t value providing an area of $\alpha/2$ in the upper tail of the t distribution with $n - 1$ degrees of freedom.

The reason the number of degrees of freedom associated with the t value in expression (8.5) is $n - 1$ concerns the use of s as an estimate of the population standard deviation σ. The expression for the sample standard deviation is

$$s = \sqrt{\frac{\Sigma(x_i - \bar{x})^2}{n - 1}}$$

Degrees of freedom refer to the number of independent pieces of information that go into the computation of $\Sigma(x_i - \bar{x})^2$. The n pieces of information involved in computing $\Sigma(x_i - \bar{x})^2$ are as follows: $x_1 - \bar{x}, x_2 - \bar{x}, \ldots, x_n - \bar{x}$. In Section 3.2 we indicated that $\Sigma(x_i - \bar{x}) = 0$ for any data set. Thus, only $n - 1$ of the $x_i - \bar{x}$ values are independent; that is, if we know

TABLE 8.3 *t* DISTRIBUTION TABLE FOR AREAS IN THE UPPER TAIL
(EXAMPLE: WITH 10 DEGREES OF FREEDOM, $t_{.025} = 2.228$)

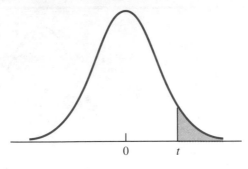

Degrees of Freedom	Upper-Tail Area (Shaded)				
	.10	.05	.025	.01	.005
1	3.078	6.314	12.706	31.821	63.657
2	1.886	2.920	4.303	6.965	9.925
3	1.638	2.353	3.182	4.541	5.841
4	1.533	2.132	2.776	3.747	4.604
5	1.476	2.015	2.571	3.365	4.032
6	1.440	1.943	2.447	3.143	3.707
7	1.415	1.895	2.365	2.998	3.499
8	1.397	1.860	2.306	2.896	3.355
9	1.383	1.833	2.262	2.821	3.250
10	1.372	1.812	2.228	2.764	3.169
11	1.363	1.796	2.201	2.718	3.106
12	1.356	1.782	2.179	2.681	3.055
13	1.350	1.771	2.160	2.650	3.012
14	1.345	1.761	2.145	2.624	2.977
15	1.341	1.753	2.131	2.602	2.947
16	1.337	1.746	2.120	2.583	2.921
17	1.333	1.740	2.110	2.567	2.898
18	1.330	1.734	2.101	2.552	2.878
19	1.328	1.729	2.093	2.539	2.861
20	1.325	1.725	2.086	2.528	2.845
21	1.323	1.721	2.080	2.518	2.831
22	1.321	1.717	2.074	2.508	2.819
23	1.319	1.714	2.069	2.500	2.807
24	1.318	1.711	2.064	2.492	2.797
25	1.316	1.708	2.060	2.485	2.787
26	1.315	1.706	2.056	2.479	2.779
27	1.314	1.703	2.052	2.473	2.771
28	1.313	1.701	2.048	2.467	2.763
29	1.311	1.699	2.045	2.462	2.756
30	1.310	1.697	2.042	2.457	2.750
40	1.303	1.684	2.021	2.423	2.704
60	1.296	1.671	2.000	2.390	2.660
120	1.289	1.658	1.980	2.358	2.617
∞	1.282	1.645	1.960	2.326	2.576

$n - 1$ of the values, the remaining value can be determined exactly by using the condition that the sum of the x_i $\bar{x}$ values must be 0. Thus, $n - 1$ is the number of degrees of freedom associated with $\Sigma(x_i - \bar{x})^2$ and hence the number of degrees of freedom for the t distribution in expression (8.5).

Let us demonstrate the small-sample interval estimation procedure by considering the training program evaluation conducted by Scheer Industries. Scheer's director of manufacturing wants to use a computer-assisted program to train the firm's maintenance employees for machine repair operations. The director expects the computer-assisted method to reduce the time needed to train employees. To evaluate the training method, the director of manufacturing requests an estimate of the population mean training time for the computer-assisted program.

Suppose management agrees to train 15 employees using the computer-assisted program. The data on training days required for each employee in the sample appear in Table 8.4. The sample mean and sample standard deviation for these data follow.

$$\bar{x} = \frac{\Sigma x_i}{n} = \frac{808}{15} = 53.87 \text{ days}$$

$$s = \sqrt{\frac{\Sigma(x_i - \bar{x})^2}{n - 1}} = \sqrt{\frac{651.73}{14}} = 6.82 \text{ days}$$

The point estimate of the population mean training time is 53.87 days. We can obtain information about the precision of this estimate by developing an interval estimate of the population mean. Because the population standard deviation is unknown, we use the sample standard deviation $s = 6.82$ days to estimate σ. With the small sample size, $n = 15$, we use expression (8.5) to develop a 95% confidence interval estimate of the population mean. If we assume that the population of training times has a normal probability distribution, the t distribution with $n - 1 = 14$ degrees of freedom provides the appropriate probability distribution for the interval estimation procedure. We see from Table 8.3 that with 14 degrees of freedom, $t_{\alpha/2} = t_{.025} = 2.145$. Using expression (8.5), we arrive at

The t distribution is based on the assumption that the population has a normal probability distribution. However, research has shown that confidence intervals based on the t distribution can be used as long as the population distribution does not differ substantially from a normal probability distribution.

$$\bar{x} \pm t_{.025} \frac{s}{\sqrt{n}}$$

$$53.87 \pm 2.145\left(\frac{6.82}{\sqrt{15}}\right)$$

$$53.87 \pm 3.78$$

TABLE 8.4   TRAINING TIME IN DAYS FOR THE COMPUTER-ASSISTED TRAINING PROGRAM AT SCHEER INDUSTRIES

CDfile
Training

Employee	Time	Employee	Time	Employee	Time
1	52	6	59	11	54
2	44	7	50	12	58
3	55	8	54	13	60
4	44	9	62	14	62
5	45	10	46	15	63

FIGURE 8.7   THE MINITAB CONFIDENCE INTERVAL FOR THE SCHEER
INDUSTRIES PROBLEM

Variable	N	Mean	StDev	SE Mean	95.0 % CI
Time	15	53.87	6.82	1.76	(50.09, 57.65)

Thus, the margin of error is 3.78 days and the 95% confidence interval estimate of the population mean is 50.09 days to 57.65 days.

Minitab can be used to provide the confidence interval for the population mean in the Scheer Industries example. In the output shown in Figure 8.7, the sample of 15 employees provides a sample mean of 53.87 days, a sample standard deviation of 6.82 days, a standard error of the mean of 1.76 days, and a 95% confidence interval from 50.09 to 57.65 days.

The Role of the Population Distribution

As we close this section, let us point out that an important consideration in developing an interval estimate of a population mean is determining what is known about the population distribution. The large-sample interval estimation procedures in Section 8.1 make no assumption about the population distribution and can be applied to a population having any distribution. The small-sample interval estimation procedures in Section 8.2 are based on the assumption that the population has a normal distribution and can be applied to a population having a normal, or near-normal distribution.

In practice, if the sample size is large ($n \geq 30$) and the form of population distribution is unknown, we rely on the procedures in Section 8.1. In this case, an interval estimate of a population mean can be constructed as follows:

σ assumed known

$$\bar{x} \pm z_{\alpha/2} \frac{\sigma}{\sqrt{n}} \tag{8.2}$$

σ estimated by s

$$\bar{x} \pm z_{\alpha/2} \frac{s}{\sqrt{n}} \tag{8.3}$$

The important thing to note is that the large-sample theory supports the use of expressions (8.2) and (8.3) for a population having *any distribution*.

For a small sample size ($n < 30$) and a normally distributed population, the procedures in Section 8.2 apply. In this case we can develop an interval estimate of a population mean as follows:

σ assumed known

$$\bar{x} \pm z_{\alpha/2} \frac{\sigma}{\sqrt{n}} \tag{8.4}$$

σ estimated by s

$$\bar{x} \pm t_{\alpha/2} \frac{s}{\sqrt{n}} \qquad (8.5)$$

In fact, for a population known to have a normal distribution, expressions (8.4) and (8.5) can be used to develop an interval estimate of a population mean in both the large-sample and small-sample cases.

In most practical applications, the form of the population distribution is unknown. Because expressions (8.2) and (8.3) apply to a population with any distribution, we make no assumption about the form of the population distribution and use (8.2) or (8.3) provided the sample size is large ($n \geq 30$). Thus, the only time it is necessary to address the assumption that the population has a normal distribution and consider using expressions (8.4) and (8.5) is when the sample size is small ($n < 30$). Figure 8.8 summarizes the interval estimation procedures covered here and provides a practical guide for computing an interval estimate of a population mean.

FIGURE 8.8   SUMMARY OF INTERVAL ESTIMATION PROCEDURES FOR A POPULATION MEAN

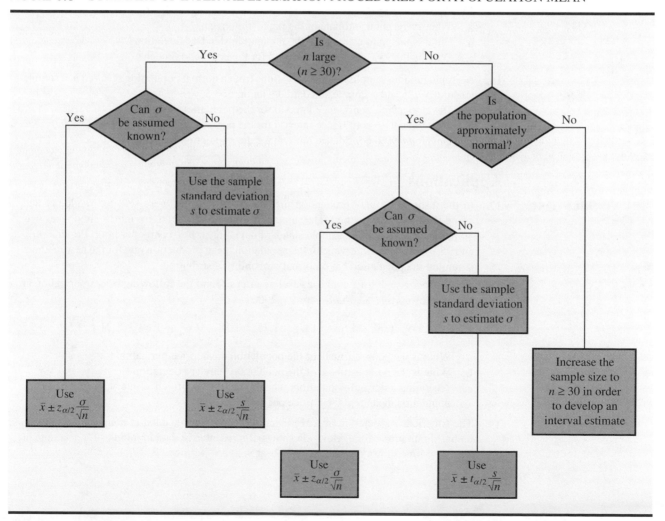

EXERCISES

Methods

13. For a t distribution with 12 degrees of freedom, find the area, or probability, in each region.
  a. To the left of 1.782
  b. To the right of -1.356
  c. To the right of 2.681
  d. To the left of -1.782
  e. Between -2.179 and $+2.179$
  f. Between -1.356 and $+1.782$

14. Find the t value(s) for each of the following cases.
  a. Upper tail area of .05 with 18 degrees of freedom
  b. Lower tail area of .10 with 22 degrees of freedom
  c. Upper tail area of .01 with 5 degrees of freedom
  d. 90% of the area is between these two t values with 14 degrees of freedom.
  e. 95% of the area is between these two t values with 28 degrees of freedom.

SELFtest   **15.** The following data collected for a sample come from a normal population: 10, 8, 12, 15, 13, 11, 6, 5.
  a. What is the point estimate of the population mean?
  b. What is the point estimate of the population standard deviation?
  c. What is the 95% confidence interval for the population mean?

16. A simple random sample of 20 observations from a normal population resulted in a sample mean of 17.25 and a sample standard deviation of 3.3.
  a. Develop a 90% confidence interval for the population mean.
  b. Develop a 95% confidence interval for the population mean.
  c. Develop a 99% confidence interval for the population mean.

Applications

SELFtest   **17.** In the testing of a new production method, 18 employees were selected randomly and asked to try the new method. The sample mean production rate for the 18 employees was 80 parts per hour and the sample standard deviation was 10 parts per hour. Provide 90% and 95% confidence intervals for the population mean production rate for the new method, assuming the population has a normal probability distribution.

18. A *USA Today* study of rental car gasoline prices found the following prices per gallon at 12 major airports (*USA Today,* April 4, 2000).

1.58	1.53	1.60	1.55	1.80	1.75	1.58	1.62	1.69	1.21	1.50	1.55

  a. What is the point estimate of the population mean price per gallon?
  b. What is the point estimate of the population standard deviation?
  c. Assuming a normal population, what is the 95% confidence interval estimate of the population mean rental car price per gallon?

CDfile
TVtime

19. The American Association of Advertising Agencies records data on nonprogram minutes on half-hour, prime-time television shows. Representative data in minutes for a sample of 20 prime-time shows on major networks at 8:30 P.M. follow.

6.0	6.6	5.8
7.0	6.3	6.2
7.2	5.7	6.4

7.0	6.5	6.2
6.0	6.5	7.2
7.3	7.6	6.8
6.0	6.2	

Assuming a normal population, provide a point estimate and a 95% confidence interval for the mean number of nonprogram minutes on half-hour, prime-time television shows at 8:30 P.M.

20. Sales personnel for Skillings Distributors submit weekly reports listing the customer contacts made during the week. A sample of 61 weekly contact reports showed a mean of 22.4 customer contacts per week for the sales personnel. The sample standard deviation was five contacts.

a. Use the large-sample case [expression (8.3)] to develop a 95% confidence interval for the mean number of weekly customer contacts for the population of sales personnel.

b. Assume that the population of weekly contact data has a normal distribution. Use the *t* distribution with 60 degrees of freedom to develop a 95% confidence interval for the mean number of weekly customer contacts.

c. Compare your answers for parts (a) and (b). Comment on why, in the large-sample case, it is permissible to develop interval estimates using the procedure in part (a) even though the *t* distribution may also be applicable.

21. Complaints about rising prescription drug prices caused the U.S. Congress to consider laws that would force pharmaceutical companies to offer prescription discounts to senior citizens without drug benefits. The House Government Reform Committee provided data on the prescription cost for some of the most widely used drugs (*Newsweek,* May 8, 2000). Assume the following data show a sample of the prescription cost in dollars for Zocor, a drug used to lower cholesterol.

110	112	115	99	100	98	104	126

Assuming a normal population, what is the 95% confidence interval estimate of the population mean cost for a prescription of Zocor?

22. The number of hours Americans sleep each night varies considerably with 12% of the population sleeping less than six hours to 3% sleeping more than eight hours (*The Macmillan Visual Almanac,* 1996). The following sample of 25 individuals reports the hours of sleep per night.

Sleep

6.9	7.6	6.5	6.2	5.3
7.8	7.0	5.5	7.6	6.7
7.3	6.6	7.1	6.9	6.0
6.8	6.5	7.2	5.8	8.6
7.6	7.1	6.0	7.2	7.7

a. What is the point estimate of the population mean number of hours of sleep each night?

b. Assuming that the population has a normal distribution, develop a 95% confidence interval for the population mean number of hours of sleep each night.

8.3   DETERMINING THE SAMPLE SIZE

In the large-sample case with σ assumed known, the interval estimate of the population mean is given by

$$\bar{x} \pm z_{\alpha/2} \frac{\sigma}{\sqrt{n}} \qquad (8.2)$$

The quantity $z_{\alpha/2}$ $(\sigma/\sqrt{n})$ is the margin of error. Thus, we see that $z_{\alpha/2}$, the population standard deviation σ, and the sample size n combine to determine the margin of error. Once we select a confidence coefficient $1 - \alpha$, $z_{\alpha/2}$ can be determined. Then, if we have a value for σ, we can determine the sample size n needed to provide any desired margin of error. Development of the formula used to compute the required sample size n follows.

Let E = the desired margin of error

$$E = z_{\alpha/2} \frac{\sigma}{\sqrt{n}}$$

If a desired margin of error is selected prior to sampling, the procedures in this section can be used to determine the sample size necessary to satisfy the margin of error requirement.

Solving for $\sqrt{n}$, we have

$$\sqrt{n} = \frac{z_{\alpha/2}\sigma}{E}$$

Squaring both sides of this equation, we obtain the following expression for the sample size.

Sample Size for an Interval Estimate of a Population Mean

$$n = \frac{(z_{\alpha/2})^2\sigma^2}{E^2} \tag{8.6}$$

This sample size provides the desired margin of error at the chosen confidence level.

In equation (8.6) E is the margin of error that the user is willing to accept, and the value of $z_{\alpha/2}$ follows directly from the confidence level to be used in developing the interval estimate. Although user preference must be considered, 95% confidence is the most frequently chosen value ($z_{.025} = 1.96$).

Finally, use of equation (8.6) requires a value for the population standard deviation σ. In most cases, σ will be unknown. However, we can still use equation (8.6) if we have a preliminary or *planning value* for σ. In practice, one of the following procedures can be chosen.

A planning value for the population standard deviation σ must be specified before the sample size can be determined. Three methods of obtaining a planning value for σ are discussed here.

1. Use the sample standard deviation from a previous sample of the same or similar units.
2. Use a pilot study to select a preliminary sample. The sample standard deviation from the preliminary sample can be used as the planning value for σ.
3. Use judgment or a "best guess" for the value of σ. For example, we might begin by estimating the largest and smallest data values in the population. The difference between the largest and smallest values provides an estimate of the range for the data. Finally, the range divided by four is often suggested as a rough approximation of the standard deviation and thus an acceptable planning value for σ.

Let us demonstrate the use of equation (8.6) to determine the sample size by considering the following example. A previous study that investigated the cost of renting automobiles in the United States found a mean cost of approximately $55 per day for renting a midsize automobile. Suppose that the organization that conducted this study would like to conduct a new study in order to estimate the population mean daily rental cost for a midsize automobile in the United States. In designing the new study, the project director specifies that the population mean daily rental cost be estimated with a margin of error of $2 and a 95% level of confidence.

Using equation (8.6), we see that the project director selected a margin of error $E = 2$. The 95% level of confidence indicates $z_{.025} = 1.96$. Thus, we only need a planning value for the population standard deviation σ in order to compute the required sample size. At this point, an analyst reviewed the sample data from the original study and found that the sample standard deviation for the daily rental cost was $9.65. Using this value as the planning value for σ, we have

Equation (8.6) provides the minimum sample size needed to satisfy the desired margin of error requirement. If the computed sample size is not an integer, round up to the next integer value to determine the recommended sample size.

$$n = \frac{(z_{\alpha/2})^2 \sigma^2}{E^2} = \frac{(1.96)^2(9.65)^2}{2^2} = 89.43$$

Thus, the sample size for the new study needs to be at least 89.43 midsize automobile rentals in order to satisfy the project director's $2 margin-of-error requirement. In cases where the computed n is not an integer, we *round up* to the next integer value; hence, the recommended sample size is 90 midsize automobile rentals.

EXERCISES

Methods

23. How large a sample should be selected to provide a 95% confidence interval with a margin of error of 5? Assume that the population standard deviation is 25.

SELFtest   **24.** The range for a set of data is estimated to be 36.
   a. What is the planning value for the population standard deviation?
   b. Using 95% confidence, how large a sample should be used to provide a margin of error of 3?
   c. Using 95% confidence, how large a sample should be used to provide a margin of error of 2?

Applications

SELFtest   **25.** Refer to the Scheer Industries example in Section 8.2. Use $\sigma = 6.82$ days as a planning value for the population standard deviation.
   a. Assuming 95% confidence, what sample size would be required to obtain a margin of error of 1.5 days?
   b. If the precision statement was made with 90% confidence, what sample size would be required to obtain a margin of error of 2 days?

26. *Bride's* magazine reported that the mean cost of a wedding is $19,000 (*USA Today,* April 17, 2000). Assume that the population standard deviation is $9,400. *Bride's* plans to use an annual survey to monitor the cost of a wedding. Use 95% confidence.
   a. What is the recommended sample size if the desired margin of error is $1000?
   b. What is the recommended sample size if the desired margin of error is $500?
   c. What is the recommended sample size if the desired margin of error is $200?

27. Annual starting salaries for college graduates with business administration degrees are believed to have a standard deviation of approximately $2000. Assume that a 95% confidence interval estimate of the mean annual starting salary is desired. How large a sample should be taken if the desired margin of error is
   a. $500?
   b. $200?
   c. $100?

28. RealFacts, a real estate research firm, provides monthly mean apartment rental costs for Los Angeles County (*Los Angeles Times,* August 1, 1999). Assume the population standard deviation of rental cost is $220 and that the desired margin of error is $50.
    a. What is the recommended sample size for a 90% confidence interval estimate of the population mean rental cost?
    b. What is the recommended sample size for a 95% confidence interval?
    c. What is the recommended sample size for a 99% confidence interval?
    d. If the desired margin of error is fixed, what happens to the sample size as the confidence level is increased?

29. The travel-to-work time for residents of the 15 largest cities in the United States is reported in the *1998 Information Please Almanac.* Suppose that a preliminary simple random sample of residents of San Francisco is used to develop a planning value of 6.25 minutes for the population standard deviation.
    a. If we want to estimate the population mean travel-to-work time for San Francisco residents with a margin of error of 2 minutes, what sample size should be used? Assume a 95% confidence.
    b. If we want to estimate the population mean travel-to-work time for San Francisco residents with a margin of error of 1 minute, what sample size should be used? Assume 95% confidence.

30. The sample standard deviation of P/E ratios for stocks listed on the New York Stock Exchange is $s = 7.8$ (*The Wall Street Journal,* March 19, 1998). Assume that we are interested in estimating the population mean P/E ratio for all stocks listed on the New York Stock Exchange today. How many stocks should be included in the sample if we want a margin of error of 2? Use 95% confidence.

8.4   INTERVAL ESTIMATION OF A POPULATION PROPORTION

In Chapter 7 we showed that a sample proportion $\bar{p}$ provides an unbiased estimator of a population proportion p and that for large samples the sampling distribution of $\bar{p}$ can be approximated by a normal probability distribution, as shown in Figure 8.9. Recall that the use of the normal distribution as an approximation of the sampling distribution of $\bar{p}$ is based on the large-sample condition that both np and $n(1 - p)$ are 5 or more. We use the sampling distribution of $\bar{p}$ to make probability statements about the sampling error whenever a sample proportion $\bar{p}$ provides the estimate of population proportion p. In this case, the sampling error is defined as the absolute value of the difference between $\bar{p}$ and p, written $|\bar{p} - p|$.

When the sample size is large, the following precision statement can be made about the sampling error.

There is a $1 - \alpha$ probability that the value of the sample proportion will provide a sampling error of $z_{\alpha/2}\sigma_{\bar{p}}$ or less.

Hence, for a proportion, the quantity $z_{\alpha/2}\sigma_{\bar{p}}$ is the margin of error.

Once we know the margin of error, $z_{\alpha/2}\sigma_{\bar{p}}$, we can subtract and add this value to $\bar{p}$ to obtain an interval estimate of the population proportion. Such an interval estimate is given by

$$\bar{p} \pm z_{\alpha/2}\sigma_{\bar{p}} \qquad\qquad (8.7)$$

FIGURE 8.9   NORMAL APPROXIMATION OF THE SAMPLING DISTRIBUTION OF $\bar{p}$
WHEN $np \geq 5$ AND $n(1 - p) \geq 5$

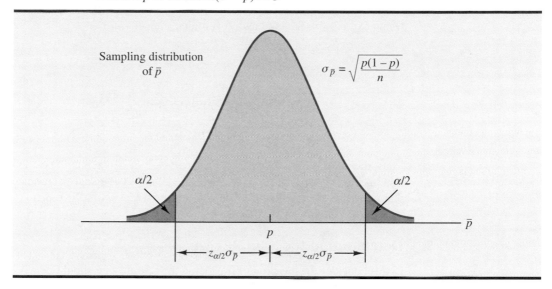

where $1 - \alpha$ is the confidence coefficient. Because the standard error of the proportion is $\sigma_{\bar{p}} = \sqrt{p(1 - p)/n}$, we can rewrite expression (8.7) as

$$\bar{p} \pm z_{\alpha/2} \sqrt{\frac{p(1 - p)}{n}} \tag{8.8}$$

To use expression (8.8) to develop an interval estimate of a population proportion p, the value of p would have to be known. Because the value of p is what we are trying to estimate, we simply substitute the sample proportion $\bar{p}$ for p. The resulting general expression for a confidence interval estimate of a population proportion follows.*

When developing confidence intervals for proportions, the quantity $z_{\alpha/2} \sqrt{\bar{p}(1 - \bar{p})/n}$ provides the margin of error.

Interval Estimate of a Population Proportion

$$\bar{p} \pm z_{\alpha/2} \sqrt{\frac{\bar{p}(1 - \bar{p})}{n}} \tag{8.9}$$

where $1 - \alpha$ is the confidence coefficient and $z_{\alpha/2}$ is the z value providing an area of $\alpha/2$ in the upper tail of the standard normal probability distribution.

The following example illustrates the computation of the margin of error and interval estimate for a population proportion. Ferrell Calvillo Communications conducted a national survey of 902 women golfers to learn how women golfers view their treatment at golf

*An unbiased estimate of $\sigma_{\bar{p}}^2$ is $\bar{p}(1 - \bar{p})/(n - 1)$, which suggests that $\sqrt{\bar{p}(1 - \bar{p})/(n - 1)}$ should be used in place of $\sqrt{\bar{p}(1 - \bar{p})/n}$ in expression (8.9). However, the bias introduced by using n in the denominator does not cause any difficulty because a large sample is generally used to estimate a population proportion. In such cases the numerical difference between the results obtained by using n and those obtained by using $n - 1$ is negligible.

courses in the United States. The survey found that 397 of the women golfers were satisfied with the availability of tee times. Thus, the point estimate of the proportion of the population of women golfers who are satisfied with the availability of tee times is 397/902 = .44. Using expression (8.9) and a 95% confidence level,

$$\bar{p} \pm z_{\alpha/2} \sqrt{\frac{\bar{p}(1 - \bar{p})}{n}}$$

$$.44 \pm 1.96 \sqrt{\frac{.44(1 - .44)}{902}}$$

$$.44 \pm .0324$$

Thus, the margin of error is .0324 and the 95% confidence interval estimate of the population proportion is .4076 to .4724. Using percentages, the survey results enable us to state that with 95% confidence between 40.76% and 47.24% of all women golfers are satisfied with the availability of tee times.

Determining the Sample Size

Let us consider the question of how large the sample size should be to obtain an estimate of a population proportion at a specified level of precision. The rationale for the sample size determination in developing interval estimates of p is similar to the rationale used in Section 8.3 to determine the sample size for estimating a population mean.

Previously in this section we pointed out that the margin of error associated with an estimate of a population proportion is $z_{\alpha/2}\sigma_{\bar{p}}$. With $\sigma_{\bar{p}} = \sqrt{p(1 - p)/n}$, the margin of error is based on the values of $z_{\alpha/2}$, the population proportion p, and the sample size n. For a confidence coefficient $1 - \alpha$, $z_{\alpha/2}$ can be determined. Then, for a specified value of the population proportion p, the margin of error is determined by the sample size n. Larger sample sizes provide a smaller margin of error and better precision.

Let $E =$ the desired margin of error

$$E = z_{\alpha/2} \sqrt{\frac{p(1 - p)}{n}}$$

Solving this equation for n provides the following formula for the sample size.

Sample Size for an Interval Estimate of a Population Proportion

$$n = \frac{(z_{\alpha/2})^2 p(1 - p)}{E^2} \tag{8.10}$$

In equation (8.10), the desired margin of error E must be specified by the user; in most cases, $E = .10$ or less. User preference also specifies the confidence level and thus the corresponding value of $z_{\alpha/2}$. Finally, because the population proportion p is unknown, the use of (8.10) requires a planning value for p. In practice, the planning value can be chosen by one of the following procedures.

1. Use the sample proportion from a previous sample of the same or similar units.
2. Use a pilot study to select a preliminary sample. The sample proportion from this sample can be used as the planning value for p.

Because the population proportion p is what we are attempting to estimate from the sample, a planning value for p must be available in order to use equation (8.10). Four ways to obtain this planning value are listed here.

3. Use judgment or a "best guess" for the value of p.
4. If none of the preceding alternatives apply, use a planning value of $p = .50$.

Let us return to the survey of women golfers and assume that the company is interested in conducting a new survey to estimate the current proportion of the population of women golfers who are satisfied with the availability of tee times. How large should the sample be if the survey director wants to estimate the population proportion with a margin of error of .025 at a 95% confidence? With $E = .025$ and $z_{\alpha/2} = 1.96$, we need a planning value of p to answer the sample size question. Using the previous survey result of $\bar{p} = .44$ as the planning value for p, equation (8.10) shows that

$$n = \frac{(z_{\alpha/2})^2 p(1 - p)}{E^2} = \frac{(1.96)^2(.44)(1 - .44)}{(.025)^2} = 1514.51$$

Thus, the sample size must be at least 1514.51 women golfers to satisfy the margin of error requirement. Rounding up to the next integer value indicates that a sample of 1515 women golfers is recommended.

The fourth alternative suggested for selecting a planning value for p is to use $p = .50$. This value of p is frequently used when no other information is available. To understand why, note that the numerator of equation (8.10) shows that the sample size is proportional to the quantity $p(1 - p)$. A larger value for the quantity $p(1 - p)$ will result in a larger sample size. Table 8.5 gives some possible values of $p(1 - p)$. Note that the largest value of $p(1 - p)$ occurs when $p = .50$. Thus, in case of any uncertainty about an appropriate planning value for p, we know that $p = .50$ will provide the largest sample size recommendation. In effect, we play it safe by recommending the largest possible sample size. If the proportion turns out to be different from the .50 planning value, the precision statement will be better than anticipated. Thus, in using $p = .50$, we guarantee that the sample size will be sufficient to obtain the desired margin of error.

Surveys that ask many questions about proportions are often designed by using a planning value of p = .50 for the sample size computation.

In the survey of women golfers example, a planning value of $p = .50$ would have provided the sample size

$$n = \frac{(z_{\alpha/2})^2 p(1 - p)}{E^2} = \frac{(1.96)^2(.50)(1 - .50)}{(.025)^2} = 1536.64$$

Thus a slightly larger sample size of 1537 women golfers would be recommended.

TABLE 8.5   SOME POSSIBLE VALUES FOR $p(1 - p)$

p	$p(1 - p)$	
.10	$(.10)(.90) = .09$	
.30	$(.30)(.70) = .21$	
.40	$(.40)(.60) = .24$	
.50	$(.50)(.50) = .25$	← Largest value for $p(1 - p)$
.60	$(.60)(.40) = .24$	
.70	$(.70)(.30) = .21$	
.90	$(.90)(.10) = .09$	

NOTES AND COMMENTS

The margin of error for estimating a population proportion is almost always .10 or less. In national public opinion polls conducted by organizations such as Gallup and Harris, a .03 or .04 margin of error is common. With such margins of error, equation (8.10) will almost always provide a sample size that is large enough to satisfy the large-sample requirements of $np \geq 5$ and $n(1 - p) \geq 5$.

EXERCISES

Methods

SELFtest

31. A simple random sample of 400 individuals provides 100 Yes responses.
  a. What is the point estimate of the proportion of the population that would provide Yes responses?
  b. What is the standard error of the proportion, $\sigma_{\bar{p}}$?
  c. Compute the 95% confidence interval for the population proportion.

32. A simple random sample of 800 elements generates a sample proportion $\bar{p} = .70$.
  a. Provide a 90% confidence interval for the population proportion.
  b. Provide a 95% confidence interval for the population proportion.

33. In a survey, the planning value for the population proportion p is .35. How large a sample should be taken to provide a 95% confidence interval with a margin of error of .05?

34. Using 95% confidence, how large a sample should be taken to obtain a margin of error for the estimation of a population proportion of .03? Assume that past data are not available for developing a planning value for p.

Applications

SELFtest

35. A *Time*/CNN poll asked 814 adults to respond to a series of questions about their feelings toward the state of affairs within the United States. A total of 562 adults responded Yes to the question: Do you feel things are going well in the United States these days? (*Time*, August 11, 1997).
  a. What is the point estimate of the proportion of the adult population that feels things are going well in the United States?
  b. At 90% confidence, what is the margin of error?
  c. What is the 90% confidence interval for the proportion of the adult population that feels things are going well in the United States?

36. A survey by the Society for Human Resource Management asked 346 job seekers why employees change jobs so frequently (*The Wall Street Journal*, March 28, 2000). The answer selected most (152 times) was "higher compensation elsewhere."
  a. What is the point estimate of the proportion of job seekers who would select "higher compensation elsewhere" as the reason for changing jobs?
  b. What is the 95% confidence interval estimate of the population proportion?

37. A survey by Wirthlin Worldwide collected data on attitudes toward the quality of customer service in retail stores. The survey found that 28% of Americans feel customer service is better today than it was two years ago (*USA Today*, January 20, 1998). If 650 adults were included in the sample, develop a 95% confidence interval for the proportion of the population of adults who feel customer service is better today than it was two years ago.

38. Audience profile data collected at the ESPN SportsZone Web site showed that 26% of the users were women (*USA Today*, January 21, 1998). Assume that this percentage was based on a sample of 400 users.
   a. Using 95% confidence, what is the margin of error associated with the estimated proportion of users who are women?
   b. What is the 95% confidence interval for the population proportion of ESPN Sportszone Web site users who are women?
   c. How large a sample should be taken if the desired margin of error is .03?

SELFtest   39. An Employee Benefit Research Institute survey explored the reasons small employers offer a retirement plan to their employees (*USA Today*, April 4, 2000). The reason "competitive advantage in recruitment/retention" was anticipated 33% of the time.
   a. What sample size is recommended if a survey goal is to estimate the proportion of small employers who offer a retirement plan primarily for "competitive advantage in recruitment/retention" with a margin of error of .03. Use 95% confidence.
   b. Repeat part (a) using 99% confidence.

40. An Associated Press poll of 1018 adults found 255 adults planned to spend less money on gifts during the 1998 holiday season compared to the previous year (ICR Media survey, November 13–17, 1998).
   a. What is the point estimate of the proportion of all adults who planned to spend less money on gifts during the 1998 holiday season?
   b. Using 95% confidence, what is the margin of error associated with this estimate?

41. An American Express retail survey found that 16% of U.S. consumers used the Internet to buy gifts during the 1999 holiday season (*USA Today*, January 18, 2000). If 1285 customers participated in the survey, what is the margin of error and what is the interval estimate of the population proportion of customers using the Internet to buy gifts? Use 95% confidence.

42. A *USA Today*/CNN/Gallup poll for the 2000 presidential campaign sampled 491 potential voters in June (*USA Today*, June 9, 2000). A primary purpose of the poll was to obtain an estimate of the proportion of potential voters who favor each candidate. Assume a planning value for the population proportion of $p = .50$ and a 95% confidence level.
   a. Using $p = .50$, what was the planned margin of error for the June poll?
   b. As the November election gets closer, better precision and smaller margins of error are desired. Assume the following margins of error are requested for surveys to be conducted during the presidential campaign. Compute the recommended sample size for each survey.

Survey	Margin of Error
September	.04
October	.03
Early November	.02
Pre-Election Day	.01

43. The League of American Theatres and Producers uses an ongoing audience tracking survey that provides up-to-date information about Broadway theater audiences (*Playbill*, Winter 1997). Every week, the League distributes a one-page survey on random theater seats at a rotation roster of Broadway shows. The survey questionnaire takes only five minutes to complete and enables audiences to communicate their views about the theater industry.

a. How large a sample should be taken if the desired margin of error on any population proportion is .04? Use 95% confidence and a planning value of $p = .50$.

b. Assume that the sample size recommended in part (a) is implemented and that during one week 445 theatergoers indicated that they do not live in New York City. What is the point estimate of the proportion of Broadway audiences that do not live in New York City?

c. Using the data in part (b), what is the 95% confidence interval for the population proportion of Broadway audiences that do not live in New York City?

SUMMARY

In this chapter we presented methods for developing a confidence interval for a population mean μ and a population proportion p. The purpose of developing a confidence interval is to give the user a better understanding of the sampling error that might be present. A wide confidence interval indicates poor precision; in such cases, the sample size can be increased to reduce the width of the confidence interval and improve the precision of the estimate.

The expression used to compute an interval estimate of a population mean depends on whether the sample size is large ($n \geq 30$) or small ($n < 30$), whether the population standard deviation can be assumed known or is estimated by the sample standard deviation s, and in some cases whether the population has a normal or approximately normal probability distribution. If the sample size is large, no assumption is required about the form of the probability distribution of the population, and $z_{\alpha/2}$ is used in the computation of the interval estimate. If the sample size is small, the population must have a normal or approximately normal probability distribution in order to develop an interval estimate of μ. If the population has a normal probability distribution, $z_{\alpha/2}$ is used in the computation of the interval estimate when σ is assumed known, whereas $t_{\alpha/2}$ is used when σ is estimated by the sample standard deviation s. Finally, if the sample size is small and the assumption of a normally distributed population is inappropriate, we recommend increasing the sample size to $n \geq 30$ in order to use the large-sample interval estimation procedure.

In addition, we showed how to determine the sample size so that interval estimates of μ and p would have a specified margin of error. In practice, the sample sizes required for interval estimates of a population proportion are generally large. Hence, we provided the large-sample interval estimation formulas for a population proportion where both $np \geq 5$ and $n(1 - p) \geq 5$.

GLOSSARY

Interval estimate   An estimate of a population parameter that provides an interval believed to contain the value of the parameter. It has the form point estimate $\pm$ margin of error.

Margin of error   The $\pm$ value added to and subtracted from a point estimate in order to develop an interval estimate of a population parameter.

Sampling error   The absolute value of the difference between the value of an unbiased point estimator, such as the sample mean $\bar{x}$, and the value of the population parameter it estimates, such as the population mean μ. In the case of a population mean, the sampling error is $|\bar{x} - \mu|$. In the case of a population proportion, the sampling error is $|\bar{p} - p|$.

Precision statement   A probability statement about the sampling error.

Confidence level   The confidence associated with an interval estimate. For example, if an interval estimation procedure provides intervals such that 95% of the intervals formed using the procedure will include the population parameter, the interval estimate is said to be constructed at the 95% confidence level.

Confidence coefficient   The confidence level expressed as a decimal value. For example, .95 is the confidence coefficient for a 95% confidence level.

t distribution   A family of probability distributions that can be used to develop an interval estimate of a population mean whenever the population standard deviation σ is estimated by the sample standard deviation s and the population has a normal or near-normal probability distribution.

Degrees of freedom   A parameter of the t distribution. When the t distribution is used in the computation of an interval estimate of a population mean, the appropriate t distribution has $n - 1$ degrees of freedom, where n is the size of the simple random sample.

KEY FORMULAS

Sampling Error When Using $\bar{x}$ as an Estimate of μ

$$|\bar{x} - \mu| \tag{8.1}$$

Interval Estimate of a Population Mean: Large-Sample Case ($n \geq 30$) with σ Assumed Known

$$\bar{x} \pm z_{\alpha/2} \frac{\sigma}{\sqrt{n}} \tag{8.2}$$

Interval Estimate of a Population Mean: Large-Sample Case ($n \geq 30$) with σ Estimated by s

$$\bar{x} \pm z_{\alpha/2} \frac{s}{\sqrt{n}} \tag{8.3}$$

Interval Estimate of a Population Mean: Small-Sample Case ($n < 30$) with σ Assumed Known

$$\bar{x} \pm z_{\alpha/2} \frac{\sigma}{\sqrt{n}} \tag{8.4}$$

Interval Estimate of a Population Mean: Small-Sample Case ($n < 30$) with σ Estimated by s

$$\bar{x} \pm t_{\alpha/2} \frac{s}{\sqrt{n}} \tag{8.5}$$

Sample Size for an Interval Estimate of a Population Mean

$$n = \frac{(z_{\alpha/2})^2 \sigma^2}{E^2} \tag{8.6}$$

Interval Estimate of a Population Proportion

$$\bar{p} \pm z_{\alpha/2} \sqrt{\frac{\bar{p}(1 - \bar{p})}{n}} \tag{8.9}$$

Sample Size for an Interval Estimate of a Population Proportion

$$n = \frac{(z_{\alpha/2})^2 p(1 - p)}{E^2} \qquad (8.10)$$

SUPPLEMENTARY EXERCISES

44. A survey of first-time home buyers found that the mean of annual household income was $50,000 (*CNBC.com,* July 11, 2000). Assume the survey used a sample of 400 first-time home buyers and that the sample standard deviation in income was $20,500.
   a. Using 95% confidence, what is the margin of error for this study?
   b. What is the 95% confidence interval for the population mean annual household income for first-time home buyers?

45. A survey conducted by the American Automobile Association showed that a family of four spends an average of $215.60 per day while on vacation. Suppose a sample of 64 families of four vacationing at Niagara Falls resulted in a sample mean of $252.45 per day and a sample standard deviation of $74.50.
   a. Develop a 95% confidence interval estimate of the mean amount spent per day by a family of four visiting Niagara Falls.
   b. Using the confidence interval from part (a), does it appear that the population mean amount spent per day by families visiting Niagara Falls differs from the mean reported by the American Automobile Association? Explain.

ActTemps

46. A survey by Accountemps asked a sample of 200 executives to provide data on the number of minutes per day office workers waste trying to locate mislabeled, misfiled, or misplaced items (*Astounding Averages,* by D. D. Dauphinais and K. Droste, 1995). Data consistent with this survey are contained in the data set ActTemps.
   a. Use ActTemps to develop a point estimate of the number of minutes per day office workers waste trying to locate mislabeled, misfiled, or misplaced items.
   b. What is the sample standard deviation?
   c. What is the 95% confidence interval for the mean number of minutes wasted per day?

47. Arthur D. Little, Inc., estimates that approximately 70% of mail received by a household is advertisements (*Time,* July 14, 1997). A sample of 20 households shows the following data for the number of advertisements received and the total number of pieces of mail received during one week.

Mail

Household	Advertisements	Total Mail	Household	Advertisements	Total Mail
1	24	35	11	13	19
2	9	14	12	16	28
3	18	30	13	20	27
4	9	12	14	17	22
5	15	28	15	21	24
6	23	33	16	21	33
7	13	20	17	15	25
8	17	20	18	15	24
9	20	23	19	18	24
10	20	25	20	12	16

    a. What is the point estimate of the mean number of advertisements received per week? What is the 95% confidence interval for the population mean?

    b. What is the point estimate of the mean number of pieces of mail received per week? What is the 95% confidence interval for the population mean?

    c. Use the point estimates in parts (a) and (b). Do these estimates agree with the statement that approximately 70% of mailings are advertisements?

48. The Money & Investing section of the *The Wall Street Journal* contains a summary of daily investment performance for stock exchanges, overseas markets, options, commodities, futures, and so on. In the New York Stock Exchange section, information is provided on each stock's 52-week high price per share, 52-week low price per share, dividend rate, yield, P/E ratio, daily volume, daily high price per share, daily low price per share, closing price per share, and daily net change. The P/E (price/earnings) ratio for each stock is determined by dividing the price of a share of stock by the earnings per share reported by the company for the most recent four quarters. A sample of 10 stocks taken from *The Wall Street Journal* (September 29, 2000) provided the following data on P/E ratios: 5, 7, 9, 10, 14, 23, 20, 15, 3, 26.

    a. What is the point estimate of the mean P/E ratio for the population of all stocks listed on the New York Stock Exchange?

    b. What is the point estimate of the standard deviation of the P/E ratios for the population of all stocks listed on the New York Stock Exchange?

    c. At 95% confidence, what is the interval estimate of the mean P/E ratio for the population of all stocks listed on the New York Stock Exchange? Assume that the population has a normal distribution.

    d. Comment on the precision of the results.

49. Many Americans who work in large offices also work at home or in the office on weekends (*USA Today*, June 18, 1997). How large a sample should be taken to estimate the population mean amount of time worked on weekends with a margin of error of 10 minutes? Use 95% confidence and assume that the planning value for the population standard deviation is 45 minutes.

50. Mileage tests are conducted for a particular model of automobile. If the desired precision is a 98% confidence interval with a margin of error of 1 mile per gallon, how many automobiles should be used in the test? Assume that preliminary mileage tests indicate the standard deviation to be 2.6 miles per gallon.

51. In developing patient appointment schedules, a medical center wants an estimate of the mean time that a staff member spends with each patient. How large a sample should be taken if the desired margin of error is two minutes at a 95% level of confidence? How large a sample should be taken for a 99% level of confidence? Use a planning value for the population standard deviation of eight minutes.

52. Annual salary plus bonus data for chief executive officers are presented in the *Business Week* 47th Annual Pay Survey (*Business Week*, April 21, 1997). A preliminary sample showed that the standard deviation is $675 with data provided in thousands of dollars. How many chief executive officers should be in a sample if we want to estimate the population mean annual salary plus bonus with a margin of error of $100,000? (Note: The desired margin of error would be $E = 100$ if the data are in thousands of dollars.) Use 95% confidence.

53. The National Center for Education Statistics reported that 47% of college students work to pay for tuition and living expenses (*The Tampa Tribune*, January 22, 1997). Assume that a sample of 450 college students was used in the study.

    a. Provide a 95% confidence interval for the population proportion of college students who work to pay for tuition and living expenses.

    b. Provide a 99% confidence interval for the population proportion of college students who work to pay for tuition and living expenses.

    c. What happens to the margin of error as the confidence is increased from 95% to 99%?

54. A *USA Today*/CNN/Gallup survey of 369 working parents found 200 who said they spend too little time with their children because of work commitments (*USA Today*, April 10, 1995).

   a. What is the point estimate of the proportion of the population of working parents who feel they spend too little time with their children because of work commitments?

   b. At 95% confidence, what is the margin of error?

   c. What is the 95% confidence interval estimate of the population proportion of working parents who feel they spend too little time with their children because of work commitments?

55. A *Time*/CNN poll of 1400 American adults asked, "Where would you rather go in your spare time?" The top response by 504 adults was a shopping mall.

   a. What is the point estimate of the proportion of adults who would prefer going to a shopping mall in their spare time?

   b. At 95% confidence, what is the margin of error associated with this estimate?

56. A well-known bank credit card firm wishes to estimate the proportion of credit cardholders who carry a nonzero balance at the end of the month and incur an interest charge. Assume that the desired margin of error is .03 at 98% confidence.

   a. How large a sample should be selected if it is anticipated that roughly 70% of the firm's cardholders carry a nonzero balance at the end of the month?

   b. How large a sample should be selected if no planning value for the population proportion could be specified?

57. In a survey, 200 people were asked to identify their major source of news information; 110 stated that their major source was television news.

   a. Construct a 95% confidence interval for the proportion of people in the population who consider television their major source of news information.

   b. How large a sample would be necessary to estimate the population proportion with a margin of error of .05 at 95% confidence?

58. A Roper Starch survey asked employees ages 18 to 29 if they would prefer better health insurance or a raise in salary (*USA Today*, September 5, 2000). Answer the following questions assuming 340 of 500 employees said they would prefer better health insurance over a raise.

   a. What is the point estimate of the proportion of employees ages 18 to 29 who would prefer better health insurance?

   b. What is the 95% confidence interval estimate of the population proportion?

59. The *1997 Statistical Abstract of the United States* reported the percentage of people 18 years of age and older who smoke. Suppose that a study designed to collect new data on smokers and nonsmokers uses a preliminary estimate of the population proportion who smoke of .30.

   a. How large a sample should be taken to estimate the proportion of smokers in the population with a margin of error of .02? Use 95% confidence.

   b. Assume that the study uses your sample size recommendation in part (a) and finds 520 smokers. What is the point estimate of the proportion of smokers in the population?

   c. What is the 95% confidence interval for the proportion of smokers in the population?

60. Although airline schedules and cost are important factors for business travelers when choosing an airline carrier, a *USA Today* survey found that business travelers list an airline's frequent flyer program as the most important factor (*USA Today*, April 11, 1995). From a sample of $n = 1993$ business travelers who responded to the survey, 618 listed a frequent flyer program as the most important factor.

   a. What is the point estimate of the proportion of the population of business travelers who believe a frequent flyer program is the most important factor when choosing an airline carrier?

   b. Develop a 95% confidence interval estimate of the population proportion.

   c. How large a sample would be required to report the margin of error of .01 at 95% confidence? Would you recommend that *USA Today* attempt to provide this degree of precision? Why or why not?

Case Problem 1   BOCK INVESTMENT SERVICES

Lisa Rae Bock started Bock Investment Services (BIS) in 1994 with the goal of making BIS the leading money market advisory service in South Carolina. To provide better service for her present clients and to attract new clients, she developed a weekly newsletter. Lisa is considering adding a new feature to the newsletter that will report the results of a weekly telephone survey of fund managers. To investigate the feasibility of offering this service, and to determine what type of information to include in the newsletter, Lisa selected a simple random sample of 45 money market funds. A portion of the data obtained is shown in Table 8.6, which reports fund assets and yields for the past seven and 30 days. Before calling the money market fund managers to obtain additional data, Lisa decided to do some preliminary analysis of the data already collected.

Managerial Report

1. Use appropriate descriptive statistics to summarize the data on assets and yields for the money market funds.
2. Develop a 95% confidence interval estimate of the mean assets, mean 7-day yield, and mean 30-day yield for the population of money market funds. Provide a managerial interpretation of each interval estimate.
3. Discuss the implication of your findings in terms of how Lisa could use this type of information in preparing her weekly newsletter.
4. What other information would you recommend that Lisa gather to provide the most useful information to her clients?

Case Problem 2   GULF REAL ESTATE PROPERTIES

Gulf Real Estate Properties, Inc., is a real estate firm located in Southwest Florida. The company, which advertises itself as "expert in the real estate market," monitors condominium sales by collecting data on location, list price, sale price, and number of days it takes to sell each unit. Each condominium is classified as *Gulf View* if it is located directly on the Gulf of Mexico or *No Gulf View* if it is located on the bay or golf course, near but not on the Gulf. Sample data from the multiple listing service in Naples, Florida, provided recent sales data for 40 Gulf View condominiums and 18 No Gulf View condominiums.* Prices are in thousands of dollars. The data are shown in Table 8.7.

Managerial Report

1. Use appropriate descriptive statistics to summarize each of the three variables for the 40 Gulf View condominiums.
2. Use appropriate descriptive statistics to summarize each of the three variables for the 18 No Gulf View condominiums.

---

*Data based on condominium sales reported in the Naples MLS (Coldwell Banker, June 2000).

TABLE 8.6   DATA FOR BOCK INVESTMENT SERVICES

CDfile
Bock

Money Market Fund	Assets ($ millions)	7-day Yield (%)	30-day Yield (%)
Amcore	103.9	4.10	4.08
Alger	156.7	4.79	4.73
Arch MM/Trust	496.5	4.17	4.13
BT Instit Treas	197.8	4.37	4.32
Benchmark Div	2755.4	4.54	4.47
Bradford	707.6	3.88	3.83
Capital Cash	1.7	4.29	4.22
Cash Mgt Trust	2707.8	4.14	4.04
Composite	122.8	4.03	3.91
Cowen Standby	694.7	4.25	4.19
Cortland	217.3	3.57	3.51
Declaration	38.4	2.67	2.61
Dreyfus	4832.8	4.01	3.89
Elfun	81.7	4.51	4.41
FFB Cash	506.2	4.17	4.11
Federated Master	738.7	4.41	4.34
Fidelity Cash	13272.8	4.51	4.42
Flex-fund	172.8	4.60	4.48
Fortis	105.6	3.87	3.85
Franklin Money	996.8	3.97	3.92
Freedom Cash	1079.0	4.07	4.01
Galaxy Money	801.4	4.11	3.96
Government Cash	409.4	3.83	3.82
Hanover Cash	794.3	4.32	4.23
Heritage Cash	1008.3	4.08	4.00
Infinity/Alpha	53.6	3.99	3.91
John Hancock	226.4	3.93	3.87
Landmark Funds	481.3	4.28	4.26
Liquid Cash	388.9	4.61	4.64
MarketWatch	10.6	4.13	4.05
Merrill Lynch Money	27005.6	4.24	4.18
NCC Funds	113.4	4.22	4.20
Nationwide	517.3	4.22	4.14
Overland	291.5	4.26	4.17
Pierpont Money	1991.7	4.50	4.40
Portico Money	161.6	4.28	4.20
Prudential MoneyMart	6835.1	4.20	4.16
Reserve Primary	1408.8	3.91	3.86
Schwab Money	10531.0	4.16	4.07
Smith Barney Cash	2947.6	4.16	4.12
Stagecoach	1502.2	4.18	4.13
Strong Money	470.2	4.37	4.29
Transamerica Cash	175.5	4.20	4.19
United Cash	323.7	3.96	3.89
Woodward Money	1330.0	4.24	4.21

Source: Barron's, October 3, 1994.

TABLE 8.7   SALES DATA FOR GULF REAL ESTATE PROPERTIES

CDfile
GulfProp

Gulf View Condominiums			No Gulf View Condominiums		
List Price	Sale Price	Days to Sell	List Price	Sale Price	Days to Sell
495.0	475.0	130	217.0	217.0	182
379.0	350.0	71	148.0	135.5	338
529.0	519.0	85	186.5	179.0	122
552.5	534.5	95	239.0	230.0	150
334.9	334.9	119	279.0	267.5	169
550.0	505.0	92	215.0	214.0	58
169.9	165.0	197	279.0	259.0	110
210.0	210.0	56	179.9	176.5	130
975.0	945.0	73	149.9	144.9	149
314.0	314.0	126	235.0	230.0	114
315.0	305.0	88	199.8	192.0	120
885.0	800.0	282	210.0	195.0	61
975.0	975.0	100	226.0	212.0	146
469.0	445.0	56	149.9	146.5	137
329.0	305.0	49	160.0	160.0	281
365.0	330.0	48	322.0	292.5	63
332.0	312.0	88	187.5	179.0	48
520.0	495.0	161	247.0	227.0	52
425.0	405.0	149			
675.0	669.0	142			
409.0	400.0	28			
649.0	649.0	29			
319.0	305.0	140			
425.0	410.0	85			
359.0	340.0	107			
469.0	449.0	72			
895.0	875.0	129			
439.0	430.0	160			
435.0	400.0	206			
235.0	227.0	91			
638.0	618.0	100			
629.0	600.0	97			
329.0	309.0	114			
595.0	555.0	45			
339.0	315.0	150			
215.0	200.0	48			
395.0	375.0	135			
449.0	425.0	53			
499.0	465.0	86			
439.0	428.5	158			

3. Compare your summary results. Discuss any specific statistical results that would help a real estate agent understand the condominium market.
4. Develop a 95% confidence interval estimate of the population mean sales price and population mean number of days to sell for Gulf View condominiums. Interpret your results.
5. Develop a 95% confidence interval estimate of the population mean sales price and population mean number of days to sell for No Gulf View condominiums. Interpret your results.
6. Assume the branch manager requested estimates of the mean selling price of Gulf View condominiums with a margin of error of $40,000 and the mean selling price of No Gulf View condominiums with a margin of error of $15,000. Using 95% confidence, how large should the sample sizes be?
7. Gulf Real Estate Properties just signed contracts for two new listings: a Gulf View condominium with a list price of $589,000 and a No Gulf View condominium with a list price of $285,000. What is your estimate of the final selling price and number of days required to sell each of these units?

Case Problem 3   METROPOLITAN RESEARCH, INC.

Metropolitan Research, Inc., a consumer research organization, conducts surveys designed to evaluate a wide variety of products and services available to consumers. In one particular study, Metropolitan was interested in learning about consumer satisfaction with the performance of automobiles produced by a major Detroit manufacturer. A questionnaire sent to owners of one of the manufacturer's full-sized cars revealed several complaints about early transmission problems. To learn more about the transmission failures, Metropolitan used a sample of actual transmission repairs provided by a transmission repair firm in the Detroit area. The following data show the actual number of miles driven for 50 vehicles at the time of transmission failure.

85,092	32,609	59,465	77,437	32,534	64,090	32,464	59,902
39,323	89,641	94,219	116,803	92,857	63,436	65,605	85,861
64,342	61,978	67,998	59,817	101,769	95,774	121,352	69,568
74,276	66,998	40,001	72,069	25,066	77,098	69,922	35,662
74,425	67,202	118,444	53,500	79,294	64,544	86,813	116,269
37,831	89,341	73,341	85,288	138,114	53,402	85,586	82,256
77,539	88,798						

Managerial Report

1. Use appropriate descriptive statistics to summarize the transmission failure data.
2. Develop a 95% confidence interval for the mean number of miles driven until transmission failure for the population of automobiles with transmission failure. Provide a managerial interpretation of the interval estimate.
3. Discuss the implication of your statistical finding in terms of the belief that some owners of the automobiles experienced early transmission failures.
4. How many repair records should be sampled if the research firm wants the population mean number of miles driven until transmission failure to be estimated with a margin of error of 5000 miles? Use 95% confidence.
5. What other information would you like to gather to evaluate the transmission failure problem more fully?

Appendix 8.1   INTERVAL ESTIMATION OF A POPULATION MEAN WITH MINITAB

We describe the use of Minitab in constructing confidence intervals for a population mean in four different cases.

Large-Sample Case With σ Assumed Known

CDfile
CJW

We illustrate using the CJW example in Section 8.1. The population standard deviation $\sigma = 20$ is assumed known. The satisfaction scores for the sample of 100 CJW customers have been entered into column C1 of a Minitab worksheet. The following steps can be used to compute a 95% confidence interval estimate of the population mean.

Step 1. Select the **Stat** pull-down menu
Step 2. Choose **Basic Statistics**
Step 3. Choose **1-Sample Z**
Step 4. When the 1-Sample Z dialog box appears:
   Enter C1 in the **Variables** box
   Enter 20 in the **Sigma** box
Step 5. Click **OK**

The Minitab default is a 95% confidence level. In order to specify a different confidence level such as 90% add the following to step 4.

   Select **Options**
   When the 1-Sample Z Options dialog box appears:
   Enter 90 in the **Confidence level** box
   Click **OK**

Large-Sample Case With σ Estimated by s

CDfile
Balance

We illustrate using the data in Table 8.2 showing the credit card balances for a sample of 85 households. The data are entered into column C1 of a Minitab worksheet. In this case the population standard deviation σ is unknown and will be estimated by the sample standard deviation s. The steps used to compute the sample standard deviation are as follow:

Step 1. Select the **Calc** pull-down menu
Step 2. Choose **Column Statistics**
Step 3. When the Column Statistics dialog box appears:
   Select **Standard deviation**
   Enter C1 in the **Input variable** box
   Enter stdev in the **Store result in** box
   Click **OK**

The output shows the sample standard deviation is 3058. This value is stored in Minitab as stdev.

The interval estimate of the population mean can now be obtained by following the steps shown for the large-sample case with σ assumed known. The only change is in step 4 where the sample standard deviation s is used to estimate σ. This change is accomplished by entering stdev in the **Sigma** box.

Small-Sample Case with σ Assumed Known

The small-sample case with σ assumed known uses the same step-by-step procedure previously described for the large-sample case with σ assumed known.

Small-Sample Case with σ Estimated by s

Training

We illustrate using the data in Table 8.4 showing the training program time in days for Scheer Industries. The data are entered in column C1 of a Minitab worksheet. In this small-sample case the population standard deviation σ is unknown and will be estimated by the sample standard deviation s. The following steps can be used to compute a 95% confidence interval estimate of the population mean.

    Step 1.   Select the **Stat** pull-down menu
    Step 2.   Choose **Basic Statistics**
    Step 3.   Choose **1-Sample t**
    Step 4.   When the 1-Sample t dialog box appears:
            Enter C1 in the **Variables** box
    Step 5.   Click **OK**

The Minitab default is a 95% confidence level. In order to specify a different confidence level such as 90% add the following to step 4.

    Select **Options**
    When the 1-Sample t dialog box appears:
    Enter 90 in the **Confidence level** box
    Click **OK**

Appendix 8.2   INTERVAL ESTIMATE OF A POPULATION MEAN WITH EXCEL

In this appendix, we develop two worksheets to use as templates for interval estimation of a population mean. The first worksheet is used for interval estimation applications based on the standard normal distribution (z), and the second worksheet is used for interval estimation applications based on the t distribution.

Using the Standard Normal Distribution

The worksheet developed here uses the standard normal distribution (z) to compute an interval estimate of a population mean. This worksheet can be applied for the following cases:

- Large-sample case with σ assumed known
- Large-sample case with σ estimated by s
- Small-sample case with σ assumed known

We will illustrate the use of this worksheet using the data on credit card balances for a sample of 85 households (Table 8.2). In this large-sample case, the population standard deviation σ is unknown and will be estimated by the sample standard deviation s.

    Refer to Figure 8.10 as we describe the worksheet. The version of the worksheet in the background shows the cell formulas used, and the version of the worksheet in the foreground shows the results of applying those formulas to the credit card data. The data are entered into cells A2:A86. Cells D4, D5, and D6 use Excel functions to compute the sample size, the sample mean, and the sample standard deviation. The user enters the desired

FIGURE 8.10   EXCEL WORKSHEET FOR INTERVAL ESTIMATE OF THE POPULATION MEAN USING
THE NORMAL DISTRIBUTION

	A	B	C	D	E	F
1	Balance		Interval Estimate of a Population Mean			
2	9619		Using the Standard Normal Distribution (z)			
3	5364					
4	8348		Sample Size	=COUNT(A2:A86)		
5	7348		Mean	=AVERAGE(A2:A86)		
6	381		Standard Deviation	=STDEV(A2:A86)		
7	2998					
8	1686		Confidence Coefficient	0.95		
9	1962		Alpha	=1-D8		
10	4920		z Value	=NORMSINV(1-D9/2)		
11	5047					
12	6921		Standard Error	=D6/SQRT(D4)		
13	5759		Margin of Error	=D10*D12		
14	8047					
15	3924		Point Estimate	=AVERAGE(A2:A86)		
16	3470		Lower Limit	=D15-D13		
17	5994		Upper Limit	=D15+D13		
18	4652					
84	3910					
85	7503					
86	1582					
87						

	A	B	C	D	E	F	G
1	Balance		Interval Estimate of a Population Mean				
2	9619		Using the Standard Normal Distribution (z)				
3	5364						
4	8348		Sample Size	85			
5	7348		Mean	5900			
6	381		Standard Deviation	3058			
7	2998						
8	1686		Confidence Coefficient	0.95			
9	1962		Alpha	0.05			
10	4920		z Value	1.960			
11	5047						
12	6921		Standard Error	331.69			
13	5759		Margin of Error	650			
14	8047						
15	3924		Point Estimate	5900			
16	3470		Lower Limit	5250			
17	5994		Upper Limit	6550			
18	4652						
84	3910						
85	7503						
86	1582						
87							

*Note: Rows 19–83 are
hidden.*

CDfile

Interval z

confidence coefficient (.95) in cell D8. The remaining cell formulas (see column D) provide the interval estimation results shown in column D of the foreground worksheet. This
worksheet is available in the file *Interval z* on the CD at the back of the book.

The worksheet in Figure 8.10 can also be used for both the large-sample and small-
sample cases with σ assumed known. In such applications, the assumed value of σ is typed
over the formula for the standard deviation in cell D6. The Excel function is not needed to
compute the sample standard deviation.

Using the *t* Distribution

The worksheet that follows uses the *t* distribution to compute an interval estimate of a
population mean. It can be applied to the small-sample case with σ estimated by *s*. We illustrate the use of this worksheet using the data on the training times for Scheer Industries
(Table 8.4). The sample size is small ($n = 15$) and the population standard deviation σ will
be estimated by the sample standard deviation *s*.

Refer to Figure 8.11 as we describe the worksheet. The data are entered into cells
A2:A16. Cells D4, D5, and D6 use Excel functions to compute the sample size, the sample
mean, and the sample standard deviation. The user enters the desired confidence coefficient
(.95) in cell D8. The remaining cell formulas provide the interval estimation results shown
in column D of the foreground worksheet. This worksheet is available in the file *Interval t*
on the CD at the back of the book.

CDfile

Interval t

FIGURE 8.11 EXCEL WORKSHEET FOR INTERVAL ESTIMATE OF THE POPULATION MEAN USING THE *t* DISTRIBUTION

	A	B	C	D	E	F
1	Training Time		Interval Estimate of a Population Mean			
2	52		Using the *t* Distribution			
3	44					
4	55		Sample size	=COUNT(A2:A16)		
5	44		Mean	=AVERAGE(A2:A16)		
6	45		Standard Deviation	=STDEV(A2:A16)		
7	59					
8	50		Confidence Coefficient	0.95		
9	54		Alpha	=1-D8		
10	62		Degrees of Freedom	=D4-1		
11	46		*t* Value	=TINV(D9,D10)		
12	54					
13	58		Standard Error	=D6/SQRT(D4)		
14	60		Margin of Error	=D11*D13		
15	62					
16	63		Point Estimate	=D5		
17			Lower Limit	=D16-D14		
18			Upper Limit	=D16+D14		
19						

	A	B	C	D	E	F
1	Training Time		Interval Estimate of a Population Mean			
2	52		Using the *t* Distribution			
3	44					
4	55		Sample size	15		
5	44		Mean	53.87		
6	45		Standard Deviation	6.82		
7	59					
8	50		Confidence Coefficient	0.95		
9	54		Alpha	0.05		
10	62		Degrees of Freedom	14		
11	46		*t* Value	2.145		
12	54					
13	58		Standard Error	1.76		
14	60		Margin of Error	3.78		
15	62					
16	63		Point Estimate	53.87		
17			Lower Limit	50.09		
18			Upper Limit	57.65		
19						

HYPOTHESIS TESTING

CONTENTS

Chapter 9

HARRIS CORPORATION*

MELBOURNE, FLORIDA

Harris Corporation, a communications equipment company, provides products and services for worldwide markets including wireless, broadcast, government, and network support systems. The company operates sales and service facilities in more than 80 countries. Many of the Harris products require medium- to high-volume production operations, including printed circuit assembly, final product assembly, and testing.

One of the company's high-volume products has an assembly called an RF deck. Each RF deck consists of 16 electronic components soldered to a machined casting that forms the plated surface of the deck. During a manufacturing run, a problem developed in the soldering process; the flow of solder onto the deck did not meet the quality criteria established for the product. After considering a variety of factors that might affect the soldering process, an engineer made the preliminary determination that the soldering problem was most likely due to defective platings.

The engineer wondered whether the proportion of defective platings in the Harris inventory exceeded that set by the supplier's design specifications. With p indicating the proportion of defective platings in the Harris inventory and p_0 indicating the proportion of defective platings set by the supplier's design specifications, the following hypotheses were formulated.

$$H_0: p \leq p_0$$
$$H_a: p > p_0$$

H_0 indicates that the Harris inventory has a defective plating proportion less than or equal to that set by the design specifications. Such a proportion would be judged acceptable, and the engineer would need to look for other causes of the soldering problem. However, H_a indicates that the Harris inventory has a defective plating proportion greater than that set by the design specifications. In that case, ex-

Harris Corporation used hypothesis testing to solve a problem in the soldering process for circuit boards. © PhotoDisc, Inc./ GettyOne Imagery.

cessive defective platings may well be the cause of the soldering problem and action should be taken to determine why the defective proportion in inventory is so high.

Tests made on a sample of platings from the Harris inventory resulted in the rejection of H_0. The conclusion was that H_a was true and that the proportion of defective platings in inventory exceeded that set by the supplier's design specifications. Further investigation of the inventory storage area led to the conclusion that the underlying problem was shelf contamination during storage. By altering the storage environment, the engineer solved the problem.

In this chapter you will learn how to formulate hypotheses about a population mean and a population proportion. Through the analysis of sample data, you will be able to determine whether a hypothesis should or should not be rejected. Appropriate conclusions and actions will be demonstrated for testing research hypotheses, testing the validity of a claim, and decision making.

*The authors are indebted to Richard A. Marshall of the Harris Corporation for providing this Statistics in Practice.

In Chapters 7 and 8 we showed how a sample could be used to develop point and interval estimates of population parameters. In this chapter we continue the discussion of statistical inference by showing how hypothesis testing can be used to determine whether a statement about the value of a population parameter should or should not be rejected.

In hypothesis testing we begin by making a tentative assumption about a population parameter. This tentative assumption is called the **null hypothesis** and is denoted by H_0. We then define another hypothesis, called the **alternative hypothesis,** which is the opposite of what is stated in the null hypothesis. The alternative hypothesis is denoted by H_a. The hypothesis testing procedure uses data from a sample to test the two competing statements indicated by H_0 and H_a.

This chapter shows how hypothesis tests can be conducted about a population mean and a population proportion. We begin by providing examples that illustrate approaches to developing null and alternative hypotheses.

9.1   DEVELOPING NULL AND ALTERNATIVE HYPOTHESES

Learning to formulate hypotheses correctly will take practice. Expect some initial confusion over the proper choice for H_0 and H_a. The examples in this section show a variety of forms for H_0 and H_a depending upon the application.

In some applications it may not be obvious how the null and alternative hypotheses should be formulated. Care must be taken to structure the hypotheses appropriately so that the hypothesis testing conclusion provides the information the researcher or decision maker wants. Guidelines for establishing the null and alternative hypotheses will be given for three types of situations in which hypothesis testing procedures are commonly employed.

Testing Research Hypotheses

Consider a particular automobile model that currently attains an average fuel efficiency of 24 miles per gallon. A product research group developed a new fuel injection system specifically designed to increase the miles-per-gallon rating. To evaluate the new system, several will be manufactured, installed in automobiles, and subjected to research-controlled driving tests. Note that the product research group is looking for evidence to conclude that the new system *increases* the mean miles-per-gallon rating. In this case, the research hypothesis is that the new fuel injection system will provide a mean miles-per-gallon rating exceeding 24; that is, $\mu > 24$. As a general guideline, a research hypothesis should be stated as the *alternative hypothesis*. Hence, the appropriate null and alternative hypotheses for the study are:

$$H_0: \mu \le 24$$
$$H_a: \mu > 24$$

Hypothesis testing is proof by contradiction. Thus, the research hypothesis is stated as the alternative hypothesis. The conclusion that the research hypothesis is true is made if the sample data contradicts the null hypothesis.

If the sample results indicate that H_0 cannot be rejected, researchers cannot conclude that the new fuel injection system is better. Perhaps more research and subsequent testing should be conducted. However, if the sample results indicate that H_0 can be rejected, researchers can make the inference that $H_a: \mu > 24$ is true. With this conclusion, the researchers have the statistical support necessary to state that the new system increases the mean number of miles per gallon. Production with the new system may begin.

In research studies such as these, the null and alternative hypotheses should be formulated so that the rejection of H_0 supports the conclusion and action being sought. The research hypothesis therefore should be expressed as the alternative hypothesis.

Testing the Validity of a Claim

As an illustration of testing the validity of a claim, consider the situation of a manufacturer of soft drinks who states that it fills two-liter containers of its products with an average of at least 67.6 fluid ounces. A sample of two-liter containers will be selected, and the contents will be measured to test the manufacturer's claim. In this type of hypothesis testing situation, we generally assume that the manufacturer's claim is true unless the sample evidence is contradictory. Using this approach for the soft-drink example, we would state the null and alternative hypotheses as follows.

$$H_0: \mu \geq 67.6$$
$$H_a: \mu < 67.6$$

If the sample results indicate H_0 cannot be rejected, the manufacturer's claim will not be challenged. However, if the sample results indicate H_0 can be rejected, the inference will be made that $H_a: \mu < 67.6$ is true. With this conclusion, statistical evidence indicates that the manufacturer's claim is incorrect and that the soft drink containers are being filled with a mean less than the claimed 67.6 ounces. Appropriate action against the manufacturer may be considered.

A manufacturer's claim is usually given the benefit of the doubt and stated as the null hypothesis. The conclusion that the claim is false can be made if the null hypothesis is rejected.

In any situation that involves testing the validity of a claim, the null hypothesis is generally based on the assumption that the claim is true. The alternative hypothesis is then formulated so that rejection of H_0 will provide statistical evidence that the stated assumption is incorrect. Action to correct the claim should be considered whenever H_0 is rejected.

Testing in Decision-Making Situations

In testing research hypotheses or testing the validity of a claim, action is taken if H_0 is rejected. In many instances, however, action must be taken both when H_0 cannot be rejected and when H_0 can be rejected. In general, this type of situation occurs when a decision maker must choose between two courses of action, one associated with the null hypothesis and another associated with the alternative hypothesis. For example, on the basis of a sample of parts from a shipment just received, a quality control inspector must decide whether to accept the shipment or to return the shipment to the supplier because it does not meet specifications. Assume that specifications for a particular part require a mean length of two inches per part. If the mean length is greater or less than the two-inch standard, the parts will cause quality problems in the assembly operation. In this case, the null and alternative hypotheses would be formulated as follows.

$$H_0: \mu = 2$$
$$H_a: \mu \neq 2$$

If the sample results indicate H_0 cannot be rejected, the quality control inspector will have no reason to doubt that the shipment meets specifications, and the shipment will be accepted. However, if the sample results indicate H_0 should be rejected, the conclusion will be that the parts do not meet specifications. In this case, the quality control inspector will have sufficient evidence to return the shipment to the supplier. Thus, we see that for these types of situations, action is taken both when H_0 cannot be rejected and when H_0 can be rejected.

Summary of Forms for Null and Alternative Hypotheses

The hypothesis tests in this chapter involve two population parameters: the population mean and the population proportion. Depending on the situation, hypothesis tests about a population parameter may take one of three forms: two use inequalities in the null hypothesis;

the third uses an equality in the null hypothesis. For hypothesis tests involving a population mean, we let μ_0 denote the hypothesized value and we must choose one of the following three forms for the hypothesis test.

$$H_0: \mu \geq \mu_0 \qquad H_0: \mu \leq \mu_0 \qquad H_0: \mu = \mu_0$$
$$H_a: \mu < \mu_0 \qquad H_a: \mu > \mu_0 \qquad H_a: \mu \neq \mu_0$$

The three possible forms of hypotheses H_0 and H_a are shown here. Note that the equality always appears in the null hypothesis H_0.

For reasons that will be clear later, the first two forms are called one-tailed tests. The third form is called a two-tailed test.

In many situations, the choice of H_0 and H_a is not obvious and judgment is necessary to select the proper form. However, as the preceding forms show, the equality part of the expression (either $\geq$, $\leq$, or $=$) *always* appears in the null hypothesis. In selecting the proper form of H_0 and H_a, keep in mind that the alternative hypothesis is often what the test is attempting to establish. Hence, asking whether the user is looking for evidence to support $\mu < \mu_0$, $\mu > \mu_0$, or $\mu \neq \mu_0$ will help determine H_a. The following exercises are designed to provide practice in choosing the proper form for a hypothesis test involving a population mean.

EXERCISES

1. The manager of the Danvers-Hilton Resort Hotel has stated that the mean guest bill for a weekend is $600 or less. A member of the hotel's accounting staff has noticed that the total charges for guest bills have been increasing in recent months. The accountant will use a sample of weekend guest bills to test the manager's claim.
   a. Which form of the hypotheses should be used to test the manager's claim? Explain.

   $$H_0: \mu \geq 600 \qquad H_0: \mu \leq 600 \qquad H_0: \mu = 600$$
   $$H_a: \mu < 600 \qquad H_a: \mu > 600 \qquad H_a: \mu \neq 600$$

   b. What conclusion is appropriate when H_0 cannot be rejected?
   c. What conclusion is appropriate when H_0 can be rejected?

SELFtest 2. The manager of an automobile dealership is considering a new bonus plan designed to increase sales volume. Currently, the mean sales volume is 14 automobiles per month. The manager wants to conduct a research study to see whether the new bonus plan increases sales volume. To collect data on the plan, a sample of sales personnel will be allowed to sell under the new bonus plan for a one-month period.
   a. Develop the null and alternative hypotheses most appropriate for this research situation.
   b. Comment on the conclusion when H_0 cannot be rejected.
   c. Comment on the conclusion when H_0 can be rejected.

3. A production line operation is designed to fill cartons with laundry detergent to a mean weight of 32 ounces. A sample of cartons is periodically selected and weighed to determine whether underfilling or overfilling is occurring. If the sample data lead to a conclusion of underfilling or overfilling, the production line will be shut down and adjusted to obtain proper filling.
   a. Formulate the null and alternative hypotheses that will help in deciding whether to shut down and adjust the production line.
   b. Comment on the conclusion and the decision when H_0 cannot be rejected.
   c. Comment on the conclusion and the decision when H_0 can be rejected.

4. Because of high production-changeover time and costs, a director of manufacturing must convince management that a proposed manufacturing method reduces costs before the new method can be implemented. The current production method operates with a mean cost of $220 per hour. A research study will measure the cost of the new method over a sample production period.
   a. Develop the null and alternative hypotheses most appropriate for this study.
   b. Comment on the conclusion when H_0 cannot be rejected.
   c. Comment on the conclusion when H_0 can be rejected.

9.2   TYPE I AND TYPE II ERRORS

The null and alternative hypotheses are competing statements about the population. Either the null hypothesis H_0 is true or the alternative hypothesis H_a is true, but not both. Ideally the hypothesis testing procedure should lead to the acceptance of H_0 when H_0 is true and the rejection of H_0 when H_a is true. Unfortunately, the correct conclusions are not always possible. Because hypothesis tests are based on sample information, we must allow for the possibility of errors. Table 9.1 illustrates the two kinds of errors that can be made in hypothesis testing.

The first row of Table 9.1 shows what can happen when the conclusion is to accept H_0. If H_0 is true, this conclusion is correct. However, if H_a is true, we make a **Type II error;** that is, we accept H_0 when it is false. The second row of Table 9.1 shows what can happen when the conclusion is to reject H_0. If H_0 is true, we make a **Type I error;** that is, we reject H_0 when it is true. However, if H_a is true, rejecting H_0 is correct.

Recall the hypothesis testing illustration discussed in Section 9.1 in which an automobile product research group developed a new fuel injection system designed to increase the miles-per-gallon rating of a particular automobile. With the current model obtaining an average of 24 miles per gallon, the hypothesis test was formulated as follows.

$$H_0: \mu \leq 24$$
$$H_a: \mu > 24$$

The alternative hypothesis, $H_a: \mu > 24$, indicates that the researchers are looking for sample evidence to support the conclusion that the population mean miles per gallon is greater than 24.

In this application, the Type I error of rejecting H_0 when it is true corresponds to the researchers claiming that the new system improves the miles-per-gallon rating ($\mu > 24$) when in fact the new system is not any better than the current system. In contrast, the Type II error of accepting H_0 when it is false corresponds to the researchers concluding that

TABLE 9.1   ERRORS AND CORRECT CONCLUSIONS IN HYPOTHESIS TESTING

		Population Condition	
		H_0 True	H_a True
Conclusion	Accept H_0	Correct Conclusion	Type II Error
	Reject H_0	Type I Error	Correct Conclusion

the new system is not any better than the current system ($\mu \leq 24$) when in fact the new system improves miles-per-gallon performance.

In practice, the person conducting the hypothesis test specifies the maximum allowable probability of making a Type I error, called the **level of significance** for the test. Common choices for the level of significance are .05 and .01. Referring to the second row of Table 9.1, note that the conclusion to *reject* H_0 indicates that either a Type I error or a correct conclusion has been made. Thus, if the probability of making a Type I error is controlled for by selecting a small value for the level of significance, we have a high degree of confidence that the conclusion to reject H_0 is correct. In such cases, we have statistical support for concluding that H_0 is false and H_a is true. Any action suggested by the alternative hypothesis H_a is appropriate.

If the sample data are consistent with the null hypothesis H_0, we will follow the practice of concluding "do not reject H_0." This conclusion is preferred over "accept H_0," because the conclusion to accept H_0 puts us at risk of making a Type II error.

Although most applications of hypothesis testing control for the probability of making a Type I error, they do not always control for the probability of making a Type II error. Hence, if we decide to accept H_0, we cannot determine how confident we can be with that decision. Because of the uncertainty associated with making a Type II error, statisticians often recommend that we use the statement "do not reject H_0" instead of "accept H_0." Using the statement "do not reject H_0" carries the recommendation to withhold both judgment and action. In effect, by never directly accepting H_0, the statistician avoids the risk of making a Type II error. Whenever the probability of making a Type II error has not been determined and controlled, we will not make the conclusion to accept H_0. In such cases, only two conclusions are possible: *do not reject H_0 or reject H_0.*

Although controlling for a Type II error in hypothesis testing is not common, it can be done. More advanced texts* describe procedures for determining and controlling the probability of making a Type II error. If proper controls have been established for this error, action based on the "do not reject H_0" conclusion can be appropriate.

NOTES AND COMMENTS

Many applications of hypothesis testing have a decision-making goal. The conclusion *reject* H_0 provides the statistical support to conclude that H_a is true and take whatever action is appropriate. The statement "do not reject H_0," although in-conclusive, often forces managers to behave as though H_0 is true. In this case, managers need to be aware of the fact that such action may be the result of a Type II error.

EXERCISES

SELFtest   5.   Americans spend an average of 8.6 minutes per day reading newspapers (*USA Today*, April 10, 1995). A researcher believes that individuals in management positions spend more than the national average time per day reading newspapers. A sample of individuals in management positions will be selected by the researcher. Data on newspaper-reading times will be used to test the following null and alternative hypotheses.

$$H_0: \mu \leq 8.6$$
$$H_a: \mu > 8.6$$

a.   What is the Type I error in this situation? What are the consequences of making this error?
b.   What is the Type II error in this situation? What are the consequences of making this error?

*See, for example, Anderson, D. R., D. J. Sweeney, and T. A. Williams, *Statistics for Business and Economics,* 8th ed. (Cincinnati: South-Western, 2002).

6. The label on a 3-quart container of orange juice claims that the orange juice contains an average of 1 gram of fat or less. Answer the following questions for a hypothesis test that could be used to test the claim on the label.
   a. Develop the appropriate null and alternative hypotheses.
   b. What is the Type I error in this situation? What are the consequences of making this error?
   c. What is the Type II error in this situation? What are the consequences of making this error?

7. Carpetland salespersons average $8000 per week in sales. Steve Contois, the firm's vice president, proposes a compensation plan with new selling incentives. Steve hopes that the results of a trial selling period will enable him to conclude that the compensation plan increases the average sales per salesperson.
   a. Develop the appropriate null and alternative hypotheses.
   b. What is the Type I error in this situation? What are the consequences of making this error?
   c. What is the Type II error in this situation? What are the consequences of making this error?

8. Suppose a new production method will be implemented if a hypothesis test supports the conclusion that the new method reduces the mean operating cost per hour.
   a. State the appropriate null and alternative hypotheses if the mean cost for the current production method is $220 per hour.
   b. What is the Type I error in this situation? What are the consequences of making this error?
   c. What is the Type II error in this situation? What are the consequences of making this error?

9.3 ONE-TAILED TESTS ABOUT A POPULATION MEAN: LARGE-SAMPLE CASE

In this section we describe how one-tailed hypothesis tests about a population mean are conducted by using a large sample. We follow the guideline that a sample size of $n \geq 30$ allows us to employ the large-sample procedures.

The Federal Trade Commission (FTC) periodically conducts studies designed to test the claims manufacturers make about their products. For example, the label on a large can of Hilltop Coffee states that the can contains at least 3 pounds of coffee. Suppose we want to check this claim by collecting a sample and conducting a hypothesis test.

The first step is to develop the null and alternative hypotheses. We begin by tentatively assuming that the manufacturer's claim is correct. If the population mean weight for coffee cans is 3 or more pounds per can, Hilltop's claim about its product is correct. However, if the population mean weight for coffee cans is less than 3 pounds per can, Hilltop's claim is incorrect.

With μ denoting the mean weight of cans for the population, the null and the alternative hypotheses are as follows.

$$H_0: \mu \geq 3$$
$$H_a: \mu < 3$$

If the sample data indicate that H_0 cannot be rejected, the statistical evidence does not support the conclusion that a label violation occurred. Hence, no action would be taken against Hilltop. However, if the sample data indicate that H_0 can be rejected, we will conclude that the alternative hypothesis, $H_a: \mu < 3$, is true. In that case, a conclusion of underfilling and a charge of a label violation would be justified.

Suppose a random sample of 36 cans of coffee is selected. If the mean filling weight, $\bar{x}$, for the sample of 36 cans is less than 3 pounds, the sample results will cast doubt on the null hypothesis $H_0: \mu \geq 3$. But how much less than 3 pounds must $\bar{x}$ be before we would be willing to risk making a Type I error and falsely accuse the company of a label violation?

FIGURE 9.1   SAMPLING DISTRIBUTION OF $\bar{x}$ FOR THE HILLTOP COFFEE STUDY WHEN THE NULL HYPOTHESIS IS TRUE ($\mu = 3$)

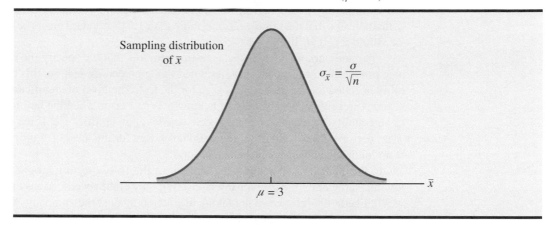

To answer this question, let us tentatively assume that the null hypothesis is true with $\mu = 3$. From the study of sampling distributions in Chapter 7, we know that whenever the sample size is large ($n \geq 30$), the sampling distribution of $\bar{x}$ can be approximated by a normal probability distribution. Figure 9.1 shows the sampling distribution of $\bar{x}$ when the null hypothesis is true at $\mu = 3$.

The value of $z = (\bar{x} - 3)/\sigma_{\bar{x}}$ is the number of standard errors $\bar{x}$ is from $\mu = 3$. For large-sample hypothesis tests about a population mean, we will use z as a **test statistic** to determine whether $\bar{x}$ deviates enough from $\mu = 3$ to justify rejecting the null hypothesis. Note that a value of $z = -1$ means that $\bar{x}$ is 1 standard error below $\mu = 3$, a value of $z = -2$ means that $\bar{x}$ is 2 standard errors below $\mu = 3$, and so on. Obtaining a value of $z < -3$ is unlikely if the null hypothesis is true. The key question is: How small must the test statistic z be before the evidence calls for a rejection of the null hypothesis?

Figure 9.2 shows that the probability of observing a value for $\bar{x}$ of more than 1.645 standard errors below the mean of $\mu = 3$ is .05. Hence, if we were to reject the null hypothesis

Recall that the standard error is the name used for the standard deviation of a point estimator ($\bar{x}$ in this case).

FIGURE 9.2   PROBABILITY THAT $\bar{x}$ IS MORE THAN 1.645 STANDARD ERRORS BELOW THE MEAN OF $\mu = 3$

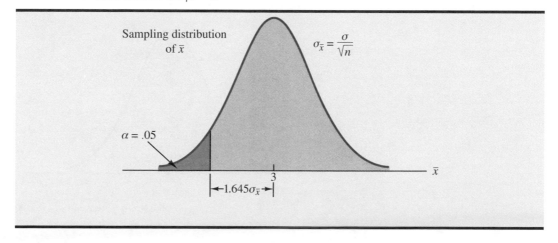

whenever the value of the test statistic $z = (\bar{x} - 3)/\sigma_{\bar{x}}$ is less than -1.645, the probability of making a Type I error would be .05. If the FTC considered .05 to be an acceptable probability of making a Type I error, we would reject the null hypothesis whenever the test statistic indicates that the sample mean is more than 1.645 standard errors below $\mu = 3$. Thus, we would reject H_0 if $z < -1.645$.

The methodology of hypothesis testing requires that we specify the maximum allowable probability of a Type I error. As noted in the preceding section, this maximum probability is called the level of significance for the test. The level of significance is denoted by α and represents the probability of making a Type I error when the null hypothesis is true as an equality. The manager must specify the level of significance. If the cost of making a Type I error is high, a small value should be chosen for the level of significance. If the cost is not high, a larger value is more appropriate.

In the Hilltop Coffee study, the director of the FTC's testing program makes the following statement: "If the company is meeting its weight specifications exactly ($\mu = 3$), I would like a 99% chance of not taking any action against the company. Although I do not want to accuse the company wrongly of underfilling its product, I am willing to risk a 1% chance of making this error."

The director's choice of $\alpha = .01$ implies a high cost of the Type I error of falsely accusing Hilltop of mislabeling.

From the director's statement, the maximum probability of a Type I error is .01. Hence, the level of significance for the hypothesis test is $\alpha = .01$. Figure 9.3 shows the sampling distributions of both $\bar{x}$ and $z = (\bar{x} - \mu)/\sigma_{\bar{x}}$ for the Hilltop Coffee example. Note that when

FIGURE 9.3   HILLTOP COFFEE REJECTION RULE HAS A LEVEL OF SIGNIFICANCE OF $\alpha = .01$

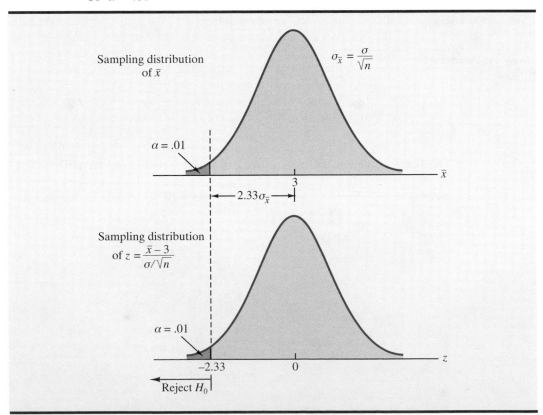

the null hypothesis is true at $\mu = 3$, the probability is .01 that $\bar{x}$ is more than 2.33 standard errors below the mean of 3. Therefore, we establish the following rejection rule.

$$\text{Reject } H_0 \text{ if } z = \frac{\bar{x} - \mu}{\sigma_{\bar{x}}} < -2.33$$

If the value of $\bar{x}$ is such that the test statistic z is in the **rejection region,** we reject H_0 and conclude that H_a is true. If the value of $\bar{x}$ is such that the test statistic z is not in the rejection region, we cannot reject H_0.

We will now continue the Hilltop Coffee study and use the sample results to draw the hypothesis testing conclusion. Two methods can be used: one based on the observed value of the test statistic and one based on the p-value criterion. We begin by using the test statistic.

Using the Test Statistic

In the large-sample case with the population standard deviation σ assumed known, the test statistic is given by

$$z = \frac{\bar{x} - \mu_0}{\sigma/\sqrt{n}} \qquad (9.1)$$

In this expression, μ_0 is the value of the population mean appearing in H_0 and n is the sample size. The sampling distribution of the test statistic z is a standard normal probability distribution; thus, the computed value of z can be used to determine whether the sample mean $\bar{x}$ falls in the rejection region. In the Hilltop coffee example, $\mu_0 = 3$ and $n = 36$. Furthermore, suppose we know from previous studies that $\sigma = .18$. Thus, once the sample mean is identified, the value of the test statistic is computed as follows.

$$z = \frac{\bar{x} - \mu_0}{\sigma/\sqrt{n}} = \frac{\bar{x} - 3}{.18/\sqrt{36}}$$

We have previously established the following rejection rule for the Hilltop hypothesis test:

$$\text{Reject } H_0 \text{ if } z < -2.33$$

The value of the test statistic that establishes the boundary of the rejection region (-2.33 in this case) is called the **critical value** for the test.

If the sample mean $\bar{x}$ provides a value of the test statistic z that is less than -2.33 (the critical value), we reject the null hypothesis $H_0: \mu \geq 3$ and conclude that the alternative hypothesis $H_a: \mu < 3$ is true. However, if the sample mean $\bar{x}$ provides a value of the test statistic z that is not in the rejection region, i.e., $z \geq -2.33$, we cannot reject $H_0: \mu \geq 3$. Note that the rejection region in Figure 9.3 is in one tail of the sampling distribution. In such cases, we say the test is a **one-tailed** test.

Suppose the sample of 36 cans provides a sample mean of $\bar{x} = 2.92$ pounds. Is $\bar{x} = 2.92$ in the rejection region? To answer this question, we compute the test statistic z.

$$z = \frac{\bar{x} - \mu_0}{\sigma/\sqrt{n}} = \frac{2.92 - 3}{.18/\sqrt{36}} = -2.67$$

Comparing $z = -2.67$ to the critical value for the test, $z = -2.33$, we see that $z = -2.67$ is less than -2.33. Thus, $z = -2.67$ is in the rejection region (see Figure 9.4) and hence we reject H_0: $\mu \geq 3$. In this case, the FTC concludes that H_a: $\mu < 3$ is true, and FTC action against Hilltop for underfilling its product is justified.

Using the *p*-Value

Another approach can be used to draw a hypothesis testing conclusion based on a probability called a **p-value.** Assuming the null hypothesis is true, the *p*-value is the probability of obtaining a sample result that is at least as unlikely as what is observed. In the Hilltop Coffee example, the rejection region is in the lower tail. The *p*-value for a lower-tailed hypothesis test is the probability of obtaining a sample mean that is less than or equal to what is observed. The *p*-value is also called the *observed level of significance.*

The p-value for a one-tailed test is always the area from the test statistic toward the rejection tail of the distribution.

In the Hilltop Coffee example, the sample mean $\bar{x} = 2.92$ pounds provided a value for the test statistic of $z = -2.67$. Because the rejection region is in the lower tail of the distribution, the *p*-value is the probability of z being less than -2.67. Using the standard normal probability distribution table, we find that the area between the mean and $z = -2.67$ is .4962. Thus the *p*-value is $.5000 - .4962 = .0038$, which is shown in Figure 9.5. This *p*-value indicates a small probability of obtaining a sample mean as small as $\bar{x} = 2.92$ when sampling from a population with $\mu = 3$.

The *p*-value can be used to make the decision in a hypothesis test by noting that if the *p*-value is *less than the level of significance* α, the value of the test statistic is in the rejec-

FIGURE 9.4 VALUE OF THE TEST STATISTIC FOR $\bar{x} = 2.92$ IS IN THE REJECTION REGION

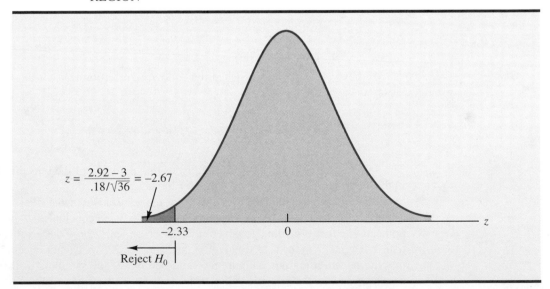

FIGURE 9.5   *p*-VALUE FOR THE HILLTOP COFFEE STUDY WHEN $\bar{x} = 2.92$ AND $z = -2.67$

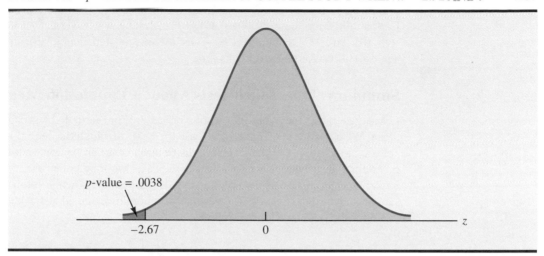

tion region. Similarly, if the *p*-value is *greater than or equal to* α, the value of the test statistic is not in the rejection region. For the Hilltop Coffee example, the fact that the *p*-value of .0038 is less than the level of significance, $\alpha = .01$, indicates that the null hypothesis should be rejected. Given the level of significance α, the *p*-value criterion for deciding whether to reject H_0 can be stated as follows.

> ### *p*-Value Criterion for Hypothesis Testing
>
> Reject H_0 if *p*-value $< \alpha$

Sometimes a researcher may simply report the p-value for a particular sample result. The user of the research findings can select any level of significance, α, he or she is willing to tolerate.

Using the *p*-value or the corresponding test statistic will always provide the same hypothesis testing conclusion. When the rejection region is in the lower tail of the sampling distribution, the *p*-value is the area under the curve less than or equal to the test statistic. When the rejection region is in the upper tail of the sampling distribution, the *p*-value is the area under the curve greater than or equal to the test statistic. For continuous sampling distributions, the *p*-value for an upper-tail rejection region is 1 minus the *p*-value for a lower-tail rejection region.

A small *p*-value indicates a sample result that is unusual given the assumption that H_0 is true. Small *p*-values lead to rejection of H_0, whereas large *p*-values indicate that the null hypothesis cannot be rejected.

Before we leave the Hilltop Coffee example, let us suppose that the sample mean for the sample of 36 coffee cans had turned out to be $\bar{x} = 2.97$ pounds. In this case the value of the test statistic would have been

$$z = \frac{\bar{x} - \mu_0}{\sigma/\sqrt{n}} = \frac{2.97 - 3}{.18/\sqrt{36}} = -1.00$$

Because $z = -1.00$ is greater than the critical value -2.33, $z = -1.00$ is not in the rejection region. Hence, the FTC cannot reject H_0. The FTC has no statistical justification to take action against Hilltop for underfilling its product.

Using the standard normal probability distribution and the test statistic value $z = -1.00$, we find an area of .3413 between the mean and $z = -1.00$. Thus, the area in the rejection tail is p-value $= .5000 - .3413 = .1587$. Because p-value $= .1587$ is greater than $\alpha = .01$, the FTC cannot reject H_0. Thus, there is no statistical justification to take action against Hilltop for underfilling its product.

Summary: One-Tailed Tests About a Population Mean

Let us generalize the hypothesis testing procedure for one-tailed tests about a population mean. We consider the large-sample case ($n \geq 30$) in which the central limit theorem enables us to assume that the sampling distribution of $\bar{x}$ can be approximated by a normal probability distribution. In the large-sample case, we may either use historical data as a basis for assuming the population standard deviation σ is known or estimate σ by using the sample standard deviation s. The general form of a lower-tailed test, where μ_0 is the stated value for the population mean, follows.

In the large-sample case, the sample standard deviation s can be used in the computation of the test statistic when the population standard deviation σ is unknown.

One-Tailed Test: Large-Sample Case ($n \geq 30$) with the Rejection Region in the Lower Tail

$$H_0: \mu \geq \mu_0$$
$$H_a: \mu < \mu_0$$

Test Statistic: σ Assumed Known

$$z = \frac{\bar{x} - \mu_0}{\sigma/\sqrt{n}} \tag{9.1}$$

Test Statistic: σ Estimated by s

$$z = \frac{\bar{x} - \mu_0}{s/\sqrt{n}} \tag{9.2}$$

Rejection Rule

Using Test Statistic: Reject H_0 if $z < -z_\alpha$
Using p-Value: Reject H_0 if p-value $< \alpha$

A second form of the one-tailed test rejects the null hypothesis when the test statistic is in the upper tail of the sampling distribution. This one-tailed test and rejection rule are summarized next (see Figure 9.6). Again, we are considering the large-sample case.

One-Tailed Test: Large-Sample Case ($n \geq 30$) with the Rejection Region in the Upper Tail

$$H_0: \mu \leq \mu_0$$
$$H_a: \mu > \mu_0$$

Test Statistic: σ Assumed Known

$$z = \frac{\bar{x} - \mu_0}{\sigma/\sqrt{n}} \tag{9.1}$$

Test Statistic: σ Estimated by s

$$z = \frac{\bar{x} - \mu_0}{s/\sqrt{n}} \tag{9.2}$$

Rejection Rule

Using Test Statistic: Reject H_0 if $z > z_\alpha$

Using p-Value: Reject H_0 if p-value $< \alpha$

FIGURE 9.6   REJECTION REGION FOR AN UPPER-TAILED HYPOTHESIS TEST ABOUT A POPULATION MEAN

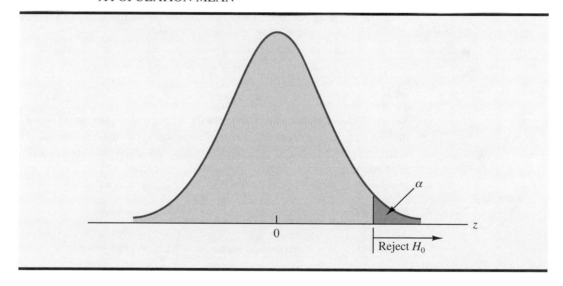

Steps of Hypothesis Testing

In conducting the Hilltop Coffee hypothesis test, we carried out the steps that can be used for any hypothesis test. A summary of the steps follows. Note that either the test statistic or the p-value may be used to draw the hypothesis testing conclusion.

Steps of Hypothesis Testing

1. Develop the null and alternative hypotheses.
2. Specify the level of significance α.
3. Select the test statistic that will be used to test the hypothesis.

Using the Test Statistic

4. Use the level of significance to determine the critical value for the test statistic and state the rejection rule for H_0.
5. Collect the sample data and compute the value of the test statistic.
6. Use the value of the test statistic and the rejection rule to determine whether to reject H_0.

Using the p-Value

4. Collect the sample data and compute the value of the test statistic.
5. Use the value of the test statistic to compute the p-value.
6. Reject H_0 if p-value $< \alpha$.

NOTES AND COMMENTS

The p-value is a measure of the likelihood of the sample results when the null hypothesis is assumed to be true. The smaller the p-value, the less likely it is that the sample results came from a situation where the null hypothesis is true. Most statistical software packages provide the p-value associated with a hypothesis test. The user can then compare the p-value to α and draw a hypothesis test conclusion without referring to a statistical table.

EXERCISES

Note to Student: Some of the hypothesis testing exercises that follow will ask you to use the test statistic and other exercises will ask you to use the p-value. Both methods will provide the same hypothesis testing conclusion. We provide exercises with both methods to give you practice using both. In an actual application, you may select either based on personal preference.

Methods

9. Consider the following hypothesis test.

$$H_0: \mu \geq 10$$
$$H_a: \mu < 10$$

A sample of 50 provided a sample mean of 9.46 and sample standard deviation of 2.
a. At $\alpha = .05$, what is the critical value for z? What is the rejection rule?
b. Compute the value of the test statistic z. What is your conclusion?

SELFtest   10. Consider the following hypothesis test.

$$H_0: \mu \leq 15$$
$$H_a: \mu > 15$$

A sample of 40 provided a sample mean of 16.5 and sample standard deviation of 7.
a. At $\alpha = .02$, what is the critical value for z, and what is the rejection rule?
b. Compute the value of the test statistic z.
c. What is the p-value?
d. What is your conclusion?

11. Consider the following hypothesis test.

$$H_0: \mu \geq 25$$
$$H_a: \mu < 25$$

A sample of 100 is used and the population standard deviation is assumed to be 12. Use $\alpha = .05$. Provide the value of the test statistic z and your conclusion for each of the following sample results.

   a. $\bar{x} = 22.0$
   b. $\bar{x} = 24.0$
   c. $\bar{x} = 23.5$
   d. $\bar{x} = 22.8$

12. Consider the following hypothesis test.

$$H_0: \mu \leq 5$$
$$H_a: \mu > 5$$

Assume the following test statistics. Compute the corresponding p-values and make the appropriate conclusions based on $\alpha = .05$.

   a. $z = 1.82$
   b. $z = .45$
   c. $z = 1.50$
   d. $z = 3.30$
   e. $z = -1.00$

Applications

SELFtest

13. Individuals filing federal income tax returns prior to March 31 had an average refund of $1056. Consider the population of "last-minute" filers who mail their returns during the last five days of the income tax period (typically April 10 to April 15).

   a. A researcher suggests that one of the reasons individuals wait until the last five days to file their returns is that on average those individuals have a lower refund than early filers. Develop appropriate hypotheses such that rejection of H_0 will support the researcher's contention.
   b. Using $\alpha = .05$, what is the critical value for the test statistic and what is the rejection rule?
   c. For a sample of 400 individuals who filed a return between April 10 and April 15, the sample mean refund was $910 and the sample standard deviation was $1600. Compute the value of the test statistic.
   d. What is your conclusion?
   e. What is the p-value for the test?

14. A Nielsen survey provided the estimate that the mean number of hours of television viewing per household is 7.25 hours per day (*New York Daily News,* November 2, 1997). Assume that the Nielsen survey involved 200 households and that the sample standard deviation was 2.5 hours per day. Ten years ago the population mean number of hours of television viewing per household was reported to be 6.70 hours. Letting $\mu =$ the population mean number of hours of television viewing per household in 1997, test the hypotheses $H_0: \mu \leq 6.70$ and $H_a: \mu > 6.70$. Use $\alpha = .01$.

   a. What is the critical value of the test statistic, and what is the rejection rule?
   b. Compute the value of the test statistic.
   c. What is your conclusion?

15. According to the National Automobile Dealers Association, the mean price for used cars is $10,192. A manager of a Kansas City used car dealership reviewed a sample of 100 recent used car sales at the dealership. The sample mean price was $9300 and the sample standard deviation was $4500. Letting μ denote the population mean price for used cars at the Kansas City dealership, test H_0: $\mu \geq 10,192$ and H_a: $\mu < 10,192$ at a .05 level of significance.
   a. What is the critical value of the test statistic, and what is the rejection rule?
   b. Compute the value of the test statistic.
   c. What is your conclusion?

16. Media Metrix, Inc., tracks Internet users in seven countries: Australia, Britain, Canada, France, Germany, Japan, and the United States. According to recent measurement figures, American home users rank first in Internet usage with a mean of 13 hours per month (*The Washington Post,* August 4, 2000). Assume that in a follow-up study involving a sample of 145 Canadian Internet users, the sample mean was 10.8 hours per month and the sample standard deviation was 9.2 hours.
   a. Formulate the null and alternative hypotheses that can be used to determine whether the sample data support the conclusion that Canadian Internet users have a population mean less than the U.S. mean of 13 hours per month.
   b. Using $\alpha = .01$, what is the critical value for the test statistic? State the rejection rule.
   c. What is the value of the test statistic?
   d. What is your conclusion?

17. Fowle Marketing Research, Inc., bases charges to a client on the assumption that telephone surveys can be completed in a mean time of 15 minutes or less. If a longer mean survey time is necessary, a premium rate is charged. Suppose a sample of 35 surveys shows a sample mean of 17 minutes and a sample standard deviation of 4 minutes. Is the premium rate justified?
   a. Formulate the null and alternative hypotheses for this application.
   b. Compute the value of the test statistic.
   c. What is the *p*-value?
   d. Using $\alpha = .01$, what is your conclusion?

18. A Channel One Network study reported that teens spend a mean of $5.72 per visit to fast-food restaurants such as McDonald's, Burger King, and Wendy's (*USA Today,* October 5, 1998). In a follow-up study, a sample of 102 teen visits to fast-food restaurants in Chicago found a sample mean of $5.98 and a sample standard deviation of $1.24.
   a. Formulate the null and alternative hypotheses that can be used to determine whether the sample data support the conclusion that teens in Chicago have a population mean expenditure of more than $5.72 per visit to fast-food restaurants.
   b. What is the value of the test statistic?
   c. What is the *p*-value?
   d. Using $\alpha = .05$, what is your conclusion?

19. The national mean sales price for new one-family homes is $181,900 (*The New York Times Almanac 2000*). A sample of 40 one-family home sales in the South showed a sample mean of $166,400 and a sample standard deviation of $33,500.
   a. Formulate the null and alternative hypotheses that can be used to determine whether the sample data support the conclusion that the population mean sales price for new one-family homes in the South is less than the national mean of $181,900.
   b. What is the value of the test statistic?
   c. What is the *p*-value?
   d. Using $\alpha = .01$, what is your conclusion?

20.   According to the National Association of Colleges and Employers, the 2000 mean annual salary of business degree graduates in accounting was $37,000 (*Time,* May 8, 2000). In a follow-up study in June 2001, a sample of 48 graduating accounting majors found a sample mean of $38,100 and a sample standard deviation of $5200.

    a.   Formulate the null and alternative hypotheses that can be used to determine whether the sample data support the conclusion that June 2001 graduates in accounting have a mean salary greater than the 2000 mean annual salary of $37,000.

    b.   What is the value of the test statistic?

    c.   What is the *p*-value?

    d.   Using $\alpha = .05$, what is your conclusion?

9.4   TWO-TAILED TESTS ABOUT A POPULATION MEAN: LARGE-SAMPLE CASE

Two-tailed tests differ from one-tailed hypothesis tests in that two-tailed tests have rejection regions in both the lower and the upper tails of the sampling distribution. Let us introduce an example to show how and why two-tailed tests are conducted.

The U.S. Golf Association (USGA) established rules that manufacturers of golf equipment must meet if their products are to be acceptable for use in USGA events. One of the rules for the manufacture of golf balls states: "A brand of golf ball, when tested on apparatus approved by the USGA on the outdoor range at the USGA Headquarters . . . shall not cover an average distance in carry and roll exceeding 280 yards. . . ." Suppose Superflight, Inc., has recently developed a high-technology manufacturing method that can produce golf balls with an average distance in carry and roll of 280 yards.

Superflight realizes, however, that if the new manufacturing process goes out of adjustment, the process may produce golf balls for which the average distance is either less than 280 yards or greater than 280 yards. In the first case, sales may decline as a result of marketing an inferior product, and in the second case, the golf balls may be rejected by the USGA for exceeding the 280-yard distance rule.

Superflight's management instituted a quality control program to monitor the manufacturing process. Periodically, a hypothesis test will be used to determine whether the manufacturing process is out of adjustment. We begin by assuming that the manufacturing process is functioning correctly, with the golf balls carrying the desired mean distance of 280 yards. The null and alternative hypotheses are as follow:

$$H_0: \mu = 280$$
$$H_a: \mu \neq 280$$

If the sample data indicate that H_0 cannot be rejected, no action will be taken to adjust the manufacturing process. However, if the sample data indicate that H_0 should be rejected, we conclude that the golf balls do not have the desired mean distance of 280 yards. In this case corrective action should be taken to adjust the manufacturing process and return it to its desired state.

The quality control team selected $\alpha = .05$ as the level of significance for the hypothesis test. Let us assume that Superflight will use a large sample each time the quality control test is performed. As a result the test statistics are

The test statistics are the same as those used for one-tailed tests in Section 9.3.

$$z = \frac{\bar{x} - \mu_0}{\sigma/\sqrt{n}}$$

if σ is assumed known, and

$$z = \frac{\bar{x} - \mu_0}{s/\sqrt{n}}$$

if σ is estimated by s.

As usual, we make the tentative assumption that the null hypothesis is true. We want to reject H_0: $\mu = 280$ when the test statistic z indicates that the sample mean distance $\bar{x}$ is significantly less than 280 yards or significantly greater than 280 yards. Thus, H_0 may be rejected for values of z in either the lower tail or upper tail of the sampling distribution. Therefore, the hypothesis test is called a **two-tailed test**.

Figure 9.7 shows the sampling distribution of z with the two-tailed rejection region for $\alpha = .05$. With two-tailed hypothesis tests, we will always determine the rejection region by placing an area or probability of $\alpha/2$ in each tail of the distribution. The values of z that provide an area of .025 in each tail can be found from the standard normal probability distribution table. We see in Figure 9.7 that $-z_{.025} = -1.96$ identifies an area of .025 in the lower tail and $z_{.025} = +1.96$ identifies an area of .025 in the upper tail. Thus, $z = -1.96$ and $z = 1.96$ are the critical values for the test and the rejection rule is as follows.

Reject H_0 if $z < -1.96$ or if $z > 1.96$

Suppose that a simple random sample of 36 golf balls provided the data in Table 9.2. For these data we obtained a sample mean of $\bar{x} = 278.5$ yards and a sample standard deviation of $s = 12$ yards. With the value $\mu_0 = 280$ from the null hypothesis and the sample standard deviation $s = 12$ used to estimate the population standard deviation σ, the value of the test statistic is

$$z = \frac{\bar{x} - \mu_0}{s/\sqrt{n}} = \frac{278.5 - 280}{12/\sqrt{36}} = -.75$$

FIGURE 9.7   REJECTION REGION FOR THE TWO-TAILED HYPOTHESIS TEST FOR SUPERFLIGHT, INC.

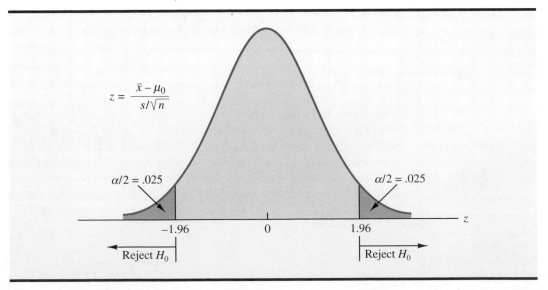

TABLE 9.2 DISTANCE DATA FOR A SIMPLE RANDOM SAMPLE OF 36 SUPERFLIGHT
GOLF BALLS

CDfile
Distance

Ball	Yards	Ball	Yards	Ball	Yards
1	269	13	296	25	272
2	300	14	265	26	285
3	268	15	271	27	293
4	278	16	279	28	281
5	282	17	284	29	269
6	263	18	260	30	299
7	301	19	275	31	263
8	295	20	282	32	264
9	288	21	260	33	273
10	278	22	266	34	291
11	276	23	270	35	274
12	286	24	293	36	277

According to the rejection rule, H_0 cannot be rejected. The sample results indicate no reason to doubt the assumption that the manufacturing process is producing golf balls with a mean distance of 280 yards.

p-Values for Two-Tailed Tests

Let us compute the *p*-value for the Superflight golf ball example. The sample mean of $\bar{x} = 278.5$ corresponds to $z = -.75$. The table for the standard normal probability distribution shows that the area between the mean and $z = -.75$ is .2734. Thus, the area in the lower tail is $.5000 - .2734 = .2266$. Looking at Figure 9.7, we see that the lower-tail portion of the rejection region has an area or probability of $\alpha/2 = .05/2 = .025$. Thus, with $.2266 > .025$, the test statistic is not in the rejection region, and the null hypothesis cannot be rejected.

One question remains: What value should we report as the *p*-value for the two-tailed test? At first glance, you may be inclined to say the *p*-value is .2266. If that is your choice, you will have to remember two different rules: one for the one-tailed test, which is to reject H_0 if the *p*-value $< \alpha$, and another for the two-tailed test, which is to reject H_0 if the *p*-value $< \alpha/2$. Alternatively, suppose we define the *p*-value for a two-tailed test as *double* the area found in the tail of the sampling distribution. Thus, for the Superflight example, we would define the *p*-value to be $2(.2266) = .4532$. The advantage of this definition of the *p*-value for a two-tailed test is that the *p*-value can be compared directly to the level of significance α. Hence, with $.4532 > .05$, we see that the null hypothesis cannot be rejected. By remembering that the *p*-value for a two-tailed test is simply double the area found in the tail of the sampling distribution, the previous rule to reject H_0 if *p*-value $< \alpha$ can be used for all hypothesis tests (lower tail, upper tail, and two-tailed).

Minitab can be used to provide hypothesis test information for a population mean. The computer output for the Superflight hypothesis test is shown in Figure 9.8. The sample mean $\bar{x} = 278.5$, the test statistic $z = -.75$ and the *p*-value $= .453$ are computed automatically. The step-by-step procedure used to obtain the Minitab output is described in Appendix 9.1.

In a two-tailed test, the p-value is found by doubling the area in the tail. The doubling of the area is done so that the p-value can be compared directly to α. As a result, the same rejection rule can be used for both one-tailed and two-tailed tests.

FIGURE 9.8   MINITAB OUTPUT FOR THE SUPERFLIGHT GOLF BALL HYPOTHESIS TEST

```
Test of mu = 280.00 vs mu not = 280.00
Variable      N      Mean    StDev    SE Mean        Z        P
Yards        36    278.50    12.00       2.00    -0.75    0.453
```

Summary: Two-Tailed Tests About a Population Mean

Let μ_0 represent the hypothesized value of the mean. The general form of the two-tailed hypothesis test about a population mean follows.

Two-Tailed Test: Large-Sample Case ($n \geq 30$)

$$H_0: \mu = \mu_0$$
$$H_a: \mu \neq \mu_0$$

Test Statistic: σ Assumed Known

$$z = \frac{\bar{x} - \mu_0}{\sigma/\sqrt{n}} \tag{9.1}$$

Test Statistic: σ Estimated by s

$$z = \frac{\bar{x} - \mu_0}{s/\sqrt{n}} \tag{9.2}$$

Rejection Rule

Using test statistic: Reject H_0 if $z < -z_{\alpha/2}$ or if $z > z_{\alpha/2}$

Using p-value: Reject H_0 if p-value $< \alpha$

Relationship Between Interval Estimation and Hypothesis Testing

In Chapter 8 we showed how to develop a confidence interval estimate of a population mean. In the large-sample case, the confidence interval estimate of a population mean corresponding to a $1 - \alpha$ confidence coefficient is given by

$$\bar{x} \pm z_{\alpha/2}\frac{\sigma}{\sqrt{n}} \tag{9.3}$$

when σ is assumed known and

$$\bar{x} \pm z_{\alpha/2}\frac{s}{\sqrt{n}} \tag{9.4}$$

when σ is estimated by s.

Conducting a hypothesis test requires us first to develop competing hypotheses about the value of a population parameter. In the case of the population mean, the two-tailed hypothesis test takes the form

$$H_0: \mu = \mu_0$$
$$H_a: \mu \neq \mu_0$$

where μ_0 is the hypothesized value for the population mean. Using the two-tailed rejection rule, we see that the region over which we do not reject H_0 includes all values of the sample mean $\bar{x}$ that are within $-z_{\alpha/2}$ and $+z_{\alpha/2}$ standard errors of μ_0. Thus, the do-not-reject region for the sample mean $\bar{x}$ in a two-tailed hypothesis test with a level of significance of α is given by

$$\mu_0 \pm z_{\alpha/2} \frac{\sigma}{\sqrt{n}} \tag{9.5}$$

when σ is assumed known and

$$\mu_0 \pm z_{\alpha/2} \frac{s}{\sqrt{n}} \tag{9.6}$$

when σ is estimated by s.

A close look at expression (9.3) and expression (9.5) provides insight about the relationship between the estimation and hypothesis testing approaches to statistical inference. Note in particular that both procedures require the computation of the values $z_{\alpha/2}$ and $\sigma/\sqrt{n}$. Focusing on α, we see that a confidence coefficient of $(1 - \alpha)$ for interval estimation corresponds to a level of significance of α in hypothesis testing. For example, a 95% confidence interval corresponds to a .05 level of significance for hypothesis testing. Furthermore, (9.3) and (9.5) show that, because $z_{\alpha/2}(\sigma/\sqrt{n})$ is the plus or minus value for both expressions, if $\bar{x}$ is in the do-not-reject region defined by (9.5), the hypothesized value μ_0 will be in the confidence interval defined by (9.3). Conversely, if the hypothesized value μ_0 is in the confidence interval defined by (9.3), the sample mean $\bar{x}$ will be in the do-not-reject region for the hypothesis $H_0: \mu = \mu_0$ as defined by (9.5). These observations lead to the following procedure for using a confidence interval to conduct a two-tailed hypothesis test.

The plus or minus value is called the margin of error in interval estimation.

A Confidence Interval Approach to Testing a Hypothesis of the Form

$$H_0: \mu = \mu_0$$
$$H_a: \mu \neq \mu_0$$

1. Select a simple random sample from the population and use the value of the sample mean $\bar{x}$ to develop the confidence interval for the population mean μ. If σ is assumed known, compute the interval estimate using

$$\bar{x} \pm z_{\alpha/2} \frac{\sigma}{\sqrt{n}}$$

If σ is estimated by s, compute the interval estimate using

$$\bar{x} \pm z_{\alpha/2} \frac{s}{\sqrt{n}}$$

2. If the confidence interval contains the hypothesized value μ_0, do not reject H_0. Otherwise, reject H_0.

For a two-tailed hypothesis test, the null hypothesis can be rejected if the confidence interval does not include μ_0.

Let us return to the Superflight golf ball study, which resulted in the following two-tailed test.

$$H_0: \mu = 280$$
$$H_a: \mu \neq 280$$

To test this hypothesis with a level of significance of $\alpha = .05$, we sampled 36 golf balls and found a sample mean distance of $\bar{x} = 278.5$ yards and a sample standard deviation of $s = 12$ yards. Using these results with $z_{.025} = 1.96$, we find that the 95% confidence interval estimate of the population mean is

$$\bar{x} \pm z_{.025} \frac{s}{\sqrt{n}}$$

$$278.5 \pm 1.96 \frac{12}{\sqrt{36}}$$

$$278.5 \pm 3.92$$

or

$$274.58 \text{ to } 282.42$$

This finding enables the quality control manager to conclude with 95% confidence that the mean distance for the population of golf balls is between 274.58 and 282.42 yards. Because the hypothesized value for the population mean, $\mu_0 = 280$, is in this interval, the hypothesis testing conclusion is that the null hypothesis, $H_0: \mu = 280$, cannot be rejected.

Note that this discussion and example pertain to two-tailed hypothesis tests about a population mean. However, the same confidence interval and two-tailed hypothesis testing relationship exists for other population parameters. The relationship can also be extended to one-tailed tests about population parameters. Doing so, however, requires the development of one-sided confidence intervals.

NOTES AND COMMENTS

1. The p-value depends on the sample outcome and whether the hypothesis test is one-tailed or two-tailed. For a lower-tailed hypothesis test, the p-value is the area under the curve to the left of the test statistic; for an upper-tailed hypothesis test, the p-value is the area under the curve to the right of the test statistic. For a two-tailed test, we first determine which tail of the sampling distribution the test statistic is in. The p-value equals twice the tail area cut off by the test statistic.

2. The interval estimation approach to hypothesis testing helps to highlight the role of the sample size. From equation (9.3) we can see that larger sample sizes n lead to narrower confidence intervals. Thus, for a given level of significance α, a larger sample is less likely to lead to an interval containing μ_0 when the null hypothesis is false. That is, the larger sample size provides a higher probability of rejecting H_0 when H_0 is false.

EXERCISES

Methods

21. Consider the following hypothesis test.

$$H_0: \mu = 10$$
$$H_a: \mu \neq 10$$

A sample of 36 provided a sample mean of 11 and sample standard deviation of 2.5.
a. At $\alpha = .05$, what is the rejection rule?
b. Compute the value of the test statistic z. What is your conclusion?

SELFtest   **22.** Consider the following hypothesis test.

$$H_0: \mu = 15$$
$$H_a: \mu \neq 15$$

A sample of 50 provided a sample mean of 14.2 and sample standard deviation of 5.
a. At $\alpha = .02$, what is the rejection rule?
b. Compute the value of the test statistic z.
c. What is the p-value?
d. What is your conclusion?

23. Consider the following hypothesis test.

$$H_0: \mu = 25$$
$$H_a: \mu \neq 25$$

For a sample of 80 and a population standard deviation of 10, compute the value of the test statistic z. Using $\alpha = .05$, specify your conclusion for each of the following sample results.
a. $\bar{x} = 22.0$
b. $\bar{x} = 27.0$
c. $\bar{x} = 23.5$
d. $\bar{x} = 28.0$

24. Consider the following hypothesis test.

$$H_0: \mu = 5$$
$$H_a: \mu \neq 5$$

Assume the following test statistics. Compute the corresponding p-values and specify your conclusions based on $\alpha = .05$.
a. $z = 1.80$
b. $z = -.45$
c. $z = 2.05$
d. $z = -3.50$
e. $z = -1.00$

Applications

SELFtest

25. The mean length of a work week for the population of workers was reported to be 39.2 hours (*Investor's Business Daily,* September 11, 2000). Suppose you took a sample of 112 workers and found a sample mean of 38.5 hours and a sample standard deviation 4.8 hours. Test the hypotheses: H_0: $\mu = 39.2$ and H_a: $\mu \neq 39.2$ with $\alpha = .05$.
    a. What are the critical values for the test statistic, and what is the rejection rule for H_0?
    b. What is the value of the test statistic?
    c. Can the null hypothesis be rejected? What is your conclusion?
    d. What is the *p*-value?

26. CNN and ActMedia provided a television channel targeted to individuals waiting in grocery checkout lines that showed news, features, and ads. The television programs were designed with an eight-minute cycle on the assumption that the population mean time a shopper stands in line at a grocery store checkout is eight minutes (*Astounding Averages,* 1995). A sample of 120 shoppers at a major grocery store showed a sample mean waiting time of 7.5 minutes with a sample standard deviation of 3.2 minutes. Test H_0: $\mu = 8$ and H_a: $\mu \neq 8$ with $\alpha = .05$.
    a. What are the critical values of the test statistic, and what is the rejection rule?
    b. Compute the value of the test statistic.
    c. What is your conclusion?

27. A production line operates with a mean filling weight of 16 ounces per container. Overfilling or underfilling presents a serious problem, which shuts down the production line if either occurs. From past data, σ is assumed to be .8 ounces. A quality control inspector samples 30 items every two hours and at that time makes the decision of whether to shut the line down for adjustment.
    a. With a .05 level of significance, what is the rejection rule for the hypothesis testing procedure?
    b. If a sample mean of $\bar{x} = 16.32$ ounces were found, what action would you recommend?
    c. If $\bar{x} = 15.82$ ounces, what action would you recommend?
    d. What is the *p*-value for parts (b) and (c)?

28. A Gallup survey found the mean charitable contribution on federal tax returns was $1075 (*USA Today,* April 10, 2000). Assume a sample of April 2001 tax returns will be used to conduct a hypothesis test designed to determine whether any change occurred in the mean charitable contributions.
    a. Formulate the null and alternative hypotheses.
    b. Assume that a sample of 200 tax returns has a sample mean of $1160 and a sample standard deviation of $840. What is the value of the test statistic?
    c. What is the *p*-value?
    d. Using $\alpha = .05$, what is your conclusion?

29. Historically, evening long-distance phone calls from a particular city have averaged 15.2 minutes per call. In a recent random sample of 35 calls, the sample mean time was 14.3 minutes per call, with a sample standard deviation of 5 minutes. Use this sample information to test whether the mean duration of long-distance phone calls has changed.
    a. Compute the value of the test statistic.
    b. What is the *p*-value?
    c. Using $\alpha = .05$, what is your conclusion?

30. The Florida Department of Labor and Employment Security reported the state mean annual wage of $26,133 (*The Naples Daily News,* February 13, 1999). A test of wages by county can be conducted to see whether the mean annual wage for the various counties differs from the state mean.

    a. Formulate the null and alternative hypotheses that can be used to determine whether the sample data from a particular county support the conclusion that the population mean annual wage for the county differs from the state mean of $26,133.

    b. A sample of 550 people in Collier County showed a sample mean annual wage of $25,457 and a sample standard deviation of $7600. Compute the value of the test statistic.

    c. What is the *p*-value?

    d. Using $\alpha = .05$, what is your conclusion?

31. At Western University the historical mean scholarship examination score of entering students is 900, with a standard deviation of 180. Each year a sample of applications is taken to see whether the examination scores are at the same level as in previous years. The null hypothesis tested is H_0: $\mu = 900$. A sample of 200 students in this year's class provided a sample mean score of 935. Use a .05 level of significance.

    a. Use a confidence interval approach to conduct a hypothesis test.

    b. Use a test statistic to test this hypothesis.

    c. What is the *p*-value?

32. An industry pays an average wage rate of $15.00 per hour. A sample of 36 workers from one company showed a mean wage of $\bar{x} = \$14.50$ and a sample standard deviation of $s = \$0.60$.

    a. A one-sided confidence interval uses the sample results to establish either an upper limit or a lower limit for the value of the population parameter. For this exercise establish an upper 95% confidence limit for the hourly wage rate paid by the company. The form of this one-sided confidence interval requires that we be 95% confident that the population mean is this value or less. What is the 95% confidence statement for this one-sided confidence interval?

    b. Use the one-sided confidence interval result to test H_0: $\mu \geq 15$. What is your conclusion? Explain.

9.5   TESTS ABOUT A POPULATION MEAN: SMALL-SAMPLE CASE

The procedures for hypothesis tests about a population mean discussed in Sections 9.3 and 9.4 were based on the central limit theorem and large-sample theory. In this section, we consider tests about a population mean using a small sample ($n < 30$). In this case the central limit theorem is not applicable, so the hypothesis testing procedures require the assumption that the population has a normal probability distribution. If this assumption is reasonable, the methodology presented in this section can be used. However, if this assumption appears unreasonable, the best alternative is to increase the sample size to $n \geq 30$ and rely on the large-sample hypothesis testing procedures presented in Sections 9.3 and 9.4.

The methodology presented in this section is based on the assumption that the population has a normal, or near-normal, distribution.

    If the population can be assumed to have a normal distribution, the sampling distribution of $\bar{x}$ is normally distributed with mean μ and standard deviation $\sigma_{\bar{x}} = \sigma/\sqrt{n}$, for any sample size. If, based on historical data or other considerations, σ can also be assumed known, then the small-sample hypothesis testing procedures are identical to the large-sample hypothesis testing procedures presented in Sections 9.3 and 9.4. The test statistic is again

When $\bar{x}$ follows a normal distribution, z follows a standard normal distribution.

$$z = \frac{\bar{x} - \mu_0}{\sigma/\sqrt{n}} \tag{9.7}$$

Because the hypothesis testing computations are identical to the computations we made previously, we shall not present a new numerical example at this time.

The small-sample hypothesis testing procedure with σ estimated by s is based on the same theory used for the small-sample interval estimation procedure presented in Section 8.2. Both use a normal population assumption and the t distribution.

Next consider the situation where the sample size is small ($n < 30$), the population is assumed to have a normal distribution and the population standard deviation σ is estimated by the sample standard deviation s. In this case, the t distribution must be used to make inferences about the value of the population mean. In using the t distribution for hypothesis tests, the test statistic is

$$t = \frac{\bar{x} - \mu_0}{s/\sqrt{n}} \tag{9.8}$$

This test statistic has a t distribution with $n - 1$ degrees of freedom.

One-Tailed Test

Let us consider an example of a one-tailed hypothesis test about a population mean for the small-sample case. The International Air Transport Association surveys business travelers to develop ratings of transatlantic gateway airports. The maximum possible rating is 10. A magazine devoted to business travel decided to classify airports according to the rating they receive. Airports with a population mean rating higher than 7 will be designated as providing superior service. Suppose a simple random sample of 12 business travelers asked to rate London's Heathrow Airport provides the following 12 ratings: 7, 8, 10, 8, 6, 9, 6, 7, 7, 8, 9, and 8. The sample mean for these data is $\bar{x} = 7.75$ and the sample standard deviation is $s = 1.215$. Assuming that the population of ratings can be approximated by a normal probability distribution, should Heathrow be designated as providing superior service?

CDfile
Heathrow

Using a .05 level of significance, we want a test to determine whether the population mean rating for the Heathrow Airport is greater than 7. The null and alternative hypotheses follow.

$$H_0: \mu \leq 7$$
$$H_a: \mu > 7$$

The Heathrow Airport will be designated as providing superior service if H_0 can be rejected.

The rejection region is in the upper tail of the sampling distribution. With $n - 1 = 12 - 1 = 11$ degrees of freedom, the t distribution table inside the front cover of the text shows that the critical value is $t_{.05} = 1.796$. Thus, the rejection rule is

$$\text{Reject } H_0 \text{ if } t > 1.796$$

Using equation (9.8) with $\bar{x} = 7.75$ and $s = 1.215$, we compute the following value for the test statistic.

$$t = \frac{\bar{x} - \mu_0}{s/\sqrt{n}} = \frac{7.75 - 7}{1.215/\sqrt{12}} = 2.14$$

Because 2.14 is greater than 1.796, the null hypothesis is rejected. At the .05 level of significance, we can conclude that the population mean rating for the Heathrow airport is greater than 7. Thus, Heathrow can be designated as providing superior service. Figure 9.9 shows that the value of the test statistic falls within the rejection region.

In the Heathrow Airport study, the rejection region was located in the upper tail of the sampling distribution. The general form of an upper-tail test about a population mean for the small-sample case when σ is unknown is the same as in the large-sample case. With μ_0

FIGURE 9.9   VALUE OF THE TEST STATISTIC ($t = 2.14$) FOR THE HEATHROW AIRPORT
HYPOTHESIS TEST IS IN REJECTION REGION

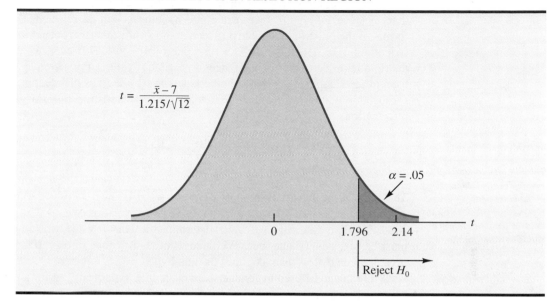

$$t = \frac{\bar{x} - 7}{1.215/\sqrt{12}}$$

$\alpha = .05$

0   1.796   2.14 t

Reject H_0

denoting the stated value for the population mean, we would state the null and alternative
hypotheses as follows:

$$H_0: \mu \leq \mu_0$$
$$H_a: \mu > \mu_0$$

The test statistic is

$$t = \frac{\bar{x} - \mu_0}{s/\sqrt{n}}$$

and the rejection rule at a level of significance α is

$$\text{Reject } H_0 \text{ if } t > t_\alpha$$

A second form of the one-tailed test for the small-sample case rejects the null hypothesis
when the test statistic is in the lower tail of the sampling distribution. In this case, the general form of the test is as follows:

$$H_0: \mu \geq \mu_0$$
$$H_a: \mu < \mu_0$$

The test statistic for the upper-tail case is the same as for the lower-tail case, given by equation (9.8). The only change is that the rejection rule now becomes

$$\text{Reject } H_0 \text{ if } t < -t_\alpha$$

The p-value can also be used to make the reject/do not reject decision in the small-sample case.

p-Values and the t Distribution

Let us consider the p-value for the Heathrow Airport hypothesis test. If the p-value is less than the level of significance α, the null hypothesis can be rejected. Unfortunately, the format of the t distribution table provided in most statistics textbooks does not contain sufficient detail to determine the exact p-value for the test. However, we can still use the t distribution table to narrow the range of possible p-values. For example, the t distribution used in the Heathrow Airport hypothesis test has 11 degrees of freedom. Referring to the t distribution table, we see that the row for 11 degrees of freedom provides the following information.

Area in Upper Tail	.10	.05	.025	.01	.005
t Value	1.363	1.796	2.201	2.718	3.106

The p-values are difficult to obtain directly from a table of the t distribution. Generally, the best that can be done with the table is to specify a range for the p-value such as between .05 and .025.

The computed value for the test statistic was $t = 2.14$. The p-value is the area in the tail corresponding to $t = 2.14$. From t distribution table information, we see 2.14 is between 1.796 and 2.201. Thus, although we cannot determine the exact p-value, we know that the p-value must be between .05 and .025. With a level of significance of $\alpha = .05$, we know that the p-value must be less than .05; thus, the null hypothesis is rejected.

Minitab can be used to conduct a small-sample hypothesis test for a population mean. The Minitab output for the Heathrow Airport hypothesis test is shown in Figure 9.10. The sample mean $\bar{x} = 7.75$, the test statistic $t = 2.14$, and the p-value = .028 are computed automatically. The step-by-step procedure used to obtain the Minitab output is described in Appendix 9.1.

Two-Tailed Test

As an example of a two-tailed hypothesis test about a population mean using a small sample, consider the following production problem. A production process is designed to fill containers with a mean filling weight of $\mu = 16$ ounces. It is undesirable for the process to underfill containers because the consumer will not receive the amount of product indicated on the container label. It is equally undesirable for the process to overfill containers; in that case, the firm loses money because the process places more product in the container than required. Quality assurance personnel periodically select a simple random sample of eight containers in order to conduct the following two-tailed hypothesis test.

$$H_0: \mu = 16$$
$$H_a: \mu \neq 16$$

If H_0 is rejected the production manager will request that the production process be stopped and that the mechanism for regulating filling weights be readjusted to ensure a mean filling

FIGURE 9.10   MINITAB OUTPUT FOR THE HEATHROW AIRPORT RATING HYPOTHESIS TEST

```
Test of mu = 7.000 vs mu > 7.000

Variable    N    Mean    StDev    SE Mean    T       P
Rating      12   7.750   1.215    0.351      2.14    0.028
```

weight of 16 ounces. Suppose a sample yields data of 16.02, 16.22, 15.82, 15.92, 16.22, 16.32, 16.12, and 15.92 ounces. We assume that the population of filling weights is approximately normally distributed and will use a level of significance of .05. What action should be taken?

The data have not been summarized, therefore we must first compute the sample mean and sample standard deviation. Doing so provides the following results.

$$\bar{x} = \frac{\Sigma x_i}{n} = \frac{128.56}{8} = 16.07 \text{ ounces}$$

and

$$s = \sqrt{\frac{\Sigma(x_i - \bar{x})^2}{n - 1}} = \sqrt{\frac{.22}{7}} = .177 \text{ ounces}$$

With a two-tailed test and a level of significance of $\alpha = .05$, $-t_{.025}$ and $t_{.025}$ are the critical values for the test. Using the table for the t distribution, we find that with $n - 1 = 8 - 1 = 7$ degrees of freedom, $-t_{.025} = -2.365$ and $t_{.025} = +2.365$. Thus, the rejection rule is

Reject H_0 if $t < -2.365$ or if $t > 2.365$

Using $\bar{x} = 16.07$ and $s = .177$, we have

$$t = \frac{\bar{x} - \mu_0}{s/\sqrt{n}} = \frac{16.07 - 16.00}{.177/\sqrt{8}} = 1.12$$

Because $t = 1.12$ is not in the rejection region, the null hypothesis cannot be rejected. The evidence is not sufficient to stop and adjust the production process.

Using the t distribution table and the row for seven degrees of freedom, we see that the computed t value of 1.12 has an upper-tail area of *more than* .10. Although the format of the t distribution table prevents us from being more specific, we can at least conclude that the two-tailed p-value is greater than $2(.10) = .20$. Because this value is greater than the .05 level of significance, we see that the p-value leads to the same conclusion; that is, do not reject H_0. The computer solution for this hypothesis test shows an exact p-value of .301.

EXERCISES

Methods

33. Consider the following hypothesis test.

$$H_0: \mu \leq 10$$
$$H_a: \mu > 10$$

A sample of 16 items provides a sample mean of 11 and sample standard deviation of 3.
a. With $\alpha = .05$, what is the rejection rule?
b. Compute the value of the test statistic t. What is your conclusion?

SELFtest   **34.** Consider the following hypothesis test.

$$H_0: \mu = 20$$
$$H_a: \mu \neq 20$$

Data from a sample of six items are: 18, 20, 16, 19, 17, 18.
a. Compute the sample mean.
b. Compute the sample standard deviation.
c. With $\alpha = .05$, what is the rejection rule?
d. Compute the value of the test statistic t.
e. What is your conclusion?

35. Consider the following hypothesis test.

$$H_0: \mu \geq 15$$
$$H_a: \mu < 15$$

A sample size of 22 provided the sample standard deviation $s = 8$. Use $\alpha = .05$. Compute the value of the test statistic t and your conclusion for each of the following sample results.
a. $\bar{x} = 13.0$
b. $\bar{x} = 11.5$
c. $\bar{x} = 15.0$
d. $\bar{x} = 19.0$

36. Consider the following hypothesis test.

$$H_0: \mu \leq 50$$
$$H_a: \mu > 50$$

Assume a sample size of 16 provided the following test statistics. Approximate the p-values in each case. What are your conclusions based on $\alpha = .05$?
a. $t = 2.602$
b. $t = 1.341$
c. $t = 1.960$
d. $t = 1.055$
e. $t = 3.261$

Applications

37. The population mean earnings per share for financial services corporations including American Express, E*Trade Group, Goldman Sachs, and Merrill Lynch was $3 (*Business Week*, August 14, 2000). In 2001, a sample of 10 financial services corporations provided the following earnings per share data:

| 1.92 | 2.16 | 3.63 | 3.16 | 4.02 | 3.14 | 2.20 | 2.34 | 3.05 | 2.38 |

a. Formulate the null and alternative hypotheses that can be used to determine whether the population mean earnings per share in 2001 differ from $3 reported in 2000.
b. Using $\alpha = .05$, what are the critical values for the test statistic, and what is the rejection rule?
c. Compute the sample mean.
d. Compute the sample standard deviation.
e. Compute the value of the test statistic.
f. What is your conclusion?
g. Approximate the p-value.

38. The average U.S. household spends $90 per day (*American Demographics,* August 1997). Assume a sample of 25 households in Corning, New York, showed a sample mean daily expenditure of $84.50 with a sample standard deviation of $14.50. Test $H_0: \mu = 90$ and $H_a: \mu \neq 90$ for the population of households in Corning. Use $\alpha = .05$.
    a. What are the critical values of the test statistic, and what is the rejection rule?
    b. Compute the value of the test statistic.
    c. What is your conclusion?
    d. Approximate the p-value.

39. On average, a housewife with a husband and two children works an estimated 55 hours or less per week on household-related activities. The hours worked during a week for a sample of eight housewives in a particular neighborhood are: 58, 52, 64, 63, 59, 62, 62, and 55. Test $H_0: \mu \leq 55$ and $H_a: \mu > 55$ for the population of housewives in that neighborhood with $\alpha = .05$.
    a. What is the critical value for the test, and what is the rejection rule?
    b. Compute the sample mean.
    c. Compute the sample standard deviation.
    d. Compute the value of the test statistic.
    e. What is your conclusion?
    f. Approximate the p-value.

40. The cost of a one-carat VS2 clarity, H color diamond from the Diamond Source USA is $4000 (*www.diasource.com,* July 2000). A midwestern jeweler makes calls to contacts in the diamond district of New York City to see whether the mean price of similar diamonds differs from $4000. The jeweler will collect cost data from 14 New York City contacts.
    a. Formulate the null and alternative hypotheses that can be used to determine whether the mean price in New York City differs from $4000.
    b. Using $\alpha = .05$, what are the critical values for the test, and what is the rejection rule?
    c. Assume the sample of 14 New York City contacts provides a sample mean price of $4120 and a sample standard deviation of $275. Compute the value of the test statistic.
    d. What is your conclusion?
    e. Approximate the p-value.

41. Callaway Golf Company's new forged titanium ERC driver has been described as "illegal" because it promises driving distances that exceed the USGA's standard. *Golf Digest* compared actual driving distances with the ERC driver and a USGA approved driver with a population mean driving distance of 280 yards. Using nine test drives, the mean driving distance by the ERC driver was 286.9 yards (*Golf Digest,* May 12, 2000). Answer the following questions assuming a sample standard deviation driving distance of 10 yards.
    a. Formulate the null and alternative hypotheses that can be used to determine whether the new ERC driver has a population mean driving distance greater than 280 yards.
    b. On average, how many yards farther did the golf ball travel with the ERC driver?
    c. Using $\alpha = .05$, what is the critical value for the test statistic, and what is the rejection rule?
    d. Compute the value of the test statistic.
    e. What is your conclusion?
    f. Approximate the p-value.

42. Joan's Nursery specializes in custom-designed landscaping for residential areas. The estimated labor cost associated with a particular landscaping proposal is based on the number of plantings of trees, shrubs, and so on to be used for the project. For cost-estimating purposes, managers use two hours of labor time for the planting of a medium-size tree. Actual times from a sample of 10 plantings during the past month follow (times in hours).

| 1.9 | 1.7 | 2.8 | 2.4 | 2.6 | 2.5 | 2.8 | 3.2 | 1.6 | 2.5 |

Using a .05 level of significance, test to see whether the mean tree-planting time exceeds two hours.

a. State the null and alternative hypotheses.
b. What is the critical value for the test, and what is the rejection rule?
c. Compute the sample mean.
d. Compute the sample standard deviation.
e. Compute the value of the test statistic.
f. What is your conclusion?
g. Approximate the p-value.

9.6   TESTS ABOUT A POPULATION PROPORTION

With the symbol p denoting the population proportion and p_0 denoting a particular hypothesized value for the population proportion, the three forms for a hypothesis test about a population proportion are as follows.

$$H_0: p \geq p_0 \qquad H_0: p \leq p_0 \qquad H_0: p = p_0$$
$$H_a: p < p_0 \qquad H_a: p > p_0 \qquad H_a: p \neq p_0$$

The first two forms are one-tailed tests, whereas the third form is a two-tailed test. The specific form used depends on the application.

Hypothesis tests about a population proportion are based on the difference between the sample proportion $\bar{p}$ and the hypothesized population proportion p_0. The methods used to conduct the tests are similar to the procedures used for hypothesis tests about a population mean. The only difference is that we use the sample proportion $\bar{p}$ and its standard error $\sigma_{\bar{p}}$ in developing the test statistic. We begin by formulating null and alternative hypotheses about the value of the population proportion. Then, using the value of the sample proportion $\bar{p}$ and its standard error $\sigma_{\bar{p}}$, we compute a value for the test statistic z. Comparing the value of the test statistic to the critical value or comparing the p-value to α enables us to determine whether the null hypothesis should be rejected.

Let us illustrate hypothesis testing for a population proportion by considering the situation faced by Pine Creek golf course. Over the past few months, 20% of the players at Pine Creek have been women. In an effort to increase the proportion of women playing, Pine Creek used a special promotion to attract women golfers. After one week, a random sample of 400 players showed 300 men and 100 women. Course managers would like to determine whether the data support the conclusion that the proportion of women playing at Pine Creek has increased.

To determine whether the promotion increased the proportion of women golfers, we state the following null and alternative hypotheses.

$$H_0: p \leq .20$$
$$H_a: p > .20$$

As usual, we begin the hypothesis testing procedure by assuming that H_0 is true with $p = .20$. Using the sample proportion $\bar{p}$ to estimate p, we next consider the sampling distribution of $\bar{p}$. Because $\bar{p}$ is an unbiased estimator of p, we know that if $p = .20$, the mean of the sampling distribution of $\bar{p}$ is .20. In addition, we know from Chapter 7 that the standard error of $\bar{p}$ is given by

$$\sigma_{\bar{p}} = \sqrt{\frac{p(1-p)}{n}}$$

With the assumed value of $p = .20$ and a sample size of $n = 400$, the standard error of $\bar{p}$ is

$$\sigma_{\bar{p}} = \sqrt{\frac{.20(1 - .20)}{400}} = .02$$

In Chapter 7 we saw that the sampling distribution of $\bar{p}$ can be approximated by a normal probability distribution if both np and $n(1 - p)$ are greater than or equal to 5. In the Pine Creek case, $np = 400(.20) = 80$ and $n(1 - p) = 400(.80) = 320$; thus, the normal probability distribution approximation is appropriate. Figure 9.11 shows the sampling distribution of $\bar{p}$.

Because the sampling distribution of $\bar{p}$ is approximately normal, the following test statistic can be used.

In hypothesis testing, a value of the population proportion, p_0, is assumed in H_0. Therefore, when H_0 is true, $\sigma_{\bar{p}}$ can be computed by using p_0 as shown in (9.10). The sample proportion, p, is not used in the computation of $\sigma_{\bar{p}}$.

Test Statistic for Tests About a Population Proportion

$$z = \frac{\bar{p} - p_0}{\sigma_{\bar{p}}} \tag{9.9}$$

where

$$\sigma_{\bar{p}} = \sqrt{\frac{p_0(1 - p_0)}{n}} \tag{9.10}$$

Suppose that $\alpha = .05$ is selected as the level of significance for the test. With the critical value $z_{.05} = 1.645$, the upper-tail rejection region for the hypothesis test (see Figure 9.12) provides the following rejection rule.

Reject H_0 if $z > 1.645$

FIGURE 9.11   SAMPLING DISTRIBUTION OF $\bar{p}$ FOR THE PROPORTION OF WOMEN GOLFERS AT PINE CREEK GOLF COURSE

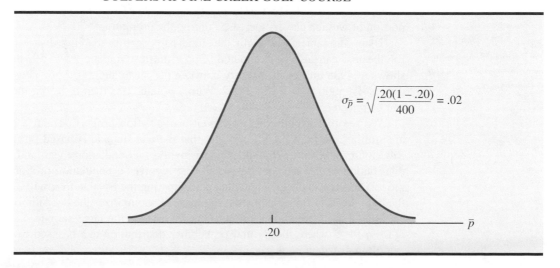

$$\sigma_{\bar{p}} = \sqrt{\frac{.20(1 - .20)}{400}} = .02$$

.20

$\bar{p}$

FIGURE 9.12   REJECTION REGION FOR THE PINE CREEK GOLF COURSE
HYPOTHESIS TEST

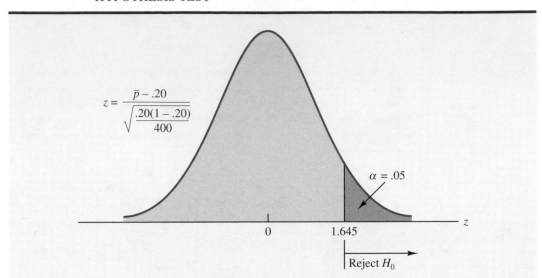

$$z = \frac{\bar{p} - .20}{\sqrt{\frac{.20(1 - .20)}{400}}}$$

$\alpha = .05$

0   1.645 z

Reject H_0

Once the rejection rule is determined, we collect the data, compute the value of the point estimator $\bar{p}$, and compute the corresponding value of the test statistic z. By comparing the value of z to the critical value ($z_{.05} = 1.645$), we can decide whether to reject the null hypothesis.

The random sample of 400 players taken during the promotion showed 100 players were women. Thus, $\bar{p} = 100/400 = .25$. With $\sigma_{\bar{p}} = .02$, the value of the test statistic is

$$z = \frac{\bar{p} - p_0}{\sigma_{\bar{p}}} = \frac{.25 - .20}{.02} = 2.5$$

Because $z = 2.5 > 1.645$, we can reject H_0. The Pine Creek managers can conclude the proportion of women players increased during the promotion.

Either the test statistic or the p-value can be used to draw the hypothesis testing conclusion.

Using the table of areas for the standard normal probability distribution, the p-value for the test can also be computed. Given the test statistic $z = 2.50$, the table of areas shows a .4938 area or probability between the mean and $z = 2.50$. Thus, the p-value for the test is $.5000 - .4938 = .0062$. With a p-value less than $\alpha = .05$, the null hypothesis can be rejected.

We see that hypothesis tests about a population proportion and a population mean are similar; the primary difference is that the test statistic is based on the sampling distribution of $\bar{x}$ when the hypothesis test involves a population mean and on the sampling distribution of $\bar{p}$ when the hypothesis test involves a population proportion. Comparing the test statistic to the critical value or comparing the p-value to α will enable us to reach the hypothesis testing conclusion. Figure 9.13 summarizes the decision rules for hypothesis tests about a population proportion. We assume the large-sample case of $np \geq 5$ and $n(1 - p) \geq 5$ where the normal probability distribution can be used to approximate the sampling distribution of $\bar{p}$.

FIGURE 9.13   SUMMARY OF REJECTION RULES FOR HYPOTHESIS TESTS ABOUT
A POPULATION PROPORTION

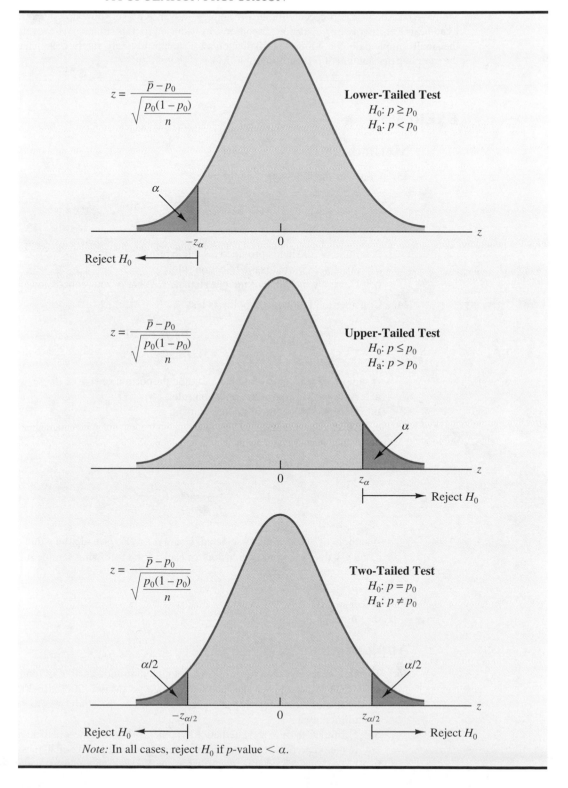

NOTES AND COMMENTS

We have not shown the procedure for small-sample hypothesis tests involving population proportions. In the small-sample case, the normal approximation of the sampling distribution of $\bar{p}$ is not applicable. More advanced texts show how hypothesis tests are conducted for this situation. However, in practice, small-sample tests are rarely conducted for a population proportion.

EXERCISES

Methods

43. Consider the following hypothesis test.

$$H_0: p \leq .50$$
$$H_a: p > .50$$

A sample of 200 items provided a sample proportion $\bar{p} = .57$.
a. At $\alpha = .05$, what is the rejection rule?
b. Compute the value of the test statistic z. What is your conclusion?

SELFtest **44.** Consider the following hypothesis test.

$$H_0: p = .20$$
$$H_a: p \neq .20$$

A sample of 400 items provided a sample proportion of $\bar{p} = .175$.
a. At $\alpha = .05$, what is the rejection rule?
b. Compute the value of the test statistic z.
c. What is the p-value?
d. What is your conclusion?

45. Consider the following hypothesis test.

$$H_0: p \geq .75$$
$$H_a: p < .75$$

A sample of 300 items was selected. Using $\alpha = .05$, provide the value of the test statistic z, the p-value, and your conclusion for each of the following sample results.
a. $\bar{p} = .68$
b. $\bar{p} = .72$
c. $\bar{p} = .70$
d. $\bar{p} = .77$

Applications

46. The Heldrich Center for Workforce Development found that 40% of Internet users received more than 10 e-mail messages per day (*USA Today,* May 7, 2000). In 2001, a similar study on the use of e-mail was repeated. The purpose of the study was to see whether use of e-mail increased.
a. Formulate the null and alternative hypotheses to determine whether an increase occurred in the proportion of Internet users receiving more than 10 e-mail messages per day.
b. Using $\alpha = .05$, what is the critical value for the test, and what is the rejection rule?

c. If a sample of 420 Internet users found 188 receiving more than 10 e-mail messages per day, what is the sample proportion and what is the value of the test statistic?

d. What is your conclusion?

SELFtest

47. A study by *Consumer Reports* showed that 64% of supermarket shoppers believed supermarket brands to be as good as national name brands in terms of product quality. To investigate whether this result applies to its own product, the manufacturer of a national name-brand ketchup product asked 100 supermarket shoppers whether they believed the supermarket brand of ketchup was as good as the national name-brand ketchup. Use the fact that 52 of the shoppers in the sample indicated that the supermarket brand was as good as the national name brand to test $H_0: p \geq .64$ and $H_a: p < .64$. Use a .05 level of significance.

a. What is the critical value, and what is the rejection rule?

b. Compute the value of the test statistic.

c. What is your conclusion?

d. What is the *p*-value?

48. Burger King sponsored what it believed to be the biggest product giveaway in fast-food history when it initiated "FreeFryDay" on Friday, January 2, 1998. Anyone who stopped at one of Burger King's 7400 restaurants received a small order of the new Burger King fries free of charge. A national taste test comparing the new Burger King fries to McDonald's fries was the basis for the Burger King promotion. Of the 500 customers who participated in the taste test, 285 expressed a taste preference for the Burger King fries (*USA Today,* December 10, 1997). Let p = the population proportion who favors the Burger King fries. Consider the hypothesis following test:

$$H_0: p \leq .50$$
$$H_a: p > .50$$

a. What is the point estimate of the population proportion that favors the Burger King fries?

b. Compute the value of the test statistic.

c. What is the *p*-value?

d. Using $\alpha = .01$, what is your conclusion?

e. Do you believe that the national taste test statistics helped Burger King's management decide to implement the "FreeFryDay" campaign? Discuss.

49. A study of driving practices in Strathcona County, Alberta, Canada, found that 48% of drivers did not stop at stop sign intersections on county roads (*Edmonton Journal,* July 19, 2000). Assume that a follow-up study two months later found that 360 of 800 drivers did not stop at stop sign intersections on county roads.

a. Formulate the null and alternative hypotheses assuming the purpose of the follow-up study is to see whether the proportion of drivers who did not stop is $p_0 = .48$.

b. Using $\alpha = .05$, what are the critical values for the test, and what is the rejection rule?

c. What is the sample proportion of drivers who do not stop?

d. Compute the value of the test statistic.

e. What is your conclusion?

50. Shell Oil office workers were asked which work schedule appealed most: working five 8-hour days or four 10-hour days (*USA Today,* September 11, 2000). Let p equal the proportion of office workers preferring the four 10-hour day alternative. Test the hypotheses $H_0: p = .50$ and $H_a: p \neq .50$ at $\alpha = .01$. A sample of 105 office workers showed that 67 workers preferred the four 10-hour day schedule.

a. What is the sample proportion preferring the four 10-hour day schedule?

b. What is the value of the test statistic?

c. What is the *p*-value?

d. What is your conclusion? Is a statistically significant preference indicated between the two alternatives?

51. Drugstore.com was the first e-commerce company to offer Internet drugstore retailing. Drugstore.com customers were provided the opportunity to buy health, beauty, personal care, wellness, and pharmaceutical replenishment products over the Internet. At the end of 10 months of operation, the company reported that 44% of orders were from repeat customers (*Drugstore.com Annual Report,* January 2, 2000). Assume that Drugstore.com will use a sample of customer orders each quarter to determine whether the proportion of orders from repeat customers has changed from the initial $p = .44$.
    a. Formulate the null and alternative hypotheses.
    b. During the first quarter a sample of 500 orders showed 205 repeat customers. What is the *p*-value? What is your conclusion using $\alpha = .05$?
    c. During the second quarter a sample of 500 orders showed 245 repeat customers. What is the *p*-value? What is your conclusion using $\alpha = .05$?

52. Microsoft Outlook is believed to be the most widely used e-mail manager. A Microsoft executive claims that Microsoft Outlook is used by at least 75% of the Internet users. A Merrill Lynch study reported 72% use Microsoft Outlook (CNBC, June 2000). Use the Merrill Lynch study to test the following hypotheses: $H_0: p \geq .75$, $H_a: p < .75$ at $\alpha = .05$.
    a. Assuming the Merrill Lynch sample size was 300 users, compute the value of the test statistic.
    b. What is the *p*-value?
    c. Should the executive's claim of at least 75% be rejected?

53. A fast-food restaurant plans a special offer that will enable customers to purchase specially designed drink glasses featuring well-known cartoon characters. If more than 15% of the customers can be expected to purchase the glasses, the special offer will be implemented. In a preliminary test set up at several locations, 88 of 500 customers purchased the glasses. Should the special glass offer be implemented? Conduct a hypothesis test that will support your decision. Use a .01 level of significance. What is your recommendation?

54. Based on rates of errors, third base is the most difficult position to play in professional baseball. Considering all third basemen, an error occurs on 4.7% of the chances (*ESPN the Magazine,* July 12, 1999). A sample of games played by all-star third baseman Brooks Robinson showed that he had 35 errors in 1182 fielding chances. Does the sample support the conclusion that Brooks Robinson makes fewer errors than the typical third baseman? Use $\alpha = .01$.
    a. What are the appropriate null and alternative hypotheses?
    b. What is the sample proportion error rate for Brooks Robinson?
    c. Compute the value of the test statistic.
    d. What is the *p*-value?
    e. What is your conclusion?

55. At least 20% of all workers are believed to be willing to work fewer hours for less pay to obtain more time for personal and leisure activities. A *USA Today*/CNN/Gallup poll with a sample of 596 respondents found 83 willing to work fewer hours for less pay to obtain more personal and leisure time (*USA Today,* April 10, 1995). Using the poll results, test H_0: $p \geq .20$ and $H_a: p < .20$ using a .05 level of significance. What is your conclusion?

SUMMARY

Hypothesis testing is a statistical procedure that uses sample data to determine whether a statement about the value of a population parameter should or should not be rejected. The hypotheses, which come from a variety of sources, must be two competing statements: a null hypothesis, H_0, and an alternative hypothesis, H_a. In some applications it is not obvious how the null and alternative hypotheses should be formulated. In Section 9.1, we suggested guidelines for developing hypotheses in the three types of situations most frequently encountered.

Figure 9.14 summarizes the test statistics used in hypothesis tests about a population mean and provides a practical guide for selecting the hypothesis testing procedure. The figure shows that the test statistic depends on whether the sample size is large, whether the population standard deviation is assumed known, and in some cases whether the population has a normal or approximately normal probability distribution. If the sample size is large ($n \geq 30$), the z test statistic is used to conduct the hypothesis test. If the sample size is small ($n < 30$), the population must have a normal or approximately normal distribution to conduct a hypothesis test about the value of μ. The z test statistic is used if σ is assumed known, whereas the t test statistic is used if σ is estimated by the sample standard deviation s. Finally, note that if the sample size is small and the assumption of a normally distributed population is inappropriate, we recommend increasing the sample size to $n \geq 30$.

FIGURE 9.14 SUMMARY OF THE TEST STATISTICS TO BE USED IN A HYPOTHESIS TEST ABOUT A POPULATION MEAN

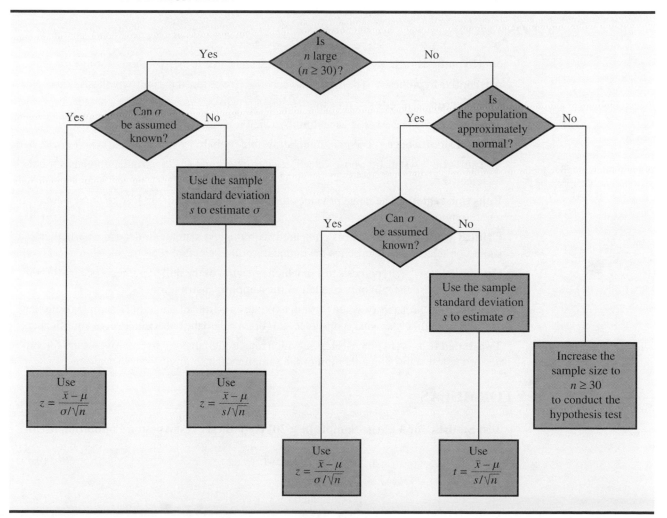

Hypothesis tests about a population proportion were developed for the large-sample case, where both $np \geq 5$ and $n(1 - p) \geq 5$. The test statistic used is

$$z = \frac{\bar{p} - p_0}{\sqrt{\dfrac{p_0(1 - p_0)}{n}}}$$

We did not consider the small-sample case for proportions because, in practice, hypothesis tests for proportions almost always involve large samples.

The rejection rule for hypothesis testing procedures involves comparing the value of the test statistic with a critical value. For lower-tail tests, the null hypothesis is rejected if the value of the test statistic is less than the critical value. For upper-tail tests, the null hypothesis is rejected if the test statistic is greater than the critical value. For two-tailed tests, the null hypothesis is rejected for values of the test statistic in either tail of the sampling distribution.

We also saw that p-values could be used for hypothesis testing. The p-value is the probability, when the null hypothesis is true, of obtaining a sample result that is at least as unlikely as what is observed. When p-values are used to conduct a hypothesis test, the rejection rule calls for rejecting the null hypothesis whenever the p-value is less than α.

GLOSSARY

Null hypothesis   The hypothesis tentatively assumed true in the hypothesis testing procedure.

Alternative hypothesis   The hypothesis concluded to be true if the null hypothesis is rejected.

Type I error   The error of rejecting H_0 when it is true.

Type II error   The error of accepting H_0 when it is false.

Level of significance   The maximum allowable probability of making a Type I error.

Test statistic   A statistic whose value is used to determine whether a null hypothesis should be rejected.

Rejection region   The range of values for the test statistic that will lead to the rejection of a null hypothesis.

Critical value   A value that is compared with the test statistic to determine whether H_0 should be rejected. It determines the boundary of the rejection region.

One-tailed test   A hypothesis test in which rejection of the null hypothesis occurs for values of the test statistic in only one tail of the sampling distribution.

p-value   The probability, when the null hypothesis is true, of obtaining a sample result that is at least as unlikely as what is observed. It is often called the observed level of significance.

Two-tailed test   A hypothesis test in which rejection of the null hypothesis occurs for values of the test statistic in either tail of the sampling distribution.

KEY FORMULAS

Test Statistic for a Large-Sample ($n \geq 30$) Hypothesis Test About a Population Mean

σ assumed known $\qquad z = \dfrac{\bar{x} - \mu_0}{\sigma/\sqrt{n}}$ $\qquad\qquad$ (9.1)

σ estimated by s $\qquad z = \dfrac{\bar{x} - \mu_0}{s/\sqrt{n}}$ $\qquad\qquad$ (9.2)

Test Statistic for a Small-Sample ($n < 30$) Hypothesis Test About a Population Mean

$$\sigma \text{ assumed known} \qquad z = \frac{\bar{x} - \mu_0}{\sigma/\sqrt{n}} \qquad\qquad (9.7)$$

$$\sigma \text{ estimated by } s \qquad t = \frac{\bar{x} - \mu_0}{s/\sqrt{n}} \qquad\qquad (9.8)$$

Test Statistic for Hypothesis Test About a Population Proportion

$$z = \frac{\bar{p} - p_0}{\sigma_{\bar{p}}} \qquad\qquad (9.9)$$

where

$$\sigma_{\bar{p}} = \sqrt{\frac{p_0(1 - p_0)}{n}} \qquad\qquad (9.10)$$

SUPPLEMENTARY EXERCISES

56. The population mean annual salary for public school teachers in the state of New York is $45,250. A sample mean annual salary of public school teachers in New York City is $47,000 (*Time*, April 3, 2000). Assume the New York City results are based on a sample of 95 teachers and the sample standard deviation was $6300.
    a. Formulate the null and alternative hypotheses that can be used to determine whether the sample data support the conclusion that public school teachers in New York City have a higher mean salary than the public school teachers in the state of New York.
    b. What is the value of the test statistic?
    c. What is the *p*-value?
    d. Using $\alpha = .01$, what is your conclusion?

57. The Buick Le Sabre is listed as having a highway fuel efficiency rating of 30 miles per gallon (U.S. Department of Energy, *Model Year 2001, Fuel Economy Guide*). A consumer interest group conducts automobile mileage tests seeking statistical evidence to show that automobile manufacturers overstate the miles-per-gallon ratings for particular models. In the case of the Buick Le Sabre, hypotheses for the test would be stated H_0: $\mu \geq 30$ and H_a: $\mu < 30$. In a sample of 50 mileage tests with the Buick Le Sabre, suppose the consumer interest group finds a sample mean highway mileage rating of 29.5 miles per gallon and a sample standard deviation of 1.8 miles per gallon. What conclusion should be drawn from the sample results? Use a .01 level of significance.

58. The chamber of commerce of a Florida Gulf Coast community advertises that area residential property is available at a mean cost of $25,000 or less per lot. Suppose a sample of 32 properties provided a sample mean of $26,000 per lot and a sample standard deviation of $2500. Using a .05 level of significance, test the validity of the chamber's claim. What is the *p*-value?

59. A bath soap manufacturing process is designed to produce a mean of 120 bars of soap per batch. Quantities over or under the standard are undesirable. A sample of 10 batches shows the following numbers of bars of soap. The population is assumed to be normal.

108	118	120	122	119	113	124	122	120	123

Using a .05 level of significance, test to see whether the sample results indicate that the manufacturing process is functioning properly.

60. The monthly rent for a two-bedroom apartment in a particular city is reported to average $550. Suppose we want to test H_0: $\mu = 550$ versus H_a: $\mu \neq 550$. A sample of 36 two-bedroom apartments is selected. The sample mean turns out to be $\bar{x} = \$562$, with a sample standard deviation of $s = \$40$.
    a. Use the value of the test statistic to draw a conclusion with $\alpha = .05$.
    b. Compute the p-value.
    c. Use the sample results to construct a 95% confidence interval for the population mean. What hypothesis testing conclusion can you draw using the confidence interval?

61. Sixty percent of Americans believe that business profits are distributed unfairly (General Social Surveys, National Opinion Research Center, University of Chicago). Suppose a sample of 40 Midwesterners showed that 27 believe business profits are distributed unfairly.
    a. Do these results justify the inference that a larger proportion of Midwesterners believe that business profits are distributed unfairly? Use $\alpha = .05$.
    b. What is the p-value?

62. An airline promotion to business travelers was based on the assumption that approximately two-thirds of business travelers use a laptop computer on overnight business trips. Sample results from an American Express online line survey found 355 of 546 business travelers use a laptop computer on overnight business trips (*The Cincinnati Enquirer,* August 31, 1998). Conduct a two-tailed hypothesis test using $\alpha = .05$ to test the validity of the assumption made for the airline promotion.
    a. What is the sample proportion?
    b. Compute the value of the test statistic.
    c. What is the p-value?
    d. Can the claim of two-thirds be rejected? Discuss.

63. In 1993 the Immigration and Naturalization service reported that 79% of foreign travelers visiting the United States stated that the primary purpose of their visit was to enjoy a vacation. In a study conducted in 2001, a sample of 500 foreign visitors showed 360 said that their primary reason for visiting the United States was to enjoy a vacation. Was the population proportion of foreign travelers vacationing in the United States in 2001 less than the proportion reported previously? Support your conclusion with a statistical test using a .05 level of significance.

64. The Gallup Organization conducted a survey of 1350 people for the National Occupational Information Coordinating Committee, a panel Congress created to improve the use of job information. A research question related to the study was: Do individuals hold jobs that they planned to hold or do they hold jobs for such reasons as chance or lack of choice? Let p indicate the population proportion of individuals who hold jobs that they planned to hold.
    a. If the hypotheses are stated H_0: $p \geq .50$ and H_a: $p < .50$, discuss the research hypothesis H_a in terms of what the researcher is investigating.
    b. The Gallup poll found that 41% of the respondents hold jobs they planned to hold. What is your conclusion at a .01 level of significance? Discuss.

65. A well-known doctor hypothesized that 75% of women wear shoes that are too small. A study of 356 women by the American Orthopedic Foot and Ankle Society found 313 women wore shoes that were at least one size too small. Test H_0: $p = .75$ and H_a: $p \neq .75$ at $\alpha = .01$. What is your conclusion?

66. The Department of Transportation reported Amtrack trains had a 78% on-time arrival record over the previous 12 months (*USA Today,* November 23, 1998). Assume that in 2001, a study found 330 of 400 Amtrack trains arrived on time. Does the sample indicate the Amtrack arrival rate has changed? Test H_0: $p = .78$ and H_a: $p \neq .78$ at $\alpha = .05$.
    a. What is the sample proportion of Amtrack trains arriving on time?
    b. Compute the value of the test statistic.

    c. What is the p-value?

    d. What is your conclusion?

67. A radio station in Myrtle Beach announced that at least 90% of the hotels and motels would be full for the Memorial Day weekend. The station advised listeners to make reservations in advance if they planned to be in the resort over the weekend. On Saturday night a sample of 58 hotels and motels showed 49 with a no-vacancy sign and nine with vacancies. What is your reaction to the radio station's claim after seeing the sample evidence? Use $\alpha = .05$ in making the statistical test. What is the p-value?

68. Environmental health indicators include air quality, water quality, and food quality. Twenty-five years ago, 47% of U.S. food samples contained pesticide residues (*U.S. News & World Report*, April 17, 2000). In a recent study, 44 of 125 food samples contained pesticide residues.

    a. What is the sample proportion?

    b. Compute the value of the test statistic.

    c. What is the p-value?

    d. Using $\alpha = .01$, what is your conclusion? Did the proportion of foods containing pesticides decline?

Case Problem 1   QUALITY ASSOCIATES, INC.

Quality Associates, Inc., a consulting firm, advises its clients about sampling and statistical procedures that can be used to control their manufacturing processes. In one particular application, a client gave Quality Associates a sample of 800 observations taken during a time in which that client's process was operating satisfactorily. The sample standard deviation for these data was .21; hence, with so much data, the population standard deviation was assumed to be .21. Quality Associates then suggested that random samples of size 30 be taken periodically to monitor the process on an ongoing basis. By analyzing the new samples, the client could quickly learn whether the process was operating satisfactorily. When the process was not operating satisfactorily, corrective action could be taken to eliminate the problem. The design specification indicated the mean for the process should be 12. The hypothesis test suggested by Quality Associates follows.

$$H_0: \mu = 12$$
$$H_a: \mu \neq 12$$

Corrective action will be taken any time H_0 is rejected.

    The following samples were collected at hourly intervals during the first day of operation of the new statistical process control procedure. These data are available in the data set Quality.

Sample 1	Sample 2	Sample 3	Sample 4
11.55	11.62	11.91	12.02
11.62	11.69	11.36	12.02
11.52	11.59	11.75	12.05
11.75	11.82	11.95	12.18
11.90	11.97	12.14	12.11
11.64	11.71	11.72	12.07
11.80	11.87	11.61	12.05

(continued)

Sample 1	Sample 2	Sample 3	Sample 4
12.03	12.10	11.85	11.64
11.94	12.01	12.16	12.39
11.92	11.99	11.91	11.65
12.13	12.20	12.12	12.11
12.09	12.16	11.61	11.90
11.93	12.00	12.21	12.22
12.21	12.28	11.56	11.88
12.32	12.39	11.95	12.03
11.93	12.00	12.01	12.35
11.85	11.92	12.06	12.09
11.76	11.83	11.76	11.77
12.16	12.23	11.82	12.20
11.77	11.84	12.12	11.79
12.00	12.07	11.60	12.30
12.04	12.11	11.95	12.27
11.98	12.05	11.96	12.29
12.30	12.37	12.22	12.47
12.18	12.25	11.75	12.03
11.97	12.04	11.96	12.17
12.17	12.24	11.95	11.94
11.85	11.92	11.89	11.97
12.30	12.37	11.88	12.23
12.15	12.22	11.93	12.25

Managerial Report

1. Conduct a hypothesis test for each sample at the .01 level of significance and determine what action, if any, should be taken. Provide the test statistic and p-value for each test.
2. Compute the standard deviation for each of the four samples. Does the assumption of .21 for the population standard deviation appear reasonable?
3. Compute limits for the sample mean $\bar{x}$ around $\mu = 12$ such that, as long as a new sample mean is within those limits, the process will be considered to be operating satisfactorily. If $\bar{x}$ exceeds the upper limit or if $\bar{x}$ is below the lower limit, corrective action will be taken. These limits are referred to as upper and lower control limits for quality control purposes.
4. Discuss the implications of changing the level of significance to a larger value. What mistake or error could increase if the level of significance is increased?

Case Problem 2   UNEMPLOYMENT STUDY

Each month the U.S. Bureau of Labor Statistics publishes a variety of unemployment statistics, including the number of individuals who are unemployed and the mean length of time the individuals have been unemployed. For November 1998, the Bureau of Labor Statistics reported that the national mean length of time of unemployment was 14.6 weeks.

The mayor of Philadelphia requested a study on the status of unemployment in the Philadelphia area. A sample of 50 unemployed residents of Philadelphia included data on the age and the number of weeks without a job. A portion of the data collected in November 1998 follows. The complete data set is available in the data file BLS.

CDfile
BLS

Age	Weeks	Age	Weeks
56	22	25	5
35	19	40	20
22	7	25	12
57	37	25	1
40	18	59	33
22	11	49	26
48	6	33	13
48	22		

Managerial Report

1. Use descriptive statistics to summarize the data.
2. Develop a 95% confidence interval estimate of the mean age of unemployed individuals in Philadelphia.
3. Conduct a hypothesis test to determine whether the mean duration of unemployment in Philadelphia is greater than the national mean duration of 14.6 weeks. Use a .01 level of significance. What is your conclusion?
4. Is there a relationship between the age of an unemployed individual and the number of weeks of unemployment? Explain.

Appendix 9.1   HYPOTHESIS TESTING WITH MINITAB

In this appendix, we describe how to conduct hypothesis tests about a population mean in both the large- and small-sample cases.

Large-Sample Case

CDfile
Distance

We illustrate the large-sample case by using the data on golf ball distances in Table 9.2. The data are entered into column C1 of a Minitab worksheet. The level of significance for the hypothesis test is $\alpha = .05$ and the population standard deviation σ is estimated by the sample standard deviation s. The following steps can be used to test the hypothesis $H_0: \mu = 280$ versus $H_a: \mu \neq 280$.

Step 1. Select the **Calc** pull-down menu
Step 2. Choose **Column Statistics**
Step 3. When the Column Statistics dialog box appears:
       Select **Standard Deviation**
       Enter C1 in the **Input variable** box
       Enter stdev in the **Store result in** box
       Click **OK**
Step 4. Select the **Stat** pull-down menu
Step 5. Choose **Basic Statistics**
Step 6. Choose **1-Sample Z**
Step 7. When the 1-Sample Z dialog box appears:
       Enter C1 in the **Variables** box
       Enter stdev in the **Sigma** box
       Enter 280 in the **Test mean** box
       Select **Options**

Step 8. Enter 95 in the **Confidence level** box*
          Select **not equal** in the **Alternative** box
          Click **OK**
Step 9. Click **OK**

In addition to the hypothesis testing results shown in Figure 9.8, the Minitab procedure provides a 95% confidence interval for the population mean.

The Superflight golf ball study used the sample standard deviation s to estimate the population standard deviation σ. In a large-sample hypothesis test where σ is assumed known, steps 1 to 3 of the preceding procedure may be skipped. In this case, simply start with step 4 and enter the appropriate value of σ in the **Sigma** box during step 7. Finally, the Superflight golf ball study involved a two-tailed hypothesis test. However, the procedure can be easily modified for a one-tailed hypothesis test by selecting the less than or greater than option in the **Alternative** box in step 8.

Small-Sample Case

Heathrow

The ratings that 12 business travelers gave for Heathrow Airport were listed in Section 9.5. The data are entered in column C1 of a Minitab worksheet. The level of significance for the test is $\alpha = .05$, and the population standard deviation σ will be estimated by the sample standard deviation s. The following steps can be used to test the hypothesis $H_0: \mu \leq 7$ against $H_a: \mu > 7$.

Step 1. Select the **Stat** pull-down menu
Step 2. Choose **Basic Statistics**
Step 3. Choose **1-Sample t**
Step 4. When the 1-Sample t dialog box appears:
          Enter C1 in the **Variables** box
          Enter 7 in the **Test mean** box
          Select **Options**
Step 5. Enter 95 in the **Confidence level** box
          Select **greater than** in the **Alternative** box
          Click **OK**
Step 6. Click **OK**

This procedure uses the sample standard deviation s to estimate the population standard deviation σ. In a small-sample hypothesis test where σ is assumed known, steps 4 through 9 of the large-sample 1-Sample Z procedure can be used with the appropriate value of σ entered in the **Sigma** box during step 7. Finally, the Heathrow Airport rating study involved a greater than hypothesis test. The preceding steps can be easily modified for other hypothesis tests by selecting the less than or not equal option in the **Alternative** box in step 5.

Appendix 9.2   HYPOTHESIS TESTING WITH EXCEL

In this appendix, we develop two worksheets that can be used as templates for hypothesis testing problems involving a population mean. One can be used for hypothesis tests using the standard normal distribution (z); the other can be used for hypothesis tests using the t distribution.

---

*Minitab provides both hypothesis testing and interval estimation results simultaneously. The user may select any confidence level for the interval estimate of the population mean: 95% confidence is suggested here.

Using the Standard Normal Distribution

The worksheet developed here uses the z value from the standard normal distribution as a test statistic. This worksheet can be applied in the following cases:

- Large-sample case with σ assumed known
- Large-sample case with σ estimated by s
- Small-sample case with σ assumed known

We illustrate the use of this worksheet for the hypothesis test involving the distance data for the Superflight golf ball study (Table 9.2). In this large-sample case ($n = 36$), the population standard deviation σ is unknown and will be estimated by the sample standard deviation s.

Refer to Figure 9.15 as we describe the test procedure. The version of the worksheet in the background shows the cell formulas used, and the version of the worksheet in the foreground shows the results of applying those formulas to the Superflight data. The data are entered into cells A2:A37. Cells D4, D5, and D6 use Excel functions to compute the sample size, the sample mean, and the sample standard deviation. The user enters the hypothesized value ($\mu_0 = 280$) into cell D8. The remaining cell formulas provide the standard error, test statistic, and p-values shown in column D of the foreground worksheet. Because it is a two-tailed hypothesis test, the p-value (Two Tail) in cell D15 is used to make the rejection decision. The p-values in cells D13 and D14 are used for one-tailed tests. This worksheet is available in the file *Hypothesis z* on the CD at the back of the book.

CDfile
Hypothesis z

The worksheet in Figure 9.15 can also be used for both large-sample and small-sample cases with σ assumed known. In such applications, the assumed value of σ is typed over the formula for the standard deviation in cell D6. The Excel function is not needed to compute the sample standard deviation.

FIGURE 9.15   EXCEL WORKSHEET FOR HYPOTHESIS TESTS USING THE NORMAL DISTRIBUTION

	A	B	C	D	E	F	G
1	Yards		Hypothesis Test About a Population Mean				
2	269		Using the Standard Normal Distribution (z)				
3	300						
4	268		Sample Size	=COUNT(A2:A37)			
5	278		Mean	=AVERAGE(A2:A37)			
6	282		Standard Deviation	=STDEV(A2:A37)			
7	263						
8	301		Hypothesized Value	280			
9	295						
10	288		Standard Error	=D6/SQRT(D4)			
11	278		Test Statistic	=(D5-D8)/D10			
12	276						
13	286		*p*-value (Lower Tail)	=NORMSDIST(D11)			
14	296		*p*-value (Upper Tail)	=1-NORMSDIST(D11)			
15	265		*p*-value (Two Tail)	=2*MIN(D13,D14)			
16	271						
34	273						
35	291						
36	274						
37	277						
38							

Note: Rows 17–33 are hidden.

	A	B	C	D	E	F	G
1	Yards		Hypothesis Test About a Population Mean				
2	269		Using the Standard Normal Distribution (z)				
3	300						
4	268		Sample Size	36			
5	278		Mean	278.5			
6	282		Standard Deviation	12.0012			
7	263						
8	301		Hypothesized Value	280			
9	295						
10	288		Standard Error	2.0002			
11	278		Test Statistic	-0.7499			
12	276						
13	286		*p*-value (Lower Tail)	0.2266			
14	296		*p*-value (Upper Tail)	0.7734			
15	265		*p*-value (Two Tail)	0.4533			
16	271						
34	273						
35	291						
36	274						
37	277						
38							

Using the *t* Distribution

The worksheet developed here uses the *t* distribution for conducting hypothesis tests about a population mean. It can be applied in the small-sample case with σ estimated by s. We illustrate the use of this worksheet for the hypothesis test involving the Heathrow Airport rating study. The sample size is small ($n = 12$) and the population standard deviation σ will be estimated by the sample standard deviation s.

Refer to Figure 9.16 as we describe the test procedure. The version of the worksheet in the background shows the cell formulas used, and the version of the worksheet in the foreground shows the results of applying those formulas to the airport rating data. The data are entered into cells A2:A13. Cells D4, D5, and D6 use Excel functions to compute the sample size, the sample mean, and the sample standard deviation. The user enters the hypothesized value ($\mu_0 = 7$) into cell D8. The remaining cell formulas provide the standard error, test statistic, degrees of freedom, and *p*-values shown in column D of the foreground worksheet. Because it is an upper-tail hypothesis test, the *p*-value (Upper Tail) in cell D15 is used to make the rejection decision. The *p*-values in cells D14 and D16 are used for lower-tail and two-tailed tests, respectively. This worksheet is available in the file *Hypothesis t* on the CD at the back of the book.

CDfile

Hypothesis t

FIGURE 9.16   EXCEL WORKSHEET FOR HYPOTHESIS TEST USING THE *t* DISTRIBUTION

	A	B	C	D	E
1	Rating		Hypothesis Tests About a Population Mean		
2	7		Using the t Distribution		
3	8				
4	10		Sample Size	=COUNT(A2:A13)	
5	8		Mean	=AVERAGE(A2:A13)	
6	6		Standard Deviation	=STDEV(A2:A13)	
7	9				
8	6		Hypothesized Value	7	
9	7				
10	7		Standard Error	=D6/SQRT(D4)	
11	8		Test Statistic	=(D5-D8)/D10	
12	9		Degrees of Freedom	=D4-1	
13	8				
14			*p*-value (Lower Tail)	=IF(D11<0,TDIST(-D11,D12,1),1-TDIST(D11,D12,1))	
15			*p*-value (Upper Tail)	=1-D14	
16			*p*-value (Two Tail)	=2*MIN(D14,D15)	
17					

	A	B	C	D	E	F
1	Rating		Hypothesis Tests About a Population Mean			
2	7		Using the t Distribution			
3	8					
4	10		Sample Size	12		
5	8		Mean	7.75		
6	6		Standard Deviation	1.2154		
7	9					
8	6		Hypothesized Value	7		
9	7					
10	7		Standard Error	0.3509		
11	8		Test Statistic	2.1376		
12	9		Degrees of Freedom	11		
13	8					
14			*p*-value (Lower Tail)	0.9721		
15			*p*-value (Upper Tail)	0.0279		
16			*p*-value (Two Tail)	0.0558		
17						

COMPARISONS INVOLVING MEANS

Chapter 10

CONTENTS

FISONS CORPORATION

ROCHESTER, NEW YORK

Fisons Corporation, Rochester, New York, is a unit of Fisons Plc., UK. Fisons opened its United States operations in 1966.

Fisons' Pharmaceutical Division uses extensive statistical procedures to test and develop new drugs. The testing process in the pharmaceutical industry usually consists of three stages: (1) preclinical testing, (2) testing for long-term usage and safety, and (3) clinical efficacy testing. At each successive stage, the chance that a drug will pass the rigorous tests decreases; however, the cost of further testing increases dramatically. Industry surveys indicate that on average the research and development for one new drug costs $250 million and takes 12 years. Hence, it is important to eliminate unsuccessful new drugs in the early stages of the testing process, as well as identify promising ones for further testing.

Statistics plays a major role in pharmaceutical research, where government regulations are stringent and rigorously enforced. In preclinical testing, a two- or three-population statistical study typically determines whether a new drug should continue to be studied in the long-term usage and safety program. The populations may consist of the new drug, a control, and a standard drug. The preclinical testing process begins when a new drug is sent to the pharmacology group for evaluation of efficacy—the capacity of the drug to produce the desired effects. As part of the process, a statistician designs an experiment that can be used to test the new drug. The design must specify the sample size and the statistical methods of analysis. In a two-population study, one sample is used to obtain data on the efficacy of the new drug (population 1), and a second sample is used to obtain data on the efficacy of a standard drug (population 2). Depending on the intended use, the new and standard drugs are tested in such disciplines as neurology, cardiology, and immunology. In most studies, the statistical method involves hypothesis testing for the difference

Statistical methods are used to test and develop new drugs. © Mark Richards/PhotoEdit.

between the means of the new drug and the standard drug. If a new drug lacks efficacy or produces undesirable effects in comparison with the standard drug, the new drug is rejected and withdrawn from further testing. Only new drugs that show promising comparisons with the standard drugs are forwarded to the long-term usage and safety testing program.

Further data collection and multipopulation studies are conducted in the long-term usage and safety testing program and in the clinical testing programs. The Food and Drug Administration (FDA) requires that statistical methods be defined prior to such testing to avoid data-related biases. In addition, to avoid human biases, some of the clinical trials are double or triple blind. That is, neither the subject nor the investigator knows what drug is administered to whom. If the new drug meets all requirements in relation to the standard drug, a new drug application (NDA) is filed with the FDA.

In this chapter you will learn how to make statistical inferences about the means of two or more populations. Techniques will be presented for analyzing independent random samples as well as matched samples.

In Chapters 8 and 9 we showed how to develop interval estimates and conduct hypothesis tests for situations involving one population mean. In this chapter we continue our discussion of statistical inference by showing how interval estimates and hypothesis tests can be developed for situations involving two or more populations. For example, we may want to develop an interval estimate of the difference between the mean starting salary for a population of men and the mean starting salary for a population of women or test a hypothesis that the mean number of hours between breakdowns is the same for four machines. We will begin our discussion by showing how an interval estimate of the difference between the means of two populations can be developed for a sampling study conducted by Greystone Department Stores, Inc.

10.1   ESTIMATION OF THE DIFFERENCE BETWEEN THE MEANS OF TWO POPULATIONS: INDEPENDENT SAMPLES

Greystone Department Stores, Inc., operates two stores in Buffalo, New York, one in the inner city and the other in a suburban shopping center. The regional manager noticed that products that sell well in one store do not always sell well in the other. The manager believes this situation may be attributable to differences in customer demographics at the two locations. Customers may differ in age, education, income, and so on. Suppose the manager asked us to investigate the difference between the mean ages of the customers who shop at the two stores.

Let us define population 1 as all customers who shop at the inner-city store and population 2 as all customers who shop at the suburban store.

μ_1 = mean of population 1 (i.e., the mean age of all customers who shop at the inner-city store)

μ_2 = mean of population 2 (i.e., the mean age of all customers who shop at the suburban store)

The difference between the two population means is $\mu_1 - \mu_2$.

To estimate $\mu_1 - \mu_2$, we will select a simple random sample of n_1 customers from population 1 and a simple random sample of n_2 customers from population 2. The simple random sample of n_1 customers selected independently of the simple random sample of n_2 customers gives us **independent simple random samples.**

$\bar{x}_1$ = sample mean age for the simple random sample of n_1 inner-city customers

$\bar{x}_2$ = sample mean age for the simple random sample of n_2 suburban customers

Because $\bar{x}_1$ is a point estimator of μ_1 and $\bar{x}_2$ is a point estimator of μ_2, the point estimator of the difference between the two population means is expressed as follows.

Point Estimator of the Difference Between Two Population Means

$$\bar{x}_1 - \bar{x}_2 \tag{10.1}$$

Thus, we see that the point estimator of the difference between two population means is the difference between the sample means of the two independent simple random samples. Figure 10.1 provides an overview of the process used to estimate the difference between two population means based on two independent simple random samples.

Assume the customer age data collected from the two independent simple random samples of Greystone customers provide the following results.

Store	Number of Customers Sampled	Sample Mean Age	Sample Standard Deviation
Inner City	36	$\bar{x}_1 = 40$ years	$s_1 = 9$ years
Suburban	49	$\bar{x}_2 = 35$ years	$s_2 = 10$ years

Using expression (10.1), we find that a point estimate of the difference between the mean ages of the two populations is $\bar{x}_1 - \bar{x}_2 = 40 - 35 = 5$ years. Thus, we are led to believe that the customers at the inner-city store have a mean age five years greater than the mean age of the suburban store customers. However, as with all point estimates, we know that five years is only one of many possible estimates of the difference between the mean ages of the two populations. If Greystone selected another simple random sample of 36 inner-city customers and another simple random sample of 49 suburban customers, the difference between the two new sample means would probably not equal five years. The sampling distribution of $\bar{x}_1 - \bar{x}_2$ is the probability distribution of the difference in sample means for all possible sets of two independent simple random samples.

FIGURE 10.1   ESTIMATING THE DIFFERENCE BETWEEN THE MEANS
OF TWO POPULATIONS

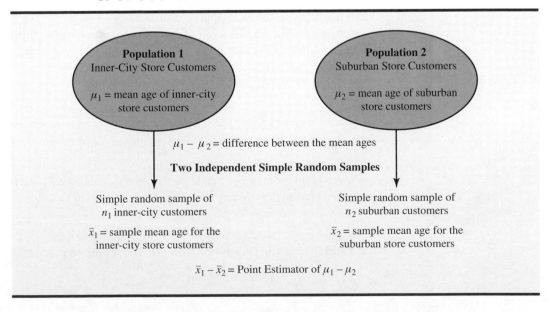

Sampling Distribution of $\bar{x}_1 - \bar{x}_2$

We can use the sampling distribution of $\bar{x}_1 - \bar{x}_2$ to develop an interval estimate of the difference between the two population means in much the same way as we used the sampling distribution of $\bar{x}$ for interval estimation with a single population mean. The sampling distribution of $\bar{x}_1 - \bar{x}_2$ has the following properties.

Sampling Distribution of $\bar{x}_1 - \bar{x}_2$

$$\text{Expected Value:} \quad E(\bar{x}_1 - \bar{x}_2) = \mu_1 - \mu_2 \tag{10.2}$$

$$\text{Standard Deviation:} \quad \sigma_{\bar{x}_1-\bar{x}_2} = \sqrt{\frac{\sigma_1^2}{n_1} + \frac{\sigma_2^2}{n_2}} \tag{10.3}$$

where

σ_1 = standard deviation of population 1
σ_2 = standard deviation of population 2
n_1 = sample size for the simple random sample
from population 1
n_2 = sample size for the simple random sample
from population 2

Distribution form: If the sample sizes are both *large* ($n_1 \geq 30$ and $n_2 \geq 30$), the sampling distribution of $\bar{x}_1 - \bar{x}_2$ can be approximated by a normal probability distribution.

Figure 10.2 shows the sampling distribution of $\bar{x}_1 - \bar{x}_2$ and its relationship to the individual sampling distributions of $\bar{x}_1$ and $\bar{x}_2$.

Let us now develop an interval estimate of the difference between the means of two populations. We consider two cases, one in which the sample sizes are large ($n_1 \geq 30$ and $n_2 \geq 30$) and another in which one or both sample sizes are small ($n_1 < 30$ and/or $n_2 < 30$). We consider the large-sample case first.

Large-Sample Case

In the large-sample case, the sampling distribution of $\bar{x}_1 - \bar{x}_2$ can be approximated by a normal probability distribution. With this approximation we can use the following expression to develop an interval estimate of the difference between the means of the two populations.

Interval Estimate of the Difference Between Two Population Means: Large-Sample Case ($n_1 \geq 30$ and $n_2 \geq 30$) with σ_1 and σ_2 Assumed Known

$$\bar{x}_1 - \bar{x}_2 \pm z_{\alpha/2}\sigma_{\bar{x}_1-\bar{x}_2} \tag{10.4}$$

where $1 - \alpha$ is the confidence coefficient

Note that to use expression (10.4) to develop an interval estimate of the difference between the means of two populations, we must know the value of $\sigma_{\bar{x}_1-\bar{x}_2}$, the standard

FIGURE 10.2 SAMPLING DISTRIBUTION OF $\bar{x}_1 - \bar{x}_2$ AND ITS RELATIONSHIP TO THE INDIVIDUAL SAMPLING DISTRIBUTION OF $\bar{x}_1$ AND $\bar{x}_2$

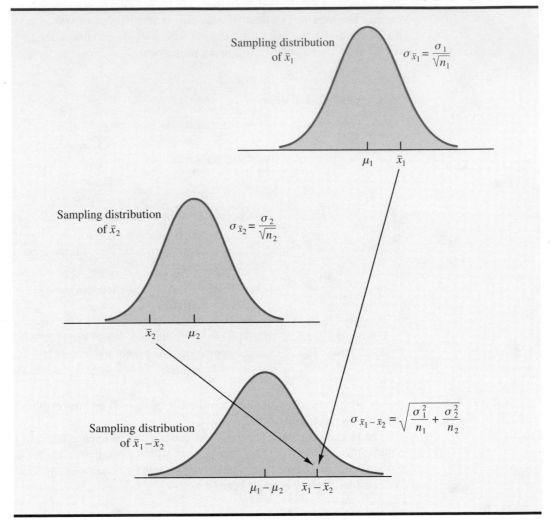

deviation of the sampling distribution of $\bar{x}_1 - \bar{x}_2$. However, equation (10.3) shows that the value of $\sigma_{\bar{x}_1 - \bar{x}_2}$ depends on the values of σ_1 and σ_2, the standard deviations of each of the populations. When the population standard deviations are unknown, we can use the sample standard deviations as estimates of the population standard deviations and estimate $\sigma_{\bar{x}_1 - \bar{x}_2}$ as follows.

Point Estimator of $\sigma_{\bar{x}_1 - \bar{x}_2}$

$$s_{\bar{x}_1 - \bar{x}_2} = \sqrt{\frac{s_1^2}{n_1} + \frac{s_2^2}{n_2}} \tag{10.5}$$

Thus, we can use the point estimator of $\sigma_{\bar{x}_1 - \bar{x}_2}$ to develop the following confidence interval estimate of the difference between the two population means.

Interval Estimate of the Difference Between Two Population Means:
Large-Sample Case ($n_1 \geq 30$ and $n_2 \geq 30$) with σ_1 and σ_2 Estimated by s_1 and s_2

$$\bar{x}_1 - \bar{x}_2 \pm z_{\alpha/2} s_{\bar{x}_1 - \bar{x}_2} \tag{10.6}$$

where $1 - \alpha$ is the confidence coefficient.

Let us use expression (10.6) to develop a confidence interval estimate of the difference between the mean ages of the two customer populations in the Greystone Department Store study. Recall that the sample mean age and sample standard deviation for the simple random sample of 36 inner-city customers are $\bar{x}_1 = 40$ years and $s_1 = 9$ years, respectively; the sample mean and sample standard deviation for the simple random sample of 49 suburban customers are $\bar{x}_2 = 35$ years and $s_2 = 10$ years, respectively. Using equation (10.5) to estimate $\sigma_{\bar{x}_1 - \bar{x}_2}$, we have

$$s_{\bar{x}_1 - \bar{x}_2} = \sqrt{\frac{(9)^2}{36} + \frac{(10)^2}{49}} = 2.07$$

With $z_{\alpha/2} = z_{.025} = 1.96$, expression (10.6) provides the following 95% confidence interval.

$$5 \pm (1.96)(2.07)$$

or

$$5 \pm 4.06$$

Thus, at a 95% level of confidence, the margin of error is 4.06 years and the interval estimate for the difference between the mean ages of the two Greystone populations is .94 years to 9.06 years.

Small-Sample Case

Let us now consider the interval estimation procedure for the difference between the means of two populations whenever one or both sample sizes are less than 30—that is, $n_1 < 30$ and/or $n_2 < 30$, which will be referred to as the small-sample case.

In Chapter 8, we presented the small-sample interval estimation procedures for a population mean. Recall that the small-sample case required the assumption that the population has a normal distribution. If the population standard deviation σ can be assumed known, the standard normal distribution z is used to develop the interval estimate. However, if the population standard deviation σ is estimated by the sample standard deviation s, the t distribution is used to develop the interval estimate.

In developing a small-sample interval estimate of the difference between two population means, we will make the assumption that both populations have a normal distribution.

If the population standard deviations σ_1 and σ_2 are assumed known, the large-sample interval estimation procedure (10.4) can be used for the small-sample case. However, if the population standard deviations σ_1 and σ_2 are estimated by the sample standard deviations s_1 and s_2, the t distribution must be used to develop a small-sample interval estimate of the difference between two population means. The details of this procedure and an example follow. We begin by making the following assumptions:

1. Both populations have normal distributions.
2. The variances of the populations are equal ($\sigma_1^2 = \sigma_2^2 = \sigma^2$).

If the sample sizes are equal, the procedure in this section provides acceptable results even if the population variances are not equal. Thus, whenever possible, a researcher should consider equal sample sizes with $n_1 = n_2$.

Given these assumptions, the sampling distribution of $\bar{x}_1 - \bar{x}_2$ is normally distributed regardless of the sample sizes. The expected value of $\bar{x}_1 - \bar{x}_2$ is $\mu_1 - \mu_2$. Because of the equal variances assumption, equation (10.3) can be written

$$\sigma_{\bar{x}_1 - \bar{x}_2} = \sqrt{\frac{\sigma^2}{n_1} + \frac{\sigma^2}{n_2}} = \sqrt{\sigma^2\left(\frac{1}{n_1} + \frac{1}{n_2}\right)} \tag{10.7}$$

The sampling distribution of $\bar{x}_1 - \bar{x}_2$ is shown in Figure 10.3.

Because equation (10.7) is based on the assumption that $\sigma_1^2 = \sigma_2^2 = \sigma^2$, we do not need separate estimates of σ_1^2 and σ_2^2. In fact, we can combine the data from the two samples to provide the best single estimate of σ^2. The process of combining the results of two independent simple random samples to provide one estimate of σ^2 is referred to as *pooling*. The **pooled variance** estimator of σ^2, denoted by s^2, is a weighted average of the two sample variances s_1^2 and s_2^2. The formula for the pooled estimator of σ^2 follows.

Pooled Estimator of σ^2

$$s^2 = \frac{(n_1 - 1)s_1^2 + (n_2 - 1)s_2^2}{n_1 + n_2 - 2} \tag{10.8}$$

FIGURE 10.3   SAMPLING DISTRIBUTION OF $\bar{x}_1 - \bar{x}_2$ FOR NORMALLY DISTRIBUTED POPULATIONS WITH EQUAL VARIANCES

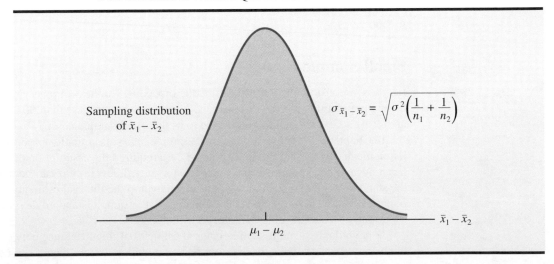

With s^2 as the pooled estimator of σ^2, we can use equation (10.7) to obtain the following estimator of $\sigma_{\bar{x}_1 - \bar{x}_2}$.

Point Estimator of $\sigma_{\bar{x}_1 - \bar{x}_2}$ When $\sigma_1^2 = \sigma_2^2 = \sigma^2$

$$s_{\bar{x}_1 - \bar{x}_2} = \sqrt{s^2 \left(\frac{1}{n_1} + \frac{1}{n_2} \right)} \tag{10.9}$$

The t distribution can now be used to compute an interval estimate of the difference between the means of the two populations. Because $n_1 - 1$ degrees of freedom are associated with the sample from population 1 and $n_2 - 1$ degrees of freedom are associated with the sample from population 2, the t distribution will have $n_1 + n_2 - 2$ degrees of freedom. The interval estimation procedure follows.

Interval Estimate of the Difference Between Two Population Means: Small-Sample Case ($n_1 < 30$ and/or $n_2 < 30$) with σ_1 and σ_2 Estimated by s_1 and s_2

$$\bar{x}_1 - \bar{x}_2 \pm t_{\alpha/2} \, s_{\bar{x}_1 - \bar{x}_2} \tag{10.10}$$

where the t value is based on a t distribution with $n_1 + n_2 - 2$ degrees of freedom and where $1 - \alpha$ is the confidence coefficient.

Let us demonstrate the interval estimation procedure for a sampling study conducted by the Clearview National Bank. Independent random samples of checking account balances for customers at two Clearview branch banks yielded the following results.

Branch Bank	Number of Checking Accounts	Sample Mean Balance	Sample Standard Deviation
Cherry Grove	12	$\bar{x}_1 = \$1000$	$s_1 = \$150$
Beechmont	10	$\bar{x}_2 = \$\ 920$	$s_2 = \$120$

Let us use these data to develop a 90% confidence interval for the difference between the mean checking account balances at the two branch banks. Suppose that checking account balances are normally distributed at both branches and that the variances of checking account balances at the branches are equal. Using equation (10.8), the pooled estimate of the population variance becomes

$$s^2 = \frac{(n_1 - 1)s_1^2 + (n_2 - 1)s_2^2}{n_1 + n_2 - 2} = \frac{(11)(150)^2 + (9)(120)^2}{12 + 10 - 2} = 18{,}855$$

Using equation (10.9), the corresponding estimate of $\sigma_{\bar{x}_1 - \bar{x}_2}$ is

$$s_{\bar{x}_1 - \bar{x}_2} = \sqrt{s^2 \left(\frac{1}{n_1} + \frac{1}{n_2} \right)} = \sqrt{18{,}855 \left(\frac{1}{12} + \frac{1}{10} \right)} = 58.79$$

The appropriate t distribution for the interval estimation procedure has $n_1 + n_2 - 2 = 12 + 10 - 2 = 20$ degrees of freedom. With $\alpha = .10$, $t_{\alpha/2} = t_{.05} = 1.725$. Thus, using expression (10.10), the interval estimate is

$$\bar{x}_1 - \bar{x}_2 \pm t_{.05}\, s_{\bar{x}_1 - \bar{x}_2}$$
$$1000 - 920 \pm (1.725)(58.79)$$
$$80 \pm 101.41$$

At a 90% confidence level, the interval estimate of the difference between the mean account balances at the two branch banks is $-\$21.41$ to $\$181.41$. The fact that the interval includes a negative range of values indicates that the actual difference between the two means, $\mu_1 - \mu_2$, may be negative. Thus, μ_2 could actually be larger than μ_1, indicating that the population mean balance could be greater for the Beechmont branch even though the results show a greater sample mean balance at the Cherry Grove branch. The fact that the confidence interval contains the value 0 can be interpreted as indicating that we do not have sufficient evidence to conclude that the population mean account balances differ between the two branches.

NOTES AND COMMENTS

1. The use of the t distribution in the small-sample case is based on the assumptions that both populations have normal distributions and $\sigma_1^2 = \sigma_2^2$. Fortunately, this procedure is a *robust* statistical procedure, meaning that it is relatively insensitive to these assumptions. For instance, if $\sigma_1^2 \neq \sigma_2^2$, the procedure provides acceptable results if n_1 and n_2 are approximately equal.

2. The t distribution is not restricted to the small-sample situation; it is applicable whenever both populations are normally distributed and the variances of the populations are equal. However, expressions (10.4) and (10.6) show how to determine an interval estimate of the difference between the means of two populations when the sample sizes are large. Thus, in the large-sample case, use of the t distribution and its corresponding assumptions are not required. We therefore do not use the t distribution until we have a small-sample case.

EXERCISES

Methods

SELFtest

1. Consider the following results for two independent random samples taken from two populations.

Sample 1	Sample 2
$n_1 = 50$	$n_2 = 35$
$\bar{x}_1 = 13.6$	$\bar{x}_2 = 11.6$
$s_1 = 2.2$	$s_2 = 3.0$

   a. What is the point estimate of the difference between the two population means?
   b. Provide a 90% confidence interval for the difference between the two population means.
   c. Provide a 95% confidence interval for the difference between the two population means.

2. Consider the following results for two independent random samples taken from two populations.

Sample 1	Sample 2
$n_1 = 10$	$n_2 = 8$
$\bar{x}_1 = 22.5$	$\bar{x}_2 = 20.1$
$s_1 = 2.5$	$s_2 = 2.0$

a. What is the point estimate of the difference between the two population means?
b. What is the pooled estimate of the population variance?
c. Develop a 95% confidence interval for the difference between the two population means.

3. Consider the following data for two independent random samples taken from two populations.

Sample 1		Sample 2	
10	7	8	7
12	7	8	4
9	9	6	9

a. Compute the two sample means.
b. Compute the two sample standard deviations.
c. What is the point estimate of the difference between the two population means?
d. What is the pooled estimate of the population variance?
e. Develop a 95% confidence interval for the difference between the two population means.

Applications

4. Gasoline prices increased substantially from 1999 to 2000. The American Automobile Association provided information on the mean cost per gallon for self-serve regular unleaded gasoline over the two years (*AAA Going Places*, May/June 2000). Assume the following results were obtained from independent samples of locations throughout the country.

2000 Cost	1999 Cost
$\bar{x}_1 = \$1.58$	$\bar{x}_2 = \$0.98$
$s_1 = \$0.12$	$s_2 = \$0.08$
$n_1 = 50$	$n_2 = 42$

a. What is the point estimate of the increase in the mean cost per gallon from 1999 to 2000?
b. What is the 95% confidence interval estimate of the increase in the mean cost per gallon from 1999 to 2000?

5. The U.S. Department of Transportation provides the number of miles that residents of the 75 largest metropolitan areas travel per day in a car. Suppose that for a simple random sample of 50 Buffalo residents the mean is 22.5 miles a day and the standard deviation is 8.4 miles a day, and for an independent simple random sample of 100 Boston residents the mean is 18.6 miles a day and the standard deviation is 7.4 miles a day.
   a. What is the point estimate of the difference between the mean number of miles that Buffalo residents travel per day and the mean number of miles that Boston residents travel per day?
   b. What is the 95% confidence interval for the difference between the two population means?

6. The International Air Transport Association surveyed business travelers to determine ratings of various international airports. The maximum possible score was 10. Suppose 50 business travelers were asked to rate the Miami airport and 50 other business travelers were asked to rate the Los Angeles airport. The rating scores follow.

CDfile
Airport

Miami

6	4	6	8	7	7	6	3	3	8	10	4	8
7	8	7	5	9	5	8	4	3	8	5	5	4
4	4	8	4	5	6	2	5	9	9	8	4	8
9	9	5	9	7	8	3	10	8	9	6		

Los Angeles

10	9	6	7	8	7	9	8	10	7	6	5	7
3	5	6	8	7	10	8	4	7	8	6	9	9
5	3	1	8	9	6	8	5	4	6	10	9	8
3	2	7	9	5	3	10	3	5	10	8		

Develop a 95% confidence interval estimate of the difference between the mean ratings of the Miami and Los Angeles airports.

7. A Cornell University study of wage differentials between men and women reported that one of the reasons wages for men are higher than wages for women is that men tend to have more years of work experience than women (*Business Week*, August 28, 2000). Assume the following sample summaries show the years of experience for each group.

Men	**Women**
$\bar{x}_1 = 14.9$ years	$\bar{x}_2 = 10.3$ years
$s_1 = 5.2$ years	$s_2 = 3.8$ years
$n_1 = 100$	$n_2 = 85$

   a. What is the point estimate of the difference between the two population means?
   b. As 95% confidence, what is the margin of error?
   c. What is the 95% confidence interval estimate of the difference between the two population means?

SELFtest

8. An urban planning group wants to estimate the difference between the mean household incomes for two neighborhoods in a large metropolitan area. Independent random samples of households in the neighborhoods provide the following results.

Neighborhood 1	Neighborhood 2
$n_1 = 8$	$n_2 = 12$
$\bar{x}_1 = \$45,700$	$\bar{x}_2 = \$44,500$
$s_1 = \$700$	$s_2 = \$850$

  a. Develop a point estimate of the difference between the mean incomes in the two neighborhoods.
  b. Develop a 95% confidence interval for the difference between the mean incomes in the two neighborhoods.
  c. What assumptions were made to compute the interval estimates in part (b)?

9. The National Association of Home Builders provided data on the cost of the most popular home remodeling projects (*USA Today,* June 17, 1997). Sample data on cost in thousands of dollars for two types of remodeling projects follow.

Kitchen	Master Bedroom
25.2	18.0
17.4	22.9
22.8	26.4
21.9	24.8
19.7	26.9
23.0	17.8
19.7	24.6
16.9	21.0
21.8	
23.6	

  a. Develop a point estimate of the difference between the population mean remodeling costs for the two types of projects.
  b. Develop a 90% confidence interval for the difference between the two population means.

10. Suppose independent random samples of 15 unionized women and 20 nonunionized women in manufacturing have been selected and the following hourly wage rates are found.

Union Workers

22.40	18.90	16.70	14.05	16.20	20.00	16.10	16.30	19.10
16.50	18.50	19.80	17.00	14.30	17.20			

Nonunion Workers

17.60	14.40	16.60	15.00	17.65	15.00	17.55	13.30	11.20
15.90	19.20	11.85	16.65	15.20	15.30	17.00	15.10	14.30
13.90	14.50							

  a. What is the point estimate of the difference between hourly wages for the two populations?
  b. What is the pooled estimate of the population variance?
  c. Develop a 95% confidence interval estimate of the difference between the two population means.
  d. Does there appear to be any difference in the mean wage rate for these two groups? Explain.

10.2   HYPOTHESIS TESTS ABOUT THE DIFFERENCE BETWEEN THE MEANS OF TWO POPULATIONS: INDEPENDENT SAMPLES

In this section we present procedures that can be used to test hypotheses about the difference between the means of two populations. The methodology is again divided into large-sample ($n_1 \geq 30$, $n_2 \geq 30$) and small-sample ($n_1 < 30$ and/or $n_2 < 30$) cases.

Large-Sample Case

As part of a study to evaluate differences in educational quality between two training centers, a standardized examination is given to individuals who are trained at the two centers. The examination scores are a major factor in assessing any quality differences between the centers. The means for the two centers follow.

μ_1 = the mean examination score for the population of individuals trained at center A

μ_2 = the mean examination score for the population of individuals trained at center B

We begin with the tentative assumption that no difference exists in the training quality provided at the two centers. Hence, in terms of the mean examination scores, the null hypothesis is $\mu_1 - \mu_2 = 0$. If sample evidence leads to the rejection of this hypothesis, we will conclude that the mean examination scores differ for the two populations. This conclusion indicates a quality differential between the two centers and that a follow-up study investigating the reasons for the differential may be warranted. The null and alternative hypotheses are written as follows.

$$H_0: \mu_1 - \mu_2 = 0$$
$$H_a: \mu_1 - \mu_2 \neq 0$$

Following the hypothesis testing procedure from Chapter 9, we make the tentative assumption that H_0 is true. Using the difference between the sample means as the point estimator of the difference between the population means, we consider the sampling distribution of $\bar{x}_1 - \bar{x}_2$ when H_0 is true. For the large-sample case, this distribution is as shown in Figure 10.4. Because the sampling distribution of $\bar{x}_1 - \bar{x}_2$ can be approximated by a normal probability distribution, the following test statistic is used.

$$z = \frac{(\bar{x}_1 - \bar{x}_2) - (\mu_1 - \mu_2)}{\sqrt{\sigma_1^2/n_1 + \sigma_2^2/n_2}} \tag{10.11}$$

If σ_1 and σ_2 are unknown, we can use the sample standard deviations s_1 and s_2 to compute the test statistic.

The value of z given by equation (10.11) can be interpreted as the number of standard deviations $\bar{x}_1 - \bar{x}_2$ is from the value of $\mu_1 - \mu_2$ specified in H_0. For $\alpha = .05$ and thus $z_{\alpha/2} = z_{.025} = 1.96$, the rejection region for the two-tailed hypothesis test is shown in Figure 10.5. Using the test statistic, the rejection rule is

Reject H_0 if $z < -1.96$ or if $z > +1.96$

FIGURE 10.4 SAMPLING DISTRIBUTION OF $\bar{x}_1 - \bar{x}_2$ WITH $H_0: \mu_1 - \mu_2 = 0$

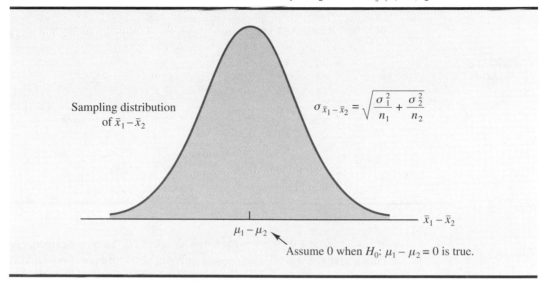

Sampling distribution of $\bar{x}_1 - \bar{x}_2$

$$\sigma_{\bar{x}_1 - \bar{x}_2} = \sqrt{\frac{\sigma_1^2}{n_1} + \frac{\sigma_2^2}{n_2}}$$

$\mu_1 - \mu_2$

$\bar{x}_1 - \bar{x}_2$

Assume 0 when $H_0: \mu_1 - \mu_2 = 0$ is true.

Let us assume that independent random samples of individuals trained at the two centers provide the examination scores in Table 10.1; summary statistics are given in Table 10.2. Using s_1 and s_2 to estimate σ_1 and σ_2, we find that the test statistic z given by equation (10.11) for the null hypothesis $H_0: \mu_1 - \mu_2 = 0$ becomes

$$z = \frac{(82.5 - 78) - 0}{\sqrt{(8)^2/30 + (10)^2/40}} = 2.09$$

FIGURE 10.5 REJECTION REGION FOR THE TWO-TAILED HYPOTHESIS TEST WITH $\alpha = .05$

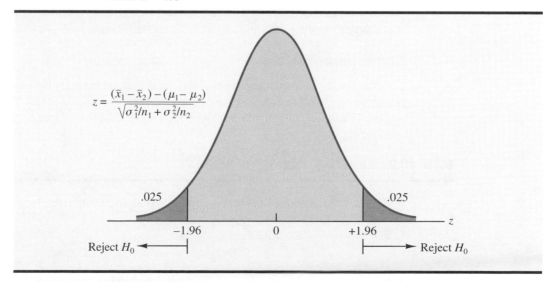

$$z = \frac{(\bar{x}_1 - \bar{x}_2) - (\mu_1 - \mu_2)}{\sqrt{\sigma_1^2/n_1 + \sigma_2^2/n_2}}$$

.025

.025

-1.96 0 $+1.96$

z

Reject H_0

Reject H_0

TABLE 10.1 EXAMINATION SCORE DATA

CDfile
ExamData

Training Center A			Training Center B			
97	83	91	64	66	91	84
90	84	87	85	83	78	85
94	76	73	72	74	87	85
79	82	92	64	70	93	84
78	85	64	74	82	89	59
87	85	74	93	82	79	62
83	91	88	70	75	84	91
89	72	88	79	78	65	83
76	86	74	79	99	78	80
84	70	73	75	57	66	76

With $z = 2.09 > 1.96$, the conclusion is to reject H_0. Thus, we can conclude that μ_1 and μ_2 are not equal and that the two centers differ in terms of educational quality.

The p-value can also be used for this hypothesis test.

With $z = 2.09$, the standard normal probability distribution table can be used to compute the p-value for this two-tailed test. With an area of .4817 between the mean and $z = 2.09$, the p-value is $2(.5000 - .4817) = .0366$; because the p-value is less than $\alpha = .05$, the p-value approach also results in the rejection of H_0.

In this hypothesis test, we wanted to determine whether the means of the two populations differed. We did not have a prior belief that one mean might be greater than or less than the other, therefore the hypotheses $H_0: \mu_1 - \mu_2 = 0$ and $H_a: \mu_1 - \mu_2 \neq 0$ were appropriate. In other hypothesis tests about the difference between the means of two populations, we may want to find out whether one mean is greater than or perhaps less than the other mean. In these cases, a one-tailed hypothesis test would be appropriate. The two forms of a one-tailed hypothesis test about the difference between two population means follow.

$$H_0: \mu_1 - \mu_2 \leq 0 \qquad H_0: \mu_1 - \mu_2 \geq 0$$
$$H_a: \mu_1 - \mu_2 > 0 \qquad H_a: \mu_1 - \mu_2 < 0$$

These hypotheses are tested by using the test statistic z given by equation (10.11). The rejection region is determined in the same way as in the one-tailed procedures presented in Chapter 9.

Small-Sample Case

Let us now consider hypothesis tests about the difference between the means of two populations for the small-sample case, that is, where $n_1 < 30$ and/or $n_2 < 30$. The procedure we will use is based on the t distribution with $n_1 + n_2 - 2$ degrees of freedom. As discussed in

TABLE 10.2 EXAMINATION SCORE RESULTS

Training Center A	Training Center B
$n_1 = 30$	$n_2 = 40$
$\bar{x}_1 = 82.5$	$\bar{x}_2 = 78$
$s_1 = 8$	$s_2 = 10$

Section 10.1, assumptions are made that both populations have normal probability distributions and that the variances of the populations are equal.

The problem that we will use to illustrate the small-sample case involves a new computer software package developed to help systems analysts reduce the time required to design, develop, and implement an information system. To evaluate the benefits of the new software package, a random sample of 24 systems analysts is selected. Each analyst is given specifications for a hypothetical information system. Then 12 of the analysts are instructed to produce the information system by using current technology. The other 12 analysts are trained in the use of the new software package and then instructed to use it to produce the information system.

This study has two populations: a population of systems analysts using the current technology and a population of systems analysts using the new software package. In terms of the time required to complete the information system design project, the population means are as follow.

$\mu_1 =$ the mean project completion time for systems analysts using the current technology

$\mu_2 =$ the mean project completion time for systems analysts using the new software package

The researcher in charge of the new software evaluation project hopes to show that the new software package will provide a shorter mean project completion time. Thus, the researcher seeks evidence to conclude that μ_2 is less than μ_1; in this case, the difference between the two population means, $\mu_1 - \mu_2$, will be greater than zero. The research hypothesis $\mu_1 - \mu_2 > 0$ is stated as the alternative hypothesis.

$$H_0: \mu_1 - \mu_2 \leq 0$$
$$H_a: \mu_1 - \mu_2 > 0$$

Suppose that the 24 analysts complete the study with the results shown in Table 10.3. Under the assumption that the variances of the populations are equal, equation (10.8) is used to compute the pooled estimate of σ^2.

$$s^2 = \frac{(n_1 - 1)s_1^2 + (n_2 - 1)s_2^2}{n_1 + n_2 - 2} = \frac{11(40)^2 + 11(44)^2}{12 + 12 - 2} = 1768$$

The test statistic for the small-sample case is

$$t = \frac{(\bar{x}_1 - \bar{x}_2) - (\mu_1 - \mu_2)}{\sqrt{s^2\left(\frac{1}{n_1} + \frac{1}{n_2}\right)}} \tag{10.12}$$

In the case of two independent random samples of sizes n_1 and n_2, the t distribution will have $n_1 + n_2 - 2$ degrees of freedom. For $\alpha = .05$, the t distribution table shows that with $12 + 12 - 2 = 22$ degrees of freedom, $t_{.05} = 1.717$. Thus, using the test statistic, the rejection region for the one-tailed test is

Reject H_0 if $t > 1.717$

TABLE 10.3 COMPLETION TIME DATA AND SUMMARY STATISTICS FOR THE SOFTWARE TESTING STUDY

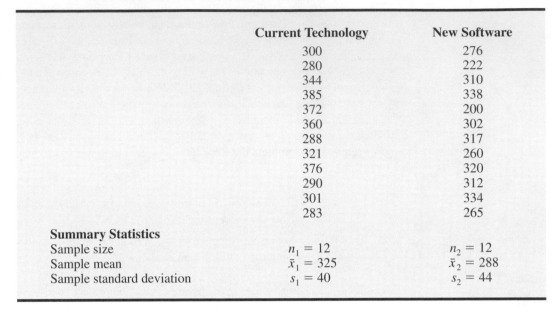

CDfile
Software

	Current Technology	New Software
	300	276
	280	222
	344	310
	385	338
	372	200
	360	302
	288	317
	321	260
	376	320
	290	312
	301	334
	283	265
Summary Statistics		
Sample size	$n_1 = 12$	$n_2 = 12$
Sample mean	$\bar{x}_1 = 325$	$\bar{x}_2 = 288$
Sample standard deviation	$s_1 = 40$	$s_2 = 44$

The sample data and equation (10.12) provide the following value for the test statistic.

$$t = \frac{(325 - 288) - 0}{\sqrt{1768\left(\dfrac{1}{12} + \dfrac{1}{12}\right)}} = 2.16$$

Checking the rejection region, we see that $t = 2.16$ allows the rejection of H_0 at the .05 level of significance. Thus, the sample results enable the researcher to conclude that $\mu_1 - \mu_2 > 0$ and that the new software package provides a smaller mean completion time.

Minitab can be used for testing hypotheses about the difference between the means of two populations. The output comparing the current and new software technology is shown in Figure 10.6. The last line of the output shows $t = 2.16$ and a p-value $= .021$. With $\alpha = .05$, the null hypothesis can be rejected. Thus, the mean completion time for the new software is less than the mean completion time with the current technology.

FIGURE 10.6 MINITAB OUTPUT FOR THE HYPOTHESIS TEST OF THE CURRENT AND NEW SOFTWARE TECHNOLOGY

```
Two sample T for Current vs New

           N       Mean      StDev     SE Mean
Current    12      325.0     40.0         12
New        12      288.0     44.0         13

Difference = mu Current - mu New
Estimate for difference:  37.0
T-Test of difference = 0 (vs >): T = 2.16  P-value = 0.021  DF = 22
Both use Pooled StDev = 42.0
```

NOTES AND COMMENTS

In hypothesis tests about the difference between the means of two populations, the null hypothesis almost always contains the assumption of no difference between the means. Hence, the following null hypotheses are possible choices.

$$H_0: \mu_1 - \mu_2 = 0$$
$$H_0: \mu_1 - \mu_2 \leq 0$$
$$H_0: \mu_1 - \mu_2 \geq 0$$

In some instances, we may want to determine whether there is a nonzero difference D_0 between the population means. The specific value chosen for D_0 depends on the application under study. However, in this case, the null hypothesis may be of the following forms.

$$H_0: \mu_1 - \mu_2 = D_0$$
$$H_0: \mu_1 - \mu_2 \leq D_0$$
$$H_0: \mu_1 - \mu_2 \geq D_0$$

The hypothesis testing computations remain the same with the exception that D_0 is used for the value of $\mu_1 - \mu_2$ in equations (10.11) and (10.12).

EXERCISES

Methods

SELFtest   **11.** Consider the following hypothesis test.

$$H_0: \mu_1 - \mu_2 \leq 0$$
$$H_a: \mu_1 - \mu_2 > 0$$

The following results are for two independent samples taken from the two populations.

Sample 1	Sample 2
$n_1 = 40$	$n_2 = 50$
$\bar{x}_1 = 25.2$	$\bar{x}_2 = 22.8$
$s_1 = 5.2$	$s_2 = 6.0$

    a. With $\alpha = .05$, what is your hypothesis testing conclusion?
    b. What is the p-value?

12. Consider the following hypothesis test.

$$H_0: \mu_1 - \mu_2 = 0$$
$$H_a: \mu_1 - \mu_2 \neq 0$$

The following results are for two independent samples taken from the two populations.

Sample 1	Sample 2
$n_1 = 80$	$n_2 = 70$
$\bar{x}_1 = 104$	$\bar{x}_2 = 106$
$s_1 = 8.4$	$s_2 = 7.6$

    a. With $\alpha = .05$, what is your hypothesis testing conclusion?
    b. What is the p-value?

13. Consider the following hypothesis test.

$$H_0: \mu_1 - \mu_2 = 0$$
$$H_a: \mu_1 - \mu_2 \neq 0$$

The following results are for two independent samples taken from the two populations. With $\alpha = .05$, what is your hypothesis testing conclusion?

Sample 1	Sample 2
$n_1 = 8$	$n_2 = 7$
$\bar{x}_1 = 1.4$	$\bar{x}_2 = 1.0$
$s_1 = 0.4$	$s_2 = 0.6$

Applications

14. Coastal areas of the United States including Cape Cod, the Outer Banks, the Carolinas, and the Gulf Coast experienced relatively high population growth rates during the 1990s. Data were collected on residents living in the coastal communities as well as on residents living in noncoastal areas throughout the United States (*USA Today*, July 21, 2000). Assume that the following sample results were obtained on the ages of individuals in the two populations:

Coastal Areas	Noncoastal Areas
$\bar{x}_1 = 39.3$ years	$\bar{x}_2 = 35.4$ years
$s_1 = 16.8$ years	$s_2 = 15.2$ years
$n_1 = 150$	$n_2 = 175$

Test the hypothesis of no difference between the mean ages of the two populations. Use $\alpha = .05$.
a. Formulate the null and alternative hypotheses.
b. What is the rejection rule?
c. What is the value of the test statistic?
d. What is your conclusion?
e. What is the p-value?

SELFtest   15. The Greystone Department Store study in Section 10.1 supplied the following data on customer ages from independent random samples taken at two store locations.

Inner-City Store	Suburban Store
$n_1 = 36$	$n_2 = 49$
$\bar{x}_1 = 40$ years	$\bar{x}_2 = 35$ years
$s_1 = 9$ years	$s_2 = 10$ years

For $\alpha = .05$, test $H_0: \mu_1 - \mu_2 = 0$ against the alternative $H_a: \mu_1 - \mu_2 \neq 0$. What is your conclusion about the mean ages of the populations of customers at the two stores? What is the p-value?

16. The Educational Testing Service conducted a study to investigate differences between the scores of male and female students on the Scholastic Aptitude Test. The study identified a random sample of 562 female and 852 male students who had achieved the same high score on the mathematics portion of the test. That is, the female and male students were viewed as having similarly high abilities in mathematics. The SAT verbal scores for the two samples follow.

Female Students	Male Students
$\bar{x}_1 = 547$	$\bar{x}_2 = 525$
$s_1 = 83$	$s_2 = 78$

Do the data support the conclusion that given a population of female students and a population of male students with similarly high mathematical abilities, the female students will have a significantly higher verbal ability? Test at a .02 level of significance. What is your conclusion?

17. A firm is studying the delivery times of two raw material suppliers. The firm is basically satisfied with supplier A and is prepared to stay with that supplier if the mean delivery time is the same as or less than that of supplier B. However, if the firm finds that the mean delivery time of supplier B is less than that of supplier A, it will begin making raw material purchases from supplier B.
   a. What are the null and alternative hypotheses for this situation?
   b. Assume that independent samples show the following delivery time characteristics for the two suppliers.

Supplier A	Supplier B
$n_1 = 50$	$n_2 = 30$
$\bar{x}_1 = 14$ days	$\bar{x}_2 = 12.5$ days
$s_1 = 3$ days	$s_2 = 2$ days

With $\alpha = .05$, what is your conclusion for the hypotheses from part (a)? What action do you recommend in terms of supplier selection?

18. Arnold Palmer and Tiger Woods are two of the best golfers to ever play the game. The question was raised as to how these two golfers would have compared if both were playing at the top of their game. The following sample data show the results of 18-hole scores during a PGA tournament competition. Palmer's scores are from his 1960 season, while Woods' scores are from his 1999 season (*Golf Magazine*, February 2000).

Palmer, 1960	Woods, 1999
$\bar{x}_1 = 69.95$	$\bar{x}_2 = 69.56$
$n_1 = 112$	$n_2 = 84$

Use the sample results to test the hypothesis of no difference between the population mean 18-hole scores for the two golfers.
   a. Assuming a population standard deviation of 2.5 for both golfers, what is the value of the test statistic?
   b. What is the p-value?
   c. Using $\alpha = .01$, what is your conclusion?

19. The mean time to locate flight information on Internet Web sites of the major airline companies is generally two to three minutes (*USA Today*, September 11, 2000). Sample results representative of the times for Delta Airlines and Northwest Airlines follow:

Delta	Northwest
$\bar{x}_1 = 2.5$ minutes	$\bar{x}_2 = 2.1$ minutes
$s_1 = .8$ minutes	$s_2 = 1.1$ minutes
$n_1 = 22$	$n_2 = 20$

a. Formulate the hypotheses if the purpose is to test for a significant difference between the mean times for the two airlines.
b. Using $\alpha = .05$, what is the rejection rule?
c. Compute the value of the test statistic.
d. What is your conclusion?
e. What can you say about the p-value?

20. Periodically, Merrill Lynch asks its customers to evaluate its financial consultants and services (2000 Merril Lynch Client Satisfaction Survey). Higher ratings on the client satisfaction survey indicate better service with 7 the maximum service rating. Independent samples of service ratings for two financial consultants are summarized here. Consultant A has 10 years of experience while consultant B has one year of experience. Using $\alpha = .05$, test to see whether the consultant with more experience achieves the higher population mean service rating.

Consultant A	Consultant B
$\bar{x}_1 = 6.82$	$\bar{x}_2 = 6.25$
$s_1 = .64$	$s_2 = .75$
$n_1 = 16$	$n_2 = 10$

a. Formulate the null and alternative hypotheses.
b. What is the rejection rule?
c. Compute the value of the test statistic.
d. What is your conclusion?
e. What can you say about the p-value?

10.3 INFERENCES ABOUT THE DIFFERENCE BETWEEN THE MEANS OF TWO POPULATIONS: MATCHED SAMPLES

Suppose a manufacturing company is considering two methods by which employees can perform a production task. To maximize production output, the company wants to identify the method with the shortest mean completion time. Let μ_1 denote the mean completion time for production method 1 and μ_2 denote the mean completion time for production method 2. With no preliminary indication of the preferred production method, we begin by tentatively assuming that the two production methods have the same mean completion time. Thus, the null hypothesis is $H_0: \mu_1 - \mu_2 = 0$. If this hypothesis is rejected, we can conclude that the mean completion times differ. In this case, the method providing the shorter mean completion time would be recommended. The null and alternative hypotheses are written as follows.

$$H_0: \mu_1 - \mu_2 = 0$$
$$H_a: \mu_1 - \mu_2 \neq 0$$

In choosing the sampling procedure that will be used to collect production time data and test the hypotheses, we consider two alternative designs. One is based on independent samples and the other is based on **matched samples.**

1. *Independent sample design:* A simple random sample of workers is selected and each worker in the sample uses method 1. A second independent simple random sample of workers is selected and each worker in this sample uses method 2. The test of the difference between means is based on the procedures in Section 10.2.
2. *Matched sample design:* One simple random sample of workers is selected. Each worker first uses one method and then uses the other method. The order of the two methods is assigned randomly to the workers, with some workers performing method 1 first and others performing method 2 first. Each worker provides a pair of data values, one value for method 1 and another value for method 2.

In the matched sample design the two production methods are tested under similar conditions (i.e., with the same workers); hence this design often leads to a smaller sampling error than the independent sample design. The primary reason is that in a matched sample design, variation between workers is eliminated as a source of sampling error.

Let us demonstrate the analysis of a matched sample design by assuming it is the method used to test the difference between the two production methods. A random sample of six workers is used. The data on completion times for the six workers are given in Table 10.4. Note that each worker provides a pair of data values, one for each production method. Also note that the last column contains the difference in completion times d_i for each worker in the sample.

The key to the analysis of the matched sample design is to realize that we consider only the column of differences. We therefore have six data values (.6, −.2, .5, .3, .0, and .6) that will be used to analyze the difference between the means of the two production methods.

Let μ_d = the mean of the *difference* values for the population of workers. With this notation, the null and alternative hypotheses are rewritten as follows.

$$H_0: \mu_d = 0$$
$$H_a: \mu_d \neq 0$$

TABLE 10.4   TASK COMPLETION TIMES FOR A MATCHED SAMPLE DESIGN

Worker	Completion Time for Method 1 (minutes)	Completion Time for Method 2 (minutes)	Difference in Completion Times (d_i)
1	6.0	5.4	.6
2	5.0	5.2	−.2
3	7.0	6.5	.5
4	6.2	5.9	.3
5	6.0	6.0	.0
6	6.4	5.8	.6

If H_0 can be rejected, we can conclude that the mean completion times differ.

The d notation is a reminder that the matched sample provides *difference* data. The sample mean and sample standard deviation for the six difference values in Table 10.4 follow.

The formulas for the sample mean and sample standard deviation use the notation d to remind the user that the data show the difference between the matched sample data values. Other than the use of the d notation, the formulas for the sample mean and sample standard deviation are the same as those used in Chapter 3.

$$\bar{d} = \frac{\Sigma d_i}{n} = \frac{1.8}{6} = .30$$

$$s_d = \sqrt{\frac{\Sigma(d_i - \bar{d})^2}{n-1}} = \sqrt{\frac{.56}{5}} = .335$$

In Chapter 9 we stated that if the population can be assumed to be normally distributed, the t distribution with $n - 1$ degrees of freedom can be used to test the null hypothesis about a population mean. Assuming difference data are normally distributed, the test statistic becomes

$$t = \frac{\bar{d} - \mu_d}{s_d/\sqrt{n}} \tag{10.13}$$

With $\alpha = .05$ and $n - 1 = 5$ degrees of freedom ($t_{.025} = 2.571$), the rejection rule for the two-tailed test becomes

$$\text{Reject } H_0 \text{ if } t < -2.571 \text{ or if } t > 2.571$$

With $\bar{d} = .30$, $s_d = .335$, and $n = 6$, the value of the test statistic for the null hypothesis $H_0: \mu_d = 0$ is

$$t = \frac{\bar{d} - \mu_d}{s_d/\sqrt{n}} = \frac{.30 - 0}{.335/\sqrt{6}} = 2.20$$

Once the difference data have been computed, the t distribution procedure for matched samples is the same as the one-population procedure described in Chapters 8 and 9.

Because $t = 2.20$ is not in the rejection region, the sample data do not provide sufficient evidence to reject H_0.

Using the 5 degrees of freedom, the t distribution table shows $t = 2.20$ is between $t_{.025} = 2.571$ and $t_{.025} = 2.015$. Thus, the one-tailed area associated with $t = 2.20$ is between .025 and .05. For a two-tailed test, we know the p-value is between .05 and .10. Because this p-value is greater than $\alpha = .05$, H_0 is not rejected. Using Minitab and the data in Table 10.4 shows p-value $= .08$.

In addition we can obtain an interval estimate of the difference between the two population means by using the single population methodology of Chapter 8. The calculation follows.

$$\bar{d} \pm t_{\alpha/2} \frac{s_d}{\sqrt{n}}$$

$$0.3 \pm 2.571 \left(\frac{.335}{\sqrt{6}} \right)$$

$$0.3 \pm .35$$

Thus, the 95% confidence interval for the difference between the means of the two production methods is $-.05$ minutes to $.65$ minutes. Note that because the confidence interval includes the value of zero, the sample data do not provide sufficient evidence to reject H_0.

NOTES AND COMMENTS

1. In the example presented in this section, workers performed the production task with first one method and then the other method. This example illustrates a matched sample design in which each sampled element (worker) provides a pair of data values. It is also possible to use different but "similar" elements to provide the pair of data values. For example, a worker at one location could be matched with a similar worker at another location (similarity based on age, education, sex, experience, etc.). The pairs of workers would provide the difference data that could be used in the matched sample analysis.
2. A matched sample procedure for inferences about two population means generally provides better precision than the independent sample approach, therefore it is the recommended design. However, in some applications the matching cannot be achieved, or perhaps the time and cost associated with matching are excessive. In such cases, the independent sample design should be used.
3. The example presented in this section had a sample size of six workers and thus was a small-sample case. The t distribution was used in both the hypothesis test and interval estimation computations. If the sample size is large $(n \geq 30)$, use of the t distribution is unnecessary; in such cases, statistical inferences can be based on the z values of the standard normal probability distribution.

EXERCISES

Methods

SELFtest   **21.** Consider the following hypothesis test.

$$H_0: \mu_d \leq 0$$
$$H_a: \mu_d > 0$$

The following data are from matched samples taken from two populations.

		Population	
Element		**1**	**2**
1		21	20
2		28	26
3		18	18
4		20	20
5		26	24

a. Compute the difference value for each element.
b. Compute $\bar{d}$.
c. Compute the standard deviation s_d.
d. Test the hypothesis using $\alpha = .05$. What is your conclusion?

22. The following data are from matched samples taken from two populations.

	Population	
Element	**1**	**2**
1	11	8
2	7	8
3	9	6
4	12	7
5	13	10
6	15	15
7	15	14

    a. Compute the difference value for each element.
    b. Compute $\bar{d}$.
    c. Compute the standard deviation s_d.
    d. What is the point estimate of the difference between the two population means?
    e. Provide a 95% confidence interval for the difference between the two population means.

Applications

SELFtest

23. A market research firm used a sample of individuals to rate the purchase potential of a particular product before and after the individuals saw a new television commercial about the product. The purchase potential ratings were based on a 0 to 10 scale, with higher values indicating a higher purchase potential. The null hypothesis stated that the mean rating "after" would be less than or equal to the mean rating "before." Rejection of this hypothesis would show that the commercial improved the mean purchase potential rating. Use $\alpha = .05$ and the following data to test the hypothesis and comment on the value of the commercial.

	Purchase Rating			**Purchase Rating**	
Individual	**After**	**Before**	**Individual**	**After**	**Before**
1	6	5	5	3	5
2	6	4	6	9	8
3	7	7	7	7	5
4	4	3	8	6	6

24. A sample of 10 international telephone calls provided the Sprint and WorldCom calling rates per minute for calls from the United States (*World Traveler,* July 2000).

Country	**Sprint**	**WorldCom**
Australia	.46	.26
Belgium	.69	.40

Country	Sprint	WorldCom
Brazil	.92	.53
Colombia	.55	.53
Denmark	.50	.26
France	.46	.26
Germany	.46	.26
Hong Kong	.92	.40
Japan	.69	.40
United Kingdom	.46	.26

Provide a 95% confidence interval estimate of the difference between the two population means.

25. The cost of transportation from the airport to the downtown area depends on the method of transportation. One-way costs for taxi and shuttle bus transportation for a sample of 10 major cities follow. Provide a 95% confidence interval for the mean cost increase associated with taxi transportation.

City	Taxi ($)	Shuttle Bus ($)	City	Taxi ($)	Shuttle Bus ($)
Atlanta	15.00	7.00	Minneapolis	16.50	7.50
Chicago	22.00	12.50	New Orleans	18.00	7.00
Denver	11.00	5.00	New York (LaGuardia)	16.00	8.50
Houston	15.00	4.50	Philadelphia	20.00	8.00
Los Angeles	26.00	11.00	Washington, D.C.	10.00	5.00

26. Rental car gasoline prices per gallon were sampled at eight major airports. Data for Hertz and National car rental companies follow (*USA Today*, April 4, 2000).

Airport	Hertz	National
Boston Logan	1.55	1.56
Chicago O'Hare	1.62	1.59
Los Angeles	1.72	1.78
Miami	1.65	1.49
New York (JFK)	1.72	1.51
New York (LaGuardia)	1.67	1.50
Orange County, CA	1.68	1.77
Washington (Dulles)	1.52	1.41

Use $\alpha = .05$ to test the hypothesis of no difference between the population mean prices per gallon for the two companies.

27. A survey was made of Book-of-the-Month-Club members to ascertain whether members spend more time watching television than they do reading. Assume a sample of 15 respondents provided the following data on weekly hours of television watching and weekly hours of reading. Using a .05 level of significance, can you conclude that Book-of-the-Month-Club members spend more hours per week watching television than reading?

CDfile
TVRead

Respondent	Television	Reading	Respondent	Television	Reading
1	10	6	9	4	7
2	14	16	10	8	8
3	16	8	11	16	5
4	18	10	12	5	10
5	15	10	13	8	3
6	14	8	14	19	10
7	10	14	15	11	6
8	12	14			

28. The 1997 price/earnings ratios and estimated 1998 price/earnings ratios for a sample of 12 stocks follow (*Kiplinger's Personal Finance Magazine,* November 1997).

CDfile
PERatio

Stock	1997 P/E Ratio	Est. 1998 P/E Ratio
Coca-Cola	40	32
Walt Disney	33	23
Du Pont	24	16
Eastman Kodak	21	13
General Electric	30	23
General Mills	25	19
IBM	19	14
Merck	29	21
McDonald's	20	17
Motorola	35	20
Philip Morris	17	13
Xerox	20	17

a. Use $\alpha = .05$ and test to see whether any change occurred in the population mean P/E ratios for the two-year period.

b. Provide a 95% confidence interval for the change in the population mean price/earnings ratios for the two-year period. What is your conclusion?

10.4 INTRODUCTION TO ANALYSIS OF VARIANCE

Sir Ronald Alymer Fisher (1890–1962) invented the branch of statistics known as experimental design. In addition to being accomplished in statistics, he was a noted scientist in the field of genetics.

In Section 10.2 we showed how a hypothesis test can be conducted to determine whether the means of two populations are equal. In this section we introduce a statistical technique called **analysis of variance** (ANOVA), which can be used to test the hypothesis that the means of three or more populations are equal. We begin our discussion of analysis of variance by considering a problem facing National Computer Products, Inc.

National Computer Products, Inc. (NCP), manufactures printers and fax machines at plants located in Atlanta, Dallas, and Seattle. To measure how much employees at these plants know about total quality management, a random sample of six employees was selected from

TABLE 10.5   EXAMINATION SCORES FOR 18 EMPLOYEES

CDfile
NCP

Observation	Plant 1 Atlanta	Plant 2 Dallas	Plant 3 Seattle
1	85	71	59
2	75	75	64
3	82	73	62
4	76	74	69
5	71	69	75
6	85	82	67
Sample mean	79	74	66
Sample variance	34	20	32
Sample standard deviation	5.83	4.47	5.66

each plant and given a quality awareness examination. The examination scores obtained for these 18 employees are listed in Table 10.5. The sample means, sample variances, and sample standard deviations for each group are also provided. Managers want to use these data to test the hypothesis that the population mean examination score is the same for all three plants.

We will define population 1 as all employees at the Atlanta plant, population 2 as all employees at the Dallas plant, and population 3 as all employees at the Seattle plant. Let

μ_1 = mean examination score for population 1

μ_2 = mean examination score for population 2

μ_3 = mean examination score for population 3

Although we will never know the actual values of μ_1, μ_2, and μ_3, we want to use the sample results to test the following hypotheses.

If H_0 is rejected, we cannot conclude that all population means are different. Rejecting H_0 indicates that at least two population means have different values.

H_0: $\mu_1 = \mu_2 = \mu_3$

H_a: Not all population means are equal

As we will demonstrate shortly, analysis of variance is a statistical procedure that can be used to determine whether the observed differences in the three sample means are large enough to reject H_0.

The two variables in the NCP example are plant location and score on the quality awareness examination. Because the objective is to determine whether the mean examination score is the same for plants located in Atlanta, Dallas, and Seattle, examination score is referred to as the dependent or **response variable** and plant location as the independent variable or **factor**. In general, the values of a factor selected for investigation are referred to as levels of the factor or **treatments**. Thus, in the NCP example the three treatments are Atlanta, Dallas, and Seattle. These three treatments define the populations of interest in the NCP example. For each treatment or plant location, the response variable is the examination score.

Assumptions for Analysis of Variance

If the sample sizes are equal, analysis of variance is not sensitive to departures from the assumption of normally distributed populations.

Three assumptions are required to use analysis of variance.

1. **For each population, the response variable is normally distributed.** Implication: In the NCP example, the examination scores (response variable) must be normally distributed at each plant.

2. **The variance of the response variable, denoted σ^2, is the same for all of the populations.** Implication: In the NCP example, the variance of examination scores must be the same for all three plants.
3. **The observations must be independent.** Implication: In the NCP example, the examination score for each employee must be independent of the examination score for any other employee.

Conceptual Overview

If the three population means are equal, we would expect the three sample means to be close together. In fact, the closer the three sample means are to one another, the more evidence we have for the conclusion that the population means are equal. Alternatively, the more the sample means differ, the more evidence we have for the conclusion that the population means are not equal. In other words, if the variability among the sample means is "small," it supports H_0; if the variability among the sample means is "large," it supports H_a.

If the null hypothesis, H_0: $\mu_1 = \mu_2 = \mu_3$, is true, we can use the variability among the sample means to develop an estimate of σ^2. First, note that if the assumptions for analysis of variance are satisfied, each sample will have come from the same normal probability distribution with mean μ and variance σ^2. Recall from Chapter 7 that the sampling distribution of the sample mean $\bar{x}$ for a simple random sample of size n from a normal population will be normally distributed with mean μ and variance σ^2/n. Figure 10.7 illustrates such a sampling distribution.

Thus, if the null hypothesis is true, we can think of each of the three sample means, $\bar{x}_1 = 79$, $\bar{x}_2 = 74$, and $\bar{x}_3 = 66$, from Table 10.5 as values drawn at random from the sampling distribution shown in Figure 10.7. In this case, the mean and variance of the three $\bar{x}$ values can be used to estimate the mean and variance of the sampling distribution. When the sample sizes are equal, as in the NCP example, the best estimate of the mean of the sampling distribution of $\bar{x}$ is the mean or average of the sample means. Thus, in the NCP example, an estimate of the mean of the sampling distribution of $\bar{x}$ is $(79 + 74 + 66)/3 = 73$.

FIGURE 10.7   SAMPLING DISTRIBUTION OF $\bar{x}$ GIVEN H_0 IS TRUE

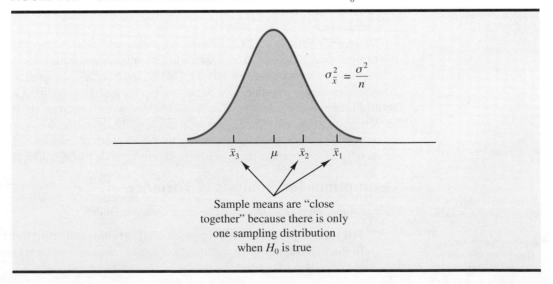

$$\sigma_{\bar{x}}^2 = \frac{\sigma^2}{n}$$

$\bar{x}_3$ μ $\bar{x}_2$ $\bar{x}_1$

Sample means are "close together" because there is only one sampling distribution when H_0 is true

We refer to this estimate as the *overall sample mean*. An estimate of the variance of the sampling distribution of $\bar{x}$, $\sigma_{\bar{x}}^2$, is provided by the variance of the three sample means.

$$s_{\bar{x}}^2 = \frac{(79 - 73)^2 + (74 - 73)^2 + (66 - 73)^2}{3 - 1} = \frac{86}{2} = 43$$

Because $\sigma_{\bar{x}}^2 = \sigma^2/n$, solving for σ^2 gives

$$\sigma^2 = n\sigma_{\bar{x}}^2$$

Hence,

$$\text{Estimate of } \sigma^2 = n\,(\text{Estimate of } \sigma_{\bar{x}}^2) = ns_{\bar{x}}^2 = 6(43) = 258$$

The result, $ns_{\bar{x}}^2 = 258$, is referred to as the *between-treatments* estimate of σ^2.

The between-treatments estimate of σ^2 is based on the assumption that the null hypothesis is true. In this case, each sample comes from the same population, and there is only one sampling distribution of $\bar{x}$. To illustrate what happens when H_0 is false, suppose the population means all differ. Note that because the three samples are from normal populations with different means, they will result in three different sampling distributions. Figure 10.8 shows that in this case, the sample means are not as close together as they were when H_0 was true. Thus, $s_{\bar{x}}^2$ will be larger, causing the between-treatments estimate of σ^2 to be larger. In general, when the population means are not equal, the between-treatments estimate will overestimate the population variance σ^2.

The variation within each of the samples also affects the conclusion we reach in analysis of variance. When a simple random sample is selected from each population, each of the sample variances provides an unbiased estimate of σ^2. Hence, we can combine or pool the individual estimates of σ^2 into one overall estimate. The estimate of σ^2 obtained in this way is called the *pooled* or *within treatments* estimate of σ^2. Because each sample variance provides an estimate of σ^2 based only on the variation within each sample, the

FIGURE 10.8 SAMPLING DISTRIBUTION FOR $\bar{x}$ GIVEN H_0 IS FALSE

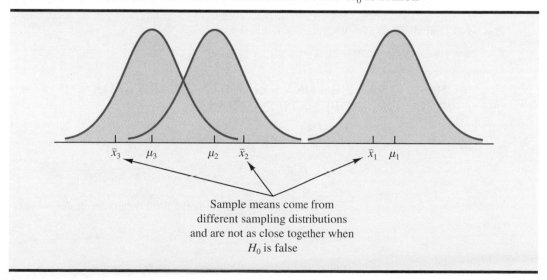

Sample means come from
different sampling distributions
and are not as close together when
H_0 is false

within-treatments estimate of σ^2 is not affected by whether the population means are equal. When the sample sizes are equal, the within-treatments estimate of σ^2 can be obtained by computing the average of the individual sample variances. For the NCP example we obtain

$$\text{Within-Treatments Estimate of } \sigma^2 = \frac{34 + 20 + 32}{3} = \frac{86}{3} = 28.67$$

In the NCP example, the between-treatments estimate of σ^2 (258) is much larger than the within-treatments estimate of σ^2 (28.67). In fact, the ratio of these two estimates is $258/28.67 = 9.00$. Recall, however, that the between-treatments approach provides a good estimate of σ^2 only if the null hypothesis is true; if the null hypothesis is false, the between-treatments approach overestimates σ^2. The within-treatments approach provides a good estimate of σ^2 in either case. Thus, if the null hypothesis is true, the two estimates will be similar and their ratio will be close to 1. If the null hypothesis is false, the between-treatments estimate will be larger than the within-treatments estimate, and their ratio will be large. In the next section we will show how large this ratio must be to reject H_0.

In summary, the logic behind ANOVA is based on the development of two independent estimates of the common population variance σ^2. One estimate of σ^2 is based on the variability among the sample means themselves, and the other estimate of σ^2 is based on the variability of the data within each sample. By comparing these two estimates of σ^2, we can determine whether the population means are equal.

NOTES AND COMMENTS

1. In Sections 10.2 and 10.3 we presented statistical methods for testing the hypothesis that the means of two populations are equal. ANOVA can also be used to test the hypothesis that the means of two populations are equal. In practice, however, analysis of variance is used only when dealing with three or more population means.

2. In Section 10.2 we discussed how to test for the equality of two population means whenever one or both sample sizes are less than 30. As part of that discussion we illustrated the process of combining the results of two independent random samples to provide one estimate of σ^2; that process was referred to as pooling, and the resulting sample variance was referred to as the pooled estimator of σ^2. In analysis of variance, the within-treatments estimate of σ^2 is simply the generalization of that concept to the case of more than two samples; that is why we also referred to the within-treatments estimator as the pooled estimator of σ^2.

10.5 ANALYSIS OF VARIANCE: TESTING FOR THE EQUALITY OF k POPULATION MEANS

Analysis of variance can be used to test for the equality of k population means. The general form of the hypothesis test is

$$H_0: \mu_1 = \mu_2 = \cdots = \mu_k$$
$$H_a: \text{Not all population means are equal}$$

where

$$\mu_j = \text{mean of the } j\text{th population}$$

We assume that a simple random sample of size n_j has been selected from each of the k populations or treatments. For the resulting sample data, let

x_{ij} = value of observation i for treatment j
n_j = number of observations for treatment j
$\bar{x}_j$ = sample mean for treatment j
s_j^2 = sample variance for treatment j
s_j = sample standard deviation for treatment j

The formulas for the sample mean and sample variance for treatment j are as follow.

$$\bar{x}_j = \frac{\sum_{i=1}^{n_j} x_{ij}}{n_j} \tag{10.14}$$

$$s_j^2 = \frac{\sum_{i=1}^{n_j} (x_{ij} - \bar{x}_j)^2}{n_j - 1} \tag{10.15}$$

The overall sample mean, denoted $\bar{\bar{x}}$, is the sum of all the observations divided by the total number of observations. That is,

$$\bar{\bar{x}} = \frac{\sum_{j=1}^{k} \sum_{i=1}^{n_j} x_{ij}}{n_T} \tag{10.16}$$

where

$$n_T = n_1 + n_2 + \cdots + n_k \tag{10.17}$$

If the size of each sample is n, $n_T = kn$; in this case equation (10.16) reduces to

$$\bar{\bar{x}} = \frac{\sum_{j=1}^{k} \sum_{i=1}^{n_j} x_{ij}}{nk} = \frac{\sum_{j=1}^{k} \sum_{i=1}^{n_j} x_{ij}/n}{k} = \frac{\sum_{j=1}^{k} \bar{x}_j}{k} \tag{10.18}$$

In other words, whenever the sample sizes are the same, the overall sample mean is just the average of the k sample means.

Because each sample in the NCP example consists of $n = 6$ observations, the overall sample mean can be computed by using equation (10.18). For the data in Table 10.5 we obtained the following result.

$$\bar{\bar{x}} = \frac{79 + 74 + 66}{3} = 73$$

If the null hypothesis is true ($\mu_1 = \mu_2 = \mu_3 = \mu$), the overall sample mean of 73 is the best estimate of the population mean μ.

Between-Treatments Estimate of Population Variance

In the preceding section, we introduced the concept of a between-treatments estimate of σ^2 and showed how to compute it when the sample sizes were equal. This estimate of σ^2 is called the *mean square due to treatments* and is denoted MSTR. The general formula for computing MSTR is

$$\text{MSTR} = \frac{\sum\limits_{j=1}^{k} n_j(\bar{x}_j - \bar{\bar{x}})^2}{k - 1} \tag{10.19}$$

The numerator in equation (10.19) is called the *sum of squares due to treatments* and is denoted SSTR. The denominator, $k - 1$, represents the degrees of freedom associated with SSTR. Hence, the mean square due to treatments can be computed by the following formula.

Mean Square Due to Treatments

$$\text{MSTR} = \frac{\text{SSTR}}{k - 1} \tag{10.20}$$

where

$$\text{SSTR} = \sum_{j=1}^{k} n_j(\bar{x}_j - \bar{\bar{x}})^2 \tag{10.21}$$

If H_0 is true, MSTR provides an unbiased estimate of σ^2. However, if the means of the k populations are not equal, MSTR is not an unbiased estimate of σ^2; in fact, in that case, MSTR should overestimate σ^2.

For the NCP data in Table 10.5, we obtain the following results.

$$\text{SSTR} = \sum_{j=1}^{k} n_j(\bar{x}_j - \bar{\bar{x}})^2 = 6(79 - 73)^2 + 6(74 - 73)^2 + 6(66 - 73)^2 = 516$$

$$\text{MSTR} = \frac{\text{SSTR}}{k - 1} = \frac{516}{2} = 258$$

Within-Treatments Estimate of Population Variance

In the preceding section we introduced the concept of a within-treatments estimate of σ^2 and showed how to compute it when the sample sizes were equal. This estimate of σ^2 is called the *mean square due to error* and is denoted MSE. The general formula for computing MSE is

$$\text{MSE} = \frac{\sum\limits_{j=1}^{k} (n_j - 1)s_j^2}{n_T - k} \tag{10.22}$$

The numerator in equation (10.22) is called the *sum of squares due to error* and is denoted SSE. The denominator of MSE is referred to as the degrees of freedom associated with SSE. Hence, the formula for MSE can also be stated as follows.

Mean Square Due to Error

$$MSE = \frac{SSE}{n_T - k} \tag{10.23}$$

where

$$SSE = \sum_{j=1}^{k}(n_j - 1)s_j^2 \tag{10.24}$$

Note that MSE is based on the variation within each of the treatments; it is not influenced by whether the null hypothesis is true. Thus, MSE always provides an unbiased estimate of σ^2.

For the NCP data in Table 10.5 we obtain the following results.

$$SSE = \sum_{j=1}^{k}(n_j - 1)s_j^2 = (6 - 1)34 + (6 - 1)20 + (6 - 1)32 = 430$$

$$MSE = \frac{SSE}{n_T - k} = \frac{430}{18 - 3} = \frac{430}{15} = 28.67$$

Comparing the Variance Estimates: The *F* Test

Let us assume that the null hypothesis is true. In that case, MSTR and MSE provide two independent, unbiased estimates of σ^2. For normal populations, the sampling distribution of the ratio of two independent estimates of σ^2 follows an *F* distribution. Hence, if the null hypothesis is true and the ANOVA assumptions are valid, the sampling distribution of MSTR/MSE is an *F* distribution with numerator degrees of freedom equal to $k - 1$ and denominator degrees of freedom equal to $n_T - k$.

If the means of the k populations are not equal, the value of MSTR/MSE will be inflated because MSTR overestimates σ^2. Hence, we will reject H_0 if the resulting value of MSTR/MSE appears to be too large to have been selected at random from an *F* distribution with degrees of freedom $k - 1$ in the numerator and $n_T - k$ in the denominator. The value of $F = $ MSTR/MSE that will cause us to reject H_0 depends on α, the level of significance. Once α is selected, a critical value can be determined. Figure 10.9 shows the sampling distribution of MSTR/MSE and the rejection region associated with a level of significance equal to α where F_α denotes the critical value.

Suppose the manager responsible for making the decision in the National Computer Products example was willing to accept a probability of making a Type I error of $\alpha = .05$. From Table 4 of Appendix B we can determine the critical *F* value by locating the value corresponding to numerator degrees of freedom equal to $k - 1 = 3 - 1 = 2$ and denominator degrees of freedom equal to $n_T - k = 18 - 3 = 15$. Thus, we obtain the critical value $F_{.05} = 3.68$. Note that this result means that if the null hypothesis is true, we will observe a value greater than 3.68 only 5% of the time. Moreover, the theory behind the analysis of variance tells us that if the null hypothesis is true, the ratio of MSTR/MSE would be

FIGURE 10.9   SAMPLING DISTRIBUTION OF F = MSTR/MSE; THE CRITICAL
VALUE FOR REJECTING THE NULL HYPOTHESIS OF EQUALITY
OF MEANS IS F_α

a value from this F distribution. Hence, the appropriate rejection rule for the NCP example
is written

$$\text{Reject } H_0 \text{ if } F = \text{MSTR/MSE} > 3.68$$

Recall that MSTR = 258 and MSE = 28.67. Because F = MSTR/MSE = 258/28.67 =
9.00 is greater than the critical value, $F_{.05}$ = 3.68, we have sufficient evidence to reject the
null hypothesis that the means of the three populations are equal. In other words, analysis
of variance supports the conclusion that the population mean examination scores at the three
NCP plants are not equal.

The p-value criterion can also be used for this hypothesis test. The usual rejection rule
applies: Reject H_0 if p-value $< \alpha$. However, because it is difficult to determine the p-value
directly from tables of the F probability distribution, a computer software package such as
Minitab or Excel is required. Appendixes 10.3 and 10.4 show the procedures that can be
used, and a discussion of the computer results for analysis of variance is provided in a subsection that follows. For the NCP example, the p-value associated with the test statistic
F = 9.00 is .003. With a p-value = .003 $< \alpha$ = .05, the null hypothesis that the means of
the three populations are equal can be rejected. A summary of the overall procedure for testing for the equality of k population means follows.

Test for the Equality of k Population Means

$$H_0: \mu_1 = \mu_2 = \cdots = \mu_k$$
$$H_a: \text{Not all population means are equal}$$

Test Statistic

$$F = \frac{\text{MSTR}}{\text{MSE}} \tag{10.25}$$

> ### Rejection Rule
>
> Using test statistic: Reject H_0 if $F > F_\alpha$
>
> Using p-value: Reject H_0 if p-value $< \alpha$
>
> where the value of F_α is based on an F distribution with $k - 1$ numerator degrees of freedom and $n_T - k$ denominator degrees of freedom.

ANOVA Table

The results of the preceding calculations can be displayed conveniently in a table referred to as the analysis of variance or **ANOVA table.** Table 10.6 shows the analysis of variance table for the National Computer Products example. The sum of squares associated with the source of variation referred to as "Total" is called the total sum of squares (SST). Note that the results for the NCP example suggest that SST = SSTR + SSE, and that the degrees of freedom associated with this total sum of squares is the sum of the degrees of freedom associated with the between-treatments estimate of σ^2 and the within-treatments estimate of σ^2.

We point out that SST divided by its degrees of freedom $n_T - 1$ is nothing more than the overall sample variance that would be obtained if we treated the entire set of 18 observations as one data set. With the entire data set as one sample, the formula for computing the total sum of squares, SST, is

$$\text{SST} = \sum_{j=1}^{k} \sum_{i=1}^{n_j} (x_{ij} - \bar{\bar{x}})^2 \tag{10.26}$$

The results we observed for the analysis of variance table for the NCP example also apply to other problems. That is,

$$\text{SST} = \text{SSTR} + \text{SSE} \tag{10.27}$$

Analysis of variance can be thought of as a statistical procedure for partitioning the total sum of squares into separate components.

In other words, SST can be partitioned into two sums of squares: the sum of squares due to treatments and the sum of squares due to error. Note also that the degrees of freedom corresponding to SST, $n_T - 1$, can be partitioned into the degrees of freedom corresponding to SSTR, $k - 1$, and the degrees of freedom corresponding to SSE, $n_T - k$. The analysis of variance can be viewed as the process of **partitioning** the total sum of squares and the degrees of freedom into their corresponding sources: treatments and error. Dividing the sum of squares by the appropriate degrees of freedom provides the variance estimates and the F value used to test the hypothesis of equal population means.

Computer Results for Analysis of Variance

Because of the widespread availability of statistical computer packages, analysis of variance computations with large sample sizes and/or a large number of populations can be performed easily. In Figure 10.10 we show output for the NCP example obtained from the Minitab computer package. The first part of the computer output contains the familiar ANOVA table format. Comparing Figure 10.10 with Table 10.6, we see that the same information is available, although some of the headings are slightly different. The heading Source is used for the source of variation column, and Factor identifies the treatments row. The sum of squares and degrees of freedom columns are interchanged, and a p-value is provided for the F test. Thus, at the $\alpha = .05$ level of significance, we reject H_0 because the p value $= 0.003 < \alpha = .05$.

FIGURE 10.10   MINITAB OUTPUT FOR THE NCP ANALYSIS OF VARIANCE

```
Analysis of Variance
Source      DF        SS        MS        F        p
Factor       2      516.0     258.0     9.00     0.003
Error       15      430.0      28.7
Total       17      946.0
                                      Individual 95% CIs For Mean
                                      Based on Pooled StDev
  Level      N       Mean      StDev  ---+---------+---------+---------+---
Atlanta      6      79.000     5.831                     (------*------)
Dallas       6      74.000     4.472              (------*-----)
Seattle      6      66.000     5.657  (-----*------)
                                      ---+---------+---------+---------+---
Pooled StDev =     5.354             63.0      70.0      77.0      84.0
```

Note that following the ANOVA table the computer output contains the respective sample sizes, the sample means, and the standard deviations. In addition, Minitab provides a figure that shows individual 95% confidence interval estimates of each population mean. In developing these confidence interval estimates, Minitab uses MSE as the estimate of σ^2. Thus, the square root of MSE provides the best estimate of the population standard deviation σ. This estimate of σ on the computer output is Pooled StDev; it is equal to 5.354. To provide an illustration of how to develop these interval estimates, we compute a 95% confidence interval estimate of the population mean for the Atlanta plant.

From our study of interval estimation in Chapter 8, we know that the general form of an interval estimate of a population mean is

$$\bar{x} \pm t_{\alpha/2} \frac{s}{\sqrt{n}} \tag{10.28}$$

where s is the estimate of the population standard deviation σ. In the analysis of variance the best estimate of σ is provided by the square root of MSE or the Pooled StDev, therefore we use a value of 5.354 for s in expression (10.28). The degrees of freedom for the t value is 15, the degrees of freedom associated with the within-treatments estimate of σ^2. Hence, with $t_{.025} = 2.131$ we obtain

$$79 \pm 2.131 \frac{5.354}{\sqrt{6}} = 79 \pm 4.66$$

TABLE 10.6   ANALYSIS OF VARIANCE TABLE FOR THE NCP EXAMPLE

Source of Variation	Sum of Squares	Degrees of Freedom	Mean Square	F
Treatments	516	2	258.00	9.00
Error	430	15	28.67	
Total	946	17		

Thus, the individual 95% confidence interval for the Atlanta plant goes from $79 - 4.66 = 74.34$ to $79 + 4.6 = 83.66$. Because the sample sizes are equal for the NCP example, the individual confidence intervals for the Dallas and Seattle plants are also constructed by adding and subtracting 4.66 from each sample mean. Thus, in the figure provided by Minitab we see that the widths of the confidence intervals are the same.

NOTES AND COMMENTS

1. The overall sample mean can also be computed as a weighted average of the k sample means.

$$\bar{\bar{x}} = \frac{n_1\bar{x}_1 + n_2\bar{x}_2 + \cdots + n_k\bar{x}_k}{n_T}$$

In problems where the sample means are provided, this formula is simpler than equation (10.16) for computing the overall mean.

2. If each sample consists of n observations, equation (10.19) can be written as

$$\text{MSTR} = \frac{n\sum_{j=1}^{k}(\bar{x}_j - \bar{\bar{x}})^2}{k-1} = n\left[\frac{\sum_{j=1}^{k}(\bar{x}_j - \bar{\bar{x}})^2}{k-1}\right]$$

$$= ns_{\bar{x}}^2$$

Note that this result is the same as presented in Section 10.4 when we introduced the concept of the between-treatments estimate of σ^2. Equation (10.19) is simply a generalization of this result to the unequal sample-size case.

3. If each sample has n observations, $n_T = kn$; thus, $n_T - k = k(n - 1)$, and equation (10.22) can be rewritten as

$$\text{MSE} = \frac{\sum_{j=1}^{k}(n-1)s_j^2}{k(n-1)} = \frac{(n-1)\sum_{j=1}^{k}s_j^2}{k(n-1)} = \frac{\sum_{j=1}^{k}s_j^2}{k}$$

In other words, if the sample sizes are the same, MSE is just the average of the k sample variances. Note that it is the same result we used in Section 10.4 when we introduced the concept of the within-treatments estimate of σ^2.

4. Confidence interval estimates for each of the k population means can be developed using

$$\bar{x} \pm t_{\alpha/2}\frac{\sqrt{\text{MSE}}}{\sqrt{n}}$$

The degrees of freedom for the t value are the degrees of freedom associated with the within-treatments estimate of σ^2.

EXERCISES

Methods

SELFtest   29. Samples of five observations were selected from each of three populations. The data obtained follow.

	Sample 1	Sample 2	Sample 3
	32	44	33
	30	43	36
	30	44	35
	26	46	36
	32	48	40
Sample mean	30	45	36
Sample variance	6.00	4.00	6.50

a. Compute the between-treatments estimate of σ^2.
b. Compute the within-treatments estimate of σ^2.

c. At the $\alpha = .05$ level of significance, can we reject the null hypothesis that the means of the three populations are equal?

d. Set up the ANOVA table for this problem.

30. Four observations were selected from each of three populations. The data obtained follow.

	Sample 1	Sample 2	Sample 3
	165	174	169
	149	164	154
	156	180	161
	142	158	148
Sample mean	153	169	158
Sample variance	96.67	97.33	82.00

a. Compute the between-treatments estimate of σ^2.

b. Compute the within-treatments estimate of σ^2.

c. At the $\alpha = .05$ level of significance, can we reject the null hypothesis that the three population means are equal? Explain.

d. Set up the ANOVA table for this problem.

31. Samples were selected from three populations. The data obtained follow.

	Sample 1	Sample 2	Sample 3
	93	77	88
	98	87	75
	107	84	73
	102	95	84
		85	75
		82	
$\bar{x}_j$	100	85	79
s_j^2	35.33	35.60	43.50

a. Compute the between-treatments estimate of σ^2.

b. Compute the within-treatments estimate of σ^2.

c. At the $\alpha = .05$ level of significance, can we reject the null hypothesis that the three population means are equal? Explain.

d. Set up the ANOVA table for this problem.

32. A random sample of 16 observations was selected from each of four populations. A portion of the ANOVA table follows.

Source of Variation	Sum of Squares	Degrees of Freedom	Mean Square	F
Treatments			400	
Error				
Total	1500			

a. Provide the missing entries for the ANOVA table.

b. At the $\alpha = .05$ level of significance, can we reject the null hypothesis that the means of the four populations are equal?

33. Random samples of 25 observations were selected from each of three populations. For these data, SSTR = 120 and SSE = 216.
    a. Set up the ANOVA table for this problem.
    b. At the α = .05 level of significance, what is the critical F value?
    c. At the α = .05 level of significance, can we reject the null hypothesis that the three population means are equal?

Applications

SELFtest

34. To test whether the mean time needed to mix a batch of material is the same for machines produced by three manufacturers, the Jacobs Chemical Company obtained the following data on the time (in minutes) needed to mix the material. Use these data to test whether the population mean times for mixing a batch of material differ for the three manufacturers. Use α = .05.

	Manufacturer	
1	**2**	**3**
20	28	20
26	26	19
24	31	23
22	27	22

35. Managers at all levels of an organization need adequate information to perform their respective tasks. One study investigated the effect the source has on the dissemination of information. In this particular study the sources of information were a superior, a peer, and a subordinate. In each case, a measure of dissemination was obtained, with higher values indicating greater dissemination of information. Using α = .05 and the following data, test whether the source of information significantly affects dissemination. What is your conclusion, and what does it suggest about the use and dissemination of information?

Superior	Peer	Subordinate
8	6	6
5	6	5
4	7	7
6	5	4
6	3	3
7	4	5
5	7	7
5	6	5

36. A study investigated the perception of corporate ethical values among individuals specializing in marketing. Using α = .05 and the following data (higher scores indicate higher ethical values), test for significant differences in perception among the three groups.

Marketing Managers	Marketing Research	Advertising
6	5	6
5	5	7
4	4	6
5	4	5
6	5	6
4	4	6

37. A study reported in the *Journal of Small Business Management* concluded that self-employed individuals experience higher job stress than individuals who are not self-employed. In this study job stress was assessed with a 15-item scale designed to measure various aspects of ambiguity and role conflict. Ratings for each of the 15 items were made using a scale with 1–5 response options ranging from strong agreement to strong dis-agreement. The sum of the ratings for the 15 items for each individual surveyed is between 15 and 75, with higher values indicating a higher degree of job stress (*Journal of Small Business Management,* October 1997). Suppose that a similar approach, using a 20-item scale with 1–5 response options, was used to measure the job stress of individuals for 15 randomly selected real estate agents, 15 architects, and 15 stockbrokers. The results obtained follow.

Stress

Real Estate Agent	Architect	Stockbroker
81	43	65
48	63	48
68	60	57
69	52	91
54	54	70
62	77	67
76	68	83
56	57	75
61	61	53
65	80	71
64	50	54
69	37	72
83	73	65
85	84	58
75	58	58

Using $\alpha = .05$, test for any significant difference in job stress among the three professions.

38. The *Business Week* Global 1000 ranks companies on the basis of their market value (*Business Week,* July 7, 1997). The following table shows the price/earnings ratios for 29 companies classified as being in the finance economic sector. An industry code of 1 indicates a banking firm, a code of 2 a financial services firm, and a code of 3 an insurance firm. At the .05 level of significance, test whether the mean price/earnings ratio is the same for these three groups of financial firms.

CDfile
MktValue

Company	Industry Code	P/E	Company	Industry Code	P/E
Citicorp	1	15	Mellon Bank	1	16
NationsBank	1	14	Fleet Financial Group	1	15
Wells Fargo	1	25	First Bank System	1	16
First Union	1	13	American Express	2	19
KeyCorp	1	14	Travelers	2	15
Chase Manhattan	1	12	Merrill Lynch	2	12
Fifth Third	1	23	MBNA	2	24
Bank of New York	1	17	Cincinnati Financial	2	19
First Chicago NBD	1	13	Franklin Resources	2	22

Company	Industry Code	P/E	Company	Industry Code	P/E
Fannie Mae	2	17	Cigna	3	12
American International Group	3	21	Lincoln National	3	13
			AFLAC	3	21
Allstate	3	14	Equitable	3	11
Marsh & McLennan	3	20	Chubb	3	20
American General	3	16	General Re	3	15

SUMMARY

In this chapter we discussed procedures for developing interval estimates and conducting hypothesis tests involving two population means. First, we showed how to make inferences about the difference between the means of two populations when independent simple random samples are selected. We considered both the large- and small-sample cases. The z values from the standard normal probability distribution are used for inferences about the difference between two population means when the sample sizes are large. In the small-sample case, if the populations are normally distributed with equal variances, the t distribution is used for inferences.

Inferences about the difference between the means of two populations were then discussed for the matched sample design. In the matched sample design each element provides a pair of data values, one from each population. The difference between the paired data values is then used in the statistical analysis. The matched sample design is generally preferred to the independent sample design because the matched-sample procedure often reduces the sampling error and improves the precision of the estimate.

Finally, we showed how analysis of variance can be used to test for differences among means of several populations. We showed that the basis for the statistical tests used in analysis of variance is the development of two independent estimates of the population variance, σ^2. By computing the ratio of these two estimates (the F statistic), we developed a rejection rule for determining whether to reject the null hypothesis that the population means are equal.

GLOSSARY

Independent simple random samples   Samples selected from two populations in such a way that the elements making up one sample are chosen independently of the elements making up the other sample.

Pooled variance   An estimate of the variance of a population based on the combination of two sample variances. The pooled variance estimate is appropriate whenever the variances of two populations are assumed equal.

Matched samples   Samples in which each data value of one sample is matched with a corresponding data value of the other sample.

Analysis of variance   A statistical technique that can be used to test the hypothesis that the means of three or more populations are equal.

ANOVA table A table used to summarize the analysis of variance computations and results. It contains columns showing the source of variation, the sum of squares, the degrees of freedom, the mean square, and the F value.

Partitioning The process of allocating the total sum of squares and degrees of freedom to the various components.

KEY FORMULAS

Point Estimator of the Difference Between the Means of Two Populations

$$\bar{x}_1 - \bar{x}_2 \tag{10.1}$$

Expected Value of $\bar{x}_1 - \bar{x}_2$

$$E(\bar{x}_1 - \bar{x}_2) = \mu_1 - \mu_2 \tag{10.2}$$

Standard Deviation of $\bar{x}_1 - \bar{x}_2$

$$\sigma_{\bar{x}_1 - \bar{x}_2} = \sqrt{\frac{\sigma_1^2}{n_1} + \frac{\sigma_2^2}{n_2}} \tag{10.3}$$

Interval Estimate of the Difference Between the Means of Two Populations: Large-Sample Case ($n_1 \geq 30$ and $n_2 \geq 30$) with σ_1 and σ_2 Assumed Known

$$\bar{x}_1 - \bar{x}_2 \pm z_{\alpha/2}\sigma_{\bar{x}_1 - \bar{x}_2} \tag{10.4}$$

Point Estimator of $\sigma_{\bar{x}_1 - \bar{x}_2}$

$$s_{\bar{x}_1 - \bar{x}_2} = \sqrt{\frac{s_1^2}{n_1} + \frac{s_2^2}{n_2}} \tag{10.5}$$

Interval Estimate of the Difference Between the Means of Two Populations: Large-Sample Case ($n_1 \geq 30$ and $n_2 \geq 30$) with σ_1 and σ_2 Estimated by s_1 and s_2

$$\bar{x}_1 - \bar{x}_2 \pm z_{\alpha/2}s_{\bar{x}_1 - \bar{x}_2} \tag{10.6}$$

Standard Deviation of $\bar{x}_1 - \bar{x}_2$ When $\sigma_1^2 = \sigma_2^2 = \sigma^2$

$$\sigma_{\bar{x}_1 - \bar{x}_2} = \sqrt{\frac{\sigma^2}{n_1} + \frac{\sigma^2}{n_2}} = \sqrt{\sigma^2\left(\frac{1}{n_1} + \frac{1}{n_2}\right)} \tag{10.7}$$

Pooled Estimator of σ_2

$$s^2 = \frac{(n_1 - 1)s_1^2 + (n_2 - 1)s_2^2}{n_1 + n_2 - 2} \tag{10.8}$$

Point Estimator of $\sigma_{\bar{x}_1 - \bar{x}_2}$ When $\sigma_1^2 = \sigma_2^2 = \sigma^2$

$$s_{\bar{x}_1 - \bar{x}_2} = \sqrt{s^2\left(\frac{1}{n_1} + \frac{1}{n_2}\right)} \tag{10.9}$$

Interval Estimate of the Difference Between the Means of Two Populations: Small-Sample Case ($n_1 < 30$ and/or $n_2 < 30$) with σ_1 and σ_2 Estimated by s_1 and s_2

$$\bar{x}_1 - \bar{x}_2 \pm t_{\alpha/2}s_{\bar{x}_1 - \bar{x}_2} \tag{10.10}$$

Test Statistic for Hypothesis Tests About the Difference Between the Means of Two Populations (Large-Sample Case)

$$z = \frac{(\bar{x}_1 - \bar{x}_2) - (\mu_1 - \mu_2)}{\sqrt{\sigma_1^2/n_1 + \sigma_2^2/n_2}} \qquad (10.11)$$

Test Statistic for Hypothesis Tests About the Difference Between the Means of Two Populations (Small-Sample Case)

$$t = \frac{(\bar{x}_1 - \bar{x}_2) - (\mu_1 - \mu_2)}{\sqrt{s^2\left(\dfrac{1}{n_1} + \dfrac{1}{n_2}\right)}} \qquad (10.12)$$

Sample Mean for Matched Samples

$$\bar{d} = \frac{\Sigma d_i}{n}$$

Sample Standard Deviation for Matched Samples

$$s_d = \sqrt{\frac{\Sigma(d_i - \bar{d})^2}{n - 1}}$$

Test Statistic for Matched Samples (Small-Sample Case)

$$t = \frac{\bar{d} - \mu_d}{s_d/\sqrt{n}} \qquad (10.13)$$

Sample Mean for Treatment j

$$\bar{x}_j = \frac{\displaystyle\sum_{i=1}^{n_j} x_{ij}}{n_j} \qquad (10.14)$$

Sample Variance for Treatment j

$$s_j^2 = \frac{\displaystyle\sum_{i=1}^{n_j}(x_{ij} - \bar{x}_j)^2}{n_j - 1} \qquad (10.15)$$

Overall Sample Mean

$$\bar{\bar{x}} = \frac{\displaystyle\sum_{j=1}^{k}\sum_{i=1}^{n_j} x_{ij}}{n_T} \qquad (10.16)$$

$$n_T = n_1 + n_2 + \cdots + n_k \qquad (10.17)$$

Mean Square Due to Treatments

$$\text{MSTR} = \frac{\text{SSTR}}{k - 1} \qquad (10.20)$$

Sum of Squares Due to Treatments

$$\text{SSTR} = \sum_{j=1}^{k} n_j(\bar{x}_j - \bar{\bar{x}})^2 \qquad (10.21)$$

Mean Square Due to Error

$$\text{MSE} = \frac{\text{SSE}}{n_T - k} \qquad (10.23)$$

Sum of Squares Due to Error

$$\text{SSE} = \sum_{j=1}^{k} (n_j - 1)s_j^2 \qquad (10.24)$$

Test Statistic for the Equality of k Population Means

$$F = \frac{\text{MSTR}}{\text{MSE}} \qquad (10.25)$$

Total Sum of Squares

$$\text{SST} = \sum_{j=1}^{k} \sum_{i=1}^{n_j} (x_{ij} - \bar{\bar{x}})^2 \qquad (10.26)$$

Partition of Sum of Squares

$$\text{SST} = \text{SSTR} + \text{SSE} \qquad (10.27)$$

SUPPLEMENTARY EXERCISES

39. Starting annual salaries for individuals with master's and bachelor's degrees in business were collected in two independent random samples. Use the following data to develop a 90% confidence interval estimate of the increase in starting salary that can be expected upon completion of a master's program.

Master's Degree	Bachelor's Degree
$n_1 = 60$	$n_2 = 80$
$\bar{x}_1 = \$40,000$	$\bar{x}_2 = \$35,000$
$s_1 = \$2,500$	$s_2 = \$2,000$

40. Mutual funds are classified as *load* or *no-load* funds. Load funds require an investor to pay an initial fee based on a percentage of the amount invested in the fund. The no-load funds do not require this initial fee. Some financial advisors argue that the load mutual funds may be worth the extra fee because these funds provide a higher mean rate of return than the no-load mutual funds. A sample of 30 load mutual funds and a sample of 30 no-load mutual funds were selected from *Barron's Lipper Mutual Funds Quarterly*, January 12, 1998. Data were collected on the annual return for the funds over a five-year period. The data are contained in the data set Mutual. The data for the first five load and first five no-load mutual funds are as follows.

Mutual

Mutual Funds—Load	Return	Mutual Funds—No Load	Return
American National Growth	15.51	Amana Income Fund	13.24
Arch Small Cap Equity	14.57	Berger One Hundred	12.13
Bartlett Cap Basic	17.73	Columbia International Stock	12.17
Calvert World International	10.31	Dodge & Cox Balanced	16.06
Colonial Fund A	16.23	Evergreen Fund	17.61

    a. Formulate H_0 and H_a such that rejection of H_0 leads to the conclusion that the load mutual funds have a higher mean annual return over the five-year period.

    b. Use the 60 mutual funds in the data set Mutual to conduct the hypothesis test. Using $\alpha = .05$, what is your conclusion?

    c. What is the p-value?

41. Samples of final examination scores for two statistics classes with different instructors provided the following results.

Instructor A	Instructor B
$n_1 = 12$	$n_2 = 15$
$\bar{x}_1 = 72$	$\bar{x}_2 = 78$
$s_1 = 8$	$s_2 = 10$

With $\alpha = .05$, test whether these data are sufficient to conclude that the mean grades for the two classes differ.

42. Figure Perfect, Inc., is a women's figure salon that specializes in weight reduction programs. Weights for a sample of clients before and after a six-week introductory program follow.

	Weight	
Client	Before	After
1	140	132
2	160	158
3	210	195
4	148	152
5	190	180
6	170	164

Using $\alpha = .05$, test to determine whether the introductory program provides a statistically significant weight loss. What is your conclusion?

43. The Asian economy faltered during the last few months of 1997. Investors anticipated that the downturn in the Asian economy would have a negative effect on the earnings of companies in the United States during the fourth quarter of 1997. The following sample data show the earnings per share for the fourth quarter of 1996 and the fourth quarter of 1997 (*The Wall Street Journal,* January 28, 1998).

CDfile
Asia

Company	Earnings 1996	Earnings 1997
Atlantic Richfield	1.16	1.17
Balchem Corp.	0.16	0.13
Black & Decker Corp.	0.97	1.02
Dial Corp.	0.18	0.23
DSC Communications	0.15	−0.32
Eastman Chemical	0.77	0.36
Excel Communications	0.28	−0.14
Federal Signal	0.40	0.29
Ford Motor Company	0.97	1.45
GTE Corp	0.81	0.73
ITT Industries	0.59	0.60
Kimberly-Clark	0.61	−0.27
Minnesota Mining & Mfr.	0.91	0.89
Procter & Gamble	0.63	0.71

a. Formulate H_0 and H_a such that rejection of H_0 leads to the conclusion that the mean earnings per share for the fourth quarter of 1997 are less than for the fourth quarter of 1996.

b. Use the data in the file Asia to conduct the hypothesis test. Using $\alpha = .05$, what is your conclusion?

44. Buyers of sport utility vehicles (SUVs) and pickup trucks find a wide choice in today's marketplace. One of the factors that is important to many buyers is the resale value of the vehicle. The following table shows the resale value (%) after two years for 10 SUVs, 10 small pickup trucks, and 10 large pickup trucks (*Kiplinger's New Cars & Trucks 2000 Buyer's Guide*).

CDfile
Trucks

Sport Utility	Resale Value	Small Pickup	Resale Value
Chevrolet Blazer LS	55	Chevrolet S-10 Extended Cab	46
Ford Explorer Sport	57	Dodge Dakota Club Cab Sport	53
GMC Yukon XL 1500	67	Ford Ranger XLT Regular Cab	48
Honda CR-V	65	Ford Ranger XLT Supercab	55
Isuzu VehiCross	62	GMC Sonoma Regular Cab	44
Jeep Cherokee Limited	57	Isuzu Hombre Spacecab	41
Mercury Mountaineer	59	Mazda B4000 SE Cab Plus	51
Nissan Pathfinder XE	54	Nissan Frontier XE Regular Cab	51
Toyota 4Runner	55	Toyota Tacoma Xtracab	49
Toyota RAV4	55	Toyota Tacoma Xtracab V6	50

Full-Size Pickup	Resale Value
Chevrolet K2500	60
Chevrolet Silverado 2500 Ext	64
Dodge Ram 1500	54
Dodge Ram Quad Cab 2500	63
Dodge Ram Regular Cab 2500	59
Ford F150 XL	58
Ford F-350 Super Duty Crew Cab XL	64
GMC New Sierra 1500 Ext Cab	68
Toyota Tundra Access Cab Limited	53
Toyota Tundra Regular Cab	58

At the $\alpha = .05$ level of significance, test for any significant difference in the mean resale value for the three types of vehicles.

45. The following data show the age of 12 top executives for major marketers of food, retail, and personal care products (*Advertising Age,* December 1, 1997).

CDfile
AgeExec

Company	Category	Executive	Age
Campbell Soup Co.	Food	Dale F. Morrison	48
General Mills	Food	Stephen W. Sanger	51
Kellogg Co.	Food	Arnold G. Langbo	59
RJR Nabisco	Food	Stephen F. Goldstone	51
Estee Lauder Cos.	Personal Care	Leonard A. Lauder	64
Gillette Co.	Personal Care	Alfred M. Zeien	67
Procter & Gamble Co.	Personal Care	John E. Pepper	59
Unilever	Personal Care	Morris Tabaksblat	59
Federated Department Stores	Retail	James W. Zimmerman	53
J.C. Penney Co.	Retail	James E. Oesterreicher	55
Sears Roebuck & Co.	Retail	Arthur C. Martinez	57
Kmart Corp.	Retail	Floyd Hall	58

At the $\alpha = .05$ level of significance, is there a significant difference in the mean age of executives for the three categories of companies?

46. A study reported in the *Journal of Small Business Management* concluded that self-employed individuals do not experience higher job satisfaction than individuals who are not self-employed. In this study, job satisfaction is measured using 18 items, each of which is rated using a Likert-type scale with 1–5 response options ranging from strong agreement to strong disagreement. A higher score on this scale indicates a higher degree of job satisfaction. The sum of the ratings for the 18 items, ranging from 18–90, is used as the measure of job satisfaction (*Journal of Small Business Management,* October 1997). Suppose that this approach was used to measure the job satisfaction for lawyers, physical therapists, cabinetmakers, and systems analysts. The results obtained for a sample of 10 individuals from each profession follow.

SatisJob

Lawyer	Physical Therapist	Cabinetmaker	Systems Analyst
44	55	54	44
42	78	65	73
74	80	79	71
42	86	69	60
53	60	79	64
50	59	64	66
45	62	59	41
48	52	78	55
64	55	84	76
38	50	60	62

At the $\alpha = .05$ level of significance, test for any difference in the job satisfaction among the four professions.

47. Crown Plaza Hotels and Resorts offered special weekend rates at their resort hotels nationwide. A sample of 30 properties from three regions of the country provided the following room rates (*USA Today,* April 14, 2000).

Resorts

West	Rate ($)	South	Rate ($)	Northeast	Rate ($)
Albuquerque	89	Atlanta	105	Albany	89
Irvine	79	Dallas	80	Boston	139
Las Vegas	119	Greenville	79	Hartford	85
Los Angeles	99	Houston	79	New York	159
Palo Alto	109	Jackson	69	Philadelphia	99
Phoenix	149	Macon	69	Pittsfield	99
Portland	79	Miami	89	Providence	149
San Francisco	139	Orlando	119	Washington	159
San Jose	99	Richmond	109	White Plains	109
Seattle	119	Tampa	119	Worchester	124

At the $\alpha = .05$ level of significance, test whether the mean rates are the same for the three regions.

48. According to the sixth annual survey of ad agency employees conducted by the accounting firm Altschuler, Melvoin & Glasser, ad agency employees can expect another banner year in compensation (*Advertising Age,* December 1, 1997). To investigate whether the annual compensation among art directors differs by region, suppose that a sample of 10 art directors was selected from each of four regions: West, South, North Central, and Northeast. The base salary ($1000s) for each of the individuals sampled follows.

ArtDir

West	South	North Central	Northeast
60.9	50.8	49.5	65.9
45.9	39.6	42.3	58.6
62.1	44.2	35.5	49.3
66.6	40.0	49.1	52.9
68.0	53.9	56.7	48.5

West	South	North Central	Northeast
65.0	45.4	41.4	52.9
49.4	61.1	51.3	52.4
62.3	42.3	49.4	48.1
62.6	38.4	42.1	46.5
57.2	38.3	55.7	45.9

At the $\alpha = .05$ level of significance, test whether the mean base salary for art directors is the same for each of the four regions.

49. The National Football League rates prospects position by position on a scale that ranges from 5 to 9. The ratings are interpreted as follows: 8.0–9.0 should start the first year; 7.0–7.9 should start; 6.0–6.9 will make the team as backup; and 5.0–5.9 can make the club and contribute. The following table shows the ratings for three positions for 40 NFL prospects (*USA Today,* April 14, 2000). Does there appear to be any significant effect on the rating due to the player's position?

CDfile
NFL

Wide Receiver		Guard		Offensive Tackle	
Name	**Rating**	**Name**	**Rating**	**Name**	**Rating**
Peter Warrick	9.0	Cosey Coleman	7.4	Chris Samuels	8.5
Plaxico Burress	8.8	Travis Claridge	7.0	Stockar McDougle	8.0
Sylvester Morris	8.3	Kaulana Noa	6.8	Chris McIngosh	7.8
Travis Taylor	8.1	Leander Jordan	6.7	Adrian Klemm	7.6
Laveranues Coles	8.0	Chad Clifton	6.3	Todd Wade	7.3
Dez White	7.9	Manula Savea	6.1	Marvel Smith	7.1
Jerry Porter	7.4	Ryan Johanningmeir	6.0	Michael Thompson	6.8
Ron Dugans	7.1	Mark Tauscher	6.0	Bobby Williams	6.8
Todd Pinkston	7.0	Blaine Saipaia	6.0	Darnell Alford	6.4
Dennis Northcutt	7.0	Richard Mercier	5.8	Terrance Beadles	6.3
Anthony Lucas	6.9	Damion McIntosh	5.3	Tutan Reyes	6.1
Darrell Jackson	6.6	Jeno James	5.5	Greg Robinson-Ran	6.0
Danny Farmer	6.5	Al Jackson	5.5		
Sherrod Gideon	6.4				
Trevor Gaylor	6.2				

50. Each month *Internet Magazine* accesses more than 100 Internet service providers (ISPs) in order to check the availability of the ISP and test the speed of the connection by measuring the time (seconds) it takes to download a number of popular Web pages. The following data show the download time for 22 free ISPs for Web sites located in the United Kingdom, United States, and Europe (*Internet Magazine,* January 2000).

CDfile
ISP

ISP Name	U.K.	U.S.	Europe
Abel Gratis	10.62	14.64	17.08
Breathe	11.67	14.14	19.86
btclick.com	12.12	16.43	21.30

(*continued*)

ISP Name	U.K.	U.S.	Europe
Bun	11.13	14.09	15.83
Cable & Wireless Life	9.99	13.07	18.43
conX	12.63	15.97	22.12
Freebeeb	11.71	15.52	19.57
Free-Online	13.77	13.98	23.35
Freeserve	10.65	13.62	25.56
FreeUK	12.20	14.96	18.95
Icom-Web	9.62	11.66	15.91
IPNet	13.82	16.70	22.86
I-way Soho	14.86	12.86	19.32
LineOne	12.01	17.82	21.88
Madasafish	13.38	15.59	19.61
NetDirect Online	11.71	15.52	19.57
Netscape Online	10.84	12.66	16.52
Screaming.net (BT Line)	13.23	15.91	23.08
Telinco Internet Services	12.83	15.34	18.76
UK Online	10.39	13.28	21.04
UKPeople	13.79	19.82	19.76
Virgin Net	12.17	15.47	21.94

At $\alpha = .05$, is there a significant difference in the mean download time for Web sites located in the three countries?

Case Problem 1   PAR, INC.

Par, Inc., manufactures golf equipment. Management believes that Par's market share could be increased with the introduction of a cut-resistant, longer-lasting golf ball. Therefore, the research group at Par investigates a new golf ball coating designed to resist cuts and provide a more durable ball. The tests with the coating show promising results.

One of the researchers voiced concern about the effect of the new coating on driving distances. Par would like the new cut-resistant ball to offer driving distances comparable to those of the current-model golf ball. To compare the driving distances for the two balls, 40 balls of both the new and current models were subjected to distance tests. The testing was performed with a mechanical hitting machine so that any difference between the mean distances for the two models could be attributed to a difference in the design. The results of the tests, with distances measured to the nearest yard, follow. These data are available in the data set Golf.

Golf

Model		Model		Model		Model	
Current	New	Current	New	Current	New	Current	New
264	277	270	272	263	274	281	283
261	269	287	259	264	266	274	250
267	263	289	264	284	262	273	253
272	266	280	280	263	271	263	260
258	262	272	274	260	260	275	270
283	251	275	281	283	281	267	263

Model		Model		Model		Model	
Current	**New**	**Current**	**New**	**Current**	**New**	**Current**	**New**
258	262	265	276	255	250	279	261
266	289	260	269	272	263	274	255
259	286	278	268	266	278	276	263
270	264	275	262	268	264	262	279

Managerial Report

1. Formulate and present the rationale for a hypothesis test that Par could use to compare the driving distances of the current and new golf balls.
2. Analyze the data to provide the hypothesis testing conclusion. What is the *p*-value for your test? What is your recommendation for Par, Inc.?
3. Provide descriptive statistical summaries of the data for each model.
4. What is the 95% confidence interval for the population mean of each model, and what is the 95% confidence interval for the difference between the means of the two populations?
5. Do you see a need for larger sample sizes and more testing with the golf balls? Discuss.

Case Problem 2   WENTWORTH MEDICAL CENTER

As part of a long-term study of individuals 65 years of age or older, sociologists and physicians at the Wentworth Medical Center in upstate New York investigated the relationship between geographic location and depression. They selected a sample of 60 individuals, all in reasonably good health: 20 individuals were residents of Florida, 20 were residents of New York, and 20 were residents of North Carolina. The researchers gave each of the individuals sampled a standardized test to measure depression. The data collected follow; higher test scores indicate higher levels of depression. These data are available in the data set Medical1.

A second part of the study considered the relationship between geographic location and depression for individuals 65 years of age or older who had a chronic health condition such as arthritis, hypertension, and/or heart ailment. The researchers identified a sample of 60 individuals with such conditions. Again, 20 were residents of Florida, 20 were residents of New York, and 20 were residents of North Carolina. The levels of depression recorded for this study follow. These data are available in the data set Medical2.

	Data from Medical1				Data from Medical2		
	Florida	**New York**	**North Carolina**		**Florida**	**New York**	**North Carolina**
	3	8	10		13	14	10
	7	11	7		12	9	12
	7	9	3		17	15	15
	3	7	5		17	12	18
	8	8	11		20	16	12

Medical1

Medical2

(continued)

Data from Medical1			Data from Medical2		
Florida	New York	North Carolina	Florida	New York	North Carolina
8	7	8	21	24	14
8	8	4	16	18	17
5	4	3	14	14	8
5	13	7	13	15	14
2	10	8	17	17	16
6	6	8	12	20	18
2	8	7	9	11	17
6	12	3	12	23	19
6	8	9	15	19	15
9	6	8	16	17	13
7	8	12	15	14	14
5	5	6	13	9	11
4	7	3	10	14	12
7	7	8	11	13	13
3	8	11	17	11	11

Managerial Report

1. Use descriptive statistics to summarize the data from the two studies. What are your preliminary observations about the depression scores?
2. Use analysis of variance on both data sets. State the hypotheses being tested in each case. What are your conclusions?
3. Use inferences about individual treatment means where appropriate. What are your conclusions?
4. Discuss extensions of this study or other analyses that you feel might be helpful.

Case Problem 3   COMPENSATION FOR ID PROFESSIONALS

For the last 10 years *Industrial Distribution* tracked compensation of industrial distribution (ID) professionals. Results for the 358 respondents in the 1997 Annual Salary Survey showed that 27% of the respondents work for companies with sales over $40 million, with the typical ID professional working for a $12 million firm. Those who work for small to mid-sized companies (between $6 million and $20 million) report higher earnings than those in larger firms. The lowest paid employees work for firms with sales of less than $1 million. The typical outside salesperson made $50,000 in 1996, and the typical inside salesperson earned just $30,000 (*Industrial Distribution,* November 1997). Suppose that a local chapter of ID professionals in the greater San Francisco area conducted a survey of its membership to study the relationship, if any, between the years of experience and salary for individuals employed in outside and inside sales positions. The survey asked respondents to specify one of three levels of years of experience: low (1–10 years); medium (11–20 years); and high (21 or more years). A portion of the data obtained follow. The complete data set, consisting of 120 observations, is available in the data set IDSalary.

Observation	Salary $	Position	Experience
1	28938	Inside	Medium
2	27694	Inside	Medium
3	45515	Outside	Low
4	27031	Inside	Medium
5	37283	Outside	Low
6	32718	Inside	Low
7	54081	Outside	High
8	23621	Inside	Low
9	47835	Outside	High
10	29768	Inside	Medium
.	.	.	.
.	.	.	.
.	.	.	.
115	33080	Inside	High
116	53702	Outside	Medium
117	58131	Outside	Medium
118	32788	Inside	High
119	28070	Inside	Medium
120	35259	Outside	Low

CDfile
IDSalary

Managerial Report

1. Use descriptive statistics to summarize the data.
2. Develop a 95% confidence interval estimate of the mean annual salary for all salespersons, regardless of years of experience and type of position.
3. Develop a 95% confidence interval estimate of the mean salary for outside salespersons. Compare your results with the national value reported by *Industrial Distribution.*
4. Develop a 95% confidence interval estimate of the mean salary for inside salespersons. Compare your results with the national value reported by *Industrial Distribution.*
5. Ignoring the years of experience, develop a 95% confidence interval estimate of the mean difference between the annual salary for outside salespersons and the mean annual salary for inside salespersons. What is your conclusion?
6. Use analysis of variance to test for any significant differences due to position. Use a .05 level of significance, and for now, ignore the effect of years of experience.
7. Use analysis of variance to test for any significant differences due to years of experience. Use a .05 level of significance, and for now, ignore the effect of position.
8. At the .05 level of significance test for any significant differences due to position, years of experience, and interaction. Use inferences about individual treatment means where appropriate.

Appendix 10.1   TWO POPULATION MEANS WITH MINITAB

We describe how to use Minitab for hypothesis tests about the difference between the means of two populations.

Large-Sample Case

We will use the data on examination scores at two training centers shown in Table 10.1. The Center A scores appear in column C1 and the Center B scores appear in column C2. Minitab does not have a two-sample hypothesis testing procedure that uses the z test statistic. However, the Minitab 2-Sample t test procedure provides a good approximation in the large-sample case. The steps necessary to use the Minitab 2-Sample t test for the training center data follow.

Step 1. Select the **Stat** pull-down menu
Step 2. Choose **Basic Statistics**
Step 3. Choose **2-Sample t**
Step 4. When the 2-Sample t dialog box appears:
  Select **Samples in different columns**
  Enter C1 in the **First** box
  Enter C2 in the **Second** box
  Make sure **Assume equal variances** is not selected
  Select **Options**
Step 5. Enter 95 in the **Confidence level** box*
  Enter 0 in the **Test Mean** box
  Enter not equal in the **Alternative** box
  Click **OK**
Step 6. Click **OK**

The Minitab output shows p-value $= .04$. With a .05 level of significance, we reject H_0.

In this large-sample case, we stated that the z test statistic should be used when population distribution is not known. However, Minitab does not provide a two-sample z test. As a result we must adapt the 2-Sample t test to our needs. For the large-sample case with s used to estimate σ, the t-value provided by Minitab is the same as the z value of 2.09. Thus, the only difference with the 2-Sample t test is that the p-value $= .04$ is slightly larger than the p-value $= .0366$ that would have been obtained using the standard normal probability distribution with $z = 2.09$. In most cases, this slight difference in the p-value does not affect the hypothesis testing conclusion.

Small-Sample Case

The Minitab 2-Sample t procedure described for the large-sample case can be used for a small-sample hypothesis test about the difference between two population means. The only difference is that **Assume equal variances** is *selected* in step 4. Finally, the **Alternative** box in step 5 may be less than, not equal, or greater than depending upon the alternative hypothesis H_a.

Matched Samples

We use the data on production times in Table 10.4 to illustrate the matched sample procedure. The completion times for method 1 are entered into column C1 and the completion times for method 2 are entered into column C2. The Minitab steps for the matched-sample hypothesis test are as follows:

Step 1. Select the **Stat** pull-down menu
Step 2. Choose **Basic Statistics**
Step 3. Choose **Paired t**

---

*Minitab provides both hypothesis testing and interval estimation results simultaneously. The user may select any confidence level for the interval estimate of the population mean: 95% is suggested here.

Step 4. When the Paired t dialog box appears:
                 Enter C1 in the **First sample** box
                 Enter C2 in the **Second sample** box
                 Select **Options**
Step 5. Enter 95 in the **Confidence level**
                 Enter 0 in the **Test Mean** box
                 Enter not equal in the **Alternative** box
                 Click **OK**
Step 6. Click **OK**

Appendix 10.2   TWO POPULATION MEANS WITH EXCEL

We describe how to use Excel for hypothesis tests about the difference between the means of two populations.

Large-Sample Case

CDfile
ExamData

We use the examination scores in Table 10.1. The label Center A is in cell A1 and the label Center B is in cell B1. The Center A scores are in cells A2:A31 and the Center B scores are in cells B2:B41. We will assume that the VAR function was used to compute the variances of the two populations. Thus, we will use $s_1^2 = (8)^2 = 64$ and $s_2^2 = (10)^2 = 100$. The steps to conduct the test follow:

Step 1. Select the **Tools** pull-down menu
Step 2. Choose **Data Analysis**
Step 3. When the Data Analysis dialog box appears:
                 Choose **z-Test: Two Sample for Means**
                 Click **OK**
Step 4. When the z-Test: Two Sample for Means dialog box appears:
                 Enter A1:A31 in the **Variable 1 Range** box
                 Enter B1:B41 in the **Variable 2 Range** box
                 Enter 0 in the **Hypothesized Mean Difference** box
                 Enter 64 in the **Variable 1 Variance** box
                 Enter 100 in the **Variable 2 Variance** box
                 Select **Labels**
                 Enter .05 in the **Alpha** box
                 Select **Output Range** and enter C1 in the box
                 Click **OK**

The value of the test statistic $z = 2.09$ appears in cell D8, and the p-value $= .0366$ appears in cell D11.

Small-Sample Case

CDfile
Software

We use the data for the software testing study in Table 10.3. The data are entered into an Excel worksheet with the label Current in cell A1 and the label New in cell B1. The completion times for the current technology are in cells A2:A13, and the completion times for the new software are in cells B2:B13. The following steps can be used to conduct a small-sample hypothesis test about the difference between two population means.

Step 1. Select **Tools** pull-down menu
Step 2. Choose **Data Analysis**

Step 3. When the Data Analysis dialog box appears:
　　　　Choose **t-Test: Two Sample Assuming Equal Variances**
　　　　Click **OK**
Step 4. When the t-Test: Two Sample Assuming Equal Variances dialog box appears:
　　　　Enter A1:A13 in the **Variable 1 Range** box
　　　　Enter B1:B13 in the **Variable 2 Range** box
　　　　Enter 0 in the **Hypothesized Mean Difference** box
　　　　Select **Labels**
　　　　Enter .05 in the **Alpha** box
　　　　Select **Output Range** and enter C1 in the box
　　　　Click **OK**

The value of the test statistic $t = 2.16$ appears in cell D10, and the one-tailed p-value = .021 appears in cell D11.

Matched Samples

Matched

We use the matched-sample completion times in Table 10.4 to illustrate. The data are entered into a worksheet with the label Method 1 in cell A1 and the label Method 2 in cell B1. The completion times for method 1 are in cells A2:A7 and the completion times for method 2 are in cells B2:B7. The Excel procedure uses the steps previously described for the small-sample case except the user chooses the **t-Test: Paired Two Sample for Means** data analysis tool in step 3. The variable 1 range is A1:A7 and the variable 2 range is B1:B7. The value of the test statistic $t = 2.196$ appears in cell D10, and the two-tailed p-value = .08 appears in cell D13.

Appendix 10.3　ANALYSIS OF VARIANCE WITH MINITAB

NCP

To illustrate how Minitab can be used to test for the equality of k population means, we show how to test whether the mean examination score is the same at each plant in the National Computer Products example introduced in Section 10.4. The examination score data are entered into the first three columns of a Minitab worksheet; column 1 is labeled Atlanta, column 2 is labeled Dallas, and column 3 is labeled Seattle. The following steps produce the Minitab output in Figure 10.10

Step 1. Select the **Stat** pull-down menu
Step 2. Choose **ANOVA**
Step 3. Choose **Oneway (Unstacked)**
Step 4. When the Oneway Analysis of Variance dialog box appears:
　　　　Enter C1-C3 in the **Responses (in separate columns)** box
　　　　Click **OK**

Appendix 10.4　ANALYSIS OF VARIANCE WITH EXCEL

NCP

To illustrate how Excel can be used to test for the equality of k population means for both of these cases, we show how to test whether the mean examination score is the same at each plant in the National Computer Products example introduced in Section 10.4. The examination score data are entered into worksheet rows 2 to 7 of columns A, B, and C as shown in Figure 10.11; note that the cells in row 1 for columns A, B, and C are labeled Atlanta, Dallas, and Seattle. The following steps are used to obtain the output shown in cells

FIGURE 10.11   EXCEL SOLUTION FOR THE NCP ANALYSIS OF VARIANCE EXAMPLE

	A	B	C	D	E	F	G	H
1	**Atlanta**	**Dallas**	**Seattle**					
2	85	71	59					
3	75	75	64					
4	82	73	62					
5	76	74	69					
6	71	69	75					
7	85	82	67					
8								
9								
10	Anova: Single Factor							
11								
12	SUMMARY							
13	*Groups*	*Count*	*Sum*	*Average*	*Variance*			
14	Atlanta	6	474	79	34			
15	Dallas	6	444	74	20			
16	Seattle	6	396	66	32			
17								
18								
19	ANOVA							
20	*Source of Variation*	*SS*	*df*	*MS*	*F*	*P-value*	*F crit*	
21	Between Groups	516	2	258	9	0.0027	3.68	
22	Within Groups	430	15	28.67				
23								
24	Total	946	17					
25								

A10:G24; the ANOVA portion of this output corresponds to the ANOVA table shown in Table 10.6.

Step 1. Select the **Tools** pull-down menu

Step 2. Choose **Data Analysis**

Step 3. Choose **Anova: Single-Factor** from the list of Analysis Tools
　　　　Click **OK**

Step 4. When the Anova: Single-Factor dialog box appears:
　　　　Enter A1:C7 in **Input Range** box
　　　　Select **Columns**
　　　　Select **Labels in First Row**
　　　　Select **Output Range** and enter A10 in the box
　　　　Click **OK**

Chapter 11

COMPARISONS INVOLVING PROPORTIONS AND A TEST OF INDEPENDENCE

CONTENTS

UNITED WAY*

ROCHESTER, NEW YORK

United Way of Greater Rochester is a nonprofit organization dedicated to improving the quality of life for all people in the seven counties it serves by meeting the community's most important human care needs.

The annual United Way/Red Cross fund-raising campaign, conducted each spring, funds hundreds of programs offered by more than 200 service providers. These providers meet a wide variety of human needs—physical, mental, and social—and serve people of all ages, backgrounds, and economic means.

Because of enormous volunteer involvement, United Way of Greater Rochester is able to hold its operating costs at just eight cents of every dollar raised.

The United Way of Greater Rochester decided to conduct a survey to learn more about community perceptions of charities. Focus-group interviews held with professional, service, and general worker groups obtained preliminary information on perceptions, which was then used to help develop the questionnaire for the survey. The questionnaire was pretested, modified, and distributed to 440 individuals; 323 completed questionnaires were obtained.

A variety of descriptive statistics, including frequency distributions and crosstabulations, were provided from the data collected. An important part of the analysis involved the use of contingency tables and chi-square tests of independence. One such statistical test determined whether perceptions of administrative expenses were independent of occupation.

The hypotheses for the test of independence were:

H_0: Perception of United Way administrative expenses is independent of the occupation of the respondent.

Providing supervised play areas for children is one of United Way's many services. © Tony Freeman/PhotoEdit.

H_a: Perception of United Way administrative expenses is not independent of the occupation of the respondent.

Two questions in the survey provided the data for the statistical test. One question obtained data on perceptions of the percentage of funds going to administrative expenses (up to 10%, 11–20%, and 21% or more). The other question asked for the occupation of the respondent.

The chi-square test at a 5% level of significance led to rejection of the null hypothesis of independence and to the conclusion that perceptions of United Way's administrative expenses did vary by occupation. Actual administrative expenses were less than 9%, but 35% of the respondents perceived that administrative expenses were 21% or more. Hence, many had inaccurate perceptions of administrative costs. In this group, production-line, clerical, sales, and professional-technical employees had more inaccurate perceptions than other groups.

The community perceptions study helped United Way of Rochester to adjust its program and fund-raising activities. In this chapter, you will learn how a statistical test of independence, such as that described here, is conducted.

*The authors are indebted to Dr. Philip R. Tyler, Marketing Consultant to the United Way, for providing this Statistics in Practice.

Many statistical applications call for a comparison of population proportions. In section 11.1, we describe statistical inferences concerning differences in the proportions for two populations. Two samples are required, one from each population, and the statistical inference is based on the two sample proportions. The second section looks at a hypothesis test comparing the proportions of a single multinomial population with the proportions stated in a null hypothesis. One sample from the multinomial population is used, and the hypothesis test is based on comparing the sample proportions with those stated in the null hypothesis. In the last section of the chapter, we show how contingency tables can be used to test for the independence of two variables. One sample is used for the test of independence, but measures on two variables are required for each sampled element. Both Sections 11.2 and 11.3 rely on the use of a chi-square statistical test.

11.1　INFERENCES ABOUT THE DIFFERENCE BETWEEN THE PROPORTIONS OF TWO POPULATIONS

Let us begin with an example involving a tax preparation firm interested in comparing the quality of work at two of its regional offices. By randomly selecting samples of tax returns prepared at each office and verifying the accuracy of the sample returns, the firm will be able to estimate the proportion of erroneous returns prepared at each office. Of particular interest is the difference between these proportions.

p_1 = proportion of erroneous returns for population 1 (office 1)
p_2 = proportion of erroneous returns for population 2 (office 2)
$\bar{p}_1$ = sample proportion for a simple random sample from population 1
$\bar{p}_2$ = sample proportion for a simple random sample from population 2

The difference between the two population proportions is given by $p_1 - p_2$. The point estimator of $p_1 - p_2$ follows.

Point Estimator of the Difference Between the Proportions of Two Populations

$$\bar{p}_1 - \bar{p}_2 \tag{11.1}$$

Thus, the point estimator of the difference between two population proportions is the difference between the sample proportions of two independent simple random samples.

Sampling Distribution of $\bar{p}_1 - \bar{p}_2$

In the study of the difference between two population proportions, $\bar{p}_1 - \bar{p}_2$ is the point estimator of interest. As we have seen in several preceding cases, the sampling distribution of the point estimator is a key factor in developing interval estimates and in testing hypotheses about the parameter of interest. The properties of the sampling distribution of $\bar{p}_1 - \bar{p}_2$ follow.

Sampling Distribution of $\bar{p}_1 - \bar{p}_2$

Expected Value: $E(\bar{p}_1 - \bar{p}_2) = p_1 - p_2$ (11.2)

The standard deviation, $\sigma_{\bar{p}_1 - \bar{p}_2}$, is also referred to as the standard error of the estimator $\bar{p}_1 - \bar{p}_2$.

Standard deviation: $\sigma_{\bar{p}_1 - \bar{p}_2} = \sqrt{\dfrac{p_1(1 - p_1)}{n_1} + \dfrac{p_2(1 - p_2)}{n_2}}$ (11.3)

where

n_1 = sample size for the simple random sample from population 1

n_2 = sample size for the simple random sample from population 2

Distribution form: If the sample sizes are large [i.e., $n_1 p_1$, $n_1(1 - p_1)$, $n_2 p_2$, and $n_2(1 - p_2)$ are all greater than or equal to 5], the sampling distribution of $\bar{p}_1 - \bar{p}_2$ can be approximated by a normal probability distribution.

Figure 11.1 shows the sampling distribution of $\bar{p}_1 - \bar{p}_2$.

Interval Estimation of $p_1 - p_2$

Suppose that independent simple random samples of tax returns from the two offices provide the following information.

Office 1	Office 2
$n_1 = 250$	$n_2 = 300$
Number of returns with errors = 35	Number of returns with errors = 27

FIGURE 11.1   SAMPLING DISTRIBUTION OF $\bar{p}_1 - \bar{p}_2$

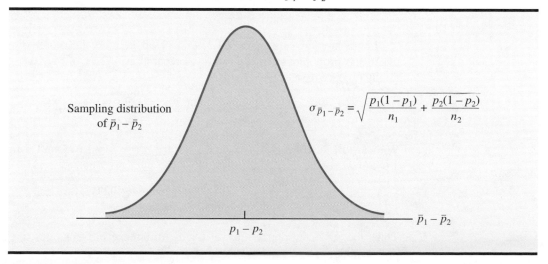

Sampling distribution of $\bar{p}_1 - \bar{p}_2$

$\sigma_{\bar{p}_1 - \bar{p}_2} = \sqrt{\dfrac{p_1(1 - p_1)}{n_1} + \dfrac{p_2(1 - p_2)}{n_2}}$

$p_1 - p_2$

$\bar{p}_1 - \bar{p}_2$

The sample proportions for the two offices follow.

$$\bar{p}_1 = \frac{35}{250} = .14$$

$$\bar{p}_2 = \frac{27}{300} = .09$$

The point estimate of the difference between the proportions of erroneous tax returns for the two populations is $\bar{p}_1 - \bar{p}_2 = .14 - .09 = .05$. Thus, we estimate that office 1 has a .05, or 5%, greater error rate than office 2.

Before developing a confidence interval for the difference between population proportions, we must estimate $\sigma_{\bar{p}_1-\bar{p}_2}$. Note that equation (11.3) cannot be used directly because p_1 and p_2 are unknown. The approach taken is to substitute $\bar{p}_1$ as an estimator of p_1 and $\bar{p}_2$ as an estimator of p_2 in equation (11.3). Doing so provides the following point estimator of $\sigma_{\bar{p}_1-\bar{p}_2}$.

Point Estimator of $\sigma_{\bar{p}_1-\bar{p}_2}$

$$s_{\bar{p}_1-\bar{p}_2} = \sqrt{\frac{\bar{p}_1(1-\bar{p}_1)}{n_1} + \frac{\bar{p}_2(1-\bar{p}_2)}{n_2}} \qquad (11.4)$$

Using equation (11.4), the following expression provides a confidence interval estimate of the difference between the proportions of two populations in the large sample case. We use $z_{\alpha/2}$ because the sampling distribution of $\bar{p}_1 - \bar{p}_2$ can be approximated by a normal distribution when the sample sizes are large.

Interval Estimate of the Difference Between the Proportions of Two Populations: Large-Sample Case with n_1p_1, $n_1(1-p_1)$, n_2p_2, and $n_2(1-p_2) \geq 5$

$$\bar{p}_1 - \bar{p}_2 \pm z_{\alpha/2}s_{\bar{p}_1-\bar{p}_2} \qquad (11.5)$$

where $1 - \alpha$ is the confidence coefficient.

Let us now use expression (11.5) to develop an interval estimate of the difference between the proportions for the two tax preparation offices in our example. Using equation (11.4), we have

$$s_{\bar{p}_1-\bar{p}_2} = \sqrt{\frac{.14(.86)}{250} + \frac{.09(.91)}{300}} = .0275$$

With a 90% confidence interval, we have $z_{\alpha/2} = z_{.05} = 1.645$ and a margin of error = 1.645(.0275). The interval estimate is

$$(.14 - .09) \pm 1.645(.0275)$$
$$.05 \pm .045$$

Thus, the 90% confidence interval for the difference in error rates at the two offices is .005 to .095.

Hypothesis Tests About $p_1 - p_2$

As an example of hypothesis tests about the difference between the proportions of two populations, let us reconsider the example concerning the error rates at two offices of the tax preparation firm. Suppose the firm simply wanted to know whether the two offices experienced a significant difference in error rates. The appropriate null and alternative hypotheses are

$$H_0: p_1 - p_2 = 0$$
$$H_a: p_1 - p_2 \neq 0$$

Figure 11.2 shows the sampling distribution of $\bar{p}_1 - \bar{p}_2$ based on the assumption of no difference between the two population proportions; that is, $p_1 - p_2 = 0$. In the large sample case, the sampling distribution is approximately normal and the test statistic for the difference between two population proportions is

$$z = \frac{(\bar{p}_1 - \bar{p}_2) - (p_1 - p_2)}{\sigma_{\bar{p}_1 - \bar{p}_2}} \tag{11.6}$$

Using $\alpha = .10$ and $z_{\alpha/2} = z_{.05} = 1.645$, the rejection rule is

Using test statistic: Reject H_0 if $z < -1.645$ or if $z > 1.645$
Using p-value: Reject H_0 if p-value $< .10$

The computation of z in equation (11.6) requires a value for the standard error of the difference between proportions $\sigma_{\bar{p}_1 - \bar{p}_2}$. Because this standard error is unknown, it must be estimated from the sample data. We may be tempted to use $\bar{p}_1$ and $\bar{p}_2$ in equation (11.4) as we did with the interval estimation procedure, but for the *special case* in which the hypotheses involve no difference between the population proportions (i.e., either $H_0: p_1 - p_2 = 0$,

FIGURE 11.2   SAMPLING DISTRIBUTION OF $\bar{p}_1 - \bar{p}_2$ WITH $H_0: p_1 - p_2 = 0$

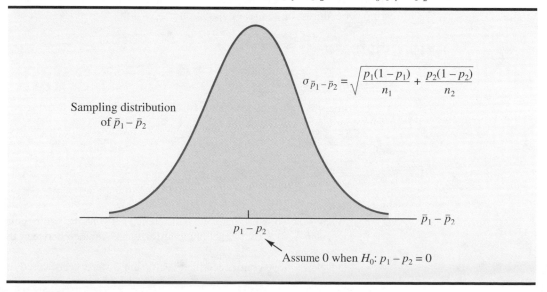

In hypothesis tests where
H_0 *is* $p_1 - p_2 = 0,$
$p_1 - p_2 \leq 0,$ *or*
$p_1 - p_2 \geq 0,$ *the 0 indicates*
no difference between the
two population proportions
p_1 *and* $p_2.$ *In this case,*
combining the two sample
proportions, $\bar{p}_1$ *and* $\bar{p}_2,$
provides one estimate of the
population proportion as in
equation (11.7). Then $s_{\bar{p}_1 - \bar{p}_2}$
can be computed as in
equation (11.8).

H_0: $p_1 - p_2 \leq 0$, or H_0: $p_1 - p_2 \geq 0$), equation (11.4) is modified to reflect the fact that when we assume H_0 to be true at the equality, we are assuming $p_1 = p_2$. When making this assumption, we combine or *pool* the two sample proportions to provide one estimate. This pooled estimator, denoted by $\bar{p}$, follows.

$$\bar{p} = \frac{n_1 \bar{p}_1 + n_2 \bar{p}_2}{n_1 + n_2} \tag{11.7}$$

With $\bar{p}$ used in place of both $\bar{p}_1$ and $\bar{p}_2$, equation (11.4) is revised to

$$s_{\bar{p}_1 - \bar{p}_2} = \sqrt{\bar{p}(1 - \bar{p})\left(\frac{1}{n_1} + \frac{1}{n_2}\right)} \tag{11.8}$$

Using equations (11.7) and (11.8), we can now proceed with a hypothesis test for the tax preparation firm example.

$$\bar{p} = \frac{250(.14) + 300(.09)}{550} = \frac{62}{550} = .113$$

$$s_{\bar{p}_1 - \bar{p}_2} = \sqrt{(.113)(.887)\left(\frac{1}{250} + \frac{1}{300}\right)} = .0271$$

The value of the test statistic is

$$z = \frac{(\bar{p}_1 - \bar{p}_2) - (p_1 - p_2)}{s_{\bar{p}_1 - \bar{p}_2}} = \frac{(.14 - .09) - 0}{.0271} = 1.85$$

Because $1.85 > 1.645$, at the .10 level of significance the null hypothesis is rejected. The area in the tail associated with $z = 1.85$ is $.5000 - .4678 = .0322$. Thus, the two-tailed p-value is $2(.0322) = .0644$, which is less than $\alpha = .10$. The sample evidence indicates a significant difference between the two population error rates.

As we saw with the hypothesis tests about differences between two population means (Chapter 10), one-tailed tests can be developed for the difference between two population proportions. The one-tailed rejection regions are established as in the one-tailed hypothesis testing procedures for a single population proportion.

EXERCISES

Methods

1. Consider the following results for two independent samples taken from two populations.

Sample 1	Sample 2
$n_1 = 400$	$n_2 = 300$
$\bar{p}_1 = .48$	$\bar{p}_2 = .36$

    a. What is the point estimate of the difference between the two population proportions?
    b. Develop a 90% confidence interval for the difference between the two population proportions.
    c. Develop a 95% confidence interval for the difference between the two population proportions.

SELFtest   **2.** Consider the hypothesis test

$$H_0: p_1 - p_2 \leq 0$$
$$H_a: p_1 - p_2 > 0$$

The following results are for two independent samples taken from the two populations.

Sample 1	Sample 2
$n_1 = 200$	$n_2 = 300$
$\bar{p}_1 = .22$	$\bar{p}_2 = .16$

    a. With $\alpha = .05$, what is your hypothesis testing conclusion?

    b. What is the p-value?

Applications

3. A *Business Week*/Harris survey asked senior executives at large corporations their opinions about the economic outlook for the future (*Business Week,* June 16, 1997). One question was "Do you think that there will be an increase in the number of full-time employees at your company over the next 12 months?" In May 1997, 220 of 400 executives answered yes, while in December 1996, 192 of 400 executives had answered yes. Provide a 95% confidence interval estimate for the difference between the proportions at the two points in time. What is your interpretation of the interval estimate?

4. A Gallup poll found that 16% of 505 men and 25% of 496 women surveyed favored a law forbidding the sale of all beer, wine, and liquor throughout the nation. Develop a 95% confidence interval for the difference between the proportion of women who favor such a ban and the proportion of men who favor such a ban.

5. A CNN/*USA Today* poll evaluated the popularity of major league baseball after the Mark McGwire and Sammy Sosa record-setting home-run chase during the 1998 season. A sample of 1082 found 682 people responding yes to the question "Are you a fan of major league baseball?" (*USA Today,* September 17, 1998). During the baseball strike of April 1995, a sample of 1008 found only 413 people responding yes to the same question.

    a. Use the sample proportions to estimate the fan support for major league baseball in 1998 and in 1995. What is the point estimate of the increase in major league baseball fan support from the strike in 1995 to the McGwire/Sosa home-run chase of 1998?

    b. Develop a 95% confidence interval estimate of the increase in fan support.

6. *Fortune* enlisted Yankelovich Partners to poll 600 adults on their ideas about marriage, divorce, and the contribution of the corporate wife to her executive husband (*Fortune,* February 2, 1998). In response to the statement, "In a divorce in a long-term marriage where the husband works outside the home and the wife is not employed for pay, the wife should be entitled to half the assets accumulated during the marriage," 279 of 300 women agreed and 255 of 300 men agreed.

    a. What are the sample proportions for the two populations, women and men?

    b. Test the hypothesis $H_0: p_1 - p_2 = 0$ using $\alpha = .05$. What is your conclusion?

    c. Provide a 95% confidence interval for the difference between the population proportions.

7. A sample of 1545 men and a sample of 1691 women were used to compare the amount of housework done by women and men in dual-earner marriages. The study showed that 67.5% of the men felt the division of housework was fair and 60.8% of the women felt the division of housework was fair (*American Journal of Sociology,* September 1994). Is the proportion of men who felt the division of housework was fair greater than the proportion of women who felt the division of housework was fair? Support your conclusion with a statistical test using a .05 level of significance.

8. In a test of the quality of two television commercials, each commercial was shown in a separate test area six times over a one-week period. The following week a telephone survey identified individuals who had seen the commercials. The individuals who had seen the commercials were asked to state the primary message in the commercials. The following results were recorded.

Commercial	Number Who Saw Commercial	Number Who Recalled Primary Message
A	150	63
B	200	60

a. Using $\alpha = .05$, test the hypothesis that there is no difference in the recall proportions for the two commercials.
b. Compute a 95% confidence interval for the difference between the recall proportions for the two populations.

9. The stock market declined in early 2000 with many stocks dropping below their 1997 highs. In fact, 81.5% of New York Stock Exchange (NYSE) stocks and 72.4% of NASDAQ stocks were trading below their 1997 highs (*Barron's,* May 22, 2000). If the data were based on 232 NYSE stocks and 210 NASDAQ stocks, test the hypothesis $H_0: p_1 - p_2 = 0$ with $\alpha = .05$. What is the *p*-value? What is your conclusion?

10. *Yahoo Internet Life* sponsored surveys in several metropolitan areas to estimate the proportion of adults using the Internet at work (*USA Today,* May 7, 2000). Results showed 40% of Washington, D.C., adults use the Internet at work, while 32% of San Francisco adults use the Internet at work. If the sample sizes are 240 and 250 respectively, do the sample results indicate that the population proportion of adults using the Internet at work in Washington, D.C., is greater than the population proportion in San Francisco? What is the *p*-value? Using $\alpha = .05$, what is the conclusion?

11.2 HYPOTHESIS TEST FOR PROPORTIONS OF A MULTINOMIAL POPULATION

The assumptions for the multinomial experiment parallel those for the binomial experiment with the exception that the multinomial experiment has three or more outcomes per trial.

In this section, we consider hypothesis tests concerning the proportion of elements in a population belonging to each of several classes or categories. In contrast to the preceding section, we deal with a single population: a **multinomial population.** The parameters of the multinomial population are the proportion of elements belonging to each category; the hypothesis tests we describe concern the value of those parameters. The multinomial probability distribution can be thought of as an extension of the binomial distribution to the case of three or more categories of outcomes. On each trial of a multinomial experiment, one and only one of the outcomes occurs. Each trial of the experiment is assumed independent, and the probabilities of the outcomes stay the same for each trial.

· As an example, consider the market share study conducted by Scott Marketing Research. Over the past year market shares stabilized at 30% for company A, 50% for company B, and 20% for company C. Recently company C developed a "new and improved" product that replaced its current entry in the market. Company C retained Scott Marketing Research to determine whether the new product will alter market shares.

In this case, the population of interest is a multinomial population; each customer is classified as buying from company A, company B, or company C. Thus, it is a multinomial population with three classifications or categories. Let us use the following notation for the proportions.

$$p_A = \text{market share for company A}$$
$$p_B = \text{market share for company B}$$
$$p_C = \text{market share for company C}$$

Scott Marketing Research conducts a sample survey and computes the proportion preferring each company's product. A hypothesis test then determines whether the new product caused a change in market shares. Assuming that company C's new product will not alter the market shares, the null and alternative hypotheses are stated as follows.

$$H_0: p_A = .30, p_B = .50, \text{ and } p_C = .20$$
$$H_a: \text{The population proportions are not}$$
$$p_A = .30, p_B = .50, \text{ and } p_C = .20$$

Sample results that lead to the rejection of H_0 provide Scott Marketing Research with evidence that the introduction of the new product affected market shares.

Let us assume that the market research firm used a consumer panel of 200 customers for the study. Each individual specified a purchase preference among the three alternatives: company A's product, company B's product, and company C's new product. The 200 responses are summarized here.

The consumer panel of 200 customers in which each individual is asked to select one of three alternatives is equivalent to a multinomial experiment consisting of 200 trials.

Observed Frequency		
Company A's Product	Company B's Product	Company C's New Product
48	98	54

We now can perform a **goodness of fit test** to determine whether the sample of 200 customer purchase preferences is consistent with the null hypothesis. The goodness of fit test is based on a comparison of the sample of *observed* results with the *expected* results under the assumption that the null hypothesis is true. Hence, the next step is to compute expected purchase preferences for the 200 customers under the assumption that $p_A = .30$, $p_B = .50$, and $p_C = .20$. Doing so provides the expected results.

Expected Frequency		
Company A's Product	Company B's Product	Company C's New Product
200(.30) = 60	200(.50) = 100	200(.20) = 40

Thus, we see that the expected frequency for each category is found by multiplying the sample size of 200 by the hypothesized proportion for the category.

The goodness of fit test now focuses on the differences between the observed frequencies and the expected frequencies. Large differences between observed and expected frequencies cast doubt on the assumption that the hypothesized proportions or market shares are correct. Whether the differences between the observed and expected frequencies are "large" or "small" is a question answered with the aid of the following test statistic.

Test Statistic for Goodness of Fit

$$\chi^2 = \sum_{i=1}^{k} \frac{(f_i - e_i)^2}{e_i} \tag{11.9}$$

where

f_i = observed frequency for category i
e_i = expected frequency for category i
k = the number of categories

Note: The test statistic has a chi-square distribution with $k - 1$ degrees of freedom provided that the expected frequencies are 5 *or more* for all categories.

Let us return to the market share data for the three companies. If the expected frequencies are all 5 or more, we can proceed with the computation of the chi-square test statistic. The calculations necessary to compute the chi-square test statistic for the Scott Marketing Research market share study are shown in Table 11.1. We see that the value of the test statistic is $\chi^2 = 7.34$.

The test for goodness of fit is always a one-tailed test with the rejection region in the upper tail of the chi-square distribution.

Suppose we test the null hypothesis that the multinomial population has the proportions of $p_A = .30$, $p_B = .50$, and $p_C = .20$ at the $\alpha = .05$ level of significance. We will reject the null hypothesis if the differences between the observed and expected frequencies are *large,* therefore we will place a rejection area of .05 in the upper tail of the chi-square distribution. Checking the chi-square distribution table (Table 3 of Appendix B), we find that with

TABLE 11.1 COMPUTATION OF THE CHI-SQUARE TEST STATISTIC FOR THE SCOTT MARKETING RESEARCH MARKET SHARE STUDY

Category	Hypothesized Proportion	Observed Frequency (f_i)	Expected Frequency (e_i)	Difference $(f_i - e_i)$	Squared Difference $(f_i - e_i)^2$	Squared Difference Divided by Expected Frequency $(f_i - e_i)^2/e_i$
Company A	.30	48	60	−12	144	2.40
Company B	.50	98	100	−2	4	0.04
Company C	.20	54	40	14	196	4.90
Total		200				7.34

$k - 1 = 3 - 1 = 2$ degrees of freedom, $\chi^2_{.05} = 5.99$. With $7.34 > 5.99$, we reject H_0. In rejecting H_0 we conclude that the introduction of the new product by company C will alter the current market share structure.

Computer software packages such as Minitab and Excel enable us to make the goodness of fit calculations and conduct the goodness of fit test using the p-value criterion. The steps for these procedures are described in Appendixes 11.1 and 11.2. Using Minitab, we find that the p-value for the Scott Marketing Research hypothesis test is .0255. Using the rejection rule, Reject H_0 if p-value $< \alpha$, we see that .0255 is less than $\alpha = .05$. Thus, we reject H_0 and conclude that the introduction of the new product will alter the current market share structure.

The p-value criterion can also be used for the goodness of fit test.

Although no further conclusions can be made as a result of the hypothesis test, we can compare the observed and expected frequencies informally to obtain an idea of how the market share structure may change. Considering company C, we find that the observed frequency of 54 is larger than the expected frequency of 40. Because the expected frequency was based on current market shares, the larger observed frequency suggests that the new product will have a positive effect on company C's market share. Comparisons of the observed and expected frequencies for the other two companies indicate that company C's gain in market share will hurt company A more than company B.

Let us summarize the general steps that can be used to conduct a goodness of fit test for any hypothesized multinomial population distribution.

Multinomial Distribution Goodness of Fit Test: A Summary

1. State the null and alternative hypotheses.

   H_0: The population follows a multinomial probability distribution with specified probabilities for each of the k categories

   H_a: The population does not follow a multinomial probability distribution with the specified probabilities for each of the k categories

2. Select a random sample and record the observed frequencies f_i for each category.
3. Assuming the null hypothesis is true, determine the expected frequency e_i for each category by multiplying the category probability by the sample size.
4. Compute the value of the test statistic.

$$\chi^2 = \sum_{i=1}^{k} \frac{(f_i - e_i)^2}{e_i}$$

5. Rejection rule:

   Using test statistic: Reject H_0 if $\chi^2 > \chi^2_\alpha$

   Using p-value: Reject H_0 if p-value $< \alpha$

   where α is the level of significance for the test and there are $k - 1$ degrees of freedom.

EXERCISES

Methods

SELFtest   **11.** Test the following hypotheses by using the χ^2 goodness of fit test.

$$H_0: p_A = .40, p_B = .40, \text{ and } p_C = .20$$
$$H_a: \text{The population proportions are not}$$
$$p_A = .40, p_B = .40, \text{ and } p_C = .20$$

A sample of size 200 yielded 60 in category A, 120 in category B, and 20 in category C. Use $\alpha = .01$ and test to see whether the proportions are as stated in H_0.

12. Suppose we have a multinomial population with four categories: A, B, C, and D. The null hypothesis is that the proportion of items is the same in every category. The null hypothesis is

$$H_0: p_A = p_B = p_C = p_D = .25$$

A sample of size 300 yielded the following results.

$$\text{A: } 85 \quad \text{B: } 95 \quad \text{C: } 50 \quad \text{D: } 70$$

Use $\alpha = .05$ to determine whether H_0 should be rejected.

Applications

SELFtest   **13.** During the first 13 weeks of the television season, the Saturday evening 8:00 P.M. to 9:00 P.M. audience proportions were recorded as ABC 29%, CBS 28%, NBC 25%, and independents 18%. A sample of 300 homes two weeks after a Saturday night schedule revision yielded the following viewing audience data: ABC 95 homes, CBS 70 homes, NBC 89 homes, and independents 46 homes. Test with $\alpha = .05$ to determine whether the viewing audience proportions have changed.

14. M&M/MARS, makers of M&M® Chocolate Candies, conducted a national poll in which more than 10 million people indicated their preference for a new color. The tally of this poll resulted in the replacement of tan-colored M&Ms with a new blue color. In the brochure "Colors," made available by M&M/MARS Consumer Affairs, the distribution of colors for the plain candies is as follows:

Brown	Yellow	Red	Orange	Green	Blue
30%	20%	20%	10%	10%	10%

In a study reported in *Chance* (no. 4, 1996), samples of 1-pound bags were used to determine whether the reported percentages were indeed valid. The following results were obtained for one sample of 506 plain candies.

Brown	Yellow	Red	Orange	Green	Blue
177	135	79	41	36	38

Use $\alpha = .05$ to determine whether these data support the percentages reported by the company.

15. One of the questions on the *Business Week* 1996 Subscriber Study was, "When making investment purchases, do you use full service or discount brokerage firms?" Survey results showed that 264 respondents use full service brokerage firms only, 255 use discount brokerage firms only, and 229 use both full service and discount firms. Use $\alpha = .10$ to determine whether there are any differences in preference among the three service choices.

16. Negative appeals have been recognized as an effective method of persuasion in advertising. A study in *The Journal of Advertising* (Summer 1997) reported the results of a content analysis of guilt advertisements in 24 magazines. The number of ads with guilt appeals that appeared in selected magazine types follow.

Magazine Type	Number of Ads with Guilt Appeals
News and opinion	20
General editorial	15
Family-oriented	30
Business/financial	22
Female-oriented	16
African-American	12

Using $\alpha = .10$ test to see whether there is a difference in the proportion of ads with guilt appeals among the six types of magazines.

17. Consumer panel preferences for three proposed store displays follow.

Display A	Display B	Display C
43	53	39

Use $\alpha = .05$ and test to see whether there is a difference in preference among the three display designs.

18. How well do airline companies serve their customers? A study showed the following customer ratings: 3% excellent, 28% good, 45% fair, and 24% poor (*Business Week,* September 11, 2000). In a similar study of service by telephone companies, assume that a sample of 400 adults found the following customer ratings: 24 excellent, 124 good, 172 fair, and 80 poor. Is the distribution of the customer ratings for telephone companies different from the distribution of customer ratings for airline companies? Test with $\alpha = .01$. What is your conclusion?

11.3   TEST OF INDEPENDENCE: CONTINGENCY TABLES

Another important application of the chi-square distribution involves using sample data to test for the independence of two variables. Let us illustrate the test of independence by considering the study conducted by the Alber's Brewery of Tucson, Arizona. Alber's manufactures and distributes three types of beer: light, regular, and dark. In an analysis of the market segments for the three beers, the firm's market research group raised the question of whether preferences for the three beers differ among male and female beer drinkers. If beer preference is independent of the gender of the beer drinker, one advertising campaign will be initiated for all of Alber's beers. However, if beer preference depends on the gender of the beer drinker, the firm will tailor its promotions to different target markets.

A test of independence addresses the question of whether the beer preference (light, regular, or dark) is independent of the gender of the beer drinker (male, female). The hypotheses for this test of independence are:

H_0: Beer preference is independent of the gender of the beer drinker

H_a: Beer preference is not independent of the gender of the beer drinker

Table 11.2 can be used to describe the situation being studied. After identification of the population as all male and female beer drinkers, a sample can be selected and each individual asked to state his or her preference for the three Alber's beers. Every individual in the sample will be classified in one of the six cells in the table. For example, an individual may be a male preferring regular beer (cell (1,2)), a female preferring light beer (cell (2,1)), a female preferring dark beer (cell (2,3)), and so on. Because we listed all possible combinations of beer preference and gender or, in other words, listed all possible contingencies, Table 11.2 is called a **contingency table.** The test of independence uses the contingency table format and for that reason is sometimes referred to as a *contingency table test.*

To test whether two variables are independent, one sample is selected and crosstabulation is used to summarize the data for the two variables simultaneously.

Suppose we select a simple random sample of 150 beer drinkers. After tasting each beer, the individuals in the sample are asked to state their preference or first choice. The crosstabulation in Table 11.3 summarizes the responses for the study. As we see, the data for the test of independence are collected in terms of counts or frequencies for each cell or category. Of the 150 individuals in the sample, 20 were men who favored light beer, 40 were men who favored regular beer, 20 were men who favored dark beer, and so on.

The data in Table 11.3 are the observed frequencies for the six classes or categories. If we can determine the expected frequencies under the assumption of independence between beer preference and gender of the beer drinker, we can use the chi-square distribution to determine whether there is a significant difference between observed and expected frequencies.

Expected frequencies for the cells of the contingency table are based on the following rationale. First we assume that the null hypothesis of independence between beer preference and gender of the beer drinker is true. Then we note that in the entire sample of 150 beer drinkers, a total of 50 prefer light beer, 70 prefer regular beer, and 30 prefer dark beer. In terms of fractions we conclude that $^{50}/_{150} = \frac{1}{3}$ of the beer drinkers prefer light beer, $^{70}/_{150} = \frac{7}{15}$ prefer regular beer, and $^{30}/_{150} = \frac{1}{5}$ prefer dark beer. If the *independence* assumption is valid, we argue that these fractions must be applicable to both male and female beer drinkers. Thus, under the assumption of independence, we would expect the sample of 80 male beer drinkers to show that $(\frac{1}{3})80 = 26.67$ prefer light beer, $(\frac{7}{15})80 = 37.33$ prefer regular beer, and $(\frac{1}{5})80 = 16$ prefer dark beer. Application of the same fractions to the 70 female beer drinkers provides the expected frequencies shown in Table 11.4.

TABLE 11.2 CONTINGENCY TABLE FOR BEER PREFERENCE AND GENDER OF BEER DRINKER

		Beer Preference		
		Light	**Regular**	**Dark**
Gender	**Male**	cell(1,1)	cell(1,2)	cell(1,3)
	Female	cell(2,1)	cell(2,2)	cell(2,3)

TABLE 11.3   SAMPLE RESULTS FOR BEER PREFERENCES OF MALE AND FEMALE
BEER DRINKERS (OBSERVED FREQUENCIES)

		Beer Preference			
		Light	Regular	Dark	Total
Gender	Male	20	40	20	80
	Female	30	30	10	70
	Total	50	70	30	150

Let e_{ij} denote the expected frequency for the contingency table category in row i and column j. With this notation, let us reconsider the expected frequency calculation for males (row $i = 1$) who prefer regular beer (column $j = 2$); that is, expected frequency e_{12}. Following the preceding argument for the computation of expected frequencies, we can show that

$$e_{12} = (7/15)80 = 37.33$$

This expression can be written slightly differently as

$$e_{12} = (7/15)80 = (70/150)80 = \frac{(80)(70)}{150} = 37.33$$

Note that 80 in the expression is the total number of males (row 1 total), 70 is the total number of individuals preferring regular beer (column 2 total), and 150 is the total sample size. Hence, we see that

$$e_{12} = \frac{(\text{Row 1 Total})(\text{Column 2 Total})}{\text{Sample Size}}$$

Generalization of the expression shows that the following formula provides the expected frequencies for a contingency table in the test of independence.

Expected Frequencies for Contingency Tables Under the Assumption of Independence

$$e_{ij} = \frac{(\text{Row } i \text{ Total})(\text{Column } j \text{ Total})}{\text{Sample Size}} \tag{11.10}$$

TABLE 11.4   EXPECTED FREQUENCIES IF BEER PREFERENCE IS INDEPENDENT
OF THE GENDER OF THE BEER DRINKER

		Beer Preference			
		Light	Regular	Dark	Total
Gender	Male	26.67	37.33	16.00	80
	Female	23.33	32.67	14.00	70
	Total	50.00	70.00	30.00	150

Using the formula for male beer drinkers who prefer dark beer, we find an expected frequency of $e_{13} = (80)(30)/150 = 16.00$, as shown in Table 11.4. Use equation (11.10) to verify the other expected frequencies shown in Table 11.4.

The test procedure for comparing the observed frequencies of Table 11.3 with the expected frequencies of Table 11.4 is similar to the goodness of fit calculations made in the previous section. Specifically, the χ^2 value based on the observed and expected frequencies is computed as follows.

Test Statistic for Independence

$$\chi^2 = \sum_i \sum_j \frac{(f_{ij} - e_{ij})^2}{e_{ij}} \qquad (11.11)$$

where

f_{ij} = observed frequency for contingency table category in row i and column j

e_{ij} = expected frequency for contingency table category in row i and column j based on the assumption of independence

Note: With n rows and m columns in the contingency table, the test statistic has a chi-square distribution with $(n - 1)(m - 1)$ degrees of freedom provided that the expected frequencies are five or more for all categories.

The double summation in equation (11.11) is used to indicate that the calculation must be made for all the cells in the contingency table.

By reviewing the expected frequencies in Table 11.4, we see that the expected frequencies are five or more for each category. We therefore proceed with the computation of the chi-square test statistic. The calculations necessary to compute the chi-square test statistic for determining whether beer preference is independent of the gender of the beer drinker are shown in Table 11.5. We see that the value of the test statistic is $\chi^2 = 6.13$.

The number of degrees of freedom for the appropriate chi-square distribution is computed by multiplying the number of rows minus 1 by the number of columns minus 1. With

TABLE 11.5   COMPUTATION OF THE CHI-SQUARE TEST STATISTIC FOR DETERMINING WHETHER BEER PREFERENCE IS INDEPENDENT OF THE GENDER OF THE BEER DRINKER

Gender	Beer Preference	Observed Frequency (f_{ij})	Expected Frequency (e_{ij})	Difference $(f_{ij} - e_{ij})$	Squared Difference $(f_{ij} - e_{ij})^2$	Squared Difference Divided by Expected Frequency $(f_{ij} - e_{ij})^2/e_{ij}$
Male	Light	20	26.67	−6.67	44.49	1.67
Male	Regular	40	37.33	2.67	7.13	0.19
Male	Dark	20	16.00	4.00	16.00	1.00
Female	Light	30	23.33	6.67	44.49	1.91
Female	Regular	30	32.67	−2.67	7.13	0.22
Female	Dark	10	14.00	−4.00	16.00	1.14
	Total	150				6.13

FIGURE 11.3   MINITAB OUTPUT FOR THE ALBER'S BREWERY TEST OF INDEPENDENCE

```
        Expected counts are printed below observed counts

                   Light      Regular       Dark      Total
            1          20           40         20         80
                    26.67        37.33      16.00

            2          30           30         10         70
                    23.33        32.67      14.00

        Total          50           70         30        150

        DF = 2,  P-Value = 0.047
```

The test for independence is always a one-tailed test with the rejection region in the upper tail of the chi-square distribution.

two rows and three columns, we have $(2 - 1)(3 - 1) = (1)(2) = 2$ degrees of freedom for the test of independence of beer preference and gender of the beer drinker. With $\alpha = .05$ for the level of significance of the test, Table 3 of Appendix B shows an upper-tail χ^2 value of $\chi^2_{.05} = 5.99$. Note that we are again using the upper-tail value because we will reject the null hypothesis only if the differences between observed and expected frequencies provide a large χ^2 value. In our example, $\chi^2 = 6.13$ is greater than the critical value of $\chi^2_{.05} = 5.99$. Thus, we reject the null hypothesis of independence and conclude that beer preference is not independent of the gender of the beer drinker.

Computer software packages such as Minitab and Excel can simplify the computations for a test of independence and provide the p-value for the test. The steps used to obtain computer results for a test of independence are presented in Appendixes 11.1 and 11.2. The Minitab output for the Alber's Brewery test of independence is shown in Figure 11.3. The p-value $= .047$ is less than $\alpha = .05$. Thus, we reject H_0 and conclude that beer preference is not independent of the gender of the beer drinker.

Although no further statistical conclusions can be made as a result of the test, we can compare the observed and expected frequencies informally to obtain an idea about the dependence between beer preference and gender. Refer to Tables 11.3 and 11.4. We see that male beer drinkers have higher observed than expected frequencies for both regular and dark beers, whereas female beer drinkers have a higher observed than expected frequency only for light beer. These observations give us insight about the beer preference differences between male and female beer drinkers.

Let us summarize the steps in a contingency table test of independence.

Test of Independence: A Summary

1. State the null and alternative hypotheses.

   H_0: The column variable is independent of the row variable
   H_a: The column variable is not independent of the row variable

2. Select a random sample and record the observed frequencies for each cell of the contingency table.

(continued)

3. Use equation (11.10) to compute the expected frequency for each cell.
4. Use equation (11.11) to compute the value of the χ^2 test statistic.
5. Rejection rule:

Using test statistic: Reject H_0 if $\chi^2 > \chi^2_\alpha$

Using p-value: Reject H_0 if p-value $< \alpha$

where α is the level of significance, with n rows and m columns providing $(n - 1)(m - 1)$ degrees of freedom.

NOTES AND COMMENTS

The test statistic for the chi-square tests in this chapter requires an expected frequency of five for each category. When a category has fewer than five, it is often appropriate to combine two adjacent categories to obtain an expected frequency of five or more in each category.

EXERCISES

Methods

SELFtest

19. The following 2×3 contingency table contains observed frequencies for a sample of 200. Test for independence of the row and column variables using the χ^2 test with $\alpha = .025$.

		Column Variable		
		A	**B**	**C**
Row Variable	**P**	20	44	50
	Q	30	26	30

20. The following 3×3 contingency table contains observed frequencies for a sample of 240. Test for independence of the row and column variables using the χ^2 test with $\alpha = .05$.

		Column Variable		
		A	**B**	**C**
	P	20	30	20
Row Variable	**Q**	30	60	25
	R	10	15	30

Applications

SELFtest

21. One of the questions on the *Business Week* 1996 Subscriber Study was, "In the past 12 months, when traveling for business, what type of airline ticket did you purchase most often?" The data obtained are shown in the following contingency table.

		Type of Flight	
		Domestic Flights	International Flights
Type of Ticket	First class	29	22
	Business/executive class	95	121
	Full fare economy/coach class	518	135

Using $\alpha = .05$, test for the independence of type of flight and type of ticket. What is your conclusion?

22. In a study of brand loyalty in the automotive industry, new car customers were asked whether the make of their new car was the same as the make of their previous car (*Business Week*, May 8, 2000). The breakdown of 600 responses shows the brand loyalty for domestic, European, and Asian cars.

		Manufacturer		
		Domestic	European	Asian
Purchased	Same Make	125	55	68
	Different Make	140	105	107

a. Test a hypothesis to determine whether brand loyalty is independent of the manufacturer. Use $\alpha = .05$. What is your conclusion?
b. If a significant difference is found, which manufacturer appears to have the greatest brand loyalty?

23. Starting positions for business and engineering graduates are classified by industry as shown in the following table.

		Industry			
		Oil	Chemical	Electrical	Computer
Degree Major	Business	30	15	15	40
	Engineering	30	30	20	20

Use $\alpha = .01$ and test for independence of degree major and industry type.

24. The results of a study conducted by Marist Institute for Public Opinion showed who men and women say is the most difficult person for them to buy holiday gifts for (*USA Today,* December 15, 1997). Suppose that the following data were obtained in a follow-up study consisting of 100 men and 100 women.

		Gender	
		Men	**Women**
Most Difficult to Buy For	Spouse	37	25
	Parents	28	31
	Children	7	19
	Siblings	8	3
	In-laws	4	10
	Other relatives	16	12

Use $\alpha = .05$ and test for independence of gender and the most difficult person to buy for. What is your conclusion?

25. Negative appeals have been recognized as an effective method of persuasion in advertising. A study in *The Journal of Advertising* (Summer 1997) reported the results of a content analysis of guilt and fear advertisements in 24 magazines. The number of ads with guilt and fear appeals that appeared in selected magazine types follows.

		Type of Appeal	
		Number of Ads with Guilt Appeals	**Number of Ads with Fear Appeals**
Magazine Type	**News and opinion**	20	10
	General editorial	15	11
	Family-oriented	30	19
	Business/financial	22	17
	Female-oriented	16	14
	African-American	12	15

Use the chi-square test of independence with a .01 level of significance to analyze the data. What is your conclusion?

26. Businesses are increasingly placing orders online. The Performance Measurement Group collected data on the rates of correctly filled electronic orders by industry (*Investor's Business Daily,* May 8, 2000). Assume a sample of 700 electronic orders provided the following results.

		Industry			
		Pharmaceutical	**Consumer**	**Computers**	**Telecommunications**
Order	**Correct**	207	136	151	178
	Incorrect	3	4	9	12

a. Test a hypothesis to determine whether order fulfillment is independent of industry. Use $\alpha = .05$. What is your conclusion?
b. Which industry has the highest percentage of correctly filled orders?

27. Three suppliers provide the following data on defective parts.

		Part Quality		
		Good	Minor Defect	Major Defect
Supplier	A	90	3	7
	B	170	18	7
	C	135	6	9

Use $\alpha = .05$ and test for independence between supplier and part quality. What does the result of your analysis tell the purchasing department?

28. A study of educational levels of voters and their political party affiliations yielded the following results.

		Party Affiliation		
		Democratic	Republican	Independent
Educational Level	Did not complete high school	40	20	10
	High school degree	30	35	15
	College degree	30	45	25

Use $\alpha = .01$ and determine whether party affiliation is independent of the educational level of the voters.

29. On the syndicated Siskel and Ebert television show the hosts often created the impression that they strongly disagreed about which movies were best. An article in *Chance* (no. 2, 1997) reported the results of ratings of 160 movies by Siskel and Ebert. Each review is categorized as Pro ("thumbs up"), Con ("thumbs down"), or Mixed.

		Ebert Rating		
		Con	Mixed	Pro
Siskel Rating	Con	24	8	13
	Mixed	8	13	11
	Pro	10	9	64

Use the chi-square test of independence with a .01 level of significance to analyze the data. What is your conclusion?

SUMMARY

In this chapter, we described statistical procedures for comparisons involving proportions and the contingency table test for independence of two variables. In the first section, we compared a proportion for one population with the same proportion from another population. We described how to construct an interval estimate for the difference between the proportions and how to conduct a hypothesis test to learn whether the difference between the proportions was statistically significant.

In the second section, we focused on a single multinomial population. There we saw how to conduct hypothesis tests to determine whether the sample proportions for the categories of the multinomial population were significantly different from the hypothesized values. The chi-square goodness of fit test was used to make the comparison.

The final section was concerned with tests of independence for two variables. A test of independence for two variables is an extension of the methodology employed in the goodness of fit test for a multinomial population. A contingency table is used to determine the observed and expected frequencies. Then a chi-square value is computed. Large chi-square values, caused by large differences between observed and expected frequencies, lead to the rejection of the null hypothesis of independence.

GLOSSARY

Multinomial population   A population in which each element is assigned to one and only one of several categories. The multinomial probability distribution extends the binomial probability distribution from two to three or more categories.

Goodness of fit test   A statistical test conducted to determine whether to reject a hypothesized probability distribution for a population.

Contingency table   A crosstabulation table used to summarize observed and expected frequencies for a test of independence.

KEY FORMULAS

Point Estimator of the Difference Between the Proportions of Two Populations

$$\bar{p}_1 - \bar{p}_2 \tag{11.1}$$

Expected Value of $\bar{p}_1 - \bar{p}_2$

$$E(\bar{p}_1 - \bar{p}_2) = p_1 - p_2 \tag{11.2}$$

Standard Deviation of $\bar{p}_1 - \bar{p}_2$

$$\sigma_{\bar{p}_1 - \bar{p}_2} = \sqrt{\frac{p_1(1 - p_1)}{n_1} + \frac{p_2(1 - p_2)}{n_2}} \tag{11.3}$$

Point Estimator of $\sigma_{\bar{p}_1 - \bar{p}_2}$

$$s_{\bar{p}_1 - \bar{p}_2} = \sqrt{\frac{\bar{p}_1(1 - \bar{p}_1)}{n_1} + \frac{\bar{p}_2(1 - \bar{p}_2)}{n_2}} \tag{11.4}$$

Interval Estimate of the Difference Between the Proportions of Two Populations: Large-Sample Case with n_1p_1, $n_1(1 - p_1)$, n_2p_2, and $n_2(1 - p_2) \geq 5$

$$\bar{p}_1 - \bar{p}_2 \pm z_{\alpha/2} s_{\bar{p}_1 - \bar{p}_2} \tag{11.5}$$

Test Statistic for Hypothesis Tests About the Difference Between the Proportions of Two Populations

$$z = \frac{(\bar{p}_1 - \bar{p}_2) - (p_1 - p_2)}{\sigma_{\bar{p}_1 - \bar{p}_2}} \tag{11.6}$$

Pooled Estimator of the Population Proportion

$$\bar{p} = \frac{n_1 \bar{p}_1 + n_2 \bar{p}_2}{n_1 + n_2} \tag{11.7}$$

Point Estimator of $\sigma_{\bar{p}_1 - \bar{p}_2}$ When $H_0: p_1 - p_2 = 0$, $H_0: p_1 - p_2 \leq 0$, or $H_0: p_1 - p_2 \geq 0$

$$s_{\bar{p}_1 - \bar{p}_2} = \sqrt{\bar{p}(1 - \bar{p})\left(\frac{1}{n_1} + \frac{1}{n_2}\right)} \tag{11.8}$$

Test Statistic for Goodness of Fit

$$\chi^2 = \sum_{i-1}^{k} \frac{(f_i - e_i)^2}{e_i} \tag{11.9}$$

Expected Frequencies for Contingency Tables Under the Assumption of Independence

$$e_{ij} = \frac{(\text{Row } i \text{ Total})(\text{Column } j \text{ Total})}{\text{Sample Size}} \tag{11.10}$$

Test Statistic for Independence

$$\chi^2 = \sum_i \sum_j \frac{(f_{ij} - e_{ij})^2}{e_{ij}} \tag{11.11}$$

SUPPLEMENTARY EXERCISES

30. A *Business Week*/Harris poll asked 1035 adults how well U.S. companies competed in the global economy, 704 respondents answered good/excellent (*Business Week*, September 11, 2000). In a similar poll of 1004 adults in 1996, 582 respondents answered good/excellent. Can the sample results be used to conclude that the proportion of adults responding good/excellent has *increased* over the four years from 1996 to 2000?
    a. State the null and alternative hypotheses.
    b. Compute the *p*-value.
    c. Using $\alpha = .01$, what is your conclusion?

31. A large automobile insurance company selected samples of single and married male policyholders and recorded the number who had made an insurance claim over the preceding three-year period.

Single Policyholders	Married Policyholders
$n_1 = 400$	$n_2 = 900$
Number making claims = 76	Number making claims = 90

   a. Using $\alpha = .05$, test to determine whether the claim rates differ between single and married male policyholders.
   b. Provide a 95% confidence interval for the difference between the proportions for the two populations.

32. Medical tests were conducted to learn about drug-resistant tuberculosis. Of 142 cases tested in New Jersey, nine were found to be drug-resistant. Of 268 cases tested in Texas, five were found to be drug-resistant. Do these data suggest a statistically significant difference between the proportions of drug-resistant cases in the two states? Test $H_0: p_1 - p_2 = 0$ at the .02 level of significance. What is the p-value and what is your conclusion?

33. In July 2001, the Harris Ad Track Research Service conducted a survey to evaluate the effectiveness of a major advertising campaign for Kodak cameras (*USA Today*, August 27, 2001). In a sample of 430 respondents, 38% thought the ads were very effective. In another sample of 285 respondents to other ad campaigns, 23% thought the ads were very effective.
    a. Estimate the number of respondents who thought the Kodak ads were very effective and the number of respondents who felt the other ads were very effective.
    b. Provide a 95% confidence interval for the difference in proportions.
    c. On the basis of your results in part (b), do you believe the Kodak advertising campaign is more effective than most advertising campaigns?

34. In June 2001, 38% of fund managers surveyed believed that the core inflation rate would be higher in one year. One month later a similar survey revealed that 22% of fund managers expected the core inflation rate to be higher in one year (*Global Research Highlights,* Merrill Lynch, July 20, 2001). Assume that the sample size was 200 in both the June and July surveys.
    a. Develop a point estimate of the difference between the June and July proportions of fund managers who felt the core inflation rate would be higher in one year.
    b. Develop hypotheses such that rejection of the null hypothesis allows us to conclude that inflation expectations diminished between June and July.
    c. Conduct a test of the hypotheses in part (b) using $\alpha = .01$. What is your conclusion?

35. In setting sales quotas, the marketing manager makes the assumption that order potentials are the same for each of four sales territories. A sample of 200 sales follows. Should the manager's assumption be rejected? Use $\alpha = .05$.

Sales Territories			
I	**II**	**III**	**IV**
60	45	59	36

36. Seven percent of mutual fund investors rate corporate stocks "very safe," 58% rate them "somewhat safe," 24% rate them "not very safe," 4% rate them "not at all safe," and 7% are "not sure." A *Business Week/*Harris poll asked 529 mutual fund investors how they would rate corporate bonds on safety. The responses are as follows.

Safety Rating	Frequency
Very safe	48
Somewhat safe	323
Not very safe	79
Not at all safe	16
Not sure	63
Total	529

Do mutual fund investors' attitudes toward corporate bonds differ from their attitudes toward corporate stocks? Support your conclusion with a statistical test using $\alpha = .01$.

37. A community park is to be opened soon. Park officials asked a sample of 140 individuals to state their preference for when they would most like to visit the park. The sample results follow.

Weekday	Saturday	Sunday	Holiday
20	20	40	60

In developing a staffing plan, should the park manager plan on the same number of individuals visiting the park each day? Support your conclusion with a statistical test using $\alpha = .05$.

38. A regional transit authority is concerned about the number of riders on one of its bus routes. In setting up the route, the assumption is that the number of riders is the same on every day from Monday through Friday. Using the following data, test with $\alpha = .05$ to determine whether the transit authority's assumption is correct.

Day	Number of Riders
Monday	13
Tuesday	16
Wednesday	28
Thursday	17
Friday	16

39. The results of *Computerworld's* Annual Job Satisfaction Survey showed that 28% of Information Systems (IS) managers are very satisfied with their job, 46% are somewhat satisfied, 12% are neither satisfied or dissatisfied, 10% are somewhat dissatisfied, and 4% are very dissatisfied (*Computerworld*, May 26, 1997). Suppose that a sample of 500 computer programmers yielded the following results.

Category	Number of Respondents
Very satisfied	105
Somewhat satisfied	235
Neither	55
Somewhat dissatisfied	90
Very dissatisfied	15

Test using $\alpha = .05$ to determine whether the job satisfaction for computer programmers is different from the job satisfaction for IS managers.

40. A sample of parts provided the following contingency table data on part quality by production shift.

Shift	Number Good	Number Defective
First	368	32
Second	285	15
Third	176	24

Use $\alpha = .05$ and test the hypothesis that part quality is independent of the production shift. What is your conclusion?

41. *The Wall Street Journal* 1996 Subscriber Study showed data on the employment status of subscribers. Sample results corresponding to subscribers of the eastern and western editions are shown here.

		Region	
		Eastern Edition	Western Edition
Employment Status	**Full-time**	1105	574
	Part-time	31	15
	Self-employed/consultant	229	186
	Not employed	485	344

Using $\alpha = .05$, test the hypothesis that employment status is independent of the region. What is your conclusion?

42. A lending institution supplied the following data on loan approvals by four loan officers. Use $\alpha = .05$ and test to determine whether the loan approval decision is independent of the loan officer reviewing the loan application.

		Loan Approval Decision	
		Approved	Rejected
Loan Officer	**Miller**	24	16
	McMahon	17	13
	Games	35	15
	Runk	11	9

43. Data on the marital status of men and women ages 20 to 29 were obtained as part of a national survey. The results from a sample of 350 men and 400 women follow. These data are representative of results published in the *U.S. Current Population Report* (*The Statistical Abstract of the United States*, 1999).

		Marital Status		
		Never Married	Married	Divorced
Gender	**Men**	234	106	10
	Women	216	168	16

a. Using $\alpha = .01$, test for independence between marital status and gender. What is your conclusion?
b. Summarize the percent in each marital status category for men and for women.

44. The following crosstabulation shows industry type and P/E ratio for 100 companies in the consumer products and banking industries.

		P/E Ratio					
		5–9	**10–14**	**15–19**	**20–24**	**25–29**	**Total**
Industry	**Consumer**	4	10	18	10	8	50
	Banking	14	14	12	6	4	50
	Total	18	24	30	16	12	100

Does there appear to be a relationship between industry type and P/E ratio? Support your conclusion with a statistical test using $\alpha = .05$.

45. The following data were collected on the number of emergency ambulance calls for an urban county and a rural county in Virginia.

		Day of Week							
		Sun	**Mon**	**Tue**	**Wed**	**Thur**	**Fri**	**Sat**	**Total**
County	**Urban**	61	48	50	55	63	73	43	393
	Rural	7	9	16	13	9	14	10	78
	Total	68	57	66	68	72	87	53	471

Conduct a test for independence using $\alpha = .05$. What is your conclusion?

46. The office occupancy rates were reported for four California metropolitan areas. Do the following data suggest that the office vacancies were independent of metropolitan area? Use a .05 level of significance. What is your conclusion?

Occupancy Status	Los Angeles	San Diego	San Francisco	San Jose
Occupied	160	116	192	174
Vacant	40	34	33	26

47. A salesperson makes four calls per day. A sample of 100 days gives the following frequencies of sales volumes.

Number of Sales	Observed Frequency (days)
0	30
1	32
2	25
3	10
4	3
Total	100

Records show sales are made to 30% of all sales calls. Assuming independent sales calls, the number of sales per day should follow a binomial probability distribution. The binomial probability function presented in Chapter 5 is

$$f(x) = \frac{n!}{x!(n-x)!} p^x(1-p)^{n-x}$$

For this exercise, assume that the population has a binomial distribution with $n = 4$, $p = .30$, and $x = 0, 1, 2, 3,$ and 4.

a. Compute the expected frequencies for $x = 0, 1, 2, 3,$ and 4 by using the binomial probability function. Combine categories if necessary to satisfy the requirement that the expected frequency is five or more for all categories.
b. Use the goodness of fit test to determine whether the assumption of a binomial distribution with $p = .30$ should be rejected. Use $\alpha = .05$. Because no parameters of the binomial distribution were estimated from the sample data, the degrees of freedom are $k - 1$ where k is the number of categories.

Case Problem   A BIPARTISAN AGENDA FOR CHANGE

In a study conducted by Zogby International for the *Democrat and Chronicle,* more than 700 New Yorkers were polled to determine whether the New York state government works. Respondents surveyed were asked questions involving pay cuts for state legislators, restrictions on lobbyists, term limits for legislators, and whether state citizens should be able to put matters directly on the state ballot for a vote (*Democrat and Chronicle,* December 7, 1997). The results regarding several proposed reforms had broad support, crossing all demographic and political lines.

Suppose that a follow-up survey of 100 individuals who live in the western region of New York was conducted. The party affiliation (Democrat, Independent, Republican) of each individual surveyed was recorded, as well as their responses to the following three questions.

1. Should legislative pay be cut for every day the state budget is late?
    Yes _____ No _____
2. Should there be more restrictions on lobbyists?
    Yes _____ No _____
3. Should there be term limits requiring that legislators serve a fixed number of years?
    Yes _____ No _____

The responses were coded using 1 for a *yes* response and 2 for a *no* response. The complete data set is available in the data set named NYReform.

CDfile
NYReform

Managerial Report

1. Use descriptive statistics to summarize the data from this study. What preliminary conclusions do you draw about the independence of the response (yes or no) and party affiliation for each of the three questions in the survey?
2. With regard to question 1, test for the independence of the response (yes or no) and party affiliation. Use $\alpha = .05$.
3. With regard to question 2, test for the independence of the response (yes or no) and party affiliation. Use $\alpha = .05$.
4. With regard to question 3, test for the independence of the response (yes or no) and party affiliation. Use $\alpha = .05$.
5. Does it appear that there is broad support for change across all political lines? Explain.

Appendix 11.1   TESTS OF GOODNESS OF FIT AND INDEPENDENCE WITH MINITAB

We describe how to use Minitab for a goodness of fit test and a test of independence.

Goodness of Fit Test

This Minitab procedure can be used for goodness of fit tests for the multinomial distribution in Section 11.2. The user must obtain the observed frequencies, calculate the expected frequencies, and enter both the observed and expected frequencies in a Minitab worksheet. Using the Scott Marketing Research example presented in Section 11.2, open a Minitab worksheet and enter the label observed in column C1. Enter the observed frequencies 48, 98, and 54 in the first three cells. Enter the label expected and the expected frequencies 60, 100, and 40 in column C2. The Minitab steps for the goodness of fit test follow.

Step 1. Select the **Calc** pull-down menu
Step 2. Choose **Calculator**
Step 3. When the Calculator dialog box appears:
       Enter ChiSquare in the **Store result in variable** box
       Enter Sum((Observed-Expected)**2/Expected) in the **Expression** box
       Click **OK**
Step 4. Select the **Calc** pull-down menu
Step 5. Choose **Probability Distributions**
Step 6. Choose **Chi-Square**
Step 7. When the Chi-Square Distribution dialog box appears:
       Select **Cumulative probability**
       Enter 2 in the **Degrees of freedom** box
       Select **Input column** and enter ChiSquare in the box
       Enter CumProb in the **Optional storage** box
       Click **OK**
Step 8. Select the **Calc** pull-down menu
Step 9. Choose **Calculator**
       When the Calculator dialog box appears:
       Enter p-value in the **Store results in variable** box
       Enter 1-CumProb in the **Expression** box
       Click **OK**

The value of the test statistic $\chi^2 = 7.34$ is shown in column C3, and the p-value $= .0255$ is shown in column C5. With $\chi^2_{.05} = 5.99$ and $\alpha = .05$, we can reject H_0.

Test of Independence

We begin with a new Minitab worksheet and enter the observed frequency data for the Alber's Brewery example from Section 11.3 into columns 1, 2, and 3, respectively. Thus, we entered the observed frequencies corresponding to a light beer preference (20 and 30) in C1, the observed frequencies corresponding to a regular beer preference (40 and 30) in C2, and the observed frequencies corresponding to a dark beer preference (20 and 10) in C3. The Minitab steps for the test of independence are as follows.

Step 1. Select the **Stat** pull-down menu
Step 2. Select the **Tables** pull-down menu
Step 3. Choose **Chi-Square Test**

Step 4. When the Chi-Square Test dialog box appears:
        Enter C1-C3 in the **Columns containing the table** box
        Click **OK**

The p-value is 0.047. With p-value $< \alpha = 0.05$, we reject H_0.

Appendix 11.2   TESTS OF GOODNESS OF FIT AND INDEPENDENCE WITH EXCEL

We describe how to use Excel for a goodness of fit test and a test of independence.

Goodness of Fit Test

This Excel procedure can be used for goodness of fit tests for the multinomial distribution in Section 11.2. The user must obtain the observed frequencies, calculate the expected frequencies, and enter both the observed and expected frequencies in an Excel worksheet. Using the Scott Marketing Research example presented in Section 11.2, open an Excel worksheet and enter the label Observed in cell A1 and the label Expected in cell B1. Then enter the observed frequencies 48, 98, and 54 in cells A2:A4 and enter the expected frequencies 60, 100, and 40 in cells B2:B4.

The χ^2 test statistic and the p-value can be computed as follows:

Step 1. Enter the following formula in cell C2

$$=(A2-B2)\char`\^2/B2$$

Step 2. Copy cell C2 to cell C3:C4
Step 3. Compute the value of χ^2 in cell C5

$$=SUM(C2:C4)$$

Step 4. Compute the p-value in cell C6

$$=CHIDIST(C5,2)$$

In step 4, the entry 2 is the degrees of freedom for the test. In the Scott Marketing Research example, the multinomial distribution goodness of fit test with $k = 3$ categories has $k - 1 = 2$ degrees of freedom. The value of the chi-square test statistic, 7.34, is in cell C5, and the p-value, .0255, is in cell C6. With $\chi^2_{.05} = 5.99$ and $\alpha = .05$, we can reject H_0.

Test of Independence

The Excel procedure for the test of independence requires the user to obtain the observed frequencies and then calculate the expected frequencies. Two tables, one with the observed frequencies and one with the expected frequencies must be entered into an Excel worksheet. Figure 11.4 shows the Excel worksheet that we developed for the Alber's Brewery example in Section 11.3. The observed frequencies appear in cells B4:D5 and the expected frequencies appear in cells B11:D12. The p-value for the test of independence is obtained by entering the following function in cell E15:

$$=CHITEST(B4:D5,B11:D12)$$

FIGURE 11.4 EXCEL WORKSHEET FOR THE ALBER'S BREWERY TEST OF INDEPENDENCE

	A	B	C	D	E	F
1	Observed Frequencies					
2		Beer Preference				
3	Gender	Light	Regular	Dark	Total	
4	Male	20	40	20	80	
5	Female	30	30	10	70	
6	Total	50	70	30	150	
7						
8	Expected Frequencies					
9		Beer Preference				
10	Gender	Light	Regular	Dark	Total	
11	Male	26.67	37.33	16	80	
12	Female	23.33	32.67	14	70	
13	Total	50	70	30	150	
14						
15				p-value=	0.047	
16						

Chapter 12

SIMPLE LINEAR REGRESSION

CONTENTS

STATISTICS IN PRACTICE: ALLIANCE DATA SYSTEMS

ALLIANCE DATA SYSTEMS*

DALLAS, TEXAS

Alliance Data Systems provides transaction processing, credit services, and marketing services for clients in the rapidly growing Customer Relationship Management (CRM) industry. The company's clients are concentrated in four industries: retail, petroleum/convenience stores, utility, and transportation. In 1983, Alliance Data began offering end-to-end credit processing services to the retail, petroleum, and casual dining industries; today they employ more than 6,500 employees who provide services to clients around the world. Operating more than 140,000 point-of-sale terminals in the United States alone, Alliance Data processes over 2.5 billion transactions annually. The company ranks second in the U.S. in private label credit services with nearly 72 million cardholders, representing 49 private label programs. Until 2001, Alliance Data Systems was a private company; in June 2001 an initial public offering was made, and the company is now listed on the New York Stock Exchange (NYSE: ADS).

One of the marketing services that Alliance Data provides is the design of direct mail campaigns and promotions. With its database containing information on the spending habits of over 100 million consumers, it is able to target those consumers most likely to benefit from a direct mail promotion. The Analytical Development Group uses regression analysis to build models used to measure and predict the responsiveness of consumers to direct marketing campaigns. Some regression models are used to predict the probability of purchase for individuals receiving a promotion, and others are used to predict the amount spent by those consumers making a purchase.

For one particular campaign, the objective was to attract new customers to a retail store chain. To predict the effect of the campaign, Alliance Data analysts selected a sample from the consumer database, sent the sampled individuals promotional materials, and then collected transaction data on the consumer's response, if any. Sample data

Alliance Data analysts discuss use of a regression model to predict sales for a direct marketing campaign. Courtesy of Alliance Data Systems.

were collected on the amount of purchase made by the consumers responding to the campaign, as well as a variety of consumer-specific variables thought to be useful in predicting sales. The consumer-specific variable that contributed most to predicting the amount purchased was the total amount of credit purchases at related stores over the past 39 months. Alliance Data analysts were able to develop the following estimated regression equation relating the amount of purchase to the amount spent at related stores.

$$\hat{y} = 26.7 + 0.00205x$$

where

$\hat{y}$ = amount of purchase

x = amount spent at related stores

Using the equation above, we would predict that someone who had spent $10,000 over the past 39 months would spend $47.20 when responding to the direct mail promotion. In this chapter, you will learn how to develop an estimated regression equation such as this.

The final model developed by Alliance Data analysts also included several other variables that increased the

*The authors are indebted to Philip Clemance, Director of Analytical Development at Alliance Data Systems, for providing this Statistics in Practice.

predictive power of the equation shown above. Some of these were the absence/presence of a bank credit card, estimated income, and the average amount spent per trip at a selected store. In the following chapter, we will learn how such additional variables can be incorporated into a multiple regression model.

Managers often base decisions on the relationship between two or more variables. For example, after considering the relationship between advertising expenditures and sales, a marketing manager might attempt to predict sales for a given level of advertising expenditures. In another case, a public utility might use the relationship between the daily high temperature and the demand for electricity to predict electricity usage on the basis of next month's anticipated daily high temperatures. Sometimes a manager will rely on intuition to judge how two variables are related. However, if data can be obtained, a statistical procedure called *regression analysis* can be used to develop an equation showing how the variables are related.

The statistical methods used in studying the relationship between two variables were first employed by Sir Francis Galton (1822–1911). Galton studied the relationship between a father's height and the son's height. Galton's disciple, Karl Pearson (1857–1936), analyzed the relationship between the father's height and the son's height for 1078 pairs of subjects.

In regression terminology, the variable being predicted is called the **dependent variable.** The variable or variables being used to predict the value of the dependent variable are called the **independent variables.** For example, in analyzing the effect of advertising expenditures on sales, a marketing manager's desire to predict sales would suggest making sales the dependent variable. Advertising expenditure would be the independent variable used to help predict sales. In statistical notation, y denotes the dependent variable and x denotes the independent variable.

In this chapter we consider the simplest type of regression analysis involving one independent variable and one dependent variable in which the relationship between the variables is approximated by a straight line. It is called **simple linear regression.** Regression analysis involving two or more independent variables is called **multiple regression** analysis; multiple regression is covered in Chapter 13.

12.1   SIMPLE LINEAR REGRESSION MODEL

Armand's Pizza Parlors chain operates Italian-food restaurants located in a five-state area. The most successful locations for Armand's are near college campuses. The managers believe that quarterly sales for these restaurants (denoted by y) are related positively to the size of the student population (denoted by x); that is, restaurants near campuses with a large population tend to generate more sales than those located near campuses with a small population. Using regression analysis, we can develop an equation showing how the dependent variable y is related to the independent variable x.

Regression Model and Regression Equation

In the Armand's Pizza Parlors example, every restaurant has associated with it a value of x (student population) and a corresponding value of y (quarterly sales). The equation that describes how y is related to x and an error term is called the **regression model.** The regression model used in simple linear regression follows.

Simple Linear Regression Model

$$y = \beta_0 + \beta_1 x + \epsilon \tag{12.1}$$

In the simple linear regression model, y is a linear function of x (the $\beta_0 + \beta_1 x$ part) plus ϵ. β_0 and β_1 are referred to as the parameters of the model, and ϵ (the Greek letter epsilon) is a random variable referred to as the error term. The error term accounts for the variability in y that cannot be explained by the linear relationship between x and y.

In Section 12.4 we will discuss the assumptions for the simple linear regression model and ϵ. One of the assumptions is that the mean or expected value of ϵ is zero. A consequence of this assumption is that the mean or expected value of y, denoted $E(y)$, is equal to $\beta_0 + \beta_1 x$; in other words, the mean value of y is a linear function of x. The equation that describes how the mean value of y is related to x is called the **regression equation.** The regression equation for simple linear regression follows.

Simple Linear Regression Equation

$$E(y) = \beta_0 + \beta_1 x \qquad\qquad (12.2)$$

The graph of the simple linear regression equation is a straight line; β_0 is the y intercept of the regression line, β_1 is the slope, and $E(y)$ is the mean or expected value of y for a given value of x. Examples of possible regression lines for simple linear regression are shown in Figure 12.1. The regression line in panel A of the figure shows that the mean value of y is related positively to x, with larger values of $E(y)$ associated with larger values of x. The regression line in panel B shows that the mean value of y is related negatively to x, with smaller values of $E(y)$ associated with larger values of x. The regression line in panel C shows the case in which the mean value of y is not related to x; that is, the mean value of y is the same for every value of x.

Estimated Regression Equation

If the values of the parameters β_0 and β_1 were known, we could use equation (12.2) to compute the mean value of y for a known value of x. Unfortunately, the parameter values are not known in practice and must be estimated by using sample data. Sample statistics (denoted b_0 and b_1) are computed as estimates of the parameters β_0 and β_1. Substituting the values of the sample statistics b_0 and b_1 for β_0 and β_1 in the regression equation, we obtain the **estimated regression equation.** The estimated regression equation for simple linear regression follows.

Estimated Simple Linear Regression Equation

$$\hat{y} = b_0 + b_1 x \qquad\qquad (12.3)$$

FIGURE 12.1   POSSIBLE REGRESSION LINES IN SIMPLE LINEAR REGRESSION

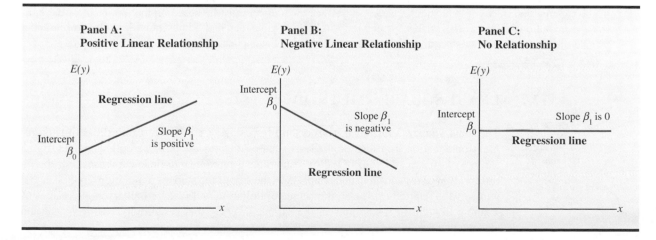

The graph of the estimated simple linear regression equation is called the *estimated regression line;* b_0 is the y intercept, b_1 is the slope, and $\hat{y}$ (pronounced y hat) *is the estimated value of y* for a given value of x. In the next section, we show how the least squares method can be used to compute the values of b_0 and b_1 in the estimated regression equation. Figure 12.2 is a summary of the estimation process for simple linear regression.

FIGURE 12.2   THE ESTIMATION PROCESS IN SIMPLE LINEAR REGRESSION

The estimation of β_0 and β_1 is a statistical process much like the estimation of μ discussed in Chapter 7. β_0 and β_1 are the unknown parameters of interest, and b_0 and b_1 are the sample statistics used to estimate the parameters.

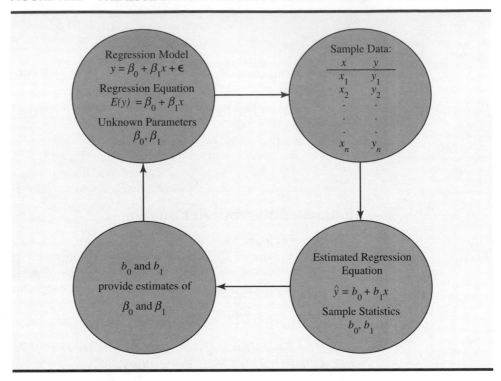

NOTES AND COMMENTS

Regression analysis cannot be interpreted as a procedure for establishing a cause-and-effect relationship between variables. It can only indicate how or to what extent variables are associated with each other. Any conclusions about cause and effect must be based on the judgment of the individual or individuals most knowledgeable about the application.

12.2   LEAST SQUARES METHOD

In simple linear regression, each observation consists of two values: one for the independent variable and one for the dependent variable.

The **least squares method** is a procedure for using sample data to find the estimated regression equation. To illustrate the least squares method, suppose we collected data from a sample of 10 Armand's Pizza Parlor restaurants located near college campuses. For the ith observation or restaurant in the sample, x_i is the size of the student population (in thousands) and y_i is the quarterly sales (in thousands of dollars). Table 12.1 summarizes the values of x_i and y_i for the 10 restaurants in the sample. We see that restaurant 1, with $x_1 = 2$ and

TABLE 12.1   STUDENT POPULATION AND QUARTERLY SALES DATA
FOR 10 ARMAND'S PIZZA PARLORS

Restaurant i	Student Population (1000s) x_i	Quarterly Sales ($1000s) y_i
1	2	58
2	6	105
3	8	88
4	8	118
5	12	117
6	16	137
7	20	157
8	20	169
9	22	149
10	26	202

$y_1 = 58$, is near a campus with 2000 students and has quarterly sales of $58,000. Restaurant 2, with $x_2 = 6$ and $y_2 = 105$, is near a campus with 6000 students and has quarterly sales of $105,000. The largest sales value is for restaurant 10, which is near a campus with 26,000 students and has quarterly sales of $202,000.

Figure 12.3 shows a scatter diagram of the data in Table 12.1. The size of the student population is shown on the horizontal axis and the value of quarterly sales is shown on the vertical axis. **Scatter diagrams** for regression analysis are constructed with values of the independent variable x on the horizontal axis and values of the dependent variable y on the vertical axis. The scatter diagram enables us to observe the data graphically and to draw preliminary conclusions about the possible relationship between the variables.

What preliminary conclusions can be drawn from Figure 12.3? Quarterly sales appear to be higher at campuses with larger student populations. In addition, for these data the relationship between the size of the student population and quarterly sales appears to be approximated by a straight line; indeed, a positive linear relationship is indicated between x and y. We therefore choose the simple linear regression model to represent the relationship between quarterly sales and student population. Given that choice, our next task is to use the sample data in Table 12.1 to determine the values of b_0 and b_1 in the estimated simple linear regression equation. For the ith restaurant, the estimated regression equation provides

$$\hat{y}_i = b_0 + b_1 x_i \tag{12.4}$$

where

$\hat{y}_i$ = estimated value of quarterly sales ($1000s) for the ith restaurant

b_0 = the y intercept of the estimated regression line

b_1 = the slope of the estimated regression line

x_i = size of the student population (1000s) for the ith restaurant

With y_i denoting the observed (actual) sales for restaurant i and $\hat{y}_i$ in equation (12.4) representing the estimated value of sales for restaurant i, every restaurant in the sample will have

FIGURE 12.3 SCATTER DIAGRAM OF STUDENT POPULATION AND QUARTERLY SALES FOR ARMAND'S PIZZA PARLORS

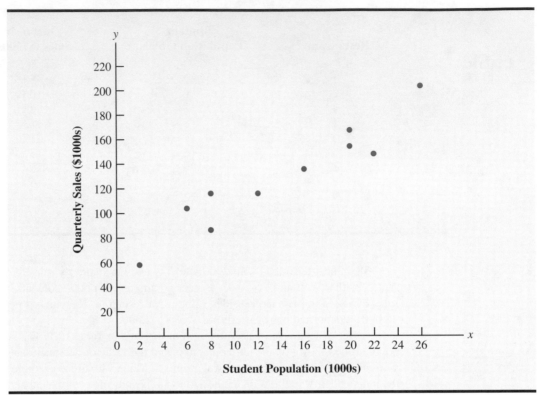

an observed value of sales y_i and an estimated value of sales $\hat{y}_i$. For the estimated regression line to provide a good fit to the data, we want the differences between the observed sales values and the estimated sales values to be small.

The least squares method uses the sample data to provide the values of b_0 and b_1 that minimize the *sum of the squares of the deviations* between the observed values of the dependent variable y_i and the estimated values of the dependent variable $\hat{y}_i$. The criterion for the least squares method is given by (12.5).

Carl Friedrich Gauss (1777–1855) proposed the least squares method.

Least Squares Criterion

$$\min \Sigma(y_i - \hat{y}_i)^2 \qquad (12.5)$$

where

y_i = observed value of the dependent variable for the ith observation

$\hat{y}_i$ = estimated value of the dependent variable for the ith observation

Differential calculus can be used to show that the values of b_0 and b_1 that minimize expression (12.5) can be found by using (12.6) and (12.7).

In computing b_1 with a calculator, carry as many significant digits as possible in the intermediate calculations. We recommend carrying at least four significant digits.

Slope and y-Intercept for the Estimated Regression Equation*

$$b_1 = \frac{\Sigma(x_i - \bar{x})(y_i - \bar{y})}{\Sigma(x_i - \bar{x})^2} \tag{12.6}$$

$$b_0 = \bar{y} - b_1\bar{x} \tag{12.7}$$

where

x_i = value of the independent variable for the ith observation
y_i = value of the dependent variable for the ith observation
$\bar{x}$ = mean value for the independent variable
$\bar{y}$ = mean value for the dependent variable
n = total number of observations

Some of the calculations necessary to develop the least squares estimated regression equation for Armand's Pizza Parlors appear in Table 12.2. With the sample of 10 restaurants, we have $n = 10$ observations. Because equations (12.6) and (12.7) require $\bar{x}$ and $\bar{y}$, we begin the calculations by computing $\bar{x}$ and $\bar{y}$.

$$\bar{x} = \frac{\Sigma x_i}{n} = \frac{140}{10} = 14$$

$$\bar{y} = \frac{\Sigma y_i}{n} = \frac{1300}{10} = 130$$

Using equations (12.6), (12.7), and the information in Table 12.2, we can compute the slope and intercept of the estimated regression equation for Armand's Pizza Parlors. The calculation of the slope (b_1) proceeds as follows.

$$b_1 = \frac{\Sigma(x_i - \bar{x})(y_i - \bar{y})}{\Sigma(x_i - \bar{x})^2}$$
$$= \frac{2840}{568}$$
$$= 5$$

The calculation of the y intercept (b_0) follows.

$$b_0 = \bar{y} - b_1\bar{x}$$
$$= 130 - 5(14)$$
$$= 60$$

---

*An alternate formula for b_1 is

$$b_1 = \frac{\Sigma x_i y_i - (\Sigma x_i \Sigma y_i)/n}{\Sigma x_i^2 - (\Sigma x_i)^2/n}$$

This form of equation (12.6) is often recommended when using a calculator to compute b_1.

TABLE 12.2 CALCULATIONS FOR THE LEAST SQUARES ESTIMATED REGRESSION EQUATION FOR ARMAND'S PIZZA PARLORS

Restaurant i	x_i	y_i	$x_i - \bar{x}$	$y_i - \bar{y}$	$(x_i - \bar{x})(y_i - \bar{y})$	$(x_i - \bar{x})^2$
1	2	58	−12	−72	864	144
2	6	105	−8	−25	200	64
3	8	88	−6	−42	252	36
4	8	118	−6	−12	72	36
5	12	117	−2	−13	26	4
6	16	137	2	7	14	4
7	20	157	6	27	162	36
8	20	169	6	39	234	36
9	22	149	8	19	152	64
10	26	202	12	72	864	144
Totals	140	1300			2840	568
	Σx_i	Σy_i			$\Sigma(x_i - \bar{x})(y_i - \bar{y})$	$\Sigma(x_i - \bar{x})^2$

Thus, the estimated regression equation is

$$\hat{y} = 60 + 5x$$

Figure 12.4 shows the graph of this equation on the scatter diagram.

The slope of the estimated regression equation ($b_1 = 5$) is positive, implying that as student population increases, sales increase. In fact, we can conclude (based on sales measured in \$1000s and student population in 1000s) that an increase in the student population of 1000 is associated with an increase of \$5000 in expected sales; that is, sales are expected to increase by \$5 per student.

If we believe the least squares estimated regression equation adequately describes the relationship between x and y, it would seem reasonable to use the estimated regression equation to predict the value of y for a given value of x. For example, if we wanted to predict sales for a restaurant to be located near a campus with 16,000 students, we would compute

Using the estimated regression equation to make predictions outside the range of the values of the independent variable should be done with caution, because outside that range we cannot be sure that the same relationship is valid.

$$\hat{y} = 60 + 5(16) = 140$$

Hence, we would predict quarterly sales of \$140,000 for this restaurant. In the following sections we will discuss methods for assessing the appropriateness of using the estimated regression equation for estimation and prediction.

NOTES AND COMMENTS

The least squares method provides an estimated regression equation that minimizes the sum of squared deviations between the observed values of the dependent variable y_i and the estimated values of the dependent variable $\hat{y}_i$. This is the least squares criterion for choosing the equation that provides the best fit. If some other criterion were used, such as minimizing the sum of the absolute deviations between y_i and $\hat{y}_i$, a different equation would be obtained. In practice, the least squares method is the most widely used.

FIGURE 12.4   GRAPH OF THE ESTIMATED REGRESSION EQUATION FOR ARMAND'S
PIZZA PARLORS: $\hat{y} = 60 + 5x$

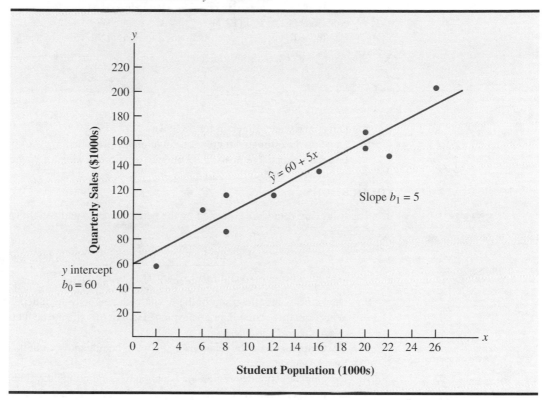

EXERCISES

Methods

1.   Given are five observations for two variables, x and y.

x_i	1	2	3	4	5
y_i	3	7	5	11	14

  a.   Develop a scatter diagram for these data.
  b.   What does the scatter diagram developed in part (a) indicate about the relationship between the two variables?
  c.   Try to approximate the relationship between x and y by drawing a straight line through the data.
  d.   Develop the estimated regression equation by computing the values of b_0 and b_1 using equations (12.6) and (12.7).
  e.   Use the estimated regression equation to predict the value of y when $x = 4$.

2.   Given are five observations for two variables, x and y.

x_i	2	3	5	1	8
y_i	25	25	20	30	16

  a.   Develop a scatter diagram for these data.
  b.   What does the scatter diagram developed in part (a) indicate about the relationship between the two variables?

    c. Try to approximate the relationship between x and y by drawing a straight line through the data.

    d. Develop the estimated regression equation by computing the values of b_0 and b_1 using equations (12.6) and (12.7).

    e. Use the estimated regression equation to predict the value of y when $x = 6$.

3. Given are five observations collected in a regression study on two variables.

x_i	2	4	5	7	8
y_i	2	3	2	6	4

    a. Develop a scatter diagram for these data.

    b. Develop the estimated regression equation for these data.

    c. Use the estimated regression equation to predict the value of y when $x = 4$.

Applications

SELFtest

4. The following data were collected on the height (inches) and weight (pounds) of women swimmers.

Height	68	64	62	65	66
Weight	132	108	102	115	128

    a. Develop a scatter diagram for these data with height as the independent variable.

    b. What does the scatter diagram developed in part (a) indicate about the relationship between the two variables?

    c. Try to approximate the relationship between height and weight by drawing a straight line through the data.

    d. Develop the estimated regression equation by computing the values of b_0 and b_1 using equations (12.6) and (12.7).

    e. If a swimmer's height is 63 inches, what would you estimate her weight to be?

5. The following data show the case sales (millions) and the media expenditures (millions of dollars) for seven major brands of soft drinks (*Superbrands '98,* October 20, 1997).

Brand	Media Expenditures ($)	Case Sales
Coca-Cola Classic	131.3	1929.2
Pepsi-Cola	92.4	1384.6
Diet Coke	60.4	811.4
Sprite	55.7	541.5
Dr. Pepper	40.2	536.9
Mountain Dew	29.0	535.6
7-Up	11.6	219.5

    a. Develop a scatter diagram for these data with media expenditures as the independent variable.

    b. What does the scatter diagram developed in part (a) indicate about the relationship between the two variables?

    c. Draw a straight line through the data to approximate a linear relationship between media expenditures and case sales.

    d. Use the least squares method to develop the estimated regression equation.

    e. Provide an interpretation for the slope of the estimated regression equation.

    f. Predict the case sales for a brand with a media expenditure of $70 million.

6.   Airline performance data for U.S. airlines were reported in *The Wall Street Journal Almanac 1998*. Data on the percentage of flights arriving on time and the number of complaints per 100,000 passengers follow.

Airline	Percentage on Time	Complaints
Southwest	81.8	0.21
Continental	76.6	0.58
Northwest	76.6	0.85
US Airways	75.7	0.68
United	73.8	0.74
American	72.2	0.93
Delta	71.2	0.72
America West	70.8	1.22
TWA	68.5	1.25

a.   Develop a scatter diagram for these data with percentage on time as the independent variable.
b.   What does the scatter diagram developed in part (a) indicate about the relationship between the two variables?
c.   Develop the estimated regression equation showing how the number of complaints per 100,000 passengers is related to the percentage of flights arriving on time.
d.   Provide an interpretation for the slope of the estimated regression equation.
e.   What is the estimated number of complaints per 100,000 passengers if the percentage of flights arriving on time is 80%?

7.   Both the Dow Jones Industrial Average (DJIA) and the Standard & Poor's 500 (S&P) indexes measure overall movement in the stock market. The DJIA is based on the price movements of 30 large companies; the S&P 500 is an index composed of 500 stocks. Some say the S&P 500 provides a better measure of stock market performance because it is broader based. The closing prices for the DJIA and the S&P 500 for 10 weeks, beginning with February 11, 2000, follow (*Barron's,* April 17, 2000).

CDfile
DowS&P

Date	DJIA	S&P
February 11	10425	1387
February 18	10220	1346
February 25	9862	1333
March 3	10367	1409
March 10	9929	1395
March 17	10595	1464
March 24	11113	1527
March 31	10922	1499
April 7	11111	1516
April 14	10306	1357

a.   Develop a scatter diagram for these data with DJIA as the independent variable.
b.   Develop the least squares estimated regression equation.
c.   Suppose the closing price for the DJIA is 11,000. Estimate the closing price for the S&P 500.

8. Mountain bikes that cost less than $1000 now contain many of the high-quality components that until recently were only available on high-cost models. Today, even sub-$1000 models often have supple suspensions, clipless pedals, and highly engineered frames. An interesting question is whether higher price still buys a higher level of handling, as measured by the bike's sidetrack capability. To measure sidetrack capability, *Outside Magazine* used a rating scale from 1 to 5, with 1 representing an average rating and 5 representing an excellent rating. The sidetrack capability and the price for 10 mountain bikes tested by *Outside Magazine* follow (*Outside Magazine Buyer's Guide*, 2001).

CDfile
MtnBikes

Manufacturer and Model	Sidetrack Capability	Price
Raleigh M80	1	600
Marin Bear Valley Feminina	1	649
GT Avalanche 2.0	2	799
Kona Jake the Snake	1	899
Schwinn Moab 2	3	950
Giant XTC NRS 3	4	1100
Fisher Paragon Genesisters	4	1149
Jamis Dakota XC	3	1300
Trek Fuel 90	5	1550
Specialized Stumpjumper M4	4	1625

a. Develop a scatter diagram for these data with sidetrack capability as the independent variable.
b. Does it appear that higher priced models have a higher level of handling? Explain.
c. Develop the least squares estimated regression equation.
d. What is the estimated price for a mountain bike if it has a sidetrack capability rating of 4?

9. A sales manager collected the following data on annual sales and years of experience.

Salesperson	Years of Experience	Annual Sales ($1000s)
1	1	80
2	3	97
3	4	92
4	4	102
5	6	103
6	8	111
7	10	119
8	10	123
9	11	117
10	13	136

a. Develop a scatter diagram for these data with years of experience as the independent variable.
b. Develop an estimated regression equation that can be used to predict annual sales given the years of experience.
c. Use the estimated regression equation to predict annual sales for a salesperson with nine years of experience.

10. *PC World* provided ratings for the top 15 notebook PCs (*PC World*, February 2000). The performance score is a measure of how fast a PC can run a mix of common business applications as compared to how fast a baseline machine can run them. For example, a PC with a performance score of 200 is twice as fast as the baseline machine. A 100-point scale was used to provide an overall rating for each notebook tested in the study. A score in the 90s is exceptional, while one in the 70s is above average. The performance scores and the overall ratings for the 15 notebooks follow.

Notebook	Performance Score	Overall Rating
AMS Tech Roadster 15CTA380	115	67
Compaq Armada M700	191	78
Compaq Prosignia Notebook 150	153	79
Dell Inspiron 3700 C466GT	194	80
Dell Inspiron 7500 R500VT	236	84
Dell Latitude Cpi A366XT	184	76
Enpower ENP-313 Pro	184	77
Gateway Solo 9300LS	216	92
HP Pavilion Notebook PC	185	83
IBM ThinkPad I Series 1480	183	78
Micro Express NP7400	189	77
Micron TransPort NX PII-400	202	78
NEC Versa SX	192	78
Sceptre Soundx 5200	141	73
Sony VAIO PCG-F340	187	77

a. Develop a scatter diagram for these data with performance score as the independent variable.
b. Develop the least squares estimated regression equation.
c. Estimate the overall rating for a new PC with a performance score of 225.

11. The following data show the gaming revenue and the hotel revenue, in millions of dollars, for 10 Las Vegas casino hotels (*Cornell Hotel And Restaurant Administration Quarterly*, October 1997).

Company	Hotel Revenue ($)	Gaming Revenue ($)
Boyd Gaming	303.5	548.2
Circus Circus Enterprises	664.8	664.8
Grand Casinos	121.0	270.7
Hilton Corp. Gaming Div.	429.6	511.0
MGM Grand, Inc.	373.1	404.7
Mirage Resorts	670.9	782.8
Primadonna Resorts	66.4	130.7
Rio Hotel & Casino	105.8	105.5
Sahara Gaming	102.4	148.7
Station Casinos	135.8	358.5

a. Develop a scatter diagram for these data with hotel revenue as the independent variable.
b. Does there appear to be a linear relationship between the two variables?
c. Develop the estimated regression equation relating the gaming revenue to the hotel revenue.
d. Suppose that the hotel revenue was $500 million. What is an estimate of the gaming revenue?

12. The following table gives the number of employees and the revenue (millions of dollars) for 20 companies (*Fortune,* April 17, 2000).

CDfile
EmpRev

Company	Employees	Revenue ($ millions)
Sprint	77,600	19,930
Chase Manhattan	74,801	33,710
Computer Sciences	50,000	7,660
Wells Fargo	89,355	21,795
Sunbeam	12,200	2,398
CBS	29,000	7,510
Time Warner	69,722	27,333
Steelcase	16,200	2,743
Georgia-Pacific	57,000	17,796
Toro	1,275	4,673
American Financial	9,400	3,334
Fluor	53,561	12,417
Phillips Petroleum	15,900	13,852
Cardinal Health	36,000	25,034
Borders Group	23,500	2,999
MCI Worldcom	77,000	37,120
Consolidated Edison	14,269	7,491
IBP	45,000	14,075
Super Value	50,000	17,421
H&R Block	4,200	1,669

a. Develop a scatter diagram for these data with number of employees as the independent variable.
b. What does the scatter diagram developed in part (a) indicate about the relationship between number of employees and revenue?
c. Develop the estimated regression equation for these data.
d. Use the estimated regression equation to predict the revenue for a firm with 75,000 employees.

13. To the Internal Revenue Service, the reasonableness of total itemized deductions depends on the taxpayer's adjusted gross income. Large deductions, which include charity and medical deductions, are more reasonable for taxpayers with large adjusted gross incomes. If a taxpayer claims larger than average itemized deductions for a given level of income, the chances of an IRS audit increase. Data (in $1000s) on adjusted gross income and the average or reasonable amount of itemized deductions follow.

Adjusted Gross Income ($1000s)	Total Itemized Deductions ($1000s)
22	9.6
27	9.6
32	10.1
48	11.1
65	13.5
85	17.7
120	25.5

a. Develop a scatter diagram for these data with adjusted gross income as the independent variable.

b. Use the least squares method to develop the estimated regression equation.

c. Estimate a reasonable level of total itemized deductions for a taxpayer with an adjusted gross income of $52,500. If this taxpayer claims total itemized deductions of $20,400, would the IRS agent's request for an audit appear justified? Explain.

14. The following data report the occupancy rates (%) and room rates ($) for the largest U.S. hotel markets (*The Wall Street Journal Almanac 1998*).

Market	Average Room Rate ($)	Occupancy Rate (%)
Los Angeles–Long Beach	75.91	67.9
Chicago	92.04	72.0
Washington	94.42	68.4
Atlanta	81.69	67.7
Dallas	74.76	69.5
San Diego	80.86	68.7
Anaheim–Santa Ana	70.04	69.5
San Francisco	106.47	78.7
Houston	66.11	62.0
Miami–Hialeah	85.83	71.2
Oahu Island	107.11	80.7
Phoenix	95.34	71.4
Boston	105.51	73.5
Tampa–St. Petersburg	67.45	63.4
Detroit	64.79	68.7
Philadelphia	83.56	70.1
Nashville	70.12	67.1
Seattle	82.60	73.4
Minncapolis–St. Paul	73.64	69.8
New Orleans	99.00	70.6

a. Develop a scatter diagram for these data with average room rate as the independent variable.

b. Develop the estimated regression equation relating the occupancy rate to the average room rate.

c. Estimate the occupancy rate for a hotel with an average room rate of $80.

12.3   COEFFICIENT OF DETERMINATION

For the Armand's Pizza Parlors example, we developed the estimated regression equation $\hat{y} = 60 + 5x$ to approximate the linear relationship between the size of the student population x and quarterly sales y. A question now is: How well does the estimated regression equation fit the data? In this section, we show that the **coefficient of determination** provides a measure of the goodness of fit for the estimated regression equation.

For the ith observation, the difference between the observed value of the dependent variable, y_i, and the estimated value of the dependent variable, $\hat{y}_i$, is called the ***i*th residual.** The ith residual represents the error in using $\hat{y}_i$ to estimate y_i. Thus, for the ith observation, the residual is $y_i - \hat{y}_i$. The sum of squares of these residuals or errors is the quantity minimized by the least squares method. This quantity, also known as the *sum of squares due to error,* is denoted by SSE.

> **Sum of Squares Due to Error**
>
> $$SSE = \Sigma(y_i - \hat{y}_i)^2 \tag{12.8}$$

The value of SSE is a measure of the error in using the estimated regression equation to estimate the values of the dependent variable in the sample.

In Table 12.3 we show the calculations required to compute the sum of squares due to error for the Armand's Pizza Parlors example. For instance, for restaurant 1 the values of the independent and dependent variables are $x_1 = 2$ and $y_1 = 58$. Using the estimated regression equation, we find that the estimated value of quarterly sales for restaurant 1 is $\hat{y}_1 = 60 + 5(2) = 70$. Thus, the error in using $\hat{y}_1$ to estimate y_1 for restaurant 1 is $y_1 - \hat{y}_1 = 58 - 70 = -12$. The squared error, $(-12)^2 = 144$, is shown in the last column of Table 12.3. After computing and squaring the residuals for each restaurant in the sample, we sum them to obtain SSE = 1530. Thus, SSE = 1530 measures the error in using the estimated regression equation $\hat{y} = 60 + 5x$ to predict sales.

Now suppose we are asked to develop an estimate of quarterly sales without knowledge of the size of the student population. Without knowledge of any related variables, we would use the sample mean as an estimate of quarterly sales at any given restaurant. Table 12.2 shows that for the sales data, $\Sigma y_i = 1300$. Hence, the mean value of quarterly sales for the sample of 10 Armand's restaurants is $\bar{y} = \Sigma y_i/n = 1300/10 = 130$. In Table 12.4 we show the sum of squared deviations obtained by using the sample mean $\bar{y} = 130$ to estimate the value of quarterly sales for each restaurant in the sample. For the ith restaurant in the sample, the difference $y_i - \bar{y}$ provides a measure of the error involved in using $\bar{y}$ to estimate sales. The corresponding sum of squares, called the *total sum of squares,* is denoted SST.

> **Total Sum of Squares**
>
> $$SST = \Sigma(y_i - \bar{y})^2 \tag{12.9}$$

TABLE 12.3   CALCULATION OF SSE FOR ARMAND'S PIZZA PARLORS

Restaurant i	x_i = Student Population (1000s)	y_i = Quarterly Sales ($1000s)	$\hat{y}_i = 60 + 5x_i$	$y_i - \hat{y}_i$	$(y_i - \hat{y}_i)^2$
1	2	58	70	−12	144
2	6	105	90	15	225
3	8	88	100	−12	144
4	8	118	100	18	324
5	12	117	120	−3	9
6	16	137	140	−3	9
7	20	157	160	−3	9
8	20	169	160	9	81
9	22	149	170	−21	441
10	26	202	190	12	144
					SSE = 1530

TABLE 12.4   COMPUTATION OF THE TOTAL SUM OF SQUARES FOR ARMAND'S PIZZA
PARLORS

Restaurant i	x_i = Student Population (1000s)	y_i = Quarterly Sales ($1000s)	$y_i - \bar{y}$	$(y_i - \bar{y})^2$
1	2	58	-72	5,184
2	6	105	-25	625
3	8	88	-42	1,764
4	8	118	-12	144
5	12	117	-13	169
6	16	137	7	49
7	20	157	27	729
8	20	169	39	1,521
9	22	149	19	361
10	26	202	72	5,184
				SST = 15,730

The sum at the bottom of the last column in Table 12.4 is the total sum of squares for Armand's Pizza Parlors; it is SST = 15,730.

In Figure 12.5 we show the estimated regression line $\hat{y} = 60 + 5x$ and the line corresponding to $\bar{y} = 130$. Note that the points cluster more closely around the estimated regression line than they do about the line $\bar{y} = 130$. For example, for the 10th restaurant in the sample we see that the error is much larger when $\bar{y} = 130$ is used as an estimate of y_{10} than when $\hat{y}_{10} = 60 + 5(26) = 190$ is used. We can think of SST as a measure of how well the observations cluster about the line $\bar{y}$ and SSE as a measure of how well the observations cluster about the $\hat{y}$ line.

To measure how much the $\hat{y}$ values on the estimated regression line deviate from $\bar{y}$, another sum of squares is computed. This sum of squares, called the *sum of squares due to regression*, is denoted SSR.

Sum of Squares Due to Regression

$$SSR = \Sigma(\hat{y}_i - \bar{y})^2 \qquad (12.10)$$

From the preceding discussion, we should expect that SST, SSR, and SSE are related. Indeed, the relationship among these three sums of squares provides one of the most important results in statistics.

SSR can be thought of as the explained portion of SST, and SSE can be thought of as the unexplained portion of SST.

Relationship Among SST, SSR, and SSE

$$SST = SSR + SSE \qquad (12.11)$$

where

SST = total sum of squares

SSR = sum of squares due to regression

SSE = sum of squares due to error

FIGURE 12.5   DEVIATIONS ABOUT THE ESTIMATED REGRESSION LINE
AND THE LINE $y = \bar{y}$ FOR ARMAND'S PIZZA PARLORS

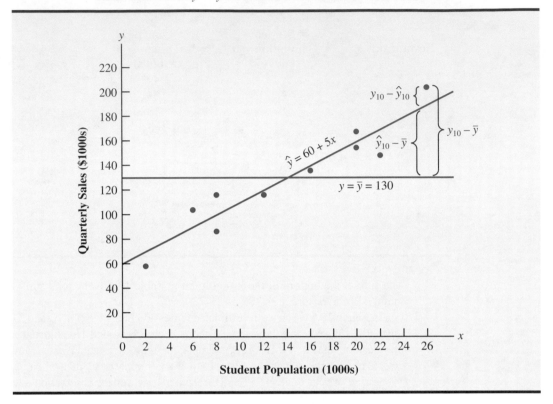

Equation (12.11) shows that the total sum of squares can be partitioned into two components, the sum of squares due to regression and the sum of squares due to error. Hence, if the values of any two of these sum of squares are known, the third sum of squares can be computed easily. For instance, in the Armand's Pizza Parlors example, we already know that SSE = 1530 and SST = 15,730; therefore, solving for SSR in equation (12.11), we find that the sum of squares due to regression is

$$SSR = SST - SSE = 15{,}730 - 1530 = 14{,}200$$

Now let us see how the three sums of squares, SST, SSR, and SSE, can be used to provide a measure of the goodness of fit for the estimated regression equation. The estimated regression equation would provide a perfect fit if every value of the dependent variable y_i happened to lie on the estimated regression line. In this case, $y_i - \hat{y}_i$ would be zero for each observation, resulting in SSE = 0. Because SST = SSR + SSE, we see that for a perfect fit SSR must equal SST, and the ratio (SSR/SST) must equal one. Poorer fits will result in larger values for SSE. Solving for SSE in (12.11), we see that SSE = SST − SSR. Hence, the largest value for SSE (and hence the poorest fit) occurs when SSR = 0 and SSE = SST.

The ratio SSR/SST, which will take values between zero and one, is used to evaluate the goodness of fit for the estimated regression equation. This ratio is called the **coefficient of determination** and is denoted by r^2.

Coefficient of Determination

$$r^2 = \frac{SSR}{SST} \tag{12.12}$$

For the Armand's Pizza Parlors example, the value of the coefficient of determination is

$$r^2 = \frac{SSR}{SST} = \frac{14,200}{15,730} = .9027$$

When we express the coefficient of determination as a percentage, r^2 can be interpreted as the percentage of the total sum of squares that can be explained by using the estimated regression equation. For Armand's Pizza Parlors, we can conclude that 90.27% of the total sum of squares can be explained by using the estimated regression equation $\hat{y} = 60 + 5x$ to predict sales. In other words, 90.27% of the variability in sales can be explained by the linear relationship between the size of the student population and sales. We should be pleased to find such a good fit for the estimated regression equation.

Correlation Coefficient

In Chapter 3 we introduced the **correlation coefficient** as a descriptive measure of the strength of linear association between two variables, x and y. Values of the correlation coefficient are always between -1 and $+1$. A value of $+1$ indicates that the two variables x and y are perfectly related in a positive linear sense. That is, all data points are on a straight line that has a positive slope. A value of -1 indicates that x and y are perfectly related in a negative linear sense, with all data points on a straight line that has a negative slope. Values of the correlation coefficient close to zero indicate that x and y are not linearly related.

In Section 3.5 we presented the equation for computing the sample correlation coefficient. If a regression analysis has already been performed and the coefficient of determination r^2 has been computed, the sample correlation coefficient can be computed as follows.

Sample Correlation Coefficient

$$r_{xy} = (\text{sign of } b_1)\sqrt{\text{Coefficient of Determination}}$$
$$= (\text{sign of } b_1)\sqrt{r^2} \tag{12.13}$$

where

$$b_1 = \text{the slope of the estimated regression equation } \hat{y} = b_0 + b_1 x$$

The sign for the sample correlation coefficient is positive if the estimated regression equation has a positive slope ($b_1 > 0$) and negative if the estimated regression equation has a negative slope ($b_1 < 0$).

For the Armand's Pizza Parlor example, the value of the coefficient of determination corresponding to the estimated regression equation $\hat{y} = 60 + 5x$ is .9027. Because the slope of the estimated regression equation is positive, (12.13) shows that the sample correlation coefficient is $+\sqrt{.9027} = +.9501$. With a sample correlation coefficient of $r_{xy} = +.9501$, we would conclude that there is a strong positive linear association between x and y.

In the case of a linear relationship between two variables, both the coefficient of determination and the sample correlation coefficient provide measures of the strength of the relationship. The coefficient of determination provides a measure between zero and one whereas the sample correlation coefficient provides a measure between -1 and $+1$. Although the sample correlation coefficient is restricted to a linear relationship between two variables, the coefficient of determination can be used for nonlinear relationships and for relationships that have two or more independent variables. In that sense, the coefficient of determination has a wider range of applicability.

NOTES AND COMMENTS

1. In developing the least squares estimated regression equation and computing the coefficient of determination, we made no probabilistic assumptions and no statistical tests for significance of the relationship between x and y. Larger values of r^2 imply that the least squares line provides a better fit to the data; that is, the observations are more closely grouped about the least squares line. But, using only r^2, we can draw no conclusion about whether the relationship between x and y is statistically significant. Such a conclusion must be based on considera-

tions that involve the sample size and the properties of the appropriate sampling distributions of the least squares estimators.

2. As a practical matter, for typical data found in the social sciences, values of r^2 as low as .25 are often considered useful. For data in the physical and life sciences, r^2 values of .60 or greater are often found; in fact, in some cases, r^2 values greater than .90 can be found. In business applications, r^2 values vary greatly, depending on the unique characteristics of each application.

EXERCISES

Methods

SELFtest

15. The data from Exercise 1 follow.

x_i	1	2	3	4	5
y_i	3	7	5	11	14

The estimated regression equation for these data is $\hat{y} = .20 + 2.60x$.
a. Compute SSE, SST, and SSR using (12.8), (12.9), and (12.10).
b. Compute the coefficient of determination r^2. Comment on the goodness of fit.
c. Compute the sample correlation coefficient.

16. The data from Exercise 2 follow.

x_i	2	3	5	1	8
y_i	25	25	20	30	16

The estimated regression equation for these data is $\hat{y} = 30.33 - 1.88x$.
a. Compute SSE, SST, and SSR.
b. Compute the coefficient of determination r^2. Comment on the goodness of fit.
c. Compute the sample correlation coefficient.

17. The data from Exercise 3 follow.

x_i	2	4	5	7	8
y_i	2	3	2	6	4

The estimated regression equation for these data is $\hat{y} = .75 + .51x$. What percentage of the total sum of squares can be accounted for by the estimated regression equation? What is the value of the sample correlation coefficient?

Applications

SELFtest

18. The following data are the monthly salaries y and the grade point averages x for students who had obtained a bachelor's degree in business administration with a major in information systems. The estimated regression equation for these data is $\hat{y} = 1790.5 + 581.1x$.

GPA	Monthly Salary ($)
2.6	3300
3.4	3600
3.6	4000
3.2	3500
3.5	3900
2.9	3600

a. Compute SST, SSR, and SSE.
b. Compute the coefficient of determination r^2. Comment on the goodness of fit.
c. What is the value of the sample correlation coefficient?

19. The data from Exercise 7 follow.

CDfile
DowS&P

Date	x = DJIA	y = S&P
February 11	10425	1387
February 18	10220	1346
February 25	9862	1333
March 3	10367	1409
March 10	9929	1395
March 17	10595	1464
March 24	11113	1527
March 31	10922	1499
April 7	11111	1516
April 14	10306	1357

The estimated regression equation for these data is $\hat{y} = -137.63 + .1489x$. What percentage of the total sum of squares can be accounted for by the estimated regression equation? Comment on the goodness of fit. What is the sample correlation coefficient?

20. The typical household income and typical home price for a sample of 18 cities follow (*Places Rated Almanac,* 2000). Data are in thousands of dollars.

City	Income	Home Price
Akron, OH	74.1	114.9
Atlanta, GA	82.4	126.9
Birmingham, AL	71.2	130.9
Bismarck, ND	62.8	92.8
Cleveland, OH	79.2	135.8
Columbia, SC	66.8	116.7
Denver, CO	82.6	161.9
Detroit, MI	85.3	145.0
Fort Lauderdale, FL	75.8	145.3
Hartford, CT	89.1	162.1
Lancaster, PA	75.2	125.9
Madison, WI	78.8	145.2
Naples, FL	100.0	173.6
Nashville, TN	77.3	125.9
Philadelphia, PA	87.0	151.5
Savannah, GA	67.8	108.1
Toledo, OH	71.2	101.1
Washington, DC	97.4	191.9

a. Use these data to develop an estimated regression equation that could be used to estimate the typical home price for a city given the typical household income.

b. Compute r^2. Would you feel comfortable using this estimated regression equation to estimate the typical home price for a city?

c. Estimate the typical home price for a city that has a typical household income of $95,000.

21. An important application of regression analysis in accounting is in the estimation of cost. By collecting data on volume and cost and using the least squares method to develop an estimated regression equation relating volume and cost, an accountant can estimate the cost associated with a particular manufacturing operation. Consider the following sample of production volumes and total cost data for a manufacturing operation.

Production Volume (units)	Total Cost ($)
400	4000
450	5000
550	5400
600	5900
700	6400
750	7000

a. Use these data to develop an estimated regression equation that could be used to predict the total cost for a given production volume.

b. What is the variable or additional cost per unit produced?

    c. Compute the coefficient of determination. What percentage of the variation in total cost can be explained by production volume?

    d. The company's production schedule shows 500 units must be produced next month. What is the estimated total cost for this operation?

22. Are company presidents and chief executive officers paid according to the profit performance of the company? The following table lists corporate data on percentage change in return on equity over a two-year period and percentage change in the pay of presidents and chief executive officers immediately after the two-year period (*Business Week*, April 21, 1997).

Company	Two-Year Change in Return on Equity (%)	Change in Executive Compensation (%)
Dow Chemical	201.3	18
Rohm & Haas	146.5	28
Morton International	76.7	10
Union Carbide	158.2	28
Praxair	−34.9	15
Air Products & Chemicals	73.2	−9
Eastman Chemical	−7.9	−20

    a. Develop the estimated regression equation with the two-year percentage change in return on equity as the independent variable.

    b. Compute r^2. Would you feel comfortable using the percentage change in return on equity over a two-year period to predict the percentage change in the pay of presidents and chief executive officers? Discuss.

    c. What is the sample correlation coefficient? Does it reflect a strong or weak relationship between return on equity and executive compensation?

12.4 MODEL ASSUMPTIONS

In conducting a regression analysis, we begin by making an assumption about the appropriate model for the relationship between the dependent and independent variable(s). For the case of simple linear regression, the assumed regression model is

$$y = \beta_0 + \beta_1 x + \epsilon$$

Then, the least squares method is used to develop values for b_0 and b_1, the estimates of the model parameters β_0 and β_1, respectively. The resulting estimated regression equation is

$$\hat{y} = b_0 + b_1 x$$

We saw that the value of the coefficient of determination (r^2) is a measure of the goodness of fit of the estimated regression equation. However, even with a large value of r^2, the estimated regression equation should not be used until further analysis of the appropriateness of the assumed model has been conducted. An important step in determining whether the assumed model is appropriate involves testing for the significance of the relationship. The tests of significance in regression analysis are based on the following assumptions about the error term ϵ.

Assumptions About the Error Term ϵ in the Regression Model

$$y = \beta_0 + \beta_1 x + \epsilon$$

1. The error term ϵ is a random variable with a mean or expected value of zero; that is, $E(\epsilon) = 0$.
   Implication: β_0 and β_1 are constants, therefore $E(\beta_0) = \beta_0$ and $E(\beta_1) = \beta_1$; thus, for a given value of x, the expected value of y is

$$E(y) = \beta_0 + \beta_1 x \qquad (12.14)$$

   As we indicated previously, equation (12.14) is referred to as the regression equation.
2. The variance of ϵ, denoted by σ^2, is the same for all values of x.
   Implication: The variance of y equals σ^2 and is the same for all values of x.
3. The values of ϵ are independent.
   Implication: The value of ϵ for a particular value of x is not related to the value of ϵ for any other value of x; thus, the value of y for a particular value of x is not related to the value of y for any other value of x.
4. The error term ϵ is a normally distributed random variable.
   Implication: Because y is a linear function of ϵ, y is also a normally distributed random variable.

Figure 12.6 is an illustration of the model assumptions and their implications; note that in this graphical interpretation, the value of $E(y)$ changes according to the specific value of x considered. However, regardless of the x value, the probability distribution of ϵ and hence the probability distributions of y are normally distributed, each with the same variance. The specific value of the error ϵ at any particular point depends on whether the actual value of y is greater than or less than $E(y)$.

At this point, we must keep in mind that we are also making an assumption or hypothesis about the form of the relationship between x and y. That is, we have assumed that a straight line represented by $\beta_0 + \beta_1 x$ is the basis for the relationship between the variables. We must not lose sight of the fact that some other model, for instance $y = \beta_0 + \beta_1 x^2 + \epsilon$, may turn out to be a better model for the underlying relationship.

12.5   TESTING FOR SIGNIFICANCE

In a simple linear regression equation the mean or expected value of y is a linear function of x: $E(y) = \beta_0 + \beta_1 x$. If the value of β_1 is zero, $E(y) = \beta_0 + (0)x = \beta_0$. In this case, the mean value of y does not depend on the value of x and hence we would conclude that x and y are not linearly related. Alternatively, if the value of β_1 is not equal to zero, we would conclude that the two variables are related. Thus, to test for a significant regression rela-

FIGURE 12.6   ASSUMPTIONS FOR THE REGRESSION MODEL

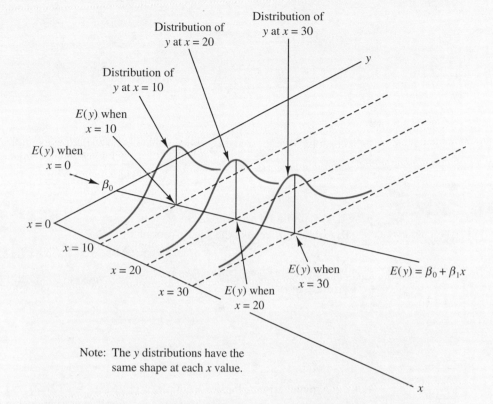

Note: The y distributions have the
same shape at each x value.

tionship, we must conduct a hypothesis test to determine whether the value of β_1 is zero. Two tests are commonly used. Both require an estimate of σ^2, the variance of ϵ in the regression model.

Estimate of σ^2

From the regression model and its assumptions we can conclude that σ^2, the variance of ϵ, also represents the variance of the y values about the regression line. Recall that the deviations of the y values about the estimated regression line are called residuals. Thus, SSE, the sum of squared residuals, is a measure of the variability of the actual observations about the estimated regression line. The **mean square error** (MSE) provides the estimate of σ^2; it is SSE divided by its degrees of freedom.

With $\hat{y}_i = b_0 + b_1 x_i$, SSE can be written as

$$SSE = \Sigma(y_i - \hat{y}_i)^2 = \Sigma(y_i - b_0 - b_1 x_i)^2$$

Every sum of squares has associated with it a number called its degrees of freedom. Statisticians have shown that SSE has $n - 2$ degrees of freedom because two parameters (β_0 and β_1) must be estimated to compute SSE. Thus, the mean square error is computed by dividing SSE by $n - 2$. MSE provides an unbiased estimator of σ^2. Because the value of MSE provides an estimate of σ^2, the notation s^2 is also used.

Estimate of σ^2

$$s^2 = \text{MSE} = \frac{\text{SSE}}{n - 2} \tag{12.15}$$

In Section 12.3 we showed that for the Armand's Pizza Parlors example, SSE = 1530; hence,

$$s^2 = \text{MSE} = \frac{1530}{8} = 191.25$$

provides an unbiased estimate of σ^2.

To estimate σ we take the square root of s^2.

Estimate of σ

$$s = \sqrt{\text{MSE}} = \sqrt{\frac{\text{SSE}}{n - 2}} \tag{12.16}$$

For the Armand's Pizza Parlors example, $s = \sqrt{\text{MSE}} = \sqrt{191.25} = 13.829$. In the following discussion, we use s to conduct tests for a significant relationship between x and y.

t Test

The simple linear regression model is $y = \beta_0 + \beta_1 x + \epsilon$. If x and y are linearly related, we must have $\beta_1 \neq 0$. The purpose of the t test is to use the sample data to conduct the following hypothesis test about the parameter β_1.

$$H_0\colon \beta_1 = 0$$
$$H_a\colon \beta_1 \neq 0$$

If H_0 is rejected, we will conclude that $\beta_1 \neq 0$ and that a statistically significant relationship exists between the two variables. However, if H_0 cannot be rejected, we will have insufficient evidence to conclude that a significant relationship exists. The properties of the sampling distribution of b_1, the least squares estimator of β_1, provide the basis for the hypothesis test.

First, let us consider what would have happened if we had used a different random sample for the same regression study. For example, suppose that Armand's Pizza Parlors used the sales records of a different sample of 10 restaurants. A regression analysis of this new sample might result in an estimated regression equation similar to our previous estimated regression equation $\hat{y} = 60 + 5x$. However, it is doubtful that we would obtain exactly the same equation (with an intercept of exactly 60 and a slope of exactly 5). Indeed, b_0 and b_1, the least squares estimators, are sample statistics that have their own sampling distributions. The properties of the sampling distribution of b_1 follow.

Sampling Distribution of b_1

Expected Value

$$E(b_1) = \beta_1$$

Standard Deviation

$$\sigma_{b_1} = \frac{\sigma}{\sqrt{\Sigma(x_i - \bar{x})^2}} \qquad (12.17)$$

Distribution Form

Normal

The standard deviation of b_1 is also referred to as the standard error of b_1.

Note that the expected value of b_1 is equal to β_1, so b_1 is an unbiased estimator of β_1.

Because we do not know the value of σ, we develop an estimate of σ_{b_1}, denoted s_{b_1}, by estimating σ with s in equation (12.17). Thus, we obtain the following estimate of σ_{b_1}.

Estimated Standard Deviation of b_1

$$s_{b_1} = \frac{s}{\sqrt{\Sigma(x_i - \bar{x})^2}} \qquad (12.18)$$

---

s_{b_1} provides an estimate of the standard error of b_1.

For Armand's Pizza Parlors, $s = 13.829$ and $\Sigma(x_i - \bar{x})^2 = 568$ (see Table 12.2). Thus, we have

$$s_{b_1} = \frac{13.829}{\sqrt{568}} = .5803$$

as the estimated standard deviation of b_1.

The t test for a significant relationship is based on the fact that the test statistic

$$\frac{b_1 - \beta_1}{s_{b_1}}$$

follows a t distribution with $n - 2$ degrees of freedom. If the null hypothesis is true, then $\beta_1 = 0$ and $t = b_1/s_{b_1}$. With b_1/s_{b_1} as the test statistic, the steps of the t test for a significant relationship are as follows.

---

t Test for Significance in Simple Linear Regression

$$H_0: \beta_1 = 0$$
$$H_a: \beta_1 \neq 0$$

Test Statistic

$$t = \frac{b_1}{s_{b_1}}$$ (12.19)

Rejection Rule

Using test statistic: Reject H_0 if $t < -t_{\alpha/2}$ or if $t > t_{\alpha/2}$

Using p-value: Reject H_0 if p-value $< \alpha$

where $t_{\alpha/2}$ is based on a t distribution with $n - 2$ degrees of freedom.

Let us conduct this test of significance for Armand's Pizza Parlors at the $\alpha = .01$ level of significance. The test statistic, equation (12.19), is

$$t = \frac{b_1}{s_{b_1}} = \frac{5}{.5803} = 8.62$$

From Table 2 of Appendix B we find that the two-tailed t value corresponding to $\alpha = .01$ and $n - 2 = 10 - 2 = 8$ degrees of freedom is $t_{.005} = 3.355$. With $8.62 > 3.355$, we reject H_0 and conclude at the .01 level of significance that β_1 is not equal to zero. The statistical evidence is sufficient to conclude that we have a significant relationship between student population and sales.

The p-value criterion can also be used to test for a significant relationship. The usual rejection rule applies: Reject H_0 if p-value $< \alpha$. However, because it is difficult to determine the p-value directly from tables of the t probability distribution, a computer software package such as Minitab or Excel is used. Appendixes 12.1 and 12.2 show the procedures that can be used; a discussion of the computer results for regression analysis is provided in Section 12.7. For Armand's Pizza Parlors, the p-value associated with the test statistic $t = 8.62$ is .000 (to three decimal places). With a p-value $= .000 < \alpha = .05$, we reject H_0 and conclude that we have a significant relationship between student population and sales.

Confidence Interval for β_1

The form of a confidence interval for β_1 is as follows:

$$b_1 \pm t_{\alpha/2} s_{b_1}$$

The point estimator is b_1 and the margin of error is $t_{\alpha/2} s_{b_1}$. The confidence coefficient associated with this interval is $1 - \alpha$, and $t_{\alpha/2}$ is the t value providing an area of $\alpha/2$ in the upper tail of a t distribution with $n - 2$ degrees of freedom. For example, suppose that we wanted to develop a 99% confidence interval estimate of β_1 for Armand's Pizza Parlors. From Table 2 of Appendix B we find that the t value corresponding to $\alpha = .01$ and $n - 2 = 10 - 2 = 8$ degrees of freedom is $t_{.005} = 3.355$. Thus, the 99% confidence interval estimate of β_1 is

$$b_1 \pm t_{\alpha/2} s_{b_1} = 5 \pm 3.355(.5803) = 5 \pm 1.95$$

or 3.05 to 6.95.

In using the t test for significance, the hypotheses tested were

$$H_0: \beta_1 = 0$$
$$H_a: \beta_1 \neq 0$$

At the $\alpha = .01$ level of significance, we can use the 99% confidence interval as an alternative for drawing the hypothesis testing conclusion for the Armand's data. Because 0, the hypothesized value of β_1, is not included in the confidence interval (3.05 to 6.95), we can reject H_0 and conclude that a significant statistical relationship exists between population and sales. In general, a confidence interval can be used to test any two-sided hypothesis about β_1. If the hypothesized value of β_1 is contained in the confidence interval, do not reject H_0. Otherwise, reject H_0.

F Test

An F test, based on the F probability distribution, can also be used to test for significance in regression. With only one independent variable, the F test will provide the same conclusion as the t test; that is, if the t test indicates $\beta_1 \neq 0$ and hence a significant relationship, the F test will also indicate a significant relationship. But with more than one independent variable, only the F test can be used to test for an overall significant relationship.

The logic behind the use of the F test for determining whether the regression relationship is statistically significant is based on the development of two independent estimates of σ^2. We have just seen that MSE provides an estimate of σ^2. If the null hypothesis $H_0: \beta_1 = 0$ is true, the sum of squares due to regression, SSR, divided by its degrees of freedom provides another independent estimate of σ^2. This estimate is called the *mean square due to regression,* or simply the *mean square regression,* and is denoted MSR. In general,

$$\text{MSR} = \frac{\text{SSR}}{\text{regression degrees of freedom}}$$

For the models we consider in this text, the regression degrees of freedom is always equal to the number of independent variables; thus,

$$\text{MSR} = \frac{\text{SSR}}{\text{number of independent variables}} \tag{12.20}$$

Because we consider only regression models with one independent variable in this chapter, we have MSR = SSR/1 = SSR. Hence, for Armand's Pizza Parlors, MSR = SSR = 14,200.

If the null hypothesis ($H_0: \beta_1 = 0$) is true, MSR and MSE are two independent estimates of σ^2 and the sampling distribution of MSR/MSE follows an F distribution with numerator degrees of freedom equal to one and denominator degrees of freedom equal to $n - 2$. Therefore, when $\beta_1 = 0$, the value of MSR/MSE should be close to one. However, if the null hypothesis is false ($\beta_1 \neq 0$), MSR will overestimate σ^2 and the value of MSR/MSE will be inflated; thus, large values of MSR/MSE lead to the rejection of H_0 and the conclusion that the relationship between x and y is statistically significant. A summary of how the F test is used to test for a significant relationship follows.

F Test for Significance in Simple Linear Regression

$$H_0: \beta_1 = 0$$
$$H_a: \beta_1 \neq 0$$

Test Statistic

$$F = \frac{MSR}{MSE} \qquad (12.21)$$

Rejection Rule

Using test statistic: Reject H_0 if $F > F_\alpha$

Using p-value: Reject H_0 if p-value $< \alpha$

where F_α is based on an F distribution with 1 degree of freedom in the numerator and $n - 2$ degrees of freedom in the denominator.

Let us conduct the F test for the Armand's Pizza Parlors example. The test statistic is

$$F = \frac{MSR}{MSE} = \frac{14{,}200}{191.25} = 74.25$$

The F test and the t test provide identical results for simple linear regression.

From Table 4 of Appendix B we find that the F value corresponding to $\alpha = .01$ with one degree of freedom in the numerator and $n - 2 = 10 - 2 = 8$ degrees of freedom in the denominator is $F_{.01} = 11.26$. With $74.25 > 11.26$, we reject H_0 and conclude at the .01 level of significance that β_1 is not equal to zero. The F test has provided the statistical evidence necessary to conclude that we have a significant relationship between student population and sales.

The p-value criterion can also be used with the F test. The usual rejection rule applies: Reject H_0 if p-value $< \alpha$. However, because it is difficult to determine the p-value directly from tables of the F probability distribution, a computer software package such as Minitab or Excel is used. Appendixes 12.1 and 12.2 show the procedures that can be used; a discussion of the computer results for regression analysis is provided in Section 12.7. For Armand's Pizza Parlors, the p-value associated with the test statistic $F = 74.25$ is .000 (to three decimal places). With a p-value $= .000 < \alpha = .05$, we reject H_0 and conclude that we have a significant relationship between student population and sales.

In Chapter 10 we covered analysis of variance (ANOVA) and showed how an **ANOVA table** could be used to provide a convenient summary of the computational aspects of analysis of variance. A similar ANOVA table can be used to summarize the results of the F test for significance in regression. Table 12.5 is the general form of the ANOVA table for simple linear regression. Table 12.6 is the ANOVA table with the F test computations performed for Armand's Pizza Parlors. Regression, Error, and Total are the labels for the three sources of variation, with SSR, SSE, and SST appearing as the corresponding sum of squares in column two. The degrees of freedom, 1 for SSR, $n - 2$ for SSE, and $n - 1$ for SST, are shown in column 3. Column 4 contains the values of MSR and MSE and column 5 contains the value of $F = MSR/MSE$. Almost all computer printouts of regression analysis include an ANOVA table.

Some Cautions About the Interpretation of Significance Tests

Rejecting the null hypothesis H_0: $\beta_1 = 0$ and concluding that the relationship between x and y is significant does not enable us to conclude that a cause-and-effect relationship is present between x and y. Concluding a cause-and-effect relationship is warranted only if

TABLE 12.5 GENERAL FORM OF THE ANOVA TABLE FOR SIMPLE LINEAR REGRESSION

In every analysis of variance table the total sum of squares is the sum of the regression sum of squares and the error sum of squares; in addition, the total degrees of freedom is the sum of the regression degrees of freedom and the error degrees of freedom.

Source of Variation	Sum of Squares	Degrees of Freedom	Mean Square	F
Regression	SSR	1	$MSR = \dfrac{SSR}{1}$	$F = \dfrac{MSR}{MSE}$
Error	SSE	$n - 2$	$MSE = \dfrac{SSE}{n - 2}$	
Total	SST	$n - 1$		

Regression analysis, which can be used to identify how variables are associated with one another, cannot be used as evidence of a cause-and-effect relationship.

the analyst has some type of theoretical justification that the relationship is in fact causal. In the Armand's Pizza Parlors example, we can conclude that there is a significant relationship between the size of the student population x and quarterly sales y; moreover, the estimated regression equation $\hat{y} = 60 + 5x$ provides the least squares estimate of the relationship. We cannot, however, conclude that changes in student population x *cause* changes in quarterly sales y just because we have identified a statistically significant relationship. The appropriateness of such a cause-and-effect conclusion is left to supporting theoretical justification and to good judgment on the part of the analyst. Armand's managers felt that increases in the student population were a likely cause of increased quarterly sales. Thus, the result of the significance test enabled them to conclude that a cause-and-effect relationship was present.

In addition, just because we are able to reject $H_0: \beta_1 = 0$ and demonstrate statistical significance does not enable us to conclude that the relationship between x and y is linear. We can state only that x and y are related and that a linear relationship explains a significant portion of the variability in y over the range of values for x observed in the sample. Figure 12.7 illustrates this situation. The test for significance calls for the rejection of the null hypothesis $H_0: \beta_1 = 0$ and leads to the conclusion that x and y are significantly related, but the figure shows that the actual relationship between x and y is not linear. Although the linear approximation provided by $\hat{y} = b_0 + b_1x$ is good over the range of x values observed in the sample, it becomes poor for x values outside that range.

TABLE 12.6 ANOVA TABLE FOR THE ARMAND'S PIZZA PARLORS PROBLEM

Source of Variation	Sum of Squares	Degrees of Freedom	Mean Square	F
Regression	14,200	1	$\dfrac{14{,}200}{1} = 14{,}200$	$\dfrac{14{,}200}{191.25} = 74.25$
Error	1,530	8	$\dfrac{1530}{8} = 191.25$	
Total	15,730	9		

FIGURE 12.7   EXAMPLE OF A LINEAR APPROXIMATION OF A NONLINEAR
RELATIONSHIP

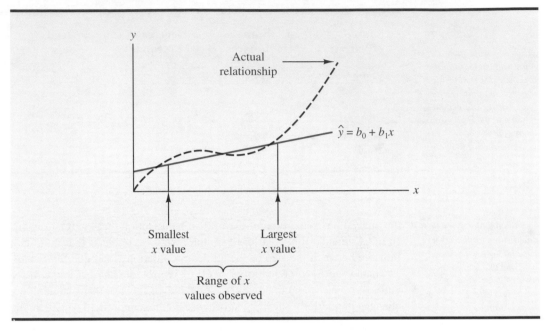

Given a significant relationship, we should feel confident in using the estimated regression equation for predictions corresponding to x values within the range of the x values observed in the sample. For Armand's Pizza Parlors, this range corresponds to values of x between 2 and 26. But unless other reasons indicate that the model is valid beyond this range, predictions outside the range of the independent variable should be made with caution. For Armand's Pizza Parlors, because the regression relationship has been found significant at the .01 level, we should feel confident using it to predict sales for restaurants where the associated student population is between 2000 and 26,000.

NOTES AND COMMENTS

1. The assumptions made about the error term (Section 12.4) allow for the tests of statistical significance in this section. The properties of the sampling distribution of b_1 and the subsequent t and F tests follow directly from these assumptions.

2. Do not confuse statistical significance with practical significance. With very large sample sizes, statistically significant results can be obtained for small values of b_1; in such cases, one must exercise care in concluding that the relationship has practical significance.

3. A test of significance for a linear relationship between x and y can also be performed by using the sample correlation coefficient r_{xy}. With ρ_{xy} denoting the population correlation coefficient, the hypotheses are as follows.

$$H_0: \rho_{xy} = 0$$
$$H_a: \rho_{xy} \neq 0$$

A significant relationship can be concluded if H_0 is rejected. However, the t and F tests presented previously in this section give the *same result* as the test for significance using the correlation coefficient. Conducting a test for significance using the correlation coefficient therefore is not necessary if a t or F test has already been conducted.

EXERCISES

Methods

SELFtest   **23.** The data from Exercise 1 follow.

x_i	1	2	3	4	5
y_i	3	7	5	11	14

    a. Compute the mean square error using equation (12.15).
    b. Compute the estimate of σ using equation (12.16).
    c. Compute the estimated standard deviation of b_1 using equation (12.18).
    d. Use the t test to test the following hypotheses ($\alpha = .05$):

$$H_0: \beta_1 = 0$$
$$H_a: \beta_1 \neq 0$$

    e. Use the F test to test the hypotheses in (d) at a .05 level of significance. Present the results in the analysis of variance table format.

24. The data from Exercise 2 follow.

x_i	2	3	5	1	8
y_i	25	25	20	30	16

    a. Compute the mean square error using equation (12.15).
    b. Compute the estimate of σ using equation (12.16).
    c. Compute the estimated standard deviation of b_1 using equation (12.18).
    d. Use the t test to test the following hypotheses ($\alpha = .05$):

$$H_0: \beta_1 = 0$$
$$H_a: \beta_1 \neq 0$$

    e. Use the F test to test the hypotheses in (d) at a .05 level of significance. Present the results in the analysis of variance table format.

25. The data from Exercise 3 follow.

x_i	2	4	5	7	8
y_i	2	3	2	6	4

    a. Compute the estimate of σ.
    b. Test for a significant relationship by using the t test. Use $\alpha = .05$.
    c. Use the F test to test for a significant relationship. Use $\alpha = .05$. What is your conclusion?

Applications

SELFtest   **26.** In Exercise 18 the data on grade point average and monthly salary were as follows.

GPA	Monthly Salary ($)	GPA	Monthly Salary ($)
2.6	3300	3.2	3500
3.4	3600	3.5	3900
3.6	4000	2.9	3600

a. Does the t test indicate a significant relationship between grade point average and monthly salary? What is your conclusion? Use $\alpha = .05$.

b. Test for a significant relationship using the F test. What is your conclusion? Use $\alpha = .05$.

c. Show the ANOVA table.

27. *Outside Magazine* tested 10 different models of day hikers and backpacking boots. The following data show the upper support and price for each model tested. Upper support was measured using a rating from 1 to 5, with a rating of 1 denoting average upper support and a rating of 5 denoting excellent upper support (*Outside Magazine Buyer's Guide*, 2001).

Boots

Manufacturer and Model	Upper Support	Price
Salomon Super Raid	2	120
Merrell Chameleon Prime	3	125
Teva Challenger	3	130
Vasque Fusion GTX	3	135
Boreal Maigmo	3	150
L.L. Bean GTX Super Guide	5	189
Lowa Kibo	5	190
Asolo AFX 520 GTX	4	195
Raichle Mt. Trail GTX	4	200
Scarpa Delta SL M3	5	220

a. Use these data to develop an estimated regression equation that could be used to estimate the price of a day hiker and backpacking boot given the upper support rating.

b. At the .05 level of significance, determine whether upper support and price are related.

c. Would you feel comfortable using the estimated regression equation developed in part (a) to estimate the price for a day hiker or backpacking boot given the upper support rating?

d. Estimate the price for a day hiker that has an upper support rating of 4.

28. Refer to Exercise 10, where an estimated regression equation relating the performance score and the overall rating for notebook PCs was developed. At the .05 level of significance, test whether these two variables are related. Show the ANOVA table. What is your conclusion?

29. Refer to Exercise 21, where data on production volume and cost were used to develop an estimated regression equation relating production volume and cost for a particular manufacturing operation. Using $\alpha = .05$, test whether the production volume is significantly related to the total cost. Show the ANOVA table. What is your conclusion?

30. Refer to Exercise 22, where the following data were used to determine whether company presidents and chief executive officers are paid on the basis of company profit performance (*Business Week*, April 21, 1997).

Company	Two-Year Change in Return on Equity (%)	Change in Executive Compensation (%)
Dow Chemical	201.3	18
Rohm & Haas	146.5	28
Morton International	76.7	10
Union Carbide	158.2	28
Praxair	−34.9	15

Company	Two-Year Change in Return on Equity (%)	Change in Executive Compensation (%)
Air Products & Chemicals	73.2	−9
Eastman Chemical	−7.9	−20

Do these data indicate a significant relationship between the two variables? Conduct the appropriate statistical test and state your conclusion. Use $\alpha = .05$.

31. Refer to Exercise 20, where an estimated regression equation was developed relating typical household income and typical home price. Test whether the typical household income for a city and the typical home price are related at the .01 level of significance.

12.6 USING THE ESTIMATED REGRESSION EQUATION FOR ESTIMATION AND PREDICTION

The simple linear regression model is an assumption about the relationship between x and y. Using the least squares method, we obtained the estimated simple linear regression equation. If the results show a statistically significant relationship between x and y, and the fit provided by the estimated regression equation appears to be good, the estimated regression equation should be useful for estimation and prediction.

Point Estimation

In the Armand's Pizza Parlors example, the estimated regression equation $\hat{y} = 60 + 5x$ provides an estimate of the relationship between the size of the student population x and quarterly sales y. We can use the estimated regression equation to develop a point estimate of the mean value of y for a particular value of x or to predict an individual value of y corresponding to a given value of x. For instance, suppose Armand's managers want a point estimate of the mean quarterly sales for all restaurants located near college campuses with 10,000 students. Using the estimated regression equation $\hat{y} = 60 + 5x$, we see that for $x = 10$ (or 10,000 students), $\hat{y} = 60 + 5(10) = 110$. Thus, a point estimate of the mean quarterly sales for all restaurants located near campuses with 10,000 students is $110,000.

Now suppose Armand's managers want to predict sales for an individual restaurant located near Talbot College, a school with 10,000 students. In this case we are not interested in the mean value for all restaurants located near campuses with 10,000 students; we are just interested in predicting quarterly sales for one individual restaurant. As it turns out, the point estimate is the same as the point estimate for the mean value of y. Hence, we would predict quarterly sales of $\hat{y} = 60 + 5(10) = 110$ or $110,000 for this one restaurant.

Interval Estimation

Confidence intervals and prediction intervals indicate the precision of the regression results. Narrower intervals indicate a higher degree of precision.

Point estimates do not provide any information about the precision associated with an estimate. For that we must develop interval estimates much like those in Chapters 8, 10, and 11. The first type of interval estimate, a **confidence interval estimate,** is an interval estimate of the *mean value of y* for a given value of x. The second type of interval estimate, a **prediction interval estimate,** is used whenever we want an interval estimate of an *individual value of y* corresponding to a given value of x. The point estimate of the mean value of y is the same as the point estimate of an individual value of y. But, the interval estimates we obtain for the two cases are different.

Confidence Interval Estimate of the Mean Value of y

The estimated regression equation provides a point estimate of the mean value of y for a given value of x. In describing the confidence interval estimation procedure, we will use the following notation.

$$x_p = \text{the particular or given value of the independent variable } x$$

$$E(y_p) = \text{the mean or expected value of the dependent variable } y$$
$$\text{when } x = x_p$$

$$\hat{y}_p = b_0 + b_1 x_p = \text{the point estimate of } E(y_p) \text{ when } x = x_p$$

Suppose we want to estimate the mean sales for all Armand's restaurants located near a campus with 10,000 students. In this case, $x_p = 10$, and $E(y_p)$ denotes the unknown mean value of sales for all restaurants where $x_p = 10$. The point estimate of $E(y_p)$ is $\hat{y}_p = 60 + 5(10) = 110$.

In general, we cannot expect $\hat{y}_p$ to equal $E(y_p)$ exactly. If we want to make an inference about how close $\hat{y}_p$ is to the true mean value $E(y_p)$, we must estimate the variance of $\hat{y}_p$. The formula for estimating the variance of $\hat{y}_p$ given x_p, denoted by $s_{\hat{y}_p}^2$, is

$$s_{\hat{y}_p}^2 = s^2 \left[\frac{1}{n} + \frac{(x_p - \bar{x})^2}{\Sigma(x_i - \bar{x})^2} \right] \tag{12.22}$$

The estimate of the standard deviation of $\hat{y}_p$ is given by the square root of equation (12.22).

$$s_{\hat{y}_p} = s \sqrt{\frac{1}{n} + \frac{(x_p - \bar{x})^2}{\Sigma(x_i - \bar{x})^2}} \tag{12.23}$$

The computational results for Armand's Pizza Parlors in Section 12.5 provided $s = 13.829$. With $x_p = 10$, $\bar{x} = 14$, and $\Sigma(x_i - \bar{x})^2 = 568$, we can use equation (12.23) to obtain

$$s_{\hat{y}_p} = 13.829 \sqrt{\frac{1}{10} + \frac{(10 - 14)^2}{568}}$$
$$= 13.829 \sqrt{.1282} = 4.95$$

The general expression for a confidence interval estimate of the mean value of y follows.

Confidence Interval Estimate of the Mean Value of y

$$\hat{y}_p \pm t_{\alpha/2} s_{\hat{y}_p} \tag{12.24}$$

where the confidence coefficient is $1 - \alpha$ and $t_{\alpha/2}$ is based on a t distribution with $n - 2$ degrees of freedom.

The margin of error associated with this internal estimate is $t_{\alpha/2}s_{\hat{y}_p}$.

Using expression (12.24) to develop a 95% confidence interval estimate of the mean quarterly sales for all Armand's restaurants located near campuses with 10,000 students, we need the value of t for $\alpha/2 = .025$ and $n - 2 = 10 - 2 = 8$ degrees of freedom. Using Table 2 of Appendix B, we have $t_{.025} = 2.306$. Thus, with $\hat{y}_p = 110$ and a margin of error of $t_{\alpha/2}s_{\hat{y}_p} = 2.306(4.95) = 11.415$, the 95% confidence interval estimate is

$$110 \pm 11.415$$

In dollars, the 95% confidence interval for the mean quarterly sales of all restaurants near campuses with 10,000 students is $110,000 ± $11,415. Therefore, the confidence interval estimate for the mean quarterly sales when the student population is 10,000 is $98,585 to $121,415.

Note that the estimated standard deviation of $\hat{y}_p$ given by equation (12.23) is smallest when $x_p = \bar{x}$ and the quantity $x_p - \bar{x} = 0$. In this case, the estimated standard deviation of $\hat{y}_p$ becomes

$$s_{\hat{y}_p} = s\sqrt{\frac{1}{n} + \frac{(\bar{x} - \bar{x})^2}{\Sigma(x_i - \bar{x})^2}} = s\sqrt{\frac{1}{n}}$$

This result implies that we can make the best or most precise estimate of the mean value of y whenever $x_p = \bar{x}$. In fact, the further x_p is from $\bar{x}$, the larger $x_p - \bar{x}$ becomes. As a result, confidence intervals for the mean value of y will become wider as x_p deviates more from $\bar{x}$. This pattern is shown graphically in Figure 12.8.

Prediction Interval Estimate of an Individual Value of y

Suppose that instead of estimating the mean value of sales for all Armand's restaurants located near campuses with 10,000 students, we want to estimate the sales for an individual restaurant located near Talbot College, a school with 10,000 students. As noted previously,

FIGURE 12.8   CONFIDENCE INTERVALS FOR THE MEAN SALES y AT GIVEN VALUES OF STUDENT POPULATION x

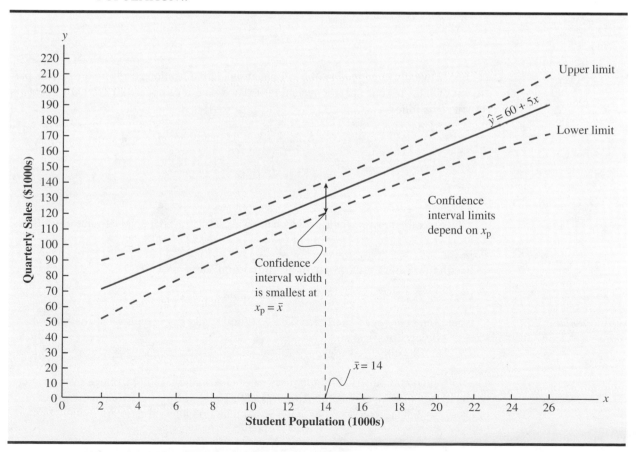

the point estimate of an individual value of y given $x = x_p$ is provided by the estimated regression equation $\hat{y}_p = b_0 + b_1 x_p$. For the restaurant at Talbot College, we have $x_p = 10$ and a corresponding estimated quarterly sales of $\hat{y}_p = 60 + 5(10) = 110$, or \$110,000. Note that this value is the same as the point estimate of the mean sales for all restaurants located near campuses with 10,000 students.

To develop a prediction interval estimate, we must first determine the variance associated with using $\hat{y}_p$ as an estimate of an individual value of y when $x = x_p$. This variance is made up of the sum of the following two components.

1. The variance of individual y values about the mean $E(y_p)$, an estimate of which is given by s^2.
2. The variance associated with using $\hat{y}_p$ to estimate $E(y_p)$, an estimate of which is given by $s_{\hat{y}_p}^2$.

The formula for estimating the variance of an individual value of y, denoted by s_{ind}^2, is

$$s_{ind}^2 = s^2 + s_{\hat{y}_p}^2$$
$$= s^2 + s^2 \left[\frac{1}{n} + \frac{(x_p - \bar{x})^2}{\Sigma(x_i - \bar{x})^2} \right]$$
$$= s^2 \left[1 + \frac{1}{n} + \frac{(x_p - \bar{x})^2}{\Sigma(x_i - \bar{x})^2} \right] \tag{12.25}$$

Hence, an estimate of the standard deviation of an individual value of y is given by

$$s_{ind} = s \sqrt{1 + \frac{1}{n} + \frac{(x_p - \bar{x})^2}{\Sigma(x_i - \bar{x})^2}} \tag{12.26}$$

For Armand's Pizza Parlors, the estimated standard deviation corresponding to the prediction of sales for one specific restaurant located near a campus with 10,000 students is computed as follows.

$$s_{ind} = 13.829 \sqrt{1 + \frac{1}{10} + \frac{(10 - 14)^2}{568}}$$
$$= 13.829 \sqrt{1.1282}$$
$$= 14.69$$

The general expression for a prediction interval estimate of an individual value of y follows.

Prediction Interval Estimate of an Individual Value of y

The margin of error associated with this interval estimate is $t_{\alpha/2} s_{ind}$.

$$\hat{y}_p \pm t_{\alpha/2} s_{ind} \tag{12.27}$$

where the confidence coefficient is $1 - \alpha$ and $t_{\alpha/2}$ is based on a t distribution with $n - 2$ degrees of freedom.

The 95% prediction interval for quarterly sales at Armand's Talbot College restaurant can be found by using $t_{.025} = 2.306$ and $s_{ind} = 14.69$. Thus, with $\hat{y}_p = 110$ and a margin of error of $t_{\alpha/2} s_{ind} = 2.306(14.69) = 33.875$, the 95% prediction interval estimate is

$$110 \pm 33.875$$

FIGURE 12.9   CONFIDENCE AND PREDICTION INTERVALS FOR SALES y AT GIVEN VALUES
OF STUDENT POPULATION x

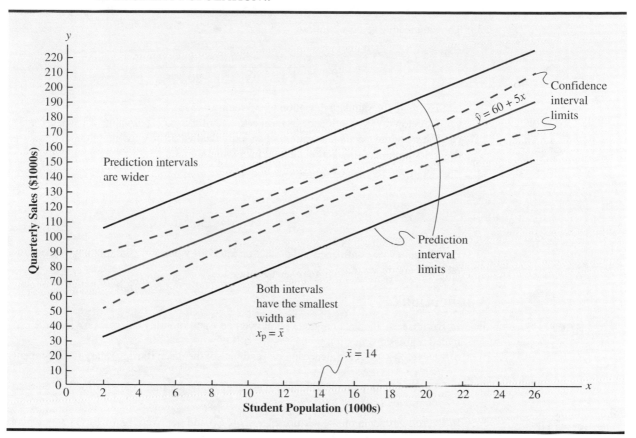

In dollars, this prediction interval is \$110,000 $\pm$ \$33,875 or \$76,125 to \$143,875. Note that the prediction interval for an individual restaurant is wider than the confidence interval for the mean sales of all restaurants located near campuses with 10,000 students (\$98,585 to \$121,415). The difference reflects the fact that we are able to estimate the mean value of y more precisely than we can an individual value of y.

Both confidence interval estimates and prediction interval estimates are most precise when the value of the independent variable is $x_p = \bar{x}$. The general shapes of confidence intervals and the wider prediction intervals are shown together in Figure 12.9.

EXERCISES

Methods

SELFtest   **32.** The data from Exercise 1 follow.

x_i	1	2	3	4	5
y_i	3	7	5	11	14

    a. Use equation (12.23) to estimate the standard deviation of $\hat{y}_p$ when $x = 4$.

    b. Use expression (12.24) to develop a 95% confidence interval estimate of the expected value of y when $x = 4$.

    c. Use equation (12.26) to estimate the standard deviation of an individual value of y when $x = 4$.

    d. Use expression (12.27) to develop a 95% prediction interval for y when $x = 4$.

33. The data from Exercise 2 follow.

x_i	2	3	5	1	8
y_i	25	25	20	30	16

    a. Estimate the standard deviation of $\hat{y}_p$ when $x = 3$.

    b. Develop a 95% confidence interval estimate of the expected value of y when $x = 3$.

    c. Estimate the standard deviation of an individual value of y when $x = 3$.

    d. Develop a 95% prediction interval for y when $x = 3$.

34. The data from Exercise 3 follow.

x_i	2	4	5	7	8
y_i	2	3	2	6	4

Develop the 95% confidence and prediction intervals when $x = 3$. Explain why these two intervals are different.

Applications

SELFtest

35. In Exercise 18, the data on grade point average x and monthly salary y provided the estimated regression equation $\hat{y} = 1790.5 + 581x$.

    a. Develop a 95% confidence interval estimate of the mean starting salary for all students with a 3.0 GPA.

    b. Develop a 95% prediction interval estimate of the starting salary for Joe Heller, a student with a GPA of 3.0.

CDfile

PCs

36. In Exercise 10, data on the performance score (x) and the overall rating (y) for notebook PCs provided the estimated regression equation $\hat{y} = 51.82 + .1452x$ (*PC World*, February 2000).

    a. Develop a point estimate of the overall rating for a PC with a performance score of 200.

    b. Develop a 95% confidence interval estimate of the mean overall score for all PCs with a performance score of 200.

    c. Suppose that a new PC developed by Dell has a performance score of 200. Develop a 95% prediction interval estimate of the overall score for this new PC.

    d. Discuss the differences in your answers to parts (b) and (c).

37. In Exercise 13, data were given on the adjusted gross income x and the amount of itemized deductions taken by taxpayers. Data were reported in thousands of dollars. With the estimated regression equation $\hat{y} = 4.68 + .16x$, the point estimate of a reasonable level of total itemized deductions for a taxpayer with an adjusted gross income of $52,500 is $13,080.

    a. Develop a 95% confidence interval estimate of the mean amount of total itemized deductions for all taxpayers with an adjusted gross income of $52,500.

    b. Develop a 95% prediction interval estimate for the amount of total itemized deductions for a particular taxpayer with an adjusted gross income of $52,500.

    c. If the particular taxpayer referred to in part (b) claimed total itemized deductions of $20,400, would the IRS agent's request for an audit appear to be justified?

    d. Using your answer to part (b), give the IRS agent a guideline as to the amount of total itemized deductions a taxpayer with an adjusted gross income of $52,500 should have before an audit is recommended.

38. Refer to Exercise 21, where data on the production volume x and total cost y for a particular manufacturing operation were used to develop the estimated regression equation $\hat{y} = 1246.67 + 7.6x$.

    a. The company's production schedule shows that 500 units must be produced next month. What is the point estimate of the total cost for next month?

    b. Develop a 99% prediction interval estimate of the total cost for next month.

    c. If an accounting cost report at the end of next month shows that the actual production cost during the month was $6000, should managers be concerned about incurring such a high total cost for the month? Discuss.

39. Nielsen Media Research collects data showing the number of households tuned in to shows that carry a particular advertisement. This information is useful to advertisers because it tells them how many consumers they are reaching. The following data show the number of household exposures in millions and the number of times the ad was aired for the week of October 27–November 2, 1997 (*USA Today,* November 17, 1997).

CDfile
Nielsen1

Advertised Brand	Times Ad Aired	Household Exposures
McDonald's	49	359.6
Burger King	42	296.1
HBO	30	271.6
Red Corner movie	26	251.1
Pizza Hut	31	229.3
Sears	20	186.9
Isuzu Rodeo	21	186.3
MCI	24	172.7
Sprint	15	166.0
JCPenney	19	162.1

    a. Use these data to develop an estimated regression equation that could be used to predict the number of household exposures given the number of times the ad is aired.

    b. Did the estimated regression equation provide a good fit? Explain.

    c. Develop a 95% confidence interval estimate of the mean number of household exposures for all ads that are aired 35 times.

    d. Suppose that Wendy's was considering airing a particular ad 35 times. Develop a 95% prediction interval estimate for the number of household exposures for this particular ad.

12.7   COMPUTER SOLUTION

Performing the regression analysis computations without the help of a computer can be quite time consuming. In this section we discuss how the computational burden can be minimized by using a computer software package such as Minitab.

    We entered Armand's student population and sales data into a Minitab worksheet. The independent variable was named Pop and the dependent variable was named Sales to assist with interpretation of the computer output. Using Minitab, we obtained the printout for Armand's Pizza Parlors shown in Figure 12.10.* The interpretation of this printout follows.

1. Minitab prints the estimated regression equation as Sales = 60.0 + 5.00 Pop.
2. A printed table shows the values of the coefficients b_0 and b_1, the standard deviation of each coefficient, the t value obtained by dividing each coefficient value by its standard deviation, and the p-value associated with the t test. Thus, to test H_0: $\beta_1 = 0$ versus H_a: $\beta_1 \neq 0$, we could compare 8.62 (located in the t-ratio column) to the appropriate critical value. This procedure is described for the t test in Section 12.5. Alternatively, we could use the p-value provided by Minitab to perform the same test. Because the p-value in this case is zero (to three decimal places), the sample results indicate that the null hypothesis (H_0: $\beta_1 = 0$) should be rejected.
3. Minitab prints the estimate of σ, $s = 13.83$, as well as information about the goodness of fit. Note that "R-sq = 90.3%" is the coefficient of determination expressed as a percentage. The output "R-Sq (adj) = 89.1%" is discussed in Chapter 13.
4. The ANOVA table is printed below the heading Analysis of Variance. Note that DF is an abbreviation for degrees of freedom and that MSR is given as 14,200 and MSE as 191. The ratio of these two values provides the F value of 74.25; in Section 12.5, we showed how the F value can be used to determine whether there is a significant relationship between Sales and Pop. Minitab also prints the p-value associated with this F test. Because the p-value is zero (to three decimal places), the relationship is judged statistically significant.
5. The 95% confidence interval estimate of the expected sales and the 95% prediction interval estimate of sales for an individual restaurant located near a campus with 10,000 students are printed below the ANOVA table. The confidence interval is (98.58, 121.42) and the prediction interval is (76.12, 143.88) as we showed in Section 12.6.

FIGURE 12.10   MINITAB OUTPUT FOR THE ARMAND'S PIZZA PARLORS PROBLEM

```
The regression equation is
Sales = 60.0 + 5.00 Pop          ←————————————     Estimated regression equation


Predictor       Coef        Stdev      t-ratio         p
Constant       60.000       9.226        6.50       0.000
Pop             5.0000      0.5803        8.62       0.000


s = 13.83       R-sq = 90.3%     R-sq(adj) = 89.1%


Analysis of Variance


SOURCE         DF           SS          MS          F          p
Regression      1         14200       14200       74.25      0.000        ←——     ANOVA table
Error           8          1530         191
Total           9         15730


      Fit Stdev.Fit          95% C.I.            95% P.I.                ←——     Interval estimates
    110.00      4.95    (  98.58, 121.42)   (  76.12, 143.88)
```

EXERCISES

Applications

SELFtest   **40.**   The commercial division of a real estate firm conducted a regression analysis of the relationship between x, annual gross rents ($1000s), and y, selling price ($1000s) for apartment buildings. Data collected on several properties recently sold provided the following output.

```
The regression equation is
Y = 20.0 + 7.21 X

Predictor         Coef       Stdev      t-ratio
Constant        20.000      3.2213         6.21
X                7.210      1.3626         5.29


Analysis of Variance

SOURCE          DF           SS
Regression       1       41587.3
Error            7
Total            8       51984.1
```

a.   How many apartment buildings were in the sample?
b.   Write the estimated regression equation.
c.   What is the value of s_{b_1}?
d.   Use the F statistic to test the significance of the relationship at a .05 level of significance.
e.   Estimate the selling price of an apartment building with gross annual rents of $50,000.

41.   The following portion of the computer output for a regression analysis relates $y = $ maintenance expense (dollars per month) to $x = $ usage (hours per week) of a particular brand of computer terminal.

```
The regression equation is
Y = 6.1092 + .8951 X

Predictor         Coef       Stdev
Constant        6.1092      0.9361
X               0.8951      0.1490


Analysis of Variance

SOURCE          DF           SS          MS
Regression       1       1575.76     1575.76
Error            8        349.14       43.64
Total            9       1924.90
```

a. Write the estimated regression equation.
b. Use a *t* test to determine whether monthly maintenance expense is related to usage at the .05 level of significance.
c. Use the estimated regression equation to predict monthly maintenance expense for any terminal that is used 25 hours per week.

42. A portion of the computer output for a regression analysis relating *x*, number of salespersons at a branch office, to *y*, annual sales at the office ($1000s) follows.

```
The regression equation is
Y = 80.0 + 50.00 X

Predictor        Coef      Stdev    t-ratio
Constant         80.0     11.333      7.06
X                50.0      5.482      9.12

Analysis of Variance

SOURCE          DF          SS          MS
Regression       1      6828.6      6828.6
Error           28      2298.8        82.1
Total           29      9127.4
```

a. Write the estimated regression equation.
b. How many branch offices were involved in the study?
c. Compute the *F* statistic and test the significance of the relationship at a .05 level of significance.
d. Predict the annual sales at the Memphis branch office. This branch has 12 salespersons.

43. The National Association of Home Builders ranks the most and least affordable housing markets, based on the proportion of homes that a family earning the median income in that market could afford to buy. Data showing the median income ($1000s) and the median sale price ($1000s) for a sample of 12 housing markets that appeared on the list of most affordable markets follow (*The Wall Street Journal Almanac 1998*).

Market	Income ($1000s)	Price ($1000s)
Syracuse, NY	41.8	76
Springfield, IL	47.7	91
Lima, OH	40.0	65
Dayton, OH	44.3	88
Beaumont, TX	37.3	70
Lakeland, FL	35.9	73
Baton Rouge, LA	39.3	85
Nashua, NH	56.9	118
Racine, WI	46.7	81
Des Moines, IA	48.3	89
Minneapolis–St. Paul, MN	54.6	110
Wilmington, DE–MD	55.5	110

a. Use these data to develop an estimated regression equation that could be used to predict the median price for a market given the median income for the market.
b. Did the estimated regression equation provide a good fit? Explain.
c. Develop a 95% confidence interval estimate of the median price for all homes sold in a market in which the median income is $40,100.
d. The median income in Binghamton, New York, was reported to be $40,100. Develop a 95% prediction interval estimate of the median sales price for homes sold in the Binghamton market.

44. Cushman & Wakefield, Inc., collects data showing the office building vacancy rates and rental rates for markets in the United States. The following data show the overall vacancy rates (%) and the average rental rates (per square foot) for the central business district for 18 selected markets (*The Wall Street Journal Almanac 1998*).

OffRates

Market	Vacancy Rate (%)	Average Rental Rate ($)
Atlanta	21.9	18.54
Boston	6.0	33.70
Hartford	22.8	19.67
Baltimore	18.1	21.01
Washington	12.7	35.09
Philadelphia	14.5	19.41
Miami	20.0	25.28
Tampa	19.2	17.02
Chicago	16.0	24.04
San Francisco	6.6	31.42
Phoenix	15.9	18.74
San Jose	9.2	26.76
West Palm Beach	19.7	27.72
Detroit	20.0	18.20
Brooklyn	8.3	25.00
Downtown, NY	17.1	29.78
Midtown, NY	10.8	37.03
Midtown South, NY	11.1	28.64

a. Develop a scatter diagram for these data; plot the vacancy rate on the horizontal axis.
b. Does there appear to be any relationship between these two variables?
c. Develop the estimated regression equation that could be used to predict the average rental rate given the overall vacancy rate.
d. Test the significance of the relationship at the .05 level of significance.
e. Did the estimated regression equation provide a good fit? Explain.
f. Predict the expected rental rate for markets with a 25% vacancy rate in the central business district.
g. The overall vacancy rate in the central business district in Ft. Lauderdale is 11.3%. Predict the expected rental rate for Ft. Lauderdale.

12.8 RESIDUAL ANALYSIS: VALIDATING MODEL ASSUMPTIONS

Residual analysis *is the primary tool for determining whether the assumed regression model is appropriate.*

As we have previously noted, the *residual* for observation i is the difference between the observed value of the dependent variable (y_i) and the estimated value of the dependent variable ($\hat{y}_i$).

Residual for Observation i

$$y_i - \hat{y}_i \tag{12.28}$$

where

y_i is the observed value of the dependent variable

$\hat{y}_i$ is the estimated value of the dependent variable

In other words, the ith residual is the error resulting from using the estimated regression equation to predict the value of y_i. The residuals for the Armand's Pizza Parlors example are computed in Table 12.7. The observed values of the dependent variable are in the second column and the estimated values of the dependent variable, obtained using the estimated regression equation $\hat{y} = 60 + 5x$, are in the third column. The corresponding residuals are in the fourth column. An analysis of these residuals will help determine whether the assumptions that have been made about the regression model are appropriate.

Let us now review the regression assumptions for the Armand's Pizza Parlors example. A simple linear regression model was assumed.

$$y = \beta_0 + \beta_1 x + \epsilon \tag{12.29}$$

This model indicates that we assumed quarterly sales (y) to be a linear function of the size of the student population (x) plus an error term ϵ. In Section 12.4 we made the following assumptions about the error term ϵ.

1. $E(\epsilon) = 0$.
2. The variance of ϵ, denoted by σ^2, is the same for all values of x.
3. The values of ϵ are independent.
4. The error term ϵ has a normal probability distribution.

These assumptions provide the theoretical basis for the t test and the F test used to determine whether the relationship between x and y is significant, and for the confidence and prediction interval estimates presented in Section 12.6. If the assumptions about the error

TABLE 12.7   RESIDUALS FOR ARMAND'S PIZZA PARLORS

Student Population x_i	Sales y_i	Estimated Sales $\hat{y}_i = 60 + 5x_i$	Residuals $y_i - \hat{y}_i$
2	58	70	-12
6	105	90	15
8	88	100	-12
8	118	100	18
12	117	120	-3
16	137	140	-3
20	157	160	-3
20	169	160	9
22	149	170	-21
26	202	190	12

term ϵ appear questionable, the hypothesis tests about the significance of the regression relationship and the interval estimation results may not be valid.

The residuals provide the best information about ϵ; hence an analysis of the residuals is an important step in determining whether the assumptions for ϵ are appropriate. Much of residual analysis is based on an examination of graphical plots. In this section we discuss a plot of the residuals against values of the independent variable x, and a plot of the residuals against the predicted values of the dependent variable $\hat{y}$.

Residual Plot Against x

A **residual plot** against the independent variable x is a graph in which the values of the independent variable are represented by the horizontal axis and the corresponding residual values are represented by the vertical axis. A point is plotted for each residual. The first coordinate for each point is given by the value of x_i and the second coordinate is given by the corresponding value of the residual $y_i - \hat{y}_i$. For a residual plot against x with the Armand's Pizza Parlors data from Table 12.7, the coordinates of the first point are $(2, -12)$, corresponding to $x_1 = 2$ and $y_1 - \hat{y}_1 = -12$; the coordinates of the second point are $(6, 15)$, corresponding to $x_2 = 6$ and $y_2 - \hat{y}_2 = 15$, and so on. Figure 12.11 is the resulting residual plot.

Before interpreting the results for this residual plot, let us consider some general patterns that might be observed in any residual plot. Three examples are shown in Figure 12.12. If the assumption that the variance of ϵ is the same for all values of x and the assumed regression model is an adequate representation of the relationship between the variables, the residual plot should give an overall impression of a horizontal band of points such as the one in panel A of Figure 12.12. However, if the variance of ϵ is not the same for all values of x—for example, if variability about the regression line is greater for larger values of x— a pattern such as the one in panel B of Figure 12.12 could be observed. In this case, the

FIGURE 12.11   PLOT OF THE RESIDUALS AGAINST THE INDEPENDENT VARIABLE x FOR ARMAND'S PIZZA PARLORS

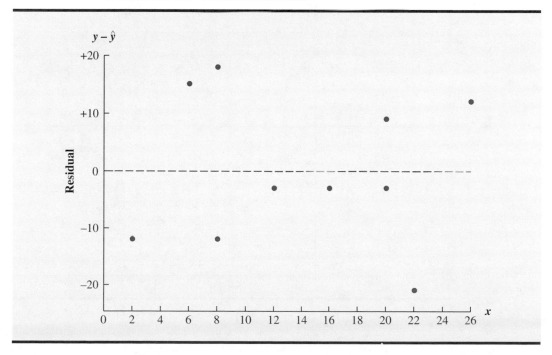

FIGURE 12.12   RESIDUAL PLOTS FROM THREE REGRESSION STUDIES

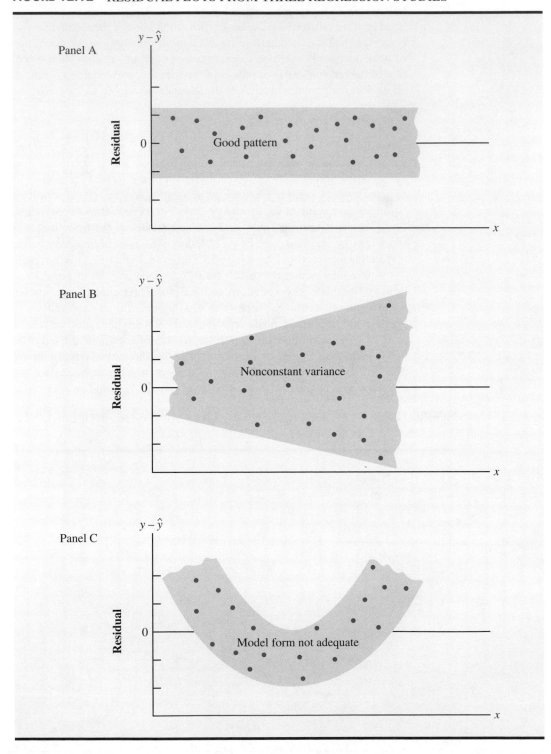

assumption of a constant variance of ϵ is violated. Another possible residual plot is shown in panel C. In this case, we would conclude that the assumed regression model is not an adequate representation of the relationship between the variables. A curvilinear regression model or multiple regression model should be considered.

Now let us return to the residual plot for Armand's Pizza Parlors shown in Figure 12.11. The residuals appear to approximate the horizontal pattern in panel A of Figure 12.12. Hence, we conclude that the residual plot does not provide evidence that the assumptions made for Armand's regression model should be challenged. At this point, we are confident in the conclusion that Armand's simple linear regression model is valid.

Experience and good judgment are always factors in the effective interpretation of residual plots. Seldom does a residual plot conform precisely to one of the patterns shown in Figure 12.12. Yet analysts who frequently conduct regression studies and frequently review residual plots become adept at understanding the differences between patterns that are reasonable and patterns that indicate the assumptions of the model should be questioned. A residual plot as shown here is one of the techniques that is used to assess the validity of the assumptions for a regression model.

Residual Plot Against $\hat{y}$

Another residual plot represents the predicted values of the dependent variable $\hat{y}$ on the horizontal axis and the corresponding residual values on the vertical axis. A point is plotted for each residual. The first coordinate for each point is given by $\hat{y}_i$ and the second coordinate is given by the corresponding value of the ith residual $y_i - \hat{y}_i$. With the Armand's data from Table 12.7, the coordinates of the first point are $(70, -12)$, corresponding to $\hat{y}_1 = 70$ and $y_1 - \hat{y}_1 = -12$; the coordinates of the second point are $(90, 15)$, and so on. Figure 12.13

FIGURE 12.13   PLOT OF THE RESIDUALS AGAINST THE PREDICTED VALUES $\hat{y}$ FOR ARMAND'S PIZZA PARLORS

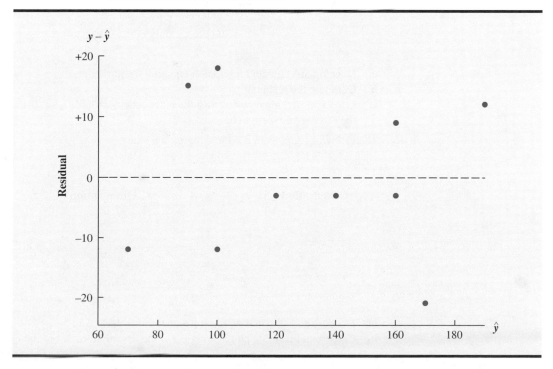

is the residual plot. Note that the pattern of this residual plot is the same as the pattern of the residual plot against the independent variable x. It is not a pattern that would lead us to question the model assumptions. For simple linear regression, both the residual plot against x and the residual plot against $\hat{y}$ provide the same pattern. For multiple regression analysis, the residual plot against $\hat{y}$ is more widely used because of the presence of more than one independent variable.

NOTES AND COMMENTS

1. We use residual plots to validate the assumptions of a regression model. If our review indicates that one or more assumptions are questionable, a different regression model and/or a transformation of the data should be considered. The appropriate corrective action when the assumptions are violated must be based on good judgment; recommendations from an experienced statistician can be valuable.

2. Analysis of residuals is the primary method statisticians use to verify that the assumptions as-

sociated with a regression model are valid. Even if no violations are found, it does not necessarily follow that the model will yield good predictions. However, if additional statistical tests support the conclusion of significance and the coefficient of determination is large, we should be able to develop good estimates and predictions using the estimated regression equation.

EXERCISES

SELFtest

Methods

45. Given are data for two variables, x and y.

x_i	6	11	15	18	20
y_i	6	8	12	20	30

   a. Develop an estimated regression equation for these data.
   b. Compute the residuals.
   c. Construct a residual plot against the independent variable x. Do the assumptions about the error terms seem to be satisfied?

46. The following data were used in a regression study.

Observation	x_i	y_i	Observation	x_i	y_i
1	2	4	6	7	6
2	3	5	7	7	9
3	4	4	8	8	5
4	5	6	9	9	11
5	7	4			

   a. Develop an estimated regression equation for these data.
   b. Construct a residual plot against x. Do the assumptions about the error term seem to be satisfied?

Applications

SELFtest   47.   Data on advertising expenditures ($1000s) and revenue ($1000s) for the Four Seasons Restaurant follow.

Advertising Expenditures	Revenue
1	19
2	32
4	44
6	40
10	52
14	53
20	54

   a.   Let x equal advertising expenditures ($1000s) and y equal revenue ($1000s). Use the method of least squares to develop a straight line approximation of the relationship between the two variables.

   b.   Test whether revenue and advertising expenditures are related at a .05 level of significance.

   c.   Construct a residual plot against the independent variable.

   d.   What conclusions can you draw from residual analysis? Should this model be used, or should we look for a better one?

48.   Refer to Exercise 9, where an estimated regression equation relating years of experience and annual sales was developed.

   a.   Compute the residuals and construct a residual plot for this problem.

   b.   Do the assumptions about the error terms seem reasonable in light of the residual plot?

49.   American Depository Receipts (ADRs) are certificates traded on the NYSE representing shares of a foreign company held on deposit in a bank in its home country. The following table shows the price/earnings (P/E) ratio and the percentage return on investment (ROE) for 10 Indian companies that are likely new ADRs (*Bloomberg Personal Finance*, April 2000).

CDfile
ADRs

Company	ROE	P/E
Bharti Televentures	6.43	36.88
Gujarat Ambuja Cements	13.49	27.03
Hindalco Industries	14.04	10.83
ICICI	20.67	5.15
Mahanagar Telephone Nigam	22.74	13.35
NIIT	46.23	95.59
Pentamedia Graphics	28.90	54.85
Satyam Computer Services	54.01	189.21
Silverline Technologies	28.02	75.86
Videsh Sanchar Nigam	27.04	13.17

   a.   Use a computer package to develop an estimated regression equation relating y = P/E and x = ROE.

   b.   Construct a residual plot against the independent variable.

   c.   Do the assumptions about the error terms and model form seem reasonable in light of the residual plot?

SUMMARY

In this chapter we showed how regression analysis can be used to determine how a dependent variable y is related to an independent variable x. In simple linear regression, the regression model is $y = \beta_0 + \beta_1 x + \epsilon$. The simple linear regression equation $E(y) = \beta_0 + \beta_1 x$ describes how the mean or expected value of y is related to x. We used sample data and the least squares method to develop the estimated regression equation $\hat{y} = b_0 + b_1 x$. In effect, b_0 and b_1 are the sample statistics used to estimate the unknown model parameters β_0 and β_1.

The coefficient of determination was presented as a measure of the goodness of fit for the estimated regression equation; it can be interpreted as the proportion of the variation in the dependent variable y that can be explained by the estimated regression equation. We reviewed correlation as a descriptive measure of the strength of a linear relationship between two variables.

The assumptions about the regression model and its associated error term ϵ were discussed, and t and F tests, based on those assumptions, were presented as a means for determining whether the relationship between two variables is statistically significant. We showed how to use the estimated regression equation to develop confidence interval estimates of the mean value of y and prediction interval estimates of individual values of y.

The chapter concluded with a section on the computer solution of regression problems and a section on the use of residual analysis to validate the model assumptions.

GLOSSARY

Dependent variable   The variable that is being predicted or explained. It is denoted by y.

Independent variable   The variable that is doing the predicting or explaining. It is denoted by x.

Simple linear regression   Regression analysis involving one independent variable and one dependent variable in which the relationship between the variables is approximated by a straight line.

Simple linear regression model   The equation that describes how y is related to x and an error term ϵ; in simple linear regression, the regression model is $y = \beta_0 + \beta_1 x + \epsilon$.

Simple linear regression equation   The equation that describes how the mean or expected value of the dependent variable is related to the independent variable; in simple linear regression, $E(y) = \beta_0 + \beta_1 x$.

Estimated simple linear regression equation   The estimate of the regression equation developed from sample data by using the least squares method. For simple linear regression, the estimated regression equation is $\hat{y} = b_0 + b_1 x$.

Least squares method   The procedure used to develop the estimated regression equation. The objective is to minimize $\Sigma(y_i - \hat{y}_i)^2$.

Scatter diagram   A graph of bivariate data in which the independent variable is on the horizontal axis and the dependent variable is on the vertical axis.

Coefficient of determination   A measure of the goodness of fit of the estimated regression equation. It can be interpreted as the proportion of the variability in the dependent variable y that is explained by the estimated regression equation.

ith residual   The difference between the observed value of the dependent variable and the value predicted using the estimated regression equation; that is, for the ith observation the ith residual is $y_i - \hat{y}_i$.

Correlation coefficient　A measure of the strength of the linear relationship between two variables (previously discussed in Chapter 3).

Mean square error　The unbiased estimate of the variance of the error term, σ^2. It is denoted by MSE or s^2.

ANOVA table　The analysis of variance table used to summarize the computations associated with the F test for significance.

Confidence interval estimate　The interval estimate of the mean value of y for a given value of x.

Prediction interval estimate　The interval estimate of an individual value of y for a given value of x.

Residual analysis　The analysis of the residuals used to determine whether the assumptions made about the regression model appear to be valid.

Residual plots　Graphical representations of the residuals that can be used to determine whether the assumptions made about the regression model appear to be valid.

KEY FORMULAS

Simple Linear Regression Model

$$y = \beta_0 + \beta_1 x + \epsilon \tag{12.1}$$

Simple Linear Regression Equation

$$E(y) = \beta_0 + \beta_1 x \tag{12.2}$$

Estimated Simple Linear Regression Equation

$$\hat{y} = b_0 + b_1 x \tag{12.3}$$

Least Squares Criterion

$$\min \Sigma(y_i - \hat{y}_i)^2 \tag{12.5}$$

Slope and y-Intercept for the Estimated Regression Equation

$$b_1 = \frac{\Sigma(x_i - \bar{x})(y_i - \bar{y})}{\Sigma(x_i - \bar{x})^2} \tag{12.6}$$

$$b_0 = \bar{y} - b_1\bar{x} \tag{12.7}$$

Sum of Squares Due to Error

$$SSE = \Sigma(y_i - \hat{y}_i)^2 \tag{12.8}$$

Total Sum of Squares

$$SST = \Sigma(y_i - \bar{y})^2 \tag{12.9}$$

Sum of Squares Due to Regression

$$SSR = \Sigma(\hat{y}_i - \bar{y})^2 \tag{12.10}$$

Relationship Among SST, SSR, and SSE

$$SST = SSR + SSE \tag{12.11}$$

Coefficient of Determination

$$r^2 = \frac{SSR}{SST} \tag{12.12}$$

Sample Correlation Coefficient

$$r_{xy} = (\text{sign of } b_1)\sqrt{\text{Coefficient of Determination}}$$
$$= (\text{sign of } b_1)\sqrt{r^2} \tag{12.13}$$

Estimate of σ^2

$$s^2 = MSE = \frac{SSE}{n - 2} \tag{12.15}$$

Estimate of σ

$$s = \sqrt{MSE} = \sqrt{\frac{SSE}{n - 2}} \tag{12.16}$$

Standard Deviation of b_1

$$\sigma_{b_1} = \frac{\sigma}{\sqrt{\Sigma(x_i - \bar{x})^2}} \tag{12.17}$$

Estimated Standard Deviation of b_1

$$s_{b_1} = \frac{s}{\sqrt{\Sigma(x_i - \bar{x})^2}} \tag{12.18}$$

t Test Statistic

$$t = \frac{b_1}{s_{b_1}} \tag{12.19}$$

Mean Square Regression

$$MSR = \frac{SSR}{\text{number of independent variables}} \tag{12.20}$$

F Test Statistic

$$F = \frac{MSR}{MSE} \tag{12.21}$$

Estimated Standard Deviation of $\hat{y}_p$

$$s_{\hat{y}_p} = s\sqrt{\frac{1}{n} + \frac{(x_p - \bar{x})^2}{\Sigma(x_i - \bar{x})^2}} \tag{12.23}$$

Confidence Interval Estimate of the Mean Value of y

$$\hat{y}_p \pm t_{\alpha/2}s_{\hat{y}_p} \tag{12.24}$$

Estimated Standard Deviation of an Individual Value of y

$$s_{ind} = s\sqrt{1 + \frac{1}{n} + \frac{(x_p - \bar{x})^2}{\Sigma(x_i - \bar{x})^2}} \tag{12.26}$$

Prediction Interval Estimate of an Individual Value of y

$$\hat{y}_p \pm t_{\alpha/2}s_{ind} \tag{12.27}$$

Residual for Observation i

$$y_i - \hat{y}_i \tag{12.28}$$

SUPPLEMENTARY EXERCISES

50. The data in the following table show the number of shares selling (millions) and the expected price (average of projected low price and projected high price) for 10 selected initial public stock offerings (*USA Today*, November 17, 1997).

CDfile
IPO

Company	Shares Selling	Expected Price ($)
American Physician	5.0	15
Apex Silver Mines	9.0	14
Dan River	6.7	15
Franchise Mortgage	8.75	17
Gene Logic	3.0	11
International Home Foods	13.6	19
PRT Group	4.6	13
Rayovac	6.7	14
RealNetworks	3.0	10
Software AG Systems	7.7	13

a. Develop an estimated regression equation with the number of shares selling as the independent variable and the expected price as the dependent variable.
b. At the .05 level of significance, is there a significant relationship between the two variables?
c. Did the estimated regression equation provide a good fit? Explain.
d. Use the estimated regression equation to estimate the expected price for a firm considering an initial public offering of 6 million shares.

51. Corporate share repurchase programs are often touted as a benefit for shareholders. But, Robert Gabele, director of insider research for First Call/Thomson Financial, has noted that many of these have been undertaken solely to acquire stock for a company's incentive options for top managers. Across all companies, existing stock options in 1998 represented

6.2 percent of all common shares outstanding. The following data show the number of shares covered by option grants and the number of shares outstanding for 13 companies (*Bloomberg Personal Finance,* January/February 2000).

CDfile

Options

Company	Shares of Option Grants Outstanding (millions)	Common Shares Outstanding (millions)
Adobe Systems	20.3	61.8
Apple Computer	52.7	160.9
Applied Materials	109.1	375.4
Autodesk	15.7	58.9
Best Buy	44.2	203.8
Fruit of the Loom	14.2	66.9
ITT Industries	18.0	87.9
Merrill Lynch	89.9	365.5
Novell	120.2	335.0
Parametric Technology	78.3	269.3
Reebok International	12.8	56.1
Silicon Graphics	52.6	188.8
Toys R Us	54.8	247.6

    a. Develop the estimated regression equation that could be used to estimate the number of shares of option grants outstanding given the number of common shares outstanding.

    b. Use the estimated regression equation to estimate the number of shares of option grants outstanding for a company that has 150 million shares of common stock outstanding.

    c. Do you believe the estimated regression equation would provide a good prediction of the number of shares of option grants outstanding? Use r^2 to support your answer.

52. *Bloomberg Personal Finance* (July/August 2001) reported that the market beta for Texas Instruments was 1.46. Market betas for individual stocks are determined by simple linear regression. For each stock, the dependent variable is its quarterly percentage return (capital appreciation plus dividends) minus the percentage return that could be obtained from a risk-free investment (the Treasury Bill rate is used as the risk-free rate). The independent variable is the quarterly percentage return (capital appreciation plus dividends) for the stock market (S&P 500) minus the percentage return from a risk-free investment. An estimated regression equation is developed with quarterly data; the market beta for the stock is the slope of the estimated regression equation (b_1). The value of the market beta is often interpreted as a measure of the risk associated with the stock. Market betas greater than 1 indicate that the stock is more volatile than the market average; market betas less than 1 indicate that the stock is less volatile than the market average. Suppose that the following figures are the differences between the percentage return and the risk-free return for 10 quarters for the S&P 500 and Horizon Technology.

S&P 500	Horizon
1.2	−0.7
−2.5	−2.0
−3.0	−5.5
2.0	4.7
5.0	1.8

S&P 500	Horizon
1.2	4.1
3.0	2.6
−1.0	2.0
.5	−1.3
2.5	5.5

a. Develop an estimated regression equation that can be used to determine the market beta for Horizon Technology. What is Horizon Technology's market beta?

b. Test for a significant relationship at the .05 level of significance.

c. Did the estimated regression equation provide a good fit? Explain.

d. Use the market betas of Texas Instruments and Horizon Technology to compare the risk associated with the two stocks.

53. The daily high and low temperatures for 20 cities follow (*USA Today*, May 9, 2000).

CDfile
HighLow

City	Low	High
Athens	54	75
Bangkok	74	92
Cairo	57	84
Copenhagen	39	64
Dublin	46	64
Havana	68	86
Hong Kong	72	81
Johannesburg	50	61
London	48	73
Manila	75	93
Melbourne	50	66
Montreal	52	64
Paris	55	77
Rio de Janeiro	61	80
Rome	54	81
Seoul	50	64
Singapore	75	90
Sydney	55	68
Tokyo	59	79
Vancouver	43	57

a. Develop a scatter diagram with low temperature on the horizontal axis and high temperature on the vertical axis.

b. What does the scatter diagram developed in part (a) indicate about the relationship between the two variables?

c. Develop the estimated regression equation that could be used to predict the high temperature given the low temperature.

d. Test for a significant relationship at the .05 level of significance.

e. Did the estimated regression equation provide a good fit? Explain.

f. What is the value of the sample correlation coefficient?

54. Jensen Tire & Auto is in the process of deciding whether to purchase a maintenance contract for its new computer wheel alignment and balancing machine. Managers feel that maintenance expense should be related to usage and have collected the following information on weekly usage (hours) and annual maintenance expense ($100s).

Weekly Usage (hours)	Annual Maintenance Expense
13	17.0
10	22.0
20	30.0
28	37.0
32	47.0
17	30.5
24	32.5
31	39.0
40	51.5
38	40.0

a. Develop the estimated regression equation that relates annual maintenance expense to weekly usage.
b. Test the significance of the relationship in part (a) at a .05 level of significance.
c. Jensen expects to use the new machine 30 hours per week. Develop a 95% prediction interval for the company's annual maintenance expense.
d. If the maintenance contract costs $3000 per year, would you recommend purchasing it? Why or why not?

55. In a manufacturing process the assembly line speed (feet per minute) was thought to affect the number of defective parts found during the inspection process. To test this theory, managers devised a situation in which the same batch of parts was inspected visually at a variety of line speeds. The following table lists the collected data.

Line Speed	Number of Defective Parts Found
20	21
20	19
40	15
30	16
60	14
40	17

a. Develop the estimated regression equation that relates line speed to the number of defective parts found.
b. At a .05 level of significance, determine whether line speed and number of defective parts found are related.
c. Did the estimated regression equation provide a good fit to the data?
d. Develop a 95% confidence interval to predict the mean number of defective parts for a line speed of 50 feet per minute.

56. A sociologist was hired by a large city hospital to investigate the relationship between the number of unauthorized days that employees are absent per year and the distance (miles) between home and work for the employees. A sample of 10 employees was chosen, and the following data were collected.

Distance to Work	Number of Days Absent
1	8
3	5
4	8
6	7
8	6
10	3
12	5
14	2
14	4
18	2

a. Develop a scatter diagram for these data. Does a linear relationship appear reasonable? Explain.
b. Develop the least squares estimated regression equation.
c. Is there a significant relationship between the two variables? Use $\alpha = .05$.
d. Did the estimated regression equation provide a good fit? Explain.
e. Use the estimated regression equation developed in part (b) to develop a 95% confidence interval estimate of the expected number of days absent for employees living 5 miles from the company.

57. The regional transit authority for a major metropolitan area wants to determine whether there is any relationship between the age of a bus and the annual maintenance cost. A sample of 10 buses resulted in the following data.

Age of Bus (years)	Maintenance Cost ($)
1	350
2	370
2	480
2	520
2	590
3	550
4	750
4	800
5	790
5	950

a. Develop the least squares estimated regression equation.
b. Test to see whether the two variables are significantly related. Use $\alpha = .05$.
c. Did the least squares line provide a good fit to the observed data? Explain.
d. Develop a 95% prediction interval for the maintenance cost for a specific bus that is four years old.

58. A marketing professor at Givens College is interested in the relationship between hours spent studying and total points earned in a course. Data collected on 10 students who took the course last quarter follow.

Hours Spent Studying	Total Points Earned
45	40
30	35
90	75
60	65
105	90
65	50
90	90
80	80
55	45
75	65

a. Develop an estimated regression equation showing how total points earned is related to hours spent studying.
b. Test the significance of the model. Use $\alpha = .05$.
c. Predict the total points earned by Mark Sweeney. He spent 95 hours studying.
d. Develop a 95% prediction interval for the total points earned by Mark Sweeney.

59. The Transactional Records Access Clearinghouse at Syracuse University reported data showing the odds of an Internal Revenue Service audit. The following table shows the average adjusted gross income reported and the percent of the returns that were audited for 20 selected IRS districts (*The Wall Street Journal Almanac 1998*).

CDfile
IRSAudit

District	Adjusted Gross Income ($)	Percent Audited
Los Angeles	36,664	1.3
Sacramento	38,845	1.1
Atlanta	34,886	1.1
Boise	32,512	1.1
Dallas	34,531	1.0
Providence	35,995	1.0
San Jose	37,799	0.9
Cheyenne	33,876	0.9
Fargo	30,513	0.9
New Orleans	30,174	0.9
Oklahoma City	30,060	0.8
Houston	37,153	0.8
Portland	34,918	0.7
Phoenix	33,291	0.7
Augusta	31,504	0.7
Albuquerque	29,199	0.6
Greensboro	33,072	0.6
Columbia	30,859	0.5
Nashville	32,566	0.5
Buffalo	34,296	0.5

a. Develop the estimated regression equation that could be used to predict the percent audited given the average adjusted gross income reported.
b. At the .05 level of significance, determine whether the adjusted gross income and the percent audited are related.
c. Did the estimated regression equation provide a good fit? Explain.
d. Use the estimated regression equation developed in part (a) to calculate a 95% confidence interval estimate of the expected percent audited for all districts with an average adjusted gross income of $35,000.

Case Problem 1   SPENDING AND STUDENT ACHIEVEMENT

Is the educational achievement level of students related to how much the state in which they reside spends on education? In many communities taxpayers ask this important question when their school districts seek to increase the amount of tax revenue spent on education. In this case, you will analyze data on spending and achievement scores in order to determine whether there is any relationship between spending and student achievement in the public schools.

The federal government's National Assessment of Educational Progress (NAEP) program is frequently used to measure the educational achievement of students. Table 12.8 shows the total current spending per pupil per year, and the composite NAEP test score for 35 states that participated in the NAEP program. The composite score is the sum of the math, science, and reading scores on the 1996 (1994 for reading) NAEP test. Pupils tested are in grade 8, except for reading, which is given to fourth-graders only. The maximum possible score is 1300. Table 12.9 shows the spending per pupil for 13 states that did not participate in relevant NAEP surveys. These data were reported in an article on spending and achievement level appearing in *Forbes* (November 3, 1997).

TABLE 12.8   SPENDING PER PUPIL AND COMPOSITE SCORES FOR STATES THAT PARTICIPATED IN THE NAEP PROGRAM

CDfile
NAEP

State	Spending per Pupil ($)	Composite Score
Louisiana	4049	581
Mississippi	3423	582
California	4917	580
Hawaii	5532	580
South Carolina	4304	603
Alabama	3777	604
Georgia	4663	611
Florida	4934	611
New Mexico	4097	614
Arkansas	4060	615
Delaware	6208	615
Tennessee	3800	618
Arizona	4041	618
West Virginia	5247	625

(continued)

TABLE 12.8   (*continued*)

State	Spending per Pupil ($)	Composite Score
Maryland	6100	625
Kentucky	5020	626
Texas	4520	627
New York	8162	628
North Carolina	4521	629
Rhode Island	6554	638
Washington	5338	639
Missouri	4483	641
Colorado	4772	644
Indiana	5128	649
Utah	3280	650
Wyoming	5515	657
Connecticut	7629	657
Massachusetts	6413	658
Nebraska	5410	660
Minnesota	5477	661
Iowa	5060	665
Montana	4985	667
Wisconsin	6055	667
North Dakota	4374	671
Maine	5561	675

TABLE 12.9   SPENDING PER PUPIL AND FOR STATES THAT DID NOT PARTICIPATE IN THE NAEP PROGRAM

State	Spending per Pupil ($)
Idaho	3602
South Dakota	4067
Oklahoma	4265
Nevada	4658
Kansas	5164
Illinois	5297
New Hampshire	5387
Ohio	5438
Oregon	5588
Vermont	6269
Michigan	6391
Pennsylvania	6579
Alaska	7890

Managerial Report

1. Develop numerical and graphical summaries of the data.
2. Use regression analysis to investigate the relationship between the amount spent per pupil and the composite score on the NAEP test. Discuss your findings.
3. Do you think that the estimated regression equation developed for these data could be used to estimate the composite scores for the states that did not participate in the NAEP program?
4. Suppose that you only considered states that spend at least $4000 per pupil but not more than $6000 per pupil. For these states, does the relationship between the two variables appear to be any different than for the complete data set? Discuss the results of your findings and whether you think deleting states with spending less than $4000 per year and more than $6000 per pupil is appropriate.
5. Develop estimates of the composite scores for the states that did not participate in the NAEP program.
6. Based upon your analyses, do you think that the educational achievement level of students is related to how much the state spends on education?

Case Problem 2   U.S. DEPARTMENT OF TRANSPORTATION

As part of a study on transportation safety, the U.S. Department of Transportation collected data on the number of fatal accidents per 1000 licenses and the percentage of licensed drivers under the age of 21 in a sample of 42 cities. Data collected over a one-year period follow.

CDfile
Safety

Percent Under 21	Fatal Accidents per 1000 Licenses	Percent Under 21	Fatal Accidents per 1000 Licenses
13	2.962	17	4.100
12	0.708	8	2.190
8	0.885	16	3.623
12	1.652	15	2.623
11	2.091	9	0.835
17	2.627	8	0.820
18	3.830	14	2.890
8	0.368	8	1.267
13	1.142	15	3.224
8	0.645	10	1.014
9	1.028	10	0.493
16	2.801	14	1.443
12	1.405	18	3.614
9	1.433	10	1.926
10	0.039	14	1.643
9	0.338	16	2.943
11	1.849	12	1.913
12	2.246	15	2.814
14	2.855	13	2.634
14	2.352	9	0.926
11	1.294	17	3.256

Managerial Report

1. Develop numerical and graphical summaries of the data.
2. Use regression analysis to investigate the relationship between the number of fatal accidents and the percentage of drivers under the age of 21. Discuss your findings.
3. What conclusion and/or recommendations can you derive from your analysis?

Case Problem 3   ALUMNI GIVING

Alumni donations are an important source of revenue for colleges and universities. If administrators could determine the factors that influence increases in the percentage of alumni who make a donation, they might be able to implement policies that could lead to increased revenues. Research shows that students who are more satisfied with their contact with teachers are more likely to graduate. As a result, one might suspect that smaller class sizes and lower student-faculty ratios might lead to a higher percentage of satisfied graduates, which in turn might lead to increases in the percentage of alumni that make a donation. Table 12.10 shows data for 48 national universities (*America's Best Colleges,* Year 2000 Edition). The column labeled % of Classes Under 20 shows the percentage of classes offered with fewer than 20 students. The column labeled Student/Faculty Ratio is the number of students enrolled divided by the total number of faculty. Finally, the column labeled Alumni Giving Rate is the percentage of alumni that made a donation to the university.

Managerial Report

1. Develop numerical and graphical summaries of the data.
2. Use regression analysis to develop an estimated regression equation that could be used to predict the alumni giving rate given the percentage of classes with fewer than 20 students.
3. Use regression analysis to develop an estimated regression equation that could be used to predict the alumni giving rate given the student-faculty ratio.
4. Which of the two estimated regression equations provides the best fit? For this estimated regression equation, perform an analysis of the residuals and discuss your findings and conclusions.
5. What conclusions and/or recommendations can you derive from your analysis?

Appendix 12.1   REGRESSION ANALYSIS WITH MINITAB

Armand's

In Section 12.7 we discussed the computer solution of regression problems by showing Minitab's output for the Armand's Pizza Parlors problem. In this appendix, we describe the steps required to generate the Minitab computer solution. First, the data must be entered in a Minitab worksheet. Student population data were entered in column C1 and quarterly sales data were entered in column C2. The variable names Pop and Sales were entered as the column headings on the worksheet. In subsequent steps, we could refer to the data by using the variable names Pop and Sales or the column indicators C1 and C2. The following steps describe how to use Minitab to produce the regression results shown in Figure 12.10.

    Step 1. Select the **Stat** pull-down menu
    Step 2. Select the **Regression** pull-down menu
    Step 3. Choose **Regression**

TABLE 12.10   DATA FOR 48 NATIONAL UNIVERSITIES

CDfile

Alumni

School	% of Classes Under 20	Student/Faculty Ratio	Alumni Giving Rate
Boston College	39	13	25
Brandeis University	68	8	33
Brown University	60	8	40
California Institute of Technology	65	3	46
Carnegie Mellon University	67	10	28
Case Western Reserve Univ.	52	8	31
College of William and Mary	45	12	27
Columbia University	69	7	31
Cornell University	72	13	35
Dartmouth College	61	10	53
Duke University	68	8	45
Emory University	65	7	37
Georgetown University	54	10	29
Harvard University	73	8	46
Johns Hopkins University	64	9	27
Lehigh University	55	11	40
Massachusetts Inst. of Technology	65	6	44
New York University	63	13	13
Northwestern University	66	8	30
Pennsylvania State Univ.	32	19	21
Princeton University	68	5	67
Rice University	62	8	40
Stanford University	69	7	34
Tufts University	67	9	29
Tulane University	56	12	17
U. of California–Berkeley	58	17	18
U. of California–Davis	32	19	7
U. of California–Irvine	42	20	9
U. of California–Los Angeles	41	18	13
U. of California–San Diego	48	19	8
U. of California–Santa Barbara	45	20	12
U. of Chicago	65	4	36
U. of Florida	31	23	19
U. of Illinois–Urbana Champaign	29	15	23
U. of Michigan–Ann Arbor	51	15	13
U. of North Carolina–Chapel Hill	40	16	26
U. of Notre Dame	53	13	49
U. of Pennsylvania	65	7	41
U. of Rochester	63	10	23
U. of Southern California	53	13	22
U. of Texas–Austin	39	21	13
U. of Virginia	44	13	28
U. of Washington	37	12	12
U. of Wisconsin–Madison	37	13	13
Vanderbilt University	68	9	31
Wake Forest University	59	11	38
Washington University–St. Louis	73	7	33
Yale University	77	7	50

Step 4. When the Regression dialog box appears:
        Enter Sales in the **Response** box
        Enter Pop in the **Predictors** box
        Click **OK**

The Minitab regression dialog box provides additional capabilities that can be obtained by selecting the desired options. For instance, to obtain a plot of the residuals against the predicted values $\hat{y}$, step 4 would be as follows:

Step 4. When the Regression dialog box appears:
        Enter Sales in the **Response** box
        Enter Pop in the **Predictors** box
        Click the **Graphs** button
    When the Regression-Graphs dialog box appears:
        Select **Regular** under Residuals for Plots
        Select **Residuals versus fits** under Residual Plots
        Click **OK**
    When the Regression dialog box appears:
        Click **OK**

Appendix 12.2 REGRESSION ANALYSIS WITH EXCEL

In this appendix we will illustrate how Excel's Regression tool can be used to perform the regression analysis computations for the Armand's Pizza Parlors problem. Refer to Figure 12.14 as we describe the steps involved. The labels Restaurant, Population, and Sales have been entered into cells A1:C1 of the worksheet. To identify each of the 10 observations, we entered the numbers 1 through 10 into cells A2:A11. The sample data have been entered into cells B2:C11. The following steps describe how to use Excel to produce the regression results.

Step 1. Select the **Tools** pull-down menu
Step 2. Choose **Data Analysis**
Step 3. Choose **Regression** from the list of Analysis Tools
Step 4. Click **OK**
Step 5. When the Regression dialog box appears:
        Enter C1:C11 in the **Input Y Range** box
        Enter B1:B11 in the **Input X Range** box
        Select **Labels**
        Select **Confidence Level**
        Enter 99 in the **Confidence Level** box
        Select **Output Range**
        Enter A13 in the **Output Range** box
          (Any upper-left-hand corner cell indicating where the output is to begin may be entered here.)
        Click **OK**

The first section of the output, titled *Regression Statistics,* contains summary statistics such as the coefficient of determination (R Square). The second section of the output, titled ANOVA, contains the analysis of variance table. The last section of the output, which is not titled, contains the estimated regression coefficients and related information. We will begin

FIGURE 12.14   EXCEL SPREADSHEET SOLUTION TO THE ARMAND'S PIZZA PARLORS PROBLEM

	A	B	C	D	E	F	G	H	I	J
1	Restaurant	Population	Sales							
2	1	2	58							
3	2	6	105							
4	3	8	88							
5	4	8	118							
6	5	12	117							
7	6	16	137							
8	7	20	157							
9	8	20	169							
10	9	22	149							
11	10	26	202							
12										
13	SUMMARY OUTPUT									
14										
15	*Regression Statistics*									
16	Multiple R	0.9501								
17	R Square	0.9027								
18	Adjusted R Square	0.8906								
19	Standard Error	13.8293								
20	Observations	10								
21										
22	ANOVA									
23		*df*	*SS*	*MS*	*F*	*Significance F*				
24	Regression	1	14200	14200	74.2484	2.55E-05				
25	Residual	8	1530	191.25						
26	Total	9	15730							
27										
28		*Coefficients*	*Standard Error*	*t Stat*	*P-value*	*Lower 95%*	*Upper 95%*	*Lower 99.0%*	*Upper 99.0%*	
29	Intercept	60	9.2260	6.5033	0.0002	38.7247	81.2753	29.0431	90.9569	
30	Population	5	0.5803	8.6167	2.55E-05	3.6619	6.3381	3.0530	6.9470	
31										

our discussion of the interpretation of the regression output with the information contained in cells A28:I30.

Interpretation of Estimated Regression Equation Output

The y intercept of the estimated regression line, $b_0 = 60$, is shown in cell B29, and the slope of the estimated regression line, $b_1 = 5$, is shown in cell B30. The label Intercept in cell A29 and the label Population in cell A30 are used to identify these two values.

In Section 12.5 we showed that the estimated standard deviation of b_1 is $s_{b_1} = .5803$. Note that the value in cell C30 is .5803. The label Standard Error in cell C28 is Excel's way of indicating that the value in cell C30 is the estimated standard error, or standard deviation, of b_1. Recall that the t test for a significant relationship required the computation of the t statistic, $t = b_1/s_{b_1}$. For the Armand's data, the value of t that we computed was $t = 5/.5803 = 8.62$. The label in cell D28, t Stat, reminds us that cell D30 contains the value of the t test statistic.

In Section 12.5 we also showed that for a significance level of $\alpha = .01$ and $n - 2 = 10 - 2 = 8$ degrees of freedom, $t_{.005} = 3.355$. With $t = 8.62 > 3.355$, we were able to conclude at the .01 level of significance that β_1 is not equal to 0. In other words, the statistical evidence is sufficient to conclude that we have a significant relationship between student population and sales. The value in cell E30 is the p-value associated with the t test for significance. Excel has displayed the p-value in cell E30 using scientific notation. To obtain the decimal value, we move the decimal point 5 places to the left, obtaining a value of .0000255. Because the p-value $= .0000255 < \alpha = .01$, we can reject H_0 and conclude that we have a significant relationship between student population and quarterly sales.

The information in cells F28:I30 can be used to develop confidence interval estimates of the y intercept and slope of the estimated regression equation. Excel always provides the lower and upper limits for a 95% confidence interval. Recall that in step 4 we selected Confidence Level and entered 99 in the Confidence Level box. As a result, Excel's Regression tool also provides the lower and upper limits for a 99% confidence interval. The value in cell H30 is the lower limit for the 99% confidence interval estimate of β_1 and the value in cell I30 is the upper limit. Thus, after rounding, the 99% confidence interval estimate of β_1 is 3.05 to 6.95. The values in cells F30 and G30 provide the lower and upper limits for the 95% confidence interval. Thus, the 95% confidence interval is 3.66 to 6.34.

Interpretation of ANOVA Output

The information in cells A22:F26 is a summary of the analysis of variance computations. The three sources of variation are labeled Regression, Residual, and Total. The label df in cell B23 stands for degrees of freedom, the label SS in cell C23 stands for sum of squares, and the label MS in cell D23 stands for mean square.

The label Significance F may be more meaningful if you think of the value in cell F24 as the observed level of significance for the F test.

In Section 12.5 we stated that the mean square error, obtained by dividing the error or residual sum of squares by its degrees of freedom, provides an estimate of σ^2. The value in cell D25, 191.25, is the mean square error for the Armand's regression output. In Section 12.5 we showed that an F test could also be used to test for significance in regression. The value in cell F24, .0000255, is the p-value associated with the F test for significance. Because the p-value $= .0000255 < \alpha = .01$, we can reject H_0 and conclude that we have a significant relationship between student population and quarterly sales. The label Excel uses to identify the p-value for the F test for significance, shown in cell F23, is *Significance F.*

Interpretation of Regression Statistics Output

The coefficient of determination, .9027, appears in cell B17; the corresponding label, R Square, is shown in cell A17. The square root of the coefficient of determination provides the sample correlation coefficient of .9501 shown in cell B16. Note that Excel uses the label Multiple R (cell A16) to identify this value. In cell A19, the label Standard Error is used to identify the value of the estimate of σ shown in cell B19. Thus, the estimate of σ is 13.8293. We caution the reader to keep in mind that in the Excel output, the label Standard Error appears in two different places. In the Regression Statistics section of the output, the label Standard Error refers to the estimate of σ. In the Estimated Regression Equation section of the output, the label Standard Error refers to s_{b_1}, the estimated standard deviation of the sampling distribution of b_1.

MULTIPLE REGRESSION

CONTENTS

Chapter 13

INTERNATIONAL PAPER*

PURCHASE, NEW YORK

International Paper is the world's largest paper and forest products company. The company has operations in nearly 50 countries, employs more than 117,000 people and exports its products to more than 130 nations. International Paper produces building materials such as lumber and plywood; consumer packaging materials such as disposable cups and containers; industrial packaging materials such as corrugated boxes and shipping containers; and a variety of papers for use in photocopiers, printers, books, and advertising materials.

Pulp mills process wood chips and chemicals to produce wood pulp. The wood pulp is then used at a paper mill to produce paper products. In the production of white paper products, the pulp must be bleached to remove any discoloration. A key-bleaching agent used in the process is chlorine dioxide, which, because of its combustible nature, is usually produced at a pulp mill facility and then piped in solution form into the bleaching tower of the pulp mill. To improve one of the processes used to produce chlorine dioxide, a study was undertaken to look at process control and efficiency. One of the aspects studied was the chemical-feed rate for chlorine dioxide production.

To produce the chlorine dioxide, four chemicals flow at metered rates into the chlorine dioxide generator. The chlorine dioxide produced in the generator flows to an absorber where chilled water absorbs the chlorine dioxide gas to form a chlorine dioxide solution. The solution is then piped into the paper mill. A key part of controlling the process involves the chemical-feed rates. Historically, the chemical-feed rates were simply set by experienced operators; this approach, however, led to overcontrol by the operators. Consequently, chemical engineers at the mill requested that a set of control equations, one for each chemical feed, be developed to aid the operators in setting the rates.

*The authors are indebted to Marian Williams and Bill Griggs for providing this Statistics in Practice. This application was originally developed at Champion International Corporation, which became part of International Paper in 2000.

Multiple regression analysis was used to develop a better bleaching process for making white paper products.
© Lester Lefkowitz/CORBIS Stockmarket.

Using multiple regression analysis, statistical analysts were able to develop an estimated multiple regression equation for each of the four chemicals used in the process. Each equation related the production of chlorine dioxide to the amount of chemical used and the concentration level of the chlorine dioxide solution. The resulting set of four equations was programmed into a microcomputer at each mill. In the new system, operators enter the concentration of the chlorine dioxide solution and the desired production rate; the computer software then calculates the chemical feed needed to achieve the desired production rate. Since the operators have begun using the control equations, the chlorine dioxide generator efficiency has increased, and the number of times the concentrations have been within acceptable ranges has increased significantly.

This Statistics in Practice discussed how multiple regression analysis could be used to develop a better bleaching process for producing white paper products. In this chapter we will discuss how statistical computer packages such as Minitab are used for such purposes. Most of the concepts introduced in Chapter 12 for simple linear regression can be directly extended to the multiple regression case.

In Chapter 12 we presented simple linear regression and demonstrated its use in developing an equation that describes the relationship between two variables. Recall that the variable being predicted or explained by the equation is called the dependent variable and the variable being used to predict or explain the dependent variable is called the independent variable. In this chapter we continue our study of regression analysis by considering situations involving two or more independent variables. This subject area is called **multiple regression analysis.** It enables us to consider more factors and thus obtain better estimates than are possible with simple linear regression.

13.1   MULTIPLE REGRESSION MODEL

Multiple regression analysis is the study of how a dependent variable y is related to two or more independent variables. In the general case, we will use p to denote the number of independent variables.

Regression Model and Regression Equation

The concepts of a regression model and a regression equation introduced in the preceding chapter apply in the case of multiple regression. The equation that describes how the dependent variable y is related to the independent variables $x_1, x_2, \ldots x_p$ and an error term is called the **multiple regression model.** We begin with the assumption that the multiple regression model has the following form.

Multiple Regression Model

$$y = \beta_0 + \beta_1 x_1 + \beta_2 x_2 + \cdots + \beta_p x_p + \epsilon \qquad (13.1)$$

In the multiple regression model, $\beta_0, \beta_1, \beta_2, \ldots, \beta_p$ are the parameters and ϵ (the Greek letter epsilon) is a random variable. A close examination of this model reveals that y is a linear function of $x_1, x_2, \ldots, x_p$ (the $\beta_0 + \beta_1 x_1 + \beta_2 x_2 + \cdots + \beta_p x_p$ part) plus an error term ϵ. The error term accounts for the variability in y that cannot be explained by the linear effect of the p independent variables.

In Section 13.4 we will discuss the assumptions for the multiple regression model and ϵ. One of the assumptions is that the mean or expected value of ϵ is zero. A consequence of this assumption is that the mean or expected value of y, denoted $E(y)$, is equal to $\beta_0 + \beta_1 x_1 + \beta_2 x_2 + \cdots + \beta_p x_p$. The equation that describes how the mean value of y is related to $x_1, x_2, \ldots, x_p$ is called the **multiple regression equation.**

Multiple Regression Equation

$$E(y) = \beta_0 + \beta_1 x_1 + \beta_2 x_2 + \cdots + \beta_p x_p \qquad (13.2)$$

Estimated Multiple Regression Equation

If the values of $\beta_0, \beta_1, \beta_2, \ldots, \beta_p$ were known, equation (13.2) could be used to compute the mean value of y at given values of $x_1, x_2, \ldots, x_p$. Unfortunately, these parameter values will not, in general, be known and must be estimated from sample data. A simple random

FIGURE 13.1   THE ESTIMATION PROCESS FOR MULTIPLE REGRESSION

In simple linear regression, b_0 and b_1 were the sample statistics used to estimate the parameters β_0 and β_1. Multiple regression parallels this statistical inference process, with b_0, b_1, b_2, . . . , b_p denoting the sample statistics used to estimate β_0, β_1, β_2, . . . , β_p.

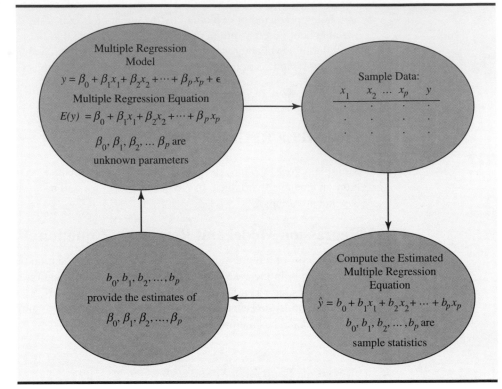

sample is used to compute sample statistics b_0, b_1, b_2, . . . , b_p that are used as the point estimators of the parameters β_0, β_1, β_2, . . . , β_p. These sample statistics provide the following **estimated multiple regression equation.**

Estimated Multiple Regression Equation

$$\hat{y} = b_0 + b_1x_1 + b_2x_2 + \cdots + b_px_p \qquad (13.3)$$

where

$$b_0, b_1, b_2, \ldots, b_p \text{ are the estimates of } \beta_0, \beta_1, \beta_2, \ldots, \beta_p$$
$$\hat{y} = \text{estimated value of the dependent variable}$$

The estimation process for multiple regression is shown in Figure 13.1.

13.2   LEAST SQUARES METHOD

In Chapter 12, we used the **least squares method** to develop the estimated regression equation that best approximated the straight line relationship between the dependent and independent variables. This same approach is used to develop the estimated multiple regression equation. The least squares criterion is restated as follows.

Least Squares Criterion

$$\min \Sigma(y_i - \hat{y}_i)^2 \tag{13.4}$$

where

y_i = observed value of the dependent variable for the ith observation

$\hat{y}_i$ = estimated value of the dependent variable for the ith observation

The estimated values of the dependent variable are computed by using the estimated multiple regression equation,

$$\hat{y} = b_0 + b_1 x_1 + b_2 x_2 + \cdots + b_p x_p$$

As expression (13.4) shows, the least squares method uses sample data to provide the values of $b_0, b_1, b_2, \ldots, b_p$ that make the sum of squared residuals [the deviations between the observed values of the dependent variable (y_i) and the estimated values of the dependent variable ($\hat{y}_i$)] a minimum.

In Chapter 12 we presented formulas for computing the least squares estimators b_0 and b_1 for the estimated simple linear regression equation $\hat{y} = b_0 + b_1 x$. With relatively small data sets, we were able to use those formulas to compute b_0 and b_1 by manual calculations. In multiple regression, however, the presentation of the formulas for the regression coefficients $b_0, b_1, b_2, \ldots, b_p$ involves the use of matrix algebra and is beyond the scope of this text. Therefore, in presenting multiple regression, we will focus on how computer software packages can be used to obtain the estimated regression equation and other information. The emphasis will be on how to interpret the computer output rather than on how to make the multiple regression computations.

An Example: Butler Trucking Company

As an illustration of multiple regression analysis, we will consider a problem faced by the Butler Trucking Company, an independent trucking company in southern California. A major portion of Butler's business involves deliveries throughout its local area. To develop better work schedules, the managers want to estimate the total daily travel time for their drivers.

Initially the managers believed that the total daily travel time would be closely related to the number of miles traveled in making the daily deliveries. A simple random sample of 10 driving assignments provided the data shown in Table 13.1 and the scatter diagram shown in Figure 13.2. After reviewing this scatter diagram, the managers hypothesized that the simple linear regression model $y = \beta_0 + \beta_1 x_1 + \epsilon$ could be used to describe the relationship between the total travel time (y) and the number of miles traveled (x_1). To estimate the parameters β_0 and β_1, the least squares method was used to develop the estimated regression equation.

$$\hat{y} = b_0 + b_1 x_1 \tag{13.5}$$

In Figure 13.3, we show the Minitab computer output from applying simple linear regression to the data in Table 13.1. The estimated regression equation is

$$\hat{y} = 1.27 + .0678 x_1$$

TABLE 13.1 PRELIMINARY DATA FOR BUTLER TRUCKING

Driving Assignment	x_1 = Miles Traveled	y = Travel Time (hours)
1	100	9.3
2	50	4.8
3	100	8.9
4	100	6.5
5	50	4.2
6	80	6.2
7	75	7.4
8	65	6.0
9	90	7.6
10	90	6.1

At the .05 level of significance, the F value of 15.81 and its corresponding p-value of .004 indicate that the relationship is significant; that is, we can reject H_0: $\beta_1 = 0$ because the p-value is less than $\alpha = .05$. Note that the same conclusion is obtained from the t value of 3.98 and its associated p-value of .004. Thus, we can conclude that the relationship between the total travel time and the number of miles traveled is significant; longer travel times are associated with more miles traveled. With a coefficient of determination (expressed as a

FIGURE 13.2 SCATTER DIAGRAM OF PRELIMINARY DATA FOR BUTLER TRUCKING

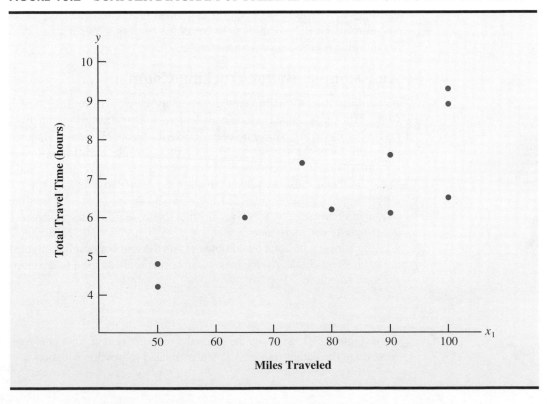

FIGURE 13.3   MINITAB OUTPUT FOR BUTLER TRUCKING WITH ONE INDEPENDENT VARIABLE

In the Minitab output the variable names Miles and Time were entered as the column headings on the worksheet; thus, x_1 = Miles and y = Time.

```
The regression equation is
Time = 1.27 + 0.0678 Miles


Predictor         Coef         Stdev      t-ratio         p
Constant         1.274         1.401         0.91     0.390
Miles          0.06783       0.01706         3.98     0.004


s = 1.002        R-sq = 66.4%      R-sq(adj) = 62.2%


Analysis of Variance


SOURCE           DF           SS           MS          F         p
Regression        1       15.871       15.871      15.81     0.004
Error             8        8.029        1.004
Total             9       23.900
```

percentage) of *R*-sq = 66.4%, we see that 66.4% of the variability in travel time can be explained by the linear effect of the number of miles traveled. This finding is fairly good, but the managers might want to consider adding a second independent variable to explain some of the remaining variability in the dependent variable.

In attempting to identify another independent variable, the managers felt that the number of deliveries could also contribute to the total travel time. The Butler Trucking data, with the number of deliveries added, are shown in Table 13.2. The Minitab computer solution with both miles traveled (x_1) and number of deliveries (x_2) as independent variables is shown in Figure 13.4. The estimated regression equation is

$$\hat{y} = -.869 + .0611x_1 + .923x_2 \tag{13.6}$$

TABLE 13.2   DATA FOR BUTLER TRUCKING WITH MILES TRAVELED (x_1) AND NUMBER OF DELIVERIES (x_2) AS THE INDEPENDENT VARIABLES

CDfile
Butler

Driving Assignment	x_1 = Miles Traveled	x_2 = Number of Deliveries	y = Travel Time (hours)
1	100	4	9.3
2	50	3	4.8
3	100	4	8.9
4	100	2	6.5
5	50	2	4.2
6	80	2	6.2
7	75	3	7.4
8	65	4	6.0
9	90	3	7.6
10	90	2	6.1

FIGURE 13.4   MINITAB OUTPUT FOR BUTLER TRUCKING WITH TWO
INDEPENDENT VARIABLES

In the Minitab output the variable names Miles, Deliv, and Time were entered as the column headings on the worksheet; thus, x_1 = Miles, x_2 = Deliv, and y = Time.

```
The regression equation is
Time = - 0.869 + 0.0611 Miles + 0.923 Deliv

Predictor         Coef         Stdev      t-ratio           p
Constant       -0.8687        0.9515        -0.91       0.392
Miles         0.061135       0.009888         6.18       0.000
Deliv          0.9234        0.2211          4.18       0.004


s = 0.5731       R-sq = 90.4%      R-sq(adj) = 87.6%


Analysis of Variance

SOURCE         DF          SS           MS          F          p
Regression      2       21.601       10.800      32.88      0.000
Error           7        2.299        0.328
Total           9       23.900
```

In the next section we will discuss the use of the coefficient of multiple determination in measuring how good a fit is provided by this estimated regression equation. Before doing so, let us examine more carefully the values of b_1 = .0611 and b_2 = .923 in equation (13.6).

Note on Interpretation of Coefficients

One observation can be made at this point about the relationship between the estimated regression equation with only the miles traveled as an independent variable and the estimated equation that includes the number of deliveries as a second independent variable. The value of b_1 is not the same in both cases. In simple linear regression, we interpret b_1 as an estimate of the change in y for a one-unit change in the independent variable. In multiple regression analysis, this interpretation must be modified somewhat. That is, in multiple regression analysis, we interpret each regression coefficient as follows: b_i represents an estimate of the change in y corresponding to a one-unit change in x_i when all other independent variables are held constant. In the Butler Trucking example involving two independent variables, b_1 = .0611. Thus, .0611 hours is an estimate of the expected increase in travel time corresponding to an increase of one mile in the distance traveled when the number of deliveries is held constant. Similarly, because b_2 = .923, an estimate of the expected increase in travel time corresponding to an increase of one delivery when the number of miles traveled is held constant is .923 hours.

EXERCISES

Note to student: The exercises involving data in this and subsequent sections were designed to be solved using a computer software package.

Methods

1. The estimated regression equation for a problem involving two independent variables and 10 observations follows.

$$\hat{y} = 29.1270 + .5906x_1 + .4980x_2$$

   a. Interpret b_1 and b_2 in this estimated regression equation.
   b. Estimate y when $x_1 = 180$ and $x_2 = 310$.

SELFtest

2. Consider the following data for a dependent variable y and two independent variables, x_1 and x_2.

x_1	x_2	y
30	12	94
47	10	108
25	17	112
51	16	178
40	5	94
51	19	175
74	7	170
36	12	117
59	13	142
76	16	211

   a. Using these data, develop an estimated regression equation relating y to x_1. Estimate y if $x_1 = 45$.
   b. Using these data, develop an estimated regression equation relating y to x_2. Estimate y if $x_2 = 15$.
   c. Using these data, develop an estimated regression equation relating y to x_1 and x_2. Estimate y if $x_1 = 45$ and $x_2 = 15$.

3. In a regression analysis involving 30 observations, the following estimated regression equation was obtained.

$$\hat{y} = 17.6 + 3.8x_1 - 2.3x_2 + 7.6x_3 + 2.7x_4$$

   a. Interpret b_1, b_2, b_3, and b_4 in this estimated regression equation.
   b. Estimate y when $x_1 = 10$, $x_2 = 5$, $x_3 = 1$, and $x_4 = 2$.

Applications

4. A shoe store has developed the following estimated regression equation relating sales to inventory investment and advertising expenditures.

$$\hat{y} = 25 + 10x_1 + 8x_2$$

   where

$$x_1 = \text{inventory investment (\$1000s)}$$
$$x_2 = \text{advertising expenditures (\$1000s)}$$
$$y = \text{sales (\$1000s)}$$

   a. Estimate sales resulting from a $15,000 investment in inventory and an advertising budget of $10,000.
   b. Interpret b_1 and b_2 in this estimated regression equation.

5. The owner of Showtime Movie Theaters, Inc., would like to estimate weekly gross revenue as a function of advertising expenditures. Historical data for a sample of eight weeks follow.

CDfile
Showtime

Weekly Gross Revenue ($1000s)	Television Advertising ($1000s)	Newspaper Advertising ($1000s)
96	5.0	1.5
90	2.0	2.0
95	4.0	1.5
92	2.5	2.5
95	3.0	3.3
94	3.5	2.3
94	2.5	4.2
94	3.0	2.5

   a. Develop an estimated regression equation with television advertising expenditures as the independent variable.
   b. Develop an estimated regression equation with both television advertising expenditures and newspaper advertising expenditures as the independent variables.
   c. Is the estimated regression equation coefficient for television advertising expenditures the same in part (a) and in part (b)? Interpret the coefficient in each case.
   d. What is the estimate of the weekly gross revenue for a week when $3500 is spent on television advertising and $1800 is spent on newspaper advertising?

6. The following table reports the curb weight, horsepower, and the speed at ¼ mile for 16 sports and GT cars (*1998 Road & Track Sports & GT Cars*).

CDfile
Auto1

Sports & GT Car	Curb Weight (lbs.)	Horsepower	Speed at ¼ mile (mph)
Acura Integra Type R	2577	195	90.7
Acura NSX-T	3066	290	108.0
BMW Z3 2.8	2844	189	93.2
Chevrolet Camaro Z28	3439	305	103.2
Chevrolet Corvette Convertible	3246	345	102.1
Dodge Viper RT/10	3319	450	116.2
Ford Mustang GT	3227	225	91.7
Honda Prelude Type SH	3042	195	89.7
Mercedes-Benz CLK320	3240	215	93.0
Mercedes-Benz SLK230	3025	185	92.3
Mitsubishi 3000GT VR-4	3737	320	99.0
Nissan 240SX SE	2862	155	84.6
Pontiac Firebird Trans Am	3455	305	103.2
Porsche Boxster	2822	201	93.2
Toyota Supra Turbo	3505	320	105.0
Volvo C70	3285	236	97.0

a. Use curb weight as the independent variable and the speed at $\frac{1}{4}$ mile as the dependent variable. What is the estimated regression equation?

b. Use curb weight and horsepower as two independent variables and the speed at $\frac{1}{4}$ mile as the dependent variable. What is the estimated regression equation?

c. The 1999 Porsche 911 Carrera has been advertised as having a curb weight of 2910 pounds and an engine with 296 horsepower. Use the results of (b) to predict the speed at $\frac{1}{4}$ mile for the Porsche 911.

7. Designers of backpacks use exotic material such as supernylon Delrin, high-density polyethylene, aircraft aluminum, and thermomolded foam to make packs that fit comfortably and distribute weight so evenly that pressure points disappear. The following data show the capacity (cubic inches), comfort rating, and price for 10 backpacks tested by *Outside Magazine*. Comfort was measured using a rating from 1 to 5, with a rating of 1 denoting average comfort and a rating of 5 denoting excellent comfort (*Outside Magazine's Buyer's Guide,* 2001).

CDfile
Backpack

Manufacturer and Model	Capacity	Comfort	Price
Camp Trails Paragon II	4330	2	190
EMS 5500	5500	3	219
Lowe Alpomayo 90+20	5500	4	249
Marmot Muir	4700	3	249
Kelly Bigfoot 5200	5200	4	250
Gregory Whitney	5500	4	340
Osprey 75	4700	4	389
Arc'Teryx Bora 95	5500	5	395
Dana Design Terraplane LTW	5800	5	439
The Works @ Mystery Ranch Jazz	5000	5	525

a. Determine the estimated regression equation that can be used to predict the price of a backpack given the capacity and the comfort rating.

b. Interpret b_1 and b_2.

c. Predict the price for a backpack with a capacity of 4500 cubic inches and a comfort rating of 4.

8. The following table gives the annual return, the safety rating (0 = riskiest, 10 = safest), and the annual expense ratio for 20 foreign funds (*Mutual Funds,* March 2000).

CDfile
ForFunds

	Safety Rating	Annual Expense Ratio (%)	Annual Return (%)
Accessor Int'l Equity "Adv"	7.1	1.59	49
Aetna "I" International	7.2	1.35	52
Amer Century Int'l Discovery "Inv"	6.8	1.68	89
Columbia International Stock	7.1	1.56	58
Concert Inv "A" Int'l Equity	6.2	2.16	131
Dreyfus Founders Int'l Equity "F"	7.4	1.80	59
Driehaus International Growth	6.5	1.88	99
Excelsior "Inst" Int'l Equity	7.0	0.90	53
Julius Baer International Equity	6.9	1.79	77
Marshall International Stock "Y"	7.2	1.49	54

(continued)

	Safety Rating	Annual Expense Ratio (%)	Annual Return (%)
MassMutual Int'l Equity "S"	7.1	1.05	57
Morgan Grenfell Int'l Sm Cap "Inst"	7.7	1.25	61
New England "A" Int'l Equity	7.0	1.83	88
Pilgrim Int'l Small Cap "A"	7.0	1.94	122
Republic International Equity	7.2	1.09	71
Sit International Growth	6.9	1.50	51
Smith Barney "A" Int'l Equity	7.0	1.28	60
State St Research "S" Int'l Equity	7.1	1.65	50
Strong International Stock	6.5	1.61	93
Vontobel International Equity	7.0	1.50	47

a. Using these data, develop an estimated regression equation relating the annual return to the safety rating and the annual expense ratio.

b. Estimate the annual return for a firm that has a safety rating of 7.5 and annual expense ratio of 2%.

9. Two experts provided subjective lists of school districts that they think are among the best in the country. For each school district the average class size, the combined SAT score, and the percentage of students who attended a four-year college were provided.

CDfile
Schools

District	Average Class Size	Combined SAT Score	% Attend Four-Year College
Blue Springs, MO	25	1083	74
Garden City, NY	18	997	77
Indianapolis, IN	30	716	40
Newport Beach, CA	26	977	51
Novi, MI	20	980	53
Piedmont, CA	28	1042	75
Pittsburg, PA	21	983	66
Scarsdale, NY	20	1110	87
Wayne, PA	22	1040	85
Weston, MA	21	1031	89
Farmingdale, NY	22	947	81
Mamaroneck, NY	20	1000	69
Mayfield, OH	24	1003	48
Morristown, NJ	22	972	64
New Rochelle, NY	23	1039	55
Newtown Square, PA	17	963	79
Omaha, NE	23	1059	81
Shaker Heights, OH	23	940	82

a. Using these data, develop an estimated regression equation relating the percentage of students who attend a four-year college to the average class size and the combined SAT score.

b. Estimate the percentage of students who attend a four-year college if the average class size is 20 and the combined SAT score is 1000.

10. *Auto Rental News* provided the following data, which show the number of cars in service (1000s), the number of locations, and the rental revenue ($ millions) for 15 car rental companies. (*The Wall Street Journal Almanac 1998*).

CDfile
CarRent

Company	Cars	Locations	Revenue
Alamo	130	171	1180
Avis	190	1130	1500
Budget	126	1052	1500
Dollar	63.5	450	560
Enterprise	315.1	2636	2060
FRCS (Ford)	55.25	1784	312.5
Hertz	250	1200	2400
National	135	935	1200
Payless	15	100	47
PROP (Chrysler)	27	1500	160
Rent-A-Wreck	10.9	460	78
Snappy	15.5	259	85
Thrifty	34	480	340
U-Save	13.5	500	95
Value	18	45	150.1

a. Determine the estimated regression equation that can be used to predict the rental revenue given the number of cars in service.

b. Provide an interpretation for the slope of the estimated regression equation developed in part (a).

c. Determine the estimated regression equation that can be used to predict the rental revenue given the number of cars in service and the number of locations.

13.3   MULTIPLE COEFFICIENT OF DETERMINATION

In simple linear regression we showed that the total sum of squares can be partitioned into two components: the sum of squares due to regression and the sum of squares due to error. The same partition applies to the sum of squares in multiple regression.

Relationship Among SST, SSR, and SSE

The sum of squares due to error is also called the residual sum of squares.

$$SST = SSR + SSE \qquad (13.7)$$

where

$$SST = \text{total sum of squares} = \Sigma(y_i - \bar{y})^2$$
$$SSR = \text{sum of squares due to regression} = \Sigma(\hat{y}_i - \bar{y})^2$$
$$SSE = \text{sum of squares due to error} = \Sigma(y_i - \hat{y}_i)^2$$

Because computing the three sums of squares is tedious, we rely on computer packages to determine these values. The analysis of variance part of the Minitab output in Figure 13.4 shows the three sums of squares for the Butler Trucking problem with two independent variables: SST = 23.900, SSR = 21.601, and SSE = 2.299. With only one independent variable (number of miles traveled), the Minitab output in Figure 13.3 shows that SST = 23.900, SSR = 15.871, and SSE = 8.029. The value of SST is the same in both cases because it does not depend on $\hat{y}$, but SSR increases and SSE decreases when a second independent variable (number of deliveries) is added. The implication is that the estimated multiple regression equation provides a better fit for the observed sample data.

In Chapter 12, we used the coefficient of determination, $r^2 = \text{SSR/SST}$, to measure the goodness of fit for the estimated regression equation. The same concept applies to multiple regression. The term **multiple coefficient of determination** indicates that we are measuring the goodness of fit for the estimated multiple regression equation. The multiple coefficient of determination, denoted R^2, is computed as follows.

Multiple Coefficient of Determination

$$R^2 = \frac{\text{SSR}}{\text{SST}} \tag{13.8}$$

The multiple coefficient of determination can be interpreted as the proportion of the variability in the dependent variable that can be explained by the estimated multiple regression equation. Hence, when multiplied by 100, it can be interpreted as the percentage of the variability in y that can be explained by the estimated regression equation.

In the two-independent-variable Butler Trucking example, with SSR = 21.601 and SST = 23.900, we have

$$R^2 = \frac{21.601}{23.900} = .904$$

Therefore, 90.4% of the variability in travel time y is explained by the estimated multiple regression equation with miles traveled and number of deliveries as the independent variables. In Figure 13.4, we see that the multiple coefficient of determination is also provided by the Minitab output; it is denoted by R-sq = 90.4%.

If an independent variable is added to the model, R^2 becomes larger even if the variable added is not statistically significant.

Figure 13.3 shows that the R-sq value for the estimated regression equation with only one independent variable, number of miles traveled (x_1), is 66.4%. Thus, the percentage of the variability in travel times that is explained by the estimated regression equation increases from 66.4% to 90.4% when number of deliveries is added as a second independent variable. In general, R^2 always increases as independent variables are added to the model.

Many analysts prefer adjusting R^2 for the number of independent variables to avoid overestimating the impact of adding an independent variable on the amount of variability explained by the estimated regression equation. With n denoting the number of observations and p denoting the number of independent variables, the **adjusted multiple coefficient of determination** is computed as follows.

The adjusted multiple coefficient of determination compensates for the number of independent variables in the model.

Adjusted Multiple Coefficient of Determination

$$R_a^2 = 1 - (1 - R^2)\frac{n - 1}{n - p - 1} \tag{13.9}$$

For the Butler Trucking example with $n = 10$ and $p = 2$, we have

$$R_a^2 = 1 - (1 - .904)\frac{10 - 1}{10 - 2 - 1} = .88$$

Thus, after adjusting for the two independent variables, we have an adjusted multiple coefficient of determination of .88. This value is provided by the Minitab output in Figure 13.4 as R-sq(adj) = 87.6%; the value we calculated differs because we used a rounded value of R^2 in the calculation.

NOTES AND COMMENTS

If the value of R^2 is small and the model contains a large number of independent variables, the adjusted coefficient of determination can take a negative value; in such cases, Minitab sets the adjusted coefficient of determination to zero.

EXERCISES

Methods

11. In Exercise 1, the following estimated regression equation based on 10 observations was presented.

$$\hat{y} = 29.1270 + .5906x_1 + .4980x_2$$

The values of SST and SSR are 6724.125 and 6216.375, respectively.
   a. Find SSE.
   b. Compute R^2.
   c. Compute R_a^2.
   d. Comment on the goodness of fit.

SELFtest   12. In Exercise 2, 10 observations were provided for a dependent variable y and two independent variables x_1 and x_2; for these data SST = 15,182.9, and SSR = 14,052.2.
   a. Compute R^2.
   b. Compute R_a^2.
   c. Does the estimated regression equation explain a large amount of the variability in the data? Explain.

13. In Exercise 3, the following estimated regression equation based on 30 observations was presented.

$$\hat{y} = 17.6 + 3.8x_1 - 2.3x_2 + 7.6x_3 + 2.7x_4$$

The values of SST and SSR are 1805 and 1760, respectively.
   a. Compute R^2.
   b. Compute R_a^2.
   c. Comment on the goodness of fit.

Applications

14. In Exercise 4, the following estimated regression equation relating sales to inventory investment and advertising expenditures was given.

$$\hat{y} = 25 + 10x_1 + 8x_2$$

The data used to develop the model came from a survey of 10 stores; for those data, SST = 16,000 and SSR = 12,000.
  a. For the estimated regression equation given, compute R^2.
  b. Compute R_a^2.
  c. Does the model appear to explain a large amount of variability in the data? Explain.

SELFtest   **15.** In Exercise 5, the owner of Showtime Movie Theaters, Inc., used multiple regression analysis to estimate weekly gross revenue (y) as a function of television advertising expenditures (x_1) and newspaper advertising expenditures (x_2). The estimated regression equation was

$$\hat{y} = 83.2 + 2.29x_1 + 1.30x_2$$

The computer solution provided SST = 25.5 and SSR = 23.435.
  a. Compute and interpret R^2 and R_a^2.
  b. When television advertising expenditures was the only independent variable, $R^2 = .653$ and $R_a^2 = .595$. Do you prefer the multiple regression results? Explain.

16. In Exercise 6, data were given on curb weight, horsepower, and the speed at $\frac{1}{4}$ mile for 16 sports and GT cars (*1998 Road & Track Sports & GT Cars*).
  a. Did the estimated regression equation that uses only curb weight to predict the speed at $\frac{1}{4}$ mile provide a good fit? Explain.
  b. Discuss the benefits of using both the curb weight and the horsepower to predict the speed at $\frac{1}{4}$ mile.

17. In Exercise 9, an estimated regression equation was developed relating the percentage of students who attend a four-year college to the average class size and the combined SAT score.
  a. Compute and interpret R^2 and R_a^2.
  b. Does the estimated regression equation provide a good fit to the data? Explain.

18. Refer to Exercise 10, where data were reported on the number of cars in service (1000s), the number of locations, and the rental revenue ($ millions) for 15 car rental companies (*The Wall Street Journal Almanac 1998*).
  a. In part (c) of Exercise 10, an estimated regression equation was developed relating the rental revenue to the number of cars in service and the number of locations. What are the values of R^2 and R_a^2?
  b. Does the estimated regression equation provide a good fit to the data? Explain.

13.4   MODEL ASSUMPTIONS

In Section 13.1 we introduced the following multiple regression model.

Multiple Regression Model

$$y = \beta_0 + \beta_1x_1 + \beta_2x_2 + \cdots + \beta_px_p + \epsilon \qquad (13.10)$$

The assumptions about the error term ϵ in the multiple regression model parallel those for the simple linear regression model.

Assumptions About the Error Term ϵ in the Multiple Regression Model
$$y = \beta_0 + \beta_1 x_1 + \cdots + \beta_p x_p + \epsilon$$

1. The error term ϵ is a random variable with mean or expected value of zero; that is, $E(\epsilon) = 0$.
   Implication: For given values of $x_1, x_2, \ldots, x_p$, the expected, or average, value of y is given by

$$E(y) = \beta_0 + \beta_1 x_1 + \beta_2 x_2 + \cdots + \beta_p x_p. \qquad (13.11)$$

   Equation (13.11) is the multiple regression equation we introduced in Section 13.1. In this equation, $E(y)$ represents the average of all possible values of y that might occur for the given values of $x_1, x_2, \ldots, x_p$.
2. The variance of ϵ is denoted by σ^2 and is the same for all values of the independent variables $x_1, x_2, \ldots, x_p$.
   Implication: The variance of y equals σ^2 and is the same for all values of x_1, $x_2, \ldots, x_p$.
3. The values of ϵ are independent.
   Implication: The size of the error for a particular set of values for the independent variables is not related to the size of the error for any other set of values.
4. The error ϵ is a normally distributed random variable reflecting the deviation between the y value and the expected value of y given by $\beta_0 + \beta_1 x_1 + \beta_2 x_2 + \cdots + \beta_p x_p$.
   Implication: Because y is a linear function of ϵ, y is also a normally distributed random variable.

To obtain more insight about the form of the relationship given by equation (13.11), consider the following two-independent-variable multiple regression equation.

$$E(y) = \beta_0 + \beta_1 x_1 + \beta_2 x_2$$

The graph of this equation is a plane in three-dimensional space. Figure 13.5 is such a graph. Note that ϵ is shown as the difference between the actual y value and the expected value of y, $E(y)$, when $x_1 = x_1^*$ and $x_2 = x_2^*$.

In regression analysis, the term *response variable* is often used in place of the term *dependent variable*. Furthermore, since the multiple regression equation generates a plane or surface, its graph is called a *response surface*.

13.5   TESTING FOR SIGNIFICANCE

In this section we show how to conduct significance tests for a multiple regression relationship. The significance tests we used in simple linear regression were a t test and an F test. In simple linear regression, both tests provide the same conclusion; that is, if the null

FIGURE 13.5   GRAPH OF THE MULTIPLE REGRESSION EQUATION WITH TWO
INDEPENDENT VARIABLES

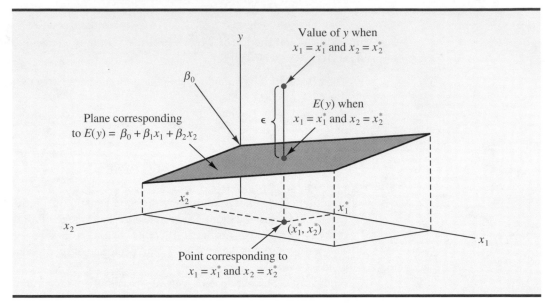

hypothesis is rejected, we conclude that $\beta_1 \neq 0$. In multiple regression, the t test and the F test have different purposes.

1. The F test is used to determine whether a significant relationship exists between the dependent variable and the set of all the independent variables; we will refer to the F test as the test for *overall significance.*
2. If the F test shows an overall significance, the t test is used to determine whether each of the individual independent variables is significant. A separate t test is conducted for each of the independent variables in the model; we refer to each of these t tests as a test for *individual significance.*

In the material that follows, we will explain the F test and the t test and apply each to the Butler Trucking Company example.

F Test

The multiple regression model as defined in Section 13.4 is

$$y = \beta_0 + \beta_1 x_1 + \beta_2 x_2 + \cdots + \beta_p x_p + \epsilon$$

The hypotheses for the F test involve the parameters of the multiple regression model.

$$H_0: \beta_1 = \beta_2 = \cdots = \beta_p = 0$$
H_a: One or more of the parameters is not equal to zero

If H_0 is rejected, we have sufficient statistical evidence to conclude that one or more of the parameters is not equal to zero and that the overall relationship between y and the set of independent variables $x_1, x_2, \ldots, x_p$ is significant. However, if H_0 cannot be rejected, we do not have sufficient evidence to conclude that a significant relationship is present.

Before describing the steps of the F test, we need to review the concept of *mean square* A mean square is a sum of squares divided by its corresponding degrees of freedom. In the multiple regression case, the total sum of squares has $n - 1$ degrees of freedom, the sum of squares due to regression (SSR) has p degrees of freedom, and the sum of squares due to error has $n - p - 1$ degrees of freedom. Hence, the mean square due to regression (MSR) is SSR/p and the mean square due to error (MSE) is SSE/$(n - p - 1)$.

$$MSR = \frac{SSR}{p} \tag{13.12}$$

and

$$MSE = \frac{SSE}{n - p - 1} \tag{13.13}$$

As discussed in Chapter 12, MSE provides an unbiased estimate of σ^2, the variance of the error term ϵ. If $H_0: \beta_1 = \beta_2 = \cdots = \beta_p = 0$ is true, MSR also provides an unbiased estimate of σ^2, and the value of MSR/MSE should be close to 1. However, if H_0 is false, MSR overestimates σ^2 and the value of MSR/MSE becomes larger. To determine how large the value of MSR/MSE must be to reject H_0, we make use of the fact that if H_0 is true and the assumptions about the multiple regression model are valid, the sampling distribution of MSR/MSE is an F distribution with p degrees of freedom in the numerator and $n - p - 1$ degrees of freedom in the denominator. A summary of the F test for significance in multiple regression follows.

F Test for Overall Significance

$$H_0: \beta_1 = \beta_2 = \cdots = \beta_p = 0$$
$$H_a: \text{One or more of the parameters is not equal to zero}$$

Test Statistic

$$F = \frac{MSR}{MSE} \tag{13.14}$$

Rejection Rule

Using test statistic: Reject H_0 if $F > F_\alpha$
Using p-value: Reject H_0 if p-value $< \alpha$

where F_α is based on an F distribution with p degrees of freedom in the numerator and $n - p - 1$ degrees of freedom in the denominator.

Let us apply the F test to the Butler Trucking Company multiple regression problem. With two independent variables, the hypotheses are written as follows.

$$H_0: \beta_1 = \beta_2 = 0$$
$$H_a: \beta_1 \text{ and/or } \beta_2 \text{ is not equal to zero}$$

Figure 13.6 is the Minitab output for the multiple regression model with miles traveled (x_1) and number of deliveries (x_2) as the two independent variables. In the analysis of variance part of the output, we see that MSR = 10.8 and MSE = .328. Using equation (13.14), we obtain the test statistic.

$$F = \frac{10.8}{.328} = 32.9$$

Note that the F value on the Minitab output is $F = 32.88$; the value we calculated differs because we used rounded values for MSR and MSE in the calculation. With a level of significance of $\alpha = .01$, Table 4 of Appendix B shows that with two degrees of freedom in the numerator and seven degrees of freedom in the denominator, $F_{.01} = 9.55$. With $32.9 > 9.55$, we reject H_0: $\beta_1 = \beta_2 = 0$ and conclude that a significant relationship is present between travel time y and the two independent variables, miles traveled and number of deliveries. The p-value = 0.000 in the last column of the analysis of variance table (Figure 13.6) also indicates that we can reject H_0: $\beta_1 = \beta_2 = 0$ because the p-value is less than $\alpha = .01$.

As noted previously, the mean square error provides an unbiased estimate of σ^2, the variance of the error term ϵ. Referring to Figure 13.6, we see that the estimate of σ^2 is MSE = .328. The square root of MSE, denoted s, is the estimate of σ, the standard deviation of the error term. Hence, we have $s = \sqrt{\text{MSE}} = \sqrt{.328} = .573$. Note that the value of s appears in the Minitab output in Figure 13.6.

Table 13.3 is the general analysis of variance (ANOVA) table that provides the F test results for a multiple regression model. The value of the F test statistic appears in the last column and can be compared to F_α with p degrees of freedom in the numerator and $n - p - 1$ degrees of freedom in the denominator to make the hypothesis testing conclusion. By reviewing the Minitab output for Butler Trucking Company in Figure 13.6, we see that Minitab's analysis of variance table contains this information. Moreover, Minitab also provides the p-value corresponding to the F test statistic.

FIGURE 13.6   MINITAB OUTPUT FOR BUTLER TRUCKING WITH TWO INDEPENDENT
VARIABLES, MILES TRAVELED (x_1) AND NUMBER OF DELIVERIES (x_2)

```
The regression equation is
Time = -0.869 + 0.0611 Miles + 0.923 Deliv


Predictor        Coef       Stdev     t-ratio        p
Constant       -0.8687      0.9515      -0.91     0.392
Miles         0.061135    0.009888       6.18     0.000
Deliv           0.9234      0.2211       4.18     0.004


s = 0.5731       R-sq = 90.4%     R-sq(adj) = 87.6%


Analysis of Variance

SOURCE           DF         SS          MS         F        p
Regression        2     21.601     10.800     32.88     0.000
Error             7      2.299      0.328
Total             9     23.900
```

TABLE 13.3   ANOVA TABLE FOR A MULTIPLE REGRESSION MODEL WITH p INDEPENDENT VARIABLES

Source	Sum of Squares	Degrees of Freedom	Mean Square	F
Regression	SSR	p	$\text{MSR} = \dfrac{\text{SSR}}{p}$	$F = \dfrac{\text{MSR}}{\text{MSE}}$
Error	SSE	$n - p - 1$	$\text{MSE} = \dfrac{\text{SSE}}{n - p - 1}$	
Total	SST	$n - 1$		

t Test

If the F test shows that the multiple regression relationship is significant, a t test can be conducted to determine the significance of each of the individual parameters. The t test for individual significance follows.

t Test for Individual Significance

For any parameter β_i

$$H_0: \beta_i = 0$$
$$H_a: \beta_i \neq 0$$

Test Statistic

$$t = \frac{b_i}{s_{b_i}} \tag{13.15}$$

Rejection Rule

Using test statistic: Reject H_0 if $t < -t_{\alpha/2}$ or if $t > t_{\alpha/2}$
Using p-value: Reject H_0 if p-value $< \alpha$

where $t_{\alpha/2}$ is based on a t distribution with $n - p - 1$ degrees of freedom.

In the test statistic, s_{b_i} is the estimate of the standard deviation of b_i. The value of s_{b_i} will be provided by the computer software package.

Let us conduct the t test for the Butler Trucking regression problem. Refer to the section of Figure 13.6 that shows the Minitab output for the t-ratio calculations. Values of b_1, b_2, s_{b_1}, and s_{b_2} are as follows.

$$b_1 = .061135 \quad s_{b_1} = .009888$$
$$b_2 = .9234 \quad s_{b_2} = .2211$$

Using equation (13.15), we obtain the test statistic for the hypotheses involving parameters β_1 and β_2.

$$t = .061135/.009888 = 6.18$$
$$t = .9234/.2211 = 4.18$$

Note that both of these t-ratio values are provided by the Minitab output in Figure 13.6. For $\alpha = .01$ and $n - p - 1 = 10 - 2 - 1 = 7$ degrees of freedom, Table 2 of Appendix B shows that $t_{.005} = 3.499$. With $6.18 > 3.499$, we reject H_0: $\beta_1 = 0$. Similarly, with $4.18 > 3.499$, we reject H_0: $\beta_2 = 0$. Note that the p-values of .000 and .004 on the Minitab output also indicate rejection of these hypotheses. Hence, both parameters are statistically significant.

Multicollinearity

We have used the term *independent variable* in regression analysis to refer to any variable being used to predict or explain the value of the dependent variable. The term does not mean, however, that the independent variables themselves are independent in any statistical sense. On the contrary, most independent variables in a multiple regression problem are correlated to some degree with one another. For example, in the Butler Trucking example involving the two independent variables x_1 (miles traveled) and x_2 (number of deliveries), we could treat the miles traveled as the dependent variable and the number of deliveries as the independent variable to determine whether those two variables are themselves related. We could then compute the sample correlation coefficient $r_{x_1 x_2}$ to determine the extent to which the variables are related. Doing so yields $r_{x_1 x_2} = .16$. Thus, we find some degree of linear association between the two independent variables. In multiple regression analysis, **multicollinearity** refers to the correlation among the independent variables.

To provide a better perspective of the potential problems of multicollinearity, let us consider a modification of the Butler Trucking example. Instead of x_2 being the number of deliveries, let x_2 denote the number of gallons of gasoline consumed. Clearly, x_1 (the miles traveled) and x_2 are related; that is, we know that the number of gallons of gasoline used depends on the number of miles traveled. Hence, we would conclude logically that x_1 and x_2 are highly correlated independent variables.

When the independent variables are highly correlated, it is not possible to determine the separate effect of any particular independent variable on the dependent variable.

Assume that we obtain the equation $\hat{y} = b_0 + b_1 x_1 + b_2 x_2$ and find that the F test shows the relationship to be significant. Then suppose we conduct a t test on β_1 to determine whether $\beta_1 \neq 0$, and we cannot reject H_0: $\beta_1 = 0$. Does this mean that travel time is not related to miles traveled? Not necessarily. What it probably means is that with x_2 already in the model, x_1 does not make a significant contribution to determining the value of y. This interpretation makes sense in our example; if we know the amount of gasoline consumed, we do not gain much additional information useful in predicting y by knowing the miles traveled. Similarly, a t test might lead us to conclude $\beta_2 = 0$ on the grounds that, with x_1 in the model, knowledge of the amount of gasoline consumed does not add much.

A sample correlation coefficient greater than +0.7 or less than −0.7 for two independent variables is a rule of thumb warning of potential problems with multicollinearity.

To summarize, in t tests for the significance of individual parameters, the difficulty caused by multicollinearity is that it is possible to conclude that none of the individual parameters are significantly different from zero when an F test on the overall multiple regression equation indicates a significant relationship. This problem is avoided when there is little correlation among the independent variables.

Statisticians have developed several tests for determining whether multicollinearity is high enough to cause problems. According to the rule of thumb test, multicollinearity is a potential problem if the absolute value of the sample correlation coefficient exceeds .7 for any two of the independent variables. The other types of tests are more advanced and beyond the scope of this text.

If possible, every attempt should be made to avoid including independent variables that are highly correlated. In practice, however, strict adherence to this policy is rarely possible. When decision makers have reason to believe substantial multicollinearity is present, they must realize that separating the effects of the individual independent variables on the dependent variable is difficult.

NOTES AND COMMENTS

Ordinarily, multicollinearity does not affect the way in which we perform our regression analysis or interpret the output from a study. However, when multicollinearity is severe—that is, when two or more of the independent variables are highly correlated with one another—we can have difficulty interpreting the results of t tests on the individual parameters. In addition to the type of problem illustrated in this section, severe cases of multicollinearity have been shown to result in least squares estimates that have the wrong sign. That is,

in simulated studies where researchers created the underlying regression model and then applied the least squares technique to develop estimates of β_0, β_1, β_2, and so on, it has been shown that under conditions of high multicollinearity the least squares estimates can have a sign opposite that of the parameter being estimated. For example, β_2 might actually be $+10$ and b_2, its estimate, might turn out to be -2. Thus, little faith can be placed in the individual coefficients if multicollinearity is present to a high degree.

EXERCISES

Methods

SELFtest

19. Exercise 1 presented the following estimated regression equation based on 10 observations.

$$\hat{y} = 29.1270 + .5906x_1 + .4980x_2$$

Here SST = 6724.125, SSR = 6216.375, s_{b_1} = .0813, and s_{b_2} = .0567.
a. Compute MSR and MSE.
b. Compute F and perform the appropriate F test. Use $\alpha = .05$.
c. Perform a t test for the significance of β_1. Use $\alpha = .05$.
d. Perform a t test for the significance of β_2. Use $\alpha = .05$.

20. Refer to the data presented in Exercise 2. The estimated regression equation for these data is

$$\hat{y} = -18.4 + 2.01x_1 + 4.74x_2$$

Here SST = 15,182.9, SSR = 14,052.2, s_{b_1} = .2471, and s_{b_2} = .9484.
a. Test for a significant relationship among x_1, x_2, and y. Use $\alpha = .05$.
b. Is β_1 significant? Use $\alpha = .05$.
c. Is β_2 significant? Use $\alpha = .05$.

21. The following estimated regression equation was developed for a model involving two independent variables.

$$\hat{y} = 40.7 + 8.63x_1 + 2.71x_2$$

After x_2 was dropped from the model, the least squares method was used to obtain an estimated regression equation involving only x_1 as an independent variable.

$$\hat{y} = 42.0 + 9.01x_1$$

a. Give an interpretation of the coefficient of x_1 in both models.
b. Could multicollinearity explain why the coefficient of x_1 differs in the two models? If so, how?

Applications

22. Exercise 4 presented the following estimated regression equation relating sales to inventory investment and advertising expenditures.

$$\hat{y} = 25 + 10x_1 + 8x_2$$

The data used to develop the model came from a survey of 10 stores; for these data SST = 16,000 and SSR = 12,000.
a. Compute SSE, MSE, and MSR.
b. Use an F test and a .05 level of significance to determine whether there is a relationship among the variables.

SELFtest 23. Refer to Exercise 5.
a. Use $\alpha = .01$ to test the hypotheses

$$H_0: \beta_1 = \beta_2 = 0$$
$$H_a: \beta_1 \text{ and/or } \beta_2 \text{ is not equal to zero}$$

for the model $y = \beta_0 + \beta_1 x_1 + \beta_2 x_2 + \epsilon$, where

$$x_1 = \text{television advertising expenditures (\$1000s)}$$
$$x_2 = \text{newspaper advertising expenditures (\$1000s)}$$

b. Use $\alpha = .05$ to test the significance of β_1. Should x_1 be dropped from the model?
c. Use $\alpha = .05$ to test the significance of β_2. Should x_2 be dropped from the model?

24. Refer to the data in Exercise 6. Use curb weight and horsepower to predict the speed of a sports and GT car at $\frac{1}{4}$ mile.
a. Use the F test to determine the overall significance of the relationship. What is your conclusion at the .05 level of significance?
b. Use the t test to determine the significance of each independent variable. What is your conclusion at the .05 level of significance?

25. A sample of 16 companies taken from the *Stock Investor Pro* database was used to obtain the following data on the price/earnings (P/E) ratio, the gross profit margin, and the sales growth for each company (*Stock Investor Pro*, American Association of Individual Investors, August 21, 1997).

CDfile
Stocks

Firm	P/E Ratio	Gross Profit Margin (%)	Sales Growth (%)
Abbott Laboratories	22.3	23.7	10.0
American Home Products	22.6	21.1	5.3
Amoco	16.7	11.0	16.5
Bristol Meyers Squibb Co.	25.9	26.6	9.4

Firm	P/E Ratio	Gross Profit Margin (%)	Sales Growth (%)
Chevron	18.3	11.6	18.4
Exxon	18.7	9.8	8.3
General Electric Company	13.1	13.4	13.1
Hewlett-Packard	23.3	9.7	21.9
IBM	17.3	11.5	5.6
Merck & Co., Inc.	26.2	25.6	18.9
Mobil	18.7	8.2	8.1
Pfizer	34.6	25.1	12.8
Pharmacia & Upjohn, Inc.	22.3	15.0	2.7
Procter & Gamble Co.	5.4	14.9	5.4
Texaco	12.3	7.3	23.7
Travelers Group, Inc.	28.7	17.8	28.7

    a. Determine the estimated regression equation that can be used to predict the price/earnings ratio given the gross profit margin and the sales growth.

    b. Use the F test to determine the overall significance of the relationship. What is your conclusion at the .05 level of significance?

    c. Use the t test to determine the significance of each independent variable. What is your conclusion at the .05 level of significance?

    d. Remove any independent variable that is not significant from the estimated regression equation. What is your recommended estimated regression equation? Compare the R^2 with the value of R^2 from part (a). Discuss the differences.

26. In Exercise 10 an estimated regression equation was developed relating the rental revenue ($ millions) to the number of cars in service (1000s) and the number of locations.

    a. Test for a significant relationship between the dependent variable and the two independent variables. Use $\alpha = .05$.

    b. Is the number of cars in service significant? Use $\alpha = .05$.

    c. Is the number of locations significant? Use $\alpha = .05$.

13.6   USING THE ESTIMATED REGRESSION EQUATION FOR ESTIMATION AND PREDICTION

The procedures for estimating the mean value of y and predicting an individual value of y in multiple regression are similar to those in regression analysis involving one independent variable. First, recall that in Chapter 12 we showed that the point estimate of the expected value of y for a given value of x was the same as the point estimate of an individual value of y. In both cases, we used $\hat{y} = b_0 + b_1 x$ as the point estimate.

In multiple regression we use the same procedure. That is, we substitute the given values of $x_1, x_2, \ldots, x_p$ into the estimated regression equation and use the corresponding value of $\hat{y}$ as the point estimate. Suppose that for the Butler Trucking example we want to use the estimated regression equation involving x_1 (miles traveled) and x_2 (number of deliveries) to develop two estimates:

    1. A *confidence interval estimate* of the mean travel time for all trucks that travel 100 miles and make two deliveries.

    2. A *prediction interval estimate* of the travel time for *one specific* truck that travels 100 miles and makes two deliveries.

TABLE 13.4 THE 95% CONFIDENCE AND PREDICTION INTERVAL ESTIMATES FOR BUTLER TRUCKING

Value of x_1	Value of x_2	Confidence Interval Lower Limit	Confidence Interval Upper Limit	Prediction Interval Lower Limit	Prediction Interval Upper Limit
50	2	3.146	4.924	2.414	5.656
50	3	4.127	5.789	3.368	6.548
50	4	4.815	6.948	4.157	7.607
100	2	6.258	7.926	5.500	8.683
100	3	7.385	8.645	6.520	9.510
100	4	8.135	9.742	7.362	10.515

Using the estimated regression equation $\hat{y} = -.869 + .0611x_1 + .923x_2$ with $x_1 = 100$ and $x_2 = 2$, we obtain the following value of $\hat{y}$.

$$\hat{y} = -.869 + .0611(100) + .923(2) = 7.09$$

Hence, the point estimate of travel time in both cases is approximately seven hours.

To develop interval estimates of the mean value of y and an individual value of y, we use a procedure similar to that for regression analysis involving one independent variable. The formulas required are beyond the scope of the text, but computer packages for multiple regression analysis will often provide confidence intervals once the values of $x_1, x_2, \ldots, x_p$ are specified by the user. In Table 13.4 we show the 95% confidence and prediction interval estimates for the Butler Trucking example for selected values of x_1 and x_2; these values were obtained using Minitab. Note that the interval estimate for an individual value of y is wider than the interval estimate for the expected value of y. This difference simply reflects the fact that for given values of x_1 and x_2 we can estimate the mean travel time for all trucks with more precision than we can predict the travel time for one specific truck.

EXERCISES

Methods

27. Exercise 1 presented the following estimated regression equation based on 10 observations.

$$\hat{y} = 29.1270 + .5906x_1 + .4980x_2$$

   a. Develop a point estimate of the mean value of y when $x_1 = 180$ and $x_2 = 310$.
   b. Develop a point estimate for an individual value of y when $x_1 = 180$ and $x_2 = 310$.

SELFtest **28.** Refer to the data in Exercise 2. The estimated regression equation for those data is

$$\hat{y} = -18.4 + 2.01x_1 + 4.74x_2$$

   a. Develop a 95% confidence interval estimate of the mean value of y when $x_1 = 45$ and $x_2 = 15$.
   b. Develop a 95% prediction interval estimate of y when $x_1 = 45$ and $x_2 = 15$.

Applications

SELFtest

29. In Exercise 5, the owner of Showtime Movie Theaters, Inc., used multiple regression analysis to estimate weekly gross revenue (y) as a function of television advertising expenditures (x_1) and newspaper advertising expenditures (x_2). The estimated regression equation was

$$\hat{y} = 83.2 + 2.29x_1 + 1.30x_2$$

   a. What is the gross revenue expected for a week when $3500 is spent on television advertising ($x_1 = 3.5$) and $1800 is spent on newspaper advertising ($x_2 = 1.8$)?
   b. Provide a 95% confidence interval estimate of the mean revenue of all weeks with the expenditures listed in part (a).
   c. Provide a 95% prediction interval estimate for next week's revenue, assuming that the advertising expenditures will be allocated as in part (a).

30. In Exercise 6, data were given on curb weight, horsepower, and speed at ¼ mile for 16 sports and GT cars (*1998 Road and Track Sports & GT Cars*).
   a. Estimate the ¼-mile speed for a 1999 Porsche 911 Carrera that has a curb weight of 2910 pounds and a horsepower of 296.
   b. Provide a 95% confidence interval estimate of the ¼-mile speed of all sports and GT cars with the characteristics listed in part (a).
   c. Provide a 95% prediction interval estimate of the ¼-mile speed for the 1999 Porsche 911 Carrera described in part (a).

31. In Exercise 9, an estimated regression equation was developed relating the percentage of students who attend a four-year college to the average class size and the combined SAT score.
   a. Develop a 95% confidence interval estimate of the mean percentage of students who attend a four-year college for a school district that has an average class size of 25 and whose students have a combined SAT score of 1000.
   b. Suppose that a school district in Conway, South Carolina, has an average class size of 25 and a combined SAT score of 950. Develop a 95% prediction interval estimate of the percentage of students who attend a four-year college.

13.7   QUALITATIVE INDEPENDENT VARIABLES

The independent variables may be qualitative or quantitative.

Thus far, the examples given involved quantitative independent variables such as student population, distance traveled, and number of deliveries. In many situations, however, we must work with **qualitative independent variables** such as gender (male, female), method of payment (cash, credit card, check), and so on. The purpose of this section is to show how qualitative variables are handled in regression analysis. To illustrate the use and interpretation of a qualitative independent variable, we consider a problem facing the managers of Johnson Filtration, Inc.

An Example: Johnson Filtration, Inc.

Johnson Filtration, Inc., provides maintenance service for water-filtration systems throughout southern Florida. Customers contact Johnson with requests for maintenance service on their water-filtration systems. To estimate the service time and the service cost, Johnson's managers want to predict the repair time necessary for each maintenance request. Hence, repair time in hours is the dependent variable. Repair time is believed to be related to two factors, the number of months since the last maintenance service and the type of repair problem (mechanical or electrical). Data for a sample of 10 service calls are reported in Table 13.5.

TABLE 13.5   DATA FOR THE JOHNSON FILTRATION EXAMPLE

Service Call	Months Since Last Service	Type of Repair	Repair Time in Hours
1	2	electrical	2.9
2	6	mechanical	3.0
3	8	electrical	4.8
4	3	mechanical	1.8
5	2	electrical	2.9
6	7	electrical	4.9
7	9	mechanical	4.2
8	8	mechanical	4.8
9	4	electrical	4.4
10	6	electrical	4.5

Let y denote the repair time in hours and x_1 denote the number of months since the last maintenance service. The regression model that uses only x_1 to predict y is

$$y = \beta_0 + \beta_1 x_1 + \epsilon$$

Using Minitab to develop the estimated regression equation, we obtained the output shown in Figure 13.7. The estimated regression equation is

$$\hat{y} = 2.15 + .304x_1 \tag{13.16}$$

At the .05 level of significance, the p-value of .016 for the t (or F) test indicates that the number of months since the last service is significantly related to repair time. R-sq = 53.4% indicates that x_1 alone explains 53.4% of the variability in repair time.

FIGURE 13.7   MINITAB OUTPUT FOR JOHNSON FILTRATION WITH MONTHS SINCE LAST SERVICE (x_1) AS THE INDEPENDENT VARIABLE

In the Minitab output the variable names Months and Time were entered as the column headings on the worksheet; thus, x_1 = Months and y = Time.

```
The regression equation is
Time = 2.15 + 0.304 Months

Predictor      Coef       Stdev     t-ratio        p
Constant      2.1473     0.6050       3.55     0.008
Months        0.3041     0.1004       3.03     0.016

s = 0.7810      R-sq = 53.4%     R-sq(adj) = 47.6%

Analysis of Variance

SOURCE        DF         SS          MS         F        p
Regression     1      5.5960      5.5960      9.17     0.016
Error          8      4.8800      0.6100
Total          9     10.4760
```

To incorporate the type of failure into the regression model, we define the following variable.

$$x_2 = \begin{cases} 0 \text{ if the type of repair is mechanical} \\ 1 \text{ if the type of repair is electrical} \end{cases}$$

In regression analysis x_2 is called a **dummy variable.** Using this dummy variable, we can write the multiple regression model as

A dummy variable is also called an indicator variable.

$$y = \beta_0 + \beta_1 x_1 + \beta_2 x_2 + \epsilon$$

Table 13.6 is the revised data set that includes the values of the dummy variable. Using Minitab and the data in Table 13.6, we can develop estimates of the model parameters. The Minitab output in Figure 13.8 shows that the estimated multiple regression equation is

$$\hat{y} = .93 + .388x_1 + 1.26x_2 \tag{13.17}$$

At the .05 level of significance, the p-value of .001 associated with the F test (F = 21.36) indicates that the regression relationship is significant. The t test part of the printout in Figure 13.8 shows that both months since last service (p-value = .000) and type of repair (p-value = .005) are statistically significant. In addition, R-sq = 85.9% and R-sq(adj) = 81.9% indicate that the estimated regression equation does a good job of explaining the variability in repair times. Thus, equation (13.17) should prove helpful in estimating the repair time necessary for the various service calls.

Interpreting the Parameters

The multiple regression equation for the Johnson Filtration example is

$$E(y) = \beta_0 + \beta_1 x_1 + \beta_2 x_2 \tag{13.18}$$

TABLE 13.6   DATA FOR THE JOHNSON FILTRATION EXAMPLE WITH TYPE OF REPAIR INDICATED BY A DUMMY VARIABLE ($x_2 = 0$ FOR MECHANICAL; $x_2 = 1$ FOR ELECTRICAL)

CDfile

Johnson

Customer	Months Since Last Service (x_1)	Type of Repair (x_2)	Repair Time in Hours (y)
1	2	1	2.9
2	6	0	3.0
3	8	1	4.8
4	3	0	1.8
5	2	1	2.9
6	7	1	4.9
7	9	0	4.2
8	8	0	4.8
9	4	1	4.4
10	6	1	4.5

FIGURE 13.8   MINITAB OUTPUT FOR JOHNSON FILTRATION WITH MONTHS
SINCE LAST SERVICE (x_1) AND TYPE OF REPAIR (x_2) AS THE
INDEPENDENT VARIABLES

*In the Minitab output the
variable names Months,
Type, and Time were
entered as the column
headings on the worksheet;
thus, x_1 = Months,
x_2 = Type, and y = Time.*

```
The regression equation is
Time = 0.930 + 0.388 Months + 1.26 Type

Predictor          Coef        Stdev    t-ratio         p
Constant         0.9305       0.4670       1.99     0.087
Months          0.38762      0.06257       6.20     0.000
Type             1.2627       0.3141       4.02     0.005

s = 0.4590      R-sq = 85.9%      R-sq(adj) = 81.9%

Analysis of Variance

SOURCE        DF          SS         MS         F          p
Regression     2      9.0009     4.5005     21.36     0.001
Error          7      1.4751     0.2107
Total          9     10.4760
```

To understand how to interpret the parameters β_0, β_1, and β_2 when a qualitative variable is present, consider the case when $x_2 = 0$ (mechanical repair). Using $E(y \mid \text{mechanical})$ to denote the mean repair time *given* a mechanical repair, we have

$$E(y \mid \text{mechanical}) = \beta_0 + \beta_1 x_1 + \beta_2(0) = \beta_0 + \beta_1 x_1 \qquad (13.19)$$

Similarly, for an electrical repair ($x_2 = 1$), we have

$$\begin{aligned} E(y \mid \text{electrical}) &= \beta_0 + \beta_1 x_1 + \beta_2(1) = \beta_0 + \beta_1 x_1 + \beta_2 \\ &= (\beta_0 + \beta_2) + \beta_1 x_1 \end{aligned} \qquad (13.20)$$

Comparing equations (13.19) and (13.20), we see that the expected repair time is a linear function of x_1 for both mechanical and electrical repairs. The slope of both equations is β_1, but the y-intercept differs. The y-intercept is β_0 in equation (13.19) for mechanical repairs and ($\beta_0 + \beta_2$) in equation (13.20) for electrical repairs. The interpretation of β_2 is that it indicates the difference between the expected repair time for an electrical repair and the expected repair time for a mechanical repair.

If β_2 is positive, the expected repair time for an electrical repair will be greater than that for a mechanical repair; if β_2 is negative, the expected repair time for an electrical repair will be less than that for a mechanical repair. Finally, if $\beta_2 = 0$, there is no difference in repair time between electrical and mechanical repairs and the type of repair is not related to the repair time.

Using the estimated multiple regression equation $\hat{y} = .93 + .388x_1 + 1.26x_2$, we see that .93 is the estimate of β_0 and 1.26 is the estimate of β_2. Thus, when $x_2 = 0$ (mechanical repair)

$$\hat{y} = .93 + .388x_1 \qquad (13.21)$$

and when $x_2 = 1$ (electrical repair)

$$\hat{y} = .93 + .388x_1 + 1.26(1)$$
$$= 2.19 + .388x_1 \tag{13.22}$$

In effect, the use of a dummy variable for type of repair has provided two equations that can be used to predict the repair time, one corresponding to mechanical repairs and one corresponding to electrical repairs. In addition, with $b_2 = 1.26$, we have learned that, on average, electrical repairs require 1.26 hours longer than mechanical repairs.

Figure 13.9 is the plot of the Johnson data from Table 13.6. Repair time in hours (y) is represented by the vertical axis and months since last service (x_1) is represented by the horizontal axis. A data point for a mechanical repair is indicated by an M and a data point for an electrical repair is indicated by an E. Equations (13.21) and (13.22) are plotted on the graph to show graphically the two equations that can be used to predict the repair time, one corresponding to mechanical repairs and one corresponding to electrical repairs.

More Complex Qualitative Variables

A qualitative variable with k levels must be modeled using k − 1 dummy variables. Care must be taken in defining and interpreting the dummy variables.

Because the qualitative variable for the Johnson Filtration example had two levels (mechanical and electrical), defining a dummy variable with zero indicating a mechanical repair and one indicating an electrical repair was easy. However, when a qualitative variable has more than two levels, care must be taken in both defining and interpreting the dummy variables. As we will show, if a qualitative variable has k levels, $k - 1$ dummy variables are required, with each dummy variable being coded as 0 or 1.

FIGURE 13.9   SCATTER DIAGRAM FOR THE JOHNSON FILTRATION REPAIR DATA
FROM TABLE 13.6

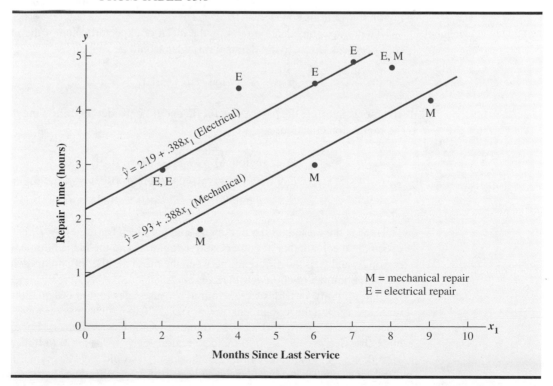

For example, suppose a manufacturer of copy machines organized the sales territories for a particular state into three regions: A, B, and C. The managers want to use regression analysis to help predict the number of copiers sold per week, using independent variables such as the number of sales personnel, advertising expenditures, and so on. Suppose the managers believe sales region is also an important factor in predicting the number of copiers sold. Because sales region is a qualitative variable with three levels, A, B and C, we need $3 - 1 = 2$ dummy variables to represent the sales region. Each variable can be coded 0 or 1 as follows.

$$x_1 = \begin{cases} 1 \text{ if sales region B} \\ 0 \text{ otherwise} \end{cases}$$

$$x_2 = \begin{cases} 1 \text{ if sales region C} \\ 0 \text{ otherwise} \end{cases}$$

With this definition, we have the following values of x_1 and x_2.

Region	x_1	x_2
A	0	0
B	1	0
C	0	1

Observations corresponding to region A would be coded $x_1 = 0$, $x_2 = 0$; observations corresponding to region B would be coded $x_1 = 1$, $x_2 = 0$; and observations corresponding to region C would be coded $x_1 = 0$, $x_2 = 1$.

The regression equation relating the mean or expected value of the number of copiers sold per week, $E(y)$, to the dummy variables would be written as

$$E(y) = \beta_0 + \beta_1 x_1 + \beta_2 x_2$$

To help us interpret the parameters β_0, β_1, and β_2, consider the following three variations of the regression equation.

$$E(y \mid \text{region A}) = \beta_0 + \beta_1(0) + \beta_2(0) = \beta_0$$
$$E(y \mid \text{region B}) = \beta_0 + \beta_1(1) + \beta_2(0) = \beta_0 + \beta_1$$
$$E(y \mid \text{region C}) = \beta_0 + \beta_1(0) + \beta_2(1) = \beta_0 + \beta_2$$

Thus, β_0 is the mean number of copiers sold per week for region A; β_1 is the difference between the mean number of copiers sold in region B and the mean number of copiers sold in region A; and β_2 is the difference between the mean number of copiers sold in region C and the mean number of copiers sold in region A.

Two dummy variables were required because sales region is a qualitative variable with three levels. But, the assignment of $x_1 = 0$, $x_2 = 0$ to indicate region A, $x_1 = 1$, $x_2 = 0$ to indicate region B, and $x_1 = 0$, $x_2 = 1$ to indicate region C was arbitrary. For example, we could have chosen $x_1 = 1$, $x_2 = 0$ to indicate region A, $x_1 = 0$, $x_2 = 0$ to indicate region B, and $x_1 = 0$, $x_2 = 1$ to indicate region C. In that case, β_1 would have been interpreted as the mean difference between regions A and B and β_2 as the mean difference between regions C and B.

The important point to remember is that when a qualitative variable has k levels, k 1 dummy variables are required in the multiple regression analysis. Thus, if the sales region example had a fourth region, labeled D, three dummy variables would be necessary with x_3 defined as follows.

$$x_3 = \begin{cases} 1 \text{ if sales region D} \\ 0 \text{ otherwise} \end{cases}$$

EXERCISES

Methods

SELFtest **32.** Consider a regression study involving a dependent variable y, a quantitative independent variable x_1, and a qualitative independent variable with two levels (level 1 and level 2).
  a. Write a multiple regression equation relating x_1 and the qualitative variable to y.
  b. What is the expected value of y corresponding to level 1 of the qualitative variable?
  c. What is the expected value of y corresponding to level 2 of the qualitative variable?
  d. Interpret the parameters in your regression equation.

33. Consider a regression study involving a dependent variable y, a quantitative independent variable x_1, and a qualitative independent variable with three possible levels (level 1, level 2, and level 3).
  a. How many dummy variables are required to represent the qualitative variable?
  b. Write a multiple regression equation relating x_1 and the qualitative variable to y.
  c. Interpret the parameters in your regression equation.

Applications

SELFtest **34.** The following regression model has been proposed to predict sales at a fast-food outlet.

$$y = \beta_0 + \beta_1 x_1 + \beta_2 x_2 + \beta_3 x_3 + \epsilon$$

where

x_1 = number of competitors within 1 mile
x_2 = population within 1 mile (1000s)
$x_3 = \begin{cases} 1 \text{ if drive-up window present} \\ 0 \text{ otherwise} \end{cases}$
y = sales ($1000s)

The following estimated regression equation was developed after 20 outlets were surveyed.

$$\hat{y} = 10.1 - 4.2x_1 + 6.8x_2 + 15.3x_3$$

  a. What is the expected amount of sales attributable to the drive-up window?
  b. Predict sales for a store with two competitors, a population of 8000 within 1 mile, and no drive-up window.
  c. Predict sales for a store with one competitor, a population of 3000 within 1 mile, and a drive-up window.

35. Refer to the Johnson Filtration problem introduced in this section. Suppose that in addition to information on the number of months since the machine was serviced and whether a mechanical or an electrical failure had occurred, the managers obtained a list showing which repairperson had performed the service. The revised data follow.

CDfile
Repair

Repair Time in Hours	Months Since Last Service	Type of Repair	Repairperson
2.9	2	Electrical	Dave Newton
3.0	6	Mechanical	Dave Newton
4.8	8	Electrical	Bob Jones
1.8	3	Mechanical	Dave Newton
2.9	2	Electrical	Dave Newton
4.9	7	Electrical	Bob Jones
4.2	9	Mechanical	Bob Jones
4.8	8	Mechanical	Bob Jones
4.4	4	Electrical	Bob Jones
4.5	6	Electrical	Dave Newton

    a. Ignore for now the months since the last maintenance service (x_1) and the repairperson who performed the service. Develop the estimated simple linear regression equation to predict the repair time (y) given the type of repair (x_2). Recall that $x_2 = 0$ if the type of repair is mechanical and 1 if the type of repair is electrical.

    b. Does the equation that you developed in part (a) provide a good fit for the observed data? Explain.

    c. Ignore for now the months since the last maintenance service and the type of repair associated with the machine. Develop the estimated simple linear regression equation to predict the repair time given the repairperson who performed the service. Let $x_3 = 0$ if Bob Jones performed the service and $x_3 = 1$ if Dave Newton performed the service.

    d. Does the equation that you developed in part (c) provide a good fit for the observed data? Explain.

36. This problem is an extension of the situation described in Exercise 35.

    a. Develop the estimated regression equation to predict the repair time given the number of months since the last maintenance service, the type of repair, and the repairperson who performed the service.

    b. At the .05 level of significance, test whether the estimated regression equation developed in (a) represents a significant relationship between the independent variables and the dependent variable.

    c. Is the addition of the independent variable x_3, the repairperson who performed the service, statistically significant? Use $\alpha = .05$. What explanation can you give for the results observed?

37. The National Football League rates prospects position by position on a scale that ranges from 5 to 9. The ratings are interpreted as follows: 8.0–9.0 should start the first year; 7.0–7.9 should start; 6.0–6.9 will make the team as backup; and 5.0–5.9 can make the club and contribute. The following table shows the position, weight, speed (for 40 yards), and ratings for 25 NFL prospects (*USA Today,* April 14, 2000).

Name	Position	Weight (pounds)	Speed (seconds)	Rating
Cosey Coleman	Guard	322	5.38	7.4
Travis Claridge	Guard	303	5.18	7.0
Kaulana Noa	Guard	317	5.34	6.8
Leander Jordan	Guard	330	5.46	6.7
Chad Clifton	Guard	334	5.18	6.3
Manula Savea	Guard	308	5.32	6.1
Ryan Johanningmei	Guard	310	5.28	6.0
Mark Tauscher	Guard	318	5.37	6.0
Blaine Saipaia	Guard	321	5.25	6.0
Richard Mercier	Guard	295	5.34	5.8
Damion McIntosh	Guard	328	5.31	5.3
Jeno James	Guard	320	5.64	5.0
Al Jackson	Guard	304	5.20	5.0
Chris Samuels	Offensive tackle	325	4.95	8.5
Stockar McDougle	Offensive tackle	361	5.50	8.0
Chris McIngosh	Offensive tackle	315	5.39	7.8
Adrian Klemm	Offensive tackle	307	4.98	7.6
Todd Wade	Offensive tackle	326	5.20	7.3
Marvel Smith	Offensive tackle	320	5.36	7.1
Michael Thompson	Offensive tackle	287	5.05	6.8
Bobby Williams	Offensive tackle	332	5.26	6.8
Darnell Alford	Offensive tackle	334	5.55	6.4
Terrance Beadles	Offensive tackle	312	5.15	6.3
Tutan Reyes	Offensive tackle	299	5.35	6.1
Greg Robinson-Ran	Offensive tackle	333	5.59	6.0

CDfile
Football

a. Develop a dummy variable that will account for the player's position.
b. Develop an estimated regression equation to show how rating is related to position, weight, and speed.
c. At the .05 level of significance, test whether the estimated regression equation developed in part (b) indicates a significant relationship between the independent variables and the dependent variable.
d. Does the estimated regression equation provide a good fit for the observed data? Explain.
e. Is position a significant factor in the player's rating? Use $\alpha = .05$. Explain.
f. Suppose a new offensive tackle prospect who weighs 300 pounds ran the 40 yards in 5.1 seconds. Use the estimated regression equation developed in part (b) to estimate the rating for this player.

38. A 10-year study conducted by the American Heart Association provided data on how age, blood pressure, and smoking relate to the risk of strokes. Assume that the following data are from a portion of this study. Risk is interpreted as the probability (times 100) that the patient will have a stroke over the next 10-year period. For the smoking variable, define a dummy variable with 1 indicating a smoker and 0 indicating a nonsmoker.

CDfile
Stroke

Risk	Age	Blood Pressure	Smoker
12	57	152	No
24	67	163	No

(continued)

Risk	Age	Blood Pressure	Smoker
13	58	155	No
56	86	177	Yes
28	59	196	No
51	76	189	Yes
18	56	155	Yes
31	78	120	No
37	80	135	Yes
15	78	98	No
22	71	152	No
36	70	173	Yes
15	67	135	Yes
48	77	209	Yes
15	60	199	No
36	82	119	Yes
8	66	166	No
34	80	125	Yes
3	62	117	No
37	59	207	Yes

a. Using these data, develop an estimated regression equation that relates risk of a stroke to the person's age, blood pressure, and whether the person is a smoker.

b. Is smoking a significant factor in the risk of a stroke? Explain. Use $\alpha = .05$.

c. What is the probability of a stroke over the next 10 years for Art Speen, a 68-year-old smoker who has blood pressure of 175? What action might the physician recommend for this patient?

SUMMARY

In this chapter, we introduced multiple regression analysis as an extension of simple linear regression analysis presented in Chapter 12. Multiple regression analysis enables us to understand how a dependent variable is related to two or more independent variables. The regression equation $E(y) = \beta_0 + \beta_1 x_1 + \beta_2 x_2 + \cdots + \beta_p x_p$ shows that the expected value or mean value of the dependent variable y is related to the values of the independent variables $x_1, x_2, \ldots, x_p$. Sample data and the least squares method are used to develop the estimated regression equation $\hat{y} = b_0 + b_1 x_1 + b_2 x_2 + \cdots + b_p x_p$. In effect $b_0, b_1, b_2, \ldots, b_p$ are sample statistics used to estimate the unknown model parameters $\beta_0, \beta_1, \beta_2, \ldots, \beta_p$. Computer printouts used throughout the chapter emphasized the fact that statistical software packages are the only realistic means of performing the numerous computations required in multiple regression analysis.

The multiple coefficient of determination was presented as a measure of the goodness of fit of the estimated regression equation. It can be interpreted as the proportion of the variation of y that can be explained by the estimated regression equation. The adjusted multiple coefficient of determination is a similar measure of goodness of fit that adjusts for the number of independent variables and thus avoids overestimating the impact of adding more independent variables.

An F test and a t test were presented as ways to determine statistically whether the relationship among the variables is significant. The F test is used to determine whether there is a significant overall relationship between the dependent variable and the set of all independent variables. The t test is used to determine whether there is a significant relationship between the dependent variable and an individual independent variable given the other independent variables in the regression model. Correlation among the independent variables, known as multicollinearity, was discussed.

The chapter concluded with a section on how dummy variables can be used to incorporate qualitative data into multiple regression analysis.

GLOSSARY

Multiple regression analysis   Regression analysis involving two or more independent variables.

Multiple regression model   The equation that describes how the dependent variable y is related to the independent variables $x_1, x_2, \ldots, x_p$ and an error term ϵ.

Multiple regression equation   The equation that describes how the expected value or mean value of the dependent variable is related to the values of the independent variables; it is $E(y) = \beta_0 + \beta_1 x_1 + \beta_2 x_2 + \cdots + \beta_p x_p$.

Estimated multiple regression equation   The estimate of the multiple regression equation developed from sample data by using the least squares method; it is $\hat{y} = b_0 + b_1 x_1 + b_2 x_2 + \cdots + b_p x_p$.

Least squares method   The method used to develop the estimated regression equation. It minimizes the sum of squared residuals (the deviations between the observed values of the dependent variable, y_i, and the estimated values of the dependent variable, $\hat{y}_i$).

Multiple coefficient of determination   A measure of the goodness of fit of the estimated multiple regression equation. It can be interpreted as the proportion of the variability in the dependent variable that can be explained by the estimated regression equation.

Adjusted multiple coefficient of determination   A measure of the goodness of fit of the estimated multiple regression equation that adjusts for the number of independent variables in the model and thus avoids overestimating the impact of adding more independent variables.

Multicollinearity   The term used to describe the correlation among the independent variables.

Qualitative independent variable   An independent variable with qualitative data.

Dummy variable   A variable, coded as 0 or 1, used to model the effect of qualitative independent variables. A dummy variable is also called an indicator variable.

KEY FORMULAS

Multiple Regression Model

$$y = \beta_0 + \beta_1 x_1 + \beta_2 x_2 + \cdots + \beta_p x_p + \epsilon \tag{13.1}$$

Multiple Regression Equation

$$E(y) = \beta_0 + \beta_1 x_1 + \beta_2 x_2 + \cdots + \beta_p x_p \tag{13.2}$$

Estimated Multiple Regression Equation

$$\hat{y} = b_0 + b_1 x_1 + b_2 x_2 + \cdots + b_p x_p \tag{13.3}$$

Least Squares Criterion

$$\min \Sigma(y_i - \hat{y}_i)^2 \qquad (13.4)$$

Relationship Among SST, SSR, and SSE

$$\text{SST} = \text{SSR} + \text{SSE} \qquad (13.7)$$

Multiple Coefficient of Determination

$$R^2 = \frac{\text{SSR}}{\text{SST}} \qquad (13.8)$$

Adjusted Multiple Coefficient of Determination

$$R_a^2 = 1 - (1 - R^2)\frac{n - 1}{n - p - 1} \qquad (13.9)$$

Mean Square Due to Regression

$$\text{MSR} = \frac{\text{SSR}}{p} \qquad (13.12)$$

Mean Square Due to Error

$$\text{MSE} = \frac{\text{SSE}}{n - p - 1} \qquad (13.13)$$

F Test Statistic for Overall Significance

$$F = \frac{\text{MSR}}{\text{MSE}} \qquad (13.14)$$

t Test Statistic for Individual Significance

$$t = \frac{b_i}{s_{b_i}} \qquad (13.15)$$

SUPPLEMENTARY EXERCISES

39. The personnel director for Electronics Associates developed the following estimated regression equation relating an employee's score on a job satisfaction test to his or her length of service and wage rate.

$$\hat{y} = 14.4 - 8.69x_1 + 13.5x_2$$

where

x_1 = length of service (years)

x_2 = wage rate (dollars)

y = job satisfaction test score (higher scores
indicate greater job satisfaction)

a. Interpret the coefficients in this estimated regression equation.

b. Develop an estimate of the job satisfaction test score for an employee who has four years of service and makes $6.50 per hour.

40. The admissions officer for Clearwater College developed the following estimated regression equation relating the final college grade point average to the student's high-school grade point average and SAT mathematics score.

$$\hat{y} = -1.41 + .0235x_1 + .00486x_2$$

where

$$x_1 = \text{high-school grade point average}$$
$$x_2 = \text{SAT mathematics score}$$
$$y = \text{final college grade point average}$$

   a. Interpret the coefficients in this estimated regression equation.
   b. Estimate the final college grade point average for a student who has a high-school grade point average of 84 and a score of 540 on the SAT mathematics test.

41. In Exercise 40, the admissions officer for Clearwater College developed the following estimated regression equation relating final college GPA to the student's SAT mathematics score and high-school GPA.

$$\hat{y} = -1.41 + .0235x_1 + .00486x_2$$

where

$$x_1 = \text{high-school grade point average}$$
$$x_2 = \text{SAT mathematics score}$$
$$y = \text{final college grade point average}$$

A portion of the Minitab computer output follows.

```
The regression equation is
Y = -1.41 + .0235 X1 + .00486 X2

Predictor            Coef            Stdev          t-ratio
Constant           -1.4053          0.4848          _____
X1                 0.023467         0.008666        _____
X2                 _____           0.001077        _____

s = 0.1298     R-sq = _____     R-sq(adj) = _____

Analysis of Variance

SOURCE          DF              SS              MS              F
Regression     _____        1.76209          _____          _____
Error          _____        _____           _____
Total            9           1.88000
```

   a. Complete the missing entries in this output.
   b. Using $\alpha = .05$, test for overall significance.
   c. Did the estimated regression equation provide a good fit to the data? Explain.
   d. Use the t test and $\alpha = .05$ to test $H_0: \beta_1 = 0$ and $H_0: \beta_2 = 0$.

42. Recall that in Exercise 39 the personnel director for Electronics Associates developed the following estimated regression equation relating an employee's score on a job satisfaction test to length of service and wage rate.

$$\hat{y} = 14.4 - 8.69x_1 + 13.5x_2$$

where

$$x_1 = \text{length of service (years)}$$
$$x_2 = \text{wage rate (dollars)}$$
$$y = \text{job satisfaction test score (higher scores indicate greater job satisfaction)}$$

A portion of the Minitab computer output follows.

```
The regression equation is
Y = 14.4 - 8.69 X1 + 13.52 X2

Predictor           Coef          Stdev        t-ratio
Constant          14.448          8.191          1.76
X1                                1.555         _____
X2                13.517          2.085         _____

s = 3.773       R-sq = _____ %  R-sq(adj) = _____ %

Analysis of Variance

SOURCE            DF            SS            MS            F
Regression         2          _____        _____        _____
Error            _____       71.17         _____
Total              7          720.0
```

a. Complete the missing entries in this output.
b. Using $\alpha = .05$, test for overall significance.
c. Did the estimated regression equation provide a good fit to the data? Explain.
d. Use the t test and $\alpha = .05$ to test $H_0: \beta_1 = 0$ and $H_0: \beta_2 = 0$.

43. A sample of 30 computer hardware companies taken from the *Stock Investor Pro* provided the following data on the price per share, book value per share, and the return on equity per share for each (*Stock Investor Pro,* American Association of Individual Investors, August 21, 1997).

Company	Price per Share	Book Value per Share	Return on Equity per Share (%)
Amdahl Corporation	12.31	4.94	−49.7
Apple Computer, Inc.	21.75	9.46	−71.8
Auspex Systems, Inc.	11.00	4.95	17.2

Company	Price per Share	Book Value per Share	Return on Equity per Share (%)
Capital Associates	3.25	4.33	5.1
Compaq Computer Corp.	65.50	9.58	20.8
Data General Corporation	35.94	8.46	13.3
Dell Computer Corporation	82.06	2.33	74.5
Digi International	15.00	7.35	−11.9
Digital Equipment Corp.	43.00	22.40	−12.9
En Pointe Technologies	14.25	4.11	18.8
Equitrac Corporation	16.25	6.83	10.7
Franklin Electronic Pbls.	12.88	9.13	9.0
Gateway 2000, Inc.	39.13	6.07	28.8
Hewlett-Packard Company	61.50	14.14	18.7
IBM	101.38	20.12	29.9
Ingram Micro, Inc.	28.75	6.35	15.1
Maxwell Technologies, Inc.	30.50	3.78	11.8
MicroAge, Inc.	27.19	12.59	9.8
Micron Electronics, Inc.	16.31	3.64	28.3
Network Computing Devices	11.88	3.56	4.0
Pomeroy Computer Resources	33.00	10.03	16.5
Sequent Computer Systems	28.19	10.64	3.3
Silicon Graphics, Inc.	27.44	9.12	−4.3
Southern Electronics Corp.	15.13	6.15	16.1
Stratus Computer, Inc.	55.50	22.38	11.1
Sun Microsystems, Inc.	48.00	6.40	26.2
Tandem Computers, Inc.	34.24	9.49	8.7
Tech Data Corporation	38.94	10.25	14.3
Unisys Corporation	11.31	0.68	1.6
Vitech America, Inc.	14.63	3.48	24.3

a. Develop an estimated regression equation that can be used to predict the price per share given the book value per share. At the .05 level of significance, test for a significant relationship.

b. Did the estimated regression equation developed in part (a) provide a good fit to the data? Explain.

c. Develop an estimated regression equation that can be used to predict the price per share given the book value per share and the return on equity per share. At the .05 level of significance, test for overall significance.

44. Following are data on price, curb weight, horsepower, time to go from 0 to 60 miles per hour, and the speed at ¼ mile for 16 sports and GT cars (*1998 Road & Track Sports & GT Cars*).

Car	Price ($1000s)	Curb Weight (lbs.)	Horse- power	0 to 60 (seconds)	Speed at ¼ mile (mph)
Acura Integra Type R	25.035	2577	195	7.0	90.7
Acura NSX-T	93.758	3066	290	5.0	108.0
BMW Z3 2.8	40.900	2844	189	6.6	93.2

(continued)

Car	Price ($1000s)	Curb Weight (lbs.)	Horse-power	0 to 60 (seconds)	Speed at ¼ mile (mph)
Chevrolet Camaro Z28	24.865	3439	305	5.4	103.2
Chevrolet Corvette Convertible	50.144	3246	345	5.2	102.1
Dodge Viper RT/10	69.742	3319	450	4.4	116.2
Ford Mustang GT	23.200	3227	225	6.8	91.7
Honda Prelude Type SH	26.382	3042	195	7.7	89.7
Mercedes-Benz CLK320	44.988	3240	215	7.2	93.0
Mercedes-Benz SLK230	42.762	3025	185	6.6	92.3
Mitsubishi 3000GT VR-4	47.518	3737	320	5.7	99.0
Nissan 240SX SE	25.066	2862	155	9.1	84.6
Pontiac Firebird Trans Am	27.770	3455	305	5.4	103.2
Porsche Boxster	45.560	2822	201	6.1	93.2
Toyota Supra Turbo	40.989	3505	320	5.3	105.0
Volvo C70	41.120	3285	236	6.3	97.0

a. Develop an estimated regression equation with price, curb weight, horsepower, and time to go from 0 to 60 mph as four independent variables to predict the speed at ¼ mile.

b. Use the F test to determine the significance of the regression results. At a .05 level of significance, what is your conclusion?

c. Use the t test to determine the significance of each independent variable. At a .05 level of significance, what is your conclusion?

d. Delete any independent variable that is not significant and provide your recommended estimated regression equation.

45. Nielsen Media Research collects data showing which advertisers get the most exposure during prime time TV on ABC, CBS, NBC, Fox, UPN, and WB networks. Data showing the number of household exposures in millions and the number of times the ad was aired for the week of April 28–May 4, 1997, follow (*USA Today,* May 5, 1997).

Nielsen

Advertised Brand	Times Ad Aired	Household Exposures
Burger King	86	616.7
McDonald's	54	439.2
Sears	33	338.0
Wendy's	28	191.7
Ford Escort	20	174.6
Austin Powers movie	14	161.3
Nissan	16	161.1
Pizza Hut	16	147.7
Saturn	16	146.3
Father's Day movie	11	138.2

a. Develop a scatter diagram with number of times the ad is aired as the independent variable and household exposures as the dependent variable. Is there anything unusual about the pattern of the points in this scatter diagram? Explain.

b. Develop the estimated regression equation showing how the number of times an ad is aired is related to the number of household exposures. Is the relationship between the two variables significant? Use a .05 level of significance.

c. Consider the addition of the independent variable BigAds, where the value of BigAds is 1 if the number of times an ad is aired is greater than 30, and 0 otherwise. Develop an estimated regression equation that can be used to predict household expenditures given the number of times an ad is aired and the dummy variable BigAds.

d. Using $\alpha = .05$, is the dummy variable added in part (c) significant?

e. What role does the dummy variable play in modeling the relationship between the number of times an ad is aired and household exposures?

46. Today's marketplace offers a wide choice to buyers of sport utility vehicles (SUVs) and pickup trucks. An important factor to many buyers is the resale value of the vehicle. The following table shows the resale value (%) after two years and the suggested retail price for 10 SUVs, 10 small pickup trucks, and 10 large pickup trucks (*Kiplinger's New Cars & Trucks 2000 Buyer's Guide*).

CDfile
Trucks

Vehicle	Type of Vehicle	Suggested Retail Price ($)	Resale Value (%)
Chevrolet Blazer LS	sport utility	19,495	55
Ford Explorer Sport	sport utility	20,495	57
GMC Yukon XL 1500	sport utility	26,789	67
Honda CR-V	sport utility	18,965	65
Isuzu VehiCross	sport utility	30,186	62
Jeep Cherokee Limited	sport utility	25,745	57
Mercury Mountaineer Monterrey	sport utility	29,895	59
Nissan Pathfinder XE	sport utility	26,919	54
Toyota 4Runner	sport utility	22,418	55
Toyota RAV4	sport utility	17,148	55
Chevrolet S-10 Extended Cab	small pickup	18,847	46
Dodge Dakota Club Cab Sport	small pickup	16,870	53
Ford Ranger XLT Regular Cab	small pickup	18,510	48
Ford Ranger XLT Supercab	small pickup	20,225	55
GMC Sonoma Regular Cab	small pickup	16,938	44
Isuzu Hombre Spacecab	small pickup	18,820	41
Mazda B4000 SE Cab Plus	small pickup	23,050	51
Nissan Frontier XE Regular Cab	small pickup	12,110	51
Toyota Tacoma Xtracab	small pickup	18,228	49
Toyota Tacoma Xtracab V6	small pickup	19,318	50
Chevrolet K2500	full-size pickup	24,417	60
Chevrolet Silverado 2500 Ext	full-size pickup	24,140	64
Dodge Ram 1500	full-size pickup	17,460	54
Dodge Ram Quad Cab 2500	full-size pickup	32,770	63
Dodge Ram Regular Cab 2500	full-size pickup	23,140	59
Ford F150 XL	full-size pickup	22,875	58
Ford F-350 Super Duty Crew Cab XL	full-size pickup	34,295	64
GMC New Sierra 1500 Ext Cab	full-size pickup	27,089	68
Toyota Tundra Access Cab Limited	full-size pickup	25,605	53
Toyota Tundra Regular Cab	full-size pickup	15,835	58

a. Develop an estimated regression equation that can be used to predict the resale value given the suggested retail price. At the .05 level of significance, test for a significant relationship.

b. Did the estimated regression equation developed in part (a) provide a good fit to the data? Explain.

c. Develop an estimated regression equation that can be used to predict the resale value given the suggested retail price and the type of vehicle.

d. Use the F test to determine the significance of the regression results. At a .05 level of significance, what is your conclusion?

Case Problem 1   CONSUMER RESEARCH, INC.

Consumer Research, Inc., is an independent agency that conducts research on consumer attitudes and behaviors for a variety of firms. In one study, a client asked for an investigation of consumer characteristics that can be used to predict the amount charged by credit card users. Data were collected on annual income, household size, and annual credit card charges for a sample of 50 consumers.

CDfile

Consumer

Income ($1000s)	Household Size	Amount Charged ($)	Income ($1000s)	Household Size	Amount Charged ($)
54	3	4016	54	6	5573
30	2	3159	30	1	2583
32	4	5100	48	2	3866
50	5	4742	34	5	3586
31	2	1864	67	4	5037
55	2	4070	50	2	3605
37	1	2731	67	5	5345
40	2	3348	55	6	5370
66	4	4764	52	2	3890
51	3	4110	62	3	4705
25	3	4208	64	2	4157
48	4	4219	22	3	3579
27	1	2477	29	4	3890
33	2	2514	39	2	2972
65	3	4214	35	1	3121
63	4	4965	39	4	4183
42	6	4412	54	3	3730
21	2	2448	23	6	4127
44	1	2995	27	2	2921
37	5	4171	26	7	4603
62	6	5678	61	2	4273
21	3	3623	30	2	3067
55	7	5301	22	4	3074
42	2	3020	46	5	4820
41	7	4828	66	4	5149

Managerial Report

1. Use methods of descriptive statistics to summarize the data. Comment on the findings.
2. Develop estimated regression equations, first using annual income as the independent variable and then using household size as the independent variable. Which variable is the better predictor of annual credit card charges? Discuss your findings.
3. Develop an estimated regression equation with annual income and household size as the independent variables. Discuss your findings.

4. What is the predicted annual credit card charge for a three-person household with an annual income of $40,000?

5. Discuss the need for other independent variables that could be added to the model. What additional variables might be helpful?

Case Problem 2   NFL QUARTERBACK RATING

The National Football League (NFL) records weekly performance statistics for individuals and teams. These data can be obtained by accessing the homepage for the NFL (www.nfl.com). For many fans, one of the most interesting statistics is the rating used to evaluate the passing performance of quarterbacks. Four categories are used as a basis for compiling a passing rating:

1. Percentage of touchdown passes per attempt
2. Percentage of completions per attempt
3. Percentage of interceptions per attempt
4. Average yards gained per attempt

To illustrate how to compute the rating, consider the performance for Steve Young, the highest rated quarterback in the NFL in 1997. For the 1997 season, Steve Young attempted 356 passes, completed 241 passes for a total of 3029 yards, and had 19 touchdown passes and 6 interceptions. Five steps are needed to compute the passing rating for Steve Young.

Step 1. Compute the ratio of the number of touchdowns (19) to the number of passes attempted (356); the value obtained is 19/356 = 0.0534. Divide this result by 0.05 to obtain the value for the touchdown component of the rating; the value obtained is 0.0534/0.05 = 1.0680.

Step 2. Compute the ratio of the number of passes completed (241) to the number of passes attempted (356); the value obtained is 241/356 = 0.6770. Subtract 0.3 from this result and divide by 0.2 to obtain the value for the second component of the rating; the value obtained is (0.6770 − 0.3)/0.2 = 1.8850.

Step 3. Compute the ratio of the number of interceptions (6) to the number of passes attempted (356); the value obtained is 6/356 = 0.0169. Subtract this value from 0.095 and divide the result by 0.04 to obtain the value for the interceptions component of the rating; the value obtained is (0.095 − 0.0169)/0.04 = 1.9525.

Step 4. Compute the ratio of the number of passing yards (3029) to the number of passes attempted (356); the value obtained is 3029/356 = 8.5084. Subtract 3 from this result and divide by 4 to obtain the value for the yards component of the rating; the value obtained is (8.5084 − 3)/4 = 1.3771.

Step 5. Add the sum of steps 1 through 4, multiply by 100 and divide by 6. The sum of steps 1 through 4 is 1.0680 + 1.8850 + 1.9525 + 1.3771 = 6.2826. After multiplying by 100 and dividing by 6 we obtain 104.7100 or 104.7; this figure is the passing rating reported by the NFL for Steve Young.

CDfile
NFL

The passing data reported by the NFL for the 1997 season are available in the data set named NFL. The labels for the columns are defined as follows:

Att   Number of passes attempted.
Comp   Number of passes completed.
Comp%   Number of passes completed divided by the number of passes attempted times 100.
Yds   Number of yards obtained passing.
Yds/Att   Number of yards obtained passing divided by the number of passes attempted.

TD   Number of touchdowns obtained passing.

TD%   Number of touchdowns divided by the number of passes attempted times 100.

Long   Longest pass completed.

Int   Number of interceptions thrown.

Int%   Number of interceptions divided by the number of passes attempted.

Rating   The quarterback passing rating.

Managerial Report

1. Use methods of descriptive statistics to summarize the data. Comment on the findings.
2. Develop an estimated regression equation that can be used to predict Int% given the value of Comp%. Discuss your findings.
3. Develop an estimated regression equation that can be used to predict Rating. Discuss your findings and comment on how your estimated regression equation relates to the previous discussion of computing passing ratings.
4. If the NFL hired you to compute the passing ratings for next year, what approach would you use? Explain.

Case Problem 3   PREDICTING STUDENT PROFICIENCY TEST SCORES

In order to predict how a school district would have scored when accounting for poverty and other income measures, *The Cincinnati Enquirer* gathered data from the Ohio Department of Education's Education Management Services and the Ohio Department of Taxation (*The Cincinnati Enquirer,* November 30, 1997). First, the newspaper obtained passage-rate data on the math, reading, science, writing, and citizenship proficiency exams given to fourth-, sixth-, ninth-, and twelfth-graders in early 1996. By combining these data, they computed an overall percentage of students that passed the tests for each district.

The percentage of a school district's students on Aid for Dependent Children (ADC), the percentage who qualify for free or reduced-price lunches, and the district's median family income were also recorded. A portion of the data collected for the 608 school districts follows. The complete data are available in the data set named Enquirer.

Enquirer

Rank	School District	County	% Passed	% on ADC	% Free Lunch	Median Income ($)
1	Ottawa Hills Local	Lucas	93.85	0.11	0.00	48231
2	Wyoming City	Hamilton	93.08	2.95	4.59	42672
3	Oakwood City	Montgomery	92.92	0.20	0.38	42403
4	Madeira City	Hamilton	92.37	1.50	4.83	32889
5	Indian Hill Ex Vill	Hamilton	91.77	1.23	2.70	44135
6	Solon City	Cuyahoga	90.77	0.68	2.24	34993
7	Chagrin Falls Ex Vill	Cuyahoga	89.89	0.47	0.44	38921
8	Mariemont City	Hamilton	89.80	3.00	2.97	31823
9	Upper Arlington City	Franklin	89.77	0.24	0.92	38358
10	Granville Ex Vill	Licking	89.22	1.14	0.00	36235
:	:	:	:	:	:	:

The data have been ranked based on the values in the column labeled % Passed; these data are the overall percentage of students passing the tests. Data in the column labeled % on ADC are the percentage of each school district's students on ADC, and the data in the column labeled % Free Lunch are the percentage of students who qualify for free or reduced-price lunches. The column labeled Median Income shows each district's median family income. Also shown for each school district is the county in which the school district is located. Note that in some cases the value in the % Free Lunch column is 0, indicating that the district did not participate in the free lunch program.

Managerial Report

Use the methods presented in this and previous chapters to analyze this data set. Present a summary of your analysis, including key statistical results, conclusions, and recommendations, in a managerial report. Include any technical material you feel is appropriate in an appendix.

Case Problem 4   ALUMNI GIVING

Alumni donations are an important source of revenue for colleges and universities. If administrators could determine the factors that could lead to increases in the percentage of alumni who make a donation, they might be able to implement policies that could lead to increased revenues. Research shows that students who are more satisfied with their contact with teachers are more likely to graduate. As a result, one might suspect that smaller class sizes and lower student-faculty ratios might lead to a higher percentage of satisfied alumni, which in turn might lead to increases in the percentage of alumni who make a donation. In Table 13.7, the column labeled Graduation Rate is the percentage of students who initially enrolled at the university and graduated. The column labeled % of Classes Under 20 shows the percentage of classes offered with fewer than 20 students. The column labeled Student-Faculty Ratio is the number of students enrolled divided by the total number of faculty. Finally, the column labeled Alumni Giving Rate is the percentage of alumni who made a donation to the university.

Managerial Report

1. Use methods of descriptive statistics to summarize the data.
2. Develop an estimated regression equation that can be used to predict the alumni giving rate given the number of students who graduate. Discuss your findings.
3. Develop an estimated regression equation that could be used to predict the alumni giving rate using the data provided.
4. What conclusions and/or recommendations can you derive from your analysis?

TABLE 13.7   DATA FOR 48 NATIONAL UNIVERSITIES

CDfile
Alumni

Schools	State	Graduation Rate	% of Classes Under 20	Student-Faculty Ratio	Alumni Giving Rate
Boston College	MA	85	39	13	25
Brandeis University	MA	79	68	8	33
Brown University	RI	93	60	8	40
California Institute of Technology	CA	85	65	3	46
Carnegie Mellon University	PA	75	67	10	28
Case Western Reserve Univ.	OH	72	52	8	31
College of William and Mary	VA	89	45	12	27
Columbia University	NY	90	69	7	31
Cornell University	NY	91	72	13	35
Dartmouth College	NH	94	61	10	53
Duke University	NC	92	68	8	45
Emory University	GA	84	65	7	37
Georgetown University	PA	91	54	10	29
Harvard University	MA	97	73	8	46
Johns Hopkins University	MD	89	64	9	27
Lehigh University	PA	81	55	11	40
Massachusetts Inst. of Technology	MA	92	65	6	44
New York University	NY	72	63	13	13
Northwestern University	IL	90	66	8	30
Pennsylvania State Univ.	PA	80	32	19	21
Princeton University	NJ	95	68	5	67
Rice University	TX	92	62	8	40
Stanford University	CA	92	69	7	34
Tufts University	MA	87	67	9	29
Tulane University	LA	72	56	12	17
U. of California–Berkeley	CA	83	58	17	18
U. of California–Davis	CA	74	32	19	7
U. of California–Irvine	CA	74	42	20	9
U. of California–Los Angeles	CA	78	41	18	13
U. of California–San Diego	CA	80	48	19	8
U. of California–Santa Barbara	CA	70	45	20	12
U. of Chicago	IL	84	65	4	36
U. of Florida	FL	67	31	23	19
U. of Illinois–Urbana Champaign	IL	77	29	15	23
U. of Michigan–Ann Arbor	MI	83	51	15	13
U. of North Carolina–Chapel Hill	NC	82	40	16	26
U. of Notre Dame	IN	94	53	13	49
U. of Pennsylvania	PA	90	65	7	41
U. of Rochester	NY	76	63	10	23
U. of Southern California	CA	70	53	13	22
U. of Texas–Austin	TX	66	39	21	13
U. of Virginia	VA	92	44	13	28
U. of Washington	WA	70	37	12	12
U. of Wisconsin–Madison	WI	73	37	13	13
Vanderbilt University	TN	82	68	9	31
Wake Forest University	NC	82	59	11	38
Washington University–St. Louis	MO	86	73	7	33
Yale University	CT	94	77	7	50

APPENDIXES

Appendix A   References and Bibliography

General

Bowerman, B. L., and R. T. O'Connell, *Applied Statistics: Improving Business Processes,* Irwin, 1996.

Freedman, D., R. Pisani, and R. Purves, Statistics, 3rd ed., W. W. Norton, 1997.

Hogg, R. V., and A. T. Craig, *Introduction to Mathematical Statistics,* 5th ed., Prentice Hall, 1994.

Hogg, R. V., and E. A. Tanis, *Probability and Statistical Inference,* 6th ed., Prentice Hall, 2001.

Joiner, B. L., and B. F. Ryan, *Minitab Handbook,* Brooks/Cole, 2000.

Miller, I., and M. Miller, *John E. Freund's Mathematical Statistics,* Prentice Hall, 1998.

Roberts, H., *Data Analysis for Managers with Minitab,* Scientific Press, 1991.

Tanur, J. M., *Statistics: A Guide to the Unknown,* 4th ed., Brooks/Cole, 2002.

Tukey, J. W., *Exploratory Data Analysis,* Addison-Wesley, 1977.

Probability

Feller, W., *An Introduction to Probability Theory and Its Application,* Vol. I, 3rd ed., Wiley, 1968.

Hogg, R. V., and E. A. Tanis, *Probability and Statistical Inference,* 6th ed., Prentice Hall, 2001.

Ross, S. M., *Introduction to Probability Models,* 7th ed., Academic Press, 2000.

Wackerly, D. D., W. Mendenhall, and R. L. Scheaffer, *Mathematical Statistics with Applications,* 6th ed., PWS, 2002.

Regression Analysis

Belsley, D. A., *Conditioning Diagnostics: Collinearity and Weak Data in Regression,* Wiley, 1991.

Chatterjee, S., and B. Price, *Regression Analysis by Example,* 3rd ed., Wiley, 1999.

Draper, N. R., and H. Smith, *Applied Regression Analysis,* 3rd ed., Wiley, 1998.

Graybill, F. A., and H. Iyer, *Regression Analysis: Concepts and Applications,* Duxbury Press, 1994.

Kleinbaum, D. G., L. L. Kupper, and K. E. Muller, *Applied Regression Analysis and Other Multivariate Methods,* 3rd ed., Duxbury Press, 1997.

Kutner, M. H., C. J. Nachtschiem, W. Wasserman, and J. Neter, *Applied Linear Statistical Models,* 4th ed., Irwin, 1996.

Mendenhall, M., and T. Sincich, *A Second Course in Statistics: Regression Analysis,* 5th ed., Prentice Hall, 1996.

Myers, R. H., *Classical and Modern Regression with Applications,* 2d ed., PWS, 1990.

TABLE 1 STANDARD NORMAL DISTRIBUTION

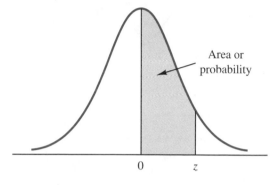

Area or probability

Entries in the table give the area under the curve between the mean and z standard deviations above the mean. For example, for $z = 1.25$ the area under the curve between the mean and z is .3944.

z	.00	.01	.02	.03	.04	.05	.06	.07	.08	.09
.0	.0000	.0040	.0080	.0120	.0160	.0199	.0239	.0279	.0319	.0359
.1	.0398	.0438	.0478	.0517	.0557	.0596	.0636	.0675	.0714	.0753
.2	.0793	.0832	.0871	.0910	.0948	.0987	.1026	.1064	.1103	.1141
.3	.1179	.1217	.1255	.1293	.1331	.1368	.1406	.1443	.1480	.1517
.4	.1554	.1591	.1628	.1664	.1700	.1736	.1772	.1808	.1844	.1879
.5	.1915	.1950	.1985	.2019	.2054	.2088	.2123	.2157	.2190	.2224
.6	.2257	.2291	.2324	.2357	.2389	.2422	.2454	.2486	.2517	.2549
.7	.2580	.2611	.2642	.2673	.2704	.2734	.2764	.2794	.2823	.2852
.8	.2881	.2910	.2939	.2967	.2995	.3023	.3051	.3078	.3106	.3133
.9	.3159	.3186	.3212	.3238	.3264	.3289	.3315	.3340	.3365	.3389
1.0	.3413	.3438	.3461	.3485	.3508	.3531	.3554	.3577	.3599	.3621
1.1	.3643	.3665	.3686	.3708	.3729	.3749	.3770	.3790	.3810	.3830
1.2	.3849	.3869	.3888	.3907	.3925	.3944	.3962	.3980	.3997	.4015
1.3	.4032	.4049	.4066	.4082	.4099	.4115	.4131	.4147	.4162	.4177
1.4	.4192	.4207	.4222	.4236	.4251	.4265	.4279	.4292	.4306	.4319
1.5	.4332	.4345	.4357	.4370	.4382	.4394	.4406	.4418	.4429	.4441
1.6	.4452	.4463	.4474	.4484	.4495	.4505	.4515	.4525	.4535	.4545
1.7	.4554	.4564	.4573	.4582	.4591	.4599	.4608	.4616	.4625	.4633
1.8	.4641	.4649	.4656	.4664	.4671	.4678	.4686	.4693	.4699	.4706
1.9	.4713	.4719	.4726	.4732	.4738	.4744	.4750	.4756	.4761	.4767
2.0	.4772	.4778	.4783	.4788	.4793	.4798	.4803	.4808	.4812	.4817
2.1	.4821	.4826	.4830	.4834	.4838	.4842	.4846	.4850	.4854	.4857
2.2	.4861	.4864	.4868	.4871	.4875	.4878	.4881	.4884	.4887	.4890
2.3	.4893	.4896	.4898	.4901	.4904	.4906	.4909	.4911	.4913	.4916
2.4	.4918	.4920	.4922	.4925	.4927	.4929	.4931	.4932	.4934	.4936
2.5	.4938	.4940	.4941	.4943	.4945	.4946	.4948	.4949	.4951	.4952
2.6	.4953	.4955	.4956	.4957	.4959	.4960	.4961	.4962	.4963	.4964
2.7	.4965	.4966	.4967	.4968	.4969	.4970	.4971	.4972	.4973	.4974
2.8	.4974	.4975	.4976	.4977	.4977	.4978	.4979	.4979	.4980	.4981
2.9	.4981	.4982	.4982	.4983	.4984	.4984	.4985	.4985	.4986	.4986
3.0	.4986	.4987	.4987	.4988	.4988	.4989	.4989	.4989	.4990	.4990

TABLE 2   *t* DISTRIBUTION

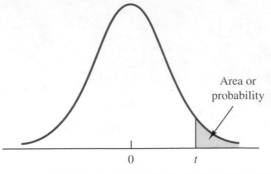

Area or probability

Entries in the table give *t* values for an area or probability in the upper tail of the *t* distribution. For example, with 10 degrees of freedom and a .05 area in the upper tail, $t_{.05} = 1.812$.

Degrees of Freedom	Area in Upper Tail				
	.10	.05	.025	.01	.005
1	3.078	6.314	12.706	31.821	63.657
2	1.886	2.920	4.303	6.965	9.925
3	1.638	2.353	3.182	4.541	5.841
4	1.533	2.132	2.776	3.747	4.604
5	1.476	2.015	2.571	3.365	4.032
6	1.440	1.943	2.447	3.143	3.707
7	1.415	1.895	2.365	2.998	3.499
8	1.397	1.860	2.306	2.896	3.355
9	1.383	1.833	2.262	2.821	3.250
10	1.372	1.812	2.228	2.764	3.169
11	1.363	1.796	2.201	2.718	3.106
12	1.356	1.782	2.179	2.681	3.055
13	1.350	1.771	2.160	2.650	3.012
14	1.345	1.761	2.145	2.624	2.977
15	1.341	1.753	2.131	2.602	2.947
16	1.337	1.746	2.120	2.583	2.921
17	1.333	1.740	2.110	2.567	2.898
18	1.330	1.734	2.101	2.552	2.878
19	1.328	1.729	2.093	2.539	2.861
20	1.325	1.725	2.086	2.528	2.845
21	1.323	1.721	2.080	2.518	2.831
22	1.321	1.717	2.074	2.508	2.819
23	1.319	1.714	2.069	2.500	2.807
24	1.318	1.711	2.064	2.492	2.797
25	1.316	1.708	2.060	2.485	2.787
26	1.315	1.706	2.056	2.479	2.779
27	1.314	1.703	2.052	2.473	2.771
28	1.313	1.701	2.048	2.467	2.763
29	1.311	1.699	2.045	2.462	2.756
30	1.310	1.697	2.042	2.457	2.750
40	1.303	1.684	2.021	2.423	2.704
60	1.296	1.671	2.000	2.390	2.660
120	1.289	1.658	1.980	2.358	2.617
∞	1.282	1.645	1.960	2.326	2.576

TABLE 3   CHI-SQUARE DISTRIBUTION

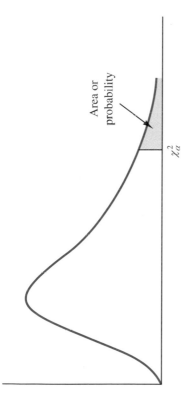

Area or probability

χ_α^2

Entries in the table give χ_α^2 values, where α is the area or probability in the upper tail of the chi-square distribution. For example, with 10 degrees of freedom and a .01 area in the upper tail, $\chi_{.01}^2 = 23.2093$.

Degrees of Freedom	Area in Upper Tail									
	.995	.99	.975	.95	.90	.10	.05	.025	.01	.005
1	$392{,}704 \times 10^{-10}$	$157{,}088 \times 10^{-9}$	$982{,}069 \times 10^{-9}$	$393{,}214 \times 10^{-8}$	.0157908	2.70554	3.84146	5.02389	6.63490	7.87944
2	.0100251	.0201007	.0506356	.102587	.210720	4.60517	5.99147	7.37776	9.21034	10.5966
3	.0717212	.114832	.215795	.351846	.584375	6.25139	7.81473	9.34840	11.3449	12.8381
4	.206990	.297110	.484419	.710721	1.063623	7.77944	9.48773	11.1433	13.2767	14.8602
5	.411740	.554300	.831211	1.145476	1.61031	9.23635	11.0705	12.8325	15.0863	16.7496
6	.675727	.872085	1.237347	1.63539	2.20413	10.6446	12.5916	14.4494	16.8119	18.5476
7	.989265	1.239043	1.68987	2.16735	2.83311	12.0170	14.0671	16.0128	18.4753	20.2777
8	1.344419	1.646482	2.17973	2.73264	3.48954	13.3616	15.5073	17.5346	20.0902	21.9550
9	1.734926	2.087912	2.70039	3.32511	4.16816	14.6837	16.9190	19.0228	21.6660	23.5893
10	2.15585	2.55821	3.24697	3.94030	4.86518	15.9871	18.3070	20.4831	23.2093	25.1882
11	2.60321	3.05347	3.81575	4.57481	5.57779	17.2750	19.6751	21.9200	24.7250	26.7569
12	3.07382	3.57056	4.40379	5.22603	6.30380	18.5494	21.0261	23.3367	26.2170	28.2995
13	3.56503	4.10691	5.00874	5.89186	7.04150	19.8119	22.3621	24.7356	27.6883	29.8194
14	4.07468	4.66043	5.62872	6.57063	7.78953	21.0642	23.6848	26.1190	29.1413	31.3193
15	4.60094	5.22935	6.26214	7.26094	8.54675	22.3072	24.9958	27.4884	30.5779	32.8013
16	5.14224	5.81221	6.90766	7.96164	9.31223	23.5418	26.2962	28.8454	31.9999	34.2672
17	5.69724	6.40776	7.56418	8.67176	10.0852	24.7690	27.5871	30.1910	33.4087	35.7185
18	6.26481	7.01491	8.23075	9.39046	10.8649	25.9894	28.8693	31.5264	34.8053	37.1564
19	6.84398	7.63273	8.90655	10.1170	11.6509	27.2036	30.1435	32.8523	36.1908	38.5822

TABLE 3 CHI-SQUARE DISTRIBUTION (*Continued*)

Degrees of Freedom	Area in Upper Tail									
	.995	.99	.975	.95	.90	.10	.05	.025	.01	.005
20	7.43386	8.26040	9.59083	10.8508	12.4426	28.4120	31.4104	34.1696	37.5662	39.9968
21	8.03366	8.89720	10.28293	11.5913	13.2396	29.6151	32.6705	35.4789	38.9321	41.4010
22	8.64272	9.54249	10.9823	12.3380	14.0415	30.8133	33.9244	36.7807	40.2894	42.7958
23	9.26042	10.19567	11.6885	13.0905	14.8479	32.0069	35.1725	38.0757	41.6384	44.1813
24	9.88623	10.8564	12.4011	13.8484	15.6587	33.1963	36.4151	39.3641	42.9798	45.5585
25	10.5197	11.5240	13.1197	14.6114	16.4734	34.3816	37.6525	40.6465	44.3141	46.9278
26	11.1603	12.1981	13.8439	15.3791	17.2919	35.5631	38.8852	41.9232	45.6417	48.2899
27	11.8076	12.8786	14.5733	16.1513	18.1138	36.7412	40.1133	43.1944	46.9630	49.6449
28	12.4613	13.5648	15.3079	16.9279	18.9392	37.9159	41.3372	44.4607	48.2782	50.9933
29	13.1211	14.2565	16.0471	17.7083	19.7677	39.0875	42.5569	45.7222	49.5879	52.3356
30	13.7867	14.9535	16.7908	18.4926	20.5992	40.2560	43.7729	46.9792	50.8922	53.6720
40	20.7065	22.1643	24.4331	26.5093	29.0505	51.8050	55.7585	59.3417	63.6907	66.7659
50	27.9907	29.7067	32.3574	34.7642	37.6886	63.1671	67.5048	71.4202	76.1539	79.4900
60	35.5346	37.4848	40.4817	43.1879	46.4589	74.3970	79.0819	83.2976	88.3794	91.9517
70	43.2752	45.4418	48.7576	51.7393	55.3290	85.5271	90.5312	95.0231	100.425	104.215
80	51.1720	53.5400	57.1532	60.3915	64.2778	96.5782	101.879	106.629	112.329	116.321
90	59.1963	61.7541	65.6466	69.1260	73.2912	107.565	113.145	118.136	124.116	128.299
100	67.3276	70.0648	74.2219	77.9295	82.3581	118.498	124.342	129.561	135.807	140.169

This table is reprinted by permission of Oxford University Press on behalf of The Biometrika Trustees from Table 8, Percentage Points of the χ^2 Distribution, by E. S. Pearson and H. O. Hartley, *Biometrika Tables for Statisticians*, Vol. 1, 3rd ed., 1966.

TABLE 4 F DISTRIBUTION

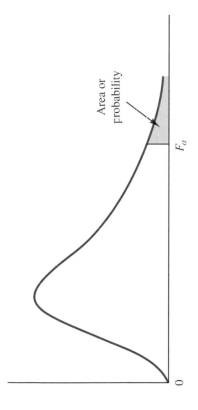

Area or probability

F_α

Entries in the table give F_α values, where α is the area or probability in the upper tail of the F distribution. For example, with 12 numerator degrees of freedom, 15 denominator degrees of freedom, and a .05 area in the upper tail, $F_{.05} = 2.48$.

Table of $F_{.05}$ Values

Denominator Degrees of Freedom	\multicolumn{19}{c}{Numerator Degrees of Freedom}

Denominator Degrees of Freedom	1	2	3	4	5	6	7	8	9	10	12	15	20	24	30	40	60	120	∞
1	161.4	199.5	215.7	224.6	230.2	234.0	236.8	238.9	240.5	241.9	243.9	245.9	248.0	249.1	250.1	251.1	252.2	253.3	254.3
2	18.51	19.00	19.16	19.25	19.30	19.33	19.35	19.37	19.38	19.40	19.41	19.43	19.45	19.45	19.46	19.47	19.48	19.49	19.50
3	10.13	9.55	9.28	9.12	9.01	8.94	8.89	8.85	8.81	8.79	8.74	8.70	8.66	8.64	8.62	8.59	8.57	8.55	8.53
4	7.71	6.94	6.59	6.39	6.26	6.16	6.09	6.04	6.00	5.96	5.91	5.86	5.80	5.77	5.75	5.72	5.69	5.66	5.53
5	6.61	5.79	5.41	5.19	5.05	4.95	4.88	4.82	4.77	4.74	4.68	4.62	4.56	4.53	4.50	4.46	4.43	4.40	4.36
6	5.99	5.14	4.76	4.53	4.39	4.28	4.21	4.15	4.10	4.06	4.00	3.94	3.87	3.84	3.81	3.77	3.74	3.70	3.67
7	5.59	4.74	4.35	4.12	3.97	3.87	3.79	3.73	3.68	3.64	3.57	3.51	3.44	3.41	3.38	3.34	3.30	3.27	3.23
8	5.32	4.46	4.07	3.84	3.69	3.58	3.50	3.44	3.39	3.35	3.28	3.22	3.15	3.12	3.08	3.04	3.01	2.97	2.93
9	5.12	4.26	3.86	3.63	3.48	3.37	3.29	3.23	3.18	3.14	3.07	3.01	2.94	2.90	2.86	2.83	2.79	2.75	2.71
10	4.96	4.10	3.71	3.48	3.33	3.22	3.14	3.07	3.02	2.98	2.91	2.85	2.77	2.74	2.70	2.66	2.62	2.58	2.54
11	4.84	3.98	3.59	3.36	3.20	3.09	3.01	2.95	2.90	2.85	2.79	2.72	2.65	2.61	2.57	2.53	2.49	2.45	2.40
12	4.75	3.89	3.49	3.26	3.11	3.00	2.91	2.85	2.80	2.75	2.69	2.62	2.54	2.51	2.47	2.43	2.38	2.34	2.30
13	4.67	3.81	3.41	3.18	3.03	2.92	2.83	2.77	2.71	2.67	2.60	2.53	2.46	2.42	2.38	2.34	2.30	2.25	2.21
14	4.60	3.74	3.34	3.11	2.96	2.85	2.76	2.70	2.65	2.60	2.53	2.46	2.39	2.35	2.31	2.27	2.22	2.18	2.13

TABLE 4 *F* DISTRIBUTION (*Continued*)

Table of $F_{.05}$ Values

Denominator Degrees of Freedom	Numerator Degrees of Freedom																		
	1	2	3	4	5	6	7	8	9	10	12	15	20	24	30	40	60	120	∞
15	4.54	3.68	3.29	3.06	2.90	2.79	2.71	2.64	2.59	2.54	2.48	2.40	2.33	2.29	2.25	2.20	2.16	2.11	2.07
16	4.49	3.63	3.24	3.01	2.85	2.74	2.66	2.59	2.54	2.49	2.42	2.35	2.28	2.24	2.19	2.15	2.11	2.06	2.01
17	4.45	3.59	3.20	2.96	2.81	2.70	2.61	2.55	2.49	2.45	2.38	2.31	2.23	2.19	2.15	2.10	2.06	2.01	1.96
18	4.41	3.55	3.16	2.93	2.77	2.66	2.58	2.51	2.46	2.41	2.34	2.27	2.19	2.15	2.11	2.06	2.02	1.97	1.92
19	4.38	3.52	3.13	2.90	2.74	2.63	2.54	2.48	2.42	2.38	2.31	2.23	2.16	2.11	2.07	2.03	1.98	1.93	1.88
20	4.35	3.49	3.10	2.87	2.71	2.60	2.51	2.45	2.39	2.35	2.28	2.20	2.12	2.08	2.04	1.99	1.95	1.90	1.84
21	4.32	3.47	3.07	2.84	2.68	2.57	2.49	2.42	2.37	2.32	2.25	2.18	2.10	2.05	2.01	1.96	1.92	1.87	1.81
22	4.30	3.44	3.05	2.82	2.66	2.55	2.46	2.40	2.34	2.30	2.23	2.15	2.07	2.03	1.98	1.94	1.89	1.84	1.78
23	4.28	3.42	3.03	2.80	2.64	2.53	2.44	2.37	2.32	2.27	2.20	2.13	2.05	2.01	1.96	1.91	1.86	1.81	1.76
24	4.26	3.40	3.01	2.78	2.62	2.51	2.42	2.36	2.30	2.25	2.18	2.11	2.03	1.98	1.94	1.89	1.84	1.79	1.73
25	4.24	3.39	2.99	2.76	2.60	2.49	2.40	2.34	2.28	2.24	2.16	2.09	2.01	1.96	1.92	1.87	1.82	1.77	1.71
26	4.23	3.37	2.98	2.74	2.59	2.47	2.39	2.32	2.27	2.22	2.15	2.07	1.99	1.95	1.90	1.85	1.80	1.75	1.69
27	4.21	3.35	2.96	2.73	2.57	2.46	2.37	2.31	2.25	2.20	2.13	2.06	1.97	1.93	1.88	1.84	1.79	1.73	1.67
28	4.20	3.34	2.95	2.71	2.56	2.45	2.36	2.29	2.24	2.19	2.12	2.04	1.96	1.91	1.87	1.82	1.77	1.71	1.65
29	4.18	3.33	2.93	2.70	2.55	2.43	2.35	2.28	2.22	2.18	2.10	2.03	1.94	1.90	1.85	1.81	1.75	1.70	1.64
30	4.17	3.32	2.92	2.69	2.53	2.42	2.33	2.27	2.21	2.16	2.09	2.01	1.93	1.89	1.84	1.79	1.74	1.68	1.62
40	4.08	3.23	2.84	2.61	2.45	2.34	2.25	2.18	2.12	2.08	2.00	1.92	1.84	1.79	1.74	1.69	1.64	1.58	1.51
60	4.00	3.15	2.76	2.53	2.37	2.25	2.17	2.10	2.04	1.99	1.92	1.84	1.75	1.70	1.65	1.59	1.53	1.47	1.39
120	3.92	3.07	2.68	2.45	2.29	2.17	2.09	2.02	1.96	1.91	1.83	1.75	1.66	1.61	1.55	1.50	1.43	1.35	1.25
∞	3.84	3.00	2.60	2.37	2.21	2.10	2.01	1.94	1.88	1.83	1.75	1.67	1.57	1.52	1.46	1.39	1.32	1.22	1.00

This table is reprinted by permission of Oxford University Press on behalf of The Biometrika Trustees from Table 18, Percentage Points of the *F* Distribution, by E. S. Pearson and H. O. Hartley, *Biometrika Tables for Statisticians*, Vol. 1, 3rd ed., 1966.

TABLE 4 *F* DISTRIBUTION (*Continued*)

Table of $F_{.025}$ Values

Denominator Degrees of Freedom	Numerator Degrees of Freedom																		
	1	2	3	4	5	6	7	8	9	10	12	15	20	24	30	40	60	120	∞
1	647.8	799.5	864.2	899.6	921.8	937.1	948.2	956.7	963.3	968.6	976.7	984.9	993.1	997.2	1,001	1,006	1,010	1,014	1,018
2	38.51	39.00	39.17	39.25	39.30	39.33	39.36	39.37	39.39	39.40	39.41	39.43	39.45	39.46	39.46	39.47	39.48	39.49	39.50
3	17.44	16.04	15.44	15.10	14.88	14.73	14.62	14.54	14.47	14.42	14.34	14.25	14.17	14.12	14.08	14.04	13.99	13.95	13.90
4	12.22	10.65	9.98	9.60	9.36	9.20	9.07	8.98	8.90	8.84	8.75	8.66	8.56	8.51	8.46	8.41	8.36	8.31	8.26
5	10.01	8.43	7.76	7.39	7.15	6.98	6.85	6.76	6.68	6.62	6.52	6.43	6.33	6.28	6.23	6.18	6.12	6.07	6.02
6	8.81	7.26	6.60	6.23	5.99	5.82	5.70	5.60	5.52	5.46	5.37	5.27	5.17	5.12	5.07	5.01	4.96	4.90	4.85
7	8.07	6.54	5.89	5.52	5.29	5.21	4.99	4.90	4.82	4.76	4.67	4.57	4.47	4.42	4.36	4.31	4.25	4.20	4.14
8	7.57	6.06	5.42	5.05	4.82	4.65	4.53	4.43	4.36	4.30	4.20	4.10	4.00	3.95	3.89	3.84	3.78	3.73	3.67
9	7.21	5.71	5.08	4.72	4.48	4.32	4.20	4.10	4.03	3.96	3.87	3.77	3.67	3.61	3.56	3.51	3.45	3.39	3.33
10	6.94	5.46	4.83	4.47	4.24	4.07	3.95	3.85	3.78	3.72	3.62	3.52	3.42	3.37	3.31	3.26	3.20	3.14	3.08
11	6.72	5.26	4.63	4.28	4.04	3.88	3.76	3.66	3.59	3.53	3.43	3.33	3.23	3.17	3.12	3.06	3.00	2.94	2.88
12	6.55	5.10	4.47	4.12	3.89	3.73	3.61	3.51	3.44	3.37	3.28	3.18	3.07	3.02	2.96	2.91	2.85	2.79	2.72
13	6.41	4.97	4.35	4.00	3.77	3.60	3.48	3.39	3.31	3.25	3.15	3.05	2.95	2.89	2.84	2.78	2.72	2.66	2.60
14	6.30	4.86	4.24	3.89	3.66	3.50	3.38	3.29	3.21	3.15	3.05	2.95	2.84	2.79	2.73	2.67	2.61	2.55	2.49
15	6.20	4.77	4.15	3.80	3.58	3.41	3.29	3.20	3.12	3.06	2.96	2.86	2.76	2.70	2.64	2.59	2.52	2.46	2.40
16	6.12	4.69	4.08	3.73	3.50	3.34	3.22	3.12	3.05	2.99	2.89	2.79	2.68	2.63	2.57	2.51	2.45	2.38	2.32
17	6.04	4.62	4.01	3.66	3.44	3.28	3.16	3.06	2.98	2.92	2.82	2.72	2.62	2.56	2.50	2.44	2.38	2.32	2.25
18	5.98	4.56	3.95	3.61	3.38	3.22	3.10	3.01	2.93	2.87	2.77	2.67	2.56	2.50	2.44	2.38	2.32	2.26	2.19
19	5.92	4.51	3.90	3.56	3.33	3.17	3.05	2.96	2.88	2.82	2.72	2.62	2.51	2.45	2.39	2.33	2.27	2.20	2.13
20	5.87	4.46	3.86	3.51	3.29	3.13	3.01	2.91	2.84	2.77	2.68	2.57	2.46	2.41	2.35	2.29	2.22	2.16	2.09
21	5.83	4.42	3.82	3.48	3.25	3.09	2.97	2.87	2.80	2.73	2.64	2.53	2.42	2.37	2.31	2.25	2.18	2.11	2.04
22	5.79	4.38	3.78	3.44	3.22	3.05	2.93	2.84	2.76	2.70	2.60	2.50	2.39	2.33	2.27	2.21	2.14	2.08	2.00
23	5.75	4.35	3.75	3.41	3.18	3.02	2.90	2.81	2.73	2.67	2.57	2.47	2.36	2.30	2.24	2.18	2.11	2.04	1.97
24	5.72	4.32	3.72	3.38	3.15	2.99	2.87	2.78	2.70	2.64	2.54	2.44	2.33	2.27	2.21	2.15	2.08	2.01	1.94
25	5.69	4.29	3.69	3.35	3.13	2.97	2.85	2.75	2.68	2.61	2.51	2.41	2.30	2.24	2.18	2.12	2.05	1.98	1.91
26	5.66	4.27	3.67	3.33	3.10	2.94	2.82	2.73	2.65	2.59	2.49	2.39	2.28	2.22	2.16	2.09	2.03	1.95	1.88
27	5.63	4.24	3.65	3.31	3.08	2.92	2.80	2.71	2.63	2.57	2.47	2.36	2.25	2.19	2.13	2.07	2.00	1.93	1.85
28	5.61	4.22	3.63	3.29	3.06	2.90	2.78	2.69	2.61	2.55	2.45	2.34	2.23	2.17	2.11	2.05	1.98	1.91	1.83
29	5.59	4.20	3.61	3.27	3.04	2.88	2.76	2.67	2.59	2.53	2.43	2.32	2.21	2.15	2.09	2.03	1.96	1.89	1.81
30	5.57	4.18	3.59	3.25	3.03	2.87	2.75	2.65	2.57	2.51	2.41	2.31	2.20	2.14	2.07	2.01	1.94	1.87	1.79
40	5.42	4.05	3.46	3.13	2.90	2.74	2.62	2.53	2.45	2.39	2.29	2.18	2.07	2.01	1.94	1.88	1.80	1.72	1.64
60	5.29	3.93	3.34	3.01	2.79	2.63	2.51	2.41	2.33	2.27	2.17	2.06	1.94	1.88	1.82	1.74	1.67	1.58	1.48
120	5.15	3.80	3.23	2.89	2.67	2.52	2.39	2.30	2.22	2.16	2.05	1.94	1.82	1.76	1.69	1.61	1.53	1.43	1.31
∞	5.02	3.69	3.12	2.79	2.57	2.41	2.29	2.19	2.11	2.05	1.94	1.83	1.71	1.64	1.57	1.48	1.39	1.27	1.00

TABLE 4 *F* DISTRIBUTION *(Continued)*

Table of $F_{.01}$ Values

Denominator Degrees of Freedom	\multicolumn{19}{c}{Numerator Degrees of Freedom}
	1	2	3	4	5	6	7	8	9	10	12	15	20	24	30	40	60	120	∞
1	4,052	4,999.5	5,403	5,625	5,764	5,859	5,928	5,982	6,022	6,056	6,106	6,157	6,209	6,235	6,261	6,287	6,313	6,339	6,366
2	98.50	99.00	99.17	99.25	99.30	99.33	99.36	99.37	99.39	99.40	99.42	99.43	99.45	99.46	99.47	99.47	99.48	99.49	99.50
3	34.12	30.82	29.46	28.71	28.24	27.91	27.67	27.49	27.35	27.23	27.05	26.87	26.69	26.60	26.50	26.41	26.32	26.22	26.13
4	21.20	18.00	16.69	15.98	15.52	15.21	14.98	14.80	14.66	14.55	14.37	14.20	14.02	13.93	13.84	13.75	13.65	13.56	13.46
5	16.26	13.27	12.06	11.39	10.97	10.67	10.46	10.29	10.16	10.05	9.89	9.72	9.55	9.47	9.38	9.29	9.20	9.11	9.06
6	13.75	10.92	9.78	9.15	8.75	8.47	8.26	8.10	7.98	7.87	7.72	7.56	7.40	7.31	7.23	7.14	7.06	6.97	6.88
7	12.25	9.55	8.45	7.85	7.46	7.19	6.99	6.84	6.72	6.62	6.47	6.31	6.16	6.07	5.99	5.91	5.82	5.74	5.65
8	11.26	8.65	7.59	7.01	6.63	6.37	6.18	6.03	5.91	5.81	5.67	5.52	5.36	5.28	5.20	5.12	5.03	4.95	4.86
9	10.56	8.02	6.99	6.42	6.06	5.80	5.61	5.47	5.35	5.26	5.11	4.96	4.81	4.73	4.65	4.57	4.48	4.40	4.31
10	10.04	7.56	6.55	5.99	5.64	5.39	5.20	5.06	4.94	4.85	4.71	4.56	4.41	4.33	4.25	4.17	4.08	4.00	3.91
11	9.65	7.21	6.22	5.67	5.32	5.07	4.89	4.74	4.63	4.54	4.40	4.25	4.10	4.02	3.94	3.86	3.78	3.69	3.60
12	9.33	6.93	5.95	5.41	5.06	4.82	4.64	4.50	4.39	4.30	4.16	4.01	3.86	3.78	3.70	3.62	3.54	3.45	3.36
13	9.07	6.70	5.74	5.21	4.86	4.62	4.44	4.30	4.19	4.10	3.96	3.82	3.66	3.59	3.51	3.43	3.34	3.25	3.17
14	8.86	6.51	5.56	5.04	4.69	4.46	4.28	4.14	4.03	3.94	3.80	3.66	3.51	3.43	3.35	3.27	3.18	3.09	3.00
15	8.68	6.36	5.42	4.89	4.56	4.32	4.14	4.00	3.89	3.80	3.67	3.52	3.37	3.29	3.21	3.13	3.05	2.96	2.87
16	8.53	6.23	5.29	4.77	4.44	4.20	4.03	3.89	3.78	3.69	3.55	3.41	3.26	3.18	3.10	3.02	2.93	2.84	2.75
17	8.40	6.11	5.18	4.67	4.34	4.10	3.93	3.79	3.68	3.59	3.46	3.31	3.16	3.08	3.00	2.92	2.83	2.75	2.65
18	8.29	6.01	5.09	4.58	4.25	4.01	3.84	3.71	3.60	3.51	3.37	3.23	3.08	3.00	2.92	2.84	2.75	2.66	2.57
19	8.18	5.93	5.01	4.50	4.17	3.94	3.77	3.63	3.52	3.43	3.30	3.15	3.00	2.92	2.84	2.76	2.67	2.58	2.49
20	8.10	5.85	4.94	4.43	4.10	3.87	3.70	3.56	3.46	3.37	3.23	3.09	2.94	2.86	2.78	2.69	2.61	2.52	2.42
21	8.02	5.78	4.87	4.37	4.04	3.81	3.64	3.51	3.40	3.31	3.17	3.03	2.88	2.80	2.72	2.64	2.55	2.46	2.36
22	7.95	5.72	4.82	4.31	3.99	3.76	3.59	3.45	3.35	3.26	3.12	2.98	2.83	2.75	2.67	2.58	2.50	2.40	2.31
23	7.88	5.66	4.76	4.26	3.94	3.71	3.54	3.41	3.30	3.21	3.07	2.93	2.78	2.70	2.62	2.54	2.45	2.35	2.26
24	7.82	5.61	4.72	4.22	3.90	3.67	3.50	3.36	3.26	3.17	3.03	2.89	2.74	2.66	2.58	2.49	2.40	2.31	2.21
25	7.77	5.57	4.68	4.18	3.85	3.63	3.46	3.32	3.22	3.13	2.99	2.85	2.70	2.62	2.54	2.45	2.36	2.27	2.17
26	7.72	5.53	4.64	4.14	3.82	3.59	3.42	3.29	3.18	3.09	2.96	2.81	2.66	2.58	2.50	2.42	2.33	2.23	2.13
27	7.68	5.49	4.60	4.11	3.78	3.56	3.39	3.26	3.15	3.06	2.93	2.78	2.63	2.55	2.47	2.38	2.29	2.20	2.10
28	7.64	5.45	4.57	4.07	3.75	3.53	3.36	3.23	3.12	3.03	2.90	2.75	2.60	2.52	2.44	2.35	2.26	2.17	2.06
29	7.60	5.42	4.54	4.04	3.73	3.50	3.33	3.20	3.09	3.00	2.87	2.73	2.57	2.49	2.41	2.33	2.23	2.14	2.03
30	7.56	5.39	4.51	4.02	3.70	3.47	3.30	3.17	3.07	2.98	2.84	2.70	2.55	2.47	2.39	2.30	2.21	2.11	2.01
40	7.31	5.18	4.31	3.83	3.51	3.29	3.12	2.99	2.89	2.80	2.66	2.52	2.37	2.29	2.20	2.11	2.02	1.92	1.80
60	7.08	4.98	4.13	3.65	3.34	3.12	2.95	2.82	2.72	2.63	2.50	2.35	2.20	2.12	2.03	1.94	1.84	1.73	1.60
120	6.85	4.79	3.95	3.48	3.17	2.96	2.79	2.66	2.56	2.47	2.34	2.19	2.03	1.95	1.86	1.76	1.66	1.53	1.38
∞	6.63	4.61	3.78	3.32	3.02	2.80	2.64	2.51	2.41	2.32	2.18	2.04	1.88	1.79	1.70	1.59	1.47	1.32	1.00

TABLE 5   BINOMIAL PROBABILITIES

Entries in the table give the probability of x successes in n trials of a binomial experiment, where p is the probability of a success on one trial. For example, with six trials and $p = .05$, the probability of two successes is .0305.

						p				
n	x	.01	.02	.03	.04	.05	.06	.07	.08	.09
2	0	.9801	.9604	.9409	.9216	.9025	.8836	.8649	.8464	.8281
	1	.0198	.0392	.0582	.0768	.0950	.1128	.1302	.1472	.1638
	2	.0001	.0004	.0009	.0016	.0025	.0036	.0049	.0064	.0081
3	0	.9703	.9412	.9127	.8847	.8574	.8306	.8044	.7787	.7536
	1	.0294	.0576	.0847	.1106	.1354	.1590	.1816	.2031	.2236
	2	.0003	.0012	.0026	.0046	.0071	.0102	.0137	.0177	.0221
	3	.0000	.0000	.0000	.0001	.0001	.0002	.0003	.0005	.0007
4	0	.9606	.9224	.8853	.8493	.8145	.7807	.7481	.7164	.6857
	1	.0388	.0753	.1095	.1416	.1715	.1993	.2252	.2492	.2713
	2	.0006	.0023	.0051	.0088	.0135	.0191	.0254	.0325	.0402
	3	.0000	.0000	.0001	.0002	.0005	.0008	.0013	.0019	.0027
	4	.0000	.0000	.0000	.0000	.0000	.0000	.0000	.0000	.0001
5	0	.9510	.9039	.8587	.8154	.7738	.7339	.6957	.6591	.6240
	1	.0480	.0922	.1328	.1699	.2036	.2342	.2618	.2866	.3086
	2	.0010	.0038	.0082	.0142	.0214	.0299	.0394	.0498	.0610
	3	.0000	.0001	.0003	.0006	.0011	.0019	.0030	.0043	.0060
	4	.0000	.0000	.0000	.0000	.0000	.0001	.0001	.0002	.0003
	5	.0000	.0000	.0000	.0000	.0000	.0000	.0000	.0000	.0000
6	0	.9415	.8858	.8330	.7828	.7351	.6899	.6470	.6064	.5679
	1	.0571	.1085	.1546	.1957	.2321	.2642	.2922	.3164	.3370
	2	.0014	.0055	.0120	.0204	.0305	.0422	.0550	.0688	.0833
	3	.0000	.0002	.0005	.0011	.0021	.0036	.0055	.0080	.0110
	4	.0000	.0000	.0000	.0000	.0001	.0002	.0003	.0005	.0008
	5	.0000	.0000	.0000	.0000	.0000	.0000	.0000	.0000	.0000
	6	.0000	.0000	.0000	.0000	.0000	.0000	.0000	.0000	.0000
7	0	.9321	.8681	.8080	.7514	.6983	.6485	.6017	.5578	.5168
	1	.0659	.1240	.1749	.2192	.2573	.2897	.3170	.3396	.3578
	2	.0020	.0076	.0162	.0274	.0406	.0555	.0716	.0886	.1061
	3	.0000	.0003	.0008	.0019	.0036	.0059	.0090	.0128	.0175
	4	.0000	.0000	.0000	.0001	.0002	.0004	.0007	.0011	.0017
	5	.0000	.0000	.0000	.0000	.0000	.0000	.0000	.0001	.0001
	6	.0000	.0000	.0000	.0000	.0000	.0000	.0000	.0000	.0000
	7	.0000	.0000	.0000	.0000	.0000	.0000	.0000	.0000	.0000
8	0	.9227	.8508	.7837	.7214	.6634	.6096	.5596	.5132	.4703
	1	.0746	.1389	.1939	.2405	.2793	.3113	.3370	.3570	.3721
	2	.0026	.0099	.0210	.0351	.0515	.0695	.0888	.1087	.1288
	3	.0001	.0004	.0013	.0029	.0054	.0089	.0134	.0189	.0255
	4	.0000	.0000	.0001	.0002	.0004	.0007	.0013	.0021	.0031
	5	.0000	.0000	.0000	.0000	.0000	.0000	.0001	.0001	.0002
	6	.0000	.0000	.0000	.0000	.0000	.0000	.0000	.0000	.0000
	7	.0000	.0000	.0000	.0000	.0000	.0000	.0000	.0000	.0000
	8	.0000	.0000	.0000	.0000	.0000	.0000	.0000	.0000	.0000

TABLE 5 BINOMIAL PROBABILITIES (*Continued*)

						p				
n	*x*	.01	.02	.03	.04	.05	.06	.07	.08	.09
9	0	.9135	.8337	.7602	.6925	.6302	.5730	.5204	.4722	.4279
	1	.0830	.1531	.2116	.2597	.2985	.3292	.3525	.3695	.3809
	2	.0034	.0125	.0262	.0433	.0629	.0840	.1061	.1285	.1507
	3	.0001	.0006	.0019	.0042	.0077	.0125	.0186	.0261	.0348
	4	.0000	.0000	.0001	.0003	.0006	.0012	.0021	.0034	.0052
	5	.0000	.0000	.0000	.0000	.0000	.0001	.0002	.0003	.0005
	6	.0000	.0000	.0000	.0000	.0000	.0000	.0000	.0000	.0000
	7	.0000	.0000	.0000	.0000	.0000	.0000	.0000	.0000	.0000
	8	.0000	.0000	.0000	.0000	.0000	.0000	.0000	.0000	.0000
	9	.0000	.0000	.0000	.0000	.0000	.0000	.0000	.0000	.0000
10	0	.9044	.8171	.7374	.6648	.5987	.5386	.4840	.4344	.3894
	1	.0914	.1667	.2281	.2770	.3151	.3438	.3643	.3777	.3851
	2	.0042	.0153	.0317	.0519	.0746	.0988	.1234	.1478	.1714
	3	.0001	.0008	.0026	.0058	.0105	.0168	.0248	.0343	.0452
	4	.0000	.0000	.0001	.0004	.0010	.0019	.0033	.0052	.0078
	5	.0000	.0000	.0000	.0000	.0001	.0001	.0003	.0005	.0009
	6	.0000	.0000	.0000	.0000	.0000	.0000	.0000	.0000	.0001
	7	.0000	.0000	.0000	.0000	.0000	.0000	.0000	.0000	.0000
	8	.0000	.0000	.0000	.0000	.0000	.0000	.0000	.0000	.0000
	9	.0000	.0000	.0000	.0000	.0000	.0000	.0000	.0000	.0000
	10	.0000	.0000	.0000	.0000	.0000	.0000	.0000	.0000	.0000
12	0	.8864	.7847	.6938	.6127	.5404	.4759	.4186	.3677	.3225
	1	.1074	.1922	.2575	.3064	.3413	.3645	.3781	.3837	.3827
	2	.0060	.0216	.0438	.0702	.0988	.1280	.1565	.1835	.2082
	3	.0002	.0015	.0045	.0098	.0173	.0272	.0393	.0532	.0686
	4	.0000	.0001	.0003	.0009	.0021	.0039	.0067	.0104	.0153
	5	.0000	.0000	.0000	.0001	.0002	.0004	.0008	.0014	.0024
	6	.0000	.0000	.0000	.0000	.0000	.0000	.0001	.0001	.0003
	7	.0000	.0000	.0000	.0000	.0000	.0000	.0000	.0000	.0000
	8	.0000	.0000	.0000	.0000	.0000	.0000	.0000	.0000	.0000
	9	.0000	.0000	.0000	.0000	.0000	.0000	.0000	.0000	.0000
	10	.0000	.0000	.0000	.0000	.0000	.0000	.0000	.0000	.0000
	11	.0000	.0000	.0000	.0000	.0000	.0000	.0000	.0000	.0000
	12	.0000	.0000	.0000	.0000	.0000	.0000	.0000	.0000	.0000
15	0	.8601	.7386	.6333	.5421	.4633	.3953	.3367	.2863	.2430
	1	.1303	.2261	.2938	.3388	.3658	.3785	.3801	.3734	.3605
	2	.0092	.0323	.0636	.0988	.1348	.1691	.2003	.2273	.2496
	3	.0004	.0029	.0085	.0178	.0307	.0468	.0653	.0857	.1070
	4	.0000	.0002	.0008	.0022	.0049	.0090	.0148	.0223	.0317
	5	.0000	.0000	.0001	.0002	.0006	.0013	.0024	.0043	.0069
	6	.0000	.0000	.0000	.0000	.0000	.0001	.0003	.0006	.0011
	7	.0000	.0000	.0000	.0000	.0000	.0000	.0000	.0001	.0001
	8	.0000	.0000	.0000	.0000	.0000	.0000	.0000	.0000	.0000
	9	.0000	.0000	.0000	.0000	.0000	.0000	.0000	.0000	.0000
	10	.0000	.0000	.0000	.0000	.0000	.0000	.0000	.0000	.0000
	11	.0000	.0000	.0000	.0000	.0000	.0000	.0000	.0000	.0000
	12	.0000	.0000	.0000	.0000	.0000	.0000	.0000	.0000	.0000
	13	.0000	.0000	.0000	.0000	.0000	.0000	.0000	.0000	.0000
	14	.0000	.0000	.0000	.0000	.0000	.0000	.0000	.0000	.0000
	15	.0000	.0000	.0000	.0000	.0000	.0000	.0000	.0000	.0000

TABLE 5   BINOMIAL PROBABILITIES (*Continued*)

						p				
n	*x*	.01	.02	.03	.04	.05	.06	.07	.08	.09
18	0	.8345	.6951	.5780	.4796	.3972	.3283	.2708	.2229	.1831
	1	.1517	.2554	.3217	.3597	.3763	.3772	.3669	.3489	.3260
	2	.0130	.0443	.0846	.1274	.1683	.2047	.2348	.2579	.2741
	3	.0007	.0048	.0140	.0283	.0473	.0697	.0942	.1196	.1446
	4	.0000	.0004	.0016	.0044	.0093	.0167	.0266	.0390	.0536
	5	.0000	.0000	.0001	.0005	.0014	.0030	.0056	.0095	.0148
	6	.0000	.0000	.0000	.0000	.0002	.0004	.0009	.0018	.0032
	7	.0000	.0000	.0000	.0000	.0000	.0000	.0001	.0003	.0005
	8	.0000	.0000	.0000	.0000	.0000	.0000	.0000	.0000	.0001
	9	.0000	.0000	.0000	.0000	.0000	.0000	.0000	.0000	.0000
	10	.0000	.0000	.0000	.0000	.0000	.0000	.0000	.0000	.0000
	11	.0000	.0000	.0000	.0000	.0000	.0000	.0000	.0000	.0000
	12	.0000	.0000	.0000	.0000	.0000	.0000	.0000	.0000	.0000
	13	.0000	.0000	.0000	.0000	.0000	.0000	.0000	.0000	.0000
	14	.0000	.0000	.0000	.0000	.0000	.0000	.0000	.0000	.0000
	15	.0000	.0000	.0000	.0000	.0000	.0000	.0000	.0000	.0000
	16	.0000	.0000	.0000	.0000	.0000	.0000	.0000	.0000	.0000
	17	.0000	.0000	.0000	.0000	.0000	.0000	.0000	.0000	.0000
	18	.0000	.0000	.0000	.0000	.0000	.0000	.0000	.0000	.0000
20	0	.8179	.6676	.5438	.4420	.3585	.2901	.2342	.1887	.1516
	1	.1652	.2725	.3364	.3683	.3774	.3703	.3526	.3282	.3000
	2	.0159	.0528	.0988	.1458	.1887	.2246	.2521	.2711	.2818
	3	.0010	.0065	.0183	.0364	.0596	.0860	.1139	.1414	.1672
	4	.0000	.0006	.0024	.0065	.0133	.0233	.0364	.0523	.0703
	5	.0000	.0000	.0002	.0009	.0022	.0048	.0088	.0145	.0222
	6	.0000	.0000	.0000	.0001	.0003	.0008	.0017	.0032	.0055
	7	.0000	.0000	.0000	.0000	.0000	.0001	.0002	.0005	.0011
	8	.0000	.0000	.0000	.0000	.0000	.0000	.0000	.0001	.0002
	9	.0000	.0000	.0000	.0000	.0000	.0000	.0000	.0000	.0000
	10	.0000	.0000	.0000	.0000	.0000	.0000	.0000	.0000	.0000
	11	.0000	.0000	.0000	.0000	.0000	.0000	.0000	.0000	.0000
	12	.0000	.0000	.0000	.0000	.0000	.0000	.0000	.0000	.0000
	13	.0000	.0000	.0000	.0000	.0000	.0000	.0000	.0000	.0000
	14	.0000	.0000	.0000	.0000	.0000	.0000	.0000	.0000	.0000
	15	.0000	.0000	.0000	.0000	.0000	.0000	.0000	.0000	.0000
	16	.0000	.0000	.0000	.0000	.0000	.0000	.0000	.0000	.0000
	17	.0000	.0000	.0000	.0000	.0000	.0000	.0000	.0000	.0000
	18	.0000	.0000	.0000	.0000	.0000	.0000	.0000	.0000	.0000
	19	.0000	.0000	.0000	.0000	.0000	.0000	.0000	.0000	.0000
	20	.0000	.0000	.0000	.0000	.0000	.0000	.0000	.0000	.0000

TABLE 5   BINOMIAL PROBABILITIES (*Continued*)

n	x	.10	.15	.20	.25	.30	.35	.40	.45	.50
2	0	.8100	.7225	.6400	.5625	.4900	.4225	.3600	.3025	.2500
	1	.1800	.2550	.3200	.3750	.4200	.4550	.4800	.4950	.5000
	2	.0100	.0225	.0400	.0625	.0900	.1225	.1600	.2025	.2500
3	0	.7290	.6141	.5120	.4219	.3430	.2746	.2160	.1664	.1250
	1	.2430	.3251	.3840	.4219	.4410	.4436	.4320	.4084	.3750
	2	.0270	.0574	.0960	.1406	.1890	.2389	.2880	.3341	.3750
	3	.0010	.0034	.0080	.0156	.0270	.0429	.0640	.0911	.1250
4	0	.6561	.5220	.4096	.3164	.2401	.1785	.1296	.0915	.0625
	1	.2916	.3685	.4096	.4219	.4116	.3845	.3456	.2995	.2500
	2	.0486	.0975	.1536	.2109	.2646	.3105	.3456	.3675	.3750
	3	.0036	.0115	.0256	.0469	.0756	.1115	.1536	.2005	.2500
	4	.0001	.0005	.0016	.0039	.0081	.0150	.0256	.0410	.0625
5	0	.5905	.4437	.3277	.2373	.1681	.1160	.0778	.0503	.0312
	1	.3280	.3915	.4096	.3955	.3602	.3124	.2592	.2059	.1562
	2	.0729	.1382	.2048	.2637	.3087	.3364	.3456	.3369	.3125
	3	.0081	.0244	.0512	.0879	.1323	.1811	.2304	.2757	.3125
	4	.0004	.0022	.0064	.0146	.0284	.0488	.0768	.1128	.1562
	5	.0000	.0001	.0003	.0010	.0024	.0053	.0102	.0185	.0312
6	0	.5314	.3771	.2621	.1780	.1176	.0754	.0467	.0277	.0156
	1	.3543	.3993	.3932	.3560	.3025	.2437	.1866	.1359	.0938
	2	.0984	.1762	.2458	.2966	.3241	.3280	.3110	.2780	.2344
	3	.0146	.0415	.0819	.1318	.1852	.2355	.2765	.3032	.3125
	4	.0012	.0055	.0154	.0330	.0595	.0951	.1382	.1861	.2344
	5	.0001	.0004	.0015	.0044	.0102	.0205	.0369	.0609	.0938
	6	.0000	.0000	.0001	.0002	.0007	.0018	.0041	.0083	.0156
7	0	.4783	.3206	.2097	.1335	.0824	.0490	.0280	.0152	.0078
	1	.3720	.3960	.3670	.3115	.2471	.1848	.1306	.0872	.0547
	2	.1240	.2097	.2753	.3115	.3177	.2985	.2613	.2140	.1641
	3	.0230	.0617	.1147	.1730	.2269	.2679	.2903	.2918	.2734
	4	.0026	.0109	.0287	.0577	.0972	.1442	.1935	.2388	.2734
	5	.0002	.0012	.0043	.0115	.0250	.0466	.0774	.1172	.1641
	6	.0000	.0001	.0004	.0013	.0036	.0084	.0172	.0320	.0547
	7	.0000	.0000	.0000	.0001	.0002	.0006	.0016	.0037	.0078
8	0	.4305	.2725	.1678	.1001	.0576	.0319	.0168	.0084	.0039
	1	.3826	.3847	.3355	.2670	.1977	.1373	.0896	.0548	.0312
	2	.1488	.2376	.2936	.3115	.2965	.2587	.2090	.1569	.1094
	3	.0331	.0839	.1468	.2076	.2541	.2786	.2787	.2568	.2188
	4	.0046	.0185	.0459	.0865	.1361	.1875	.2322	.2627	.2734
	5	.0004	.0026	.0092	.0231	.0467	.0808	.1239	.1719	.2188
	6	.0000	.0002	.0011	.0038	.0100	.0217	.0413	.0703	.1094
	7	.0000	.0000	.0001	.0004	.0012	.0033	.0079	.0164	.0312
	8	.0000	.0000	.0000	.0000	.0001	.0002	.0007	.0017	.0039

TABLE 5 BINOMIAL PROBABILITIES (*Continued*)

						p				
n	*x*	.10	.15	.20	.25	.30	.35	.40	.45	.50
9	0	.3874	.2316	.1342	.0751	.0404	.0207	.0101	.0046	.0020
	1	.3874	.3679	.3020	.2253	.1556	.1004	.0605	.0339	.0176
	2	.1722	.2597	.3020	.3003	.2668	.2162	.1612	.1110	.0703
	3	.0446	.1069	.1762	.2336	.2668	.2716	.2508	.2119	.1641
	4	.0074	.0283	.0661	.1168	.1715	.2194	.2508	.2600	.2461
	5	.0008	.0050	.0165	.0389	.0735	.1181	.1672	.2128	.2461
	6	.0001	.0006	.0028	.0087	.0210	.0424	.0743	.1160	.1641
	7	.0000	.0000	.0003	.0012	.0039	.0098	.0212	.0407	.0703
	8	.0000	.0000	.0000	.0001	.0004	.0013	.0035	.0083	.0176
	9	.0000	.0000	.0000	.0000	.0000	.0001	.0003	.0008	.0020
10	0	.3487	.1969	.1074	.0563	.0282	.0135	.0060	.0025	.0010
	1	.3874	.3474	.2684	.1877	.1211	.0725	.0403	.0207	.0098
	2	.1937	.2759	.3020	.2816	.2335	.1757	.1209	.0763	.0439
	3	.0574	.1298	.2013	.2503	.2668	.2522	.2150	.1665	.1172
	4	.0112	.0401	.0881	.1460	.2001	.2377	.2508	.2384	.2051
	5	.0015	.0085	.0264	.0584	.1029	.1536	.2007	.2340	.2461
	6	.0001	.0012	.0055	.0162	.0368	.0689	.1115	.1596	.2051
	7	.0000	.0001	.0008	.0031	.0090	.0212	.0425	.0746	.1172
	8	.0000	.0000	.0001	.0004	.0014	.0043	.0106	.0229	.0439
	9	.0000	.0000	.0000	.0000	.0001	.0005	.0016	.0042	.0098
	10	.0000	.0000	.0000	.0000	.0000	.0000	.0001	.0003	.0010
12	0	.2824	.1422	.0687	.0317	.0138	.0057	.0022	.0008	.0002
	1	.3766	.3012	.2062	.1267	.0712	.0368	.0174	.0075	.0029
	2	.2301	.2924	.2835	.2323	.1678	.1088	.0639	.0339	.0161
	3	.0853	.1720	.2362	.2581	.2397	.1954	.1419	.0923	.0537
	4	.0213	.0683	.1329	.1936	.2311	.2367	.2128	.1700	.1208
	5	.0038	.0193	.0532	.1032	.1585	.2039	.2270	.2225	.1934
	6	.0005	.0040	.0155	.0401	.0792	.1281	.1766	.2124	.2256
	7	.0000	.0006	.0033	.0115	.0291	.0591	.1009	.1489	.1934
	8	.0000	.0001	.0005	.0024	.0078	.0199	.0420	.0762	.1208
	9	.0000	.0000	.0001	.0004	.0015	.0048	.0125	.0277	.0537
	10	.0000	.0000	.0000	.0000	.0002	.0008	.0025	.0068	.0161
	11	.0000	.0000	.0000	.0000	.0000	.0001	.0003	.0010	.0029
	12	.0000	.0000	.0000	.0000	.0000	.0000	.0000	.0001	.0002
15	0	.2059	.0874	.0352	.0134	.0047	.0016	.0005	.0001	.0000
	1	.3432	.2312	.1319	.0668	.0305	.0126	.0047	.0016	.0005
	2	.2669	.2856	.2309	.1559	.0916	.0476	.0219	.0090	.0032
	3	.1285	.2184	.2501	.2252	.1700	.1110	.0634	.0318	.0139
	4	.0428	.1156	.1876	.2252	.2186	.1792	.1268	.0780	.0417
	5	.0105	.0449	.1032	.1651	.2061	.2123	.1859	.1404	.0916
	6	.0019	.0132	.0430	.0917	.1472	.1906	.2066	.1914	.1527
	7	.0003	.0030	.0138	.0393	.0811	.1319	.1771	.2013	.1964
	8	.0000	.0005	.0035	.0131	.0348	.0710	.1181	.1647	.1964
	9	.0000	.0001	.0007	.0034	.0016	.0298	.0612	.1048	.1527
	10	.0000	.0000	.0001	.0007	.0030	.0096	.0245	.0515	.0916
	11	.0000	.0000	.0000	.0001	.0006	.0024	.0074	.0191	.0417
	12	.0000	.0000	.0000	.0000	.0001	.0004	.0016	.0052	.0139
	13	.0000	.0000	.0000	.0000	.0000	.0001	.0003	.0010	.0032
	14	.0000	.0000	.0000	.0000	.0000	.0000	.0000	.0001	.0005
	15	.0000	.0000	.0000	.0000	.0000	.0000	.0000	.0000	.0000

TABLE 5   BINOMIAL PROBABILITIES (*Continued*)

						p				
n	x	.10	.15	.20	.25	.30	.35	.40	.45	.50
18	0	.1501	.0536	.0180	.0056	.0016	.0004	.0001	.0000	.0000
	1	.3002	.1704	.0811	.0338	.0126	.0042	.0012	.0003	.0001
	2	.2835	.2556	.1723	.0958	.0458	.0190	.0069	.0022	.0006
	3	.1680	.2406	.2297	.1704	.1046	.0547	.0246	.0095	.0031
	4	.0700	.1592	.2153	.2130	.1681	.1104	.0614	.0291	.0117
	5	.0218	.0787	.1507	.1988	.2017	.1664	.1146	.0666	.0327
	6	.0052	.0301	.0816	.1436	.1873	.1941	.1655	.1181	.0708
	7	.0010	.0091	.0350	.0820	.1376	.1792	.1892	.1657	.1214
	8	.0002	.0022	.0120	.0376	.0811	.1327	.1734	.1864	.1669
	9	.0000	.0004	.0033	.0139	.0386	.0794	.1284	.1694	.1855
	10	.0000	.0001	.0008	.0042	.0149	.0385	.0771	.1248	.1669
	11	.0000	.0000	.0001	.0010	.0046	.0151	.0374	.0742	.1214
	12	.0000	.0000	.0000	.0002	.0012	.0047	.0145	.0354	.0708
	13	.0000	.0000	.0000	.0000	.0002	.0012	.0045	.0134	.0327
	14	.0000	.0000	.0000	.0000	.0000	.0002	.0011	.0039	.0117
	15	.0000	.0000	.0000	.0000	.0000	.0000	.0002	.0009	.0031
	16	.0000	.0000	.0000	.0000	.0000	.0000	.0000	.0001	.0006
	17	.0000	.0000	.0000	.0000	.0000	.0000	.0000	.0000	.0001
	18	.0000	.0000	.0000	.0000	.0000	.0000	.0000	.0000	.0000
20	0	.1216	.0388	.0115	.0032	.0008	.0002	.0000	.0000	.0000
	1	.2702	.1368	.0576	.0211	.0068	.0020	.0005	.0001	.0000
	2	.2852	.2293	.1369	.0669	.0278	.0100	.0031	.0008	.0002
	3	.1901	.2428	.2054	.1339	.0716	.0323	.0123	.0040	.0011
	4	.0898	.1821	.2182	.1897	.1304	.0738	.0350	.0139	.0046
	5	.0319	.1028	.1746	.2023	.1789	.1272	.0746	.0365	.0148
	6	.0089	.0454	.1091	.1686	.1916	.1712	.1244	.0746	.0370
	7	.0020	.0160	.0545	.1124	.1643	.1844	.1659	.1221	.0739
	8	.0004	.0046	.0222	.0609	.1144	.1614	.1797	.1623	.1201
	9	.0001	.0011	.0074	.0271	.0654	.1158	.1597	.1771	.1602
	10	.0000	.0002	.0020	.0099	.0308	.0686	.1171	.1593	.1762
	11	.0000	.0000	.0005	.0030	.0120	.0336	.0710	.1185	.1602
	12	.0000	.0000	.0001	.0008	.0039	.0136	.0355	.0727	.1201
	13	.0000	.0000	.0000	.0002	.0010	.0045	.0146	.0366	.0739
	14	.0000	.0000	.0000	.0000	.0002	.0012	.0049	.0150	.0370
	15	.0000	.0000	.0000	.0000	.0000	.0003	.0013	.0049	.0148
	16	.0000	.0000	.0000	.0000	.0000	.0000	.0003	.0013	.0046
	17	.0000	.0000	.0000	.0000	.0000	.0000	.0000	.0002	.0011
	18	.0000	.0000	.0000	.0000	.0000	.0000	.0000	.0000	.0002
	19	.0000	.0000	.0000	.0000	.0000	.0000	.0000	.0000	.0000
	20	.0000	.0000	.0000	.0000	.0000	.0000	.0000	.0000	.0000

TABLE 6   VALUES OF $e^{-\mu}$

μ	$e^{-\mu}$	μ	$e^{-\mu}$	μ	$e^{-\mu}$
.00	1.0000				
.05	.9512	2.05	.1287	4.05	.0174
.10	.9048	2.10	.1225	4.10	.0166
.15	.8607	2.15	.1165	4.15	.0158
.20	.8187	2.20	.1108	4.20	.0150
.25	.7788	2.25	.1054	4.25	.0143
.30	.7408	2.30	.1003	4.30	.0136
.35	.7047	2.35	.0954	4.35	.0129
.40	.6703	2.40	.0907	4.40	.0123
.45	.6376	2.45	.0863	4.45	.0117
.50	.6065	2.50	.0821	4.50	.0111
.55	.5769	2.55	.0781	4.55	.0106
.60	.5488	2.60	.0743	4.60	.0101
.65	.5220	2.65	.0707	4.65	.0096
.70	.4966	2.70	.0672	4.70	.0091
.75	.4724	2.75	.0639	4.75	.0087
.80	.4493	2.80	.0608	4.80	.0082
.85	.4274	2.85	.0578	4.85	.0078
.90	.4066	2.90	.0550	4.90	.0074
.95	.3867	2.95	.0523	4.95	.0071
1.00	.3679	3.00	.0498	5.00	.0067
1.05	.3499	3.05	.0474	6.00	.0025
1.10	.3329	3.10	.0450	7.00	.0009
1.15	.3166	3.15	.0429	8.00	.000335
1.20	.3012	3.20	.0408	9.00	.000123
				10.00	.000045
1.25	.2865	3.25	.0388		
1.30	.2725	3.30	.0369		
1.35	.2592	3.35	.0351		
1.40	.2466	3.40	.0334		
1.45	.2346	3.45	.0317		
1.50	.2231	3.50	.0302		
1.55	.2122	3.55	.0287		
1.60	.2019	3.60	.0273		
1.65	.1920	3.65	.0260		
1.70	.1827	3.70	.0247		
1.75	.1738	3.75	.0235		
1.80	.1653	3.80	.0224		
1.85	.1572	3.85	.0213		
1.90	.1496	3.90	.0202		
1.95	.1423	3.95	.0193		
2.00	.1353	4.00	.0183		

TABLE 7 POISSON PROBABILITIES

Entries in the table give the probability of x occurrences for a Poisson process with a mean μ. For example, when $\mu = 2.5$, the probability of four occurrences is .1336.

					μ					
x	0.1	0.2	0.3	0.4	0.5	0.6	0.7	0.8	0.9	1.0
0	.9048	.8187	.7408	.6703	.6065	.5488	.4966	.4493	.4066	.3679
1	.0905	.1637	.2222	.2681	.3033	.3293	.3476	.3595	.3659	.3679
2	.0045	.0164	.0333	.0536	.0758	.0988	.1217	.1438	.1647	.1839
3	.0002	.0011	.0033	.0072	.0126	.0198	.0284	.0383	.0494	.0613
4	.0000	.0001	.0002	.0007	.0016	.0030	.0050	.0077	.0111	.0153
5	.0000	.0000	.0000	.0001	.0002	.0004	.0007	.0012	.0020	.0031
6	.0000	.0000	.0000	.0000	.0000	.0000	.0001	.0002	.0003	.0005
7	.0000	.0000	.0000	.0000	.0000	.0000	.0000	.0000	.0000	.0001

					μ					
x	1.1	1.2	1.3	1.4	1.5	1.6	1.7	1.8	1.9	2.0
0	.3329	.3012	.2725	.2466	.2231	.2019	.1827	.1653	.1496	.1353
1	.3662	.3614	.3543	.3452	.3347	.3230	.3106	.2975	.2842	.2707
2	.2014	.2169	.2303	.2417	.2510	.2584	.2640	.2678	.2700	.2707
3	.0738	.0867	.0998	.1128	.1255	.1378	.1496	.1607	.1710	.1804
4	.0203	.0260	.0324	.0395	.0471	.0551	.0636	.0723	.0812	.0902
5	.0045	.0062	.0084	.0111	.0141	.0176	.0216	.0260	.0309	.0361
6	.0008	.0012	.0018	.0026	.0035	.0047	.0061	.0078	.0098	.0120
7	.0001	.0002	.0003	.0005	.0008	.0011	.0015	.0020	.0027	.0034
8	.0000	.0000	.0001	.0001	.0001	.0002	.0003	.0005	.0006	.0009
9	.0000	.0000	.0000	.0000	.0000	.0000	.0001	.0001	.0001	.0002

					μ					
x	2.1	2.2	2.3	2.4	2.5	2.6	2.7	2.8	2.9	3.0
0	.1225	.1108	.1003	.0907	.0821	.0743	.0672	.0608	.0550	.0498
1	.2572	.2438	.2306	.2177	.2052	.1931	.1815	.1703	.1596	.1494
2	.2700	.2681	.2652	.2613	.2565	.2510	.2450	.2384	.2314	.2240
3	.1890	.1966	.2033	.2090	.2138	.2176	.2205	.2225	.2237	.2240
4	.0992	.1082	.1169	.1254	.1336	.1414	.1488	.1557	.1622	.1680
5	.0417	.0476	.0538	.0602	.0668	.0735	.0804	.0872	.0940	.1008
6	.0146	.0174	.0206	.0241	.0278	.0319	.0362	.0407	.0455	.0504
7	.0044	.0055	.0068	.0083	.0099	.0118	.0139	.0163	.0188	.0216
8	.0011	.0015	.0019	.0025	.0031	.0038	.0047	.0057	.0068	.0081
9	.0003	.0004	.0005	.0007	.0009	.0011	.0014	.0018	.0022	.0027
10	.0001	.0001	.0001	.0002	.0002	.0003	.0004	.0005	.0006	.0008
11	.0000	.0000	.0000	.0000	.0000	.0001	.0001	.0001	.0002	.0002
12	.0000	.0000	.0000	.0000	.0000	.0000	.0000	.0000	.0000	.0001

TABLE 7 POISSON PROBABILITIES (*Continued*)

					μ					
x	3.1	3.2	3.3	3.4	3.5	3.6	3.7	3.8	3.9	4.0
0	.0450	.0408	.0369	.0344	.0302	.0273	.0247	.0224	.0202	.0183
1	.1397	.1304	.1217	.1135	.1057	.0984	.0915	.0850	.0789	.0733
2	.2165	.2087	.2008	.1929	.1850	.1771	.1692	.1615	.1539	.1465
3	.2237	.2226	.2209	.2186	.2158	.2125	.2087	.2046	.2001	.1954
4	.1734	.1781	.1823	.1858	.1888	.1912	.1931	.1944	.1951	.1954
5	.1075	.1140	.1203	.1264	.1322	.1377	.1429	.1477	.1522	.1563
6	.0555	.0608	.0662	.0716	.0771	.0826	.0881	.0936	.0989	.1042
7	.0246	.0278	.0312	.0348	.0385	.0425	.0466	.0508	.0551	.0595
8	.0095	.0111	.0129	.0148	.0169	.0191	.0215	.0241	.0269	.0298
9	.0033	.0040	.0047	.0056	.0066	.0076	.0089	.0102	.0116	.0132
10	.0010	.0013	.0016	.0019	.0023	.0028	.0033	.0039	.0045	.0053
11	.0003	.0004	.0005	.0006	.0007	.0009	.0011	.0013	.0016	.0019
12	.0001	.0001	.0001	.0002	.0002	.0003	.0003	.0004	.0005	.0006
13	.0000	.0000	.0000	.0000	.0001	.0001	.0001	.0001	.0002	.0002
14	.0000	.0000	.0000	.0000	.0000	.0000	.0000	.0000	.0000	.0001

					μ					
x	4.1	4.2	4.3	4.4	4.5	4.6	4.7	4.8	4.9	5.0
0	.0166	.0150	.0136	.0123	.0111	.0101	.0091	.0082	.0074	.0067
1	.0679	.0630	.0583	.0540	.0500	.0462	.0427	.0395	.0365	.0337
2	.1393	.1323	.1254	.1188	.1125	.1063	.1005	.0948	.0894	.0842
3	.1904	.1852	.1798	.1743	.1687	.1631	.1574	.1517	.1460	.1404
4	.1951	.1944	.1933	.1917	.1898	.1875	.1849	.1820	.1789	.1755
5	.1600	.1633	.1662	.1687	.1708	.1725	.1738	.1747	.1753	.1755
6	.1093	.1143	.1191	.1237	.1281	.1323	.1362	.1398	.1432	.1462
7	.0640	.0686	.0732	.0778	.0824	.0869	.0914	.0959	.1002	.1044
8	.0328	.0360	.0393	.0428	.0463	.0500	.0537	.0575	.0614	.0653
9	.0150	.0168	.0188	.0209	.0232	.0255	.0280	.0307	.0334	.0363
10	.0061	.0071	.0081	.0092	.0104	.0118	.0132	.0147	.0164	.0181
11	.0023	.0027	.0032	.0037	.0043	.0049	.0056	.0064	.0073	.0082
12	.0008	.0009	.0011	.0014	.0016	.0019	.0022	.0026	.0030	.0034
13	.0002	.0003	.0004	.0005	.0006	.0007	.0008	.0009	.0011	.0013
14	.0001	.0001	.0001	.0001	.0002	.0002	.0003	.0003	.0004	.0005
15	.0000	.0000	.0000	.0000	.0001	.0001	.0001	.0001	.0001	.0002

					μ					
x	5.1	5.2	5.3	5.4	5.5	5.6	5.7	5.8	5.9	6.0
0	.0061	.0055	.0050	.0045	.0041	.0037	.0033	.0030	.0027	.0025
1	.0311	.0287	.0265	.0244	.0225	.0207	.0191	.0176	.0162	.0149
2	.0793	.0746	.0701	.0659	.0618	.0580	.0544	.0509	.0477	.0446
3	.1348	.1293	.1239	.1185	.1133	.1082	.1033	.0985	.0938	.0892
4	.1719	.1681	.1641	.1600	.1558	.1515	.1472	.1428	.1383	.1339

TABLE 7 POISSON PROBABILITIES (*Continued*)

					μ					
x	5.1	5.2	5.3	5.4	5.5	5.6	5.7	5.8	5.9	6.0
5	.1753	.1748	.1740	.1728	.1714	.1697	.1678	.1656	.1632	.1606
6	.1490	.1515	.1537	.1555	.1571	.1587	.1594	.1601	.1605	.1606
7	.1086	.1125	.1163	.1200	.1234	.1267	.1298	.1326	.1353	.1377
8	.0692	.0731	.0771	.0810	.0849	.0887	.0925	.0962	.0998	.1033
9	.0392	.0423	.0454	.0486	.0519	.0552	.0586	.0620	.0654	.0688
10	.0200	.0220	.0241	.0262	.0285	.0309	.0334	.0359	.0386	.0413
11	.0093	.0104	.0116	.0129	.0143	.0157	.0173	.0190	.0207	.0225
12	.0039	.0045	.0051	.0058	.0065	.0073	.0082	.0092	.0102	.0113
13	.0015	.0018	.0021	.0024	.0028	.0032	.0036	.0041	.0046	.0052
14	.0006	.0007	.0008	.0009	.0011	.0013	.0015	.0017	.0019	.0022
15	.0002	.0002	.0003	.0003	.0004	.0005	.0006	.0007	.0008	.0009
16	.0001	.0001	.0001	.0001	.0001	.0002	.0002	.0002	.0003	.0003
17	.0000	.0000	.0000	.0000	.0000	.0001	.0001	.0001	.0001	.0001

					μ					
x	6.1	6.2	6.3	6.4	6.5	6.6	6.7	6.8	6.9	7.0
0	.0022	.0020	.0018	.0017	.0015	.0014	.0012	.0011	.0010	.0009
1	.0137	.0126	.0116	.0106	.0098	.0090	.0082	.0076	.0070	.0064
2	.0417	.0390	.0364	.0340	.0318	.0296	.0276	.0258	.0240	.0223
3	.0848	.0806	.0765	.0726	.0688	.0652	.0617	.0584	.0552	.0521
4	.1294	.1249	.1205	.1162	.1118	.1076	.1034	.0992	.0952	.0912
5	.1579	.1549	.1519	.1487	.1454	.1420	.1385	.1349	.1314	.1277
6	.1605	.1601	.1595	.1586	.1575	.1562	.1546	.1529	.1511	.1490
7	.1399	.1418	.1435	.1450	.1462	.1472	.1480	.1486	.1489	.1490
8	.1066	.1099	.1130	.1160	.1188	.1215	.1240	.1263	.1284	.1304
9	.0723	.0757	.0791	.0825	.0858	.0891	.0923	.0954	.0985	.1014
10	.0441	.0469	.0498	.0528	.0558	.0588	.0618	.0649	.0679	.0710
11	.0245	.0265	.0285	.0307	.0330	.0353	.0377	.0401	.0426	.0452
12	.0124	.0137	.0150	.0164	.0179	.0194	.0210	.0227	.0245	.0264
13	.0058	.0065	.0073	.0081	.0089	.0098	.0108	.0119	.0130	.0142
14	.0025	.0029	.0033	.0037	.0041	.0046	.0052	.0058	.0064	.0071
15	.0010	.0012	.0014	.0016	.0018	.0020	.0023	.0026	.0029	.0033
16	.0004	.0005	.0005	.0006	.0007	.0008	.0010	.0011	.0013	.0014
17	.0001	.0002	.0002	.0002	.0003	.0003	.0004	.0004	.0005	.0006
18	.0000	.0001	.0001	.0001	.0001	.0001	.0001	.0002	.0002	.0002
19	.0000	.0000	.0000	.0000	.0000	.0000	.0000	.0001	.0001	.0001

					μ					
x	7.1	7.2	7.3	7.4	7.5	7.6	7.7	7.8	7.9	8.0
0	.0008	.0007	.0007	.0006	.0006	.0005	.0005	.0004	.0004	.0003
1	.0059	.0054	.0049	.0045	.0041	.0038	.0035	.0032	.0029	.0027
2	.0208	.0194	.0180	.0167	.0156	.0145	.0134	.0125	.0116	.0107
3	.0492	.0464	.0438	.0413	.0389	.0366	.0345	.0324	.0305	.0286
4	.0874	.0836	.0799	.0764	.0729	.0696	.0663	.0632	.0602	.0573

TABLE 7 POISSON PROBABILITIES (*Continued*)

					μ					
x	7.1	7.2	7.3	7.4	7.5	7.6	7.7	7.8	7.9	8.0
5	.1241	.1204	.1167	.1130	.1094	.1057	.1021	.0986	.0951	.0916
6	.1468	.1445	.1420	.1394	.1367	.1339	.1311	.1282	.1252	.1221
7	.1489	.1486	.1481	.1474	.1465	.1454	.1442	.1428	.1413	.1396
8	.1321	.1337	.1351	.1363	.1373	.1382	.1388	.1392	.1395	.1396
9	.1042	.1070	.1096	.1121	.1144	.1167	.1187	.1207	.1224	.1241
10	.0740	.0770	.0800	.0829	.0858	.0887	.0914	.0941	.0967	.0993
11	.0478	.0504	.0531	.0558	.0585	.0613	.0640	.0667	.0695	.0722
12	.0283	.0303	.0323	.0344	.0366	.0388	.0411	.0434	.0457	.0481
13	.0154	.0168	.0181	.0196	.0211	.0227	.0243	.0260	.0278	.0296
14	.0078	.0086	.0095	.0104	.0113	.0123	.0134	.0145	.0157	.0169
15	.0037	.0041	.0046	.0051	.0057	.0062	.0069	.0075	.0083	.0090
16	.0016	.0019	.0021	.0024	.0026	.0030	.0033	.0037	.0041	.0045
17	.0007	.0008	.0009	.0010	.0012	.0013	.0015	.0017	.0019	.0021
18	.0003	.0003	.0004	.0004	.0005	.0006	.0006	.0007	.0008	.0009
19	.0001	.0001	.0001	.0002	.0002	.0002	.0003	.0003	.0003	.0004
20	.0000	.0000	.0001	.0001	.0001	.0001	.0001	.0001	.0001	.0002
21	.0000	.0000	.0000	.0000	.0000	.0000	.0000	.0000	.0001	.0001

					μ					
x	8.1	8.2	8.3	8.4	8.5	8.6	8.7	8.8	8.9	9.0
0	.0003	.0003	.0002	.0002	.0002	.0002	.0002	.0002	.0001	.0001
1	.0025	.0023	.0021	.0019	.0017	.0016	.0014	.0013	.0012	.0011
2	.0100	.0092	.0086	.0079	.0074	.0068	.0063	.0058	.0054	.0050
3	.0269	.0252	.0237	.0222	.0208	.0195	.0183	.0171	.0160	.0150
4	.0544	.0517	.0491	.0466	.0443	.0420	.0398	.0377	.0357	.0337
5	.0882	.0849	.0816	.0784	.0752	.0722	.0692	.0663	.0635	.0607
6	.1191	.1160	.1128	.1097	.1066	.1034	.1003	.0972	.0941	.0911
7	.1378	.1358	.1338	.1317	.1294	.1271	.1247	.1222	.1197	.1171
8	.1395	.1392	.1388	.1382	.1375	.1366	.1356	.1344	.1332	.1318
9	.1256	.1269	.1280	.1290	.1299	.1306	.1311	.1315	.1317	.1318
10	.1017	.1040	.1063	.1084	.1104	.1123	.1140	.1157	.1172	.1186
11	.0749	.0776	.0802	.0828	.0853	.0878	.0902	.0925	.0948	.0970
12	.0505	.0530	.0555	.0579	.0604	.0629	.0654	.0679	.0703	.0728
13	.0315	.0334	.0354	.0374	.0395	.0416	.0438	.0459	.0481	.0504
14	.0182	.0196	.0210	.0225	.0240	.0256	.0272	.0289	.0306	.0324
15	.0098	.0107	.0116	.0126	.0136	.0147	.0158	.0169	.0182	.1094
16	.0050	.0055	.0060	.0066	.0072	.0079	.0086	.0093	.0101	.0109
17	.0024	.0026	.0029	.0033	.0036	.0040	.0044	.0048	.0053	.0058
18	.0011	.0012	.0014	.0015	.0017	.0019	.0021	.0024	.0026	.0029
19	.0005	.0005	.0006	.0007	.0008	.0009	.0010	.0011	.0012	.0014
20	.0002	.0002	.0002	.0003	.0003	.0004	.0004	.0005	.0005	.0006
21	.0001	.0001	.0001	.0001	.0001	.0002	.0002	.0002	.0002	.0003
22	.0000	.0000	.0000	.0000	.0001	.0001	.0001	.0001	.0001	.0001

TABLE 7 POISSON PROBABILITIES (*Continued*)

	μ									
x	9.1	9.2	9.3	9.4	9.5	9.6	9.7	9.8	9.9	10
0	.0001	.0001	.0001	.0001	.0001	.0001	.0001	.0001	.0001	.0000
1	.0010	.0009	.0009	.0008	.0007	.0007	.0006	.0005	.0005	.0005
2	.0046	.0043	.0040	.0037	.0034	.0031	.0029	.0027	.0025	.0023
3	.0140	.0131	.0123	.0115	.0107	.0100	.0093	.0087	.0081	.0076
4	.0319	.0302	.0285	.0269	.0254	.0240	.0226	.0213	.0201	.0189
5	.0581	.0555	.0530	.0506	.0483	.0460	.0439	.0418	.0398	.0378
6	.0881	.0851	.0822	.0793	.0764	.0736	.0709	.0682	.0656	.0631
7	.1145	.1118	.1091	.1064	.1037	.1010	.0982	.0955	.0928	.0901
8	.1302	.1286	.1269	.1251	.1232	.1212	.1191	.1170	.1148	.1126
9	.1317	.1315	.1311	.1306	.1300	.1293	.1284	.1274	.1263	.1251
10	.1198	.1210	.1219	.1228	.1235	.1241	.1245	.1249	.1250	.1251
11	.0991	.1012	.1031	.1049	.1067	.1083	.1098	.1112	.1125	.1137
12	.0752	.0776	.0799	.0822	.0844	.0866	.0888	.0908	.0928	.0948
13	.0526	.0549	.0572	.0594	.0617	.0640	.0662	.0685	.0707	.0729
14	.0342	.0361	.0380	.0399	.0419	.0439	.0459	.0479	.0500	.0521
15	.0208	.0221	.0235	.0250	.0265	.0281	.0297	.0313	.0330	.0347
16	.0118	.0127	.0137	.0147	.0157	.0168	.0180	.0192	.0204	.0217
17	.0063	.0069	.0075	.0081	.0088	.0095	.0103	.0111	.0119	.0128
18	.0032	.0035	.0039	.0042	.0046	.0051	.0055	.0060	.0065	.0071
19	.0015	.0017	.0019	.0021	.0023	.0026	.0028	.0031	.0034	.0037
20	.0007	.0008	.0009	.0010	.0011	.0012	.0014	.0015	.0017	.0019
21	.0003	.0003	.0004	.0004	.0005	.0006	.0006	.0007	.0008	.0009
22	.0001	.0001	.0002	.0002	.0002	.0002	.0003	.0003	.0004	.0004
23	.0000	.0001	.0001	.0001	.0001	.0001	.0001	.0001	.0002	.0002
24	.0000	.0000	.0000	.0000	.0000	.0000	.0000	.0001	.0001	.0001

	μ									
x	11	12	13	14	15	16	17	18	19	20
0	.0000	.0000	.0000	.0000	.0000	.0000	.0000	.0000	.0000	.0000
1	.0002	.0001	.0000	.0000	.0000	.0000	.0000	.0000	.0000	.0000
2	.0010	.0004	.0002	.0001	.0000	.0000	.0000	.0000	.0000	.0000
3	.0037	.0018	.0008	.0004	.0002	.0001	.0000	.0000	.0000	.0000
4	.0102	.0053	.0027	.0013	.0006	.0003	.0001	.0001	.0000	.0000
5	.0224	.0127	.0070	.0037	.0019	.0010	.0005	.0002	.0001	.0001
6	.0411	.0255	.0152	.0087	.0048	.0026	.0014	.0007	.0004	.0002
7	.0646	.0437	.0281	.0174	.0104	.0060	.0034	.0018	.0010	.0005
8	.0888	.0655	.0457	.0304	.0194	.0120	.0072	.0042	.0024	.0013
9	.1085	.0874	.0661	.0473	.0324	.0213	.0135	.0083	.0050	.0029
10	.1194	.1048	.0859	.0663	.0486	.0341	.0230	.0150	.0095	.0058
11	.1194	.1144	.1015	.0844	.0663	.0496	.0355	.0245	.0164	.0106
12	.1094	.1144	.1099	.0984	.0829	.0661	.0504	.0368	.0259	.0176
13	.0926	.1056	.1099	.1060	.0956	.0814	.0658	.0509	.0378	.0271
14	.0728	.0905	.1021	.1060	.1024	.0930	.0800	.0655	.0514	.0387

TABLE 7   POISSON PROBABILITIES (*Continued*)

					μ					
x	11	12	13	14	15	16	17	18	19	20
15	.0534	.0724	.0885	.0989	.1024	.0992	.0906	.0786	.0650	.0516
16	.0367	.0543	.0719	.0866	.0960	.0992	.0963	.0884	.0772	.0646
17	.0237	.0383	.0550	.0713	.0847	.0934	.0963	.0936	.0863	.0760
18	.0145	.0256	.0397	.0554	.0706	.0830	.0909	.0936	.0911	.0844
19	.0084	.0161	.0272	.0409	.0557	.0699	.0814	.0887	.0911	.0888
20	.0046	.0097	.0177	.0286	.0418	.0559	.0692	.0798	.0866	.0888
21	.0024	.0055	.0109	.0191	.0299	.0426	.0560	.0684	.0783	.0846
22	.0012	.0030	.0065	.0121	.0204	.0310	.0433	.0560	.0676	.0769
23	.0006	.0016	.0037	.0074	.0133	.0216	.0320	.0438	.0559	.0669
24	.0003	.0008	.0020	.0043	.0083	.0144	.0226	.0328	.0442	.0557
25	.0001	.0004	.0010	.0024	.0050	.0092	.0154	.0237	.0336	.0446
26	.0000	.0002	.0005	.0013	.0029	.0057	.0101	.0164	.0246	.0343
27	.0000	.0001	.0002	.0007	.0016	.0034	.0063	.0109	.0173	.0254
28	.0000	.0000	.0001	.0003	.0009	.0019	.0038	.0070	.0117	.0181
29	.0000	.0000	.0001	.0002	.0004	.0011	.0023	.0044	.0077	.0125
30	.0000	.0000	.0000	.0001	.0002	.0006	.0013	.0026	.0049	.0083
31	.0000	.0000	.0000	.0000	.0001	.0003	.0007	.0015	.0030	.0054
32	.0000	.0000	.0000	.0000	.0001	.0001	.0004	.0009	.0018	.0034
33	.0000	.0000	.0000	.0000	.0000	.0001	.0002	.0005	.0010	.0020
34	.0000	.0000	.0000	.0000	.0000	.0000	.0001	.0002	.0006	.0012
35	.0000	.0000	.0000	.0000	.0000	.0000	.0000	.0001	.0003	.0007
36	.0000	.0000	.0000	.0000	.0000	.0000	.0000	.0001	.0002	.0004
37	.0000	.0000	.0000	.0000	.0000	.0000	.0000	.0000	.0001	.0002
38	.0000	.0000	.0000	.0000	.0000	.0000	.0000	.0000	.0000	.0001
39	.0000	.0000	.0000	.0000	.0000	.0000	.0000	.0000	.0000	.0001

Summations

Definition

$$\sum_{i=1}^{n} x_i = x_1 + x_2 + \cdots + x_n \tag{C.1}$$

Example for $x_1 = 5$, $x_2 = 8$, $x_3 = 14$;

$$\sum_{i=1}^{3} x_i = x_1 + x_2 + x_3$$
$$= 5 + 8 + 14$$
$$= 27$$

Result 1

For a constant c:

$$\sum_{i=1}^{n} c = \underbrace{(c + c + \cdots + c)}_{n \text{ times}} = nc \tag{C.2}$$

Example for $c = 5$, $n = 10$:

$$\sum_{i=1}^{10} 5 = 10(5) = 50$$

Example for $c = \bar{x}$

$$\sum_{i=1}^{n} \bar{x} = n\bar{x}$$

Result 2

$$\sum_{i=1}^{n} cx_i = cx_1 + cx_2 + \cdots + cx_n$$
$$= c(x_1 + x_2 + \cdots + x_n) = c\sum_{i=1}^{n} x_i \tag{C.3}$$

Example for $x_1 = 5$, $x_2 = 8$, $x_3 = 14$, $c = 2$:

$$\sum_{i=1}^{3} 2x_i = 2\sum_{i=1}^{3} x_i = 2(27) = 54$$

Result 3

$$\sum_{i=1}^{n} (ax_i + by_i) = a\sum_{i=1}^{n} x_i + b\sum_{i=1}^{n} y_i \tag{C.4}$$

Example for $x_1 = 5$, $x_2 = 8$, $x_3 = 14$, $a = 2$, $y_1 = 7$, $y_2 = 3$, $y_3 = 8$, $b = 4$:

$$\sum_{i=1}^{3}(2x_i + 4y_i) = 2\sum_{i=1}^{3}x_i + 4\sum_{i=1}^{3}y_i$$
$$= 2(27) + 4(18)$$
$$= 54 + 72$$
$$= 126$$

Double Summations

Consider the following data involving the variable x_{ij}, where i is the subscript denoting the row position and j is the subscript denoting the column position:

		Column		
		1	**2**	**3**
Row	1	$x_{11} = 10$	$x_{12} = 8$	$x_{13} = 6$
	2	$x_{21} = 7$	$x_{22} = 4$	$x_{23} = 12$

Definition

$$\sum_{i=1}^{n}\sum_{j=1}^{m}x_{ij} = (x_{11} + x_{12} + \cdots + x_{1m}) + (x_{21} + x_{22} + \cdots + x_{2m})$$
$$+ (x_{31} + x_{32} + \cdots + x_{3m}) + \cdots + (x_{n1} + x_{n2} + \cdots + x_{nm}) \quad \textbf{(C.5)}$$

Example:

$$\sum_{i=1}^{2}\sum_{j=1}^{3}x_{ij} = x_{11} + x_{12} + x_{13} + x_{21} + x_{22} + x_{23}$$
$$= 10 + 8 + 6 + 7 + 4 + 12$$
$$= 47$$

Definition

$$\sum_{i=1}^{n}x_{ij} = x_{1j} + x_{2j} + \cdots + x_{nj} \quad \textbf{(C.6)}$$

Example:

$$\sum_{i=1}^{2}x_{i2} = x_{12} + x_{22}$$
$$= 8 + 4$$
$$= 12$$

Shorthand Notation

Sometimes when a summation is for all values of the subscript, we use the following shorthand notations:

$$\sum_{i=1}^{n}x_i = \sum_i x_i \quad \textbf{(C.7)}$$

$$\sum_{i=1}^{n}\sum_{j=1}^{m}x_{ij} = \sum\sum x_{ij} \quad \textbf{(C.8)}$$

$$\sum_{i=1}^{n}x_{ij} = \sum_i x_{ij} \quad \textbf{(C.9)}$$

Chapter 1

2. a. 9
   b. 4
   c. Qualitative: country and room rate
      Quantitative: number of rooms and overall score
   d. Country is nominal; room rate is ordinal; number of rooms and overall score are ratio

4. a. 10
   b. *Fortune* 500 largest U.S. corporations
   c. $14,227.59 million
   d. $14,227.59 million

6. Questions a, c, and d are quantitative
   Questions b and e are qualitative

8. a. 2013
   b. Qualitative
   c. Percentages
   d. 563 or 564

10. a. Quantitative; ratio
   b. Qualitative; nominal
   c. Qualitative; ordinal
   d. Qualitative; nominal
   e. Quantitative; ratio

12. a. All visitors to Hawaii
   b. Yes
   c. Questions 1 and 4 provide quantitative data
      Questions 2 and 3 provide qualitative data

14. a. 4
   b. All are quantitative
   c. Time series

16. a. Product taste tests and test marketing
   b. Specially designed statistical studies

18. a. 40%
   b. Qualitative

20. a. 56% and $387,325
   b. 3.73
   c. $387,325

22. a. All adult viewers reached by the station
   b. Viewers contacted in the telephone survey

24. a. Correct
   b. Incorrect
   c. Correct
   d. Incorrect
   e. Incorrect

Chapter 2

2. a. .20
   b. 40
   c/d.

Class	Frequency	Percent Frequency
A	44	22
B	36	18
C	80	40
D	40	20
Total	200	100

4. a. Qualitative
   b.

TV Show	Frequency	Percent Frequency
Millionaire	24	48
Frasier	15	30
Chicago Hope	7	14
Charmed	4	8
Total	50	100

   d. Millionaire has the largest market share; Frasier is second

6. a.

Book	Frequency	Percent Frequency
7 Habits	10	16.66
Millionaire	16	26.67
Motley	9	15.00
Dad	13	21.67
WSJ Guide	6	10.00
Other	6	10.00
Total	60	100.00

   b. First 5: *Millionaire, Dad, 7 Habits, Motley, WSJ Guide*
   c. 48.33%

8. a.

Position	Frequency	Relative Frequency
P	17	.309
H	4	.073
1	5	.091
2	4	.073
3	2	.036
S	5	.091
L	6	.109
C	5	.091
R	7	.127
Totals	55	1.000

b. Pitcher
c. 3rd base
d. Right field
e. Infielders 16 to outfielders 18

10. a. Quality of service classifications
b.

Rating	Frequency	Relative Frequency
3	2	.03
4	4	.07
5	12	.20
6	24	.40
7	18	.30
Totals	60	1.00

12.

Class	Cumulative Frequency	Cumulative Relative Frequency
≤19	10	.20
≤29	24	.48
≤39	41	.82
≤49	48	.96
≤59	50	1.00

14. a/b.

Class	Frequency	Percent Frequency
6.0–7.9	4	20
8.0–9.9	2	10
10.0–11.9	8	40
12.0–13.9	3	15
14.0–15.9	3	15
Totals	20	100

16. a.

Stock Price ($)	Frequency	Relative Frequency	Percent Frequency
10.00–19.99	10	.40	40
20.00–29.99	4	.16	16
30.00–39.99	6	.24	24
40.00–49.99	2	.08	8
50.00–59.99	1	.04	4
60.00–69.99	2	.08	8
Total	25	1.00	100

b.

Earnings per Share ($)	Frequency	Relative Frequency	Percent Frequency
−3.00 to −2.01	2	.08	8
−2.00 to −1.01	0	.00	0
−1.00 to −0.01	2	.08	8
0.00 to 0.99	9	.36	36
1.00 to 1.99	9	.36	36
2.00 to 2.99	3	.12	12
Total	25	1.00	100

18. a. Lowest salary: $93,000
   Highest salary: $178,000
b.

Salary ($1000s)	Frequency	Relative Frequency	Percent Frequency
91–105	4	0.08	8
106–120	5	0.10	10
121–135	11	0.22	22
136–150	18	0.36	36
151–165	9	0.18	18
166–180	3	0.06	6
Total	50	1.00	100

c. 20/50
d. 24%

20. a. 48.9%
   b. 51.1%
   c. 43.4%
   d. 97.075 million
   e. 46.6125 million

22.

5	7 8
6	4 5 8
7	0 2 2 5 5 6 8
8	0 2 3 5

24. Leaf Unit = 10

```
11 | 6
12 | 0 2
13 | 0 6 7
14 | 2 2 7
15 | 5
16 | 0 2 8
17 | 0 2 3
```

26. Leaf Unit = .1

```
0 | 4 7 8 9 9
1 | 1 2 9
2 | 0 0 1 3 5 5 6 8
3 | 4 9
4 | 8
5 |
6 |
7 | 1
```

28. a.

```
0 | 5 8
1 | 1 1 3 3 4 4
1 | 5 6 7 8 9 9
2 | 2 3 3 3 5 5
2 | 6 8
3 |
3 | 6 7 7 9
4 | 0
4 | 7 8
5 |
5 |
6 | 0
```

b.

2000 P/E Forecast	Frequency	Relative Frequency
5–9	2	6.7
10–14	6	20.0
15–19	6	20.0
20–24	6	20.0
25–29	2	6.7
30–34	0	0.0
35–39	4	13.3
40–44	1	3.3
45–49	2	6.7
50–54	0	0.0
55–59	0	0.0
60–64	1	3.3
Total	30	100.0

30. b. Negative relationship

32. a.

Sales/ Margins/ ROE	EPS Rating					Total
	0–19	20–39	40–59	60–79	80–100	
A				1	8	9
B		1	4	5	2	12
C	1		1	2	3	7
D	3	1		1		5
E		2	1			3
Total	4	4	6	9	13	36

b.

Sales/ Margins/ ROE	EPS Rating					Total
	0–19	20–39	40–59	60–79	80–100	
A				11.11	88.89	100
B		8.33	33.33	41.67	16.67	100
C	14.29		14.29	28.57	42.86	100
D	60.00	20.00		20.00		100
E		66.67	33.33			100

Higher EPS ratings seem to be associated with higher ratings on Sales/Margins/ROE

34. No apparent relationship

36. a.

Vehicle	Frequency	Percent Frequency
F-Series	17	34
Silverado	12	24
Taurus	8	16
Camry	7	14
Accord	6	12
	50	100

b. Ford F-Series Pickup and Chevrolet Silverado

38. a.

Movie	Frequency	Percent Frequency
Blair Witch Project	159	36.0
Phantom Menace	89	20.2
Beloved	85	19.3
Primary Colors	57	12.9
Truman Show	51	11.6
Total	441	100.0

c. 56.2%

40. a/b

Closing Price	Freq.	Rel. Freq.	Cum. Freq.	Cum. Rel. Freq.
0–9.99	9	.225	9	.225
10–19.99	10	.250	19	.475
20–29.99	5	.125	24	.600
30–39.99	11	.275	35	.875
40–49.99	2	.050	37	.925
50–59.99	2	.050	39	.975
60–69.99	0	.000	39	.975
70–79.99	1	.025	40	1.000
Totals	40	1.000		

42.

Income ($)	Frequency	Relative Frequency
18,000–21,999	13	0.255
22,000–25,999	20	0.392
26,000–29,999	12	0.235
30,000–33,999	4	0.079
34,000–37,999	2	0.039
Total	51	1.000

44. a. High Temperatures

```
3 |
4 |
5 | 7
6 | 1  4  4  4  4  6  8
7 | 3  5  7  9
8 | 0  1  1  4  6
9 | 0  2  3
```

b. Low Temperatures

```
3 | 9
4 | 3  6  8
5 | 0  0  0  2  4  4  5  5  7  9
6 | 1  8
7 | 2  4  5  5
8 |
9 |
```

c. The range of low temperatures is below the range of high temperatures

d. 8 cities

e.

	Frequency	
Temperature	High Temp.	Low Temp.
30–39	0	1
40–49	0	3
50–59	1	10
60–69	7	2
70–79	4	4
80–89	5	0
90–99	3	0
Total	20	20

46. a.

	Satisfaction Score						
Occupation	30–39	40–49	50–59	60–69	70–79	80–89	Total
Cabinetmaker			2	4	3	1	10
Lawyer	1	5	2	1	1		10
Physical Therapist			5	2	1	2	10
Systems Analyst		2	1	4	3		10
Total	1	7	10	11	8	3	40

b.

	Satisfaction Score						
Occupation	30–39	40–49	50–59	60–69	70–79	80–89	Total
Cabinetmaker			20	40	30	10	100
Lawyer	10	50	20	10	10		100
Physical Therapist			50	20	10	20	100
Systems Analyst		20	10	40	30		100
Total	1	7	10	11	8	3	40

c. Cabinetmakers seem to have the highest job satisfaction scores; lawyers seem to have the lowest

48. b.

Year	Freq.	Fuel	Freq.
1973 or before	247	Elect.	149
1974–79	54	Nat. Gas	317
1980–86	82	Oil	17
1987–91	121	Propane	7
Total	504	Other	14
		Total	504

50. a. Crosstabulation of market value and profit

Market Value ($1000s)	Profit ($1000s)				Total
	0–300	300–600	600–900	900–1200	
0–8000	23	4			27
8000–16,000	4	4	2	2	12
16,000–24,000		2	1	1	4
24,000–32,000		1	2	1	4
32,000–40,000		2	1		3
Total	27	13	6	4	50

b.

Market Value ($1000s)	Profit ($1000s)				Total
	0–300	300–600	600–900	900–1200	
0–8000	85.19	14.81	0.00	0.00	100
8000–16,000	33.33	33.33	16.67	16.67	100
16,000–24,000	0.00	50.00	25.00	25.00	100
24,000–32,000	0.00	25.00	50.00	25.00	100
32,000–40,000	0.00	66.67	33.33	0.00	100

c. A positive relationship is indicated between profit and market value; as profit goes up, market value goes up

52. b. A positive relationship is demonstrated between market value and stockholders' equity

Chapter 3

2. 16, 16.5

4. 59.727, 57, 53

6. a. 91.45, 87.5, 120
  b. 66.3, 69.5, 70
  c. 500 @ $50
  d. Yes

8. a. 34.75, 25
  b. 34.5
  c. 25.5, 43.5
  d. 27

10. a. 48.33, 49; do not report a mode
  b. 45, 55

12. *City:*   mean = 15.58, median = 15.9,
            mode = 15.3
  Country: mean = 18.92, median = 18.7,
            mode = 18.6 and 19.4

14. a. $639
  b. 98.8 pictures
  c. 110.2 minutes

16. 16, 4

18. a. 22
  b. 75.2
  c. 8.67
  d. 4.87

20. a. Range = 32, IQR = 10
  b. 92.75, 9.63

22. *Dawson:* range = 2, s = .67
    Clark: range = 8, s = 2.58

24. a. 161, 92.5; 56, 19.5
  b. 2705.38, 52.01; 290.85, 17.05
  c. 56.38, 25.56
  d. Greater for 500 @ $50

26. *Quarter-milers:* s = .056, Coef. of Var. = 5.8
    Milers: s = .130, Coef. of Var. = 2.9

28. a. 95%
  b. Almost all
  c. 68%

30. .20, 1.50, 0, −.50, −2.20

32. a. 34%
  b. 81.5%
  c. 16%

34. a. −.95
  b. 3.90
  c. Labor cost in part (b) is an outlier

36. a. 100; 13.88 or approximately 14
  b. 16%
  c. 11.1 and 10.77; no outliers

38. 15, 22.5, 26, 29, 34

40. 5, 8, 10, 15, 18

42. a. 5, 9.6, 14.5, 19.2, 52.7
  b. Limits: −4.8, 33.6
  c. 41.6 is an outlier
    52.7 is an outlier

44. a. 105.79, 52.7
  b. 15.7, 78.3
  c. Silicon Graphics, Toys R Us
  d. 26.73; much greater

46. a. 37.48, 23.67
  b. 7.91, 51.92
  c. Limits: −58.11, 117.94
    Russia and Turkey are outliers

48. b. There appears to be a positive linear relationship between x and y
  c. s_{xy} = 26.5
  d. r_{xy} = .693

50. −.91; negative relationship

52. a. .92
  b. Strong positive linear relationship

54. a. 3.69
  b. 3.175

56. a. 2.50
  b. Yes

58. 10.74, 25.63, 5.06

60. a. 138.52, 129, 0
  b. No, much more
  c. 95, 169
  d. 467, 74

e. 9271.01, 96.29

f. Yes, the $467 value

62. a. 18.57, 16.5

b. 53.49, 7.31

c. Quantex

d. 1.15

e. $-.90$

f. No, according to z-scores

64. 7195.5, 7019; 7,165,941; 2676.93

66. a. Public: 32; auto: 32

b. Public: 4.64; auto: 1.83

c. Auto has less variability

68. a. 400, 624, 836, 999, 1278

b. *Limits:* 61.5, 1561.5

c. No outliers

70. b. .9856; strong positive relationship

72. b. .75; positive relationship

74. a. 817

b. 833

76. 51.5, 227.37, 15.08

Chapter 4

2. 20 ways

4. b. (H,H,H), (H,H,T), (H,T,H), (H,T,T),
(T,H,H), (T,H,T), (T,T,H), (T,T,T)

c. $\frac{1}{8}$

6. .40, .26, .34; relative frequency method

8. a. 4: Commission Positive—Council Approves,
Commission Positive—Council Disapproves,
Commission Negative—Council Approves,
Commission Negative—Council Disapproves

10. a. .60

b. .09

c. .78

d. 86

e. $1.53 billion

12. a. 1,906,884

b. 1/1,906,884

c. 1/80,089,128

14. a. $\frac{1}{4}$

b. $\frac{1}{2}$

c. $\frac{3}{4}$

16. a. 36

c. $\frac{1}{6}$

d. $\frac{5}{18}$

e. No; $P(\text{odd}) = P(\text{even}) = \frac{1}{2}$

f. Classical

18. a. $P(0) = .05$

b. $P(4 \text{ or } 5) = .20$

c. $P(0, 1, \text{ or } 2) = .55$

20. a. .112

b. .086

c. .49

22. a. .40, .40, .60

b. .80, yes

c. $A^c = (E_3, E_4, E_5)$; $C^c = (E_1, E_4)$;
$P(A^c) = .60$; $P(C^c) = .40$

d. (E_1, E_2, E_5); .60

e. .80

24. a. .05

b. .70

26. a. .30, .23

b. .17

c. .64

28. a. .698

b. .302

30. a. .67

b. .80

c. No

32. a.

	Single	Married	Total
Under 30	.55	.10	.65
30 or Over	.20	.15	.35
Total	.75	.25	1.0

b. Higher probability of under 30

c. Higher probability of single

d. .55

e. .8462

f. No

34. a. .44

b. .15

c. .0225

d. .0025

e. .136

f. .106

36. a. .

Occupation	Satisfaction Score					
	Under 50	50–59	60–69	70–79	80–89	Total
Cabinetmaker	.000	.050	.100	.075	.025	.250
Lawyer	.150	.050	.025	.025	.000	.250
Physical Therapist	.000	.125	.050	.025	.050	.250
Systems Analyst	.050	.025	.100	.075	.000	.250
Total	.200	.250	.275	.200	.075	1.000

b. .075

c. .20

d. .25

e. .15

f. .60

g. .275

38. a. 52/190 = .2737
   b. .0125
   c. .3684

40. a. .10, .20, .09
   b. .51
   c. .26, .51, .23

42. a. .21
   b. Yes

44. .6754

46. a. .68
   b. 52
   c. 10

48. a. .61
   b. 18–34 and 65+
   c. .30

50. a. 76
   b. .24

52. b. .2022
   c. .4618
   d. .4005

54. a. .49
   b. .44
   c. .54
   d. No
   e. Yes

56. a. .25
   b. .125
   c. .0125
   d. .10
   e. No

58. 3.44%

60. a. .0625
   b. .0132
   c. Three

Chapter 5

2. a. x = time in minutes to assemble product
   b. Any positive value: $x > 0$
   c. Continuous

4. $x = 0, 1, 2, \ldots, 12$

6. a. $0, 1, 2, \ldots, 20$; discrete
   b. $0, 1, 2, \ldots$; discrete
   c. $0, 1, 2, \ldots, 50$; discrete
   d. $0 \leq x \leq 8$; continuous
   e. $x > 0$; continuous

8. a.

x	1	2	3	4
$f(x)$	.15	.25	.40	.20

   c. $f(x) \geq 0$, $\Sigma f(x) = 1$

10. a.

x	1	2	3	4	5
$f(x)$	.05	.09	.03	.42	.41

   b.

x	1	2	3	4	5
$f(x)$	.04	.10	.12	.46	.28

   c. .83
   d. .28
   e. Senior executives more satisfied

12. a. Yes
   b. .65

14. a. .05
   b. .70
   c. .40

16. a. 5.20
   b. 4.56, 2.14

18. a. $E(x) = 2.3$, same
   b. $\text{Var}(x) = 1.23$, $\sigma = 1.11$

20. a. 166
   b. −94; concern is to protect against the expense of a big accident

22. a. 445
   b. 1250 loss

24. a. Medium: 145; large: 140
   b. Medium: 2725; large: 12,400

26. a. $f(0) = .3487$
   b. $f(2) = .1937$
   c. .9298
   d. .6513
   e. 1
   f. $\sigma^2 = .9000$, $\sigma = .9487$

28. a. .3292
   b. .6422
   c. .0182

30. a. Probability of a defective part must be .03 for each trial; trials must be independent
   c. 2
   d.

Number of defects	0	1	2
Probability	.9409	.0582	.0009

32. a. .90
   b. .99
   c. .999
   d. Yes

34. a. .0634
   b. .0634
   c. .9729

38. a. $f(x) = \dfrac{3^x e^{-3}}{x!}$
   b. .2241
   c. .1494
   d. .8008

40. a. .1952
b. .1048
c. .0183
d. .0907

42. a. .0009
b. .9927
c. .9698
d. .8271

44. a. $\mu = 1.25$
b. .2865
c. .3581
d. .3554

46. a. .50
b. .067
c. .4667
d. .30

48. a. .50
b. .3333

50. a. .01
b. .07
c. .92
d. .07

52. a. .5333
b. .6667
c. .7778
d. $n = 7$

54. a. $f(x) \geq 0$ and $\Sigma f(x) = 1$
b. 3.64, .6704
c. Appears overvalued

56. a. .0364
b. .4420
c. 48
d. 6.7882

58. a. .9510
b. .0480
c. .0490

60. a. 328
b. 13.91
c. 13.91

62. .1912

64. a. .2240
b. .5767

66. a. .4667
b. .4667
c. .0667

Chapter 6

2. b. .50
c. .60
d. 15
e. 8.33

4. b. .50
c. .30
d. .40

6. a. .40
b. .64
c. .68

10. a. .3413
b. .4332
c. .4772
d. .4938

12. a. .2967
b. .4418
c. .3300
d. .5910
e. .8849
f. .2389

14. a. $z = 1.96$
b. $z = .61$
c. $z = 1.12$
d. $z = .44$

16. a. $z = 2.33$
b. $z = 1.96$
c. $z = 1.645$
d. $z = 1.28$

18. a. .2451
b. .1170
c. 69.48 minutes or more

20. a. .025
b. 5.16%
c. 33.72 or more

22. a. .4194
b. $517.44 or more
c. .0166

24. a. 902.75, 114.185
b. .1841
c. .1977
d. 1,091 million

26. a. .5276
b. .3935
c. .4724
d. .1341

28. a. .3935
b. .2231
c. .3834

30. a. 50 hours
b. .3935
c. .1353

32. a. $f(x) = 30e^{-30x}$
b. .0821
c. .7135

34. a. $63,000
b. $43,800 or less

c. 12.92%
d. $87,675

36. a. $3229
   b. .2244
   c. $12,383 or more

38. a. .0228
   b. $50

40. a. 38.3%
   b. 3.59% better, 96.41% worse
   c. 38.21%

42. $\mu = 19.23$ ounces

44. a. $\frac{1}{7}$ minute
   b. $f(x) = 7e^{-7x}$
   c. .0009
   d. .2466

46. a. 2 minutes
   b. .2212
   c. .3935
   d. .0821

Chapter 7

2. 22, 147, 229, 289

4. a. IBM, Microsoft, Intel, GE, AT&T
   b. 252

6. 2782, 493, 825, 1807, 289

8. Washington, Clemson, Oklahoma, Colorado, USC, and Wisconsin

10. Finite, infinite, infinite, infinite, finite

12. a. .50
   b. .3667

14. a. .19
   b. .32
   c. .79

16. .80

18. a. 2000
   b. 5
   c. Normal with $E(\bar{x}) = 200$ and $\sigma_{\bar{x}} = 5$
   d. The probability distribution of $\bar{x}$

20. 3.54, 2.50, 2.04, 1.77
   $\sigma_{\bar{x}}$ decreases as n increases

22. a. Only for $n = 30$ and $n = 40$
   b. $n = 30$; normal with $E(\bar{x}) = 400$
      and $\sigma_{\bar{x}} = 9.13$
      $n = 40$; normal with $E(\bar{x}) = 400$
      and $\sigma_{\bar{x}} = 7.91$

24. a. Normal with $E(\bar{x}) = 51,800$ and $\sigma_{\bar{x}} = 516.40$
   b. $\sigma_{\bar{x}}$ decreases to 365.15
   c. $\sigma_{\bar{x}}$ decreases as n increases

26. a. Normal with $E(\bar{x}) = 1.20$ and $\sigma_{\bar{x}} = .014$
   b. .8414
   c. .5222

28. a. .5036, .6212, .7888, .9232, .9876
   b. Higher probability withing ± 250

30. a. Normal with $E(\bar{x}) = 166,500$ and $\sigma_{\bar{x}} = 4200$
   b. .9826
   c. .7660, .4514, .1896
   d. Increase the sample size

32. a. n/N .01; no
   b. 1.29, 1.30; little difference
   c. .8764

34. a. .6156
   b. .8530

36. a. .6156
   b. .7814
   c. .9488
   d. .9942
   e. Higher probability with larger n

38. a. Normal with $E(\bar{p}) = .76$ and $\sigma_{\bar{p}} = .0214$
   b. .8384
   c. .9452

40. a. Normal with $E(\bar{p}) = .25$ and $\sigma_{\bar{p}} = .0306$
   b. .6730
   c. .8968

42. a. Normal with $E(\bar{p}) = .15$ and $\sigma_{\bar{p}} = .0505$
   b. .4448
   c. .8389

44. 112, 145, 73, 324, 293, 875, 318, 618

46. a. Normal with $E(\bar{x}) = 31.5$ and $\sigma_{\bar{x}} = 1.70$
   b. .4448
   c. .9232

48. a. 707
   b. .50
   c. .8414
   d. .9544

50. a. 625
   b. .7888

52. a. Normal with $E(\bar{p}) = .305$ and $\sigma_{\bar{p}} = .0326$
   b. .7814
   c. .4582

54. a. .9606
   b. .0495

56. a. 48
   b. Normal, $E(\bar{p}) = .25$, $\sigma_{\bar{p}} = .0625$
   c. .2119

Chapter 8

2. a. 30.60 to 33.40
   b. 30.34 to 33.66
   c. 29.81 to 34.19

4. 62

6. 362.80 to 375.20

8. a. 11,769 to 12,231
   b. 11,725 to 12,275
   c. 11,638 to 12,362
   d. Width increases to be more confident

10. 7.25 to 8.25

12. a. 3.8
   b. .81
   c. 2.99 to 4.61

14. a. 1.734
   b. -1.321
   c. 3.365
   d. -1.761 and 1.761
   e. -2.048 and 2.048

16. a. 15.97 to 18.53
   b. 15.71 to 18.79
   c. 15.14 to 19.36

18. a. 1.58
   b. .1474
   c. 1.49 to 1.67

20. a. 21.15 to 23.65
   b. 21.12 to 23.68
   c. Intervals are essentially the same

22. a. 6.86
   b. 6.54 to 7.18

24. a. 9
   b. 35
   c. 78

26. a. 340
   b. 1358
   c. 8487

28. a. 53
   b. 75
   c. 129
   d. Must increase n

30. 59

32. a. .6733 to .7267
   b. .6682 to .7318

34. 1068

36. a. .4393
   b. .3870 to .4916

38. a. .0430
   b. .2170 to .3030
   c. 822

40. a. .2505
   b. .0266

40. a. .0442
   b. 601, 1068, 2401, 9604

44. a. 2009
   b. 47,991 to 52,009

46. a. 49.8
   b. 15.99
   c. 47.58 to 52.02

48. a. 13.2
   b. 7.8
   c. 7.62 to 18.78
   d. Wide interval; larger n desirable

50. 37

52. 176

54. a. .5420
   b. .0508
   c. .4912 to .5928

56. a. 1267
   b. 1509

58. a. .68
   b. .6391 to .7209

60. a. .3101
   b. .2898 to .3304
   c. 8219; No, this sample size is unnecessarily large

Chapter 9

2. a. $H_0: \mu \le 14$
      $H_a: \mu > 14$

4. a. $H_0: \mu \ge 220$
      $H_a: \mu < 220$

6. a. $H_0: \mu \le 1$
      $H_a: \mu > 1$
   b. Claiming $\mu > 1$ when it is not true
   c. Claiming $\mu \le 1$ when it is not true

8. a. $H_0: \mu \ge 220$
      $H_a: \mu < 220$
   b. Claiming $\mu < 220$ when it is not true
   c. Claiming $\mu \ge 220$ when it is not true

10. a. Reject H_0 if $z > 2.05$
   b. 1.36
   c. .0869
   d. Do not reject H_0

12. a. .0344; reject H_0
   b. .3264; do not reject H_0
   c. .0668; do not reject H_0
   d. Approximately 0; reject H_0
   e. .8413; do not reject H_0

14. a. 2.33; reject if $z > 2.33$
   b. 3.11
   c. Reject H_0

16. a. $H_0: \mu \ge 13$
      $H_a: \mu < 13$
   b. Reject if $z < -2.33$
   c. -2.88
   d. Reject H_0

18. a. $H_0: \mu \le 5.72$
      $H_a: \mu > 5.72$

b. 2.12
c. .0170
d. Reject H_0

20. a. $H_0: \mu \leq 37{,}000$
    $H_a: \mu > 37{,}000$
b. 1.47
c. .0708
d. Do not reject H_0

22. a. Reject H_0 if $z < -2.33$ or $z > 2.33$
b. 1.13
c. .2584
d. Do not reject H_0

24. a. .0718; do not reject H_0
b. .6528; do not reject H_0
c. .0404; reject H_0
d. Approximately 0; reject H_0
e. .3174; do not reject H_0

26. a. Reject H_0 if $z < -1.96$ or if $z > 1.96$
b. -1.71
c. Do not reject H_0

28. a. $H_0: \mu = 1075$
    $H_a: \mu \neq 1075$
b. $z = 1.43$
c. .1528
d. Do not reject H_0

30. a. $H_0: \mu = 26{,}133$
    $H_a: \mu \neq 26{,}133$
b. -2.09
c. .0366
d. Reject H_0

32. a. 14.66 or less
b. Reject H_0

34. a. 18
b. 1.41
c. Reject H_0 if $t < -2.571$ or $t > 2.571$
d. -3.47
e. Reject H_0

36. a. .01; reject H_0
b. .10; do not reject H_0
c. Between .025 and .05; reject H_0
d. Greater than .10; do not reject H_0
e. Approximately 0; reject H_0

38. a. Reject H_0 if $t < -2.064$ or $t > 2.064$
b. -1.90
c. Do not reject H_0
d. It is between .05 and .10

40. a. $H_0: \mu = 4000$
    $H_a: \mu \neq 4000$
b. Reject H_0 if $t < -2.160$ or if $t > 2.160$
c. 1.63
d. Do not reject H_0
e. It is between .10 and .20

42. a. $H_0: \mu \leq 2$
    $H_a: \mu > 2$
b. Reject H_0 if $t > 1.833$
c. 2.4
d. .516
e. 2.45
f. Reject H_0
g. It is between .01 and .025

44. a. Reject H_0 if $z < -1.96$ or $z > 1.96$
b. -1.25
c. .2112
d. Do not reject H_0

46. a. $H_0: p \leq .40$
    $H_a: p > .40$
b. Reject H_0 if $z > 1.645$
c. 1.99
d. Reject H_0

48. a. .57
b. 3.13
c. Less than .001
d. Reject H_0
e. Yes

50. a. .6381
b. 2.83
c. .0046
d. Reject H_0

52. a. -1.20
b. .1151
c. Do not reject H_0

54. a. $H_0: p \geq .047$
    $H_a: p < .047$
b. .0296
c. -2.82
d. .0024
e. Reject H_0

56. a. $H_0: \mu \leq 45{,}250$
    $H_a: \mu > 45{,}250$
b. 2.71
c. .0034
d. Reject H_0

58. $z = 2.26$, p-value $= .0119$
Reject H_0

60. a. $z = 1.80$; do not reject
b. p-value $= .0718$
c. 548.93 to 575.07; do not reject

62. a. .6502
b. $-.98$
c. .3270
d. Do not reject H_0

64. a. Show $p < .50$
b. $z = -6.62$; reject H_0

66. a. .825
b. 2.17

c. .03

d. Reject H_0

68. a. 352

b. -2.64

c. .0041

d. Reject H_0

Chapter 10

2. a. 2.4

b. 5.27

c. .09 to 4.71

4. a. .60

b. .56 to .64

6. $-.51$ to 1.27

8. a. 1200

b. 438 to 1962

c. Populations normal with equal variances

10. a. 2.18

b. 4.41

c. .71 to 3.65

12. a. $z = -1.53$; do not reject H_0

b. .1260

14. a. $H_0: \mu_1 - \mu_2 = 0$

$H_a: \mu_1 - \mu_2 \neq 0$

b. Reject if $z < -1.96$ or $z > 1.96$

c. 2.18

d. Reject H_0

e. .0292

16. $z = 4.99$, p-value ≈ 0

Reject H_0

18. a. 1.08

b. .2802

c. Do not reject H_0

20. a. $H_0: \mu_1 - \mu_2 \leq 0$

$H_a: \mu_1 - \mu_2 > 0$

b. Reject H_0 if $t > 1.711$

c. 2.07

d. Reject H_0

e. Approximately .025

22. a. 3, -1, 3, 5, 3, 0, 1

b. 2

c. 2.0282

d. 2

e. .07 to 3.93

24. .16 to .35

26. $t = 1.63$; do not reject H_0

28. a. $t = 7.34$; reject H_0

b. 4.96 to 9.21

30. a. MSTR = 268

b. MSE = 92

c. Cannot reject H_0 because $F = 2.91 < F_{.05} = 4.26$

d.

Source of Variation	Sum of Squares	Degrees of Freedom	Mean Square	F
Treatments	536	2	268	2.91
Error	828	9	92	
Total	1364	11		

32. a.

Source of Variation	Sum of Squares	Degrees of Freedom	Mean Square
Treatments	1200	3	400
Error	300	60	5
Total	1500	63	

b. Reject H_0 because $F = 80 > F_{.05} = 2.76$

34. Reject H_0 because $F = 10.63 > F_{.05} = 4.26$

36. Significant difference;

$F = 7.00 > F_{.05} = 3.68$

38. Significant difference;

p-value $= .015$

40. a. $H_0: \mu_1 - \mu_2 \leq 0$

$H_a: \mu_1 - \mu_2 > 0$

b. $z = .59$; do not reject H_0

c. .2776

42. $t = 2.29$; reject H_0

44. Significant difference; $F = 18.59$

p-value $= .000 < \alpha = .05$

46. Significant difference; $F = 4.87$

48. Significant difference; $F = 8.74$

50. Significant difference; $F = 93.16$

Chapter 11

2. a. $\bar{p} = .184$, $s_{\bar{p}_1 - \bar{p}_2} = .0354$, $z = 1.69$; reject H_0

b. .0455

4. .04 to .14

6. a. .93, .85

b. $z = 3.13$, reject H_0

c. $.08 \pm .05$

8. a. $z = 2.33$; reject H_0

b. .02 to .22

10. p-value $= .0322$; reject H_0

12. $\chi^2 = 15.33$, $\chi^2_{.05} = 7.81473$; reject H_0

14. $\chi^2 = 29.51$, $\chi^2_{.05} = 11.07$; reject H_0

Percentage figures are not as reported

16. $\chi^2 = 10.69$, $\chi^2_{.10} = 9.24$; reject H_0

18. $\chi^2 = 16.31$, $\chi^2_{.01} = 11.34$; reject H_0

20. $\chi^2 = 19.78$, $\chi^2_{.05} = 9.48773$; reject H_0

22. $\chi^2 = 7.36$, $\chi^2_{.05} = 5.99$; reject H_0

24. $\chi^2 = 13.43$, $\chi^2_{.05} = 11.0705$; reject H_0

26. $\chi^2 = 7.85$, $\chi^2_{.05} = 7.81473$; reject H_0

28. $\chi^2 = 13.42$, $\chi^2_{.01} = 13.2767$; reject H_0

30. a. $H_0: p_1 - p_2 \leq 0$
   $H_a: p_1 - p_2 > 0$
b. $z = 4.70$; p-value ≈ 0
c. Reject H_0

32. .0174; reject H_0

34. a. .16
b. $H_0: p_1 - p_2 \leq 0$
   $H_a: p_1 - p_2 > 0$
c. $z = 3.49$; reject H_0

36. $\chi^2 = 41.69$, $\chi^2_{.01} = 13.2767$; reject H_0

38. $\chi^2 = 7.44$, $\chi^2_{.05} = 9.48773$; do not reject H_0

40. $\chi^2 = 8.11$, $\chi^2_{.05} = 5.99147$; reject H_0

42. $\chi^2 = 2.21$, $\chi^2_{.05} = 7.81473$; do reject H_0

44. $\chi^2 = 9.76$, $\chi^2_{.05} = 9.48773$; reject H_0

46. $\chi^2 = 7.78$, $\chi^2_{.05} = 7.81473$; do not reject H_0

Chapter 12

2. b. There appears to be a linear relationship between x and y
d. $\hat{y} = 30.33 - 1.88x$
e. 19.05

4. b. There appears to be a linear relationship between x and y
d. $\hat{y} = -240.5 + 5.5x$
e. 106 pounds

6. c. $\hat{y} = 6.02 - .07x$
e. .42

8. b. yes
c. $\hat{y} = 490.21 + 204.24x$
d. 1307

10. b. $\hat{y} = 51.82 + .145x$
c. 84.4

12. c. $\hat{y} = 1293 + .3165x$
d. 25,031

14. b. $\hat{y} = 49.63 + 2.455x$
c. 69.3%

16. a. SSE = 6.3325, SST = 114.80, SSR = 108.47
b. $r^2 = .945$
c. $r = -.9721$

18. a. SSE = 85,135.14, SST = 335,000,
   SSR = 249,864.86
b. $r^2 = .746$
c. $r = +.8637$

20. a. $\hat{y} = -48.11 + 2.3325x$
b. $r^2 = .82$
c. \$173,500

22. a. $\hat{y} = -1.02 + .13x$
b. $r^2 = .3631$
c. $r = +.6026$

24. a. 2.11
b. 1.453
c. .262
d. Significant
   $t = -7.18 < -t_{.05} = -3.182$
e. Significant
   $F = 51.41 > F_{.05} = 10.13$

26. a. Significant
   $t = 3.43 > t_{.025} = 2.776$
b. Significant
   $F = 11.74 > F_{.05} = 7.71$

28. They are related because $F = 20.17 > F_{.05} = 4.67$

30. No significant relationship

32. a. 1.11
b. 7.07 to 14.13
c. 2.32
d. 3.22 to 17.98

34. Confidence interval: $-.4$ to 4.98
   Prediction interval: -2.27 to 7.31

36. a. 80.859
b. 78.58 to 83.14
c. 72.92 to 88.80

38. a. \$5046.67
b. \$3815.10 to \$6278.24
c. Not out of line

40. a. 9
b. $\hat{y} = 20.0 + 7.21x$
c. 1.3626
d. Significant relationship because $F = 28 > F_{.05} = 5.59$
e. \$380,500

42. a. $\hat{y} = 80.0 + 50.0x$
b. 30
c. Significant relationship because $F = 83.17 > F_{.05} = 4.20$
d. \$680,000

44. b. Yes
c. $\hat{y} = 37.1 - .779x$
d. Significant relationship; p-value $= 0.003$
e. $r^2 = .434$; not a good fit
f. \$12.28 to \$22.91
g. \$17.49 to \$39.05

46. a. $\hat{y} = 2.32 + .64x$
b. No; the variance does not appear to be the same for all values of x

48. b. Yes

50. a. $\hat{y} = 9.26 + .711x$
b. Significant relationship

c. $r^2 = .744$; good fit
d. $13.53

52. a. Market beta = 95
   b. Significant relationship
   c. $r^2 = .470$; not a good fit
   d. Texas Instruments has a higher risk

54. a. $\hat{y} = 10.5 + .953x$
   b. Significant relationship; p-value = .000
   c. $2874 to $4952
   d. Yes

56. a. Negative linear relationship
   b. $\hat{y} = 8.10 - .344x$
   c. Significant relationship; p-value = .002
   d. $r^2 = .711$; reasonably good fit
   e. 5.2 to 7.6 days

58. a. $\hat{y} = 5.85 + .830x$
   b. Significant relationship; p-value = .000
   c. 84.65 points
   d. 65.35 to 103.96

Chapter 13

2. a. $\hat{y} = 45.06 + 1.94x_1$; $\hat{y} = 132.36$
   b. $\hat{y} = 85.22 + 4.32x_2$; $\hat{y} = 150.02$
   c. $\hat{y} = -18.37 + 2.01x_1 + 4.74x_2$; $\hat{y} = 143.18$

4. a. $255,000

6. a. Speed = 49.8 + .0151 Weight
   b. Speed = 80.5 - .00312 Weight + .105 Horsepwr

8. a. Return = 247 - 32.8 Safety + 34.6 ExpRatio
   b. 70.2

10. a. Revenue = 33.3 + 7.98 Cars
    b. Increase of 1000 cars will increase revenue by $7.98 million
    c. Revenue = 106 + 8.94 Cars - .191 Location

12. a. .926
    b. .905
    c. Yes

14. a. .75
    b. .68

16. a. No, $R^2 = .311$
    b. Multiple regression analysis

18. a. $R^2 = .942$, $R_a^2 = .932$
    b. The fit is good

20. a. Significant; p-value = .000
    b. Significant; p-value = .000
    c. Significant; p-value = .002

22. a. SSE = 4000, $s^2 = 571.43$, MSR = 6000
    b. Significant; $F = 10.50 > F_{.05} = 4.74$

24. a. Reject H_0: $\beta_1 = \beta_2 = 0$; p-value = .000
    b. Weight: Cannot reject H_0: $\beta_1 = 0$; p-value = .386
       Horsepower: Reject H_0: $\beta_2 = 0$; p-value = .000

26. a. Significant; p-value = .000
    b. Significant; p-value = .000
    c. Not significant; p-value = .087

28. a. 132.16 to 154.16
    b. 111.13 to 175.18

30. a. Speed = 72.6 + .0968 Horsepwr; estimate of speed is 101.29
    b. 99.490 to 103.089
    c. 94.596 to 107.984

32. a. $x_2 = 0$ if level 1; $x_2 = 1$ if level 2
       $E(y) = \beta_0 + \beta_1 x_1 + \beta_2 x_2$
    b. $E(y) = \beta_0 + \beta_1 x_1$
    c. $E(y) = \beta_0 + \beta_1 x_1 + \beta_2$
    d. $\beta_2 = E(y \mid \text{level 2}) - E(y \mid \text{level 1})$

34. a. $15,300
    b. $56,100
    c. $41,600

36. a. $\hat{y} = 1.86 + 0.291$ Months + 1.10 Type - 0.609 Person
    b. Significant; p-value = .002 < α = .05
    c. Person is not significant

38. a. $\hat{y} = -91.8 + 1.08$ Age + .252 Pressure + 8.74 Smoker
    b. Significant; p-value = .010 < α = .05
    c. 95% prediction interval is 21.35 to 47.18 or a probability of .2135 to .4718; quit smoking and begin some type of treatment to reduce his blood pressure

40. b. 3.19

42. b. Significant; $F = 22.79 > F_{.05} = 5.79$
    c. $R_a^2 = .861$; good fit
    d. Both are significant

44. a. Speed = 97.6 + .0693 Price - .00082 Weight + .0590 Horsepwr - 2.48 Zero60
    b. Significant relationship
    c. Price and Weight are not significant
    d. Speed = 103 + .0558 Horsepwr - 3.19 Zero60

46. a. Resale% = 38.8 + .000766 Price
    b. Not a good fit; R-Sq = 36.7%
    c. Resale% = 42.6 + 9.09 Type 1 + 7.92 Type 2 + .000341 Price
       where Type 1 = 1 if a full-size pickup and Type 2 = 1 if a sport utility vehicle
    d. Significant relationship; p-value corresponding to $F = 14.79 = .000 < \alpha = .05$

Chapter 1

2. a. 9
   b. 4
   c. Country and room rate are qualitative variables; number of rooms and the overall score are quantitative variables
   d. Country is nominal; room rate is ordinal; number of rooms is ratio; overall score is interval

3. a. Average number of rooms = 808/9 = 89.78 or approximately 90 rooms
   b. Average score = 732.1/9 = 81.3
   c. 2 of 9 are located in England; approximately 22%
   d. 4 of 9 have a room rate of $$; approximately 44%

4. a. 10
   b. *Fortune* 500 largest U.S. industrial corporations
   c. Average revenue = $142,272.9/10 = $14,227.29 million
   d. Using the sample average, statistical inference would let us estimate the average revenue for the population of 500 corporations as $14,227.29 million

13. a. Quantitative, earnings in billions of dollars
   b. Time series with 6 observations
   c. Earnings
   d. Time series shows an increase; an increase would be expected in 2003, but it appears that the rate of increase is slowing

Chapter 2

3. a. 360° × 58/120 = 174°
   b. 360° × 42/120 = 126°
   c.

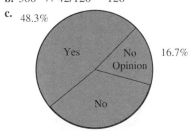

48.3%   Yes   No Opinion 16.7%   No   35%

   d.

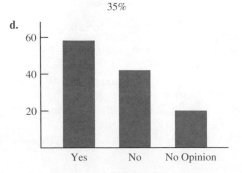

7.

Rating	Frequency	Relative Frequency
Outstanding	19	.38
Very good	13	.26
Good	10	.20
Average	6	.12
Poor	2	.04

Management should be pleased with these results: 64% of the ratings are very good to outstanding, and 84% of the ratings are good or better; comparing these ratings to previous results will show whether the restaurant is making improvements in its customers' ratings of food quality

12.

Class	Cumulative Frequency	Cumulative Relative Frequency
≤19	10	.20
≤29	24	.48
≤39	41	.82
≤49	48	.96
≤59	50	1.00

15. a/b.

Waiting Time	Frequency	Relative Frequency
0–4	4	.20
5–9	8	.40
10–14	5	.25
15–19	2	.10
20–24	1	.05
Totals	20	1.00

c/d.

Waiting Time	Cumulative Frequency	Cumulative Relative Frequency
≤4	4	.20
≤9	12	.60
≤14	17	.85
≤19	19	.95
≤24	20	1.00

e. 12/20 = .60

23. Leaf unit = .1

```
 6 | 3
 7 | 5  5  7
 8 | 1  3  4  8
 9 | 3  6
10 | 0  4  5
11 | 3
```

25.

```
 9 | 8  9
10 | 2  4  6  6
11 | 4  5  7  8  8  9
12 | 2  4  5  7
13 | 1  2
14 | 4
15 | 1
```

29. a.

		y		
		1	**2**	**Total**
	A	5	0	5
x	**B**	11	2	13
	C	2	10	12
	Total	18	12	30

b.

		y		
		1	**2**	**Total**
	A	100.0	0.0	100.0
x	**B**	84.6	15.4	100.0
	C	16.7	83.3	100.0

c.

		y	
		1	**2**
	A	27.8	0.0
x	**B**	61.1	16.7
	C	11.1	83.3
	Total	100.0	100.0

d. *A* values are always in *y* = 1
   B values are most often in *y* = 1
   C values are most often in *y* = 2

32. a.

Sales/ Margins/ ROE	EPS Rating					
	0–19	**20–39**	**40–59**	**60–79**	**80–100**	**Total**
A				1	8	9
B		1	4	5	2	12
C	1		1	2	3	7
D	3	1		1		5
E		2	1			3
Total	4	4	6	9	13	36

b.

Sales/ Margins/ ROE	EPS Rating					
	0–19	**20–39**	**40–59**	**60–79**	**80–100**	**Total**
A				11.11	88.89	100
B		8.33	33.33	41.67	16.67	100
C	14.29		14.29	28.57	42.86	100
D	60.00	20.00		20.00		100
E		66.67	33.33			100

Higher EPS ratings seem to be associated with higher ratings on Sales/Margins/ROE; of those companies with an "A" rating on Sales/Margins/ROE, 88.89% of them had an EPS Rating of 80 or higher; of the eight companies with a "D" or "E" rating on Sales/Margins/ROE, only 1 had an EPS rating above 60

Chapter 3

3. Arrange data in order: 15, 20, 25, 25, 27, 28, 30, 34

$$i = \frac{20}{100}(8) = 1.6; \text{ round up to position 2}$$

20th percentile = 20

$$i = \frac{25}{100}(8) = 2; \text{ use positions 2 and 3}$$

$$25\text{th percentile} = \frac{20 + 25}{2} = 22.5$$

$$i = \frac{65}{100}(8) = 5.2; \text{ round up to position 6}$$

65th percentile = 28

$$i = \frac{75}{100}(8) = 6; \text{ use positions 6 and 7}$$

$$75\text{th percentile} = \frac{28 + 30}{2} = 29$$

8. a. $\bar{x} = \frac{\Sigma x_i}{n} = \frac{695}{20} = 34.75$

   Mode = 25 (appears three times)

b. Data in order: 18, 20, 25, 25, 25, 26, 27, 27, 28, 33, 36, 37, 40, 40, 42, 45, 46, 48, 53, 54

Median (10th and 11th positions)

$$\frac{33 + 36}{2} = 34.5$$

At home workers are slightly younger

c. $i = \frac{25}{100}(20) = 5$; use positions 5 and 6

$$Q_1 = \frac{25 + 26}{2} = 25.5$$

$i = \frac{75}{100}(20) = 15$; use positions 15 and 16

$$Q_3 = \frac{42 + 45}{2} = 43.5$$

d. $i = \frac{32}{100}(20) = 6.4$; round up to position 7

32nd percentile = 27
At least 32% of the people are 27 or younger

17. Range = $34 - 15 = 19$
Arrange data in order: 15, 20, 25, 25, 27, 28, 30, 34

$i = \frac{25}{100}(8) = 2$; $Q_1 = \frac{20 + 25}{2} = 22.5$

$i = \frac{75}{100}(8) = 6$; $Q_3 = \frac{28 + 30}{2} = 29$

IQR = $Q_3 - Q_1 = 29 - 22.5 = 6.5$

$\bar{x} = \frac{\Sigma x_i}{n} = \frac{204}{8} = 25.5$

x_i	$(x_i - \bar{x})$	$(x_i - \bar{x})^2$
27	1.5	2.25
25	−.5	.25
20	−5.5	30.25
15	−10.5	110.25
30	4.5	20.25
34	8.5	72.25
28	2.5	6.25
25	−.5	.25
		242.00

$$s^2 = \frac{\Sigma(x_i - \bar{x})^2}{n - 1} = \frac{242}{8 - 1} = 34.57$$

$$s = \sqrt{34.57} = 5.88$$

18. a. Range = $190 - 168 = 22$

b. $\bar{x} = \frac{\Sigma x_i}{n} = \frac{1068}{6} = 178$

$s^2 = \frac{\Sigma(x_i - \bar{x})^2}{n - 1}$

$= \frac{4^2 + (-10)^2 + 6^2 + 12^2 + (-8)^2 + (-4)^2}{6 - 1}$

$= \frac{376}{5} = 75.2$

c. $s = \sqrt{75.2} = 8.67$

d. $\frac{s}{\bar{x}}(100) = \frac{8.67}{178}(100) = 4.87$

27. Chebyshev's theorem: *at least* $(1 - 1/z^2)$

a. $z = \frac{40 - 30}{5} = 2$; $(1 - \frac{1}{2}^2) = .75$

b. $z = \frac{45 - 30}{5} = 3$; $(1 - \frac{1}{3}^2) = .89$

c. $z = \frac{38 - 30}{5} = 1.6$; $(1 - \frac{1}{1.6}^2) = .61$

d. $z = \frac{42 - 30}{5} = 2.4$; $(1 - \frac{1}{2.4}^2) = .83$

e. $z = \frac{48 - 30}{5} = 3.6$; $(1 - \frac{1}{3.6}^2) = .92$

40. Arrange data in order: 5, 6, 8, 10, 10, 12, 15, 16, 18

$i = \frac{25}{100}(9) = 2.25$; round up to position 3

$Q_1 = 8$
Median (5th position) = 10

$i = \frac{75}{100}(9) = 6.75$; round up to position 7

$Q_3 = 15$
5-number summary: 5, 8, 10, 15, 18

43. a. Arrange data in order low to high

$i = \frac{25}{100}(21) = 5.25$; round up to 6th position

$Q_1 = 1872$
Median (11th position) = 4019

$i = \frac{75}{100}(21) = 15.75$; round up to 16th position

$Q_3 = 8305$
5-number summary: 608, 1872, 4019, 8305, 14,138

b. IQR = $Q_3 - Q_1 = 8305 - 1872 = 6433$
Lower limit: $1872 - 1.5(6433) = -7777$
Upper limit: $8305 + 1.5(6433) = 17,955$

c. No; data are within limits

d. $41,138 > 27,604$; 41,138 would be an outlier; data value should be reviewed and corrected

e.

47. b. There appears to be a negative linear relationship between x and y

c.

x_i	y_i	$x_i - \bar{x}$	$y_i - \bar{y}$	$(x_i - \bar{x})(y_i - \bar{y})$
4	50	−4	4	−16
6	50	−2	4	−8
11	40	3	−6	−18
3	60	−5	14	−70
16	30	8	−16	−128
40	230	0	0	−240

$\bar{x} = 8;\ \bar{y} = 46$

$$s_{xy} = \frac{\Sigma(x_i - \bar{x})(y_i - \bar{y})}{n - 1} = \frac{-240}{4} = -60$$

The sample covariance indicates a negative linear association between x and y

d. $r_{xy} = \dfrac{s_{xy}}{s_x s_y} = \dfrac{-60}{(5.43)(11.40)} = -.97$

The sample correlation coefficient of $-.97$ is indicative of a strong negative linear relationship

55. a.

f_i	M_i	$f_i M_i$
4	5	20
7	10	70
9	15	135
5	20	100
25		325

$$\bar{x} = \frac{\Sigma f_i M_i}{n} = \frac{325}{25} = 13$$

b.

f_i	M_i	$(M_i - \bar{x})$	$(M_i - \bar{x})^2$	$f_i(M_i - \bar{x})^2$
4	5	−8	64	256
7	10	−3	9	63
9	15	2	4	36
5	20	7	49	245
25				600

$$s^2 = \frac{\Sigma f_i(M_i - \bar{x})^2}{n - 1} = \frac{600}{25 - 1} = 25$$

$$s = \sqrt{25} = 5$$

56. a.

Grade x_i	Weight w_i
4(A)	9
3(B)	15
2(C)	33
1(D)	3
0(F)	0
	60 credit hours

$$\bar{x} = \frac{\Sigma w_i x_i}{\Sigma w_i} = \frac{9(4) + 15(3) + 33(2) + 3(1)}{9 + 15 + 33 + 3}$$

$$= \frac{150}{60} = 2.5$$

b. Yes

Chapter 4

2. $\dbinom{6}{3} = \dfrac{6!}{3!3!} = \dfrac{6 \cdot 5 \cdot 4 \cdot 3 \cdot 2 \cdot 1}{(3 \cdot 2 \cdot 1)(3 \cdot 2 \cdot 1)} = 20$

ABC	ACE	BCD	BEF
ABD	ACF	BCE	CDE
ABE	ADE	BCF	CDF
ABF	ADF	BDE	CEF
ACD	AEF	BDF	DEF

6. $P(E_1) = .40$, $P(E_2) = .26$, $P(E_3) = .34$
The relative frequency method was used

9. $\dbinom{50}{4} = \dfrac{50!}{4!46!} = \dfrac{50 \cdot 49 \cdot 48 \cdot 47}{4 \cdot 3 \cdot 2 \cdot 1} = 230,300$

10. a. Use the relative frequency approach
$P(\text{California}) = 1434/2374 = .60$

  b. Number not from 4 states
  $= 2374 - 1434 - 390 - 217 - 112$
  $= 221$
  $P(\text{Not from 4 states}) = 221/2374 = .09$

  c. $P(\text{Not in early stages}) = 1 - .22 = .78$

  d. Estimate of number of Massachusetts' companies in early stage of development $= (.22)390 \approx 86$

  e. If we assume the size of the awards did not differ by state, we can multiply the probability an award went to Colorado by the total venture funds disbursed to get an estimate
  Est. of Colo. funds $= (112/2374)(\$32.4)$
  $\qquad\qquad\qquad = \$1.53$ billion

  Authors' Note: The actual amount going to Colorado was $1.74 billion

15. a. $S = $ (ace of clubs, ace of diamonds, ace of hearts, ace of spades)

  b. $S = $ (2 of clubs, 3 of clubs, . . . , 10 of clubs, J of clubs, Q of clubs, K of clubs, A of clubs)

  c. There are 12; jack, queen, or king in each of the four suits

  d. For (a): $4/52 = 1/13 = .08$
  For (b): $13/52 = 1/4 = .25$
  For (c): $12/52 = .23$

17. a. (4, 6), (4, 7), (4, 8)

  b. $.05 + .10 + .15 = .30$

  c. (2, 8), (3, 8), (4, 8)

  d. $.05 + .05 + .15 = .25$

  e. .15

23. a. $P(A) = P(E_1) + P(E_4) + P(E_6)$
  $\qquad = .05 + .25 + .10 = .40$
  $P(B) = P(E_2) + P(E_4) + P(E_7)$
  $\qquad = .20 + .25 + .05 = .50$
  $P(C) = P(E_2) + P(E_3) + P(E_5) + P(E_7)$
  $\qquad = .20 + .20 + .15 + .05 = .60$

  b. $A \cup B = \{E_1, E_2, E_4, E_6, E_7\}$
  $P(A \cup B) = P(E_1) + P(E_2) + P(E_4) + P(E_6) + P(E_7)$
  $\qquad = .05 + .20 + .25 + .10 + .05$
  $\qquad = .65$

c. $A \cap B = \{E_4\}$, $P(A \cap B) = P(E_4) = .25$

d. Yes, they are mutually exclusive

e. $B^c = \{E_1, E_3, E_5, E_6\}$

$P(B^c) = P(E_1) + P(E_3) + P(E_5) + P(E_6)$
$= .05 + .20 + .15 + .10$
$= .50$

28. Let B = rented a car for business reasons
P = rented a car for personal reasons

a. $P(B \cup P) = P(B) + P(P) - P(B \cap P)$
$= .540 + .458 - .300$
$= .698$

b. $P(\text{Neither}) = 1 - .698 = .302$

30. a. $P(A \mid B) = \dfrac{P(A \cap B)}{P(B)} = \dfrac{.40}{.60} = .6667$

b. $P(B \mid A) = \dfrac{P(A \cap B)}{P(A)} = \dfrac{.40}{.50} = .80$

c. No, because $P(A \mid B) \neq P(A)$

33. a.

	Reason for Applying			
	Quality	**Cost/ Convenience**	**Other**	**Total**
Full-time	.218	.204	.039	.461
Part-time	.208	.307	.024	.539
Total	.426	.511	.063	1.000

b. A student is most likely to cite cost or convenience as the first reason (probability = .511); school quality is the first reason cited by the second largest number of students (probability = .426)

c. $P(\text{quality} \mid \text{full-time}) = .218/.461 = .473$

d. $P(\text{quality} \mid \text{part-time}) = .208/.539 = .386$

e. For independence, we must have $P(A)P(B) = P(A \cap B)$; from the table

$P(A \cap B) = .218$, $P(A) = .461$, $P(B) = .426$

$P(A)P(B) = (.461)(.426) = .196$

Because $P(A)P(B) \neq P(A \cap B)$, the events are not independent

39. a. Yes, because $P(A_1 \cap A_2) = 0$

b. $P(A_1 \cap B) = P(A_1)P(B \mid A_1) = .40(.20) = .08$
$P(A_2 \cap B) = P(A_2)P(B \mid A_2) = .60(.05) = .03$

c. $P(B) = P(A_1 \cap B) + P(A_2 \cap B) = .08 + .03 = .11$

d. $P(A_1 \mid B) = \dfrac{.08}{.11} = .7273$

$P(A_2 \mid B) = \dfrac{.03}{.11} = .2727$

42. M = missed payment
D_1 = customer defaults
D_2 = customer does not default
$P(D_1) = .05$, $P(D_2) = .95$, $P(M \mid D_2) = .2$, $P(M \mid D_1) = 1$

a. $P(D_1 \mid M) = \dfrac{P(D_1)P(M \mid D_1)}{P(D_1)P(M \mid D_1) + P(D_2)P(M \mid D_2)}$

$= \dfrac{(.05)(1)}{(.05)(1) + (.95)(.2)}$

$= \dfrac{.05}{.24} = .21$

b. Yes, the probability of default is greater than .20

Chapter 5

1. a. Head, Head (H, H)
Head, Tail (H, T)
Tail, Head (T, H)
Tail, Tail (T, T)

b. x = number of heads on two coin tosses

c.

Outcome	Values of x
(H, H)	2
(H, T)	1
(T, H)	1
(T, T)	0

d. Discrete; it may assume 3 values: 0, 1, and 2

3. Let: Y = position is offered
N = position is not offered

a. $S = \{(Y, Y, Y), (Y, Y, N), (Y, N, Y), (Y, N, N), (N, Y, Y),$
$(N, Y, N), (N, N, Y), (N, N, N)\}$

b. Let N = number of offers made; N is a discrete random variable

c.

Experimental Outcome	(Y, Y, Y)	(Y, Y, N)	(Y, N, Y)	(Y, N, N)	(N, Y, Y)	(N, Y, N)	(N, N, Y)	(N, N, N)
Value of N	3	2	2	1	2	1	1	0

7. a. $f(x) \geq 0$ for all values of x
$\Sigma f(x) = 1$; therefore, it is a proper probability distribution

b. Probability $x = 30$ is $f(30) = .25$

c. Probability $x \leq 25$ is $f(20) + f(25) = .20 + .15 = .35$

d. Probability $x > 30$ is $f(35) = .40$

8. a.

x	$f(x)$	
1	3/20 =	.15
2	5/20 =	.25
3	8/20 =	.40
4	4/20 =	.20
	Total	1.00

b.

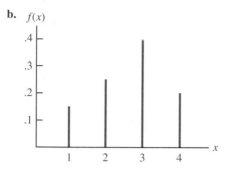

c. $f(x) \geq 0$ for $x = 1, 2, 3, 4$
$\Sigma f(x) = 1$

16. a.

y	f(y)	yf(y)
2	.20	.40
4	.30	1.20
7	.40	2.80
8	.10	.80
Totals	1.00	5.20

$$E(y) = \mu = 5.20$$

b.

y	y − μ	(y − μ)²	f(y)	(y − μ)²f(y)
2	−3.20	10.24	.20	2.048
4	−1.20	1.44	.30	.432
7	1.80	3.24	.40	1.296
8	2.80	7.84	.10	.784
			Total	4.560

$$Var(y) = 4.56$$
$$\sigma = \sqrt{4.56} = 2.14$$

18. a/b.

x	f(x)	xf(x)	(x − μ)	(x − μ)²	(x − μ)²f(x)
0	.01	.00	−2.3	5.29	.0529
1	.23	.23	−1.3	1.69	.3887
2	.41	.82	−0.3	0.09	.0369
3	.20	.60	0.7	0.49	.0980
4	.10	.40	1.7	2.89	.2890
5	.05	.25	2.7	7.29	.3645
	E(x) = 2.30			Var(x) = 1.2300	
					σ = 1.11

The expected value, $E(x) = 2.3$, of the probability distribution is the same as the average reported in the *1997 Statistical Abstract of the United States*
$Var(x) = 1.23$ television sets squared
$\sigma = \sqrt{1.23} = 1.11$ television sets

25. a.

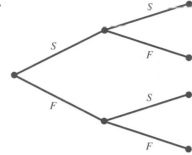

b. $f(1) = \binom{2}{1}(.4)^1(.6)^1 = \dfrac{2!}{1!1!}(.4)(.6) = .48$

c. $f(0) = \binom{2}{0}(.4)^0(.6)^2 = \dfrac{2!}{0!2!}(1)(.36) = .36$

d. $f(2) = \binom{2}{2}(.4)^2(.6)^0 = \dfrac{2!}{2!0!}(.16)(.1) = .16$

e. $P(x \geq 1) = f(1) + f(2) = .48 + .16 = .64$

f. $E(x) = np = 2(.4) = .8$
$Var(x) = np(1 - p) = 2(.4)(.6) = .48$
$\sigma = \sqrt{.48} = .6928$

30. a. Probability of a defective part being produced must be .03 for each trial; trials must be independent

b. Let D = defective
G = not defective

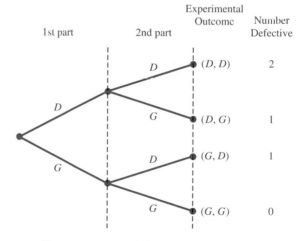

c. Two outcomes result in exactly one defect

d. $P(\text{no defects}) = (.97)(.97) = .9409$
$P(1 \text{ defect}) = 2(.03)(.97) = .0582$
$P(2 \text{ defects}) = (.03)(.03) = .0009$

39. a. $f(x) = \dfrac{2^x e^{-2}}{x!}$

b. $\mu = 6$ for 3 time periods

c. $f(x) = \dfrac{6^x e^{-6}}{x!}$

d. $f(2) = \dfrac{2^2 e^{-2}}{2!} = \dfrac{4(.1353)}{2} = .2706$

e. $f(6) = \dfrac{6^6 e^{-6}}{6!} = .1606$

f. $f(5) = \dfrac{4^5 e^{-4}}{5!} = .1563$

40. a. $\mu = 48(5/60) = 4$

$f(3) = \dfrac{4^3 e^{-4}}{3!} = \dfrac{(64)(.0183)}{6} = .1952$

b. $\mu = 48(15/60) = 12$

$f(10) = \dfrac{12^{10} e^{-12}}{10!} = .1048$

c. $\mu = 48(5/60) = 4$; one can expect four callers to be waiting after 5 minutes

$f(0) = \dfrac{4^0 e^{-4}}{0!} = .0183$; the probability none will be waiting after 5 minutes is .0183

d. $\mu = 48(3/60) = 2.4$

$f(0) = \dfrac{2.4^0 e^{-2.4}}{0!} = .0907$; the probability of no interruptions in 3 minutes is .0907

46. a. $f(1) = \dfrac{\binom{3}{1}\binom{10-3}{4-1}}{\binom{10}{4}} = \dfrac{\left(\dfrac{3!}{1!2!}\right)\left(\dfrac{7!}{3!4!}\right)}{\dfrac{10!}{4!6!}}$

$= \dfrac{(3)(35)}{210} = .50$

b. $f(2) = \dfrac{\binom{3}{2}\binom{10-3}{2-2}}{\binom{10}{2}} = \dfrac{(3)(1)}{45} = .067$

c. $f(0) = \dfrac{\binom{3}{0}\binom{10-3}{2-0}}{\binom{10}{2}} = \dfrac{(1)(21)}{45} = .4667$

d. $f(2) = \dfrac{\binom{3}{2}\binom{10-3}{4-2}}{\binom{10}{4}} = \dfrac{(3)(21)}{210} = .30$

50. $N = 60, n = 10$

a. $r = 20, x = 0$

$f(0) = \dfrac{\binom{20}{0}\binom{40}{10}}{\binom{60}{10}} = \dfrac{(1)\left(\dfrac{40!}{10!30!}\right)}{\dfrac{60!}{10!50!}}$

$= \left(\dfrac{40!}{10!30!}\right)\left(\dfrac{10!50!}{60!}\right)$

$= \dfrac{40 \cdot 39 \cdot 38 \cdot 37 \cdot 36 \cdot 35 \cdot 34 \cdot 33 \cdot 32 \cdot 31}{60 \cdot 59 \cdot 58 \cdot 57 \cdot 56 \cdot 55 \cdot 54 \cdot 53 \cdot 52 \cdot 51}$

$\approx .01$

b. $r = 20, x = 1$

$f(1) = \dfrac{\binom{20}{1}\binom{40}{9}}{\binom{60}{10}} = 20\left(\dfrac{40!}{9!31!}\right)\left(\dfrac{10!50!}{60!}\right)$

$\approx .07$

c. $1 - f(0) - f(1) = 1 - .08 = .92$

d. Same as the probability one will be from Hawaii; in part (b) it was equal to approximately .07

Chapter 6

1. a.

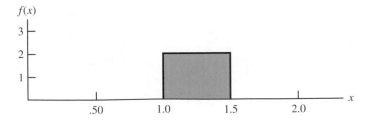

b. $P(x = 1.25) = 0$; the probability of any single point is zero because the area under the curve above any single point is zero

c. $P(1.0 \le x \le 1.25) = 2(.25) = .50$

d. $P(1.20 < x < 1.5) = 2(.30) = .60$

4. a.

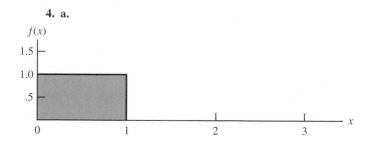

b. $P(.25 < x < .75) = 1(.50) = .50$
c. $P(x \leq .30) = 1(.30) = .30$
d. $P(x > .60) = 1(.40) = .40$

13. a. $.6879 - .0239 = .6640$
b. $.8888 - .6985 = .1903$
c. $.9599 - .8508 = .1091$

15. a. Look in the table for an area of $.5000 - .2119 = .2881$; $z = .80$ cuts off an area of .2119 in the upper tail; thus, for an area of .2119 in the lower tail, $z = -.80$
b. Look in the table for an area of $.9030/2 = .4515$; $z = 1.66$
c. Look in the table for an area of $.2052/2 = .1026$; $z = .26$
d. Look in the table for an area of $.4948$; $z = 2.56$
e. Look in the table for an area of $.1915$; because the value we are seeking is below the mean, the z value must be negative; thus, $z = -.50$

18. a. Find $P(x \geq 60)$

At $x = 60$, $z = \dfrac{60 - 49}{16} = \dfrac{11}{16} = .69$

$P(x < 60) = .7549$
$P(x \geq 60) = 1 - P(x < 60) = 1 - .7549 = .2451$

b. Find $P(x \leq 30)$

At $x = 30$, $z = \dfrac{30 - 49}{16} = -1.19$

$P(x \leq 30) = .5000 - .3830$
$\qquad\qquad = .1170$

c. Find z-score so that $P(z \geq z\text{-score}) = .10$
A z-score of 1.28 cuts off 10% in upper tail; now, solve for corresponding value of x

$1.28 = \dfrac{x - 49}{16}$

$x = 49 + (16)(1.28)$
$\quad = 69.48$

So, 10% of subscribers spend 69.48 minutes or more reading *The Wall Street Journal*

27. a. $P(x \leq x_0) = 1 - e^{-x_0/3}$
b. $P(x \leq 2) = 1 - e^{-2/3} = 1 - .5134 = .4866$
c. $P(x \geq 3) = 1 - P(x \leq 3) = 1 - (1 - e^{-3/3})$
$\qquad\qquad = e^{-1} = .3679$
d. $P(x \leq 5) = 1 - e^{-5/3} = 1 - .1889 = .8111$
e. $P(2 \leq x \leq 5) = P(x \leq 5) - P(x \leq 2)$
$\qquad\qquad = .8111 - .4866 = .3245$

29. a.

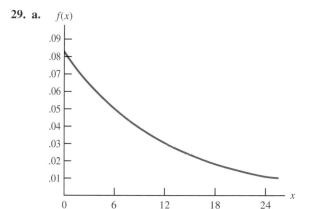

b. $P(x \leq 12) = 1 - e^{-12/12} = 1 - .3679 = .6321$
c. $P(x \leq 6) = 1 - e^{-6/12} = 1 - .6065 = .3935$
d. $P(x \geq 30) = 1 - P(x < 30)$
$\qquad\qquad = 1 - (1 - e^{-30/12})$
$\qquad\qquad = .0821$

Chapter 7

1. a. AB, AC, AD, AE, BC, BD, BE, CD, CE, DE
b. With 10 samples, each has a $\frac{1}{10}$ probability
c. E and C because 8 and 0 do not apply; 5 identifies E; 7 does not apply; 5 is skipped because E is already in the sample; 3 identifies C; 2 is not needed because the sample of size 2 is complete

3. 459, 147, 385, 113, 340, 401, 215, 2, 33, 348

11. a. $\bar{x} = \dfrac{\Sigma x_i}{n} = \dfrac{54}{6} = 9$

b. $s = \sqrt{\dfrac{\Sigma(x_i - \bar{x})^2}{n - 1}}$

$\Sigma(x_i - \bar{x})^2 = (-4)^2 + (-1)^2 + 1^2 + (-2)^2 + 1^2 + 5^2$
$\qquad\qquad = 48$

$s = \sqrt{\dfrac{48}{6 - 1}} = 3.1$

13. a. $\bar{x} = \dfrac{\Sigma x_i}{n} = \dfrac{465}{5} = 93$

b.

x_i	$(x_i - \bar{x})$	$(x_i - \bar{x})^2$
94	+1	1
100	+7	49
85	−8	64
94	+1	1
92	−1	1
Totals 465	0	116

$$s = \sqrt{\frac{\Sigma(x_i - \bar{x})^2}{n - 1}} = \sqrt{\frac{116}{4}} = 5.39$$

19. a. The sampling distribution is normal with:

$$E(\bar{x}) = \mu = 200$$

$$\sigma_{\bar{x}} = \frac{\sigma}{\sqrt{n}} = \frac{50}{\sqrt{100}} = 5$$

For +5, $(\bar{x} - \mu) = 5$,

$$z = \frac{\bar{x} - \mu}{\sigma_{\bar{x}}} = \frac{5}{5} = 1$$

Area = .3413 × 2 = .6826

b. For ±10, $(\bar{x} - \mu) = 10$,

$$z = \frac{\bar{x} - \mu}{\sigma_{\bar{x}}} = \frac{10}{5} = 2$$

Area = .4772 × 2 = .9544

25. a.

$$\sigma_{\bar{x}} = \frac{\sigma}{\sqrt{n}} = \frac{4000}{\sqrt{60}} = 516.40$$

$$z = \frac{52,300 - 51,800}{516.40} = +.97$$

Area = .3340 × 2 = .6680

b. $$\sigma_{\bar{x}} = \frac{\sigma}{\sqrt{n}} = \frac{4000}{\sqrt{120}} = 365.15$$

$$z = \frac{52,300 - 51,800}{365.15} = +1.37$$

Area = .4147 × 2 = .8294

34. a. $E(\bar{p}) = .40$

$$\sigma_{\bar{p}} = \sqrt{\frac{p(1 - p)}{n}} = \sqrt{\frac{(.40)(.60)}{200}} = .0346$$

$$z = \frac{\bar{p} - p}{\sigma_{\bar{p}}} = \frac{.03}{.0346} = .87$$

Area = .3078 × 2 = .6156

b. $$z = \frac{\bar{p} - p}{\sigma_{\bar{p}}} = \frac{.05}{.0346} = 1.45$$

Area = .4265 × 2 = .8530

37. a.

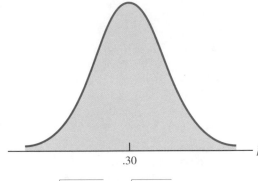

$$\sigma_{\bar{p}} = \sqrt{\frac{p(1 - p)}{n}} = \sqrt{\frac{.30(.70)}{100}} = .0458$$

The normal distribution is appropriate because $np = 100(.30) = 30$ and $n(1 - p) = 100(.70) = 70$ are both greater than 5

b. $P(.20 \leq \bar{p} \leq .40) = ?$

$$z = \frac{.40 - .30}{.0458} = 2.18$$

Area = .4854 × 2 = .9708

c. $P(.25 \leq \bar{p} \leq .35) = ?$

$$z = \frac{.35 - .30}{.0458} = 1.09$$

Area = .3621 × 2 = .7242

Chapter 8

2. Use $\bar{x} \pm z_{\alpha/2}(\sigma/\sqrt{n})$ with the sample standard deviation s used to estimate σ
 a. $32 \pm 1.645 (6/\sqrt{50})$
   32 ± 1.4; 30.6 to 33.4
 b. $32 \pm 1.96(6/\sqrt{50})$
   32 ± 1.66; 30.34 to 33.66
 c. $32 \pm 2.76(6/\sqrt{50})$
   32 ± 2.19; 29.81 to 34.19

5. a. $1.96\sigma/\sqrt{n} = 1.96 (5.00/\sqrt{49}) = 1.40$
 b. 24.80 ± 1.40; 23.40 to 26.20

15. a. $\bar{x} = \frac{\Sigma x_i}{n} = \frac{80}{8} = 10$

 b. $s = \sqrt{\frac{\Sigma(x_i - \bar{x})^2}{n - 1}} = \sqrt{\frac{84}{8 - 1}} = 3.46$

c. With 7 degrees of freedom, $t_{.025} = 2.365$

$$\bar{x} \pm t_{.025}\frac{s}{\sqrt{n}}$$

$$10 \pm 2.365\frac{3.46}{\sqrt{8}}$$

$$10 \pm 2.90; 7.10 \text{ to } 12.90$$

17. At 90%, $80 \pm t_{.05}(s/\sqrt{n})$ with degrees of freedom = 17

$$t_{.05} = 1.740$$
$$80 \pm 1.740(10/\sqrt{18})$$
$$80 \pm 4.10; 75.90 \text{ to } 84.10$$

At 95%, $80 \pm t_{.025}(10/\sqrt{18})$ with degrees of freedom = 17

$$t_{.025} = 2.110$$
$$80 \pm 2.110 (10/\sqrt{18})$$
$$80 \pm 4.97; 75.03 \text{ to } 84.97$$

24. a. Planning value of $\sigma = \dfrac{\text{Range}}{4} = \dfrac{36}{4} = 9$

b. $n = \dfrac{z_{.025}^2 \sigma^2}{E^2} = \dfrac{(1.96)^2(9)^2}{(3)^2} = 34.57$; use $n = 35$

c. $n = \dfrac{(1.96)^2(9)^2}{(2)^2} = 77.79$; use $n = 78$

25. a. Use $n = \dfrac{z_{\alpha/2}^2 \sigma^2}{E^2}$

$$n = \dfrac{(1.96)^2(6.82)^2}{(1.5)^2} = 79.41; \text{ use } n = 80$$

b. $n = \dfrac{(1.645)^2(6.82)^2}{(2)^2} = 31.47$; use $n = 32$

31. a. $\bar{p} = \dfrac{100}{400} = .25$

b. $\sqrt{\dfrac{\bar{p}(1-\bar{p})}{n}} = \sqrt{\dfrac{.25(.75)}{400}} = .0217$

c. $\bar{p} \pm z_{.025}\sqrt{\dfrac{\bar{p}(1-\bar{p})}{n}}$

$$.25 \pm 1.96(.0217)$$
$$.25 \pm .0424; .2076 \text{ to } .2924$$

35. a. $\bar{p} = 562/814 = .6904$

b. $1.645\sqrt{\dfrac{.6904(1-.6904)}{814}} = .0267$

c. $.6904 \pm .0267; .6637 \text{ to } .7171$

39. a. $n = \dfrac{1.96^2 p(1-p)}{E^2}$

$$n = \dfrac{1.96^2(.33)(.67)}{(.03)^2} = 943.75; \text{ use } n = 944$$

b. $n = \dfrac{2.576^2(.33)(.67)}{(.03)^2} = 1630.19$; use $n = 1631$

Chapter 9

2. a. $H_0: \mu \le 14$
$H_a: \mu > 14$

b. No evidence that the new plan increases sales

c. The research hypothesis $\mu > 14$ is supported; the new plan increases sales

5. a. Rejecting $H_0: \mu \le 8.6$ when it is true

b. Accepting $H_0: \mu \le 8.6$ when it is false

10. a. $z = 2.05$
Reject H_0 if $z > 2.05$

b. $z = \dfrac{x - \mu}{s/\sqrt{n}} = \dfrac{16.5 - 15}{7/\sqrt{40}} = 1.36$

c. Area for $z = 1.36 = .4131$
p-value $= .5000 - .4131 = .0869$

d. Do not reject H_0

13. a. $H_0: \mu \ge 1056$
$H_a: \mu < 1056$

b. Reject H_0 if $z < -1.645$

c. $z = \dfrac{\bar{x} - \mu}{s/\sqrt{n}} = \dfrac{910 - 1056}{1600/\sqrt{400}} = -1.83$

d. Reject H_0; conclude $\mu < 1056$

e. p-value $= .5000 - .4664 = .0336$

22. a. Reject H_0 if $z < -2.33$ or $z > 2.33$

b. $z = \dfrac{\bar{x} - \mu}{\sigma/\sqrt{n}} = \dfrac{14.2 - 15}{5/\sqrt{50}} = 1.13$

c. p-value $= 2(.5000 - .3708) = .2584$

d. Do not reject H_0

25. a. Reject H_0 if $z < -1.96$ or $z > 1.96$

b. $z = \dfrac{\bar{x} - \mu_0}{s/\sqrt{n}} = \dfrac{38.5 - 39.2}{4.8/\sqrt{112}} = -1.54$

c. Do not reject H_0

d. p-value $= 2(.5000 - .4382) = .1236$

34. a. $\bar{x} = \dfrac{\Sigma x_i}{n} = \dfrac{108}{6} = 18$

b. $s = \sqrt{\dfrac{\Sigma(x_i - \bar{x})}{n-1}} = \sqrt{\dfrac{10}{6-1}} = 1.41$

c. Reject H_0 if $t < -2.571$ or $t > 2.571$

d. $t = \dfrac{\bar{x} - \mu}{s/\sqrt{n}} = \dfrac{18 - 20}{1.41/\sqrt{6}} = -3.47$

e. Reject H_0; conclude H_a is true

37. a. $H_0: \mu = 3.00$
$H_a: \mu \ne 3.00$

b. Reject H_0 if $t < -2.262$ or if $t > 2.262$

c. $\bar{x} = \Sigma x_i/n = \dfrac{28}{10} = 2.80$

d. $s = \sqrt{\dfrac{\Sigma(x_i - \bar{x})^2}{n-1}} = .70$

e. $t = \dfrac{\bar{x} - \mu_0}{s/\sqrt{n}} = \dfrac{2.80 - 3.00}{.70/\sqrt{10}} = -.90$

f. Do not reject H_0

g. $t_{.10} = 1.383$; p-value greater than $2(.10) = .20$

44. a. Reject H_0 if $z < -1.96$ or $z > 1.96$

b. $\sigma_{\bar{p}} = \sqrt{\dfrac{.20(.80)}{400}} = .02$

$z = \dfrac{\bar{p} - p}{\sigma_{\bar{p}}} = \dfrac{.175 - .20}{.02} = -1.25$

c. p-value $= 2(.5000 - .3944) = .2112$

d. Do not reject H_0

47. a. Reject H_0 if $z < -1.645$

b. $\bar{p} = 52/100 = .52$

$\sigma_{\bar{p}} = \sqrt{\dfrac{p(1 - p)}{n}} = \sqrt{\dfrac{.64(1 - .64)}{100}} = .0480$

$z = \dfrac{\bar{p} - p}{\sigma_{\bar{p}}} = \dfrac{.52 - .64}{.0480} = -2.50$

c. Reject H_0; conclude less than 64% agree

d. p-value $= .5000 - .4938 = .0062$

Chapter 10

1. a. $\bar{x}_1 - \bar{x}_2 = 13.6 - 11.6 = 2$

b. $s_{\bar{x}_1 - \bar{x}_2} = \sqrt{\dfrac{s_1^2}{n_1} + \dfrac{s_2^2}{n_2}} = \sqrt{\dfrac{(2.2)^2}{50} + \dfrac{3^2}{35}} = .595$

$2 \pm 1.645(.595)$

$2 \pm .98$ or 1.02 to 2.98

c. $2 \pm 1.96(.595)$

2 ± 1.17, or $.83$ to 3.17

8. a. $\bar{x}_1 - \bar{x}_2 = 45{,}700 - 44{,}500 = 1200$

b. Pooled variance

$s^2 = \dfrac{7(700)^2 + 11(850)^2}{18} = 632{,}083$

$s_{\bar{x}_1 - \bar{x}_2} = \sqrt{632{,}083\left(\dfrac{1}{8} + \dfrac{1}{12}\right)} = 362.88$

With 18 degrees of freedom $t_{.025} = 2.101$,

$1200 \pm 2.101(362.88)$

1200 ± 762, or 438 to 1962

c. Populations are normally distributed with equal variances

11. a. $s_{\bar{x}_1 - \bar{x}_2} = \sqrt{\dfrac{s_1^2}{n_1} + \dfrac{s_2^2}{n_2}} = \sqrt{\dfrac{(5.2)^2}{40} + \dfrac{6^2}{50}} = 1.18$

$z = \dfrac{(\bar{x}_1 - \bar{x}_2) - (\mu_1 - \mu_2)}{s_{\bar{x}_1 - \bar{x}_2}}$

$= \dfrac{(25.2 - 22.8)}{1.18} = 2.03$

Reject H_0 if $z > 1.645$; therefore reject H_0; conclude H_a is true and $\mu_1 > \mu_2$

b. p-value $= .5000 - .4788 = .0212$

15. $H_0: \mu_1 - \mu_2 = 0$

$H_a: \mu_1 - \mu_2 \neq 0$

Reject H_0 if $z < -1.96$ or if $z > 1.96$

$z = \dfrac{(\bar{x}_1 - \bar{x}_2) - 0}{\sqrt{\sigma_1^2/n_1 + \sigma_2^2/n_2}} = \dfrac{40 - 35}{\sqrt{(9)^2/36 + (10)^2/49}}$

$= 2.41$

p-value $= 2(.5000 - .4920) = .0160$

Reject H_0; customers at the two stores differ in terms of mean ages

21. a. $1, 2, 0, 0, 2$

b. $\bar{d} = \dfrac{\Sigma d_i}{n} = \dfrac{5}{5} = 1$

c. $s_d = \sqrt{\dfrac{\Sigma(d_i - \bar{d})^2}{n - 1}} = \sqrt{\dfrac{4}{5 - 1}} = 1$

d. With 4 degrees of freedom, $t_{.05} = 2.132$; reject H_0 if $t > 2.132$

$t = \dfrac{\bar{d} - \mu_d}{s_d/\sqrt{n}} = \dfrac{1 - 0}{1/\sqrt{5}} = 2.24$

Reject H_0; conclude $\mu_d > 0$

23. d = rating after − rating before

$H_0: \mu_d \leq 0$

$H_a: \mu_d > 0$

With 7 degrees of freedom, reject H_0 if $t > 1.895$; when $\bar{d} = .63$ and $s_d = 1.3025$,

$t = \dfrac{\bar{d} - \mu_d}{s_d/\sqrt{n}} = \dfrac{.63 - 0}{1.3025/\sqrt{8}} = 1.36$

Do not reject H_0; we cannot conclude that seeing the commercial improves the potential to purchase

29. a. $\bar{\bar{x}} = (30 + 45 + 36)/3 = 37$

$\text{SSTR} = \sum_{j=1}^{k} n_j(\bar{x}_j - \bar{\bar{x}})^2$

$= 5(30 - 37)^2 + 5(45 - 37)^2 + 5(36 - 37)^2$

$= 570$

$\text{MSTR} = \dfrac{\text{SSTR}}{k - 1} = \dfrac{570}{2} = 285$

b. $\text{SSE} = \sum_{j=1}^{k}(n_j - 1)s_j^2$

$= 4(6) + 4(4) + 4(6.5) = 66$

$\text{MSE} = \dfrac{\text{SSE}}{n_T - k} = \dfrac{66}{15 - 3} = 5.5$

c. $F = \dfrac{\text{MSTR}}{\text{MSE}} = \dfrac{285}{5.5} = 51.82$

$F_{.05} = 3.89$ (2 degrees of freedom numerator and 12 denominator)

Because $F = 51.82 > F_{.05} = 3.89$, we reject the null hypothesis that the means of the three populations are equal

d.

Source of Variation	Sum of Squares	Degrees of Freedom	Mean Square	F
Treatments	570	2	285	51.82
Error	66	12	5.5	
Total	636	14		

34.

	Mfg 1	Mfg 2	Mfg 3
Sample mean	23	28	21
Sample variance	6.67	4.67	3.33

$$\bar{\bar{x}} = (23 + 28 + 21)/3 = 24$$

$$\text{SSTR} = \sum_{j=1}^{k} n_j(\bar{x}_j - \bar{\bar{x}})^2$$

$$= 4(23 - 24)^2 + 4(28 - 24)^2$$
$$+ 4(21 - 24)^2 = 104$$

$$\text{MSTR} = \frac{\text{SSTR}}{k-1} = \frac{104}{2} = 52$$

$$\text{SSE} = \sum_{j=1}^{k} (n_j - 1)s_j^2$$

$$= 3(6.67) + 3(4.67) + 3(3.33) = 44.01$$

$$\text{MSE} = \frac{\text{SSE}}{n_T - k} = \frac{44.01}{12 - 3} = 4.89$$

$$F = \frac{\text{MSTR}}{\text{MSE}} = \frac{52}{4.89} = 10.63$$

$F_{.05} = 4.26$ (2 degrees of freedom numerator and 9 denominator)

Because $F = 10.63 > F_{.05} = 4.26$, we reject the null hypothesis that the mean time needed to mix a batch of material is the same for each manufacturer

Chapter 11

2. a. $\bar{p} = \dfrac{n_1 \bar{p}_1 + n_2 \bar{p}_2}{n_1 + n_2} = \dfrac{200(.22) + 300(.16)}{200 + 300} = .184$

$$s_{\bar{p}_1 - \bar{p}_2} = \sqrt{(.184)(.816)\left(\frac{1}{200} + \frac{1}{300}\right)} = .0354$$

Reject H_0 if $z > 1.645$

$$z = \frac{(.22 - .16) - 0}{.0354} = 1.69$$

Reject H_0

b. p-value $= (.5000 - .4545) = .0455$

11. Expected frequencies: $e_1 = 200(.40) - 80$
$$e_2 = 200(.40) = 80$$
$$e_3 = 200(.20) = 40$$

Actual frequencies: $f_1 = 60, f_2 = 120, f_3 = 20$

$$\chi^2 = \frac{(60 - 80)^2}{80} + \frac{(120 - 80)^2}{80} + \frac{(20 - 40)^2}{40}$$

$$= \frac{400}{80} + \frac{1600}{80} + \frac{400}{40}$$

$$= 5 + 20 + 10 = 35$$

$\chi^2_{.01} = 9.21034$, with $k - 1 = 3 - 1 = 2$ degrees of freedom

Because $\chi^2 = 35 > 9.21034$, reject the null hypothesis; that is, the population proportions are not as stated in the null hypothesis

13. $H_0: p_{\text{ABC}} = .29, p_{\text{CBS}} = .28, p_{\text{NBC}} = .25, p_{\text{IND}} = .18$
H_a: The proportions are not
$$p_{\text{ABC}} = .29, p_{\text{CBS}} = .28, p_{\text{NBC}} = .25, p_{\text{IND}} = .18$$

Expected frequencies: $300(.29) = 87, 300(.28) = 84$
$$300(.25) = 75, 300(.18) = 54$$
$$e_1 = 87, e_2 = 84, e_3 = 75, e_4 = 54$$

Actual frequencies: $f_1 = 95, f_2 = 70, f_3 = 89, f_4 = 46$

$\chi^2_{.05} = 7.81$ (3 degrees of freedom)

$$\chi^2 = \frac{(95 - 87)^2}{87} + \frac{(70 - 84)^2}{84} + \frac{(89 - 75)^2}{75}$$

$$+ \frac{(46 - 54)^2}{54} = 6.87$$

Do not reject H_0; there is no significant change in the viewing audience proportions

19. H_0: The column variable is independent of the row variable

H_a: The column variable is not independent of the row variable

Expected frequencies:

	A	B	C
P	28.5	39.9	45.6
Q	21.5	30.1	34.4

$$\chi^2 = \frac{(20 - 28.5)^2}{28.5} + \frac{(44 - 39.9)^2}{39.9} + \frac{(50 - 46.5)^2}{45.6}$$

$$+ \frac{(30 - 21.5)^2}{21.5} + \frac{(26 - 30.1)^2}{30.1} + \frac{(30 - 34.4)^2}{34.4}$$

$$= 7.86$$

$\chi^2_{.025} = 7.37776$, with $(2 - 1)(3 - 1) = 2$ degrees of freedom

Because $\chi^2 = 7.86 > 7.37776$, reject H_0; that is, conclude that the column variable is not independent of the row variable

21. H_0: Type of ticket purchased is independent of the type of flight

H_a: Type of ticket purchased is not independent of the type of flight

Expected Frequencies:

$e_{11} = 35.59$ $e_{12} = 15.41$

$e_{21} = 150.73$ $e_{22} = 65.27$

$e_{31} = 455.68$ $e_{32} = 197.32$

Ticket	Flight	Observed Frequency (f_i)	Expected Frequency (e_i)	$(f_i - e_i)^2/e_i$
First	Domestic	29	35.59	1.22
First	International	22	15.41	2.82
Business	Domestic	95	150.73	20.61
Business	International	121	65.27	47.59
Full-fare	Domestic	518	455.68	8.52
Full-fare	International	135	197.32	19.68
Totals		920		100.43

$\chi^2_{.05} = 5.99$ with $(3 - 1)(2 - 1) = 2$ degrees of freedom

Because $100.43 > 5.99$ we reject H_0; type of ticket purchased is not independent of the type of flight

Chapter 12

1. a.

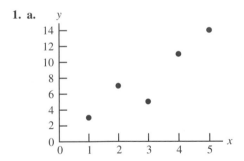

b. There appears to be a linear relationship between x and y

c. Many different straight lines can be drawn to provide a linear approximation of the relationship between x and y; in part (d) we will determine the equation of a straight line that "best" represents the relationship according to the least squares criterion

d. Summations needed to compute the slope and y-intercept:

$\Sigma x_i = 15$, $\Sigma y_i = 40$, $\Sigma(x_i - \bar{x})(y_i - \bar{y}) = 26$, $\Sigma(x_i - \bar{x})^2 = 10$

$$b_1 = \frac{\Sigma(x_i - \bar{x})(y_i - \bar{y})}{\Sigma(x_i - \bar{x})^2} = \frac{26}{10} = 2.6$$

$b_0 = \bar{y} - b_1\bar{x} = 8 - (2.6)(3) = 0.2$

$\hat{y} = 0.2 - 2.6x$

e. $\hat{y} = .2 + 2.6x = .2 + 2.6(4) = 10.6$

4. a.

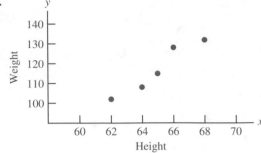

b. It indicates there may be a linear relationship between the variables

c. Many different straight lines can be drawn to provide a linear approximation of the relationship between x and y; in part (d) we will determine the equation of a straight line that "best" represents the relationship according to the least squares criterion

d. Summations needed to compute the slope and y-intercept:

$\Sigma x_i = 325$, $\Sigma y_i = 585$, $\Sigma(x_i - \bar{x})(y_i - \bar{y}) = 110$, $\Sigma(x_i - \bar{x})^2 = 20$

$$b_1 = \frac{\Sigma(x_i - \bar{x})(y_i - \bar{y})}{\Sigma(x_i - \bar{x})^2} = \frac{110}{20} = 5.5$$

$b_0 = \bar{y} - b_1\bar{x} = 117 - (5.5)(65) = -240.5$

$\hat{y} = -240.5 + 5.5x$

e. $\hat{y} = -240.5 + 5.5(63) = 106$

The estimate of weight is 106 pounds

15. a. $\hat{y}_i = .2 + 2.6x_i$ and $\bar{y} = 8$

x_i	y_i	$\hat{y}_i$	$y_i - \hat{y}_i$	$(y_i - \hat{y}_i)^2$	$y_i - \bar{y}$	$(y_i - \bar{y})^2$
1	3	2.8	.2	.04	−5	25
2	7	5.4	1.6	2.56	−1	1
3	5	8.0	−3.0	9.00	−3	9
4	11	10.6	.4	.16	3	9
5	14	13.2	.8	.64	6	36
				SSE = 12.40		SST = 80

$$\text{SSR} = \text{SST} - \text{SSE} = 80 - 12.4 = 67.6$$

b. $r^2 = \dfrac{\text{SSR}}{\text{SST}} = \dfrac{67.6}{80} = .845$

The least squares line provided a good fit; 84.5% of the variability in y has been explained by the least squares line

c. $r = \sqrt{.845} = +.9192$

18. a. The estimated regression equation and the mean for the dependent variable:

$\hat{y} = 1790.5 + 581.1x$, $\bar{y} = 3650$

The sum of squares due to error and the total sum of squares:

$\text{SSE} = \Sigma(y_i - \hat{y}_i)^2 = 85,135.14$

$\text{SST} = \Sigma(y_i - \bar{y})^2 = 335,000$

Thus, SSR = SST − SSE

$$= 335,000 - 85,135.14 = 249,864.86$$

b. $r^2 = \dfrac{SSR}{SST} = \dfrac{249,864.86}{335,000} = .746$

The least squares line accounted for 74.6% of the total sum of squares

c. $r = \sqrt{.746} = +.8637$

23. a. $s^2 = MSE = \dfrac{SSE}{n-2} = \dfrac{12.4}{3} = 4.133$

b. $s = \sqrt{MSE} = \sqrt{4.133} = 2.033$

c. $\Sigma(x_i - \bar{x})^2 = 10$

$$s_{b_1} = \dfrac{s}{\sqrt{\Sigma(x_i - \bar{x})^2}} = \dfrac{2.033}{\sqrt{10}} = .643$$

d. $t = \dfrac{b_1 - \beta_1}{s_{b_1}} = \dfrac{2.6 - 0}{.643} = 4.04$

$t_{.025} = 3.182$ (3 degrees of freedom)

Because $t = 4.04 > t_{.05} = 3.182$, we reject $H_0: \beta_1 = 0$

e. $MSR = \dfrac{SSR}{1} = 67.6$

$$F = \dfrac{MSR}{MSE} = \dfrac{67.6}{4.133} = 16.36$$

$F_{.05} = 10.13$ (1 degree of freedom numerator and 3 denominator)

Because $F = 16.36 > F_{.05} = 10.13$, we reject $H_0: \beta_1 = 0$

Source of Variation	Sum of Squares	Degrees of Freedom	Mean Square	F
Regression	67.6	1	67.6	16.36
Error	12.4	3	4.133	
Total	80	4		

26. a. $s^2 = MSE = \dfrac{SSE}{n-2} = \dfrac{85,135.14}{4} = 21,283.79$

$$s = \sqrt{MSE} = \sqrt{21,283.79} = 145.89$$

$$\Sigma(x_i - \bar{x})^2 = .74$$

$$s_{b_1} = \dfrac{s}{\sqrt{\Sigma(x_i - \bar{x})^2}} = \dfrac{145.89}{\sqrt{.74}} = 169.59$$

$$t = \dfrac{b_1 - \beta_1}{s_{b_1}} = \dfrac{581.08 - 0}{169.59} = 3.43$$

$t_{.025} = 2.776$ (4 degrees of freedom)

Because $t = 3.43 > t_{.025} = 2.776$, we reject $H_0: \beta_1 = 0$

b. $MSR = \dfrac{SSR}{1} = \dfrac{249,864.86}{1} = 249,864.86$

$$F = \dfrac{MSR}{MSE} = \dfrac{249,864.86}{21,283.79} = 11.74$$

$F_{.05} = 7.71$ (1 degree of freedom numerator and 4 denominator)

Because $F = 11.74 > F_{.05} = 7.71$, we reject $H_0: \beta_1 = 0$

c.

Source of Variation	Sum of Squares	Degrees of Freedom	Mean Square	F
Regression	29,864.86	1	29,864.86	11.74
Error	85,135.14	4	21,283.79	
Total	335,000	5		

32. a. $s = 2.033$

$\bar{x} = 3, \Sigma(x_i - \bar{x})^2 = 10$

$$s_{\hat{y}_p} = s\sqrt{\dfrac{1}{n} + \dfrac{(x_p - \bar{x})^2}{\Sigma(x_i - \bar{x})^2}}$$

$$= 2.033\sqrt{\dfrac{1}{5} + \dfrac{(4-3)^2}{10}} = 1.11$$

b. $\hat{y} = .2 + 2.6x = .2 + 2.6(4) = 10.6$

$\hat{y}_p \pm t_{\alpha/2}s_{\hat{y}_p}$

$10.6 \pm 3.182(1.11)$

10.6 ± 3.53, or 7.07 to 14.13

c. $s_{ind} = s\sqrt{1 + \dfrac{1}{n} + \dfrac{(x_p - \bar{x})^2}{\Sigma(x_i - \bar{x})^2}}$

$$= 2.033\sqrt{1 + \dfrac{1}{5} + \dfrac{(4-3)^2}{10}} = 2.32$$

d. $\hat{y}_p \pm t_{\alpha/2}s_{ind}$

$10.6 \pm 3.182(2.32)$

10.6 ± 7.38, or 3.22 to 17.98

35. a. $s = 145.89, \bar{x} = 3.2, \Sigma(x_i - \bar{x})^2 = .74$

$\hat{y} = 290.54 + 581.08x = 290.54 + 581.08(3)$

$\quad = 2033.78$

$$s_{\hat{y}_p} = s\sqrt{\dfrac{1}{n} + \dfrac{(x_p - \bar{x})^2}{\Sigma(x_i - \bar{x})^2}}$$

$$= 145.89\sqrt{\dfrac{1}{6} + \dfrac{(3 - 3.2)^2}{.74}} = 68.54$$

$\hat{y}_p \pm t_{\alpha/2}s_{\hat{y}_p}$

$2033.78 \pm 2.776(68.54)$

2033.78 ± 190.27, or \$1843.51 to \$2224.05

b. $\hat{y} = 290.54 + 581.08x = 290.54 + 581.08(3)$
$\qquad = 2033.78$

$$s_{ind} = s\sqrt{1 + \frac{1}{n} + \frac{(x_p - \bar{x})^2}{\Sigma(x_i - \bar{x})^2}}$$

$$= 145.89\sqrt{1 + \frac{1}{6} + \frac{(3 - 3.2)^2}{.74}} = 161.19$$

$\qquad \hat{y}_p \pm t_{\alpha/2}s_{ind}$
$\qquad 2033.78 \pm 2.776(161.19)$
$\qquad 2033.78 \pm 447.46$, or \$1586.32 to \$2481.24

40. a. 9

b. $\hat{y} = 20.0 + 7.21x$

c. 1.3626

d. SSE = SST − SSR = 51,984.1 − 41,587.3 = 10,396.8

MSE = 10,396.8/7 = 1485.3

$$F = \frac{MSR}{MSE} = \frac{41,587.3}{1485.3} = 28.0$$

$F_{.05} = 5.59$ (1 degree of freedom numerator and 7 denominator)

Because $F = 28 > F_{.05} = 5.59$, we reject $H_0: \beta_1 = 0$

e. $\hat{y} = 20.0 + 7.21(50) = 380.5$, or \$380,500

45. a. $\Sigma x_i = 14$, $\quad \Sigma y_i = 76$, $\quad \Sigma(x_i - \bar{x})(y_i - \bar{y}) = 200$,
$\Sigma(x_i - \bar{x})^2 = 126$

$$b_1 = \frac{\Sigma(x_i - \bar{x})(y_i - \bar{y})}{\Sigma(x_i - \bar{x})^2} = \frac{200}{126} = 1.5873$$

$b_0 = \bar{y} - b_1\bar{x} = 15.2 - (1.5873)(14) = -7.0222$

$\hat{y} = -7.02 + 1.59x$

b.

x_i	y_i	$\hat{y}_i$	$y_i - \hat{y}_i$
6	6	2.52	3.48
11	8	10.47	-2.47
15	12	16.83	-4.83
18	20	21.60	-1.60
20	30	24.78	5.22

c.

$y - \hat{y}$

With only five observations, it is difficult to determine whether the assumptions are satisfied; however, the plot does suggest curvature in the residuals, which would indicate that the error term assumptions are not satisfied; the scatter diagram for these data also indicates that the underlying relationship between x and y may be curvilinear

47. a. Let x = advertising expenditures and y = revenue

$\hat{y} = 29.4 + 1.55x$

b. SST = 1002, SSE = 310.28, SSR = 691.72

$$MSR = \frac{SSR}{1} = 691.72$$

$$MSE = \frac{SSE}{n - 2} = \frac{310.28}{5} = 62.0554$$

$$F = \frac{MSR}{MSE} = \frac{691.72}{62.0554} = 11.15$$

$F_{.05} = 6.61$ (1 degree of freedom numerator and 5 denominator)

Because $F = 11.15 > F_{.05} = 6.61$, we conclude that the two variables are related

c.

x_i	y_i	$\hat{y}_i = 29.40 + 1.55x_i$	$y_i - \hat{y}_i$
1	19	30.95	-11.95
2	32	32.50	-.50
4	44	35.60	8.40
6	40	38.70	1.30
10	52	44.90	7.10
14	53	51.10	1.90
20	54	60.40	-6.40

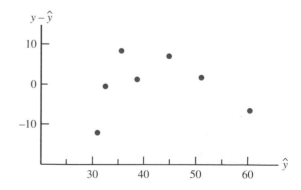

d. The residual plot leads us to question the assumption of a linear relationship between x and y; even though the relationship is significant at the $\alpha = .05$ level, it would be extremely dangerous to extrapolate beyond the range of the data

Chapter 13

2. a. The estimated regression equation is
$\hat{y} = 45.06 + 1.94x_1$
An estimate of y when $x_1 = 45$ is
$\hat{y} = 45.06 + 1.94(45) = 132.36$

b. The estimated regression equation is
$\hat{y} = 85.22 + 4.32x_2$
An estimate of y when $x_2 = 15$ is
$\hat{y} = 85.22 + 4.32(15) = 150.02$

c. The estimated regression equation is
$\hat{y} = -18.37 + 2.01x_1 + 4.74x_2$
An estimate of y when $x_1 = 45$ and $x_2 = 15$ is
$\hat{y} = -18.37 + 2.01(45) + 4.74(15) = 143.18$

5. a. The Minitab output is shown in Figure E13.5a
b. The Minitab output is shown in Figure E13.5b
c. It is 1.60 in part (a) and 2.29 in part (b); in part (a) the coefficient is an estimate of the change in revenue due to a one-unit change in television advertising expenditures; in part (b) it represents an estimate of the change in revenue due to a one-unit change in television advertising expenditures when the amount of newspaper advertising is held constant
d. Revenue = 83.2 + 2.29(3.5) + 1.30(1.8) = 93.56 or $93,560

12. a. $R^2 = \dfrac{\text{SSR}}{\text{SST}} = \dfrac{14,052.2}{15,182.9} = .926$

FIGURE E13.5a

```
The regression equation is
Revenue = 88.6 + 1.60 TVAdv

Predictor       Coef       Stdev      t-ratio        p
Constant      88.638       1.582        56.02    0.000
TVAdv         1.6039       0.4778        3.36    0.015

s = 1.215       R-sq = 65.3%     R-sq(adj) = 59.5%

Analysis of Variance

SOURCE          DF          SS          MS         F         p
Regression       1       16.640      16.640     11.27     0.015
Error            6        8.860       1.477
Total            7       25.500
```

FIGURE E13.5b

```
The regression equation is
Revenue = 83.2 + 2.29 TVAdv + 1.30 NewsAdv

Predictor       Coef       Stdev      t-ratio        p
Constant      83.230       1.574        52.88    0.000
TVAdv         2.2902       0.3041         7.53    0.001
NewsAdv       1.3010       0.3207         4.06    0.010

s = 0.6426      R-sq = 91.9%     R-sq(adj) = 88.7%

Analysis of Variance

SOURCE          DF          SS          MS         F         p
Regression       2       23.435      11.718     28.38     0.002
Error            5        2.065       0.413
Total            7       25.500
```

b. $R_a^2 = 1 - (1 - R^2)\dfrac{n-1}{n-p-1}$

$= 1 - (1 - .926)\dfrac{10-1}{10-2-1} = .905$

c. Yes; after adjusting for the number of independent variables in the model, we see that 90.5% of the variability in y has been accounted for

15. a. $R^2 = \dfrac{SSR}{SST} = \dfrac{23.435}{25.5} = .919$

$R_a^2 = 1 - (1 - R^2)\dfrac{n-1}{n-p-1}$

$= 1 - (1 - .919)\dfrac{8-1}{8-2-1} = .887$

b. Multiple regression analysis is preferred because both R^2 and R_a^2 show an increased percentage of the variability of y explained when both independent variables are used

19. a. $MSR = \dfrac{SSR}{p} = \dfrac{6216.375}{2} = 3108.188$

$MSE = \dfrac{SSE}{n-p-1} = \dfrac{507.75}{10-2-1} = 72.536$

b. $F = \dfrac{MSR}{MSE} = \dfrac{3108.188}{72.536} = 42.85$

$F_{.05} = 4.74$ (2 degrees of freedom numerator and 7 denominator)

Because $F = 42.85 > F_{.05} = 4.74$, the overall model is significant

c. $t = \dfrac{b_1}{s_{b_1}} = \dfrac{.5906}{.0813} = 7.26$

$t_{.025} = 2.365$ (7 degrees of freedom)
With $t = 7.26 > t_{.025} = 2.365$, β_1 is significant

d. $t = \dfrac{b_2}{s_{b_2}} = \dfrac{.4980}{.0567} = 8.78$

With $t = 8.78 > t_{.025} = 2.365$, β_2 is significant

23. a. $F = 28.38$

$F_{.01} = 13.27$ (2 degrees of freedom numerator and 1 denominator)

Because $F > F_{.01} = 13.27$, reject H_0
Alternatively, the p-value of .002 leads to the same conclusion

b. $t = 7.53$

$t_{.025} = 2.571$

Because $t > t_{.025} = 2.571$, β_1 is significant and x_1 should not be dropped from the model

c. $t = 4.06$

$t_{.025} = 2.571$

With $t > t_{.025} = 2.571$, β_2 is significant and x_2 should not be dropped from the model

28. a. Using Minitab, the 95% confidence interval is 132.16 to 154.15

b. Using Minitab, the 95% prediction interval is 111.15 to 175.17

29. a. See Minitab output in Figure E13.5b.
$\hat{y} = 83.230 + 2.2902(3.5) + 1.3010(1.8) = 93.588$ or $93,588

b. Using Minitab: 92.840 to 94.335, or $92,840 to $94,335

c. Using Minitab: 91.774 to 95.401, or $91,774 to $95,401

32. a. $E(y) = \beta_0 + \beta_1 x_1 + \beta_2 x_2$

where $x_2 = \begin{cases} 0 \text{ if level 1} \\ 1 \text{ if level 2} \end{cases}$

b. $E(y) = \beta_0 + \beta_1 x_1 + \beta_2(0) = \beta_0 + \beta_1 x_1$

c. $E(y) = \beta_0 + \beta_1 x_1 + \beta_2(1) = \beta_0 + \beta_1 x_1 + \beta_2$

d. $\beta_2 = E(y \mid \text{level 2}) - E(y \mid \text{level 1})$
β_1 is the change in $E(y)$ for a 1-unit change in x_1 holding x_2 constant

34. a. $15,300, because $b_3 = 15.3$

b. $\hat{y} = 10.1 - 4.2(2) + 6.8(8) + 15.3(0)$
$= 10.1 - 8.4 + 54.4$
$= 56.1$
Sales prediction: $56,100

c. $\hat{y} = 10.1 - 4.2(1) + 6.8(3) + 15.3(1)$
$= 10.1 - 4.2 + 20.4 + 15.3$
$= 41.6$
Sales prediction: $41,600

Index

Data Files Available on CD-ROM

Chapter 1

Fortune	Exercises 4 and 5
Hotel	Exercises 2 and 3
Norris	Table 1.5
Shadow	Table 1.1

Chapter 2

ApTest	Table 2.10
Audit	Table 2.5
BwBooks	Exercise 6
Casino	Exercise 35
Client	Exercise 10
Computer	Exercise 21
Comstock	Exercise 40
Consolid	Case Problem
Crosstab	Exercise 29
Fortune	Table 2.18
HighLow	Exercise 44
IBD	Table 2.15
Income	Exercise 42
JobSat	Exercise 27
Names	Exercise 5
Nielsen	Exercise 4
OccupSat	Exercise 46
PEforcast	Exercise 28
Restaurant	Table 2.11
RevEmps	Exercise 47
Scatter	Exercise 30
Shadow	Exercise 41
SoftDrink	Table 2.1
Spending	Exercise 17
Stereo	Table 2.14
Stocks	Table 2.9
Vehicles	Exercise 36
Wageweb	Exercise 18

Chapter 3

AcctSal	Exercise 5
Asian	Case Problem 3
Cameras	Exercise 14
Cities	Exercise 69
Consolid	Case Problem 1
Crime	Exercise 23
Discount	Exercises 6 & 24
DowS&P	Exercise 52
Eat	Exercise 60
Exam	Exercise 67
Health	Case Problem 2
HighLow	Exercise 53
Income	Exercise 65
Injury	Exercise 45
Mortgage	Exercise 63
Music	Exercise 7
NBA	Exercise 36
Notebook	Exercise 19
Options	Exercise 44

PCs	Exercise 51
ReEquity	Exercise 42
Retainer	Exercise 61
Salary	Table 3.1
Speakers	Exercise 37
Stereo	Table 3.7
Wageweb	Exercise 35
Websites	Exercise 9
World	Exercise 46

Chapter 4

Judge	Case Problem

Chapter 7

EAI	Section 7.1
MetAreas	Appendix 7.1, 7.2

Chapter 8

ActTemps	Exercise 46
Auto	Case Problem 3
Balance	Table 8.2
Bock	Case Problem 1
CJW	Section 8.1
FastFood	Exercise 12
GulfProp	Case Problem 2
Interval z	Figure 8.10
Interval t	Figure 8.11
Mail	Exercise 47
Miami	Exercise 11
Training	Table 8.4
Sleep	Exercise 22
TVtime	Exercise 19
Workers	Exercise 9

Chapter 9

BLS	Case Problem 2
Distance	Table 9.2
Heathrow	Section 9.5
Interval z	Figure 9.15
Interval t	Figure 9.16
Quality	Case Problem 1

Chapter 10

AgeExec	Exercise 45
Airport	Exercise 6
ArtDir	Exercise 48
Asia	Exercise 43
ExamData	Table 10.1
Golf	Case Problem 1
IDSalary	Case Problem 3
ISP	Exercise 50
Matched	Table 10.4
Medical1	Case Problem 2
Medical2	Case Problem 2
MktValue	Exercise 38
Mutual	Exercise 40
NCP	Table 10.5

NFL	Exercise 49
PERatio	Exercise 28
Resorts	Exercise 47
SatisJob	Exercise 46
Software	Table 10.3
Stress	Exercise 37
Trucks	Exercise 44
TVRead	Exercise 27
Union	Exercise 10

Chapter 11

NYReform	Case Problem

Chapter 12

ADRs	Exercise 49
Alumni	Case Problem 3
Armand's	Table 12.1
Boots	Exercise 27
Casino	Exercise 11
Cities	Exercise 20
DowS&P	Exercises 7 and 19
EmpRev	Exercise 12
HighLow	Exercise 53
HomeBldg	Exercise 43
Hotel	Exercise 14
IPO	Exercise 50
IRSAudit	Exercise 59
MtnBikes	Exercise 8
NAEP	Case Problem 1
Nielsen1	Exercise 39
OffRates	Exercise 44
Options	Exercise 51
PCs	Exercises 10 and 36
Safety	Case Problem 2

Chapter 13

Alumni	Case Problem 4
Auto1	Exercise 6
Auto2	Exercise 44
Backpack	Exercise 7
Butler	Tables 13.1 and 13.2
CarRent	Exercise 10
Computer	Exercise 43
Consumer	Case Problem 1
Enquirer	Case Problem 3
Exer2	Exercise 2
Football	Exercise 37
ForFunds	Exercise 8
Johnson	Table 13.6
NFL	Case Problem 2
Nielsen	Exercise 45
Repair	Exercise 35
Schools	Exercise 9
Showtime	Exercise 5
Stocks	Exercise 25
Stroke	Exercise 38
Trucks	Exercise 46